AIR RAID!

AIR RAID!

The enemy air offensive against East Anglia 1939~45

Michael J.F. Bowyer

 PSL **Patrick Stephens, Wellingborough**

Front cover painting *Symbolic representation of a German bomber releasing its load over East Anglia, by James Leech.*

First published in 1986

British Library Cataloguing in Publication Data

Bowyer, Michael J.F.
Air raid: the enemy air offensive against East
Anglia 1939–45. — (Air raid; 1)
1. World War, 1939–45 — Aerial operations,
German   2. Bombing, Aerial — England — East
Anglia — History
I. Title   II. Series
940.54′21   D760.8.D2/

ISBN 0–85059–685–8

*Patrick Stephens Limited is part of the
Thorsons Publishing Group*

Photoset in 10 on 11 pt Times by Avocet Marketing Services, Aylesbury, Bucks. Printed in Great Britain on 115 gsm Fineblade coated cartridge, and bound, by Anchor Brendon Limited, Tiptree, Colchester, for the publishers, Patrick Stephens Limited, Denington Estate, Wellingborough, Northants, NN8 2QD, England.

Contents

Preface and acknowledgements   7
Glossary of terms and abbreviations   12
Realities   15
Chapter 1   The amateurs   21
Chapter 2   The professionals   25
Chapter 3   By the seaside   29
Chapter 4   Look out, there's a mine!   37
Chapter 5   Midsummer nights' madness   46
Chapter 6   From out of the clouds   59
Chapter 7   Those most fateful days   68
Chapter 8   Big bangs   86
Chapter 9   Against the people   97
Chapter 10   The Romans have come!   113
Chapter 11   The lights of perverted science   117
Chapter 12   In the bleak, cruel winter   120
Chapter 13   Unhappy New Year   128
Chapter 14   Clouds, clouds, go *away!*   141
Chapter 15   Into the spring   156
Chapter 16   On the move   168
Chapter 17   Towards a respite   184
Chapter 18   The sacking of Norwich   211
Chapter 19   Many targets, great and small   227
Chapter 20   Facing the unexpected   250
Chapter 21   Six faces of the foe   260
Chapter 22   From Capricorn to Overlord   289
Chapter 23   Final fling   315
Chapter 24   The reckoning   327
Appendix 1   Ministry of Home Security assessment of German weapons thought to have fallen on East Anglia May 1940– May 1945   330
Appendix 2   Metric tonnages of bombs dropped on East Anglia (number of days of attacks bracketed). Excludes unclassified bombs   331
Appendix 3   Areas most heavily attacked   332
Appendix 4   Attacks on major East Anglian towns   332

Appendix 5 Fieseler Fi 103/FZG-76/V-1 flying bomb incidents
in East Anglia 1944–1945   333
Appendix 6 Heinkel He 111 FZG-76 launchers claimed in combat
by Mosquitoes   334
Appendix 7 A-4 long-range rocket incidents in East Anglia 1944–1945 334
Appendix 8 Locations of anti-aircraft guns and searchlights
in East Anglia   337
Appendix 9 Regional maps showing Rural Districts, airfields and
main centres of enemy activity   343
Select index   349

Preface and acknowledgements

There is no question about it. If you lived through the Second World War you will never forget the experience, and will often recall events which for the majority of people are something to be read about, or to be seen in pictures. If you experienced the East Anglian war as I did, then you had the best ringside seat from which to view the air war in Europe. This volume tells of the German air activity over the Eastern Counties.

For that purpose East Anglia is being looked upon as the counties of Cambridgeshire, Norfolk, Suffolk and Essex north of a line joining the River Blackwater-Chelmsford-Stansted and crossing Hertfordshire via Royston to the Al road at Biggleswade, thence to Peterborough and north to the Wash. Some of the activity involving Bedfordshire has been included, since aircraft from more truly 'East Anglia' strayed that way before usually recrossing the eastern counties. Chelmsford, many would say, is not in East Anglia. Yet it was often involved in raids upon the region, and again has been included for the sake of completeness and also because attacks upon the city were in no way related to those on London.

The Ministry of Home Security viewed the area as part of Region 4, including the whole of Essex, Hertfordshire and Bedfordshire. Fighter Command split East Anglia roughly along the line Bawdsey-Duxford so that north of that division became 12 Group territory, 11 Group defending the south. Their divisions roughly equated those of the Army's gunners.

It is now almost impossible to stand upon the sites where the bombs fell and believe that such things really did happen, that places where holidaymakers swarm, the Saturday crowds bustle, the cows graze or new houses stand (mine included) were subjected in some instances to most horrific events. It is hard to stand in a shop and believe that flying glass cut some to ribbons in that very place, and that others may have died from blast which hurled them against a wall before withdrawing them through a plate glass window. If that shocks you, then that was, and is, the reality of war. Tackling a burning incendiary bomb may, in retrospect, have seemed quite a novelty event until one recalls its explosive variants, the Firepots cracking away, the awful phosphor bombs. One may, if old enough, still 'see' the image of an alarming chandelier flare hovering, portent of doom. Still it is possible to visualize the sight and sound of a mine and its swishing parachute, a spooky combination which could reduce a small town to waste in a gigantic flash. It is equally hard to stand in a Suffolk field where the hideous wartime 'butterflies' settled and believe that such bestial objects could have fallen among the ripening corn. Shop in Newmarket High Street and no longer is there more than a trace of a ghastly Tuesday afternoon. Visit the yearly Suffolk Show and the idea of a Dornier crew strafing the area is barely within imagining.

Facing such things was the highly disciplined population, who were not only so because schooling had been tough. Most knew hardship all their lives, were happy with fewer material things than people today. Knowledge of foreigners was still largely scant, for few travelled far and the media as it now exists was waiting to be invented. So, in many respects, it may have been easier to face the foe than it would be now when so many know so much comfort and own so much. Not only that, many only in their forties had already experienced a most ghastly war in France and viewed air raids as nothing compared with what they had seen. Air attack had been built up as something as bad as could ever be, with whole cities disappearing in a flash. Only at the end of the war could that have happened, but there were times when towns we knew and loved burnt their hearts out — and ours.

Not only did the Luftwaffe take away the buildings which had been a part of life, it stole a way of living. Whilst the changes took some years to become complete, it is true that the war set in chain the removal of much that was an accepted part of life. It pushed away the lamplighter active by the street gas lamps in 1939, the milk man delivering into a jug from his churn, the horse and cart, sugar in the old blue bag and the corner shop grocer dipping his little shovel into the sack of rice to be used only for the rice pudding and never some fancy foreign dish. Blasted away the village pump when the water was laid on to the nearby aerodrome — airfield was a nasty name the Americans delivered! Revealed in the tumbled little houses much wallpaper whose design had altered little since Victoria's time, and the piano whose place was being overtaken by less demanding means of making music.

Social change was certainly brought about by air raids, great removers of class barriers and prejudice. Splendid humour laced them, and so did singing troubles away. Rationing, which in retrospect seems an impossible thing to cope with, one took as just a fact of life. Nobody seemed to starve, and indeed many seem to have survived barely harmed. There was, too, the adventure of getting 'a little extra' by some fairly harmless activity which nowadays would probably result in a psychological study, maybe a visit from a social worker! Fortunately, most of us were guarded from statistics although some opinion polls might have brought much fun, although probably never as much as Lord Haw Haw. One felt quite cheated when the BBC announcer as ever preceded the bulletin with his own name to prove its genuine quality. Haw Haw was for ever providing the latest news about things one was never told by the BBC, and which one's experience classed as untrue.

Air Raid!, however, is not a social study, but an account of the air attacks upon East Anglia. It is based upon personal experience and official documentation — local and national — of events of forty years ago.

Apart from my recollections and collection of material from the war years and additions since made, I have received help from many sources. Some idea of the readiness of others to help may be gauged from the fact that when *The Gorleston Advertiser* carried my request for memories from any who lived at or near Great

Yarmouth during the war I received within ten days nearly 300 letters. I had hoped to meet all who replied to this and other requests, but there were so many that it proved quite impossible. All had interesting stories or advice to offer, and still more telephoned their recollections. I have woven into the book as many of the contributions as possible.

Official records to which I have referred fall into several categories. There are those prepared for the Ministry of Home Security and now held within the Public Record Office's collection of Home Office documents within Classes H0198, H0199, H0201 and H0202. These give varying amounts of detail, and in drawing items from them I acknowledge Crown Copyright. More localized records tend to give a more intimate picture than such material, and for much of the war I was fortunate in being able to copy the Daily Damage Reports for Region 4 which give invaluable detail, and which seem not to have survived elsewhere.

All East Anglian county authorities maintain flourishing County Record Offices in which records of air attack may be found. Each county recorded the effects of air attacks in its own manner, but fortunately all the East Anglian County Record Offices have something to offer and usually plenty. In the case of Cambridge Borough various items concerning attacks are held by Michael Petty and his team in the Central Library's Cambridgeshire Collection. The Suffolk records are split between West Suffolk at Bury St Edmunds and East Suffolk at Ipswich. The latter cover a vast amount of activity in extensive detail, even to the extent of including police reports. Essex records are held at Chelmsford and consist of detailed daily and consolidated reports. Since I already had much relating to Norfolk I had but a brief confirmatory glance at the listing of attacks within that county now held in Norwich. Sadly, the Cambridgeshire records have long since been disposed of, but Michael Farrar gave me as much help as possible. To all of the patient and extremely helpful archivists and librarians whom I met during my research I extend my most grateful thanks.

Major libraries within East Anglia's main towns hold a variety of interesting useful local histories, some have extensive photograph collections and most hold local newspapers. All are worth consulting for items concerning the raids for, despite wartime censorship, there are many reports to examine. In particular I would like to extend my thanks to the Reference Department of Lowestoft Library and the Local Studies sections in Clacton and Norwich Central Libraries.

On the military side I again drew from the recordings I made at the time as well as from various Official documents, including those now held at the Public Record Office within Classes AIR22, AIR24, AIR25 and AIR27. The search within these documents has covered a very extensive field. Many years ago I was fortunate enough to examine much Luftwaffe material prior to its return to Germany. This I have been able to set against the British version of German operations. In relevant instances I acknowledge Crown Copyright. Ever his highly helpful self has been my close friend Gerrit Zwanenburg, at all times ready to contribute much relating to operations flown from bases in the Netherlands.

In respect of industrial undertakings which came under attack I was fortunate in being able to obtain details and photographs and extend my thanks for their help to Mrs K.M.P. Mathews of Boulton & Paul, Mr E. Longbottom, Mr Vernon Howlett and Mrs E. Mandall Hall of Rowntree Mackintosh and Mr

William C.C. Gaymer of Gaymer's Cider, Attleborough.

Obtaining photographs has meant a wide search. Within the German Bundesarchiv collection in Koblenz I managed to locate a number of photographs of aircraft likely to have operated over East Anglia and record my thanks for being able to use these. To Mr Tony Kemp of the Eastern Daily Press I am much indebted for the loan of precious prints depicting the results of raids upon Norwich. Recently reprinted was the book *Port War* packed with splendid photographs of Lowestoft taken by Ford Jenkins. For permission to use some of these I record my thanks to Miss N.J. Rhodes and Ford Jenkins Ltd. Yarmouth is shown in photographs from assorted sources, and airfield and aircraft photographs have also come from the RAF Museum where Mr Reginald Mack as ever went to considerable lengths to help.

To Mr John Strangward I express my most sincere gratitude for the help so generously given during the proof stage of *Air Raid!*

A host of people offered items for this volume and provided far more material for inclusion than space allowed. So, if you contacted me including an item which does not appear, please do not think that I was not grateful for your help. In particular I would like to thank J.R. Aldridge, Blanche M. Allen, Mr Ashman, Mrs E. Ashman (née Keable), Ulf Balke, Jim Balwin, Frank C. Beaumont, Alan Beeton, R.G. Berry, George Bowyer, Ruby Bowyer, D.F. Brock, Barbara Buckton, Dr J.A. Charles, Mike Cheesman, Molly Colgan, Bob Collis and the Norfolk & Suffolk Aviation Museum at Flixton, near Bungay, S.T. Cox, I.G. Crane, Mrs J.E. Daly for the unique photographs of Newmarket, Mrs E.I. Deterding, Mrs J.M. Dixon, J.M. Dryhurst, C.A. Emms, Derrick G. Foster for the copy of *Constable's County* carrying his most useful article relating to wartime Ipswich, A.M. Fryatt, G.W.E. Gardiner, Dorothy Gray, Mrs A.E. Girling, Arthur Guy, Mary K. Gurney, Dorothy M. Halifax, Charles Hall, Olive Halliday, Mervyn Hambling, Mrs Iris Harpour, B.R.J. Harvey, Laurence Haylock for his careful artwork, Mr L.G. Healey, Colin Henderson, H.R. Hicks, Florence E. Hines, E.H. King, Mrs M. King, Peter King, D.P. Lane, Mrs Margaret Lindley, Mrs C. Lister, Mr K. Loveday, Mrs D. Maddison, Mrs M.S. Mobbs, Mr R.H. Myhill, L.K. Newling, R. Nugent, Dave Osborne of the *Halstead Gazette* and Essex County Newspapers, L.A. Pearce, Miss Sally Pearce, Cecil B. Pettit, Mrs H. Pretty, Mr G. Pulford, Reg Rainer, Ken Ransome for most useful help relating to crashed enemy aircraft, Evelyn Read, R.A. Redfern, D. Roberts, Betty and Peter Ross, interested in Sheringham's past, G. Sambrooke-Sturgess for his memories of extraordinary events in Norwich, Mr E. Sizeland, Don Smith, Mr R. Snowdon, Mrs V.M. Swaine, A.E. Tunbridge, Jack Turner, Jim Watts, W. Walford for first loan of the history of the bombing of Yarmouth, Mr C.W. Weedon, J. Whitsun for the Fiat BR20 photograph sent along by his friend Arthur E. Smith, Percy Woodcock, J.R. Wylie and my friend of many years (and many books!), Gerrit Zwanenburg.

Finally, before you tackle it, here are some brief guidelines relating to *Air Raid!* Many of those to whom I spoke during the writing of the book remembered events as summer, winter, mid-afternoon, 'when it was dark'. I have tried wherever possible to be precise with local times and dates to help place events, even though this does not make for light reading. Secondly, the precise places where bombs fell were often not recorded, especially if they dropped on to open country causing little or no damage. Without doubt many unexploded bombs have never been found and to look for them nowadays in a spirit of adventure would be *extremely* foolhardy. *Any* weapons found should never be touched, and the police should be informed immediately. Often, a stick of bombs fell across several parishes, from a town into the country. For that reason there are many references to local government districts in this book, maps of which show where most of the bombs fell.

Finally, a personal request. Nearly half a century has passed since the sounds of Dorniers, Heinkels, Ju 88s and many more heralded frightening moments. It was hard to realize that aboard them were people, and many like ourselves caught in terrifying situations not of their choice or making. If you happen to be one of those, who knew our eastern skies in bad times for us all, and would like to recall the events from a very different seat than mine, then do please write!

Michael J. F. Bowyer
Cambridge, August 1985

Glossary of terms and abbreviations

AA Anti-aircraft.

AB Abwurf Behalter — 'throwing out container', ie, metal container for forced ejection of fire bombs or anti-personnel bombs.

ABB As above, with 'B = Brandbomben' added. Where the following number was that of an HE bomb, then the container occupied the same bomb bay stowage space as the bomb, eg ABB500.

AC Aircraftsman.

AFS Auxiliary Fire Service.

AI Airborne Interception radar (carried in aircraft).

ARP Air Raid Precautions.

BEF British Expeditionary Force.

B Bayerische Flugzeugwerke — see also Me.

Blenheim 1f Blenheim 1 bomber modified into an auxiliary fighter.

BM1000 Bombe Minen — air drop mine Type 'G'.

B1 Brandebombe 1 kg — standard incendiary bomb, often found in its E = Elektron version, sometimes with nose or tail explosive, (indicated by 'Z' inscribed on bomb, for fuze).

Bogey Enemy aircraft.

Brand C.50A/C.250A Phosphorus component oil bomb.

BSB, BSK/BK German bomb containers (see ABB).

Bury Refers in all cases to Bury St Edmunds — 'Bury' to East Anglians!

Butterfly bomb See SD2.

CHL Chain Home Low-Flying radar station.

Container See ABB.

CWS Co-operative Wholesale Society.

Do Dornier aircraft.

Do 17Z-2 Dornier 17 bomber Verzion Zwei (ie, Mk 2) sub-series 2.

Do 217 Dornier 17, redesigned, ie, Type 2.

3.(F)/122 Number 3 Staffel, 122 Reconnaissance Gruppe.

Firepot Incendiary bomb, see Sprengbrand C. 50.

Flam C250C, C500 Oil bomb, 'Flammenbombe' = flame bomb. Some oil bombs utilized a KC250 Container intended for chemical weapons. KC = Kampstoff Cylindrisch.

FN (Convoy) Convoy sailing from the Thames to the Firth of Forth.

FS (Convoy) Convoy sailing from the Firth of Forth to the Thames.

GDA Gun Defended Area.

Geschwader Luftwaffe equivalent organization to an RAF Group.

Gruppe (Gr) Luftwaffe equivalent organization to an RAF Wing. See KG (Kampfgeschwader).

Hostile (act) Enemy aircraft were technically 'hostile' only after having made an attack.

HE High explosive (bomb).

He Heinkel aircraft.

IAZ Inner Artillery Zone, the AA-defended central London area.

IBEN Incendiary Bomb Explosive Nose.

IBSEN Incendiary Bomb with Separating Explosive Nose.

Identity letters
(Luftwaffe) Throughout this book there are references to Luftwaffe aircraft such as *U5+DK*. The '*U5*' component identified the Geschwader, '*D*' the individual aircraft and '*K*' the Staffel (or squadron) within the Gruppe. See also Staffel.

IE RAF squadrons were organized on a basis of usually twelve aircraft called their Initial or Immediate Equipment.

IR Backing the IR was the Immediate Reserve, usually four aircraft. Thus a squadron's strength comprised its IE + IR.

Ju Junkers aircraft.

KG Kampfgeschwader — Luftwaffe equivalent organization to an RAF Bomber Group.

Kg Kilogramme, equivalent to 2.2046 lb.

KGr. Kampfgruppe — Bomber Group.

Kü.Fl.Gr. Küstenfliegergruppe — Coastal Group.

LAA Light anti-aircraft (gun).

LDV Local Defence Volunteers (renamed Home Guard).

LG Lehrgeschwader — operational training geschwader. Operational training in German bomber groups was also undertaken by their IVth Gruppe, entitled for example IV/KG77.

LMB Air-dropped mine.

LMG Light machine-gun.

Lodger squadron RAF squadron temporarily sighted at a station not under the same controlling Group as the squadron.

Luftflotte German air fleet.

LV Light vessel (Trinity House light ship).

LZ balloon Low-zone kite (barrage) balloon, flying to 6,000 ft.

Me/Bf Messerschmitt. During the war the Messerschmitt 109 was generally, if erroneously, called the Me 109 and not correctly the Bf 109 (see also Bf).

MC Military Cross.

MT Metric Tonne, 1,000 kg or 0.9842 of a British ton.

MU Maintenance Unit.

NJG Nachtgeschwader — night fighter geschwader.

Ob.d.L. Oberkommando der Luftwaffe—Luftwaffe High Command.

Phosphor bomb 'Brand C.50' — fire bomb with a phosphorus/rubber solution filling.

Q-Site Dummy airfield lit at night to distract enemy attacks from real airfields.

RD Rural District — Local Government administrative area, within a county, a system existent from 1894 to 1974 — with some adjustments. A high proportion of bombs aimed at East Anglia fell in open country, one salvo sometimes crossing two, even three parishes. Therefore there are references to such events under the Rural District in which they occurred. Rural Districts are listed within their counties in Appendix 2.

Red Alert Four alert states existed for the Civil Defence organization throughout the war. 'Red' meant attack imminent, sirens to be sounded; 'White' meant no enemy activity in the area; 'Yellow' was a precautionary state and 'Purple' meant enemy activity imminent.

RGA Royal Garrison Artillery.

SB1000 Spreng Behalter — explosive cylinder, parachute bomb.

SC (bomb) Spreng Cylindrisch — explosive cylinder, standard HE bomb designation.

SD (bomb) Spreng Dickwandig — explosive thick-walled fragmentation bomb, eg, SD1700.

SD1, 2, 10 1 kg, 2 kg and 10 kg anti-personnel bombs. SD2 = 'butterfly bomb'.

Section (of fighters) Usually two RAF fighters, three normally being called a 'Flight'.

Sector Designated air space under control of a permanent fighter station which might have jurisdiction over others.

SKG Schnelles Kampfgeschwader — fast bomber geschwader, eg, SKG 10.

SLC See page 157.

SNIB Steel-nosed incendiary bomb.

Sprengbrand C.50 Firepot, explosive incendiary bomb scattering many components.

Stab Staff (Flight, usually).

Staffel Luftwaffe equivalent of a British squadron, comprised three Ketten (Flights), each of three aircraft. Three Staffeln (27 aircraft) comprised a Gruppe, three of which (106 aircraft) nominally armed a Geschwader. The aircraft within each Gruppe carried their Staffel letter in a colour allocated to the Staffel, that colour sometimes being applied to aircraft spinners along with the Gruppe colour. Staffel letters/colours and Gruppe allocation were: Geschwader Stab, *A*, green letter; Geschwader, *B* to *F*, green letters; I Gruppe, *I*, white, *H*, Staffel 1., white, *K*, Staffel 2., red, *L*, Staffel 3., yellow; II Gruppe, *II*, red; *M*, Staffel 4., white, *N*, Staffel 5., red, *P*, Staffel 6., yellow; III Gruppe, *III*, yellow; *R*, Staffel 7., white, *S*, Staffel 8., red, *T*, Staffel 9., yellow; IV Gruppe, *IV*, blue — usually the operational training element; *U*, Staffel 10., white, *V*, Staffel 11., red, and *W*, Staffel 12., yellow. Large units extended to V Gruppe: *X*, Staffel 13., white, *Y*, Staffel 14., red and *Z*, Staffel 15., yellow.

NB: The identity markings of an aircraft did not always relate to its operating crew, so that a Do 17Z of 8./KG2 might well be operating with 9./KG2 or even another Gruppe. Thus, misconceptions can arise as to why unit identities are sometimes quoted 'wrongly'. From 1943 the Staffel number was sometimes boldly painted on the tails of bombers, by which time the use of coloured letters was uncommon. Indeed, missing letters, no letters, merely one letter, perhaps only a white outline or full identity in white on the tail, were all typical features.

TA Territorial Army.

Times quoted All are Local Times, ie. GMT, BST, DBST as appropriate.

Tonne Metric tonne (*qv*).

UP Unrotating Projectile.

UX (HE, etc) Unexploded.

Wekusta Wettererkundungsstaffel — weather reconnaissance staffel.

WNr Werke Nummer — German aircraft's constructor's number, given sometimes preceding the aircraft identity letters. Some preceded by aircraft type, eg. *088* for Ju 88.

Yarmouth All East Anglians would surely know Great Yarmouth affectionately as 'Yarmouth'!

Zenit flight Weather reconnaissance sortie.

ZG Zerstorergeschwader — long-range fighter geschwader.

Realities

'Oh Hell!', I yelled.

'Don't you ever let me hear you say...' Dad's remaining words disappeared within a thunderous din accompanied by an earthquake which rocked the old oak mantelpiece, set the light shade a-dancing and propelled cousin Cecil from his fireside 'box'. Bad language before a lady, though, was certainly of more import than this mere air raid. Such an attitude was to become the hallmark of the nation as it faced the terror. Mum's response of 'That was near', 'poor souls' and 'thank God we are safe' would soon re-echo through the land, for we had been a part, and a close one, of the first serious air raid on England.

Surprisingly, it left me feeling neither scared nor fortified, but almost relieved that Hitler had at last come — or at least sent a representative. Captain Norman Macmillan, MC, AFC, writing in *The Daily Mail* of 1 February 1935, and imagining a raid on Liverpool, had forecast that 'simultaneously, at a signal, 5,000 bombs containing 1,250 tons of high explosive will drop along the whole length of dockland and burst into a sheet of flame. Next will come the heavy bombers with one- and two-ton bombs. They will come in droves, a hundred at a time, to seek the special spots destined for destruction. Over the buildings of the city succeeding waves will pass, dropping delay-action bombs that penetrate roofs and ceilings until they explode on the lowest floor.' Similarly we had been warned of the horror of air attack by public display, leaflet, film and even cigarette card.

When it really came, a streamlined Heinkel on a hot summer night destroying small, precious homes nearby, it was nothing like the forecast nightmare. Very close, yet still distant enough, the noise louder than anyone had warned of, it made one realize one's powerlessness to intervene. Spanish refugee children had related spine-chilling tales of airborne death; yet they had survived, and now so had we — but it had been a most unpleasant experience with a horrific aftermath for many.

Luckier than the Spaniards, we had our well-organized and brave 'ARP' to hand, Civil Defence in remote, official parlance. We also had a fine array of council officials caring for us, showing a kind face. Cambridge Borough Council proved its benevolence by building a collection of air raid shelters for the affluent to copy. Emphasizing a thoughtful nature, it had even sited them on Council property — the Borough Cemetery. 'From the cradle to the grave — via the shelter,' commented one wit! What ghoulish mind had sited them thus, introducing the comic and macabre so evident in all air raids? Lavish too were those shelters, ideal for even our nasty, nuclear age.

Important council men in 1938 revealed to us the mysterious 'incendiary bomb', introducing the ARP's most important antidote — sand. When an attempt to extinguish burning thermite proved none too successful, 'He'd do better by covering it with a dustbin,' said a nearby know-all, summing up the popular attitude to the forecast holocaust. Council officials wedded to writing letters were suddenly appointed to face complicated weapons and terrifying situations — not to mention a population largely hostile to spending on ALL defence. When it appeared that the local authorities were advocating the use of water buckets by the million, hessian sandbags by the multi-million and countless souls to fill them, there was understandably an air of incredulity. Without them, though, Britain would have suffered much worse when hostilities came, even though the zinc or enamel buckets were soon brimming with fag ends and pavements were littered with sand. Passing children never could resist a poke at a bag, already under great pressure from higher bags.

It was in July 1935, while the nation was celebrating King George V's Silver Jubilee, that the Home Office outlined to local authorities measures necessary to safeguard the civilian population against air attack. Particular emphasis was laid upon the possibility of gas attack when, late in 1937, plans were publicly discussed in the face of vociferous, ill-informed opposition. In 1938 in major East Anglian towns, Chief Wardens were appointed, independent of the police. By March 1938 for instance, Colchester had recruited 800 ARP volunteers, men and women, in the month when recruitment began of Special Constables who were to give sterling service most courageously. In addition to street Wardens, decontamination workers, auxiliary firemen, first aid and rescue workers, staff for mobile canteens, ambulance workers, drivers and messengers were needed, and nearly all would be volunteers. Overseeing them would be the Report Centre staff to direct them to 'incidents'. A high proportion of the ARP force comprised quite elderly men and women who volunteered for tasks demanding vast surges of immense courage when dealing with appalling acts of cruelty. They would endure horrific moments when friends were engulfed by roaring conflagrations or walls tottered and, without flinching, take enormous risks. And the backbone of the force was always the Air Raid Warden.

Proudly radiating importance, he or she donned a black tin helmet and arm band. A raid warning whistle and wooden rattle were sometimes supplemented by a handbell, producing a warlike rag and bone merchant yelling a warning street cry. Such folk never spoke of 'sirens', but wallowed in a colourful world of 'yellow', 'purple' and 'red' warnings denoting the state of their affairs. They professed plentiful knowledge of 'Jerry' and of bombs, proudly leaking it to lower folk. And, when the moon was high, and passing unsynchronized Heinkels made one distinctly uneasy, the ARP 'wizard' apparently contacted their crews to confirm general belief that every enemy alien soaring over Cambridge had sometime partaken of its University life and spied from Norwich Cathedral prior to hostilities. Besides providing the KGB with faithful sons, Cambridge apparently educated every Luftwaffe airman who flitted by on Hitler's behalf between 1939 and 1945.

A wartime innovation was the establishment in 1941 of a lesser-trained, virtually enrolled group of defenders, the fire watchers. People who actually

*The education value of cigarette cards pre-war was enormous. W.D. & H.O. Wills
produced an 'Air Raid Precautions' series. Examples depict a 'refuge room', gas mask,
stirrup pump and ARP badge.*

seemed to enjoy their places of work would now 'protect' them overnight from incendiary attack, thereby safeguarding the boss' possessions and, in some cases, even take care of the great man's secretary. Then, when the enemy came, all performed courageously.

For senior ARP men, moments of immense power came upon receipt of a 'red' warning. Impressively they sounded their assorted and overgrown 'horns', briefly sharing a secret and sending lesser mortals scampering fast to the safety of their burrows. When, however, the enemy persistently refused to appear, that activity declined.

Easily overlooked remains the merciless campaign the Luftwaffe appeared to wage upon Britain's countryside. No statistics will ever portray the desecration of rural England — something its Preservation Council was powerless to halt. A vast majority of bombs dropped in East Anglia fell in 'open country' — all too often synonymous with a near miss upon a farmhouse and the death of prized, indeed loved, animals. Bombs intended for airfields usually overshot on to fields, village greens, churches and 'pubs', and frequently far from intended targets. Much has been made in post-war literature of the inaccuracy of RAF bombing; that of the Luftwaffe was incredibly bad, ten-mile misses being far from uncommon. Tour the countryside and one may occasionally observe a copse nesting in a deep hollow and enjoying the fertility of a misplaced mine.

Mines? How can one forget them, dangling terrifyingly from spooky parachutes which delighted in hanging from trees and launching amazing rumours. Coloquially known as 'land mines', they were in reality adapted sea mines which, upon exploding, produced a tremendous, hollow bang and blast over wide areas. Gently arriving, many failed to detonate, adding to the aura surrounding them. Extensive areas then needed to be cleared while tremendously brave bomb disposal experts moved in to neutralize the weapon. ARP men could, meanwhile, assert great power and knowledge, write reports in

Vicarage Terrace, Cambridge, in 1940.
Did I really stand on the right-hand side
pavement corner not very long after those
bombs fell?

profusion, call WVS women to feed their thousands — amazingly well in a time of dire food shortage — so that the good prospered. And, as one gazed, distantly, upon a mighty mine, one quaked at its mystique wondering whether this cataclysmic cylinder was one of those magnetic contraptions which exploded at the mere sight of the metal on one's braces. Adding to the novelty effect, the government remained silent on the entire subject of mines.

No wartime East Anglian can surely ever forget the constant rain of the smelly 1 kg incendiary bombs which produced dazzling firework displays. Luckily, these highly potent, dangerous little beasts took great delight in depositing themselves upon heathland, grassland and hedgerows and usually seemed to avoid villages and aerodromes. Come the mornings and there were enough bomb tails for many villagers to acquire a trophy from night-time adventures. Those first upon the scene were often rewarded with a dangerous live specimen, a souvenir to be tucked away in the garden shed and occasionally exhibited in great secrecy until the owner came to his senses. Such activities undoubtedly led to curious official fire-bomb counts by conscientious officials who recorded the number of tails or bomb holes discovered, apparently unaware that incendiaries were usually dropped in standardized container loads. Firebomb trophies were even placed upon mantelpieces, but the usual souvenir thereabouts was a slice of metal from a high-explosive bomb rooted from the crater among the 'ex-hollyhocks' of Gran's blasted cottage — in which Gran would probably continue to resolutely reside.

Aside from such aspects of air raids there was, overwhelmingly, the malignancy of it all, the impossibility of escape and the exposure of one's home, the ultimate invasion of privacy, to an army of strangers. In a flash one's entire world could disintegrate and many deeply loved, instantly be no more. The dusty smell of shattered buildings, that curious sweet aroma from incendiaries and a sickly stench of fire became commonplace. Often the poorest suffered most, housed as they were close to factories, railways and docklands — all legitimate targets. Broken windows, lost tiles and smashed-in doors abounded, each a mighty personal tragedy on a cold winter's night. Fearsome events arose when, with water pipes frozen, incendiaries showered upon highly combustible buildings. Come the dawn many confronted a pile of rubble called 'home' and the realization that friends had simply vanished — and all too often a deeply cherished pet to whom official shelter was denied.

Night attacks, especially from low levels, were undoubtedly the more frightening. Major raids are the subjects of many written accounts, yet a few bombs along the High Street of a small town on market day generated proportionately far more fear, revulsion and damage. The threshold to fear is soon crossed. To be exposed to a strafing Do 17 'flying pencil' was, I can categorically state, not a satisfying experience.

Nevertheless, sombre events daily in evidence throughout the war were often mixed with the unusual and humorous. Even when the bombing was at its worst it was never long before a good round of community singing became coupled with a strong dose of the contempt with which all self-respecting citizens viewed Mein Führer and his miserymen.

No air attack has yet subjugated the civilian population's will to resist. There was no way in which Britain could have been terrorized into submission — even by the tonnes of bombs the Luftwaffe hurled upon East Anglia.

Chapter 1
The amateurs

The First of September 1939 was a memorable Friday, warm, clear, and laced with disturbing news bulletins informing, misinforming and increasingly worrying concerning invasion of Poland. Would the Ju 86Ks soon destroy all that we, too, cherished? Impossible — until we heard that thousands of city children were being shuttled into the safe countryside, would desperately need love, security and safety. Unbelievable, it now seems, that most could not name sights common in the green and yellowing fields as they passed in the trains conveying them to places with quaint names. Simultaneously, over three days, 7,000 from Thames-side towns were shipped to Yarmouth on pleasure steamers. Then they were dispersed into Norfolk.

By mid-afternoon many children had reached their destinations while German bombers pulverized the Poles, some of whom were courageously making cavalry charges against tanks. Rumour said that the Luftwaffe was dive-bombing civilians with fearsome din, great accuracy and tremendous fercocity. Alarming, indeed.

Upon seeing evacuee children standing homeless and forlorn, just praying that the coming ordeal would not be too bad, my mother became one among the thousands who accepted two. What followed was amazing for it was soon obvious that our life styles were very different. Within moments of arrival they hid their travel rations, including 6d tins of the then-common corned beef — but which they had never before encountered. My mother, deciding that a secret 'contraband search' was advisable, persuaded me to lead the boys to the local sweet emporium. Poor Mr Waller! Obviously sensing that the army of newcomers might too readily relieve him of his precious goodies, he had closed early leaving only a courageous slot machine to face them.

For its operation I proffered coins to my young friends. They needed only one, and by carefully inserting it demonstrated a simple technique for rapidly relieving the contraption of its entire contents. Mr Wrigley's gum flowed forth like water for Moses. It was incredible, and I marvelled at their 'skill' while watching out for PC 99. I also assumed that Fulham's sweet sellers merely performed a social service.

Arriving home, war likely, I joined Dad in trying to black-out the windows. Using old clothes, possibly Victorian even, we eventually achieved it, although there was no way that the complex process could be repeated nightly. What a blessing that the 'ancients' adored black! Elsewhere dark red curtains, chintz of

Top *Frantic digging of air raid slit trenches in Old Chesterton, Cambridge in October 1938* (Cambridgeshire Collection).

Above *More solid were the concrete-braced shelters built on 'waste ground' between the Brunswick School and Auckland Road, Cambridge* (Cambridgeshire Collection).

every hue, old coats and table cloths — the sort protecting every table top's shiny surface from the ravages of battered Dinky toys — were forced against the windows to prevent Hitler finding us. Only total blackout could achieve that, we gathered.

'You'll have to do something about the light coming from under your door!' yelled Mr Clarke, lying on his tummy. He represented a new breed proving his worth in astonishing manner, the Air Raid Warden, often hilarious and always important. Dad, confronting him with some comment about '...in the '14-'18 war...', eventually appeased him by using a rolled copy of the '*Evening News*' thus making us invisible to the outside world. Mr Clarke responded by informing us that Hitler would not now find us. That was most comforting.

Our task on the morrow was to make doubly certain of that. Dad and I hastened to a timber merchant where, for a mere nothing, we purchased giant planks then steered them home on wobbling bicycles. Mum, facing a task of far less ease, took the evacuees fishing.

Using a bakelite-cased, fierce, steel-sprung ruler, I measured the plentiful windows at the rear of the house. Dad, manipulating a saw which still gives me excellent service, soon constructed light-proof window screens while Mum, using her treadle sewing machine, produced some curtains for upstairs use. Heavy the wooden screens were, but nightly until blackout restrictions were lifted in 1944, they were wedged into place. How well they would have withstood a close blast remains conjectural. Scientifically, we painted them white to deflect any heat, but Mr Clarke maintained that it would enable Hitler to find us after all. We took that chance, hiding within our home-built fortress. Most people had similar experiences with their blackout.

The Third of September was an overcast day befitting the grim event for which it would be remembered. Although less hectic than those immediately past, it radiated an awful sense of foreboding. My mother did her best to prevent the evacuees from knowing that the war had started; to me she emotionally recalled her brother resting by Paschendaele Ridge, expressing relief that I was, for the moment, too young to soar aloft. As to the war, all that anyone could do was accept whatever the crazy, pushing politicians forced upon us. That feature of life, at least, remains.

Dad and I were 'digging for victory', but only against the weeds in his huge garden, while Mr Chamberlain announced the worst. Soon afterwards, a few Blenheim IVs trudged westwards, breaking an alarming silence. Apart from a speedily multiplying number of soldiers, searchlights settling in unlikely places and legions of sandbags, there was little evidence that hostilities had commenced. By lunchtime the popular belief that the Luftwaffe would instantly annihilate us had proven wrong. Hitler had not 'missed the bus', he had boarded the wrong one. The afternoon passed as in peacetime for we took the customary Sunday drive in our black Hillman Minx, CCE337. Its course included Newmarket, Dad proving to me that there really were *LN*-coded Wellingtons sheltering near the racecourse Grandstand, to the fascination of swarms of onlookers.

Darkness found us nervous and waiting to be attacked. It was very late, exceptionally quiet, when we at last braved bed, by torchlight because upstairs blackout posed major problems. Would it ever again be safe to sleep, I wondered?

Shortly after midnight came the alarm, warning of impending disaster, a sort of terrifying relief. In the south sirens had wailed just after war began, but not in East Anglia — not our part anyway. But now, Hitler's hoards were surely approaching. In pitch darkness my parents hurriedly dressed then rushed into my room to hand me a pair of trousers — Sunday best, naturally. Mustn't face a stranger when poorly dressed. In the ensuing haste and pitch darkness I tried them on — over my head — as we all three raced to devote our attention to the evacuees.

Gas masks at the ready, we clustered in the hall, said to be the safest place in a raid. Aeroplanes were approaching — most fascinating, and frightening. The most commonly pictured German aircraft had been Ju 86Ks — 'K' for Krieg being widely used as a suitable suffix for any bomber based upon an airliner — as all German bombers were said to be. Soon we would have the He 111K yet never the Do 17K for that, from the start, was just 'The Flying Pencil'. Of the Ju 88 almost nothing was known, even by the experts. What, then, was mumbling overhead now? I remain uncertain, but as three passed by I reckoned them by sound to be Tiger-powered Whitleys which seems feasible. Relief came after

The Munich Crisis brought throughout the land the mass filling of sandbags mostly to protect buildings and windows but also for the numerous anti-aircraft machine-guns which appeared at most unlikely places. This Lewis gun was situated near the Cambridge Drill Hall (Cambridgeshire Collection).

thirty minutes when the 'All Clear' wailed. More correctly there were 'All Clears' for the sirens, set at various spots, had their individual calls. Although it had been a false alarm I subsequently lay awake pondering the realization that air attacks upon us were likely. Just what would they be like?

Next day an ARP man surveyed our house, telling us that it would be safe enough in an air raid, adding that if we wanted a shelter we would have to build our own. 'You can hide in this cupboard under these stairs,' he added, 'shelter in the hall or your middle room which will survive all but a direct hit.' He was, I think, a trifle over-confident.

In one respect I had, since the Munich Crisis, been in a privileged postion, for which I shall always remain indebted to 'the Borough Council'. For reasons best known to themselves they had selected me and two other youngsters to become the first in Cambridge to be covered by gas masks. The head master, courageously explaining to our school why I was worth saving, said the reason was that I was 'sensible'. Secretly I thought it was because we were related to the Mayor. As soon as the head master had gone I tried my gas mask on my best friend, Barbara Robinson. When he returned and glimpsed my activity he said that I was 'not sensible' but that, as I had 'breathed in it', I must keep the gas mask. I have continued to obey his word.

Armed with the gruesome object, hiding behind Dad's shutters, putting our trust in the ever-watchful ARP men and their piles of sand, we faced the Nazis. The Government and the Services were also doing something, on rather a bigger, much more expensive and more menacing scale. Well, they were The Professionals.

Chapter 2
The professionals

East Anglia's air defence was administered by Nos 11 and 12 (Fighter) Groups, the former guarding north Essex and leaving 12 Group defending the remainder. No 12 Group was formed under Air Commodore J.H.S.Tyssen, MC, at Uxbridge on 1 April 1937. After moving to Hucknall on 15 May 1937, it assumed control of Duxford, home of the 24 Gauntlets of 19 and 66 Squadrons. At a time of deep concern lest the Germans should attack during the 1937 Coronation celebrations, the defence of East Anglia virtually depended upon just two squadrons. Martlesham Heath joined 12 Group, along with 64 Squadron and its two-seat Demons, on 11 October 1937. Next month Air Commodore T.E.B. Howe became Group Commander and was soon followed by Air Commodore Trafford Leigh Mallory, DSO, the wartime commander.

Backing the fighters were the guns and searchlights of No 2 Anti-Aircraft Division (or Northern Division) formed 10 December 1936, largely from field units of the 46th North Midland Division, Territorial Army. The southern part of East Anglia was defended by the 1st AA Division centred on the defence of London, its hub the Inner Artillery Zone (IAZ). All were pathetically equipped, the 1st Division with 120 searchlights when it needed 1,000 and with 3-in naval guns which for anti-aircraft purposes were outdated by 1918. Some of those would now 'defend' Harwich.

The cost of providing the Services with modern equipment horrified much of the nation, defence plans going ahead against enormous public outcry. Government response was an attempt to placate both parties and it produced the worst possible outcome. In East Anglia, where the most important two Groups of Bomber Command were established, the defences were almost nil.

Expense of anti-aircraft defence, particularly of Vital Points, was thrashed out on 22 April 1937, a scheme being drawn up for 300 sets of twin 40 mm Bofors gun sites (or double that number of Lewis guns). The Committee of Imperial Defence decided in the case of East Anglia that the only civilian installations worth the expense of being defended were the King's Lynn Oil depot, the Shell and Anglo American Oil Company at Ipswich and Norwich Power Station. Each could have four 40 mm Swedish-designed Bofors to defend them against low-level attack, the possiblity of which seemed more likely than high level raids. A scheme whereby local workers, 38-55 year-olds of the National Defence Battery, defended their place of work, was promoted. Wearing government-provided overalls, perhaps a steel helmet, drilling on private premises to save expenditure on drill halls, and attending three weekend camps a year for a payment of £2 annually (but only for those 'certified efficient'), seemed a most attractive notion to the politicians. Even the expense of that came under scrutiny — on 3 August 1937 King's Lynn was taken from the list and Norwich soon after. Harwich would have three or four twin-barrelled guns at Copperas Wood, three or four at Wrabness to discourage low level attack, possibly six static 3-in guns and three twin-barrels in the hands of a battery of the 12th LAA Brigade. A handful of 3-in guns at Landguard was also to be provided. Fortunately encouraged, and destined to perform brilliantly, was the Observer Corps, which plotted for guns and fighters, visually, the movements of all aircraft throughout the coming hostilities.

After starving the AA defences of money and equipment for years the Committee of Imperial Defence, in November 1937, decided to give it top priority, and increase licence production of the Swedish 40 mm Bofors light AA gun. The twin-barrelled 2-pdr would go into production in 1939 and 300 3-in naval guns (hopelessly outdated) would be surrendered by the Navy to the Army. Anti-aircraft guns needed anti-aircraft sites, usually near towns. At that the public outcry was tremendous with protesters having a grand time backed by foolish local councils which, if all else failed, pointed out the noise nuisance of guns. Under the welter of opposition the public's protection had to be sited in undesirable operational positions to enable politicians to survive. The authorities feared the idiotic protests might discourage recruitment to the TA which was to man the guns and searchlights, but by January 1938 the 2nd AA division had 45 per cent of its planned manpower.

The Operations Room, HQ 12 Group, came into use on 17 May 1938, supervising among others Duxford's Sector Control. Nos 64 and 213 Squadrons moved to 12 Group's newest station, Wittering, on 18 May. Debden had opened in 11 Group on 22 April 1937 and received 73, 80 and 87 Squadrons in June, Demon turret fighters of 29 Squadron replacing 73 Squadron in November 1937. In April 1938 Gladiators of 85 Squadron took the place of 80 Squadron's Gladiators.

The arrival of Spitfires at Duxford in late summer 1938 was a great forward step. Firstly 19 Squadron re-equipped, but no Spitfires were operational when the Munich Crisis developed. Stations in 12 Group mobilized at noon on 24 September 1938, constant watch then commencing in HQ Ops Room. Anti-aircraft personnel of the TA, also mobilized, were sent to their chosen sites, facing enormous problems in establishing searchlights and guns ready for action. By the 28th the crisis was at its peak. Ammunition belts were loaded, aircraft stood refuelled protected by sandbag walls. Tin-hatted Servicemen were plentiful, the soldiers bell-tented and slithering around on wet grass in disturbed meadows. Stores for them were a mighty problem, nobody it seems had thought of the Unions' attitude to long hours in the national interest. Anti-aircraft guns at airfields were merely Lewis or Vickers guns, the Bofors not yet available.

Not until 1 October 1938 was high readiness relaxed, after Mr Chamberlain's crafty postponement of the fight, and the TA returned to more peaceful style by 14 October. Many civilians readily resumed their normal lives, although air raid trench shelters dug in parks were to remain. Indeed, some were soon concrete-lined like those in Chapel Field Gardens, Norwich. Recruiting for the ARP services though soon fell away once more.

The closing weeks of 1938 brought more equipment changes, 66 Squadron having its full complement of Spitfires (fourteen Initial Equipment (IE) and four Immediate Reserve (IR)) by 19 December. At Wittering, No 23 Squadron was then receiving Blenheim Ifs. Both 85 and 87 Squadrons at Debden had been flying Hurricanes since the summer and in December, 29 Squadron also began re-arming with Blenheim Ifs.

Putting the AA forces on to a readiness footing was difficult because of their large TA manning level. May 1939 saw a searchlight belt, 'Couverture', stretching from Newcastle to London (protecting the Midlands) and thence to Portsmouth. It was constantly manned by 1,000 officers and 22,000 other ranks of the TA arranged in four contingents so that each manned the line on a monthly basis during which for half the time they stood down so that fifty per cent operational manning was achieved — very useful for training purposes, especially of fighter pilots. The Government adopted a particularly mean attitude to the soldiers, claiming that although many might lose pay at their civilian work places they lived better than at home...and so they gave them no additional pay! In contrast the militias, just being conscripted, received all possible perks — naturally, for political reasons. Never, indeed, never does it pay to be a volunteer in Britain!

Britain's defences were tested when, on 11 August 1939, the annual Home Defence Exercise commenced involving all of East Anglia. Duxford was packed with fighters including resident Spitfires, 504 Squadron's Hurricanes and 64 Squadron's Blenheims, the latter flying by night from goose neck flare-lined grass runways. Wittering's Blenheims similarly practised at night, aided by searchlights. Manned by companies of the Regiment of Royal Artillery, the small searchlight sites were set in clusters of three, about 10,000 yd apart during the exercise and in wartime. A Central Operations Room passed details of targets to battery HQs which passed details to relevant companies. Final decision to light the 90 cm unit was given by the site commander and depended upon the weather. On a cloudy night a searchlight using diffuse light could well aid a fighter, whereas summer haze could reduce effectiveness. Sixteen men manned each site, three handling the light, others the generator and control system and sound locators. In the early war period there were about 20 searchlight companies in East Anglia, about 60 searchlights.

On 24 August 1939 No 19 Squadron, East Anglia's spearhead of defence, placed a Battle Flight at half hour readiness, and soon on a war footing. At 10:10 on 1 September, mobilization complete, Duxford was informed that the bombing of Polish towns without any warning had commenced at 05:30. By then the TA-manned AA guns of Nos 107-108 and 117-121 Batteries were sited, in Troops, at nineteen RAF Stations in East Anglia.

Commencement of the State of War found 'A' Flight, 66 Squadron, vacating Duxford for the advanced base, Watton, where six Spitfires — sometimes the entire squadron — stood by daily to protect the bomber bases, a task shared with 611 Squadron.

Throughout the first wartime day high readiness states were maintained, then in the early hours of 4 September unidentified aircraft were located by Bawdsey radar heading for Felixstowe and Harwich. Air raid warnings sounded over the whole of East Anglia, and at 02:50 11 Group scrambled six Spitfires (*K9863-9865, K9867, K9870* and *K9932*) of 74 Squadron which searched for an hour before the raiders were declared 'friendlies'. Another alarm came on 5 September, North Weald's 56 Squadron being called to readiness at 03:00. At 12:15 both Nos 151 and 604 Squadrons were scrambled, again to meet non-existent foes.

Such was not the case when, at 06:40 on 6 September, Hurricanes of 56 Squadron hurriedly left North Weald and, led by the Commanding Officer, manned the Harwich-Colchester patrol line at 11,000 ft, with the squadron's 'B' Flight taking up station near Ipswich. Meanwhile, Spitfires of 74 Squadron had again 'scrambled'. The cause of the alarm had been the detection by a listening station of a Heinkel He 111 at the easternmost limit of the Thames Estuary, the first enemy aircraft to approach England. After circling it had turned north and, under the call sign 'THW', continued its reconnaissance flight fifty miles out to sea, causing sirens to sound throughout East Anglia at 07:30. 'All Clear' sounded at 09:00 allowing thousands, who on their ways to work had hurried to the shelters, to proceed — albeit duly chastened at what could overtake them. By the time the raider turned away, north-east off Cromer at 09:27, tragedy had overtaken the defenders.

At 07:10 two reserves joined 56 Squadron, tagging on half a mile behind at 1,000 ft below. Tragically, two Spitfires (*K9683* and *K9685*) of 74 Squadron misidentified them, shooting down *L1980* and killing Pilot Officer Hulton-Harrop and causing Pilot Officer Rose to force land *L1985* in a field near Wherstead. The rest of 56 Squadron was immediately recalled, no enemy aircraft being in their area.

Enemy failure to attack was causing many parents to retrieve evacuated children. Disturbing tales of harsh treatment abounded in the big cities, whereas most of the children had never tasted such a good life as was being lavished upon them. Our evacuees' father informed us that, on the second Sunday of the war, he would rescue them from 'sleeping on a pile of straw like all country yokels do'. Upon his arrival we fed him well, pleaded that he left the boys with us. Then we took him to their room whereupon he sampled the feather bed and to the amazement of all — not least his sons — he promptly fell asleep muttering about the terrible bus ride to Cambridge. When he awoke he snatched the children from our care and, with barely a word of thanks, dragged them off as they cried, pleaded, screamed to stay. Such sorrowful scenes were quite common. It had been fun having the children, and we wrote time and again imploring the parents to bring them out of Fulham. From there, silence. Countless times we were to wonder if...

Strange was the twilight period which had already descended upon the nation as it slid into an unexpectedly quiet war. The forecast raids did not come, so the Government dreamed up an after-Christmas treat, rationing. It gave everyone time to stock up for the bad days sure to come, and Dad acquired half an over-salted pig and a squadron of productive hens. Blackout was firmly insisted upon, just in case Hitler did begin to search for us. Entertainment, savagely slaughtered when war began, suddenly was seen as vital to maintaining morale and cinemas were soon once more portraying the good life as few had ever known it. But amid the sandbags, and propaganda stories from France of possible 'washing on the Siegfried Line', there came the early torpedoing of the liner *Athenia*, then HMS *Courageous*. The war was very much under way at sea, and off East Anglia.

Chapter 3
By the seaside

With incredible speed, holidaymakers had vacated the East Anglian seaside resorts as war drew near. Children and such adults as could be spared from the towns were also evacuated. They had good cause to leave because, during September 1939, several enemy aircraft, probably He 111s of KG26, ventured fairly close to the Sheringham-Gt Yarmouth front, and at least one journeyed a little way out to sea between Orford Ness and Clacton. Precisely how many participated is uncertain, but they were all engaged upon maritime and weather reconnaissance. Doubtless they reported that escorted convoys — 'FN' sailing from Methil to Southend and 'FS' in the reverse direction — sailed about twenty miles off shore.

East coast radar stations, poorly equipped for control of fighters protecting shipping, were unable to locate low-flying reconnaisance aircraft. Fighter pilots were untrained for shipping protection which required slow flying and lengthy duration when only short-range interceptors were available. To achieve the best possible cover, flights of fighters were moved from Debden, Duxford and Wittering to Martlesham Heath, Watton, Bircham Newton and West Raynham. Horsham St Faith later served Duxford. Even so, cover of only five miles seaward was Fighter Command's responsibility, although deeper sorties took place. During such events, then, what types of enemy aircraft might be encountered?

They were the Dornier Do 17, Dornier 215, Heinkel He 111, Junkers Ju 88 and Messerschmitt 110, of which the most impressive in official opinion was the Me 110. No self-respecting Englishman then spoke of a Bf 110! Feared most was its normal range, estimated to be 960 miles (actually a mere 565 miles). Other intelligence assessments were more accurate, giving its top speed as 350 mph at 15,000 ft (actually 349 mph at 22,967 ft and 294 mph at sea level), its cruising speed as 300 mph (301 mph at 22,967 ft) and service ceiling as 30,000 ft (32,800 ft). When encountered it showed poor manoeuvrability, making it outclassed by Spitfires and Hurricanes. Four '110s had impressively been displayed at Augsburg in August 1938 and the Richthofen Geschwader two months later received some. The British assessment of October 1939 considered the aircraft, of which 200 (five Gruppen) were believed to be in service, to be underpowered.

The He 111 was credited with a 4,400 lb bomb load, range of 1,650 miles at 200 mph and a ceiling of 23,000 ft — all slightly optimistic figures. Mid-1939 estimates were of 20 Gruppen (780 aircraft) having He 111s, with production running at 200 a month and the type arming two-thirds of the bomber force.

Of the finest German bomber, the Ju 88, very little was known, yet it was already operational. First flown in 1936, it was discovered as a bomber by the British in 1938 and reported to be in production that summer. Göring told the British Ambassador in September 1938 that the Ju 88 was 'well in advance of any other bomber', claiming a range of 1,865 miles with a 6,615 lb bomb load, at the time of the Nuremberg Rally. A world record of 621 miles carrying a two-ton load at an average speed of 321.26 mph was claimed in March 1939, and at the outbreak of war the RAF credited the Ju 88 with a top speed of 329 mph carrying a 4,400 lb load for 1,240 miles. Its dive-bombing capability was known but not before October 1939 was its existence publicized in Britain.

Ten pre-production Ju 88A-Os were built early in 1939 and 60 Ju 88A-1s that year. Rechlin's small Ju 88 trials unit became 1./KG25 in August 1939. A month later, rejuvenated as 1./KG30, it became operational at Westerland, Sylt, with

Left *Recognition cards: There was scarcely any aircraft recognition material available to the Services when the war started. Depicted here is an item from a 1939 handbook showing the non-existent He 111 Mk V (sometimes called Va) with an incorrect wing planform.*

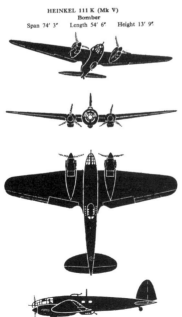

HEINKEL 111 K (Mk V)
Bomber
Span 74' 3"   Length 54' 6"   Height 13' 9"

Left *Two great leaps forward in aircraft recognition came in 1941 when the first issue of* The Aeroplane Spotter *appeared and then in February 1941 the first public handbook, a Penguin Special by R.A. Saville Sneath illustrated by official silhouettes including this Heinkel 111 K (Mk V). Raid spotters made widespread use of the booklet — at the height of low-level attacks on the area. But obviously the officials were not letting the Germans or the roof watchers know that they knew as much as they did.*

Top *Messerschmitt Bf 110 being inspected* (Bundesarchiv 403/329/33).
Above *Messerschmitt 110 recognition sheet of 1939 vintage.*
Below *An He 111 drops its bomb load* (Bundesarchiv 317/43/17).

A Heinkel He 115 floatplane — possibly the first German aircraft type to operate close to East Anglia (Bundesarchiv 78/7/30A).

an anti-shipping role shared with KG26's He 111s. Actual top speed of the Ju 88A was around 290 mph at 19,600 ft and it cruised at 230 mph at 17,400 ft. Its service ceiling was 26,900 ft, range about 1,100 miles.

Unexpected was the use of slow-flying Dornier Do 18 flying-boats, production of which ceased in September 1939. Closer to shore came gawky Heinkel He 115 floatplanes cruising at 180 mph. Fully loaded, their range was about 1,200 miles and they could carry bombs and torpedoes. Marine aircraft operated from Sylt and Borkum, at least a dozen Do 18s being based at Hornum.

Intelligence authorities calculated that Luftflotte II (HQ Brunswick) held 324 Heinkel 111s within three Kampfgeschwader, KG26 with a Gruppe at Lübeck and others at Lüneburg and Phalsburg, KG27 with Gruppen at Langenhagen, Wunsdorf and Delmenhorst, and KG28 spread between Fritzlar and Gutersloh. He 111s of KG4 (home bases Gotha, Erfurt and Nordhausen) were soon being detached to north-west Germany, supplementing aircraft based there for operations against Britain and North Sea shipping. Luftflotte II was thought to hold 72 dive-bombers and 312 fighters. Germany's four Luftflotten, plus a force in Prussia, were thought to hold 205,000 personnel and 3,241 aircraft. At the outbreak of war the actual figures were 1,180 bombers (1,008 serviceable), 1,179 fighters, 240 maritime aircraft and 262 long-range reconnaissance aircraft, all part of the grand total of 4,161 of which 3,699 were serviceable. Pre-war RAF belief was that the Luftwaffe would attempt to destroy our will to fight by launching massive attacks on large towns, but soon it was thought that aircraft factories might be prime targets. Instead the Luftwaffe Operations Staff was pressing for heavy attacks on British ports. Inland raids would, they argued, prevent any possibility of an early peaceful settlement.

In East Anglia the RAF's fighter force on 3 September 1939 comprised the following stations and squadrons: Wittering, 23 Squadron (twelve Blenheim 1fs) and 213 Squadron (fourteen Hurricane 1s); Duxford, 19 Squadron and 66 Squadron (each with sixteen Spitfires) and 611 Squadron (eighteen Spitfires); and Debden, 29 Squadron (twelve Blenheim 1fs) and 17 Squadron (eighteen

Hurricanes). No 85 Squadron was preparing for a move to France. Something like a half of these were ready for action.

In accordance with plans, early enemy operations were all directed against shipping. At 17:25 on 14 September, three enemy aircraft were found about 110 miles east of St Abbs Head. They continued southerly to about thirty miles east of the North Foreland before turning for Terschelling. Another was located about 110 miles east of Cromer, heading for Borkum. All were thought to be Do 18s, and others were known to have operated well north of East Anglia where much of the early fighting was to take place. To increase the northern defences, 611 Squadron moved to Digby on 10 October, making way for the formation at Duxford of No 222 Squadron soon equipped with Blenheim 1f long-range auxiliary fighters. It was believed that the Luftwaffe might put on a show to celebrate Trafalgar Day, for which reason 19 Squadron temporarily moved to Catterick and returned to Duxford on 27 October. To bolster the coastal defences, 56 Squadron on 22 October vacated North Weald for Martlesham where 504 Squadron, based at Debden, maintained detachments.

The maritime bomber force facing the British in early September was actually composed of 65 Heinkel 111s of KG26 and twenty Ju 88As of I/KG30. They were under the control of General Hans Ferdinand Geisler whose original brief to attack British warships was now extended to include raids on merchant ships and naval auxiliaries.

Nine enemy ventures off Cromer were reported during October, three off Lowestoft, three off Orford Ness, two off Southwold and one off Felixstowe. Some raiders were undoubtedly recorded twice during one sortie, others not at all. In every case the Luftwaffe kept well away from the shore as on 30 October when at 08:03 a 'bogey' was logged ten miles east of Lowestoft where it appeared to be conducting a line search. The fifth enemy aircraft noted that day operated fifty miles north-east of Yarmouth.

East Anglia's fighter force received its first major boost in October. Three Blenheim 1f squadrons formed in the area, No 222 at Duxford and two lodger squadrons, Nos 236 and 254, on the bomber station at Stradishall. Both squadrons moved on 9 December, No 236 to Martlesham and 254 to Sutton Bridge. All classed as 'Trade Protection Squadrons' (ie, convoy escort squadrons), they had received their Operations Orders on 7 December, the day a Polish destroyer was attacked in the North Sea. Next day 12 Group squadrons began covering the Lowestoft and Yarmouth herring fishers, six Spitfires of 66 Squadron being scrambled when an enemy aircraft attacked trawlers. Very likely this attack, given wide publicity at the time as an attempt to sink harmless fishing boats, was made in the belief that they were minesweepers, or part of the trawler screen placed to supplement CHL station capability.

'Kipper Patrols' over the fishing fleet, in which Wittering's 23 Squadron had taken part from West Raynham, were viewed by Fighter Command as a diversion from its role. The intention that the Blenheims would summon short-range fighters as needed displeased Dowding, who considered the protection of 'FN'/'FS' convoys Coastal Command's job. No 254 was switched to Bircham Newton on 8 January 1940 and 236 to North Coates on 29 February 1940. Duxford's 222 Squadron, however, remained in Fighter Command, becoming operational on 20 December for maritime and night fighting around East Anglia's shore.

By day 213 Squadron was also deploying to West Raynham to assist protecting shipping in the Wash and was alerted when an unidentified aircraft passed in cloud over Cromer. In the expectant conditions of the time it was at once declared 'hostile', and soon called a 'Heinkel'. Details of 'Cromer's Heinkel' spread far, fast and wide until almost the whole country had been placed under 'Red Alert'. Very soon it was 'observed' simultaneously over Bristol and Liverpool, after somehow having enjoyed a mystery tour embracing Windsor and Wiltshire. As it supposedly hurried along the Bristol Channel it amazingly multiplied itself, transforming, before an unimaginative soul, into a flock of large birds. Finally came reports that it had been brought down, by forces unknown, soon after leaving our western shores.

Such events typified the goings-on of this period, but in reality the enemy was still mainly out to sea — until 13 November when a Do 18 came creeping closer than usual. Under Bawdsey radar control, 'B' Flight of 56 Squadron scrambled Blue Section from Martlesham, to engage. The three Hurricanes, *L1990* (Flight Lieutenant Soden), *L1992* (Pilot Officer Down) and *L2076* (Pilot Officer Illingworth) found the flying-boat forty miles east of Southwold and damaged it before it escaped into cloud. This was the closest East Anglia's fighters had yet come to success.

More sightings, reported sightings and shooting occured on 17 November — all amid grand rumour. At 09:44, 56 Squadron at Martlesham and 79 Squadron at Manston scrambled after He 111s which had sneaked along the Dutch and Belgian coasts undiscovered, and were then found off the Thames Estuary and believed to be trying to reach London. Into this disturbing development was suddenly injected a call from an Observer Corps post that a 'Heinkel' had sneaked across the North Wales coast. Sirens at once wailed in thirteen major north-west towns and as the 'raider' journeyed unseen over Liverpool and Merseyside their AA guns blazed away. A similar welcome greeted it over Manchester where it was reported as turning away. A section of Hurricanes soon scrambled from Digby to defend its new reckoned target, Finningley. From the Coventry area another note of novelty was injected when an unusual aeroplane was spotted bearing the identity letters *OTW*. Expanding excitement soon placed raiders over March and York before all magically evaporated.

The cause of the excitement? One of three 'friendlies' later discovered to have been, astonishingly, a poor old Walrus amphibian which had been so frightened over Manchester that it turned away in terror!

Within this and similar episodes there was the certainty that few Servicemen or civilians could identify 'our' aeroplanes or 'theirs'. Just how poor aircraft recognition was at sea became clear when, off Hunstanton, the crew of HMS *Fleetwood* on 27 October had reported five British aircraft as 'hostile' and the order to 'fire' was given. That afternoon HMS *Halcyon* reported nine aircraft attacking a convoy forty miles north-east of Cromer. What could be believed?

Attempting to remove the dangers, Fighter Command commissioned wooden scale models of ten types of German aircraft, followed by a contract for 2,500 black bakelite copies for issue to the Forces. A more sensible policy would have been to employ Frog and Skybird, highly successful kit manufacturers, to supply the Services, but officials never take the easy path. The arrival of the rough

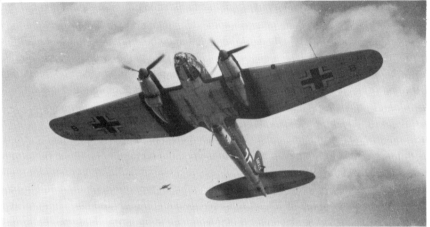

Top *From the* Royal Eagle, *evacuees disembark at Lowestoft on 1 September 1939* (Ford Jenkins Photography).

Above *Fortunately the evacuees never had such a frightening view of a He 111. But the throb of the Heinkels' unsychronized engines was a nightly event in 1940–1941 (Bundesarchiv 343/698/22).*

Bottom *British impression of the Heinkel 115 floatplane.*

models set going a 'billet room industry', the carving of wooden replicas of aircraft to pass away hours of boredom. Therein was created much of the lasting interest in military aircraft.

The professional modellers had been cold-shouldered, but officialdom was unable to ignore the increasing number of civilians interested in aircraft. Demands to be able to distinguish friend from foe soon resulted in the public production of material far superior to anything officially available. The latter, first assembled in 1938, consisted of poor quality tiny silhouettes and awful doctored pictures; all useless. The first worthwhile, praiseworthy attempt to improve the whole identification business came from a most unlikely quarter, *The Daily Mirror*, whose staff produced a small booklet entitled *Spot Them in the Air*. An immediate sell-out, it contained good silhouettes and details of British and German aircraft. Needless to say, it was unacceptable for official use and it was spring 1940 before its Government equivalent appeared — including silhouettes of secret British aircraft not due to appear for many months!

Enemy reconnaissance flights, meanwhile, had continued with Aufkl. Gr. 122, Munster-based, being active over the southern half of the North Sea. Dornier 18s late in November had shadowed the 3rd Destroyer Flotilla which was subsequently attacked by six aircraft of Staffel 2./Ku.Fl.Gr. 606 operating from Sylt. But no engagements took place — until 20 November.

At 09:40 an enemy aircraft was detected off Dover. Hurricanes of Manston's 79 Squadron took off to engage and this time *L1715* (Flying Officer Davies) and *L1718* (Flight Sergeant Brown) found a Do 17. Desperately it manoeuvred to escape before it was shot into the sea. Around midday, a high flier over the English Channel turned north-west and crossed into Sussex. Then it swung eastwards, clearly intent upon a photo-reconnaissance sortie before leaving the country along the Thames Estuary. Again 79 Squadron was ordered up, but patrolling between Canterbury and Margate saw nothing. The quarry was further north, where 74 Squadron was waiting to pounce.

At 12:45 three of the squadron's Spitfires, *K9932* (Flying Officer Measures), *K9864* (Pilot Officer Temple-Harris) and *K9870* (Sergeant Flinders) spotted a He 111 at 27,000 ft flying easterly at 270 mph fifteen miles from Southend. As they attacked, the bomber dived so steeply that parts of an engine cowling were torn away. Using cloud cover it passed over Ramsgate then Margate before flying north into Essex, close to Ipswich and out to sea near Felixstowe. Engine trouble and battle damage overcame the Heinkel when it was 100 miles out. Three of the crew were rescued from their dinghy and taken aboard the destroyer HMS *Gipsy*, a generous gesture soon ungratefully rewarded.

While the rescue was under way a Section of 56 Squadron had been vectored from Martlesham to a flying-boat twenty miles east of Felixstowe, possibly co-operating with the Heinkel. Squadron Leader Knowles (*L1984*) and Flying Officer Holden (*L1988*) fired at it, but the enemy fast found cloud refuge. Another raider which also escaped had, the same day, tried to bomb HMS *Boadicea* six miles east of Cromer. At the time He 111s of both KG26 and KG4 (each holding about 78 aircraft) were available for operations, KG4 moving detachments forward from Erfurt for the task.

By all reckoning it had been a memorable day, East Anglia's first certain enemy intruder having been effectively dealt with. Already, and unknown though, a far more serious threat had developed.

Chapter 4
Look out, there's a mine!

Almost all enemy air attacks so far had taken place in daylight. Not surprisingly, discovery of considerable activity low off the Essex coast and over the Firth of Forth during the evening of 18 November was a major event. Unsure of what was happening, Fighter Command ordered 'Red Alert' for coastal towns, but after thirty minutes the enemy had gone. The weather was unsuitable for the intended task. Previous information indicated that night operations were likely, and fighter pilots had practised night flying.

At 18:15 on 20 November night activity again occurred, off Southend, the North Foreland and over Harwich harbour. Enemy aircraft also operated by Dungeness, and off Dover whose AA guns twice fired at them. In every case the aircraft had flown below 3,000 ft making precise runs over recognized shipping lanes. Quickly it was established that all were He 115Bs of Staffel 3./Kustenfliegerstaffel 906, a coastal reconnaissance squadron. Something special was under way.

Daylight on 21 November 1939 brought a visitor from F./122 gathering information about weather conditions in the southern North Sea. This suggested more night sorties. Response to them was rapid. No 928 Squadron, Balloon Command, Bristol-based was, on 22 November, ordered to haul down its LZ Kite Balloons and prepare to move in two groups to RAF Felixstowe. It is unlikely that the enemy knew of this, but an early morning reconnoitring high-flying aircraft — possibly a Do 17P — was located over Suffolk. Although 56 Squadron was ordered to engage, the enemy aircraft escaped, presumably with many photographs.

Conditions right, He 115s came a third time, during the early evening of 22 November, from both Borkum and Sylt, arriving off the east coast when tidal conditions were as required. Included was 3./Ku. Fl. Gr. 106 making its debut, operating over the Thames Estuary. During an alert, watchers at Southend saw two objects fall into the water, and in the early hours of 23 November, with the tide low, a menacing, cylindrical object was observed. An urgent call resulted in the arrival of mine experts from HMS *Vernon* who, with enormous courage and primitive tools, disarmed the weapon. Later that day HMS *Gipsy*, rescuer of the crew of the He 111 shot down on the 20th, was sunk off Harwich by a similar mine.

Since the commencement of hostilities it had been suspected that the Germans might use mines triggered off by a ship's magnetic field. Such 'magnetic mines' were used by the Royal Navy in 1918. Sowing them was a problem and British development — and countermeasures to deal with them — had been neglected due, as usual, to insufficient defence expenditure. Cheap defence spending is money totally wasted.

Having discovered the danger of the seaplane forays, how could it be nullified? Sweeping the mines by employing large magnets, and other ideas, were worth exploring, but destruction of the minelayers, and prevention of their activity in vulnerable areas, were essential. Fighter and Coastal Commands increased patrols over estuaries and coastal shipping lanes in the hope that during the current moon period the Heinkels would be warned off. Night flying accident rates soared, and the chance of intercepting a low-flying aircraft at night was poor. The enemy was neither discouraged nor destroyed, so other defensive measures were necessary.

At Harwich, a Gun Defended Area (GDA) in the 1st AA Division, the arrival of a train load of personnel and an assortment of the strange vehicles of 928 Squadron was one answer. Rapid deployment was demanded with eight winches and six balloons being sited on either side of the River Stour. No 30 Group instructed that the six balloons on either shore must be raised on 25 November and five more would fly from barges anchored in the river. Within a few weeks the deployment consisted of 'A' Flight (North Side) with five shore sites and three waterborne, and 'B' Flight (HQ at Albert Hall House, Harwich) flying three balloons from land and five from fixed barges. Later provision was made for moving the waterborne balloons, all of which were the large Low Zone type highly susceptible to weather damage and very vulnerably sited at Harwich. Flying them at about 4,500 ft was, however, an immediate discouragement to mining of the harbour. To prevent minelaying by aircraft, No 952 Squadron moved to Sheerness taking fifty balloons which were deployed on barges to protect the Yantlet Dredged Channel.

So alarming was the mine threat that on 25 November Blenheims of 23 Squadron flew a dusk sweep hoping to catch minelayers heading for our shores. Success being nil, a dozen Blenheim 1fs of 25 and 601 Squadrons set off from Bircham Newton on 28 November to strafe the seaplanes at their lair. Again, little was achieved. For a while the minelayers retained the upper hand, proven on the 30th when the SS *Sheaf Crest* (2,730 tons) was mined at 51° 32' N/01° 26' E.

Little doubt remained that He 115s were mining shipping lanes along the east coast, and final proof arrived early on 6 December. Activity began late on 5 December, poor weather grounding fighters. One minelayer, of 3./Ku. Fl. Gr. 506, encountered icing and bad weather in which the crew of three lost their bearings. In error they crossed the Norfolk coast near Cromer and, as they turned seawards again at about 03:00, their Heinkel skimmed low over Sheringham's gas holder before smashing into the sea seventy yards from the tideline. Pilot error, panic or engine trouble had brought down the aircraft, which broke apart upon impact. At around 05:00 the body of Oberfeldwebel Emil Rödel, the observer, was washed ashore. The receding tide revealed an aircraft broken into two reasonably intact parts, although both engines had been wrenched out. Of the gunner and pilot no trace was found. Their collapsible rubber boat in its canvas cover remained in its stowage. Although a novel find, far more interesting were the aircraft's fuel tanks snugly protected by fire- and puncture-resistant rubberized material. Such covers had been under development since 1914, but British tests had met with little success, making this find of enough value to cause some of the material to be rushed to Farnborough for examination.

Throughout 6 December a technical investigation team combed the aircraft for useful items while personnel from 54 MU Cambridge gathered the pieces now strewn along a mile and a half of beach. Rapid analysis of the Heinkel's weapon racks revealed it able to carry an 8-ft long, 25-in diameter mine, a store of about 930 lb. Where that load had been dropped none could tell, but on 8 December the 751-ton *Corea* was sunk by a mine half a mile north of Cromer LV (light vessel). Two more ships became mine victims on 12 December, the 496-ton *Marwick Head* sunk half a mile south of Caister Buoy and *King Egbert* of 4,535 tons mined four miles south-west of Happisburgh Lightvessel.

Remnants of He 115 Werke Nr *2081*, *BB* the only fuselage lettering decipherable, reached 54 MU's Cambridge depot on 19 December, and were placed by the southern perimeter fence yet still visible for those who made the effort! Intelligence sources had already established that the aircraft belonged to Staffel 3./Ku. Fl. Gr. 506 normally Sylt-based but which of late had been receiving new equipment during Baltic training. The aircraft's full coding may have been *S4+BB*. Almost at once the remains were transferred by LEP Transport to Orford Ness for testing. To 54 MU throughout the war came similar remains of enemy aircraft shot down in the area. Formed as No 3 Salvage Centre, the unit had moved to a tiny site by Barnwell Bridge, Cambridge, on 23 September before settling on 10 November at its wartime home opposite the Cambridge Borough Cemetery where those show-piece pre-war air raid shelters were now all flooded.

If the He 115 can carry mines, the Navy enquired, what about the He 111? Investigation of the example brought down at Haddington, east of Dalkeith, on 28 October showed it to have four vertical bomb stowage cells on either side of a fuselage walkway, each able to hold a 550 lb bomb. The reconnaissance variant had instead four vertical tanks on the starboard side with cameras occupying the rest of the bomb bay. Mines could be carried externally only.

The usefulness of mining operations as cover for covert operations was not lost to either side. Late on 12 December two Blenheims of 29 Squadron hurriedly left Debden to investigate the activity around a seaplane reported to have alighted off Frinton. One was to illuminate the scene with a flare for the other to attack, but searchlights lit it in error. The weather was very poor so both Blenheims abandoned the operation. Sergeant Bloor (*L6741*) returned safely to Debden, whereas wherever Flight Sergeant Packer took *L6740* bad weather prevented a landing. The aircraft finally crashed in Great Chesterford Park, Packer being killed. His gunner, Leading Aircraftsman Jones, was found many hours later seriously injured. Their squadron was currently using Mildenhall and Martlesham as advanced bases.

There was no doubt that mining was increasing so on 12 December Bomber Command initiated 'security patrols' designed to halt He 115s operating in darkness out of Borkum and Sylt. Again, their ineffectiveness was soon evident for during the evening of 15 December at least fourteen mining aircraft operated.

If the enemy was prepared to mine indiscriminately, then surely bombing of any ships was likely. Indeed, a KG30 Ju 88 had attempted to bomb a merchant

Dornier Do 17P-1 4U+DL *of Aufklärungsgruppe (Reconnaissance Group) 123. Aircraft of this type certainly reconnoitred East Anglia during the first year of the war* (Bundesarchiv 340/159/14).

ship off Cromer on 6 December. Warships were fair game, whereas attacks upon merchant ships, fishing boats and particularly lightships, caused immediate — if illogical — public outrage. One official claimed that such practices were 'in keeping with German pedigree'. Whether the prevention of fishing differed from Britain's announced food blockade of Germany is questionable. One might reasonably argue that sustenance of civilians producing weapons made merchant shipping a legitimate target. Irrespective of the moral viewpoint, the Luftwaffe's anti-shipping campaign was very clearly under way in a few days, and continued off East Anglia into 1943. On 17 December a morning attack using 50 kg HE bombs was made upon a small motor boat and three trawlers, possibly in the belief that they were naval vessels. Other ships were machine-gunned, their crews sustaining casualties. He 115s, He 111s, Ju 88s and, less frequently, Do 18s were used for such operations.

In addition to its December anti-shipping campaign, the Luftwaffe made a few more exploratory flights over Britain. Among them was reputedly a sortie on 10 December by a Do 17 along the course of the River Ouse to Ely, although a dozen fighters failed to find the raider. On 27 December another Do 17 reconnoitred the Yarmouth area, cruising at 20,000 ft. With its destruction feasible, fighters were again despatched but missed their quarry through confused ground control.

During January 1940 anti-shipping operations continued, three enemy aircraft seeking targets off Norfolk on the 2nd. Atrociously cold weather made life difficult for all, but fighter pilots tried to protect coastal shipping, their patrols extended fifteen miles seaward and were usually made by flights of three aircraft. On both 6 and 7 January reconnaissance flights were flown by F./122 from Munster, and next day 504 Squadron moved to Martlesham, relieving 17 Squadron. On the 9th 'A' Flight of 610 Squadron, Wittering-based, moved from detachment at Bircham Newton where 213 Squadron was still operational, and two sections of 610 Squadron increased Martlesham's force. A section of 23 Squadron was constantly based at Digby for night operations against minelayers.

Positioning fighters near the coast had become essential, and its value was obvious on 9 January. Between 09:30 and 12:00, He 111s of II/KG26 from Schleswig operated between Lowestoft and Aberdeen and assaulted ten British and four Danish ships. One Heinkel strafed the SS *Delphinus* before delivering two bombing attacks, and the SS *Oakgrove* (1,985 tons) was sunk about fifteen miles south-east of Cromer Knoll LV. SS *Reculver*, a 683-ton Trinity House tender, was three times strafed off Yarmouth and, badly holed, limped into port. Ten miles away the SS *Upminster* (1,013 tons), a coaster outward-bound from London, was bombed and strafed by two He 111s. It foundered at 53° 03'N/01° 29'E with the loss of its crew.

Similar attacks came on 11 January off the north-east coast before the day's main event unfolded. At 08:15 Spitfires of 'A' Flight, 66 Squadron, and flown by Sergeant Cameron (*N3029*) and Sergeant Stone (*N3036*), were patrolling twenty miles east of Cromer when they spotted a He 111 circling a zig-zagging cargo ship. As soon as the bomber crew saw the Spitfires they jettisoned their bombs and fled, pursued by 66 Squadron. All three Spitfires fired, and two were hit by the Heinkel's gunfire. Short of fuel, Sergeant Stone forced-landed near Happisburgh. The bomber made off flying very close to the water, its port propeller turning slowly. With very low fuel states the other two Spitfires were nursed home. Next morning a Danish newspaper informed interested parties that a battle-scarred Heinkel of KG26 had crash-landed at Skaerbaek, South Jutland, and was promptly set on fire by its crew.

Throughout January anti-shipping operations continued. At 16:20 on 13 January three aircraft set about seventeen ships and three destroyers escorting them seven miles off Aldeburgh, the bursting of eleven bombs being clearly heard in the town. At midnight on 21 January a Staffel of KG30's Ju 88s operating east of the Thames Estuary attacked nine ships while further north more of KG30 and II/KG26 were busy. Over 24 hours they attemped to sink 25 vessels. Gradually, the weather became extremely cold, so much snow having fallen that by the 28th all eastern fighter aerodromes — except North Coates and Martlesham — were closed, preventing assistance being given to a ship attacked north-east of Cromer that day.

The enemy now took full advantage of the British predicament, mounting a large anti-shipping operation. On 30 January seventeen He 111s of II/KG26 roamed between Texel — 65 miles east of Cromer—and thence to the Shetlands, attacking thirty ships, two of them light vessels. From one, *East Dugeon*, there was only one survivor. Once ashore he recalled that initially the crew was not unduly alarmed, having survived previous air attacks. This time nine bombs were aimed at the lightship, and the crew took to their small boat. Nobody came to their rescue and it was early next day when, having endured intense cold, their lifeboat reached land. By then only two men had strength to row, and at a critical moment a wave capsized the boat, hurling all its exhausted occupants into the raging sea. Only John James Richard Sanders of Northgate Street, Yarmouth, survived.

Tragedy also overtook Hall Brothers' 4,300-ton SS *Royal Crown* sailing to the USA via Dover when it was bombed thirteen miles off Southwold. One of the three HEs aimed at the ship scored a direct hit amidships, setting the vessel ablaze. Four men died in the attack, others having lucky escapes when the He 111 returned to machine-gun the crew. A lifeboat was launched and, carrying nineteen survivors, eventually drifted ashore. Soaked and intensely cold, the crew broke into an unoccupied bungalow for rest and warmth before announcing themselves.

At 12:30 another 4,000-tonner was bombed off Lowestoft. A further vessel was assaulted near Hammonds Knoll and 25 miles east of Cromer a Norwegian oil tanker was discovered by 23 Squadron burning and sinking. A British destroyer rescued the crew.

Analysis of reported enemy air activity off the East Coast towns between 3 September 1939 and 31 January 1940 revealed the following number of approaches to these points:

	9.39	10.39	11.39	12.39	1.40
Over the Wash	—	—	—	1	—
Cromer	1	9	3	1	6
Sheringham	1	—	—	2	—
Yarmouth	1	1	3	5	4
Lowestoft	—	3	2	3	1
Southwold	—	2	2	5	3
Aldeburgh	—	—	2	3	3
Orford Ness	1	3	4	2	—
Felixstowe	1	1	8	7	5
Harwich	—	—	1	4	4
Walton-on-the-Naze	—	1	6	4	2
Clacton	1	1	13	4	—
Thames Estuary	—	1	2	6	2

Despite wintry conditions, the Luftwaffe vigorously pursued its anti-shipping campaign, strafing the *Voreda* on 1 February. Two days later two of 24 Heinkels operating over the North Sea were seen near Southwold at 11:09, and another ventured close to Lowestoft. The day brought the first really concentrated assault on a convoy, sixteen of the vessels being attacked including five of neutral nations. One ship was sunk, one abandoned and five damaged. Fighters brought into action claimed to have damaged three KG26 attackers.

Both Gruppen of KG26 had 48 aircraft assigned to them, their bases being: Gruppe I, Lübeck; Gruppe II, Schwerin. KG30 consisted only of Gruppe I armed with 39 Ju 88s and based near Hamburg. All used Westerland, Sylt, as an advanced operating base, and were supported by Bomber Recce Group 122, Munster. Its aircraft set out before the bombers, radioing to shore or airborne aircraft details of shipping positions, enabling KG26/30 to tackle them.

Shipping raids were attempted on most days in the first half of February 1940, mainly north of East Anglia. Tactics laid down for cloud-cover shipping strikes, usually by flights of up to three aircraft dropping 50 kg and 250 kg HEs, were now clearly exposed. Upon sighting the quarry one aircraft flew low, assessing the ship's defences. Then came shallow-dive attacks delivered always stern to bow with a level-out as low as fifty feet for bombing, usually followed by strafing. Generally very few HEs would be dropped.

The remainder of February witnessed fewer forays, but included nine night sorties on the 22nd/23rd flown between the Thames and Newcastle. Only one ship was attacked. Damage was sustained by an Italian vessel on the 27th when two British ships were also bombed and a couple of He 111s shot down at sea. Sailing from Dover to Hartlepool on 29 February, the Genoa-registered *Maria Rosa* was mined fourteen miles north-east of Cross Light. Within moments the ship was burning, and eleven of the 39 crew were killed in the incident. Other ships mined off East Anglia that month were the *British Triumph* (8,501 tons, at 53° 06'N/01° 25'E on the 13th), *Clan Morrisson* (5,936 tons, at 53° 07'N/01° 22'E on the 14th) and *Jevington Court* (4,544 tons, 53° 08'N/01° 22'E on the 24th). Fighter protection was being given to light vessels by 29 Squadron's Blenheims.

Firmer airfield surfaces for fighters were now allowing ready movement to forward bases. Generally, 19 and 66 Squadrons used Horsham, 213, 222 and 610 Wittering or Bircham Newton. Martlesham remained Debden's forward base, and Digby's squadrons took care of shipping passing north from the Wash.

Intensive anti-shipping operations evolved over the first seven days of March. On the 1st, eight attacks resulted in a sinking, and two more next day. On the 6th, six ships and two lightships were raided by ten He 111s operating between Yarmouth and Aberdeen. As darkness closed in, trawlers in particular were selected for bombing and strafing, eleven more being subjected to similar attention at dusk next day. Mines claimed the *Chevy Chase* (2,719 tons, at 53° 18'N/01° 13'E on the 9th) and *Gardenia* (3,745 tons, at 53° 04'N/01° 33'E on the 12th).

Two interesting new developments were now taking place. Firstly, there was a very considerable increase in training by German bomber groups, a new departure being much night flying by KG4. Its significance was not yet possible to assess. Secondly, a new fighter, the Boulton Paul Defiant, East Anglian-born, began its operational career when 264 Squadron (which had been working up at Martlesham) placed its 'A' Flight at Wittering on 22 March 1940. The same day a determined but unsuccessful attempt was made to sink the Cromer Knoll LV. The Defiants moved to Bircham Newton in the belief that they could be very useful defending shipping, but the aircraft was not ready for operations and on the 27th all returned to Martlesham. Other equipment changes concerned 229 Squadron whose Hurricanes became operational on 26 March, and 222 Squadron now using Spitfires.

Enemy anti-shipping activity was tailing off as the Scandinavian adventure took precedence. Nevertheless, 213 and 222 Squadrons nearly caught a raider off Skegness on 29 March, and when two He 115s approached a convoy on 2 April 504 Squadron shot one into the sea.

Although the Norwegian Campaign required much of the enemy's strength, mine-laying continued, there being sixteen aircraft thus engaged on 22 April, four of them operating two miles off Felixstowe within the front North Foreland-Great Yarmouth.

Soon after dawn on 29 April radio signals were intercepted from a Zenit flight (weather reconnaissance) by F. /122 flying from Munster via Terschelling to the Thames Estuary. Repeatedly the aircraft (call sign '5IF') radioed details of conditions from positions it had passed — 06:45, 65 miles east of Lowestoft; 07:20, eight miles west of Lowestoft; 07:30, fifteen miles south of King's Lynn, and eventually from the Farne Islands. It had pioneered a route to be frequently followed by such flights in 1940.

Night mining continued. If public doubt remained that the enemy frequently ventured close to our shores, proof was spectacularly afforded late on 30 April, in the first major air raid incident on land during the war.

Fourteen tracks had been discovered over the Thames Estuary and more off the Tyne and Humber mouths. Then, soon after 23:00 could be heard the sound of a very low-flying aircraft heading from the sea towards Clacton where no air raid warning had been sounded. There seems little doubt that the crew had become disorientated and, not realizing they were very low close to land, nearly crashed into the cliffs at Marine Parade East, hit a chimney stack on a house, bounced, then reduced another house to a pile of rubble. The next two houses were seriously damaged as the Heinkel 111 ended its sortie at 23:08 on a plot of clear land on the west side of Victoria Road, at its junction with Skelmersdale Road and Albert Gardens. Moments later one of the two 1,500 lb charge alloy case mines aboard exploded, producing a crater 25 ft across and five feet deep. Although no property caught fire, part of the aircraft was burnt, luckily before there was much leakage of coal gas. Nothing like this had happened before. Not only did it rock Clacton, it disturbed the whole of Britain whose newspapers carried dramatic photographs and, unusually, named the site. Experts flocked in from far to view the effects of this huge blast.

It had occurred in a smart residential area of mostly two-storey semi-detached houses, 582 properties being variously harmed. Of 56 seriously damaged, nine were flattened and a further fourteen suffered major structural damage. Even half a mile away the blast was fierce enough to shatter five plate glass windows. Much brickwork had been thrown a long way, and an uprooted tree was hurled on to a roof. Most amazing of all was the very low loss of life, even bearing in mind that many people had left the coastal town. Out of six fatalities, four were Germans who were buried with full military honours. Of 156 people injured, 34 needed hospital treatment, 91 received treatment at first aid posts and 29 casualties were helped by a mobile first aid unit.

An engine from the aircraft, reasonably intact, lodged itself by the bay window of a bungalow, and nearby was the dark green/light blue rear fuselage which, by its letters *1T+EL* (*E* in yellow), confirmed that a new Geschwader was mining. Radio intelligence heard three aircraft calling up for landing at Marx — and no reply to the airfield's call to another. It was the Clacton machine, and it was of 3./KG28.

With so much debris and shattered glass; with ARP, first aid and hospital services fully stretched; it was little wonder that for some time there was no realization that a second mine lay unexploded in the wreckage. At 13:00 on 1 May Service personnel ordered civilians, many of whom were staying with their damaged houses, to evacuate the area immediately. Also forced to leave were rescue workers scouring the wreckage for any people possibly buried. Soon after 14:00 the magnetic mine was taken away, having been rendered safe very quickly.

The crash of the Heinkel was not the only incident of the night. At 00:16 a German aircraft was plotted near Mistley, following the Stour towards the sea. AA guns at Landguard Point fired without evidence of success, but a burning aircraft was reported soon after to have crashed in the sea off Walton-on-the-Naze.

More mining took place in May, the intense propaganda 'scoop' provided by the Clacton explosion having no effect upon the campaign. Media and public reaction in wartime mattered little. On 3/4 May KG28 operated another four aircraft from Marx, an additional thirteen aircraft in all placing mines in the North Sea and off Holland. Reconnaissance and Zenit flights were stepped up, one briefly crossing Norfolk's shore on 4 May. The same region was violated again on 7 May by two late afternoon flights, reconnaissance sorties which penetrated to Norwich and King's Lynn. Entry to Suffolk was also made. On the 9th, an aircraft, call sign HDC, flew a late afternoon coastal reconnaissance including an incursion to Norwich. Such flights involved Do 17s of KG76 as well as those of (F)/122, the three Gruppen of the former being at standby for possible attacks on south and south-east England.

By 16 May all the Luftwaffe's long-range bomber groups had reached the western front to first subdue the Dutch and then consolidate for the bombing to come. Each of the three Staffeln of each Gruppe had been ordered first to provide formations of twelve aircraft for raids on Holland. Then, on 19 May, Harwich guns fired at an emeny aircraft leaving East Anglia at night. How much longer before the countryside echoed to the sound of Heinkels and reverberated to the bombs of the Luftwaffe?

It is hard to imagine that a minelayer He 111 crashed here in Clacton in April 1940; a plaque on the wooden seat commemorates the event, though.

Chapter 5
Midsummer nights' madness

East Anglia's fighter force was quickly re-aligned to meet likely challenges arising from the Blitzkrieg, 222 Squadron's Spitfires moving to Digby on 10 May, and Blenheims commencing defensive coastal night sorties on the 11th. No 23 Squadron guarded Norfolk's shores while No 29 Squadron patrolled between Lowestoft and the Blackwater Estuary. Daybreak on 15 May brought two high-flying Do 17Zs of KG76 to survey Norfolk, adding urgency to the move of 66 Squadron which arrived at Horsham St Faith the next day.

News of Rotterdam's sacking, of refugees being machine-gunned, and the screaming of Stukas with which news broadcasts were laced, brought the uppermost thought of 'Who next?' Returning, dishevelled remnants of the BEF did nothing to increase confidence. Surprisingly, nobody called for pre-war pacifists and disarmers to be forced to view these awful scenes, the fruits of their labours. As the torn, weaponless, BEF struggled home, the Luftwaffe rumbled on to French airfields, preparing Britain's decimation. A brutal period in our history was about to begin.

East Anglia's first bombs were five HEs which fell, at 00:32, on 22 May into the sea between Landguard Point and Felixstowe Pier. A further eight exploded an hour later near the Cork lightship.

The first bomb to fall on East Anglian soil was a solitary HE which burst harmlessly at 01:55 in the south-east corner of a field west of Butley Church, close to Bentwaters airfield. Its crater was professionally pronounced to be three feet deep and thirteen feet in diameter. Such measurements — made whenever possible — gave clues to sizes and types of weapons, and suggested the first bomb to be a 50 kg HE, probably dropped by a He 111. Blast from two others, which fell at 05:16 in the sea off Felixstowe, smashed six windows of houses in Manor Terrace.

Early on 25 May German-based Heinkel 111s, probably of KG27, then based at Stuttgart/Grosenheim, Echterndingen and Bonn, attempted to bomb partially lit West Raynham airfield. Eighteen HEs fell at 00:35 in open ground near the aerodrome, causing no damage. Another bomb exploded harmlessly near Harleston. Such events — often distant, mysterious, unwelcome thuds, encouraged the obvious questions of 'why?', 'where?', 'who?' and 'where next?' The answer, this time, was in a field at Willow Farm, Langley, Loddon, where, at 01:20, two HEs fell killing a cow and injuring a pony, the first animals to so suffer in East Anglia. Another bomb fell at Aylsham, and one of seven at Burgh St

Peter exploded in a tree twenty feet above ground level, the blast damaging two bungalows. Two more dropped at Raveningham, the spread suggesting targets that the raiders were unable to locate. At 01:45, the first Essex bombing, at Wickford near Southend, resulted in a bungalow and fourteen other houses being damaged by a 50 kg HE.

The next, small scale raids, came on 2 June. At 02:00 an HE at Strumpshaw, seven miles east of Norwich, caused the first serious injury due to bombing in East Anglia. A concerted attack upon RAF Mildenhall was also attempted that night. The Luftwaffe knew plenty about that bomber station for, in 1937, its senior officers had been entertained there. Now their colleagues were displaying their gratitude by hurling 23 50 kg HEs at the aerodrome. No damage was caused — this time.

The Fifth of June was a hot, beautiful day. There were many like that in 1940. So extensive was the air activity over France that Fighter Command's plotting staff in their stuffy, underground operations room could barely cope. Meanwhile, a mile and a half off Landguard Point, the *Sweep II*, a sludge vessel of 145 tons, was mined — a reminder that minelayers were probably still busy. As dusk fell it became certain that Britain was in for a hard night, for radar and radio stations were detecting abnormal enemy activity. The Germans were coming, in strength and in anger, determined to extend their influence into the night sky between the Orkneys and the Isle of Wight. Over six hours, 134 individual sorties were plotted, ports and airfields emerging clearly as targets. The big attack was at last under way.

He 111s were mainly being used, one of which, Raid X37, crossed the Norfolk coast at 00:26, dropped fifteen HEs near Swanton Morley airfield killing two horses, then flew off, lights on to confuse the defences. Bombs also fell close to Bircham Newton, and another near Horsham St Faith aerodrome. An HE fell at the Buxton/Spixworth road junction at 00:35 and another Norfolk incident occurred at North Tuddenham where, at 01:22, eight more HEs were dropped. Several parachute flares released over Stoke Holy Cross drifted over Norwich, possibly the first released over Britain, and gave the inhabitants a preview of a typical overture to forthcoming raids.

The deepest penetration of East Anglia resulting in bombing was to Duxford, Cambridgeshire. Nearby, a shower of incendiaries, the first to fall in England, was unloaded at 00:11 on to a barley field at New Farm, Newton, and burst with a brilliant glow visible for many miles. Piles of ash, plenty of smoke and a distinctive smell long lingered among any experiencing such events. The RAF reckoned that between sixty and 100 small cylindrical bombs had fallen, while the police count suggested 150-200 and ARP officials 100. Soon after dawn, by which time the dew had turned the ash into something resembling the outpouring from a volcano, plenty of officials from London invaded the farm to view the new arrivals. All apparently agreed that one load of incendiaries had spread over 500 sq yd.

Precise details will ever remain uncertain in respect of many incidents. Without holes to count, the extent of weapon drop was often underestimated and types uncertain. Luftwaffe units kept monthly operations summaries, but few survived the war. Corroboration or correction of accepted figures is sometimes possible—just.

Memory of the events is a very different matter, many remaining unforgettable. Mine, of the first incendiaries, is of an intense bluish-white glare in the south-western sky which died away as suddenly as it arose — and to the unmistakable sound of a hurrying Heinkel. That eerie glow, lasting a few moments, was caused by a shoal of 1 kg thermite bombs — designed to produce rapid heat and showers of fragments. This basic weapon used thoughout the war, later with modifications, comprised a 1.96-in diameter cylinder 8.3 in long attached to a 4.75-in-long tail giving limited stability and guidance. Very small, these bombs had curious ballistics which caused them, when released from a container, to spread over a wide area — as was the intention. Weapon casing was of a flammable magnesium alloy with the detonator at the forward end. Around its compartment were small holes covered by insulating tape until arming took place immediately prior to dropping. Bombs often failed to strike the ground in the manner needed to explode the detonator, which was intended to clout a primer and ignite the filling. Many live incendiaries would usually be found in a drop zone. Mercifully, they did not easily explode when souvenir hunters gathered them. A common, harmless activity was the collection of tail units from ignited bombs. Little wonder the authorities rarely knew how many incendiaries fell in any raid. Strangely, they rarely related the numbers to the types of containers found or likely to have been used.

Incendiaries were normally aluminium in colour, sometimes sprayed yellow-green overall. The Germans knew the basic type as the B1 (ie, Brandbombe ['fire-bomb'] 1kg), the B1 E having an 'Elektron' nose. For early operations, 1 kg incendiaries were carried in BSK 36 containers designated 'Container Type A' by the British. Roughly cylindrical, 3 ft 7 in long and of 8-in diameter, usually aluminium in colour, they contained up to 36 incendiaries and were used exclusively for 'Brandbomben'. No containers were located after the Newton drop. Incendiaries fell at 03:50 the same night around Iredale Approved School, Stifford, two miles north-west of Tilbury, Essex. These were the first two fire raids to be released on England, but previous drops had occurred in Scotland.

During 6/7 June, 170 night intrusions were made into England between Yorkshire and Hampshire, and a new problem — the unexploded HE bomb—came to East Anglia. Six raids penetrated at around 15,000 ft between 21:30 and 01:00. After flying around Yarmouth, Raid 73 attempted to bomb Feltwell and instead bombed the airfield's Q-Site with eight HEs and incendiaries. A crater 45 ft across and 6 ft deep was the largest yet produced in the area. Raid X12 crossed the coast and flew over Pulham, north of Feltwell and East Dereham before, in attempting to bomb Marham, it dropped five HEs on Church Farm, Foulden, then left the country over Cromer. A third Raid, El, passed south of Norwich and via Bury, Newmarket and Ely to arrive over Upwood where Blenheims were night flying and the flare path was lit. Fifteen 50 kg HEs landed on open ground, but one airman was killed and two injured. The warning was sounded twenty minutes later, after an incorrect assessment of enemy intentions. Another five bombs (one UX) were dropped near Mildenhall, and both Depwade RD and Loddon RD each collected three UXHEs. In towns, UXBs, although producing considerable problems, were more easily discovered than in open country. There, locating them was very difficult. Bombs in fields can never naturally become harmless, and indeed become more unstable as years pass. They must *never* be tampered with if found.

Almost all the HEs dropped had been of 50 kg calibre, but late on 6 June an enemy aircraft which came in over Lowestoft dropped four HEs, including possibly the first 250 kg HE, and probably the heaviest yet to fall, in the lane to Patrick's Farm, Bedfield, Suffolk. Another fell nearby, at Monk Soham and was exploded by a bomb disposal team two days later.

On 7/8 June, Heinkels attempted more airfield attacks. Raid X10 mistook the bombing range west of Honington for the airfield, plastering it with ten HEs, while Raid X15 which passed in over Wells at 23:35 flew via Holkam to Bircham Newton whose Q-Site and nearby Searchlight Site 21321 received seven HEs before the bomber dropped five bombs in fields north-east of Rudham then left over Cromer at 23:55. In a circuit beginning off Sheringham at 00:05 a Heinkel headed for Wittering via Digby then doubled back to drop eight HEs near Cottesmore. After circling it then ran up on Peterborough and placed five HEs in Bridge Street and Bishop's Road, breaking many windows and producing slight structural damage, after which it again circled Wittering before leaving the country over Yarmouth.

Shortly after dusk a fog belt descended along the coast between Spurn Head and Essex and gradually drifted inland, becoming as much as six miles wide. It was into these conditions that there strayed a Heinkel He 115 (probably a B-1). FF Searchlight Company, FF22 detachment, was ordered to attempt to illuminate the aircraft as it tried to find a way out towards the south-west. Moments after switching on, the intruder, at only 300 ft, was brilliantly lit and, completely dazzled, the pilot crashed the floatplane at 23:31 in the grounds of The Old Rectory, Eyke, three miles from Woodbridge. For half an hour it burnt, only an engine then remaining intact. To the east was a crater twenty feet wide and four feet deep caused, presumably, by a 925 kg LMB III mine, the parachute of which was resting on some nearby bushes. Two of the crew had been killed, but the very tall third member, a Leutnant, seriously injured and still wearing his parachute harness, was found suspended from a tree. He courageously struggled with his captors but was to die in East Suffolk and Ipswich Hospital on Sunday, 9 June 1940.

Collation of a complete list of enemy intrusions over East Anglia is now impossible, but it is certain that daylight reconnaissance flights were being made, several occurring on 8 June. Next night, 41 HEs were accounted for in Cambridgeshire's part of Newmarket RD. On 10/11 June two night reconnaissance flights crossed East Anglia, five HEs falling in Hartismere RD before poor weather conditions closed in. When operations were resumed on 18/19 June they resulted in events ever to remember.

'A bomber's moon', 'twas called, and it shone brilliantly this night from a cloudless sky baring the virgin landscape for any high-flying passing rapist. Such wartime nights contained a terribly unnerving sense of defencelessness only slightly lessened by the blackout. In winter they seemed to intensify the incredible cold immediately preceding dawn. In June the warmth of the summer sun lingered through the night, encouraging memories of carefree hours spent roaming cowslip meadows and past happy days by the sea.

Dreams were alarmingly shattered for many shortly before 23:00 when the first Heinkels of KG 4, controlled by Schiphol, and KG27 from the Lille region, penetrated the 12 Group area. By 03:00, when activity ceased, 139 flights had been tracked over Britain making the night's activity the most intensive yet. Despatched were sixteen He 111s of I/KG27, twelve of II/KG27, twelve of

III/KG27 and ten of II/KG4 to attack various places in south and east England, particularly airfields and the LNER network. Another 21 He 111s of I and III/KG4 were sent to destroy oil tanks at Thameshaven, so that 71 aircraft set out for England.

Reasonable warning and a full moon, ideal for night fighter operations, were about to be put to good use. Warned of the approaching Heinkels, Blenheims of 29 Squadron, Debden, were ordered to intercept. Squadron Leader McLean took off at 22:50, and from Duxford a 19 Squadron Spitfire (*N3198*) flown by Flight Sergeant Steere, hurried off at 23:15. Sergeant Steere's squadron had returned from Hornchurch and 11 Group on 5 June. Three nights later, Flying Officer Petra and Pilot Officer Haynes tried a night interception sortie, but without the slightest success on that dark night. Successful single-seater fighter night interceptions were later achieved, although two motors and four eyes — not to mention ample radar guidance — proved preferable. Nevertheless, 19 Squadron was, in the moonlight, about to prove that the premier Spitfire squadron was a force to be reckoned with. Meanwhile, Wittering's 23 Squadron Blenheims were also getting airborne. By then the He 111s, including some from Merville where only 29 days previously Debden's Hurricanes had been briefly placed, were invading East Anglia.

Intent upon destroying aerodromes, they were entering over Clacton and Wells-next-Sea, making use for navigation purposes of coastal features. The leader passed over Clacton at precisely 23:00 and the ninth aircraft at 23:15, all flying high. Suddenly the last one was played upon by searchlight beams and part of its load was released. Three HEs exploded damaging houses in King's Cliff Avenue, Medina Road and Salisbury Road, Holland-on-Sea. Too late the raid warning now sounded. Chelmsford's sirens, too, wailed at 23:18.

The leading bombers were already well inland and, just after 23:00, news was flashed to Bury St Edmunds ARP Centre that bombs had fallen at Rougham Rectory and by its churchyard. A likely explanation for an 'unprovoked attack on a Suffolk village' was that the Heinkel's crew had discovered a 29 Squadron Blenheim (*L1376*) close at hand. Squadron Leader McLean and his gunner, Pilot Officer Watson, later reported that they had attempted to intercept three bombers east of Bury. All were too fast for the rudimentary Blenheim fighter upon which one Heinkel's crew had fired.

Eight other He 111s used Sheringham as their entry point. Sergeant Close in Blenheim *YP:S* of 23 Squadron located Raid 75 held in the beams of Searchlight Company 220 and at once attacked. The Heinkel's gunners returned the fire and the burning Blenheim crashed at Terrington St Clement. Flight Lieutenant Duke-Woolley, with AC Bell as his gunner, had left Wittering at 22:38 in Blenheim *YP:L*; they were immediately ordered to the scene of Close's engagement. Very soon they located a He 111 of 4./KG4, which at 00:15 was brought down into shallow water in Blakeney Creek. Coastguards captured the crew, two officers, a Sergeant and an Airman, one of whom was wounded.

News of the Rougham bombing was just being given to Major A. G. Bailey-Hawkes, Deputy Sub-Controller, Newmarket ARP, in Graham House at 23:07, when suddenly its doors and windows were violently shaken. More HEs had fallen, on Side Hill immediately east of Newmarket.

By midnight a number of raiders, flying mainly at 15,000 ft and above, had penetrated to the Wellington bomber bases, the nineteen 50 kg HEs intended for

Stradishall falling around Hargrave, six miles south-west of Bury. There, the Germans shattered a house, scarred farmland, scored a hit at the side of the Rectory wherein the vicar's daughter was injured by flying glass, and removed the porch from the village church. Ten minutes later three more HEs fell on Lodge Farm, Rede, five miles north-east of Stradishall. Simultaneously, eighteen HEs were dropped in Fersfield Street, Bressingham, damaging a cottage.

Marham, too, had come under attack, one of the Sheringham raiders inbound dropping fourteen bombs near King's Lynn. A further thirteen (six UXHEs) were dropped at Narborough by Raid 87X. Six exploded in Docking RD, eighteen in Depwade RD. By midnight enemy activity had become audible over much of East Anglia, and particularly Suffolk. The bombing had been the most intensive yet in Britain. Another eight HEs exploded at Culford, four miles north-west of Bury, as the attackers hopelessly tried to neutralize Mildenhall. But six fighter squadrons, Nos 19, 23, 29, 66, 74 and 604, were now searching for the foe in the dangerous moonlight. Among them were five of Duxford's Spitfires ordered up at 00:20 and flown on individualistic sorties by Flying Officer Petra, Flight Lieutenant Clouston, Flying Officer Bell and Flying Officer Lawson in an attempt to intercept the Mildenhall raid. Some of KG4's crews had been ordered to attack railway installations, and the result of that was the first serious loss of life in the bombing campaign upon Britain.

A 'Red' warning at 23:30 had encouraged some Cambridge dwellers to leave their beds, but the general belief was that 'it would never happen to anywhere as lovely as Cambridge', a town 'too beautiful' to be bombed. Surely, the enemy would not risk retaliation against Heidelberg, it was argued. Perhaps the attack upon Cambridge was unintentional, maybe fighter activity provoked it? More likely, the huge Mill Road Bridge area's railway complex was clearly visible in the moonlight, and an irresistible target. The truth may never be known, but the outcome remains indelible.

Moments before midnight came the strange sound of the unsynchronized revving of a Heinkel's engines. Accompanying a shallow dive there was a piercing unmistakable whistle. Bombs were falling, hurtling overhead — and very low. Before I could come to terms with such a frightening reality, two colossal detonations occurred. There was a rush of air, a swinging lamp shade and the shuddering of a home whose windows violently rattled and whose shutters were severely shaken. Amid the alarm was the amazing sight of the swinging salted carcase of the pig which Dad had acquired to ensure that Hitler could not starve us during any invasion attempt. What we had so long awaited had come, and it was nothing quite like I had imagined. Mum said that it was 'close'. She avoided saying what we were all really thinking...one or two moments sooner and... But surely more bombs would follow? A Merlin-engined fighter — and certainly not a Spitfire — raced overhead, so maybe we were safe now.

The road where we lived was already packed with people being shepherded by an excited ARP warden who was furiously blowing his whistle and, for good measure, swinging his rattle, thus both warning us of a possible onslaught and prejudging a gas attack! Furthermore, he unleashed a thundering impact upon our front door which frightened us all. Then, through the letter box, he yelled insistence that we retreat to the safety of the Brunswick School's shelters.

Where homes once stood, a jumbled array marks the spot of destruction in Vicarage Terrace (Cambridgeshire Collection).

I promptly pointed out that an 'expert' had pronounced our house 'safe', but the warden's demands were impossible to resist. In any case, a chance to glimpse the action outside was an attraction too tempting to miss, and we quickly set off from our precious home — after Dad had duly checked the door and window catches. Mum, however, already had the kettle in action for the inevitable cup of tea, a splendid answer to the Luftwaffe. 'There's no time for that,' said the warden. As Dad set off for the shelter he looked like a miniature holidaymaker because he was carrying precious documents (and money?) in a small, leather attaché case. Mum was almost certainly praying as we hurried across the caretaker's estate while cousin Cecil, awaiting his call by the RAF, was encouragingly forecasting imminent and terrible disasters. That was making him tremendously popular among others who had left their beds with alacrity, for once eager to heed the call of the sirens. War had become real, a doorstep event, yet in our brief journey all I noticed was a distant bright glow to the south.

Barely were we underground when Mr Clover, the Chief Warden, made a prestigious appearance to enquire of our discomfort before calmly issuing an unofficial communiqué that sounded as totally uninformative as a real one: 'Bombs have fallen. There have been casualties. I am not permitted to tell you any more.'

'Yes, Mrs Bowyer, there have been serious casualties.'

'Where did they drop?', called someone.

'I am not permitted to say, yet,' said Mr Clover as other ARP men nodded in agreement. Just then an ordinary person rushed into our concrete hideaway shouting, 'They've got Vicarage Terrace'.

'Where's Vicarage Terrace?', I called — only to be met by a hail of sharp glances from appalled faces, all of which had instantly detected that already I was planning an early sortie to view the scene. Such morbidity no youth must be permitted to contemplate. 'Wait until you are 21' (and thereby have served three years in the Services), their faces all were stating, while above ground the action by some marginally older than I was intense.

Rescue services were frantically active at a row of small, terraced houses smashed in the glow of cruel moonbeams. 'He saw lights reflected off St Matthew's Church windows', went the tale, 'and thought it was a signal.' Unlikely, but viciously he had destroyed homes Victorian, typical of hundreds of thousands soon to be brutally broken—and not only in Britain.

Recently an interesting aspect of the incident has revealed itself. A young boy living at the 'Dog and Pheasant' close to Vicarage Terrace, has recalled how his family were awaiting the start of Mum's birthday, 19 June, when the bombs fell... at precisely two minutes to midnight. While the adults did their best at the ghastly scene he ran to Gwydir Street to summon help. Total disbelief greeted him and a refusal, he claimed, to make a report of the incident from the word of a mere child. Not so easily thwarted, he telephoned the police from their call box on the side of the Beaconsfield Hall. According to official accounts, Vicarage Terrace was bombed at 00:15. Strange, because the large oak clock on our mantelpiece recorded the event at midnight, and it kept fairly good time.

Not only Cambridge had been attacked. Ten enemy aircraft passed over the Ely area between 23:40 and 01:40. Eight HEs fell at 00:12 from 20,000 ft, at West Fen, Ely, killing one civilian, damaging a hut and killing thirty cattle. Death among animals had been uncatered for in one's calculations, yet vast numbers were to die in homes, on farms or in the fields.

At 00:20 another ten HEs fell in the vicinity of St John's Road, Ely, and by the Millpits, breaking windows. A further seven exploded near the Old Bridge River Bank, and on Chapel Farm, Benwick. Ten minutes later two were dropped in Dykemoor Drove and at 00:40 another seven slightly damaged the railway line at Badgeney, March, falling in a field by Death Drove. At 00:45, 215 Company's searchlights were illuminating He 111s over Downham and Fordham, and five minutes later nine HEs were dropped, this time in Delph Terrace, Chatteris, at the cemetery by 'The Little Nightlayer' and at The Dock. Simultaneously, a He 111 was being engaged by Feltwell's AA guns, an event they repeated at 01:50. Another He 111 illuminated by the 205th Company released seven HEs on to Berner's Heath bombing range at 00:56, and five HEs were dropped in Newton Park near Harston, close to the HQ of the London Scottish Regiment in camp in the area.

More bombs had fallen in Essex — four at 00:40 in a field at Wodensford, Great Canfield, and another four in an oat field near Little Henham. At Westfield Cottages, opposite Harlow Road sugar beet factory, Bury St Edmunds, Suffolk, three HEs had broken windows and caused two minor casualties. Debden's 29 Squadron was trying hard to thwart the attackers. *L8509* had taken off at 00:10, and Pilot Officer Barnwell left for a two-hour patrol in *L6636*. Several He 111s were attracted by Debden's lights and one of these was discovered by Pilot Officer Humphries (*L1375*) of 29 Squadron. He poured his ammunition into the He 111', setting its port engine on fire. Although the Blenheim's hydraulics were damaged, it landed safely at Debden whereas the Heinkel crashed at Springfield Road, Chelmsford, after it was also engaged by a 74 Squadron Spitfire. Three of its crew died.

Barnwell then engaged a Heinkel, illuminated over Debden at 01:00 by searchlights. Starboard engine blazing, it crashed after its rear gunners had managed to damage the Blenheim. Barnwell's fate, and that of his gunner,

Sergeant Long, remains speculative. Two more raiders were engaged off the Stour Estuary and *L6636* never returned. Anti-aircraft guns were also in action in the Landguard Point area at 01:13. Barnwell's body was later washed ashore at Walton-on-the-Naze.

Cambridge having received no more enemy attention, visitors to our shelter began whispering about returning to their homes. Suddenly, the Head Warden, Mr Clover, rushed in with stupendous news. 'They've shot the blighter down, killed them all.' Amid the euphoria a lone, excited youth cried 'Where?'. 'Ah, son, that's a military secret.' The secret lasted seconds before, smiling with knowledge, he announced 'Fulbourn', and added that 'A Spitfire shot it down'. 'A Spitfire?' Pull the other one! No Spitfire would be likely to do that at night. 'German pilot was up at the Varsity before the war', said another warden. What excellent communications these chaps had with the other side!

Yet, against all the odds, it WAS indeed a 19 Squadron Spitfire pilot, Flying Officer Petra in *L1032*, who had downed a Heinkel. Depending upon eyesight and know-how to guide him, he had achieved the almost impossible in the vast night sky.

Those four pilots of 19 Squadron (Flying Officer Petra, Flight Lieutenant Clouston in *R6625*, Flying Officer Bell in *K9807*, Flying Officer Lawson in *N3198*) were airborne for about an hour seeking raiders around Mildenhall and Honington. At 01:25 AA guns at Wattisham had opened fire, and a few minutes later a salvo of bombs burst one mile from Honington. Searchlights of 206 Company illuminated the He 111 which then circled, firing down the beams. Petra located his He 111 at 01:20 near Newmarket and followed as it turned towards its target, Honington, near Bury St Edmunds. The Heinkel, *5J+AM* of 4./KG4 had taken off from Merville and crossed the Norfolk coast at 16,000 ft. Soon afterwards, it was located by searchlights and in taking evasive action had dived even to 3,000 ft, turning and climbing, but was repeatedly illuminated.

Just as Petra was about to fire, a Blenheim arrived on the scene. Sheering to one side, Petra switched on his landing light to illuminate the bomber for attack and poured in tracer during a wide deflection shot. Then, as smoke gushed from one of the bomber's engines, 204 Company's searchlights disastrously illuminated the Spitfire at 01:36. Immediately, the Heinkel's gunners fired, for the lights had revealed its position. The belly gunner fired down the beam of searchlight number 20426 while the upper gunner put explosive bullets into the Spitfire's fuel tank. Petra baled out of his instantly blazing fighter, face and hands terribly badly burned. After landing he was rushed to Bury hospital. His Spitfire clouted the roof of Thurston House, before crashing in its garden not far from Whelnetham railway station.

Although doomed, the blazing Heinkel turned west in an attempt to escape. The crew jettisoned seventeen 50 kg HEs, thirteen of them exploding on Warren Hill and four on Side Hill, east of Newmarket, injuring a person in Chippenham Lodge. Realizing recovery was impossible, three of the crew baled out, leaving their dead colleague in the burning bomber. As it passed over, low, some soldiers enterprisingly engaged it with rifles and their light machine-gun, but it was well out of range. Very little of the He 111 was recognizable in the cornfield where, at 01:48, it crashed, north of the junction of the A11 and Balsham-Fulbourn road. None of the crew captured by the LDV, two officers and a very unhappy infantryman who claimed to have 'gone along for the experience' had, apparently, ever visited Cambridge—and they were not responsible for the Vicarage Terrace bombing.

At the time of that crash Flying Officer Bell, told to investigate a raider over Newmarket, found another Heinkel 111 lit by searchlights and chased it. Ten minutes earlier, and in the same area, Squadron Leader O'Brien flying Blenheim *YP:H* of 23 Squadron had also attacked a He 111. After he fired several long bursts from 100 to 50 yd, smoke gushed from the enemy's starboard engine as he broke off the engagement. Then the Blenheim entered an uncontrollable spin so Pilot Officer King, navigator, baled out only to be killed instantly by a propeller. O'Brien baled out too, but his air gunner, Corporal Little, was killed when the Blenheim crashed.

Whether O'Brien's Heinkel was that chased almost to Colchester by Flying Officer Bell remains speculative. But he did follow one in that direction, riddling it with machine-gun fire as he closed from 200 to 50 yd. The bomber lost height and probably jettisoned its load over south Essex. Eventually the Heinkel was ditched off Margate.

Pilot Officer Kells (*L1508*) of 29 Squadron had followed a He 111 to Felixstowe where searchlights picked it out for him to shoot into the sea, close to where Barnwell was reckoned to have downed a Heinkel. Pilot Officer Humphries (*L1375*) of 29 Squadron was then vectored to the area, clearly being used as an exit point, and found another bomber dodging searchlight beams near Harwich. Humphries fired two bursts and claimed the raider destroyed. Another claim made at 01:13 by AA gunners at Harwich was later confirmed, this too a He 111 brought down in the sea. As a parting gesture the last He 111 to leave East Anglia dropped bombs around Clacton at 02:50. An empty house in Salisbury Road received a direct hit, fifteen bombs fell on fields at Giles Farm, Sladbury Lane, two exploded on marshland and others in fields at Thorpe. The total of eleven raiders claimed destroyed was later reduced to seven — five He 111s and two probables. That remains a remarkably high score, much of the success engineered by skilled searchlight crews working in remarkably bright moonlight.

A dawn survey of the night's nationwide activity suggested that 127 HEs and another fourteen UXHEs had fallen. Relatively little damage had been caused, although some of the forty HEs and a few incendiaries in Essex had hit oil wharves on Canvey Island/Thameshaven at 23:25. Others had fallen at Rivenhall at 23:20, causing a slight casualty. Dunmow RD had recorded four bombs and Saffron Walden RD another two. Four HEs had dropped in Huntingdon RD late on 18 June and one in St Neots RD where an UXHE was also found. 'All Clear' was sounded throughout East Anglia at around 03:15.

As the bombers were homeward-bound, details of the Cambridge tragedy unfolded, the most serious bombing event in Britain so far. Clearly, it was not the number of bombs that brought greatest damage and distress, but the positions of explosions. The manner and angle at which they struck, materials forming buildings, the latter's proximity, blast patterns, shock waves and their deflection along with a host of other variables, all controlled the amount of damage.

Calibre of the Cambridge bombs, probably 50 kg, was never proven. Two close craters were found, the larger nine feet deep. The bombs demolished Nos 1 to 6, Vicarage Terrace, the larger crater marking where houses 3 and 5 had stood. Houses 7-10 were seriously damaged, and various walls remained. Across the street the eight-foot high wall surrounding St Matthew's Vicarage was largely demolished. Many slates were blown off roofs to the rear of the Terrace, and St Matthew's Church had many windows smashed. Gas, water mains and a sewer near the craters had fractured, and another main had burst fifty yards away in Sturton Street. This hazardous damage brought much concern, for if reproduced widely it would cause serious health hazards.

Rescue services had acted very efficiently. It was from Gwydir Street AFS station that, at 00:20, the first official report of the incident reached the Civil Defence Control Centre in the Guildhall and requested an ambulance. At 00:26 ARP Post 7A (St Matthews) reported a small fire at Vicarage Terrace. A full report of the incident was at the Control Centre by 00:40 and a call put out for more ambulances when the extent of the casualties was clear. Among the many who helped to retrieve the dead and injured from the wrecked homes were several Cameron Highlanders. Mr and Mrs Dear in one of the houses had escaped almost uninjured, whereas their beloved child was killed. Both Palmer children also died. When the final tally was made three men, a woman and five children under sixteen years old were found to have been killed. A woman and two men were seriously injured and six women and a child slightly hurt. Daybreak revealed widespread damage in a closely packed Victorian housing area. If two bombs could do that, what of a major attack?

Inescapable at the scene was the smell of dust pervading the air, something one came to associate with air raids. A poor old piano resting on the shattered pavement would clearly never sing again, and even sadder were the remains of a doll whose dismembered body rested close to the wooden poles placed on familiar X-shaped supports, which all councils used, closing off the end of the street. Were the Germans making all this effort, suffering grim losses, just to break the children's dolls and smash the homes and lives of the none too well-to-do?

The children I knew not, but that total war was virtually on our doorstep I understood only too well. ARP men, people we had long regarded as figures of fun, had performed most courageously and tirelessly, learning as they undertook their thankless task. Not only had awful events taken place in Cambridge for, during the night, other Britons had suffered too. But the night's prime targets, the railways and East Anglia's bomber airfields, had remained completely unharmed. For that reason the bombers would obviously return.

During the morning I wandered across Midsummer Common, by the Cam, wondering what the outcome of the war would be. Suddenly I realized that something was missing — of course, the Midsummer Fair. It had been arriving the previous day and now it had all gone. Pointless, that, for there was no longer a place in which to hide. That, yes that, was the new truth.

*   *   *

Considering the number of sorties flown over Britain, relatively few bombs had been dropped, crews being told to bomb only prescribed targets, and nearly all sorties had taken place in darkness. There was, however, one daylight attempt, at 20:12 on 21 June, to bomb Parkeston Quay.

Resumption of operations over East Anglia came on 21/22 June. Of 26 bombing incidents, most serious was the first of 52 raids on Ipswich where sirens sounded at 23:05 as bombs fell in adjacent rural areas. At 00:20 a He 111 at

18,000 ft laid a 700-yd stick of bombs across the northern part of the town. The first exploded in front of a detached house in Dale Hall Lane, close to a sandbag-protected room used as a shelter, and killed Mr and Mrs Anderson and their maid, Miss Crawford. Six neighbouring houses were damaged. Other bombs (four of which remained UX) did little damage, but one produced a 24-ft-deep, 7-ft-wide crater in Waterburn Road.

Following the raid a most interesting item was found in the town centre, a 14-in long 1.5-in diameter black cardboard 'organ pipe' once attached to a bomb tail. All bombs whistled whilst falling but the addition of this tube produced a shrill scream of unchanging note, a cheap, effective, night terror weapon.

That was not the only novelty of the night. At Rede, Suffolk, three oil bombs, the first in East Anglia, produced craters 3 ft deep by 2 ft wide and damaged farm buildings. These were possibly the first oil bombs used on Britain, although others fell at about this time near Melton Ross, Brigg, Lincolnshire.

Within a 250 kg HE bomb case was a container carrying 16 gal of a heavy, tarry liquid, heavy oil or petroleum mix. Centrally placed was 1.25 kg of TNT mixed with charcoal and magnesium powder packed in a 4.75-in diameter tube 2.5 in long. Measuring overall 5 ft 3 in long by 14.5 in diameter, the bomb was filled immediately before the operation, by which time it weighed about 110 kg. Initially it was known as the KC250 GB, later the Flam C250C (Flam = Flammenbomben). Later versions were fuzed to ignite just prior to target penetration, so that their contents spread further than the usual twenty yard radius. The intention was for the oil bomb to penetrate strong roofing which resisted 1 kg incendiaries. Initial use against rural areas led to the belief that it was intended for use against crops.

Extensive operations by about eighty He 111s controlled from Lille resulted in Smallborough RD receiving 26 HEs (one UX), and Docking RD sixteen. The Suffolk coastal region reported nine incidents including six HEs at Hollesley, four HEs and a few incendiaries at Branfield, five HEs near Martlesham, HEs at Marcus Road and Fort Lodge, Felixstowe, and four UXHEs at Bungay. Nine UX bombs fell near Harwich and ten HEs betwen Jaywick and Brightlingsea.

From Marx and Westerland, further sea mining took place. Most of the effort appeared to be devoted to night operational training and reconnaissance during which many airfields were overflown. German bombers were active around Colchester, Orford Ness, Harleston and Winterton, near all of which bombs had fallen. As they headed for their bases urgent calls were made, for KG4 to land at Schiphol and KG27 (particularly busy over Norfolk and Suffolk and whose aircraft used included *1G+LR*, *1G+AP*, *BP*, *DP*, *FP*, *GP* and *HP*) to return to Munster/Handorf or Gutersloh due to fog in the Lille area. All were back by 03:30.

A Zenit flight from the south coast to Lincolnshire — via East Anglia—took place on 24 June. Thus there was little surprise when III/KG4 followed next night, on 24/25 June, its principal targets being industrial. Nevertheless, attempts — in which KG27 took part — were again made to bomb Debden, Duxford, Coltishall, Mildenhall, Bircham Newton and Wittering. Two bombs fell at Bradwell, near Yarmouth, and four on Wicken Farm, Tattersett, along with Norfolk's first incendiaries. More of those burnt at Whitehall Farm, Syderstone, at 00:15. The Halstead area received its first bombing, an HE dropping in Chapel Street, Steeple Bumpstead, damaging four houses. North-west Essex too experienced its first raid when seventeen HEs (eleven in fields) fell around Wimbish (close to Debden) and disturbed the police house. On to Mildenhall's Q-Site, Tuddenham, fifteen HEs (two UX) proved its value, ten actually exploding on the site. Crews manning these intentionally lit targets were housed in shelters — with overruns possible hazards. Fog again greeted the bombers on their return and while KG27 landed at Merville most of KG4 put down at Jever. About fifty He 111s had operated, many not bombing. It was believed that they were helping to co-ordinate planning and timing of the likely invasion, such activities preceding the attack on the Low Countries.

A sophisticated night assault by seventy aircraft commenced shortly before midnight on 25/26 June. In part one, seventy HEs and over 500 incendiaries were scattered over the Midlands, part two including anti-shipping operations along the east coast from Scotland to the Wash. Incendiaries were dropped shortly after 01:00 at Stiffkey, and at Rudham where a heath fire was started. Three groups of raids by KG27 crossed the East Anglian coast around midnight on 27/28 June, just as fog was building. HEs fell near St Neots, Peterborough, March and Winterton. About 200 incendiaries were distributed over Newmarket Heath. Raid 42 released flares near Saxmundham at 00:06 before dropping four HEs near Snape, Alderton and Pelgrave. Raid 80 soon arrived but did not bomb, probably due to the misty conditions. A third attack in the area, presumably against Orford Ness, resulted in eleven HEs in fields near Alderton at 02:23. At 01:00 an enemy aircraft circled Clacton where no alert was in force. Searchlights failed to illuminate the raider, whose bombs were placed on a searchlight battery near Half Way Garage by the Colchester road. Others fell in front of Crossley House, east of the pier, at Weeley, Bentley, and incendiaries ignited in Hartley Woods.

Although thick cloud impeded German efforts during the closing nights of June, further attempts were made to cripple Honington, Harwich and Coltishall. Mining took place off Harwich on the 28th/29th and Pilot Officer D.A. Williams with Pilot Officer Atkinson of 23 Squadron claimed a He 111.

Dunwich received nine HEs along with a load of incendiaries at 00:45. One bomb damaged church tiles and windows, and two chicken huts on Hospital Farm suffered. Incendiary damage was the most yet experienced, and resulted from three fires. At 06:40 another nine HEs and a swarm of incendiaries fell on Surlingham from high level. Seven bombs had delayed action fuzing and one exploded, bringing down the walls of a carriage shed.

The scale of attack had varied little, a count for 29/30 June indicating that 101 HEs had fallen. Some 100 incendiaries burnt in open country around Norwood Chase and March marshalling yard. Another twelve at Grays Moor showed that railways were targeted. About twenty enemy aircraft operated over East Anglia that night, including a few from Villacoublay venturing here for the first time. One, call sign 'OZ4T8', released its bombs eight miles east of Cardington at 00:23.

Early on 1 July raiders came from Merville, north-west Germany and Aalborg but soon deterioration in weather and the passing of the moon period reduced enemy effort. In such conditions, could the offensive be continued? The answer was emphatically 'Yes', for the clouds gave a similar cloak to darkness. For East Anglians yet another, often very frightening, phase of the war was about to begin.

Chapter 6
From out of the clouds

On 2 July a dramatic increase in the scale of Luftwaffe operations was ordered by the German High Command. An all-out bombing campaign upon the British Isles, vicious enough to force surrender, was to be unleashed upon the morrow. Daylight attacks would now be made, and cloud cover, permitting sneak sorties, would be fully exploited. Lone, concealed intruders with a choice of listed targets achieved more success than night attackers of the period. Often the bomber would unleash its load and be gone before any warning sounded. Resultant civilian casualties and damage could be quite high, while indiscriminate machine-gunning poured high terror into the situation. Failure to destroy such evil perpetrators always generated intense civilian fury, especially when the aircraft was boldly displayed before disappearing into cloud. If, however, its crew was brazen enough to attempt a preparatory or secondary run over a well-defended area, then the hazardous nature of such activity was then, as now, hideously exhibited. Whenever in my experience such an intruder appeared it did so to the infuriating cry, 'Where are the fighters?', and too often it was voiced by those who had begrudged even a farthing for 'defence'.

At 12:55 on 3 July the first cloud cover daylight attack on East Anglia took place when Raid 72, a Do 17Z of KG77, broke cloud to place nineteen HEs on Tinker's Farm and the sea wall at Walberswick. This was but an overture, for the main attack of the day was delivered against the fringes of Suffolk and Essex between 16:00 and 17:00. It opened with attacks on the Bawdsey-Harwich front, the first bombs falling from a cloud-scudding Dornier 17Z at 16:00 between Walton and Oakley, and all burst in water. At 16:05, five HEs fell near a searchlight post at Bawdsey and moments later another fifteen exploded by Orford Road, Tunstall Heath, by which time the defences were engaging the violator over Leiston. At 16:15 the action switched to Felixstowe over which, heading south-west, another low-flying Dornier was chased by four fighters. Its load of three HEs was jettisoned in the sea opposite Reed Pond about twenty yards from the shore. At the same time, eight bombs were aimed on to Frinton, four undershooting into the sea and the others exploding on the front without causing casualties. More bombs were dropped at Wrabness, nine fell on the shore and in the sea at Dovercourt at 16:47 and the phase ended when six HEs were dropped north of Walton by a Ju 88. In all of these raids little damage had been caused and no lives lost. There were, however, two punishing attacks within the same period, the worst yet experienced by East Anglians.

Clapham Road, Lowestoft, on 3 July 1940, moments after the bombs fell by the Co-op. The scene was captured by Ford Jenkins who maintained a photographic record of wartime Lowestoft. The book, Port War *(Panda Books), contains many of the pictures.*

At 15:27 the ARP HQ in Ipswich received a 'yellow' warning, but no alert had been sounded when Raid 40 raced in low from the north-east to place twenty 50 kg bombs in a line extending 1,200 yd across a residential area. AA guns opened fire as people quickly took shelter. Miraculously, only three bombs exploded in dwellings; the fifth hit a semi-detached house, the tenth fell by a bungalow and the thirteenth almost demolished a two-storey house whilst only slightly injuring its inmate. One person was killed, seventeen were injured and eighteen had slight wounds. Additionally, two houses were badly damaged, four moderately so, one slightly and another 149 suffered blast damage. The targets being attacked were uncertain, but may have been public utilities.

The other town viciously assaulted was Lowestoft where many owed their lives to the prompt action of a lady at the Services Department who, on her own initiative, ordered the crash warning to be sounded at the lighthouse. A Do 17Z came in low from the sea and flew north-westerly over the town prior to making its bomb run, by which time people had taken cover. Then it returned, flying roughly along Clapham Road line preparing a bombing run. On turning, it dropped two HEs in the sea, one on the beach, two on the sea wall, one close to a pile driver, two on the Denes and one by a gun emplacement. Another burst by a shelter before the ninth smashed a cottage. A woman and two children were killed instantly, the other occupant having a miraculous escape. A steep bank brought the bomber on to its final run from which the first bomb fell in the entrance to an Anderson Shelter. The next dropped on the railway at Clapham Road before one—possibly two—hit the pavement by the 150-ft frontage CWS (Co-Op) store which immediately erupted into flames. A UXHE lodged itself in a nearby alleyway, another bomb exploded on a courtyard between the Technical College and public library, one fell at a lock-up garage and two more nearby.

Vicious onslaught had come to a town where, but a year before, many would have been happily enjoying the sea and sand. The disfiguring bomb craters seemed unbelievably incongruous. The vulnerablility of coastal towns to 'tip and run' raiders was immediately obvious, and resulted in no mean alarm. A local resident was killed outside the local 'Co-Op', a quite unbelievable thing to happen. But soon many a familiar soul would die similarly in horrific circumstances on a summer's day, by the sea. That's what air raids were all about, and they were unacceptably uncivilized.

Almost instantly, the friendly local Co-Op had become an inferno in the basement of which, a shelter for ninety, many shoppers had taken cover as the first bombs fell. Within three minutes the fire brigade was in action then, from the conflagration, two Co-Op vans emerged, driven by two anonymous naval ratings displaying immense bravery. Prompt, courageous action by the fire brigade also enabled the basement to be safely cleared. Within the hour familiar landmarks began to crumble as demolition parties removed the shell of the familiar shop and unsafe parts of the Technical College.

Casualties totalled four killed, five seriously wounded and twenty needing treatment, and would have been higher had not many shoppers taken cover in time. It was always sensible to take cover, but many came to ignore that maxim because alerts often sounded and no bombs fell.

A problem at both towns was that, during daylight, many ARP workers were at their work places. At Ipswich there was a desperate call for them, and only by hurrying to their posts could they ever relieve the overworked police force. Throughout the war this problem remained, demanding total dedication and immense courage from those who suddenly left their workmates to face indescribable scenes of horror. Now that the bombing had commenced, gone, for ever, was the ridicule of the comic who cried 'put that light out'. Instead he often came glowing with the light of help and courage.

The Ipswich and Lowestoft 'terror attacks' were the most serious cloud cover raids within the raid period 09:30 to 05:45 on 3/4 July. In Blyth RD, nineteen HEs had fallen, twelve each in Mitford and Launditch RD and Dunmow RD. Apart from four small night raids (in which 23 bombs had fallen at Great Canfield and High Roding, Essex) all bombing had taken place in daylight, 26 towns and villages in Kent and Sussex, and sixteen in Essex and Suffolk, having been attacked. The proximity of airfields, communications targets, harbours, radar stations and ground defences within twenty miles of the coast suggested that these were the intended targets which many bombs overshot.

From the enemy's point of view the most successful attack involved Mistley Quay, Manningtree, on to which a Ju 88 dropped its load at 23:00. Two bombs landed by the railway track, three burst on railway sidings, one burrowed deep beside a house and spectacular disaster overtook Brooks Flour Mill where a store containing 3,000 tins of oil cake — £75,000 worth — was destroyed in a huge fire which blazed for three days. The *Bijou*, a 98-ton sailing barge, sank and its wreckage can still be seen at low tide.

Review of operation areas between 25 June and 5 July (when Lowestoft was subjected to its second attack) showed that most frequently bombed had been South Wales (nine times), Hampshire (six times) with Humberside, Tyneside and East Anglia each being subjected to special attention on four occasions. Bombing appeared to be spasmodic, to no specific pattern, and obvious targets were seemingly ignored — perhaps to delude the defenders. July's night activity fell away as the moon period waned.

Having decided to initiate large-scale day bombing, the Luftwaffe exposed itself to fighter and AA defences. Raid 73 chanced it by crossing in over Happisburgh on 7 July to drop three bombs near West Raynham. Next day the action was mainly over Suffolk. Shotley's AA guns were, at 09:47, first to engage an aircraft heading for Ipswich. Then at 10:00 a He 111H of I/KG53 began circling low around Clacton and after thirty minutes dropped five bombs on fields near Lamdermere. As it retreated seawards, listeners on the shore heard three bursts of machine-gun fire coming from Hurricanes of 17 Squadron covering Convoy 'Ancient'. The Heinkel fell into the sea.

Ipswich came under attack when, at 10:25, a Do 17Z broke cloud, dived through AA fire and dropped a stick of ten bombs extending a quarter of a mile across the dock area. The first bounced off the quay into the water, the second of 250 kg clouted a gantry and warehouse wall before resting by a railway line, the next penetrated a warehouse wall, number four immersed itself in malt, the next shot through a church roof to lodge in flagstones, the sixth splashed into a garden pond, the seventh halted by a footpath and three others slid into the river. Only the third had exploded, but there was little doubt that the failure of the bombs to explode was unintentional. Another enemy aircraft crossed in towards Ipswich at 10:28, but 85 Squadron's Hurricanes chased it out to sea and destroyed the He 111H-2 of Stab./KG1 at 10:30, six miles out from Felixstowe. None of the crew survived. At 13:45 five HEs fell on Horsey Island, and more south-west of Harwich that afternoon. At 23:15 another attempt to bomb Ipswich was driven off by AA fire, then Raid 40 circled to the north-east before unloading ten HEs in the Bond's Corner, Grundisburgh/Clopton area, this being the third time bombs had fallen there, possibly intended for Martlesham. Two hours later incendiaries and four HEs fell west of Saxmundham. While such activity took place, mining was continuing in east coast estuaries, mainly now being carried out by (F)/106, Ku. Fl. Gr. 506 and KG28, sometimes supported by (F)/126.

Facing daylight intrusions were detachments of Nos 17 and 85 Hurricane Squadrons at Martlesham. Spitfires of 66 Squadron had since 29 May been at Coltishall where on 9 July a new 242 Squadron, equipped with Hurricanes and commanded by the indomitable Squadron Leader Douglas Bader, became operational. No 19 Squadron was available at Duxford and at Fowlmere, and guarding the northern flank were Wittering's squadrons.

A tempting target particularly at risk now, and throughout hostilities, was Norwich. Its sirens had not sounded when, just after 17:00 on 9 July, Raid 40, a Do 17Z, sneaked over the coast at 6,000 ft and north-east of Norwich teamed up with Raid 44. Flying in line astern, they glided in at 2,000 ft, their target the Boulton & Paul Riverside Works where the workers were just coming off shift. The first two of the total of twenty bombs exploded with great ferocity in the constructional engineering shop causing the roof to cave in as it rushed to replace the air expelled by blast. Wire mesh netting caught 75 per cent of the falling glass, but asbestos fragments fluttered through to the floor. Amazingly no one was injured, but bombs three to five (one UX) crashed into the steel framing of the wire-weaving workshop, damaging machines and even passing through $\frac{1}{4}$ in steel plates. Here the casualties were ten killed, 68 wounded. Two other bombs burst on the railway lines out of Thorpe Station. Fortunately, production was only briefly halted. From Colman's Carrow Road factory the workforce was leaving as the bombs fell. An airburst caused over twenty horrific casualties.

Above *Crosses mark the impact points of seven bombs, from the railway lines and across the Boulton & Paul works, resulting from the attack on the factory at Norwich made on 9 July 1940* (Boulton & Paul).

Right *Production clearly interrupted after a precision attack on Boulton & Paul's factory in 1940* (Boulton & Paul).

Bombs from the second aircraft aimed at Barnard's Iron Works at Mousehold caused widespread damage. Two workers leaving the factory were instantly killed, and many others had miraculous escapes when a gunner strafed them, killing one woman. Two houses were bombed, one large of eighteenth century origin whose timbers were shattered and one wall collapsed. What remained surprising was the resilience of many buildings.

Spitfires of 66 Squadron quickly 'scrambled' to intercept the retreating Dorniers, closing rapidly upon one and firing as it sped out over Winterton.

They used all their ammunition, but it escaped. Some retribution was exacted when, forty miles off the Stour at 17:15, Hurricanes of 17 Squadron shot down a Heinkel He 111H-3 of I/KG53 interfering with Convoy 'Ancient'.

After dusk about thirty bombers operated mainly over East Suffolk dropping fifteen HEs on Lemon's Farm, Ringsfield, and machine-gunning a searchlight camp on nearby Low Farm. Ten minutes later ten HEs fell at Hinton, Blythburgh. Two aircraft were burnt out when eleven HEs were dropped on West Raynham where a corner of No 1 Hangar was hit. Dornier 17s were responsible, one of which crossed the coast at Southwold at 05:15 and dropped eighteen HEs by the Woodbridge-Felixstowe road where it skirted Martlesham aerodrome upon which five bombs landed. Eight 50 kg HEs exploded by Hadleigh's Whitehorse Inn, cracking a corner of the building. At 05:08, Raid 29 attacked Honington.

Another phase of activity commenced at 06:15 on 10 July, and continued spasmodically to 02:14 on 11 July. In its final hour alone 170 HEs and a few incendiaries were reported in East Anglia. Weybourne received fifteen HEs at 07:15, the largest a 250 kg bomb which replaced a scullery with a 30 ft by 12 ft crater. Others exploded in gardens, among greenhouses and by the main road. RAF Honington was attacked and this time 66 Squadron claimed the Do 17Z off Winterton. Also shot down off Norfolk that day, by 242 Squadron, was a He 111H-2 of III/KG53.

The Eleventh of July proved to be a disastrous day. In the early hours HEs and incendiaries intended for Debden fell around Arkesden and Newport, Essex, but rain and low cloud were more ideal for lone day raiders, an aspect the enemy was about to exploit. Raid 30, the first of about twelve which operated between Cromer and Lowestoft and attacked from below 1,000 ft, was intercepted by three 85 Squadron Hurricanes led by Squadron Leader Peter Townsend. Return fire from the Do 17Z of II/KG2 forced him to bale out, his Hurricane crashing off Harwich.

The first major incident followed at 06:10 when Raid 22, a Do 17Z, circled Cromer twice before machine-gunning the town and releasing fourteen 50 kg HEs. Beach Station caught the brunt of the first two, the second bursting in the kitchens of an adjacent house, killing a person in a bedroom and injuring two others. Mr George Baker, in Cromer at the time, recalls that in Central Road Mrs King was killed and that across the road a splinter sliced off a man's thumb. A UXHE fell near the cinema in Hans Place and another bomb exploded behind Munday's, the newsagent in Church Street and now known as Hewitt's, killing Edward Munday and his sister, Elizabeth. The most amazing episode, recalls George, was at Brunswick House where a bomb came in through a toilet window, hurtled downstairs, was jumped over by an astonished boy and finally came to rest in the basement. Joyce's Cafe on the East Promenade (now replaced by The Rocket House) was destroyed but luckily six bombs failed to explode. The aircraft's crew had cause to regret machine-gunning the lifeboat and station for not long after they and their aircraft were shot into the sea. Another Do 17 machine-gunned Wells at 06:55.

Preparing its run-in at that time was another Do 17Z, of I/KG3, its target Great Yarmouth which was to become the most frequently raided town in East Anglia. Air raid warnings sounded at Yarmouth a staggering 2,046 times, 219 times it was bombed and 217 of its residents were to die over four years of war.

Just what it meant to be a victim of these early raids was movingly and most graphically recalled for me by Mrs E.A. Ashman (née Keable), still living in the area.

'My home, where I then lived with my parents and two brothers, at 68 Wolseley Road, Southtown, was the first building to be bombed in the town, at 06:30 on 11 July. The enemy 'plane flew in quite low, the weather being dull, rainy and visibility very poor. Seven bombs were dropped, 50 kg type. Three fell in the built-up area, four across the marshes killing eight cows and a horse. Two houses received direct hits and were demolished. Four people were killed and three injured.

'My father was downstairs in the kitchen making tea. We often jokingly said, "You'll die making tea", but little did we think this would come true. But it happened that way for he was dead from internal injuries by the time of his arrival at hospital. It seemed ironic that he had spent three years in Flanders during the 1914-1918 War, in the thick of the fighting, only to die in his own home from German bombs.

'My teenage brother was asleep in bed at the back of the house when the bomb came. He pulled the eiderdown over his head and landed, still in bed and unhurt, at the bottom of the garden! I was in bed in the front room, my mother in the middle bedroom. We had to wait for the police to rescue us because the stairs were gone. We were not hurt, apart from shock and being cut by glass. My ten-year-old brother had been evacuated.

'I was twenty years old at the time, my wedding planned for 14 July 1940. My wedding cake was ruined, my wedding dress slightly damaged and oil marked. Dad was buried on 13 July, at St Mary's Southtown Church, and I was married Sunday afternoon, 14 July, in the same church and with tremendous help and moral support from friends and neighbours.'

At 22:10 another major incident came about when the Ipswich Dock area was attacked, eighteen bombs falling instead around private dwellings over a distance of three-quarters of a mile. Harbour installations completely escaped, but the rear wall of a house was demolished, foundations were damaged and one bomb exploded in the roof of a house from which two people on the ground floor had a miraculous escape. There were no serious casualties, but there was the task of filling giant holes in gardens and fields.

The Twelfth of July was another memorable day. For the first time a formation raid entered the East Anglia region, the day's only major operation. Shortly after 07:00 reports filtered to Fighter Command indicating that He 111s of III/KG53 and Do 17Zs of II/KG2 were formating over France. Moving northerly as Raid 31, they soon passed along the east coast through 11 Group area some way off shore, and entered 12 Group zone at 08:24 — by which time they clearly had 'FN' Convoy 'Booty', towards which they were closing off Suffolk, as their target. Since the size of the enemy force and its exact intentions were uncertain, the defenders' response was too limited to be really effective.

At 08:48, 'A' Flight, 17 Squadron, ordered to protect the convoy, went into action as pairs of He 111s commenced shallow dive attacks from 8,000 ft on ships a little way north of Felixstowe. Pilot Officer K. Manger and Sergeant G. Griffiths were the first Hurricane pilots to score, shooting down a HE 111H-2 off Orford Ness. Hurricanes of 85 Squadron shot down another Heinkel and Pilot Officer P. E. Pitman and Sergeant D. Fopp damaged another. The battle cost

Sergeant L. Jowitt's aircraft, which at 09:00 fell into the sea off Felixstowe. By then 17 Squadron had turned its attention on to the Dorniers, claiming its first victim at 09:05. Unlike the Heinkels, the Dorniers held their formation and when reinforcement arrived, eleven Hurricanes of 151 Squadron from North Weald, they faced concentrated return fire which shot down Flying Officer J. H. L. Allan, and damaged two other Hurricanes. Flying Officer Count M. B. Czernin and Pilot Officer D. W. H. Halman of 17 Squadron claimed a retiring Dornier at 09:32. Although six Defiants of 264 Squadron and three Hurricanes of 242 Squadron had been sent on patrol, they did not participate in the fight. With hindsight a strong attack on the unprotected bombers — which sank the 2,162-ton *Hornchurch* off Aldeburgh — would have been worthwhile.

Night-time on 14/15 July brought the next major activity. Between 19:45 and 02:00 mining took place from the Wash to Flamborough Head, and in a second phase from 23:50 to 02:00 another 27 aircraft were plotted mining between North Foreland and Orford Ness, thus endangering much of the east coast convoy route. Proximity of the minelayers brought Norwich three warnings during a night in which a few bombs fell near Harwich.

A low pressure system over England reduced activity between 16 and 19 July, but it was not only that which resulted in only ten more incidents in East Anglia during the month. The Luftwaffe was preparing for its onslaught on the south. No 12 Group awaited further convoy raids, placing 19 Squadron's cannon-armed Spitfires on patrol from Coltishall and Martlesham. They searched for their first quarry, unsuccessfully, on 20 July.

Anti-shipping operations had continued, and at 00:01 on 18 July an aircraft flown by Oberleutnant Westhaus struck a cable within 928 Squadron's Harwich balloon barrage. Urgently he called his base stating that he was ditching. Nothing further was heard of the aircraft. That night ships were bombed off Felixstowe, HEs fell for the first time between Colchester and Braintree and at 00:35 an HE fell at Bawdsey Manor. Another five were dropped at Felixstowe, on the north side of Walton Avenue and on open ground. Early on the 19th Marx-based He 111s mined the convoy route off Suffolk. On the 21st five HEs dropped near Parkeston Station, one causing closure of the line. Incendiaries burnt on Barling Marshes, Essex, and late on the 22nd more were dropped, on marshes near Bawdsey, but all of these were relatively small raids.

Before July closed there were several quite spectacular, small-scale operations. Raid 81 came in at 06:06 on the 19th to bomb Norwich. Seven bombs on Norwich Aero Club's premises at Mousehold reduced them to memory. Another crashed through a 6-in thick cement balcony on corporation flats, one smashed through a manhole cover to sever 28 ft of piping underground before blowing the next manhole cover sky high! More bombs fell in Magdalen Close, at Nos 78–80 Bull Close, injuring two, and the twelfth bomb exploded by Hingles furniture shop, Botolph Street.

In the afternoon of 23 July, the day on which Flight Lieutenant G.S. Powell-Sheddon of 242 Squadron was first to destroy one of 4(F)./122's Ju 88s which recently had begun the daily weather reconnaissance along the east coast, a Ju 88 broke cloud in an attempt to bomb Harleston. It made off before 242 Squadron could catch it. At 16:48 a Do 17Z came out of cloud and this time the results were spectacular in the extreme. Its target was RAF Pulham, the one-time airship station, now a weapons store. Below the 700-ft cloud base the Do 17 delivered a stick of sixteen 50 kg HEs. Two penetrated the 700-ft long by 180-ft wide steel airship shed, exploding within. Another burst in the roof, the fourth on a pile of 500 lb bomb cases. A fifth shot through the roof and a sixth entered a hangar annexe. Vast amounts of groaning air disturbed within the gigantic hangar blew out 450 of its 1,248 panes of glass, sufficient to allow the blast to escape and for the colossal steel structure to survive.

Attacks upon moving trains were rare, but Raid 47, which flew to Colchester via Bury late in the afternoon of 24 July, struck at the track south-east of Colchester, bombing from about 750 ft alongside the railway where two trains were passing, and adding to the alarm by using screamer-attached bombs.

Another raid intended to cause considerable alarm was delivered upon Norwich early on 30 July. Raid X15 crossed in near Yarmouth at 05:37, hurried to Attlebridge then flew to Norwich over which it circled before its first bomb run, circled again and attacked targets bombed on previous occasions. The bomber dropped twenty HEs shortly after 06:00 and fled to Kessingland before the warning could be given. Three HEs burst in the River Wensum, the parking area at Surrey Street Bus Station was hit and a water main burst close by. Other bombs exploded to the rear of the 'George IVth' public house, on houses in Victoria Terrace where ten were killed, in Compass Street where No 3 received a direct hit, in Lorne Place and Argyle Street and on the printing department at Colman's Carrow Lane Works.

Despite the effects of attacks on land targets, the emphasis on shipping raids remained strong. At 14:05 on 29 July a Do 17Z of Stab./KG2, seeking shipping 45 miles east of Felixstowe, was mauled so badly by 85 Squadron Hurricanes guarding Convoy 'Agent' that it forced-lanced at St Inglevert. With evidence of the convoy's position to hand, He 111s of I/KG53 set off to attack it. This time the fighters were better deployed, 17 Squadron attacking the southern flank and bringing down a raider while to the north 66 Squadron went into action. 'A' Flight (*K9944, N3043* and *N3044*) scored first, shooting down an He 111H-2 24 miles south-east of Lowestoft. Then it was the turn of *L1083, N3121* and *R6689* to destroy another, fourteen miles east of Hammond's Knoll. Little wonder the Heinkels soon made off. Nevertheless, anti-shipping operations were paying dividends, for HMS *Wren*, a 1,120-ton destroyer, was bombed and sunk off Aldeburgh on 27 July, and on the 29th two ships were mined, the *Clam Monroe* (5,952 tons at 51^0 52'N/01^0 48'E) and *Moidart* (1,292 tons at 51^0 59'N/01^0 49'E).

Increased day and night bombing and the sudden attacks from low clouds brought to a head an issue troubling the public and the authorities, bombing attacks delivered when no public warning had been sounded. In official quarters there was belief that the enemy was attempting, with brief pernicious attacks widely spread, to cause the entire country to be placed under 'Red' alert thus bringing confusion and tremendous disruption to industry. Clearly that was unacceptable, and brought to the forefront the question of when to alert the public. To avoid too many and lengthy alerts, the sirens would be sounded only when attack seemed likely and taking cover was prudent. Skill was required in making such forecasts, and mistakes inevitably came about — indeed, had already occurred. Some failures to give warnings were due to the attackers avoiding detection, and warnings which came after bombing indicated the likelihood of further activity. As to the certainty of the latter, there could be no doubt. August was going to bring fierce action for our skies.

Chapter 7
Those most fateful days

Not until late August did attacks upon East Anglia vastly increase. Instead, there was a non-stop widespread effort. On 31 July / 1 August a few raids operated over Suffolk, bombs falling near Wattisham, Martlesham, Newmarket and Felixstowe. At sea, He 115s of Ku. Fl. Gr. 106 and '506 mined coastal waters. An unplotted Ju 88 crept around the outskirts of Norwich and at 15:15 on Thursday 1 August, dived low from the south-west and placed two HEs and incendiaries on to Boulton & Paul's large, aged, wood-working and paint shop which instantly erupted in flames. Nine workers were killed and twenty injured as the truss roof and its corrugated iron covering collapsed and the steel frame buckled. Destroyed too were the box making and sheet metal shops, canteen, offices and boardroom, and only the fine work of the ARP staff saved much more of the factory from destruction. Another three HEs fell on Thorpe Station, but only one exploded. As the Ju 88 sped into cloud its gunner machine-gunned Prince of Wales Road and the station area, killing and injuring more people. Total casualties were high, amounting to thirteen killed, 59 injured and 72 with slight wounds.

Meanwhile, Ju 88s of KG30 and He 111s of KG4, from Schiphol, were taking off, bound for Convoy 'Pilot' passing along the Norfolk coast. From 18:00 they made 1½ hours of repeated attempts to sink the ships. No 242 Squadron hastened to their aid, Sergeant Richardson (*P3087*) shooting down a Ju 88. Another, badly damaged by Flying Officer Christie, crash-landed at Aalborg. Although fighters had driven off the raiders, seventeen more sorties by He 111s and Do 17s were flown against the convoy after dark. Next morning at 11:15, off Norfolk, 19 Squadron led by Flight Lieutenant Clouston intercepted a marauding He 111.

Recent casualty figures brought a brief alteration to public raid warning policy leading to unnecessary alerts on a lavish scale. Reduced activity due to poor weather was soon followed by a reversion to the previous system. Another problem was being caused by high flying reconnaissance aircraft. They gave a clue to areas of enemy interest and, since these aircraft rarely carried bombs, were often unmolested. One high flier on 4 August entered the country via Gloucestershire, flew to Preston, Pocklington, Kirton, Wittering and Duxford before leaving over the Thames Estuary. Misty weather had prevented photography.

Bombs fell at Freckenham, near Kennett, and at Stuntney from Raid 4 and

Dense smoke rises from an intense fire at Boulton & Paul's Riverside factory in Norwich on 1 August 1940 (Boulton & Paul).

also in Clare RD (twelve and two UXHEs) and Cosford RD (seven and six UXHEs) on 4/5 August. More discouragement to the ceaseless mining and anti-shipping campaign came at 06:15 on 6 August when a Do 17Z of 7./KG53 was disposed of by 85 Squadron. Nevertheless, at 22:45 on 8 August a passing Do 18 is recorded as having fired upon a searchlight camp near Bawdsey from a mere 300 ft, and that night 27 HEs were dropped in the Southwold area.

Activity increased on 9/10 August, after a Zenit flight tracked from Schiphol to Flushing via Mildenhall and London. An attempt was made to shoot down balloons guarding Harwich, and shortly after midnight bombs fell near Stowmarket, Harleston, Framlingham and Alwalton. Off Southwold a dozen fell in the sea. The town suffered a pernicious attack during the afternoon when two heavy bombs fell in Lorne Road, demolishing three unoccupied houses. So ferocious was the assault that debris hurled into the road was, in places, piled ten feet high. Only 41 HEs were dropped on Britain in daylight on the 10th. Raid 37 bombed Hethersett, possibly in error for the nearby Stoke Holy Cross radar station, killing two pheasants and bringing telephone wires down before dropping three HEs not far from Norwich football ground and damaging a shed at Colman's. Attacks on airfields at Bircham Newton, Horsham St Faith and Watton by KG4 were made after darkness before bad weather once more limited operations, on 11 August, to an unsuccessful midday attempt by a few Do 17s of 9./KG2 escorted by Bf 110s of 1. and 2./ZG26 and Erpro. Gr. 210 to bomb Convoy 'Booty' off Harwich. Spitfires of 74 Squadron engaged them, Squadron Leader Mungo Park claiming a Bf 110 and the rest of the squadron two more. Six Hurricanes of 17 Squadron laid claim to another Bf 110 and Hurricanes of 85 Squadron led by Squadron Leader Peter Townsend damaged another. Three Dorniers were also damaged. Two Spitfires were, however, shot down off Clacton.

Activity then fell away again, only 51 HEs being known to have fallen in East Anglia during the next four days. At 22:23 on the 12th three HEs brought down the roof and smashed the windows of Nettlestead church. Two cottages were also damaged and two horses were killed. A He 111 trying to bomb Bircham Newton dropped nineteen HEs at Docking on the 13th and nine HEs which came down at 02:00 on 14 August on White House Farm, Bulcamp, Blyth. They proved of considerable interest because one had an incendiary device attached.

During a pass across Felixstowe at 17:33 a stick of fourteen HEs was dropped, the first exploding outside the main post office and the second opposite a butcher's shop at No 24 Station Road. Outside Butlin's amusement park cafe a bomb which had not at first exploded now did so, while another fell in the promenade gardens opposite and one exploded on the beach. At the Cavendish Hotel serious damage was caused by a bomb in its car park. A UXHE rested behind No 41 Chaucer Road, while others exploded in the gardens of Nos 11, 10/12 and 22/24 Highfield Road. A delayed action bomb settled at 27, Leopold Road, while in Cobbold Road a car was destroyed at No 91 and damage caused at No 30. Despite the extensive spread of the salvo, only one person was injured. Four other HEs exploded on the sports field of HMS *Ganges*, three on the shore nearby and others close to HMS *Cardiff* anchored in the Haven.

All East Anglian raids in this period were loosely related to 'The Battle of Britain', but not until 15 August did the first large scale daylight raid on an East Anglian airfield take place. Five major attacks were launched by day, beginning with the bombing of Dover and Hawkinge at around 11:00. Attempts to attack bomber bases in Yorkshire followed, before mid-afternoon saw a surprising development.

Precisely what overtook Martlesham remains open to question. Official sources, and their interpreters, differ and local witnesses both confirm and deny the use of Ju 87 dive bombers. According to the records of the AA gunners the raid was carried out at '15:10 by two attacking forces. First were nine Ju 87s approaching in two vee formations. Four came from the east in line astern and attacked dropping eight 250 kg bombs as they dived from 5,000 to 2,000 ft. A second attack was carried out by six Bf 110s dropping incendiaries and HEs from an average of 4,000 ft.' Some who are adamant concerning Ju 87 involvement claim that the dive-bombers concentrated their effort on a radio station. Whatever the truth, the defenders were taken by surprise.

From a confused situation, about a dozen low flying Bf 110s of Erprobungsgruppe 210—more used to attacking shipping, and now each carrying two 50 kg bombs—raced along the Essex coast. A few Bf 109Es provided cover at 20,000 ft. Just before the raiders turned sharply across the coast three Hurricanes of 17 Squadron, Martlesham, were scrambled, but too late to halt rooftop delivery of eighteen bombs (two of them oil bombs) on their airfield, damaging the Officers' Mess, the Station Workshops and a hangar and putting the airfield out of action for 48 hours. Another four HEs and five incendiaries landed on Leeches Farm, the Manse, the Baptist Chapel at Windcross and at Waldringfield. As the '110s turned for home the Hurricanes, reinforced by four more, were engaging the top cover. Over Felixstowe Flight Lieutenant W. J. Harper claimed a Bf 109 before he was shot down, suffering leg and face burns as a consequence. All the Bf 110s escaped, but three Hurricanes of 1 Squadron sent as reinforcements were shot down.

Not since 26 July had the Luftwaffe bombed north-west Essex, but at 17:37 on 15 August a sharp attack was delivered by one aircraft upon the railway installation at Elsenham where the five HEs dropped killed one person and injured another. At Broxted the 11,000-volt overhead cable was cut, one bomb destroyed five lengths of track. Despite the presence of a UXB, a gang courageously repaired the smashed lines. Eight other UXHEs were also discovered in open ground. The same day the *Brixton* (1,557 tons) was mined at position 52⁰06'N/ 01⁰49'E.

The Luftwaffe was extremely active on 16 August off the Norfolk coast seeking shipping, although no bombs were dropped. As seven Spitfires of No 19 Squadron were returning to Duxford from Coltishall in the early evening they were suddenly ordered to intercept Raid X42 approaching Clacton on their way home from raiding targets by the Thames. A force of He 111s, over which fifty fighters, Bf 109s and Bf 110s of ZG26 provided cover, faced the Spitfires which directed their attention on to the '110s. Flight Sergeant G. E. Unwin (*R6776*) destroyed one and Sergeant J. A. Potter (*R6761*) shot down another, while two more were damaged. Sergeant Roden's Spitfire (*R6904*) was badly damaged in the fight. Scores might have been higher had the cannon in six Spitfires not suffered stoppages. Numerous incidents were a by-product of this raid, including incendiaries on Harwich beach at 17:30 and damage to its Guildhall, also an HE near Manningtree station. The following night, bombing was reported from many areas, among them Halstead RD where 200 incendiaries, 21 HE and two UXHE fell, and Saffron Walden where 36 HE and one UXHE were dropped.

As the Luftwaffe conserved its strength for daylight raids, operations were reduced, yet still they brought distressing moments — as at 04:00 on 18 August when an enemy aircraft machine-gunned parts of East Suffolk including Leiston, searchlights and Mr S. Snowden's Wood Farm. Night bombing of Home Farm, Bedingfield, seriously damaged the nearby church. Some fifteen bombs fell near Leiston and many incendiaries on Harwich.

The Nineteenth of August brought a furious enemy into twenty areas of East Anglia, particularly in daylight. During the 24 hours ended 06:00 on 20 August, Norwich sirens had warned eight times, and Colchester was alerted from 16:59 to 18:48. Near Newmarket, thirteen HEs fell, 28 in Deben RD and 45 more north of Norwich. Direct hits were scored on two houses in Wellesley Road, Clacton, at 01:00, and two bombs had fallen in Skelmersdale Road. Several dropped in the railway yard did not explode. Then, at 17:15 on 19 August, a load of incendiaries set fire to the Eastern National Castle Road bus garage. A single raider which, at 14:15, had dive-bombed Coltishall, released five HEs on to an incomplete hangar, slightly damaging it and killing four and injuring 25 men before leaving over Cromer. At 16:15 a Heinkel 111 using cloud cover bombed Honington, scoring hits on the barrack square. Spitfires of 66 Squadron chased it to thirty miles east of Cromer. That morning the squadron had shot down, off Aldeburgh, a Bf 110D of 2./Erpro. Gr. 210. More success attended 19 Squadron too, three Spitfire Ibs (*R6882, R6897* and *R6911*) destroying a Do 17Z of 7./KG2 off Suffolk at 18:20. At 17:45 nineteen HEs (three UX) were unloaded on to Colchester's Moler Brick Works, Brown's Timber Yard and Spottiswood Printing Works. Many people, luckily, had taken cover. Nightfall brought intensive activity — and particularly over the Midlands where extensive use was made of parachute flares for target identification. Bombers returning from the Midlands unloaded some of their loads on to East Anglia where, yet again, airfields at Honington and Watton were attacked, also Harleston and Stowmarket.

Some particularly pointless, sharp attacks were at this time directed upon Southwold. Bf 110s of 2./Erpro. Gr.210 bombed and machine-gunned the town at 15:40 on 20 August, dropped nine HEs—two behind cottages in Hotson

Above *'To my right, beyond Karl, I could see Debden flugplatz. We were on course for Duxford. Behind me was splendid, impressive might.'* (Bundesarchiv 341/456/14).

Below *The rest of KG2's Dornier 17Zs follow Hans, on a beautiful summer's morning. Intent upon destroying Duxford?* (Bundesarchiv 341/456/11).

Road—and incendiaries on tennis courts by the pier and Reydon Field. Spitfires of 66 Squadron failed to intercept them. As Hotson Road was being cleared, another fast raid developed, thirteen bombs falling. Services already on hand rescued three people from a partly demolished house. Another next to the Grand Hotel was severely damaged, and yet another in Hotson Road. No warning had been possible because electricity had been cut in the first raid.

During daylight on the 20th, twelve areas of East Anglia were raided by single aircraft and Norwich received six Red warnings. Green Section, 257 Squadron, thirty miles east of Clacton at 08:45, spotted a Do 17 at 8,000 ft over a convoy. Flying Officer Mitchell (*V7294*) attacked first, then Pilot Officer Cappons (*V7296*), before the Dornier entered cloud, smoke pouring from its port engine.

At 18:00 No 257 Squadron spotted another Dornier 17Z of 7./KG2, off Southwold. This time Mitchell silenced the enemy rear gunner before the aircraft fled into cloud. Another Do 17Z bombed Great Yarmouth before a warning was possible. Ferry Hill electricity sub-station was hit, and Mr S. Wright of Gorleston suffered burns. Three other people were injured, and the resident of 55 Cliff Hill (in which area some of the 50 kg bombs dropped) was killed. Many of the twenty bombs fell in the harbour, demolishing ten buildings to the west and damaging ten more.

Ample cloud cover on 21 August allowed Raid 42 to sneak in over the Norfolk coast at 08:00 to place five bombs on Married Quarters at RAF Bircham Newton. Another intruder bombed Stradishall in a type of attack which was to continue over many months; it was well dealt with on this occasion when Sub-Lieutenant Gardner of 242 Squadron at 12:20 destroyed a Do 17 of 4./KG3 eight miles west of Harleston.

Lowestoft's third bombing came at 16:12 on the 21st, when a Do 17Z distributed a dozen 50 kg HEs, five over the Belvedere Road area and on to an air raid shelter at the Zephyr Engineering Works where four were killed and three injured. Other HEs fell in the harbour, on shore, at Harvey-Wilsons'. In all six people were killed, seven seriously injured. Activity was over a wide area and during the day 28 HEs were directed against shipping off Southwold where, at 15:30, two 500 kg bombs damaged unoccupied houses in Lorne Road. Near Newmarket eighteen HEs fell, plus twenty in Weyland RD, 26 (two UX) in Deben and 22 (of which only one exploded) in Depwade.

Losses were, however, not entirely one way — 611 Squadron shot down a KG3 Do 17Z-3 from which only a wheel and one body were found after it crashed in the sea off Brancaster Staithe. No 66 Squadron damaged a Do 17 fifteen miles north-east of Yarmouth, but undoubtedly the highlight was the bagging by Flying Officer R. E. P. Brooker (Hurricane *P3513*) of 56 Squadron of a Do 17Z-3 of 8./KG2. During an air test he was vectored to the aircraft over Claydon, setting its port engine alight. Police Superintendent D. G. Foster recalls that the crew of four baled out, one landing at Sproughton and another within a short distance of the wreckage, in open land on the south side of Stonelodge Lane, Gippeswyk Park. The other two touched down on the rooftops of houses in the Harland Street and Waterside works areas of Ipswich. Luckily for them they were quickly in official hands, for they were confronted, according to a report of the time, by 'a certain hostile attitude among the public', some of whom were housewives brandishing carving knives — and surely a few garden forks?

After a relatively quiet night, about a dozen Dorniers operated off Norfolk and Suffolk between 09:00 and noon against shipping, which resulted in seventeen HEs on marshland 300 yd south of Blundell's Hotel, Aldeburgh.

At 09:13 on 23 August, Raid 22, a lone Do 17Z, approached Duxford from the south-east at 3,000 ft. Duxford's 3-in guns at AA Site 'B' promptly engaged it with five rounds, nearby Bofors firing eight. Between them they crippled the machine before 310's Hurricanes could engage it. Near Babraham the crew jettisoned ten HEs, all UX, before their aircraft forced-landed almost intact at Layer Farm, Wickhambrook. More anti-shipping operations took place that morning leading to fifteen HEs on East Bergholt marshes. Next night, the 23rd/24th, bombs were dropped near King's Lynn, Halesworth and twenty at Gorleston where machine-gunning took place.

A ferocious battle broke out over central and southern Essex between 15:30 and 17:25 on 24 August, 19 Squadron's Spitfires being among the fighters ordered to engage fifty Bf 109s/110s covering bombers attacking North Weald. Bombs fell at many places, 56 at Hornchurch and some near Barnston, Dunmow, as the fighting spread, resulting in incendiaries burning at Rivenhall. The local Spitfire squadrons did well, Squadron Leader B. J. E. Lane (*R6919*) claiming a Bf 110 and Sergeant B. J. Jennings another two. At 16:04 a He 111 of III/KG53 crashed, killing its crew, on Hill Farm, Layer, five miles south-west of Colchester; and a Bf 110 crashed on Bury's Farm, Great Warley. No 310 Squadron arrived too late to participate.

Between 20:30 and 03:30 on the 25th/26th August, two target types were attacked — industrial in the Midlands, airfields in the east — including Bircham Newton, Bury St Edmunds, Duxford, Feltwell, Newmarket, Wyton, Marham, West Raynham and Upwood. Raid 18 approached Newmarket from the south-east at 10,000 ft and at 01:08 began bombing with a salvo near the gasworks and into open country. It circled before returning on a reciprocal course. Raid 85 made a similar run, from King's Lynn at 10,000 ft, for what also appears to have been a briefed target, albeit an unusual one: The Maltings, Great Ryburgh, near Fakenham. For the following account of the raid I am indebted to Mr L. Snowden, and to Mr E. Sizeland, whose personal experiences of the bombing could surely never be forgotten.

'The attack happened in the late evening, just as dusk had fallen, but for some time before that the very distinctive sound of enemy aircraft had been heard. At that time I and nine other chaps in the Parish formed two crews (part time) of the NFS, and when we heard the air raid warning one crew used to go to the station—the Mill House—and the other would be on call—if needed.

'When he came in, the bomber was holding a more or less easterly course, and was seen by folk at the western end of the village. This was an incendiary raid, some of the bombs falling on open farm land to the west of The Maltings, others directly on them—we never knew how many — and the rest in meadows and fields by the river.

'The Warden and watchman formed a squad to search The Maltings, but failed to locate anything suspicious, and after a while when all was quiet they decided to call off the search. That, of course, should not have happened, for an hour or two anyway.

'A chap who was watching from his upper window suddenly saw flames coming from No 4 Roof and raised the alarm only a few minutes after the search had been called off. Probably the reason why no sign of fire had been found was that for two or three years No 4 House had been used by a farm company for storage. At the time it was filled with tons of cocksfoot seed, to a depth of about 3 ft. Incendiaries could have buried themselves in that and taken some time to burn through. The bottom floor of the house was used as a builders' store, and lots of old and new timber there soon became involved in the fire. Some years before the war the old wooden roof of No 4 Kiln had, luckily, been replaced.

'The first Brigade to arrive was Fakenham's, followed by more from Dereham, Reepham, Massingham and Lynn. Very soon they had exhausted all water at the site, so they ran hoses under the railway tracks and across meadows to the river—which all took time. It was obvious now that nothing could be done to save Nos 4 and 5 Houses as so much of their interiors were composed of wood as dry as tinder. Soon there was an inferno — and the fire was visible for miles around. Indeed, one Ryburgh man, a porter at a Norwich station, told his mates that he thought it was his home on fire; he guessed right, his parents lived on the site. It was several days before the fire was brought under control, relief fire crews being repeatedly changed. Us local part-timers had our normal work to do during the day, then for a week or more we went afterwards to the fire.'

Clearly, the firemen faced terrifying moments as when parts of the building collapsed, showering sparks high and making attractive beacons. The worst collapse came when No 5 Kiln roof fell, complete with its six large cupolas, causing an almighty crash like an explosion. Such malt as was left in silos and barley in bins was ruined and mostly ploughed in. As for the walls, Royal Engineers drilled holes for the intention was to demolish them. Instead, they had a reprieve and remain to this day. Members of the brigades in the area all agree, this was probably the biggest fire they have ever attended. Of that there can surely be no doubt — it took seven weeks for the fire to be finally doused. For their fine work the part-timers at Ryburgh received a special commendation from the firm and a monetary award.

Another small-scale, specialized attack was directed against Cambridge late on 25 August. The target, playing an increasingly useful part in the war effort, was the Unicam Instrument Works in Arbury Road where sights and periscopes for submarines were assembled. This raid, the first of several, consisted of an incendiary shower which fell on nearby farmland, damaging a cow shed.

Around 02:20 on the 26th a second Heinkel 111, which approached via Royston and St Ives, dropped at least four 50 kgs over a wide area. Firstly, a bomb exploded in a meadow at Manor Farm, Arbury Road, Cambridge, killing one of Alice Cardinal's cows and damaging a stable and ten house exteriors. A UXHE rested in a field farmed by Bill Downham, and two bombs damaged eight houses in Leys Avenue. A second set of bombs from a third He 111, which ran in from St Neots, crossed the railway installations on the south side of Hills Road Bridge, Cambridge, the first exploding in Pemberton Terrace, the next on Foster's Farm in Shaftesbury Avenue, one on Purbeck Road playing fields and two in Homerton College grounds. Damage was slight. Bombs fell in sixteen areas of East Anglia that night, among them 22 (four UX) in Gipping RD, fifteen in Walsingham RD, a load of incendiaries near Debden and nine HEs at Bishop's Stortford, which was being attacked for the first time.

The only noticeable evidence in East Anglia of the massive day raids being made by the Luftwaffe over the south was an evening sky drenched by high clouds. More correctly they were decayed vapour trails, remnants of the high fighting during the big day raids south. Neutralization of the fighter aerodromes was, for the Germans, an essential pre-invasion requisite. There were precious few in East Anglia, whose bomber airfields were to be pulverized immediately prior to any troop landing. Destruction of fighter stations north of London was becoming more urgent and, although at extreme range for fighter cover, the Luftwaffe commenced the task on 26 August. For the first time a large formation headed our way.

Radar stations plotted fighters and bombers congregating over Lille in the early afternoon, combined groups from St Omer and Calais soon heading on a northerly track. Two bomber formations, Do 17Zs of II/KG2, from Saint Léger, and II/KG3 based at Antwerp/Duerne, were being shielded on their seaward flank by Bf 110s of ZG26 and ZG76. Part of the formation turned off, heading along the River Crouch to approach Hornchurch from the north-west while fourteen Dorniers escorted by twenty Bf 110s made for the Blackwater Estuary. Near Braintree, Hurricanes of No 1 Squadron, RCAF, intercepted the Bf 110s which were on a northerly track and on the western flank of the bombers. A fierce engagement ensued as a result of which Bf 110-D *3U+CM* of 4./ZG26 crashed at Baldwin's Farm, Great Tey, the crew being killed. Soon after, a second fighter specially modified for extra long-range escort, Bf 110C-4 *2N+AK* of 9./ZG76, crashed and burnt furiously on Crabtree Farm, Great Bentley, and again the crew died. The battle cost the Canadians Flying Officer R. L. Edwards (*P3974*) but it resulted in many of the German fighters being forced to turn south for their fuel state was none too good. The Canadians continued to harry them, but their inexperience cost two more of their number. They had, at 15:18, brought down Do 17Z-3 *U5+LR* of 7./KG2, which exploded to fall over two fields at Highams Farm, Thaxted, two of the crew baling out to become PoWs. A second Dornier was certainly brought down before the formation bombed. AA Command records list it as falling to 111 Squadron near Clacton, far from the run-in track and even further from the exit route. It was more likely Do 17Z-3 W Nr *1207* of 7./KG2, which apparently fell to No 1 Squadron, RCAF, and made a belly landing at Whepstead in Suffolk. Whatever the truth, it was beyond doubt twelve Do 17Zs in three 'vics' of four, line astern, that approached Debden at 15:20 flying at 15,000 ft. That they lost height before bombing seems certain, from eye witnesses. Doubtless those with the best, certain recollection must be the crew of a Lysander flying north across Debden at 1,500 ft just as the first bombs burst!

Although intelligence sources had warned, at around 13:00, that an attack on Debden was possible, most of its Hurricanes were away when the attack came. At 15:00, 19 Squadron, Fowlmere, and 310 Squadron, Duxford, had therefore frantically been ordered to defend Debden. There was insufficient time to position them to thwart the bombing of the airfield and, by the time they were ready, over 160 bombs had been released over the aerodrome and the surrounding area. But all had not been lost for, with the bombers now at about 4,000 ft, Debden's Bofors guns started firing and very quickly split the formation. Site M4 banged off a rapid six rounds among the raiders, and some of the Dorniers abruptly swung in a southerly direction, the others towards the north-west. Site M3 also fired and scored a direct hit on *U5+TR* which curled away spewing black smoke to crash at Cole End after its crew had all baled out.

Bullet holes in the Dornier testified to fighter attack too.

Twenty Bf 110s also crossed the airfield quite low, by which time there was general confusion. A Hurricane tried to take off, but seventeen large craters on the landing ground, and a direct hit on the metalled runway intersection, meant trouble. The AA gunners were to persistently claim that an enemy aircraft exploded and fluttered down in three pieces to the north-west, but there is no evidence of that. Of the effectiveness of the rapid bombing at 15:23 there was, however, plenty of proof.

Four bombs exploded close to the watch office, four on the parade ground. One stick had fallen alongside the protected transmitting station, removing its aerial and thus seriously damaging the station's operational capability. Power was also cut to the Operations Room where the lights went out until alternative power could be generated — which took some time to arrange. One wing of the Sergeants' Mess was badly damaged, the front entrance to the NAAFI demolished and a barrack block destroyed. One damaged hangar had lost its windows. The MT Section had received a direct hit, WAAF quarters were damaged and Equipment Sections, electricity and water supplies were disrupted. Casualties were miraculously low: five killed (three of them of 257 Squadron sheltering in trenches) and fourteen injured.

Analysis of the bombing showed that incendiaries had fallen on the south-east corner of the site without causing any fires. One PoW claimed that the operational load per aircraft was ten 50 kg HEs, but clearly that was untrue. Crater sizes suggested the use of bombs in the ratio of ten 250 kg HEs, fifteen 50 kg HEs and 25 incendiaries.*

At Duxford 'take cover' had been ordered at 15:00 for it was feared that it, too, was about to be attacked. When the formation was split some of Debden's bombing overran to within a few miles of Duxford, bombs bursting behind trees on the southern fringing hills where, a little over a year ago, Blenheims had pretended to be shot down on Empire Air Day.

There is no doubt that the AA gunners did a fine job, but unhappily for their inhabitants Wimbish was plastered at 15:20, then Arkesden (west of Newport), while HEs fell in Rockell's Meadow at Duddenhoe End, at Elmdon, Langley south of Duxford and at Thaxted.

Mr K. Loveday, then a twelve-year-old living at Littlebury Green, was helping bring in the harvest for Mr A. Dukes at Elmdon Lee when a stick of bombs began bursting in the field. 'We all dived to the foot of a large beech tree, but I wanted to see what was happening, so raised my head and saw the last few bombs bursting and dirt flying into the air. My head was pushed down again by the men with me, then we all dived into a nearby brook for better cover! The bombs fell quite close to Rockell's New Farm, a short distance along the B1039 road. I remember racing to see what had happened, after we finished work — at 8 pm. The last bomb had exploded within the field where Mr Clark and Mr Starling

---

* The Do 17Z-2 normally carried a 1,000 kg bomb load. It had four bomb cells, each of which could accommodate one 250 kg, two 100 kg or four 50 kg HEs, or equivalent containers. The He 111H carried a 2,000 kg load distributed over eight cells, each containing one 250 kg, two 100 kg, four 50 kg HEs or containers. The Ju 88A carried, usually, two 500 kg, four 250 kg or 32 50 kg HEs or incendiaries. Specially modified, the He 111H-4 could carry two 1,000 kg or one 1,800 kg on an external rack.

were cutting corn with a tractor and binder. The old International tractor carried two or three shrapnel holes to the end of its days. The bomb craters were small except for one large one in which dead animals were later to be buried. And to think, it all took place on a bright Monday afternoon in August.'

Meanwhile, close to Debden aerodrome, the road through Elder Street had been blocked by a 15-ft wide crater, west of Burnt Home Farm, and a smaller one to the west. Another was on the roadside, and a UXB resided opposite RAF Debden's favourite, the Beehive Cafe. Nearby, four houses had been demolished and the road to Saffron Walden was blocked by a UXB on Cement Works Hill. Several fields were blazing, and at Higham Farm, Wimbish, three UXBs were soon located. By 29 August the total of 'ripe apples' (ie, UXBs) found by 46 BDS was twenty, and there were probably more.

Fowlmere's Spitfires had been vectored too late to Debden whereas 310 Squadron was sent further south to engage retiring attackers. Breaking cloud near Harlow, the Czechs saw the Do 17s with Bf 110s giving top cover; 310 was well placed for action. Quickly the Dorniers jettisoned their bombs, fifty of them along with incendiaries falling on to Little Hallenbury, damaging property and killing a mother who had just collected her child from the village school — and who had not taken cover. More bombs fell on Hatfield Broad Oak, White Roding and Good Easter during the Dorniers' hasty flight towards Foulness. Four miles north of Chelmsford, twenty HEs and incendiaries exploded at 15:35. More dropped near Tiptree and at least one UXB at Danbury, five miles east of Chelmsford. One Dornier apparently tried a lone escape towards the north-east, for incendiaries fell at Finchingfield around 16:14. The precise extent of the bombing was impossible to ascertain, totals indicating that 100 HEs and 67 UXBs were released in Saffron Walden RD, sixteen in Dunmow RD, fifteen (and one UX) around Chelmsford and nine near Bishop's Stortford.

Since only Squadron Leader G. D. M. Blackwood, 310 Squadron's commander, had VHF in his Hurricane, controlling their fight was not easy. He singled out a Dornier, but return fire hit his forward tank forcing him to bale out near Wickham Bishop. Pilot Officer E. Fechtner claimed a Bf 110 but the inexperienced Czech squadron was badly mauled. Sergeant Pilot E. M. Prchal chased a Do 17 some fifteen miles out from Harwich, then a Bf 109 engaged him, a cannon shot nearly blowing the wing off his Hurricane. He forced-landed near Upminster.

Flight Lieutenant G. L. Sinclair was lucky to make base, his aircraft's cockpit cover being drenched with oil. Pilot Officer Obergman, shot down over Southminster, baled out and landed 30 yd from the burning wreck of his Hurricane. For Debden and 310 Squadron it had been a sobering afternoon, but three Bf 110s had been shot down for certain, their remains being visible around Chelmsford.

If the enemy could not knock out the northern fighter stations by day then it would have to be by night and on 27/28 August, seventeen attacks were identified, the sharpest around Chelmsford where fourteen bombs fell, and in south Cambridgeshire where 22 bombs (eight UX) dropped during two incidents. Bombing was also reported from near Duxford, Harleston, Halesworth and Stoke Holy Cross. When dawn broke, Duxford was wreathed in thick fog, the first since winter. Might such weather bring a respite? Sea mist could, on the other hand, shield enemy troops landing.

Since June, such a prospect had loomed ever larger. Strangely sited concrete pillboxes were constructed, and thousands of wooden posts, festooned with ropes, wires and strings were erected upon areas which might serve as landing grounds for Ju 52s. East coast amusement parks became mini-fortresses, and mines were plentiful upon many a playground shore. 'Dad's Army' was at its classic, busiest and most important best. Equipped with little more than ex-Italian rifles and arm-bands, but rich with determination to defend every garden, the Local Defence Volunteers were backed by an equally strong-willed population whose intention to win the war was being immensely strengthened by Göring's terrorists. It was amazing how the bombing ingrained an iron will never to be beaten. Giving such decision stupendous support, there came the Prime Minister's unforgettable speeches. Delivered at 9 o'clock when the sun was still bright, and the sky seemingly always a brilliant blue in Double Summer Time, they bolstered courage enormously. '...we will NEVER surrender', he thundered; and he meant it. To have heard Sir Winston Churchill deliver his breathtaking lines, packed with phrases which echo still, remains for me and, I am certain, for many more, a treasured memory of that most momentous summer.

After his words had passed into history the silence which seemed to dominate the land while he was speaking was always shattered for me in a similar manner. Although Hitler had found us and bombed our neighbours, he had caused everyone to think decisively of victory. 'You heard what he said', my father would always say, and within moments Dad and I would be adding to the number of petrol-filled bottles in the garden shed. I really do think we would have thrown them at Hitler had he ever dared to darken our street!

* * *

Every day, at dawn and dusk, two Lysanders left Cambridge Airport, their crews scanning the East Anglian coast for signs of an enemy's landing. These 'Lyssies', dispersed on the corner of the airfield nearest to Cherry Hinton and by Teversham Lane, showed signs of a battering in France. They were tempting targets and, at 23:50 on 28 August, they came under attack. Over 100 incendiaries were scattered across Cherry Hinton by a Ju 88 and three 50 kg HEs cratered a Coldham's Lane field near 16 Squadron's Lysanders. Four more HEs did little damage to the Norman Cement Works, and another bomb exploded at Shelford Bottom. Although wide by then, the aim was good at the start. More accurate was that of 66 Squadron when, on 30 August, three Spitfires (*N3043, N3049* and *R6715* (shot down by return fire)) destroyed Raid 78, a Do 215 of 4./Aufkl.Gr.Ob.d.L, W Nr *0036:G2+JH*, off Yarmouth after a long chase. From the lost Spitfire, Pilot Officer Pickering was taken aboard a lightship. After Monday's raid on Debden it seemed certain that Duxford's turn must soon come, even though enemy escort fighters would be operating at extreme range. The wait was short.

Soon after daybreak on Saturday, 31 August, a hot, clear day, the Luftwaffe assembled over France a task force comprising Dornier 17Zs of KG2 covered by Bf 110s of ZG26. A northerly course led the bombers across the Thames Estuary and on reaching the Blackwater at 08:07 they turned inland, one group tracking slightly west of the other which passed over Chelmsford. Very likely the latter were soon using the main railway line to Cambridge as a navigational aid. It was clear to the defenders that Debden and Duxford were about to be attacked, but in case somewhere else was at risk the sirens sounded over a wide area. In Cambridge, the warning at 08:15 came as a great surprise to many then on their way to work. And as the sirens wailed, 19 Squadron's Spitfires went quickly to protect Debden, 310 Squadron being scrambled soon after in the defence of Duxford.

As the leading Raid 29 approached its target, Duxford's 3-in guns were brought to readiness. Living in Stonehill Road, Great Shelford, at the time was Mr L.A. Pearce who vividly remembers the next few moments. 'Being on a hill gave me a very good view of the Duxford area. Saturday, 31 August, was indeed a lovely day — clear blue sky, already very warm when at breakfast we were suddenly shaken by gunfire. Upon running outside I saw shell bursts in the Duxford direction for the battery by the Thriplow road was firing. There was also the sound of machine-gun fire.' Duxford's B Site had opened fire at 08:31, the enemy predicted as flying at 14,500 ft.

'I picked out the raiders heading towards the Foxton area where they turned, appearing to follow the railway line towards me. The AA guns were still firing, but not very near the target. I counted twenty aircraft in the formation and all appeared to be Dorniers, although I am not certain regarding the first vic. They were in formation in a tight oblong box as they passed by unmolested by fighters or AA fire.' Already most had bombed.

Within moments of the warning in Cambridge, Duxford's heavy AA guns opened fire bringing an alarming rush to the shelters by thousands. Such gunfire had not previously been heard here. Within seconds heavy explosions had encouraged empty streets. There seems no doubt that the gunners had done extremely well, their report stating that 'five rounds burst in and around the formation, which broke and dropped bombs'. Driven off track to the north-east and away from their intended turn-in point for attack, and possibly surprised at facing heavy guns, the bomber crews released their bombs in order to make a faster withdrawal.

Just as the first bombs fell, someone rushed into our shelter in panic and flipped down its anti-gas blanket. That did nothing for morale as the shelter, some eight miles from the bombing, shook with considerable convulsions as, at 08:30, between 120 and 150 HEs exploded in the Meldreth district in a more or less continuous line, with craters at 50-yd intervals, the lines being roughly 100 yd apart. Starting at Manor Farm, Fowlmere, near little-harmed farm buildings, a group of about fifty craters crossed a clover field in a north-westerly direction making extremely shallow craters in the clunch before, at the end of the salvo, they became deeper. There, a group of men working on a watercress bed were breakfasting in a shed whose windows and roof were damaged. The bomb line continued through stubble, orchard and grassland until it reached the Cambridge-Royston road, alongside which a bomb fell 100 yd south of the Fowlmere turn, forcing single-line traffic. Across a stubble field the bomb line continued, crossing the Cambridge-Hitchin railway lines, passing close to the Cam Blue Lias Cement Works and continuing to about half way between Meldreth and Shepreth stations. Miraculously, the track escaped damage. Onwards, the bomb line continued, across a grass field and through an orchard to the Meldreth-Shepreth Road. One bomb in the middle of that close to a small bridge hurled a large chunk of concrete towards a cottage, but it remained undamaged. And still the bombs fell, alongside a stream till it entered the river. A few fell north of the confluence, in Barrington Parish. Official assessment was that 206 HEs and four UXHEs had been dropped in South Cambridgeshire and an undetermined number of incendiaries.

It had all happened so very fast. In Shepreth the present Mrs King was a scared little girl whose mother had just prepared father's breakfast when aircraft were heard. 'Ours', thought Dad. Then the doors and windows shook and the family got behind a door—complete with cat and dog. 'We heard a bomb pass the window between ours and next door, and it landed in a field at the bottom of our garden', she recalls. 'I remember a boy picking up the remains of a bomb which fell on his father's land. It looked like silk inside.'

Colin Henderson remembers that morning well: 'The Fowlmere Road from Tyrell's Hall Park to Station Road was largely full of military vehicles moving out of the park. The Northumberland Regiment had been camping there during the past weeks. My family had a smallholding at Shepreth and that morning after breakfast I cycled along Station Road, turned right down our field roadway when, suddenly, out of the blue, it all burst forth. I jumped off the bike and dived into the deep (and dry) ditch by our plantation, and was scared to death. There was an awful racket in the trees above, too noisy for birds and what I shall always think were bullets. All around, in the distance bombs could be heard exploding and in the orchard next to me an incendiary bomb fell. The attack ended as quickly as it started, but while it was on the 8:35 Cambridge-King's Cross train pulled into the station. When the attack was over I went from the ditch to the edge of the wood and saw two columns of smoke. Two incendiaries had fallen in our barley field, fortunately cut. But each bomb had fallen on to a sheaf, and I will always be amazed how thoroughly they were consumed, with hardly an ear left.'

The incendiaries fell erratically, eastwards of the HEs, some at Fowlmere, others on Barrington Green. But most were among stooks and sheaves around Shepreth where fields were decorated by small fires from which columns of smoke ascended vertically in the still, morning air.

Meanwhile, the enemy formation was on its way home, swinging on to a reciprocal course, and crossing Shepreth Junction close to Long Road, Cambridge, then turned south over the 'Gogs'. In so doing one of the Dorniers dropped incendiaries at Shelford Bottom, recalls Mr Pearce, 'and in the field at the corner of the A604 and Hinton Way, I found about a dozen craters'. Some of the HEs had burst in a field farmed by Mr Long and his wife Dora, sister of Alice Cardinal who had but lately lost a cow through bombing. Mr Pearce found that Nunton Way had a direct hit about 150 yd from the crossroads, and on the opposite side of the A604 some horses had been killed. This incident probably marked the point at which 19 Squadron attacked the enemy force.

The Spitfire pilots, patrolling at 20,000 ft south-east of Duxford, had spotted the formation heading for home and engaged the enemy as they swung south of Fulbourn. Over the next few minutes Flight Lieutenant Clouston (*R6888*) claimed one enemy aircraft, Pilot Officer Burgoyne (*R6890*) and Sergeant Cox (*R6924*) each laying claim too. German records indicate the loss of only one Bf 110D, W Nr *3396:U8+HS* of 8./ZG26 which came down in Essex. For 19 Squadron this was a disastrous engagement due to spent cartridges jamming the cannon mechanism. Flying Officer Coward (*X4231*) was shot down and suffered serious foot injuries, Flying Officer Brinsden (*R6958*) baled out of his aircraft over Newton and Flying Officer Aerberhardt (*R6912*) was killed when his damaged Spitfire overturned on landing.

Debden and the countryside around was bombed at 08:39, about 160 HEs and incendiaries being released. The fourteen Dorniers, flying at 15,000 ft in vics astern as Raid 37, had followed the Duxford attackers. Approaching from the south, their formation abruptly turned east and then headed north-west on the bomb run. Since fighters were in the area the AA guns did not fire. At the moment for bombing the lead Dornier released a bright flare and the bombs were dropped. They fell from south of the Newport road across the camp north-westwards, the incendiaries being scattered on the north side of the landing ground. Damage was extensive, but much of it involved buildings hit in the previous raid, including the Sergeants' Mess, NAAFI and R/T Transmitter. Station Sick Quarters received a direct hit and half a barrack block was demolished. The Airmen's Mess, garages and a hangar were all damaged. There were three fatalities and twelve injured. It was a much more effective attack than the previous one because it reduced operational capability far more.

As for civilian damage, two houses at Elder Street were burnt out and there were numerous UXBs in the area, one thought to be at the Friend's School in Saffron Walden. The surrounding region was evacuated quickly, but the scare proved a false alarm. Another did lie in Maltings Field, Station Road, Saffron Walden, and bombs had also exploded in Audley End Park. More UXBs were found at Wimbish, on the north edge of Rowney Wood and south of Elder Street. An official estimate was that 35 HEs had dropped in Saffron Walden RD, eleven within the town, which also received incendiaries.

After bombing, the Dorniers turned anti-clockwise in line astern and re-formed under the protection of about twenty Bf 110s which had stood off to the west during the bombing. On the way home one Dornier placed ten HEs and incendiaries on to Colchester's Spittal and Fambridge Roads at 08:40. A water main in Hythe broke, flooding the sewage works, and incendiaries on Plaxman's caused a small fire. Others set a house in Brook Steet ablaze and two houses were demolished. In Roman Road a UXB resulted in sixty houses being without gas. Six other UXBs were dropped just south of High Roding.

However, the enemy had still to face 257 Squadron which had left Martlesham at 08:30, led by Flight Lieutenant Berisford, and taken position over Clacton at 18,000 ft. Thus, the squadron was well placed for an interception and broke up the fifty-Messerschmitt formation with head-on attacks. During the sharp engagement at 09:10 in the Maldon-Burnham area, where a few HEs were dropped, Pilot Officer Henderson (*P3708*) shot down two Bf 110s before baling out of his burning aircraft and being rescued, face and hands burnt, from the sea near Brightlingsea. Flight Lieutenant Berisford (*P3705*), Flying Officer Mitchell (*L1706*) and Pilot Officer Cochrane (*P3709*) each claimed a Bf 110. Pilot Officer Gundry (*P3704*) chased another to the south coast, met a huge enemy formation on return, and put a few shots into a Bf 110. Pilot Officer Moffett (*R4903*) was shot down and killed. Two of the Dorniers which participated in the raid, Do 17Z-2 W Nr *3483:U5+CN* of II/KG2 and *U5+AD* of Stab.III/KG2 were brought down, the first by 19 Squadron, the second by 111 Squadron off Felixstowe.

As 19 Squadron was landing at Fowlmere, the 'All Clear' sounded in

Cambridge at 08:57. It was then that I spotted my intrepid friend, Walter Horn, mounting his cycle. With captured Italian rifle (grenade attachment firmly in place) slung across his back, he was smartly clad in his smooth denim Local Defence Volunteer uniform. Walter had a ten-minute cycle ride home to collect his gun, extended by an order to take cover. Now, as he set off for his post, the 'All Clear' came. Parachutists had not descended to seize the sandbagged emplacement along with Chesterton railway viaduct; but the day was young and plenty of action was to follow. No 310 Squadron had taken no part in the battle and was already back at Duxford.

At 10:50 the sirens wailed once more amid expectation that the Luftwaffe was to attack Duxford again, which 19 Squadron patrolled until 11:25; no attack materialized, however. Sergeant Walter Horn had hurried from his place at the 'Pitt Press' and was well on the way to his outpost when the 'All Clear' sounded at 11:19. A third warning came at 13:30 and once more Walter tried to reach his post in time. How cruel fate can be: the 'All Clear' sounded at 13:57. One then felt bound to snatch as much as possible of a glorious summer afternoon for peaceful contemplation of all that was being so cruelly spoilt in the world around us.

At 14:53 three Spitfires of 66 Squadron (*K9823, N3032* and *N3035*) claimed a Do 215 PR aircraft after a chase from Norwich to twenty miles south-east of Felixstowe. Our final warning came at 18:25, local squadrons patrolling in reserve as Walter made one more journey to his bridge which, by now, surely he would have admitted was a trifle too far! Yet his day's duty was far from over. As dusk reluctantly fell, he mounted his high bike and, for the fifth time, set off for the sandbagged emplacement guarding Chesterton Viaduct, in case some ill-behaved 'nuns' tried to hi-jack the LNER. I know he thought back upon 'quite a day'. I know *I* did, for the thought that the Germans might destroy dear old Duxford, on a bright summer day, was quite unacceptable. Some defiant retort was necessary so, before going to bed, Dad and I put the shutters in place then filled even more bottles with petrol and torn shirts. Thank goodness the incendiaries never found them!

Whilst the big raids grabbed public attention, daylight attacks on coastal shipping had continued. On 2 September another three of 66 Squadron (*K9823, N3060* and *R6689*) destroyed a He 111 six miles north-east of Smith's Knoll LV. Apart from ten HEs which fell in Gipping RD, 2 September was a quiet, if uneasy, day with the squadrons at advanced alert states. Shortly after midnight raiders penetrated to Bedfordshire, dropping bombs at Stagsden, Renhold, Castle Mills, Keysoe and Little Staughton, supplementing HEs with a few incendiaries.

The assumption that the Luftwaffe would again try for Duxford meant that any intrusion into airspace north of London attracted 12 Group Squadrons into action. On 3 September, when 611 Squadron was covering 19 Squadron's re-equipment with non-cannon Spitfires, 310 Squadron intercepted Do 17s heading for Colchester over North Weald. The Davey Paxman Co iron works at Colchester was hit and a 32-in water main fractured. The Czechs, who lost one aircraft, claimed two Do 17s, five Bf 110s and a possible sixth. Also engaged was 17 Squadron which lost three aircraft flown respectively by Squadron Leader Miller, who forced-landed at North Weald; Sergeant D. Fopp who, seriously burned, baled out near Brentwood; and Flying Officer D. W. H. Hanson, killed — shot down over Foulness by a Dornier. A further three Hurricanes were lost by

46 Squadron, and 257 Squadron returned without Pilot Officer C. A. Bon-Seigneur (*P3578*) or Pilot Officer D. W. Hunt (*L1703*), who crashed near Chelmsford at 10:30. Pilot Officer K. C. Gundry (*P3704*) landed at Martlesham with part of his aircraft's tailplane shot off by cannon fire, and Sergeant Nettles' (*P3705*) starboard wing and fuel tank were badly damaged. Eventually the enemy aircraft reckoned shot down included: one Do 17Z-2 W Nr *3450:U5+AN* in the River Crouch by Flying Officer Hanson, and five Bf 110s of 1./ZG2 (W Nr *2146: 3M+BF, 3120:3M+CB, 2133:3M+HL, 2065:3M+EK* and *3113:3M+EL*). Two more Bf 110Ds shot down by Spitfire Ibs of 19 Squadron were *3310:3U+EP* of 6./ZG26 and *3225:3U+KR* of 7./ZG26.

Limited night activity followed on 3/4 September, thirteen HEs with incendiaries dropping by Felixstowe's boating lake, in Sea Road and Mill Lane at 20:38, HEs and incendiaries dropped on Harwich at 01:00, starting a fire at Cliff House where, at 05:30, firemen still attending the incident were machine-gunned. High explosives fell in King George Avenue, on allotments at Parkeston and damaged the railway line to Dovercourt. Eight more and incendiaries were dropped at Braintree. With Merseyside the main target on the 4th/5th, enemy aircraft traversed East Anglia at about 18,000 ft. At 03:30 bombs fell on Peartree Farm, Higham, Bedfordshire, and that night a Heinkel 111 came down at Wantisden, Rendlesham.

Daylight saw two major raids on England. At 09:25, twenty-minute air raid alerts were held in many East Anglian towns as enemy aircraft produced an unexpected operation against the new Bradwell Bay airfield. Duxford's 19 and 310 Squadrons were committed on 6 September to Leigh Mallory's 'Big Wing' concept after intelligence indicated that major daylight raids on Debden and Duxford would not be repeated. Nuisance raids were another matter and on 6 September lone bombers attacked Cromer and Lowestoft. Early the next night, intruders operated against Wittering, Marham and Norwich.

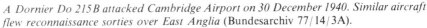

A Dornier Do 215B attacked Cambridge Airport on 30 December 1940. Similar aircraft flew reconnaissance sorties over East Anglia (Bundesarchiv 77/14/3A).

There was no daylight enemy activity over East Anglia on 8 September, but the following night's bombing included six HEs in the Halstead area, over 100 incendiaries in Blyth RD and two HEs at Bromham, near Bedford. Almost the entire country spent the night under Red Alert, and fifty minelayers of KG4 and Gruppe 126 operated along the East Coast. About 220 bombers raided Britain while Ku.Fl.Gr. 1/906 and 2/906 sought shipping well out to sea.

Early on 10 September, incendiaries fell on the Moler Works at Colchester, and over its Hythe district. Great Yarmouth received a raid warning at 10:34 on the 10th but so often did the sirens sound, and nothing seem to happen, that many people were no longer taking shelter. Luckily that was not true this time for, at 11:35, a bomber crossed the town from north to south dropping HEs, the first in the river mouth, the second on the fish curing yard opposite Toby's and another in Admiralty Road, damaging a naval store at the back of the Nelson Monument. Two women were killed, three people were injured and four houses were damaged.

A reconnaissance aircraft toured East Anglian airfields before dropping bombs near Mildenhall, and ten miles north of Happisburgh three Spitfires of 74 Squadron, led by Flight Lieutenant J. C. Mungo Park, damaged an Erpro. 210 Bf 110. Others engaged a He 111 off Lowestoft and a Ju 88 north-east of Ipswich which, from low level and without warning, had dropped four HEs and an oil bomb over a space of a mile on the town. At Bolton Lane/Sloane Street, St Margaret's Green, one of the bombs caused the fracture of a water main from which a column of water spurted high. Early in the afternoon, Pilot Officer B. V. Draper of 74 Squadron claimed a Ju 88 some forty miles south-east of Yarmouth, again after it had bombed the town in a west-east pass. Five HEs and an oil bomb were dropped, the latter in the grounds of the naval barracks; one of the bombs in Nelson Gardens, Marine Parade, hurled glass from windows in Wellington Pier causing a dozen minor casualties.

As the night blitz developed, lengthy, lone daylight reconnaissance and damage assessment flights by high-flying Do 215s and Ju 88s were operated, as on the 13th when from Wales-Sheffield-Humber-the Wash an aircraft passed Chelmsford where thirteen HEs fell.

One of the few night raiders brought down at this time was He 111 W Nr *4321* which crashed at 02:30 on 14 September, at Downhill Estate, Bishop's Stortford, after encountering anti-aircraft fire. Around 15:25 on this cloudy day bombs were dropped on Yarmouth, Clacton, Ipswich, Southwold and West Suffolk.

Limited night bombing of airfields again took place on 14/15 September before Duxford's fighters played a busy part in the hectic engagements on the 15th, the first 'Battle of Britain Day'. The only enemy activity over East Anglia the next night involved route marker flares out to sea. Two operations were mounted against the area on the 16th, the first mid-afternoon and the second around 22:00 . During the early phase ten HEs fell in fields immediately west of Henlow aerodrome. Half an hour later four more bombs dropped south-west of a railway bridge near Lower Standon, Bedfordshire. A Do 17 arrived over East Wretham just as 311 Squadron was moving in, and was driven off by anti-aircraft fire. It then attacked Honington at 15:55, and the gunners there shot down the bomber. Bombing over East Anglia was widespread, indiscriminate to most people, generally accepted as a calculated risk one lived with — until a novel weapon brought widespread concern.

Chapter 8
Big bangs

On 17/18 September, visibly and audibly, 'the big banger' burst upon London and the south-east. Reports, secret and coded, were rushed to the Ministry of Home Security confirming that a new weapon, the parachute mine, had come into use. An 'indiscriminate form of aerial attack against the morale of the people', to quote a Ministerial pronouncement, it produced extensive blast effect over a radius of as much as two miles. As property-destroying weapons, mines were of less value, but they could destroy windows, tiles and slates over vast areas.

News of the first arrival came from ARP workers on the East Coast where a cylinder, estimated to be 8 ft long by 2 ft 6 in in diameter, was spotted before it exploded to produce a crater they claimed was 100 ft in diameter. By the early hours of 18 September, 21 mine incidents had been notified to London, some involving two weapons. Only nine had exploded so that investigation of the mines' characteristics — very hazardous — was possible.

Not their least alarming feature was the frightening, sinister sight and swishing sound of a mine descending. That first report was quite accurate for most of them were 8 ft 8 in long, a smaller version being 5 ft 8 in in length. Both had a diameter of 2ft 2 in and they were dark green in colour. They arrived suspended from a sea green artificial silk parachute of about 27-ft diameter, the larger LMB mine being known to the British as Type C, the smaller as Type D. Both had hemispherical nose cones, and at the rear a bowl-shaped cap into which was packed the parachute, vital for control of descent and landing. As the mine left the aircraft the bowl was snatched away allowing the parachute to billow, reducing descent speed to about 40 mph.

Apart from the conventional Type F parachute, two others constructed from 2-in strips of khaki-coloured artificial silk were later employed. One had silk ribbons radiating from an apex to form a lattice structure, the other variant having three strips arranged circumferentially. For the former a silk drogue was necessary for deployment. Later types of parachute improved the weapon's limited accuracy.

The sight of a mine dangling from its parachute — such as was seen on 18 September in London's Shoreditch High Street — was, to say the least, menacing. Precise investigation revealed the LMB Type C mine to have a nominal weight of 1,000 kg, a body length of 104 in and a maximum diameter of 26 in. The tail bowl's diameter was 23.5 in, its maximum depth 15 in, so that it brought the mine's overall length to 119 in. LMA Type D was a 500 kg weapon with a 67 in-long body 26 in in diameter with bowl dimensions as for the larger mine giving an overall length of 82 in. Whereas the Type C was steel-cased and very destructive, Type D had an aluminium case giving it an extremely high charge/weight ratio for heavy blast effect, though this was considerable with either type, as was particularly clear at Petts Wood and Rochester on the first night of use.

While the extent of the night's mine campaign was being considered, the Luftwaffe made a few incursions into East Anglia using conventional weapons, nine HEs being dropped on Lakenheath Warren at 09:30 on the 18th. Another raider dropped ten bombs south of Hammer Hill, Haynes, Essex. A further attempt was made to bomb Mildenhall before darkness fell, and two oil bombs and 22 HEs (and two UXs) were dropped near Chelmsford.

Throughout that day the threat from mines brought increasing concern. The few that had exploded illustrated their enormous potential and public belief was strong that those which had not exploded would do so very easily if approached. So serious was the situation that at 11:20 on 18 September a news flash was sent from the Ministry of Home Security to all Civil Defence Regional HQs stating that a 'number of magnetic mines are suspected of having been dropped in urban areas' and that some had not exploded. No motor vehicle was to be brought near, and every effort made to prevent any vibration near the weapons. The Royal Navy was investigating what seemed to be something very new, and all persons were ordered to be evacuated from areas where the weapons fell. No details of the new projectiles were, however, given to the ARP authorities — but the official belief that these were magnetic mines was not true. They were modified standard sea mines.

Meanwhile, more conventional operations continued, while nine mines fell in the London area and Kent. During the night of 18/19 September Norwich was bombed but next day the defenders notched up two notable successes. Beginning in June the Luftwaffe had commenced daily weather and maritime reconnaissance flights along the East Coast, employing Do 17s and later Ju 88s about forty to fifty miles off shore and making closer incursions to observe shipping movements. Up to four such flights operated daily — for much of the war — but their distance from shore made interception none too easy. However, on 19 September Hurricanes of 17 Squadron operating off Suffolk came upon a Ju 88 of 4(F)./121, and engaged it. What followed seems never to have been unravelled, but a Ju 88 belly landed on Oakington — in the middle of an anti-invasion exercise—and turned out to be W Nr *0362:7A+FM*, from Caen, a Dessau-built Ju 88 reconnaissance aircraft accepted by the Luftwaffe on 8 August 1940 and which, having a few .303-in holes in the port engine, must have suffered a power loss and the crew total disorientation. All four became PoWs. There can be little doubt that this was 17 Squadron's Ju 88. There were three cameras in the bomb bay, but no bomb racks or sights. The cameras were removed and in an unusual twist subsequently used in Oakington's PR Spitfires.

Another Ju 88A-1, W Nr *2151:32+GH* of KG 77, wearing a large *P* on the port side of its fin and having white spinners, crashed in Culford Park, Bury St Edmunds, at 11:00. In mist, rain and low cloud, the bomber had attacked Upwood and was retiring across Suffolk when it was caught by a Section of 302 Squadron. Flown by Flight Lieutenant Riley, Flying Officer Kolowski and

German bombs, containers, incendiaries and other weapons

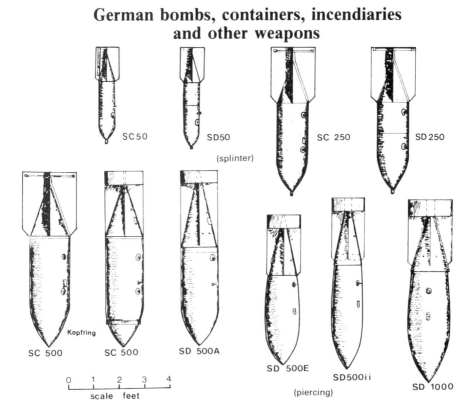

A. Smaller types of German high explosive (HE) bomb. SC (Spreng Cylindrisch) types were thin steel case bombs distinctively marked by a yellow band on the tail fins or tail cone, the latter sometimes being yellow overall. Commonly used were the 50, 250, 500 and 1,000 kg variants. A retarder ring ('Kopfring') was sometimes added to the SC50, SC250, and SC500 weapons. Steel spikes (Stabbomben) preventing ricochet were a feature only of bombs specifically built for them. SD (Spreng Dickwandig) types were medium case bombs whose heavier steel walling caused a greater blast and heavy fragmentation effect. Most Common were 50, 250 and 500 kg weapons, and identifiable by red tail markings. All these bombs could be fitted with a variety of fuzes, some causing lengthy delayed action.

	Body length	Body diameter	Length overall including tail
SC50	28.25 to 30	8	43 to 45
SC250	46 to 47.5	14.5	64 to 66
SC500	54 to 56	18.5	78 to 79
SD50*	23.5	8	42.5 to 43
SD250*	33.5	14.5	63.5
SD500A*	53	17.5	80
SD500E	43.5	15.5	68
SD500ii	54	15.5	78
SD1000	58	19.75	82

The last three mentioned were 'armour' piercing weapons for use against 'hard' targets including ships, and were also known by a PC (Panzer Cylindrisch) prefix in place of SD. They could be identified by blue markings.

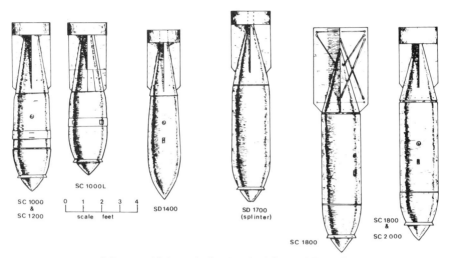

SC 1000L

SC 1000 & SC 1200

0 1 2 3 4
scale feet

SD 1400

SD 1700 (splinter)

SC 1800

SC 1800 & SC 2000

B. Larger types of German high explosive bomb. SC and SD prefixes also identified these weapons which had similar colours. Kopfrings were permanently fitted to all but the SD 1,400 kg bomb. By mid-war many German bombs had a circular addition to the tail vanes.

Dimensions of weapons (inches)

	Body length	Body diameter	Length overall including tail
SC1000/1200*	74.5	26	112.5
SD/PC1400	76.5	22	111
SD1700	92	25.5	?
SC1800	104.5	26	147 (long tail)
SC2000	104.5	26	136.5 (short tail)

* These bombs could be fitted with a screwed-in steel 15- or 24-in extension rod.

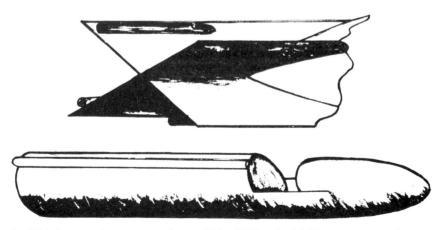

C. Whistle to produce a scream from a falling HE bomb. Of this most common form up to four examples could be clipped to bomb fins as shown. It consisted of a metal tube 11 in long and 1.5 in diameter to which a 4-in long wooden nose was attached by two nails. Possibly fitted to one bomb dropped in June 1940, but first found after a raid on Ipswich.

Flight Lieutenant Jastrzebski, the fighters were lucky to locate and destroy the raider.

During the day over 500 incendiaries fell in Saffron Walden RD, and in Hartismere 150, also an oil bomb and eleven HEs (one UX). The main bombing events, though, took place after dark when more mines arrived. Their use in rural areas had little value, yet many were released over the countryside. But at Chelmsford, with a variety of industrial targets, in the region of which two were now sown, they had more purpose. Only one exploded. The other, which came down at 04:30 at Springfield, north-east of Chelmsford, stayed dormant. A third, in Melford RD, did not explode either.

The Luftwaffe had a none-too-successful night for He 111P-2 *G1+LK* of I/KG55, seriously damaged by London's AA guns, was brought down at Thorley, Bishop's Stortford, at 23:15. Three of the crew died, the other became a prisoner.

Daylight on 20 September attracted few enemy aircraft but after nightfall activity was on a much increased scale. Around Duxford, 41 HEs dropped. Another eighteen fell on Queach Farm, Blakenham, Suffolk, and at 01:15 four HEs at Poplar Hill, Stowmarket. But again it was parachute mines that brought most concern. One fell in Blyth RD, and another at Great Cornard, resting a mile south-south-east of Sudbury and 150 yd from a road. These, and another at Scalby, near Scarborough, were the first dropped well away from London. The 68th mine arrived 450 yd south of Wysing Grange, Bourn, Cambridgeshire, and being of the smaller type, aroused considerable interest, being possibly the first Type D to be found. Its rounded nose had slightly penetrated the ground, but the aluminium tail section was fully intact. Ten HEs came down at the same time. By dawn over 100 mines had in all been reported.

The most alarming incident in East Anglia happened at 03:25 on 21 September when the 93rd reported mine drifted into a stonemason's yard in the vicinity of Cemetery Road, Ipswich, a centrally sited area of the town, and only partially exploded, demolishing a house, seriously damaging 25 more and blast-damaging 150. An ARP team with incredible courage used a stirrup pump to extinguish a blazing harness on the mine. Most of the mine lay exposed on the surface, its parachute alongside. Although a naval BDS team worked all day they were unable to render it safe. They had no choice but to detonate it *in situ*, the local population having been evacuated before dawn. The force of the explosion far exceeded expectations and a crater 50 ft wide and 25 ft deep resulted. Damage was tremendous, seventy more houses being totally demolished, 750 damaged and many windows in the main street 650 yd away were shattered.

At 03:35 another mine drifted down at Rushmere St Andrew, a mile and a half to the east. It fell upon open ground by 'Brackenside', Camberley Road, where Mr and Mrs Halliday lived, and caused damage over a wide area, extending as far as Foxhall Road. Olive Halliday recalls how 'my husband and I were extremely fortunate not to be injured — due, I think, to us having taken a small mattress into the kitchen, placing it on the floor directly behind the stairs. All windows were blown in, the floors and the blanket covering us had glass all over them, and there were knife-like splinters embedded in walls. In spite of the destruction, vases were still standing on window-sills and I remember a teapot standing on the kitchen table — minus handle and spout! I can still recall the "swishing" sound of the parachute descending, although at the time I did not realize what it was. Our roof was lifted and replaced itself, and inner walls leant at acute angles.'

Another mine exploded at Burnham, Essex, while unexploded mines came down at Lawn Hall, North End on the A130 eight miles north-west of Chelmsford and at Gally Wood two miles south of Chelmsford. At 21:55 yet another exploded at Church Farm, Ashfield, producing a crater 46 ft by 20 ft and damaging houses. Rumours about the mines were widespread. Certainly the 'hollow bang' sound upon detonation was extremely loud, the shock wave tremendous. That so few exploded, however, added to their mystique, fuelling general belief that these were 'magnetic mines' which would easily explode in close proximity to metal objects. That belief was long-lasting in official circles too.

Early in the mining campaign, Region 4 Headquarters in St Regis, a block of requisitioned flats in Chesterton Road, Cambridge, received a report of a mine at Litlington, behind a row of cottages. The Cambridgeshire Civil Defence Officer, George Bowyer, cautiously viewed the site — in the company of a local 'Bobby'. Mine and parachute were only too evident as they crept towards the unwelcome visitor. Gone from their pockets metallic objects, and from the constable's tunic his buttons. Also, having metal items fitted within their braces, they had decided that safety was of more import than the chance of immodesty, and hoped... Cautiously they ventured into the garden where the green mine rested in a cabbage patch. Suddenly a shattering noise overcame them. The Constable had taken insufficient precautions — his police whistle crashed on to the ground! Luckily the mine neither heard nor apparently cared, and later surrendered peacefully to a disposal squad. Such events, though, evoked no humour until long after the event; no weapon was trivial — not even the smallest.

During the night of 21/22 September East Anglia had received more attention in addition to eight parachute mines, after leaders of a steady stream of bombers from Holland crossed the Essex coast from 20:09 heading for London. Followers came from Belgian bases.

At Ilford, at 21:40 on 22 September, there was a hideous demonstration of just how destructive a mine could be when one demolished 100 houses literally in a flash. In East Anglia, one on Lord Butler's farm, near Saffron Walden, did not explode until 14:30 on the 23rd. Another mine fell in Blyth RD without exploding.

Around 16:00 on Sunday the 22nd a quite different phase of activity returned to the fore when, under cover of mist and rain, several low-flying hostiles entered East Anglia from Hertfordshire. First to rock from enemy bombs were railway sheds, track and outhouses at Royston. Another aircraft placed ten bombs on the west side of Fowlmere airfield, destroying a 19 Squadron Spitfire (*X4351*). Its Red Section immediately responded by placing a few shots into the fleeing annoyance.

Subsequent night activity over East Anglia and Lincolnshire aroused considerable British interest because of an apparent three-phase pattern. The first lasted from 21:00 to 22:30, the second from 01:45 to 02:11 and the third from 03:00 to 05:45. Raiders crossed in at between 10,000 and 15,000 ft apart from some which uncharacteristically approached at 2,000 ft. From this, and the phases of operations, it was concluded that the night's activity was planned to interrupt RAF bomber operational take-off and landing phases with a central period for the interruption of night flying training. This appears to have been the first occasion when such a co-ordinated plan was operated, its significance only being confirmed much later.

The night of 23/24 September was a very busy one, the main target being Manchester. Four parachute mines floated down around Poslingford, West Suffolk — quite near Stradishall — and two exploded. Another fell in North Witchford, one on Household Farm, Benwick, Isle of Ely, and a further one at Chilton Street, West Suffolk, a mile north-west of Clare. Upon exploding, the latter brought extensive damage to cottages.

Nine HEs dropped on Braintree before local activity reached a climax around 02:00 with a sharp attack on the Bury St Edmunds area, the highlight a direct hit on an ammunition dump. Airfields were again the main target, in particular Mildenhall. A parachute mine settled alongside the junction of the Thetford/Ipswich railway line, halting traffic until the weapon's safe removal shortly before 08:00.

At 04:15 the Bury St Edmunds area again came under attack, three bombs with tail 'screamers' signalling their approach with an individualistic sound to explode by Bury station, and another near air raid shelters between St Andrews Street and Prospect Row. Tail whistles fitted to HE bombs were of at least three types, one a black cardboard tube resembling an organ pipe, another an adaptation of a bayonet scabbard. Both about 14 in long by $1\frac{1}{2}$ in in diameter, the former had a vent some 4 in from the pointed tip, the latter a number of cuts to increase the range of tones within the scream. One attachment was sufficient for each bomb. A further variant was a hollow metal tube, its nose blocked by a wooden bung nailed in place. Often, the screamer was found intact near the bomb's impact point.

Four parachute flares had been released over Callis Hall Road to mark the opening of the Bury attack. Only two ignited, then incendiaries were distributed in a cemetery near Bury Barracks. Five minutes later the first three HEs were dropped north-east of the town, only two exploding. At 04:00 another three produced craters near Langton Church and on the playing fields of the East Anglian School. The attack was resumed at 04:25 when a parachute mine slipped into the garden of No 35 Queen's Road without exploding. Behind a house in Fornham Road a bomb exploded, and three more near the sugar beet factory before screaming bombs burst near the railway station breaking windows in the general and parcels offices. This was the most elaborate night attack yet upon any Suffolk town.

Air raids always produced a splendid crop of rumours and unlikely stories, and none bettered those following the discovery, after the Bury raid, of great quantities of a fine cotton wool-like substance on trees, telephone wires and generally floating around after the Germans had gone. News spread fast — the enemy had dropped a secret weapon. 'Guncotton' suggested one and 'phosphorus thread' another. But it was late summer and, as any East Anglian must know, that is in particular spider time, and it did not take long for the intelligence men to name the real culprits. Obviously Fifth Columnist spiders who must have enjoyed mixing a supply of the incredible with their inimitable gossamer ...

Further inland, too, the enemy had been active. A Red Alert sounded in

Cambridge at 03:40, and within a quarter of an hour two oil bombs had fired crops next to Cherry Hinton Hall, fairly close to the aerodrome. All then quietened on this very clear night, and well I recall my mother and I helping older residents living near us, and who regularly took shelter, back to their homes when, without any warning, there came a tremendous explosion. A high-flying Ju 88 which had approached Cambridge from the south was now scampering away. Obviously its target was Cambridge railway installations, and again the bombs had fallen wide. The first made a crater 8 ft across by 4 ft deep just inside Fenner's Cricket Ground and demolished a wall by Mortimer Road. The blast effect was incredible, and mainly caused, I reckoned at the time, by a second bomb on the University Tennis Courts 20 yd from Gresham Road and a third which exploded in the garden of No 49, Hills Road, close to the line dividing it from Lyndewode Road. Despite their brown sticky paper protection, thousands of windows were smashed and slates in profusion shaken or blown from roofs over an amazingly wide area — particularly from houses in Mortimer Road, Willis Road, Mill Road, Gresham Road, Glisson Road, Mawson Road, Regent Street, Harvey Road, St Paul's Road, Lyndewode Road and Tenison Road where, at No 27, an oil bomb landed appropriately in a coal place, starting a fire which was rapidly extinguished.

Two further bombs had fallen at Cherry Hinton Hall, causing blast damage to greenhouses. The hall was private property, and it was some time before the craters were located. Their size caused astonishment for one was 50 ft across and 8 ft deep, in the centre of which, to the amazement of its discoverers, was a most splendid crop of mushrooms enjoying new-found fertility. The Head Warden for that area Mr R. H. Myhill, is still insistent that the craters would have provided an excellent basis for a rock garden, or lily pool, and a novel war memorial. The tremendous noise made by these bombs — particularly the final two, probably of 500 kg — was followed by yet another common wartime tale. 'They must have been British.' The Germans, short of bombs thanks to the blockade of Germany, were having to use unexploded, superior British bombs! Another popular tale was that the Germans dropped lots of 'dud, sand-filled bombs because they were too stupid to load the right ones'. That took a lot of believing.

Slight activity off the coast during daylight on 24 September resulted in 74 Squadron engaging a Do 17 ten miles off Sheringham, but without success. Anti-shipping activity continued after dark, but the main concern again surrounded the dropping of parachute mines. Four (one UX) and three HEs came down near Braintree and another four (one UX) at Bacon End, Stoke-by-Clare, along with two oil bombs and five HEs. During the night 31 HEs (six UX) fell in the Downham Market area, and over 200 incendiaries outside Saffron Walden. Mine Incident 168 involved an unexploded example 200 yd south of the A120 two miles south of Dunmow, while another two exploded near White Roding, Essex.

Low cloud and rain on 25 September permitted lone raiders using cloud cover to reach well inland, including Bedfordshire. Two bombs exploded harmlessly on Cranfield aerodrome just after midday, but at 15:53 a major incident at Henlow resulted in eight bombs hitting the camp and six exploding in Station Road, Lower Standon. Two Henlow hangars suffered blast damage, casualties amounting to three Servicemen killed, six seriously and three slightly injured. Four civilians were also wounded.

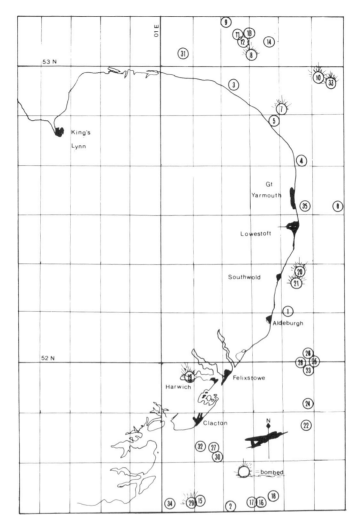

British merchant ships sunk by bombs or mines (probably air mines) off East Anglia. During 1939–40. Day/month follows map key number. Tonnage (bracketed) follows name. Ships mined unless otherwise indicated.

1939 1 10.9 *Magdapur* (8,641); **2** 13.11 *Ponzano* (1,346); **3** 8.12 *Corea* (751); **4** 12.12 *Marwich Head* (496); **5** 12.12 *King Egbert* (4,535); **6** 19.12 *City of Kobe* (4,373).

1940 7 9.1 *Oakgrove* (1,985); **8** 10.1 *Upminster* (689); **9** 12.1 *Granta* (2,719); **10** 30.1 *Voreda* (7,216); **11** 13.2 *British Triumph* (8,501); **12** 13.2 *Clan Morrison* (5,936); **13** 24.2 *Jevington Court* (4,544); **14** 12.3 *Gardenia* (3,745); **15** 20.3 *Hawnby* (5,380); **16** 24.4 *Stokesley* (1,149); **17** 20.4 *Hawnby* (5,380); **18** 8.6 *Hardingham* (5,415); **19** 3.7 *Bijou* (98, sailing barge) bombed Mistley Quay; **20** 12.7 *Hornchurch* (2,162); **21** 15.7 *Heworth* (2,855); **22** 26.7 *Hayton* (1,189); **23** 29.7 *Moidart* (1,262); **24** 29.7 *Clan Monroe* (5,952); **25** 3.8 *Wychwood* (2,794); **26** 15.8 *Brixton* (1,557); **27** 5.10 *Adaptity* (372); **28** 17.10 *Frankrig* (1,361); **29** 7.11 *Astrologer* (1,673); **30** 9.11 *Baltrader* (1,699); **31** 15.11 *Amenity* (297); **32** 18.11 *Ability* (293); **33** 15.11 *Blue Galleon* (712); **34** 24.11 *Ryal* (367); **35** 24.11 *Thomas M* (310).

Above *Sea mine, parachute-delivered, being winched aboard a trolley and destined for a Ju 88 of 5./KG54* (Bundesarchiv 375/2710/27).
Below *He 111s flew many anti-shipping sorties off East Anglia during 1939-1941. Seen here are two marauders of KG1, the 'Hindenburg' Geschwader* (Bundesarchiv 385/587/15).

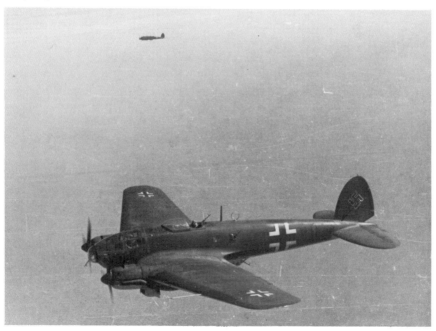

Airfield attacks continued after dark. A mine intended for Stradishall deposited itself on Home Farm without exploding and another two, along with two oil bombs, fell wide of Debden. A mine dropped near Dunmow, two exploded in Chesterton RD and more along with two containers of incendiaries in Cosford RD. A seventh mine lay unexploded at Heveringham, Suffolk. At Moat Farm, Theberton, a mine exploded blowing tiles off the farmhouse, but the most gripping event of the night happened at Peasenhall where, at 22:03, two mines came down, one 400 yd south of High House Farm and another, which did not explode, near Goodwyns Farm. For three days the gruesome object lay in the field awaiting neutralization. Easier said than done because, before that could take place, the mine needed to be rolled over. That task was courageously performed by Sub-Lieutenant John Easton, RN, who shifted the D-Mine (made 30 August 1940) and then extracted the detonator. Bravery indeed.

Again making use of cloud, the Luftwaffe operated on 26 September, two aircraft bombing Lowestoft from 1,000 ft placing eighteen 50 kg HEs in a line over the Herring Basin and on into the sea. Two bombs hit the North Pier extension, one exploded in the Fish Market, four in the Herring Basin and one on the corner of Beach Road.

Bad weather over the Continent reduced activity on 27/28 September although twenty HEs (and three UXs) were dropped in Downham RD. Incendiaries fell at Duxford the next night but activity was mainly by intruders and against Lincolnshire airfields. Shortly before midnight on the 29th, eighteen HEs dropped in South Cambs, and seventeen near Bury (three UX). The most serious incident was again at Lowestoft where eighteen HEs exploded on Waveney Dock and the harbour. Serious damage was caused to two houses, offices, a water main and telephone wires. Twelve civilians were killed and nine injured.

Cloud covered East Anglia on the 30th allowing further deep penetrations by the Luftwaffe. A He 111 which raided Baldock was subsequently tracked as far as Cannock where it reputedly dropped an agent by parachute. That evening, Ipswich received eleven bombs.

Two mines await external loading on a Heinkel He 111 (Bundesarchiv 478/457/3A).

Chapter 9
Against the people

Autumn brought increasingly ferocious night attacks upon major British cities, cloudy days providing ample oportunities for hit and run bombardment. No 74 Squadron's engagement of a He 111 off Cromer on 1 October was a reminder of continuous anti-shipping operations. Such would be October's pattern.

The Second of October was ideal for cloud cover penetration to Upwood, Wyton and industrial targets around Bedford. But one bomber at least did not achieve its aim, for Do 17Z W Nr *3423:U5+FA* of Stab./KG2 was intercepted heading inland. Hurricanes of 17 Squadron forced it down near Pulham at 09:05, the crew being taken prisoner.

Persistent low cloud and rain continued to be exploited over the next two days, the afternoon of 3 October bringing several bombers to Bedfordshire where eighteen HEs fell at Winfield, north-west of Luton. Five bombs exploded near Sandy before a second attack on Bedfordshire developed late in the afternoon. Five HEs were dropped near Oakley and four close to Biggin Farm, Tempsford. Before the day was out an oil bomb and twenty HEs had fallen at Braintree, four oil bombs and two HEs (one UX) in Huntingdon RD and eight in Chesterton RD where incendiaries were inaccurately directed at Chiver's jam factory.

Next day's activity was mostly over East Coast towns and airfields, and at 10:10 Squadron Leader Stanford Tuck of 257 Squadron shot down Ju 88A-1 W Nr *3160:3Z+HL* of 1./KG77 ten miles east of Orford Ness. That unit had recently replaced its Do 17s with Ju 88s. Subsequent bombing was off Yarmouth, and at 12:30 in Aldeburgh where houses Nos 8, 10 and 12 Lee Road were demolished. The Roman Catholic Church in Fawcett Road was considerably damaged, 170 houses needed repairs and an oil bomb fell in Crag Path. Incendiaries dropped around Frinton and Walton, and eleven HEs (one UX) landed east of Maltings, Tunstall. On to Honington came bombs from a Do 17 which was subsequently destroyed by 11 Group fighters. Dornier 17Zs were now the most common enemy aircraft operating over East Anglia, and another was destroyed off Harwich by 74 Squadron on 5 October.

Enemy crews on 5/6 October particularly sought airfields, among them Coltishall, Bury, Mildenhall and Wittering, all of which went unscathed. Four oil bombs intended for Newmarket Heath ignited between Slade Farm on the east and Reach Road on the west, by the Devil's Ditch at Reach. Some 300 incendiaries were also dropped. When officials arrived to assess the quantity they visited the obvious place to take a census, the local school, where children in attendance admitted to collecting 213 tails!

Most incendiaries had easily been extinguished using a few loads of soil. In two cases they had penetrated roofs, one setting fire to bedding before a neighbour climbed on to a roof, then poked the bomb through a ceiling into a large dish which was promptly carried outside. The other was extinguished by a householder who climbed on to rafters with a garden hose which his wife held fast on a water tap. Such 'help yourself' fire fighting was typical of the approach by many to air raids, and particularly in rural East Anglia where to many they were a wretched nuisance! Most fire bombs were rendered harmless, or discovered in inconsequential resting places.

Two 500 kg HEs at Yarmouth on 5 October, were certainly far more harmful. A warning sounded at 19:44 but not until 23:35 did the large bombs explode, 300 yd north of Beach Station about 40 yd from the railway track. They produced giant craters 50 ft across and 25 ft deep. No casualties were caused, but windows were broken over a 500-yd radius. Another unusual item was an oil bomb, which exploded some 200 ft above the ground at Coddenham. There were few such air bursts, which would clearly have been very effective against certain targets.

There seemed to be a slight increase in the number of enemy aircraft now being brought down. At 00:54 on 6 October a Ju 88A, W Nr *4079*, of 9./KG30 crashed near Manor Farm, Colmworth. Two of the crew were found dead. Another bomber was brought down in daylight on the 6th. Further attempts were made to put airfields out of use, a midday sortie to Debden resulting in a III/KG76 Do 17Z-3 W Nr *4221:F1+FN*, being destroyed by 17 Squadron not far from the aerodrome. Other activity resulted in Ufford being machine-gunned at 13:50 before a Dornier placed seven HEs on to Framlingham, demolishing the School House, killing Mrs Harvey and damaging 64 houses. Another Dornier positioned a salvo south of Newmarket without causing damage.

Whereas many enemy aircraft passed over East Anglia on 7/8 October heading for the Midlands, the next night brought attacks throughout the region. One group of bombers mounted a sharp raid upon Duxford without scoring any hits on the aerodrome. Its Q-Site, unlit, was bombed at 03:00, and three bombs on Fowlmere satellite caused no damage. Raids on South Cambs resulted in 38 HEs being dropped, making a total of 338 HEs and 24 UXBs so far. Other centres of interest during the night were Weyland RD (44 HEs), Clare (fifteen HEs and one UX) and Thedwastre RD (21 HEs, three UX). Fresh attacks developed around 04:20, four HEs on Fallowfields Park Gate Farm, Wickhambrook, announcing yet another attempt to cripple Stradishall.

A curious aspect of night bombing in rural areas was highlighted on 8/9 October; although having no particular significance within the war effort, they were sometimes subjected to heavy bombing due to erroneous belief. Small Army encampments sometimes explained such onslaughts, but the delivery of 29 HEs on to Balsham between 22:15 and 06:15 was certainly strange. The action commenced with two oil bombs and ended with a hefty load of 25 HEs at Valley Farm. In Cambridgeshire that night bombs fell quite some way from airfields, as this complete listing illustrates: at 20:30, four HEs at Milton and Soham; at 21:40, eight HEs and incendiaries at Linton, one HE at Weston Colville and one HE, followed by 150 incendiaries at 22:00, at West Wickham; at 21:50, four HEs at Chippenham; at 03:20, eight HEs at Fowlmere; at 03:30, one parachute mine

'Vergeltungsflug nach Norwich.' According to the German caption, an SC1000 HE bomb soon to fall in revenge upon Norwich (Bundesarchiv 85/17/0).

at Shudy Camps; at 04:10, three HEs at Newton; and at 05:30, three HEs at Hardwick and eight HEs plus an oil bomb at Caldecote.

The night of 9/10 October brought more ineffective attempts to put Duxford out of use. At Mildenhall, Henlow and Cardington, too, the Luftwaffe was cheated out of success. Nine bombs fell at Woodbridge and on the 10th/11th more were aimed at Duxford. Yarmouth, though, was hit for the tenth time when, on the 11th/12th at 20:55, a low-level pass to the north-west resulted in HEs on the pleasure gardens and three on the beach. After circling, the raider headed south-west dropping another ten 50 kg HEs, two on the sea front damaging two houses and injuring Private R. A. Richardson, Northumberland Fusiliers, who later died of his wounds.

The events around Harwich harbour on 12 October were astonishing. Shortly after 20:00, a Ju 88 collided with a balloon cable and crashed into the water two miles south-west of Landguard Point. None of the crew survived, and the wreck was taken to HMS *Ganges* for examination. At this time there were 24 balloons (ten waterborne) in the area. An hour and a half later another Ju 88 inbound to intrude upon airfields was held in searchlights which dazzled the pilot, forcing him into the sea. Two Ju 88s brought down in quick succession without a shot being fired was no common achievement.

Warnings widely sounded in East Anglian towns around midday on 13 October were connected with activity mainly over Essex. A second attack materialized shortly before 19:00, towns raided including Chelmsford where, at 19:30, the home of the Mayor received a direct hit which killed him, along with the Mayoress, their sons, two grandchildren and the house maid.

Night activity lasted until 06:00 on the 14th. The main attack was on Liverpool, transit to and return from which led to long warning periods in the eastern counties. Such became more common as the winter deepened. There was always fear that mingled into the main force might be small scale raids on East

No alert in progress, a blinding flash, a gas main instantly erupted, and a very substantially built house in Barrow Road, Cambridge, was overcome (Cambridgeshire Collection).

Anglian targets, and also the risk of bombers unloading 'hang-ups' or choosing secondary targets. As these nightly processions, often hundreds strong, made their way along 'Knickebein' beams, participating types were easily identified by their engine notes — 'oom-pahing' Heinkels, Anson-like clattering Dorniers and rushing Ju 88s. When darkness came earlier the eastern warning sounded around 19:00, sometimes sooner. The first raiders would pass over some twenty minutes later at about 18,000 ft, placing them above heavy AA fire levels. 'All Clear' would sound after many hours, in mid-winter, with daybreak.

About 300 enemy aircraft operated over Britain on 13/14 October, eighty against London. Following a heavy raid, rumours of exotic weapons such as miles of wire dropped to engulf the population and said to festoon trees and chimney pots, excessive damage including the flattening of Liverpool Street Station and horrific casualties in cinemas and Underground stations, were widespread. Some had some foundation in fact, as on the 14th when Wood Green tube station was hit by a large bomb, the crater of which extended into a nearby tunnel; fourteen people were killed outright and 51 seriously injured. News of the horrifying bombing of a block of flats in Stoke Newington spread widely. Over 150 people were sheltering in its basement, two compartments of which were deluged with debris while another section was flooded. As for the wire story, the British Parachute and Cable device provided sound basis for rumour. (PAC comprised a shell which burst releasing a wire attached to a parachute, which was fired in an attempt to ensnare an enemy aircraft.)

Between 19:00 and 21:05 on the 14th, seventy London raiders crossed the coast between Shoeburyness and Orford, a second phase from 23:00 entering the Midlands via the Wash and Wittering-Peterborough area. Weyland RD received 23 HEs before East Anglia was clear at 01:00.

Although airfields in Bedfordshire, Cambridgeshire and Suffolk were prescribed targets for 15/16 October, there was little local evidence of that. This was a night to be remembered for the variety of events that developed. Each brought poignant tragedies, every one dwarfing those which largely feed the media of the 1980s. Take, for instance, the experience which suddenly confronted a Cambridge ARP warden that evening when, without warning, a heavy bomb from a He 111 fell close by.

He 111 1H + EP *of 6./KG26 about to take aboard SC500 HEs. Additional aerials are connected with 'Knickebein'* (Bundesarchiv 321/883/10).

'The bomb dropped in Barrow Road when we were at dinner. The front door was blown in, and as I grabbed my tin hat and went out I wondered what I should find.

'I was given the task of visiting each house in The Sector in case of injury, and was horrified to see, in a few minutes, a Barrow Road house go up in flames. Very shortly we could see the rafters burning and sparks were falling, in Bentley Road, on our tin hats. I heard that the householder was found behind the window curtains, as if he'd been looking out; the bomb had hit the gas main nearby. His wife, in the kitchen, escaped harm.

'The plane circled a bit then went off, though someone said "If he sees the fire he'll come back and drop another". He didn't.

'At one house all the windows had been sucked out on to the terrace. I rang the doorbell, and a dear old lady opened the door. I asked if they were all right, and did she know that her windows were shattered? She replied, airily, "Oh yes! We're *quite* all right", adding "I think you're wonderful, would you like a cup of tea?" I thanked her, but explained that I had to go around the other houses. *She* was wonderful!

'Though I found no other damage, and most people seemed to be in bed, I had a narrow escape in one garden. They had a sunken pool about three feet down, walled round, and I nearly fell into it in the dim light. Anti-climax: after some hours we did get a cup of tea — at the post.'

No 19 Barrow Road had been reduced to rubble by a 500 kg HE, the heaviest ever to fall on Cambridge and fortunately still of unusual calibre. No 17 had been seriously damaged. The large, Long Road area marshalling yards were probably the intended target. Just before the explosion a Ju 88A-1, W Nr *0317:4D+DM* of Stab. II/KG30, mining specialists, had crashed by the Much Hadham Road one mile west of Bishop's Stortford, a blazing victim of the guns of the IAZ. The presence of minelayers was emphasized later in the night when four parachute mines fell in Saffron Walden RD, another near Halstead and two (one UX) near Braintree. Two more were released near Clacton at 03:30, one landing in Smees sand pit, Melbourne Road, the other (UX) on allotments in London Road.

Just past midnight two groups of bombs were aimed at the railway near Chesterton Viaduct. An oil bomb and an HE burst on open ground, Fen Road, and then two HEs dropped at 00:20 at Fen Ditton where Cecil B. Pettit lived. For him this was a night of awful tragedy, as he recalls.

'I lived in a small cottage on a half acre of ground in the Green End area of Fen Ditton almost opposite the 'Harvest Home' public house. Caretaker at the Village Hall, I married in the local church in June 1935, my only son being buried in the cemetery, after premature birth, in 1937.

'There was a blinding flash when the bombs fell seemingly aimlessly and I at once found myself removing tiles from my immediate surrounds. I saw the full moon above and, with my arms around my wife, ran rather panic stricken to my brother-in-law's home 60 yd away. Eventually I was taken to Addenbrooke's Hospital, and after four days and nights during which time I endured the kind of pain the more recent Brighton bomb recipients must have experienced, my left eye was extracted.

'Although I was the only named casualty, many others suffered — among them my 37-year-old wife who contracted cancer and, after two terrible operations, died in 1943. The bombs had reduced my home to a heap of rubble and my 'war service' was spent re-building my life. Furniture purchased was itemized by War Damage officials who allowed only for essentials. In return for loads of brick rubble a village farmer supplied me with manure for the garden where I was to spend many happy hours.' Now nearly eighty years old, Mr Pettit is again happily married — to a lady who suffered similar misfortune elsewhere.

Off Shotley Spit, 750 yd from the Naval Pier, the arrival in flames of He 111H-4 W Nr *6955:1T+BB* caused no mean excitement and questioning. It had come under fire from the guns around, but balloons were also flying. A deflated example was found at Grimston Hall Farm, Trimley, raising questions as to whether the Heinkel had clouted a cable. Investigations also suggested that despite its KG28 identity letters it was being flown by a crew of 2./KG26.

Birmingham was the main target on the 15th/16th, approach and withdrawal being made over the South Coast. Mine droppers were, however, busy in the early hours of the 16th, four mines falling in Saffron Walden RD, another near Halstead and two (one UX) near Braintree. Close to Bishop's Stortford, thirteen HEs were dropped.

During small-scale operations on 16/17 October, airfields in Cambridgeshire, Bedfordshire and Suffolk figured in the bombing. A Ju 88A was brought down at 19:20, on fire, at Much Hadham, after its crew had baled out. Less fortunate were those aboard a Heinkel 111 for all were killed when it crashed at night into the sea off Shotley. Hurricanes of 242 Squadron next day intercepted an enemy aircraft off Lowestoft, but failed to 'bag' it. The squadron patrolling over Yarmouth had a disastrous engagement with a Do 17 whose return fire hit Pilot Officer Brown's *P3207* preventing him from being able to close the throttle. Pilot Officer Campbell (*V6575*) did not return from the action. Two raids were also plotted off Harwich, but the most evident enemy activity was that of a Do 215 which, after reconnoitring London, turned its attention to East Anglian airfields and towns.

In avenging the loss of the Heinkel, Shotley was bombed in daylight on 19 October before more cloudy weather set in, reducing the level of activity over East Anglia. On the 20th thirteen HEs and three oil bombs fell in South Cambs RD, Dunmow RD had eight HEs and an oil bomb, and Frinton/Walton twelve HEs possibly intended for an explosives works fairly near.

One of the most amazing flights of the period was that of Do 17Z W Nr *2783:7T+AH* flown by a crew of 1./606. Late on 20 October they left Lanvioc/Poulmiac and flew over the Irish Sea, intending to reconnoitre Liverpool. Turning inland too soon they arrived instead over Shrewsbury where they encountered a magnetic storm which put the radio out of use following a heavy static discharge. They turned about and over Chippenham, Wiltshire, another discharge disabled their compass. In the belief they were still on course for home they soon discovered that they were not over Cherbourg but had been heading north, so they turned through what they judged to be 180 degrees. Over Salisbury they again encountered a storm. Believing they were over France, at about 2,700 ft, and running out of fuel, the crew baled out.

It was at 08:00 that the Do 17 *7T+AH* bearing two bullet holes in its fuselage was discovered fairly intact at Erwarton, near Nesscreak, seven miles south-east of Ipswich. Surprise greeted the find — until the crew which had abandoned it so far away explained their arrival after lengthy interrogation.

On 21 October a Do 17Z following the railway line loosed off a few rounds of machine-gun fire as it raced low over Hills Road Bridge, Cambridge. Such strafing was still uncommon. Bombing of the railway at Girtford, Bedfordshire, then closed the route until evening. More bombs were then ineffectively aimed at Duxford, and others fell at Newmarket, Burnham (Norfolk), Rattlesden (twenty HEs on Chestnut and Peggs Farms, two UX on Brooks Farm), Biggleswade (nine HEs), Dunmow RD (35 HEs), Saffron Walden RD (200 incendiaries and thirty HEs, five UX), Bishop's Stortford RD (two oil bombs, one UX) and Thedwastre RD (eighteen HEs two UX). The amount of activity was typical for the period. Two mines which exploded next night at Park Farm, Wivenhoe, caused only slight damage.

In hazy conditions on 24 October a long range photo-reconnaissance flight over the Midlands was attempted by Do 215 W Nr *0060:L2+KS* of 3./Auflk1.Gr.Ob.d.L. Near Banbury it was intercepted and damaged by Hurricanes of No 1 Squadron who forced it away from Coventry, its main target. Three Hurricanes of 17 Squadron flown by Flying Officer Czernin (*V7408*), Pilot Officer Fajtl (*V6553*) and Sergeant Hogg (*P2972*) took off at 11:50 and were vectored on to the Dornier which they shot down and which burnt itself out 200 yd off the A1 near 'The Crown' public house, Wyboston. Two of the crew baled out, one parachute not opening.

Enemy activity was certainly producing unusual and interesting highlights, for Do 215s were comparatively rare over Britain. Another unlikely visitor was Bf 110C-5 W Nr *2257:S6+MC* of 2 (F)./122, probably on a shipping search, brought down by 72 squadron north-east of Yarmouth at 14:05 on 25 October. At 09:10 on 27 October the Luftwaffe provided for the residents of Harwich two large bundles of reading matter. Whereas the RAF delivered many millions of propaganda leaflets, it was an activity which the Luftwaffe rarely indulged in, making these leaflets most prized items. At 12:50 on the same day a Ju 88 dive-bombed the *Harvest Gleamer*, a trawler, half a mile off Southwold. An hour later the ship sank, three men having died. Seven were rescued.

None of these events, though, proved as noteworthy as that which unfurled at Ipswich on 27 October. At 16:40 a most extensive operation developed, directed against airfields in eastern England. The overture was spectacular, for it consisted of a high-speed low-level strike from the north-east by about at least 22

Bf 109E fighter-bombers on Martlesham. Damage was caused to the Battery Room, but otherwise it was to civilian property — four bombs exploded at Mill Hill Farm and four houses were damaged. Three of the eighteen bombs which exploded landed near Foxhall radio station, and additional bombing resulted in two HEs falling at Playford, one at Little Bealings and two at St Audrey's Hospital at Ufford where a patient was killed and eighteen others were injured. He 111s and Do 17s sought out Mildenhall, where twelve HEs were dropped and a hangar, the cookhouse, sick quarters and a barrack block were hit, while a UXB rested by the water tower. Two were killed and ten injured. Another fourteen HEs at West Row caused no damage. Feltwell was raided, and at Honington a hangar hit along with other buildings and three aircraft. More were killed and one injured, a dozen HEs and three bombs also falling on Manor Farm nearby. At Newmarket Heath nineteen HEs fell mainly around the Grandstand and Stalls at 17:55. Bury was machine-gunned, bombs fell near Marham church and more at West Raynham and a hangar was burnt out at Mousehold. Two Blenheims were destroyed at Great Massingham, the LNER track being blocked by a UXB. At Coltishall an attacking He 111 was brought down by ground fire, and other incidents took place at Newmarket and Woodbridge Mental Hospital. The activity was quite costly for the Luftwaffe. Two Do 17Zs of III/KG53 were damaged by 1 Squadron near Feltwell, one at around 16:30; Do 17Z W Nr *1150:F1+HR* of III/KG76 was shot down in the Stour by 17 Squadron at 17:00, and 85 Squadron shot down a He 111H-2 of I/KG1, *5541:V4+HW* at 18:10, the aircraft crashing at Salt Fleet, Norfolk. Certainly it was a busy evening, and it became even more memorable for an event at Ipswich which produced widespread concern.

At 18:23, as most airfield attackers headed home, a solitary Do 17 flew low over southern Ipswich to the sound, apparently, of machine-gun fire. Mr D. F. Brock, then living at Ipswich, says, 'I can vividly recall how, just at dusk on a day of low cloud and intermittent drizzle, I was putting my bike in the shed when I heard the all too familiar noise of an approaching Jerry. A Do 17, he was just below cloud level and heading north-north-east. I saw "things" falling from the aircraft which I took to be leaflets of some sort as there were so many.' Near Felixstowe the raider was engaged by AA guns, its engines spluttering as it headed out to sea. It was not long before some very small craters, broken windows and smashed roof tiles were discovered.

'Then came curious stories of broken trolley bus overhead wires, electric cables and telephone wires down, below which most strange small metal plates were found. Five small explosions had also occurred at Manson's Field, Poplar Farm, Sproughton, where later five unexploded items were discovered. There appeared little structural damage to property. Soon the source of the trouble was located — small, cylindrical bombs to which vanes were attached.'

Police and ARP personnel immediately scoured Ipswich to seek for what were obviously alarming weapons. An Inspector, Sergeant, Constable and a Special Constable were being shown how the bomb's centre wire unscrewed, when the weapon was dropped and exploded. The Inspector lost an eye, the Sergeant and the 'Special' each lost a leg, and the Constable died shortly after from fragmentation effect akin to gunshot. Extremely alarming was the discovery that the newcomers had been distributed over a civilian housing area a mile long and a quarter-mile wide. The search for unexploded examples, which in the blackout could have caused horrific casualties, was frantic. Mr G. Pulford, a member of Portman Road Rescue Squad, went to the corner of Hatfield Road and Nacton Road where several bombs were resting in gutters and on roofs. More, he recalls, were found in gardens. That they were released over a town was bad enough. To have sown them over a civilian housing estate was a dastardly deed.

Miraculously, casualties were limited. One bomb exploded 8 ft up the side wall of a house making a $1\frac{1}{2}$ ft hole, and causing only one slight casualty. Mr Brock's neighbour, Mr Quinton, had been killed. Locations of unexploded bombs were found during the night, and a lot of small craters by and in the river Orwell. By the next day confirmation arrived that more of these pernicious little brutes had, at 21:07, been cast over Kelsale two miles north of Saxmundham. Reports then surfaced that two days previously two strange contraptions had been found in Blyth RD.

At about 07:00 on 28 October in a small enclosed yard behind a shop an explosion occurred as the owners were examining a strange object. Six people were killed, two wounded and a small corrugated iron roof was peppered with small fragments. Three bombs were recovered from the river, morning finds proving that the bombs had fallen over a two-mile-long strip. Some had air-burst, probably causing the initial casualties. At about 13:00 the inevitable happened, two children who found one of the strange bombs in woodland were injured as they explored it. Within an hour all schools commanded their children to stay away from the weapons and not disturb them. This was insufficient warning; the whole population was at risk. At 16:00 a phonogram was flashed to all controllers in the Eastern Region — under NO circumstances must the bombs be touched, and any found must be guarded. Disturbance fuzing was suspected. For killing children these were ideal weapons, so that their use in an urban situation was a most criminal act, and totally inexcusable. Even if the intention was to festoon the dock area with the bombs, delivery in darkness was wickedly irresponsible.

It was essential to obtain examples of the bombs for examination—easier said than done, for any slight disturbance exploded them. With judicious use of long poles, unexploded bombs were collected for examination. Shaped like a small tin, the bomb was enclosed in a grey or grey-green case which opened in the form of two petals attached to the explosive container by 5 in of wire. Circular panels on either end of the bomb also opened adjacent to the petals, the four items retarding the bomb's fall. Eight revolutions of the vanes set the striker, and four revolutions freed a clock which started from impact. Retardation by the clock mechanism ranged from three seconds to a maximum of thirty minutes, the fuze also allowing an air burst, an impact burst or longer delay through a disturbance setting achieved by a spring and compression. Test firing proved the bomb, aided by a yellow TNT charge, to hurl fragments, up to 50 ft. Fully extended the bomb and cable measured $9\frac{1}{4}$ in long, the covered bomb being $3\frac{1}{4}$ in in diameter.

There being high casualty risk from these 'butterfly bombs', the BBC on the evening of 30 October carried a special announcement stating that, 'Reports have been received of enemy planes dropping small objects about the size of a Mills bomb or fifty-cigarette tin with wire attached. The public are warned not to handle such objects, which should be reported to the police or wardens.'

By then it was known that these anti-personnel bombs had a 2 kg charge. The issue of details to ARP Controllers sparked off reports of other unusual small weapons. Three very small pear-shaped bombs had been reported from Luton on 14 October, found at the scene of damage. Lengthy consideration led to the conclusion that these also were anti-personnel bombs, known as SD1, 1 kg impact fuze weapons 6¾ in long and of 2 in maximum diameter. They looked most curious because of their six or eight fins. Another report was of a brass cylinder painted aluminium in colour, 2¾ in long and of 2 in diameter and weighing 1¼ lb picked up in Shunting Road, South Poplar. Naval sources reported small 6-in-long shells of 3 in diameter and dropped from small containers carrying from six to ten, which killed six men on 28 October.

By Friday, 1 November, the Bomb Disposal Service and the Navy had at Ipswich dealt with 54 of the 2 kg weapons. It was believed that more had fallen, many air-bursting. The Ministry of Home Security recorded the total dropped and found on land intact or exploded as 165, and listed a further sixty as unexploded along with ten in Samford RD on 27 October. There can be little doubt that the true number dropped was in excess of this. What was never finally established was whether 26 unexplained small bombs dropped in St Faiths/Aylsham RD on 31 August were really anti-personnel weapons, although it was now strongly suspected.

Known to the Germans as the SD2, the 2 kg 'butterfly bomb' had a Type 67 fuze handling up to thirty minutes' delayed action. It could be replaced by a vibration fuze. The bombs were known to be capable of burying themselves in soft ground leaving their vanes flush. As important as anything was the discovery of a dark green 3 ft 7½ in long and 8 in diameter AB23 container which revealed its load as 23 SD2s. It was known to the British as Container Type 'J'. From the evidence to hand the Ipswich attack may have amounted to as many as 230 bombs — which meant that at least five were unaccounted for and might have fallen in the river. In later attacks many fewer bombs were found than were assumed to have been dropped. While no intact containers were recovered, from remains it was found that the containers opened after release at a height set for a fuze, the method of delivery being covered by the designation AB (ie, *Abwurf* = throwing out and *Behalter* = a container). The container split open horizontally and was superseded by the Type 'M' AB-70-3 or the more streamlined AB-70-5, either 3 ft 4 in or 3 ft 7½ in long and of 8 in diameter, able to carry 22 or 23 SD 2s. SD2s could also be carried in the rarely used AB 24t (Type 'K') which accommodated 24.

The question now was where would the SD2s be used again? The assumption was, against airfields. Yet when a second dusk attack by groups of one to six aircraft began at 17:40 on 29 October, conventional weapons were employed. About forty incidents were reported from Honington, Newmarket (where a cottage was destroyed), Mildenhall (fourteen HEs), Matlask (where three Do 17s damaged huts and caused six casualties), Wattisham (where several aircraft were damaged along with the hospital, equipment and other buildings) and in the Mitford-and-Launditch RD where 74 HEs fell (five UX). Northgate Street in Bury St Edmunds, and Newmarket Heath were machine-gunned, luckily with neither damage nor casualties.

While the investigation into the SD2 attack proceeded there was plenty of other enemy activity. A mile off Orford Ness at 07:55 on 28 October, Do 17Z-2 *2544:5K+CH* of I/KG53 was shot down by 17 Squadron, two of whose aircraft fired mid-morning at another Do 17. It was also a Dornier which circled Bungay

SC50 HEs await loading on to a Do 17Z, U5 + HT, *in the winter of 1940–1941* (Bundesarchiv 346/845017).

and at 11:24 callously released three HEs on the town. Two bombs in Earsham Street started a fire in Wightman's Drapery, ten shops and 25 houses were damaged. The one fatal casualty was a six-week-old baby; eight people were injured. The Walton area was raided at 14:50, the B1034 road being closed by a 14-ft crater a little way west of Walton Church.

Intruder activity developed during the evening. A He 111 heading homewards was illuminated for a minute over Harwich by Searchlight 201 and the crew, soon disorientated, abandoned their aircraft, *A1+LT*, which crashed into the Stour one mile west of Parkeston Quay at 23:30. During the evening Raid 76 had visited Bassingbourn, unloading two HEs and incendiaries there.

In a repeat of the dusk assault on airfields a similar operation came on 29 October, nine airfields being featured. The first three bombers crossed the East Anglian coast at 17:45 and at 18:00 they set about Wattisham, putting twenty HEs in a line across the aerodrome. One released incendiaries over Great Bricett village and Cottage Farm, Offton. From a blazing Wattisham hangar a burning Blenheim was courageously pushed through flames and glass fragments. Five men were injured in the attack there. Also damaged were the NAAFI, SHQ and the MT Section. Not until next morning was the arrival of SD2s on the flying ground discovered, after they had taken the lives of Flight Sergeant Fisher and a civilian. Another six were located at Park Farm, Wattisham.

Three Dorniers reached Newmarket at 18:00 and, after circling several times, machine-gunned the town, bombed the Heath and outskirts of the town. One stick of HEs fell across Terrace House Paddocks to Stratton Avenue damaging the Stud Groom's home, two cottages wherein one person was killed, houses in Cockford's Road and near the Station. Another dozen HEs exploded in paddocks north-west of the Heath, and fourteen more around Cavenham. Mildenhall was also attacked with fourteen HEs and at 18:23 Coltishall was strafed by a Ju 88. He 111 H-3 *3296:V4+DH* which had also attempted to bomb Coltishall never reached home.

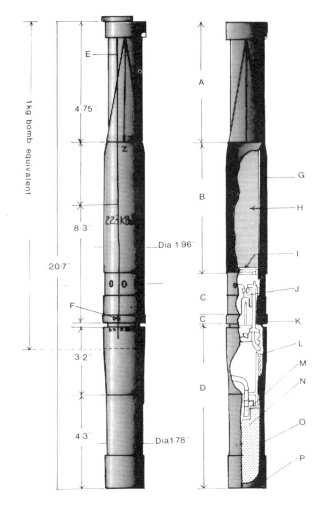

Left 1kg incendiary bomb with explosive nose attached (IBEN). To the conventional 1 kg bomb an explosive component is added in a steel extension. The normal 1 kg incendiary had a nose detonator aft of which was a series of holes covered with insulating tape until the weapon became 'live'. The first alteration was the addition of a small explosive charge in a tiny chamber within the tail unit, the second being the fitting of a steel nose plug adding about 12 oz to the weight of the bomb — useful for better penetration. Some of the latter type had a small charge of explosive in the nose, and were known as Type B1 EZ.B or B1.3 EZ.B. **Right** Illustrated in cut-away form is the incendiary bomb with an explosive nose. Parts shown are: A—tail unit; B—incendiary unit; C—fuze section; D—delayed action explosive unit; E (left)—the arming wire in position; F—the safety pin attached; G—the inflammable alloy casing; H—main incendiary filling; I—primer cap for firing main incendiary charge; J—detonator mechanism which fires cap of G and leads also to activation of the time fuze (L) and explosives detonator (K) which fires the explosive (N) within its steel container covered by a nose fairing (P). Perhaps the complexity of operation, and indeed the crudity of the basic bomb, explains why so many incendiaries did not ignite. Introduced in 1940.

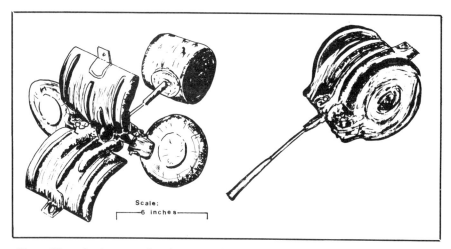

Scale:
6 inches

Above Three basic types of anti-personnel bombs were dropped upon East Anglia, of which the most notorious was the SD2 'butterfly bomb' depicted here. Weighing 2 kg, the cylindrical bomb was 3.5 in long and 3.25 in in diameter. Upon being released, usually from an AB23 container, the grey-green (or dark red, or yellow) wings opened and the two ends covering the bomb became vanes which set the device spinning at the end of a 5 in long arming cable which set the fuze live. Three fuze settings allowed for explosion three seconds after release or on impact, up to thirty minutes or activation by disturbance.

Right The SD1 weighed about 1 kg, had a maximum diameter of 2 in and was 6.75 in long overall. It had six or eight fins, was yellow or green overall and had an impact fuze. First reports of use came from Luton, but there was never official confirmation and they might well have been examples of a version of French origin.

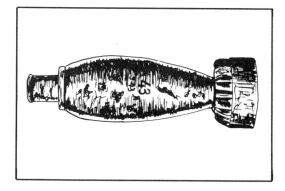

Right Larger was the equally pernicious SD10A dropped late in the war. In length 21 ⅝ in and of about 3.5 in diameter, its olive green casing was 0.6 in thick. The Type II had an inner case, the space between the two being filled with ¼ in steel cubes set in concrete.

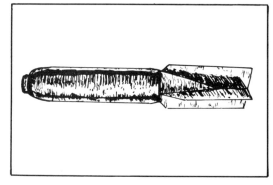

Late afternoon on 30 October saw twelve raiders seeking shipping off Harwich where, in the evening, minelayers were active. Debden was raided during the night, and a large fire was started at Clacton. Early next morning East Dereham was bombed and villages south-west of Norwich were machine-gunned.

Another Ju 88A-1 *088 50008:L1+GS* entered East Anglia from the south, reconnoitred the Manchester area then attempted exit over Skegness. There, it was intercepted by No 1 Squadron. Badly shot about, it pursued an erratic course to Sutton Bridge where two of the crew baled out before the aircraft headed south. Then an engine seized, bringing it down intact at Stuntney, near Ely.

Midday on the 31st saw the start of a series of mixed attacks. At 13:01 six HEs near a Bassingbourn hangar brought no casualties. Over Duxford at the same time a Do 17 was engaged with nineteen rounds of 3-in shells from B-Site guns, another 22 being fired by Bofors without effect at a Dornier crossing at 8,000 ft.

A potentially valuable attack was directed at Claydon Cement Works, a solitary HE hitting the disused electrics shops at 13:25. This was possibly dropped by the same Ju 88 from which, as it passed over Stradbroke, a small object fell. It was a tin of 'Lyon's Assorted Toffeeskotch, Made in London'. One local commentator is said to have remarked, 'Wonder why the blighter 'et 'em?' Another said, 'I thought we could all trust Joe Lyons!' Well, if nothing else, it proved that those bombarding us were not all that different from us, and indeed underlined the stupidity of what was going on around. Soon after, four HEs dropped on Yarmouth, landing in North Drive, Middle Market Road, Nettle Hill and Regent Road, injuring eight people.

In the evening eighteen HEs straddled Freeman's Farm, Rattlesden — alarming enough, but even more worrying was a container of SD2s in Samford RD along with five HEs. Indiscriminate dropping of those would have been an horrific development. Otherwise the night was comparatively quiet apart from sixteen HEs at North Brink, Wisbech.

November's raids retained the mixed pattern, although bombing of Ely sugar beet factory from 10,000 ft at 07:10 was unusual. The nineteen bombs dropped (nine on the factory) injured sixteen workers, damaged workshops and the boiler house and put the factory out of use for a month. At 07:45 lone attacks on airfields began with another damaging assault on Wattisham. Ten HEs were scattered across the camp from east of the Married Quarters to the top hangar. Three MQ houses were demolished, a bomb fell by the SHQ and another outside the Guardroom, but most horrific of all, two barrack blocks were hit, in one instance causing the reinforced top floor to collapse on to the ground floor. Nine people were killed, nineteen seriously wounded. But this time the perpetrator did not go free, 17 Squadron putting it into the sea off Orford at 08:00. Grundisburgh area was machine-gunned at 07:48 before six HEs exploded in Gulpher Road, Felixstowe, and incidents also developed during the day at Debden (seventeen HEs, and two UX), Horsham St Faith (thirteen HEs), Blyth RD (eleven HEs) and Chelmsford (sixteen HEs). At 21:15 Raid 16 aimed for Cambridge airport but succeeded only in dropping an HE at Fulbourn and another two on the Gogs at 21:15. Later, Raid 21 placed two on Fowlmere landing ground.

Another dusk operation against airfields was mounted on 3 November. Two Ju 88s crossed Stradishall at 17:17, 1,000 yd apart, one so low that hangars shielded it from AA fire. Ten HEs fell, setting two hangars on fire and damaging the Sergeants' Mess, while the Operations Room was machine-gunned. A barrack block was damaged and an Anson set on fire. As one of the '88s sped across the airfield a map fluttered down to the feet of the late Kenneth Beales. It showed that the aircraft had crossed the coast three miles south of Dunwich, headed for Diss and made for Stradishall. Although Stradishall's 3 in AA guns fired three rounds, no hits were scored on the Ju 88s. Simultaneously, two He 111s machine-gunned Martlesham.

Wattisham suffered harsh treatment at 17:25 when two Ju 88s managed to place five HEs on Hangars 1 and 2, the latter burning for a while. Council houses at Creeting St Peter were machine-gunned and at 17:35 another He 111 fired at traffic on the A123 road and then upon Martlesham. Over the following half hour machine-gunning took place at Stradbroke, Dennington, Framlingham, Rushmere, Aldeburgh and Shotley.

As the bombers raced for home an ominous south-north run over Ipswich by a Do 17 resulted in another load of anti-personnel bombs dropping, this time on the edge of a council estate, over an ARP cleansing station and others on a road and private houses. This was a much smaller release than the previous one. Estimates suggested that nine bomb clusters had then fallen, and possibly more than one aircraft had taken part. Six bombs in the second Ipswich attack fell at right angles to those in the first. Damage to overhead trolley bus wires, cables and telephone lines was repeated, 57 SD2s having burst. Another eighteen UX examples were located.

Bombs intended for the Shell Mex-BP installation at Cliff Quay, Ipswich, dropped on a domestic area at 22:10 on the 3rd. An Anderson Shelter behind No 32 Fletcher Road was hurled into the next door garden, the rear of No 255 Landseer Road was smashed and the front blown off No 253. The side of another house was demolished, the occupants making an amazing escape through a window. Of the eighteen HEs dropped, ten fell on open ground.

On 5 November low cloud and rain gave excellent cover to low-flying Dorniers. Brief warnings were now sounding during daylight, Cambridge, for instance, having three this day. Unlikely as it now seems, the operation of the Rustat Road waterworks siren was in error, 'All Clear' becoming the warning and the latter the 'All Clear'. Most confusing! Notable events the same day occurred at Aldeburgh where, at 16:30, three attackers placed twenty HEs on the Victoria Road and Park Road areas, at Horsham St Faith (twenty HEs and three UX), Halstead RD (seventeen HEs and one UX) with Gipping and Blyth RD each receiving sixteen HEs. Another eight fell in Newmarket RD, seven more near

At Aldeburgh on 6 November, nineteen HEs and one UX fell, and South Cambs RD received eleven (one UX). HEs were still the most common weapons dropped, the oil bomb in St Neots RD, along with twelve HEs (one UX) being an example of the less common.

During 7 November there was little enemy activity until about 12:00 when a convoy soon to pass Clacton called for fighter protection. Two squadrons of fighters were scrambled and soon found themselves facing over fifty enemy aircraft. Half an hour later Ju 87 Stukas dive-bombed the convoy from 5,000 ft, and two ships were sunk. Apart from this, enemy activity was limited, the most noteworthy night event being the dropping of nineteen bombs in the Braintree area.

On 8 November a raid on east coast shipping led to one of the fiercest engagements off the East Anglian coast. At 13:00 eight Hurricanes of 257 Squadron took off to patrol over a northbound convoy when, to the south-east, they saw bomb splashes and heard 17 Squadron entering a fight. By the time they had arrived all the enemy aircraft had left, and two ships could be seen sinking. Closing in at 6,000 ft, 17 Squadron's pilots had seen Ju 87s dive bombing, protected by about thirty fighters. 17 Squadron tore into the Stukas, which were easy prey, and within five minutes claimed fifteen and six damaged. A resounding victory was hailed at the time as the most successful against Stukas since 16 August. Royal Navy gunners also claimed success and 17 Squadron maintained that some Bf 109s were shot down off Clacton. The claim of fifteen Ju 87s was certainly inflated, but no accurate score appears to have been authenticated. Two ships were sunk, and the Hurricane of Sergeant Page, 257 Squadron, came down at Hythe Road, Spelling Minnis, and was burnt out.

On the same day intruders placed twenty HEs in Downham RD, fifteen at Colchester, twelve at Swaffham and five (with eleven UX) at Wymondham. An evening low flier crept in unobserved, bombed Mildenhall, and on the way out put four HEs on Honington. Alert ground defences brought down the Ju 88 (probably *V4+ER*), its crew of four being killed when it was burnt out alongside a hangar. Before the day was out Southwold's Constitutional Club had been destroyed, forty houses nearby damaged and three people injured.

A Heinkel 111 operating in cloud conditions mid-morning on 9 November dropped bombs near Bury before heading north to circle Church Fenton and Leconfield in Yorkshire for some considerable time before leaving via the Humber. Under 12 Group surveillance during its journey south, it machine-gunned coal barges and minesweepers off Mablethorpe before attacking Wainfleet railway station. Foolishly, the crew cut across Norfolk and eight miles off Yarmouth Spitfires of 72 Squadron destroyed the Heinkel.

A Do 17 was later damaged off Aldeburgh. That aircraft and its companions from 13:30 made cloud cover penetrations into Norfolk, Suffolk and Cambridgeshire, dropping bombs near Mildenhall, Feltwell, Ely, King's Lynn and Horsham St Faith (nine HE). After dark a raid developed in the Duxford area, forty HEs (three UX), nine oil bombs and incendiaries falling. Another five HEs (two UX) came down near Debden. At 17:55 eleven HEs exploded in a beet field near the Red Cross, south of Cambridge. That evening thirteen HEs also fell near Dunmow. Recent dusk raids on airfields were clearly specially organized although it was some while before details were obtained from prisoners. On 10 November individual sorties were identified as Ju 88C night fighter-bombers seeking air activity, machine-gunning and bombing airfields. Such activity ceased by 22:50, by which time incidents had occurred at Bedford, Cambridge, Henlow, Royston, Wittering and Norwich. Additionally, incendiaries and three oil bombs fell at Ipswich and seventeen HEs (fourteen UX) in Samford RD. Yarmouth at 16.56 also received attention by a bomber flying at 1,000 ft which placed a 500 kg HE in the Royal Naval Hospital grounds, injuring two people.

Cloud cover day raids, anti-shipping operations, armed reconnaissance flights, and in particular dusk and night attacks upon airfields, the significance of which was uncertain, had taken place throughout the month. What was about to commence had been expected and provided material for rumour and humour.

Chapter 10
The Romans have come!

There's no point in hiding it, wartime Britain was unimpressed with its Italian adversaries. Their uniforms converted them into operatic-like figures, martial gondoliers who once produced splendid ice cream, who must dream of the grand days of Rome which still keeps many a teacher in business. Their leader, Benito Mussolini — fat, unpleasant and with a comic name — had hijacked an excitable, appealing nation.

When Mussolini stabbed the Allies in the back during June 1940 he hoped for spoils from broken France. He did not expect RAF Wellingtons promptly on his doorstep. Neither did he forget nor forgive Britain, and he became determined to avenge an insult. His airmen would blast the British in their hearths. Initial skirmishes over Africa did not bode well for such activities, and when thousands of Italian soldiers became prisoners, and their rifles joined our Home Guard, it was hardly surprising that the battered British had a poor opinion of their new foe. The ultimate insult came when some of the Italian hardware was passed to the OTCs' boy soldiers!

The Germans managed to keep their partners well away from the Battle of Britain, realizing how an injection of hasty temperament could be disastrous for the Luftwaffe. By September Mussolini had put so much pressure on his Ally that the Germans agreed to his air force operating from Belgium — while they kept at a distance.

Completely untrained and unprepared for operations in northern Europe, the problems the Regia Aeronautica would face became clear as aircraft, moving to Belgium, frequently lost their way and forced-landed. Luftwaffe personnel were even less benevolent when explaining those landings! Eventually forty or so Fiat BR.20s of the 98⁰ Gruppo and 99⁰ Gruppo, 43⁰ Stormo reached Melsbroek and Chievres, fifty Fiat CR.42 biplane fighters of 18⁰ Gruppo, 55⁰ and 56⁰ Stormo, arrived at Eech/Charleroi from Turin/Miafiori, and 48 Fiat G.50s of 20⁰ Gruppo moved into Ursel. Each fighter Gruppo was divided into three squadrons, and a few Cant Z.1007*bis* bombers rolled in for use as exotic transports. Weeks of training preceded operations during which the Italian Press expressed the joy of the Italian people that the formation known as the Corps Aero Italiano in Belgium would be able to repay Great Britain directly for the bombing of Northern Italy.

Night attacks were clearly safer, yet the bomber force was even less prepared for those. Nevertheless, in hasty style, sixteen bomber crews on 25 October mounted a night raid on Harwich. One bomber came to grief on take-off, two became hopelessly lost, and residents of Harwich knew nothing of the venture. Following a day foray by 24 BR.20s of 43⁰ Stormo towards Ramsgate on 29 October, eight Italian aircraft again unsuccessfully attempted, on 5 November, a night raid on Harwich. The Italians, though, wanted something more spectacular, a big daylight raid to prove themselves. For Operation No 8 they chose to attack a convoy off Harwich, and ideally on 11 November, Armistice Day.

Morning Luftwaffe fighter sweeps over Kent, two attacks upon Channel shipping and an inland raid near Dungeness were laid on before, around 13:30, radar located two formations from Chievres approaching Convoy 'Booty' off Harwich. Ten Fiat BR.20s, 242ᵃ Squadriglia's vic of five leading those of the 243ᵘ were coming in at 12,000 ft, escorted by forty CR.42s. Hurricanes of Nos 17, 46 and 257 Squadrons were immediately 'scrambled', thirty in all, and vectored on to the raid. The BR.20's top speed was 255 mph at 13,500 ft, maximum bomb load was 3,550 lb, and range 1,350 miles carrying 2,200 lb of bombs. For this raid they flew at 200 mph, each carrying three 550 lb bombs. The Fiat CR.42s, each with only two 12.7 mm guns, had a top speed of 270 mph at 13,100 ft, a service ceiling of 32,000 ft and a range of 485 miles at around 15,000 ft, and were very manoeuvrable.

The leading bombers and the fighters drew ahead, allowing the Hurricane pilots time to select attack profiles. Flight Lieutenant 'Cowboy' Blatchford (*V6962*) led 257 Squadron into battle and soon had claimed two BR.20s at sea, and two CR.42s damaged. Pilot Officers North (*V6864*) and Mortimer (*P2835*) claimed another bomber, while Pilot Officer Pniak (Polish) and Pilot Officer Kay (*V6880*) brought down a BR.20 which, at 14:00 crashed three-quarters of a mile north of Bromeswell rifle range. Pniak, and Pilot Officers Andrews and King, claimed two BR.20s at sea. No 46 Squadron reckoned to have destroyed two more bombers and two fighters. These claims, inflated, came about because of the ease with which the formations were broken apart.

As regards claims for enemy fighters, Sergeant Barnes (*V6863*) and Sergeant Lucan (*R4088*) reckoned on one at sea and Flight Lieutenant Blatchford damaged two before, running out of ammunition and finding himself close to a CR.42, he closed in to hit the upper mainplane with his propeller, which damaged two of its blades.

As soon as they had landed, 257's pilots hurried to Bromeswell to inspect BR.20M *MM22621*. Mottled dark green, brown and purplish grey on its upper surfaces, and light blue below, the aircraft carried on its nose a cross half black and half red bearing the number *243*. Badly damaged, this was the only Italian bomber brought down in Britain during the war. Crashed with its engines running, the captain, Pietro Appiani, then aged 22, stated that he thought the fuel tanks were holed. With the crew of five had come a photographer, whose pictures doubtless would have been universally unpopular at home. Luckily for the victors, the excellent supply of vino with which the Italians were proposing to celebrate their homeward flight was still intact ...but the usual story was that 'Customs men' had 'removed it'. Arthur E. Smith, later of 115 Squadron, visited the wreck around which bars of chocolate were also found. Officials discouraged consumption — 'might be poisoned'.

Two Fiat CR.42 fighters came down on land. One, *MM5701*, unit identity

Top *On Orford's shore a Fiat CR 42 fighter tipped on to its nose after forced landing. Repaired, then registered BT474, it became a common East Anglian sight during demonstration flights from Duxford* (RAF Museum). **Above** *It is now exhibited in the RAF Museum* (Author).

Below *The other Italian CR 42 which came down, MM6976, crashed near Corton railway station. The pilot had lost his way home* (Ford Jenkins Photography).

95*13 (ie, No 13 of the 95ᵈ Squadriglia) and flown by Sergeant Pietro Salvadadon, aged 23, forced-landed at 14:30 on shingle at Orford Ness range. Its camouflage was a sand shade mottled green, the underside silvery blue. Taken to RAE for investigation, and later to Duxford for tactical trials, it became *BT474*. Surprisingly it survives, exhibited in Hendon's Battle of Britain Museum.

Sergeant Major Antonio Lazzari, flying *MM6976:85*16* crashed 400 yd north of Corton railway station at 14:50. His aircraft, too, had pale blue propeller blades, a yellow engine cowling and a unit badge. Originally five CR.42s and eight BR.20s were reckoned as brought down; the authenticated totals were three of each. No British fighters were lost but another ten Italian fighters were damaged when landing!

Fiat BR.20s approached the Thames Estuary on 17 November, protected by Luftwaffe Bf 109s, for the Germans feared for their Allies. The Italians attempted at least seven more BR.20 night attacks upon East Anglian coastal targets: Harwich received six aircraft on 17 November, twelve on the 20th, eleven on 14 December, six on the 21st and four on the 22nd; nine bombers visited Lowestoft, Yarmouth and Ipswich on 29 November, and five returned to Ipswich on 5 January 1941.

During the Lowestoft raid seven 100 kg HEs dropped at 18:38, no alert being in force. No 1 CWS factory was slightly damaged by three bombs, one hitting a cast iron column, the second exploding on a concrete floor and the most damaging detonating in a roof causing the collapse of three trusses. The Harwich raid of 21 December commenced at 17:47 with six HEs. At 17:55 two fell in Dovercourt and at 18:05 one at Harwich. Some bombs had dropped near Kings Head Street and Market Street causing ten casualties. Damaged seriously were fifteen houses and shops, another thirty showing various scars.

At Ipswich on 21 December four HEs were dropped at 17:55, also seven 43 lb incendiaries with semi-armour piercing noses, revealing the Italian connection. Unusual was the penetrative capability of the bombs for at No 109 Bixley Road, a UX buried itself 30 in deep in the garden and at No 85 one burst into flames even though it was buried 3 ft deep. At No 62 Bixley Road one fell 6 ft from a lady holding a linen basket. After lying flat for a few minutes she hurried to the front of the house, as the bomb burst. She soon put it out with handfuls of soil. At No 60 Princethorpe Road, a bomb bounced off a kitchen dresser and on to the floor. Others fell in the garden of No 22 Princethorpe Road and outside No 20; by No 45 Cheltenham Road, and on the school playing fields in Cobblestone Road where the HEs also dropped. At Ness Farm near Ipswich two large incendiaries burnt for 28 minutes.

That there were lone daylight cloud cover ventures is certain, a Fiat BR.20 being seen over Ipswich by Mr D. F. Brock. Clacton, too, was probably a target on 27 November, a dusk raid was attempted off Southwold and there remain strong suspicions of night penetrations to Bedford and Huntingdonshire. Certainly some very strange-sounding engines were heard overhead at this time.

The offensive was, however, too difficult to sustain. The Italian bombers left for sunnier climes in early 1941, the fighters in April before the Fiat G.50s had shown themselves. Of the Italian effort, there had not been much to worry about.

Chapter 11
The lights of perverted science

By winter 1940 the grim bombing campaign was taking a heavy toll of life, limb and living. Turning the darkness to light, nightly came the bombs and mines and, irrationally, as much fear was generated by the widely sown but almost harmless parachute flares. The sight of one dormant, bearing strange printing and foreign words few understood, seemed never for the faint-hearted. To watch a burning chandelier flare's downward drift, coupled with the passage of its sower, was not one of life's more enjoyable moments.

Flares served either for target illumination or route markers, the latter burning red, green or yellow. Target lighting flares burnt white with a blueish tint. In 1944 Luftwaffe pathfinders employed special ground and sky markers. Although first dropped in June 1940, the initial use of flares for target exposure appears to have taken place on 5/6 August 1940 when six gave sufficient light to bare the Isle of Sheppey, although it would be wrong to imagine the area brightly lit.

Such single flares, which burnt for about ten minutes, were each contained in aluminium alloy cases 3 ft 3 in long by 8 in diameter. By November 1940 examples from six manufacturers had been found, most being made by Nicolaus Werke. Either they were dropped singly or in packs of four, suspended from a silk or artificial silk parachute 10 ft in diameter. By December 1940 parachutes of about 14 ft diameter were being used to increase drift time. They were red, white or dull green in colour and when discovered often led to the belief that a parachute mine had fallen. The flares were packed in paper lined tubes, the total four-flare item weighing 76 lb. Later variations included a small flare of which ten could be carried in an ABB500 container, along with SD.2 APBs, and a $13\frac{1}{4}$-in-long flare with parachute attached, 41 of which could be dropped from a Mark 250-LK container. Little wonder, then, that they so often caused consternation.

If flares were an alarming sight, however, they in no way equalled that moment when searchlights began sweeping the sky and the gun flashes really did turn night into day. It was surely then time to take cover for the intensely hot, heavy shrapnel fell in shoals.

Whilst the Army manned the searchlights and AA guns throughout the war (until the RAF Regiment took on most airfield defence), overall direction was by Fighter Command. One AA Corps controlled guns and searchlights within two Fighter Groups. Under the three Corps the force was divided into twelve

Divisions plus an independent one for Orkney and Shetland. No 2 Division was responsible roughly for the 12 Group area of East Anglia and No 6 Division for parts of Suffolk and the whole of Essex. Under Divisional HQ were the Brigades, Regiments, some Battalion HQs, AA and searchlight Batteries, AA sites and Searchlight Companies. The latter took their designations from the Sector Station, eg, DX013 = Duxford Sector, first Company, light three, although the organization and designations were very complex, extensive and expensive in manpower.

Heavy AA guns, never very common in East Anglia, were intended to break up enemy formations. A battery usually consisted of eight 3-in ex-Naval guns, or 3.7-in static or mobile guns. They were normally dispersed to avoid attack and for administrative reasons were sited in two groups of four which were still able to mount a hefty punch. Such guns throughout the war were found around Harwich and Ipswich, at certain airfields during 1940 and in 1942 at other towns likely to be heavily bombed.

Light anti-aircraft batteries held sixteen 40 mm Swedish-designed Bofors guns, each gun equipping a site as an entity. The intention was for them to engage raiders before they could reach their bomb release point. The number of guns defending any vulnerable point depended upon its importance, but was usually a Troop of four. Each site under the Detachment Commander had a team of four men manning the gun, three the Kerrison predictor, two controlling the ammunition and one the power generator. Yet of 331 men on a Light AA Battery, only 128 were operationally employed.

During 1941 'Z' UP (Unrotating Projectile) rocket projector Regiments became operational with twin-rocket projectors in batteries of 64 which took up considerable space. Later nine-barrel projectors were set in batteries of twelve. The plan was for all rockets to be fired simultaneously at low or high levels to form a box containing the enemy. The amount of shrapnel falling from the 3-in weapons after one firing was considerable. To release Regular troops, the Home Guard very competently manned the local '101 Battery' of these weapons from 1943 at Cambridge, Chelmsford, Colchester and Peterborough, despite obvious complications of pay and status.

For months prior to the war searchlights were a common sight, a few bell tents and a small wooden hutted encampment being a sight so much part of the early wartime scene in the countryside. By 1941 the normal three-searchlight cluster had a 150 cm Master Projector controlled by SLC equipment and two 90 cm satellite lights, the three sited about 600 yd apart being simultaneously exposed. Clusters were placed at 10,000-yd intervals throughout the region to illuminate continuously the Aircraft Fighting Zone, with increased concentrations in vulnerable areas. Battery HQ decided from information received which cluster(s) (up to three) would engage a target, although the final decision rested with the Site Commander. Cloud conditions were always to be considered, haze too. While Sound Locators remained in use the Gun Laying radar carpet was by 1941 aiding the searchlight crews. Although radar came to nullify much of the need for searchlights, they remained a useful aid to fighters—especially when in 1944 the enemy dropped 'Düppel'. Searchlight crews always tried to hold the target in the beam's trailing edge, thus avoiding blotting it out for the fighter. A searchlight Battery consisted of four officers and 126 men manning 24 projectors, each working unit comprising three operators, three controllers, three generator mechanics, two spotters and a Detachment Commander and his Deputy. Many sites also had a light machine-gun.

In summer 1941 when the intensity of raids fell away questions were raised as to the value of having 300,000 men manning AA positions. To release many of them over 70,000 ATS personnel took on non-firing duties, but the changes took some time to implement. The Baedecker raids brought more heavy guns to East Anglia, then a total re-organization followed in autumn 1942, East Anglia coming under 5 AA Group (north) and 9 AA Group (south). In April 1943 the Command's strength was set at 2,291 guns and 1,850 lights manned by 180,000 men and 77,000 women.

Discouragement of formation attacks and prevention of bombing — and not the destruction of enemy aircraft — was the prime purpose of the AA guns. Nevertheless, they achieved notable, spectacular destruction of raiders on a number of occasions. In September 1940 it was reckoned that one raider was shot down for every 20,000 rounds fired at night, improving to one per 7,000 by November. By day it took but 250 rounds and one Battery averaged a score of one hit in sixty shots. In November 1940 1,421 heavy guns, 55! Bofors and 4,519 others were deployed. It is impossible to know how many enemy aircraft were destroyed by AA guns since a number of damaged machines crashed far off-shore. During the 1944 V-1 campaign the gunners achieved stupendous success on the East Anglian coast.

The machinations within the AA defence of the UK were complex, and the reader is recommended to turn to the fascinating writings of its wartime commander, General Sir Frederick Pile, for details. Meanwhile, with Christmas 1940 approaching, let us return to the wartime days.

Parachute flares being loaded, probably on a lead illuminator Ju 88 (Bundesarchiv 493/3366/30).

Chapter 12
In the bleak, cruel winter

With the war going badly, morale remained surprisingly high. High explosive and incendiary bombs seemed to rain at random over East Anglia, and mines floated down at unlikely places, in the eerie flarelight. Unpleasantly, an extremely cold winter was closing in. Nothing seemed in our favour, and only when fog covered Britain did the Luftwaffe fail to hammer on the door. Irregularly it visited us in daylight — cloud conditions permitting even the dropping of a mine at 15:11 on 10 November on Royston Heath. Another day raid involved Wisbech where at 15:25 on 11 November, HEs demolished several houses, killing two and seriously injuring another two people. In East Anglia airfields continued to attract most of the enemy's attention.

Around 04:00 on 11 November a few Ju 88Cs had come in among our returning bombers. One reached Mildenhall — after dropping bombs near Honington — and two landing Wellingtons were lucky not to be attacked. A home-bound Ju 88 machine-gunned West Raynham, six bombs fell near Marham and another ten in Blyth RD. Shipping off Southwold was attacked at dusk, then Norwich had its fourth alert of the day. Incendiaries caused a fire at Victoria Goods Station. In misty conditions at 11:15, HEs near Colchester's second railway bridge caused several hours' closure of the Ipswich line.

Foggy weather on 12/13 November prevented operations until shortly before dawn when airfield intruders roamed at between 3,000 and 7,000 ft. Morning reconnaissance flights to the Midlands crossed East Anglia, their significance obvious later. During the night there was more intruder activity, mainly north of Cambridge and around Newmarket. Another attempt to interfere with a convoy was made on 14 November near Clacton by four Bf 110s of I/Erpro.210. Hurricanes of 257 Squadron at 11:05, ordered to patrol that area at 15,000 ft, were soon inconclusively engaging six Bf 109s.

Around 19:00 on the clear, moonlit night of the 14th/15th, sirens wailed over much of East Anglia. About half an hour later high flying Dutch-based bombers began trekking north-westwards, and in Cambridge we were aware of a non-stop stream passing overhead. What we did not know was that this was merely an accessory to the main element crossing in over the south coast. Some of the 350 bombers operating passed over Bedford, through which one of the 'Knickebein' beams led to Coventry. Indeed, at 21:20 a parachute mine exploded at Bedford, extensively damaging over 100 houses and injuring thirteen people. Two more exploded in Samford RD. North Witchford and Ely RD each received nine

HEs and Blyth RD another fourteen. These were merely incidental to the main onslaught and, largely free of interference, most attackers found their main target, the city of Coventry where soon melting lead from the roof of the cathedral dripped down its mediaeval walls like greying tears.

By contrast, the 15th/16th November was quieter, East Anglia attracting the most activity. Some 48 HEs (three UX) fell in South Cambridgeshire RD, in Deben 21 HEs (one UX) and near Braintree five parachute mines, two of which did not explode. At 19:30 two HEs hit Little Barford power station near St Neots. Ten 50 kg bombs and a KC250 oil bomb had been dropped, one bursting on the boiler house roof and another on the corner of a building. At Elsworth in the early hours of the 16th ten HEs badly damaged four houses in Brook Street, and rescue operations had to be mounted. Next night HEs again fell over widely separated areas — eleven in Chesterton RD, 21 in South Cambs, thirteen in Dunmow RD, seven (one UX) near Docking and two parachute mines (one UX) in Ely RD. No 25 Squadron, during the evening of 16 November, claimed a He 111 near Colchester.

Fighter-bombers again appeared on 17 November. No 257 Squadron patrolling off Harwich battled with six Bf 109s. Flight Lieutenant Blatchford (*V6962*) and Pilot Officer Kay each claimed a Bf 109, but Pilot Officer Matthews (*P2835*) was injured by a cannon shell and Sergeant Henson was shot down. Bf 110s were operating against shipping, and the crew was rescued from one which came down in the sea off Aldeburgh.

Below *Ju 88s were numerous during the Coventry raid. W Nr 4634 is the nearer aircraft* (Bundesarchiv 376/2735/18).
Bottom *He 111s were also busy and led the raid. This example of KG55 externally carries an SC1000 HE* (Bundesarchiv 346/846/13).

Another convoy was attacked at 13:28 in hazy weather on 19 November between Lowestoft and Yarmouth, and a member of HMT *Star of Pentland*'s crew was killed. Despite extensive fog on 19/20 November, the largest number of Luftwaffe sorties in one night so far was flown, Birmingham being the main target. Bombing was distributed widely over East Anglia. Near Downham Market two mines were dropped (one UX) along with twenty HEs, eleven HEs fell in Cambridgeshire and forty in Chesterton RD. Next night activity was again extensive, the Midlands once more the main target until around 02:30 when heavy rain halted the proceedings. Activity then switched to East Anglia where from 03:15 another series of raids developed and bombs fell near Wittering. Three mines fell, one at 03:03 demolishing poultry houses at Pretty's Poultry Farm near Lowestoft. Another dropped 255 yd east of the Oulton-Somerleyton Road, seriously damaging six houses and slightly damaging 180 more. The third came down at Laxford at 04:55 by Ubbeston Low Road, damaging the church and seven houses. Windows in Akeham church were broken by an HE bomb. Over a dozen incidents were reported in East Anglia, two dozen HEs falling in Cambridgeshire and eight in Newmarket RD, while March marshalling yards were bombed, as was Bury St Edmunds. Ely RD received eight HEs, King's Lynn eight (one UX), Swaffham nine and Downham Market RD fifteen.

A low-flying bomber attacked Yarmouth at 08:38 on the 21st. Diving fast, it placed a dozen 50 kg HEs on to the north part of the town, from Salisbury Road to Eastcourt Road, four bombs landing at the infirmary which was in use as a barracks. Casualties amounted to one killed and three injured. Three houses were demolished and six more had to be pulled down. Half an hour later Hurricanes of 17 Squadron damaged a Do 17Z off Felixstowe. During the afternoon a dozen HEs landed at Walton-on-the-Naze between Saville Street, Stanley Road and Mill Lane, demolishing a furniture store and two cottages. At Mersea a parachute mine produced an 80-ft crater.

Only about forty enemy aircraft operated on the night of 21/22 November, but this was sufficient nevertheless to keep East Anglia under alert from 19:30 to 08:30. Attacks were carried out in Chesterton RD (41 HEs), on Chivers Farm, Sedge Fen Lakenheath (twenty HEs), Debden (25 HEs), Hartismere, where another mine fell, Yarmouth where twelve bombs were dropped, Bury St Edmunds, Mutford RD (four parachute mines), Saffron Walden RD (35 HEs — five UX and over 200 incendiaries), Dunmow (sixteen HEs and incendiaries) and Downham RD where another two mines and four HEs were dropped.

On 22/23 November wave after wave of bombers heavily bombed Birmingham, some approaching along a radio beam crossing southern East Anglia. One raider dropped incendiaries and ten HEs on open ground at Colchester's Mile End area. A particularly active phase then developed between about 05:50 and 06:50. Near Docking ten UXHEs fell, near St Neots eighteen HEs (one UX), at Frinton twelve HEs, in Dunmow RD 23 HEs (one UX), in Chesterton RD fourteen HEs and another 25 in South Cambs. During the morning of the 23rd, a strong enemy bomber force approached an East coast convoy and was soon driven off by the appearance of Hurricanes of 17 and 257 Squadrons. Before the fog closed in around 22:00 that night, 26 HEs were dropped in Huntingdon RD, nineteen (six UX) in Halstead RD and ten at Felixstowe.

Bombing during the remaining nights of November was much reduced, partly due to the enemy approaching targets from the Irish Sea to avoid fog over England. Colchester was twice bombed during the evening of 24 November, first at around 18:30 when five HEs exploded near Kingsford Lodge, Layer Road, damaging two houses. The second attack came moments before midnight when ten HEs and incendiaries fell harmlessly at Mile End. Around dawn on 25 November the Luftwaffe launched hit-and-run raids on coastal areas, nine HEs falling at West Bergholt at 06:25 hitting seven houses and causing two casualties. Around 07:35 ten HEs and incendiaries fell at Great and Little Clacton and half an hour later more incendiaries fell on Frinton's golf course. By then fighters were searching for the attackers and at about 08:45 two Hurricanes of 17 Squadron engaged a Do 17 seven miles off Felixstowe without a certain kill. Later that day bombs also fell in Samford and Dunmow RDs. Particularly impressive was the 50-ft crater, 25 ft deep, which was produced on Bassingbourn's Q-Site on 28 November. One of the busiest nights over East Anglia was 29/30 November when 350 enemy aircraft operated (120 against London) and 46 HEs (five UX) were dropped near Norman Cross, seventeen (two UX) near Saffron Walden, ten HEs and incendiaries near Dunmow. During daylight on 29 November a Do 215 was intercepted over East Anglia by 222 Squadron and chased to Calais by Flight Lieutenant van Mentz who was then rewarded with a successful engagement.

At the end of November 1940 an official survey of the number of bombing incidents reported from East Anglia and the whole of Essex over the preceding three months showed:

	9-30 September	October	November
Bedfordshire	20	94	62
Cambridgeshire	31	95	49
East Suffolk	53	65	86
Essex	120	400	186
Huntingdonshire	16	15	13
Isle of Ely	29	5	24
Norfolk	50	116	106
West Suffolk	67	55	28

Much of December 1940's weather was too poor for large scale operations. On 1/2 December when London raids were routed in over Harwich, only four enemy night sorties operated over East Anglia to attack Cranfield and Newmarket Heath aerodromes without success. In thick mist just after dusk, a raider attacked Norwich before leaving to the south. Newmarket Heath was again attacked at 17:14 on 3 December, by a Do 17 which dived from 6,000 ft machine-gunning as it sped away towards Burwell. Then it turned and dropped eighteen bombs which undershot on to fields flanking the railway linking Burwell and Fordham close to where the B1103 road crossed the track upon which two bombs exploded, ripping it apart for 50 yd. A passenger train had just stopped at Exning Halt and two RAF personnel who leaned out were injured by machine-gun fire from the Dornier.

Few attacks took place on 5 December although Stowmarket and Yarmouth were bombed and a trawler ten miles off Lowestoft was attacked, Spitfires of 222 Squadron sent to its protection having no success. Another engagement involved Pilot Officer Humphrey of 266 Squadron who chased a Ju 88 out over the Wash, then followed a He 111 which he shot down off the Scheldt mouth. At night twelve HEs fell on Lowestoft's North Pier and destroyed two houses.

Only two hostiles operated over East Anglia on 7 December, one to recconnoitre the Midlands, the other to drop four HEs shortly after noon near Yarmouth's scenic railway. The most memorable event of 8 December involved Takeley, Essex. An alert sounded at 17:40, enemy aircraft thereafter spasmodically operating in the area. Unexpectedly a stick of four HEs were, at midnight, released across the sleeping village, demolishing four cottages. Eight occupants asleep on ground floors were buried, seven of them being killed. Over 100 incendiaries had added to the horror before more HEs caused minor damage in the area. One relatively small incident had produced unexpected grief on a large scale in a small community.

Over Norfolk a Ju 88C for two hours patrolled airfields, dropping bombs south of Bircham Newton and machine-gunning Bodney. Raiders from the south unsuccessfully attacked Upwood, Bury St Edmunds and Wyton. Squadron Leader Stanford Tuck (*V6864*) on 9 December located a Do 17 out to sea and promptly shot it down. He had just landed when three Hurricanes patrolling Martlesham at 17:10 spotted a Do 17 attempting to dive-bomb the airfield. They engaged it, but the aircraft escaped after firing shots into Hurricane *V7607*. Limited night activity occurred over Halstead RD, 200 incendiaries and two HEs fell near Saffron Walden and more incendiaries at Colchester, Dunmow and Melford.

At 16:05 on 10 December, HEs demolishing Nos 16,18 and 21 The Parade, Walton, injured three soldiers. The following night proved quiet until around 06:30 when Ju 88s accompanied returning RAF bombers. No airfields were damaged, but bombs fell close to Bircham Newton, Coltishall, Norwich and Wittering. At Wymondham six HEs (one UX) were dropped, and incendiaries in Cosford RD.

The next day, 12 December, was far busier, two-phase raids being mounted against Birmingham. Bombs also fell over a wide area of the east. Three oil bombs, four HEs and a few incendiaries were delivered on Ipswich, eighteen HEs in Debden. A most unlikely event overtook Great Abington, a few miles south of Cambridge, where a 50 kg bomb passed through its small brick bridge over the river, producing a 3-ft crater into which half the arch collapsed, causing great inconvenience, not to mention annoyance!

Mines continued to spasmodically drift down. One exploded in Chelmsford RD on 13 December, and on the 14th/15th two landed, on Lower Farm and Daisy Farm, near Great Holland, closing the nearby railway. That night, the largest number of bombs dropped, 45, was in Woodbridge RD. Operations were again being reduced by foggy weather, but bombs nevertheless fell in Hartismere, Lothingland, Gipping and Freebridge RDs, also on Yarmouth where at 03:13 a UXHE in King Street became the 106th HE to fall upon the town.

Consistency of bombing policy was not easy to discern at the time, although airfields, ports and military concentrations were main targets. Railway installations too attracted much attention, the 08:45 raid upon Audley End station on 16 December clearly being to a specific plan embracing the use of HE, incendiary and oil weapons. Later that morning three Bf 110s circled Clacton bombing north of the town during a speedy pass.

Further bad weather halted operations until 20 December when two parachute mines dropped in Launditch RD failed to explode. Early on the 21st another two mines (and two UX) dropped in Forhoe and HEs in Depwade RD and at Norwich. Much activity was generated next night as a large force crossed East Anglia between 18:00 and 01:00 en route for Liverpool. At 07:25 on the 21st six enemy aircraft, which had joined a returning RAF bomber force, operated over Forhoe RD, and other bombs fell in Depwade RD and at Norwich again.

For the Birmingham raid of 22/23 December, enemy aircraft were routed mainly from and to the south coast, little activity taking place over East Anglia apart from thirteen HEs dropped in South Cambs RD. About thirty enemy aircraft mined between Yarmouth and Withernsea, only five briefly crossing the coast.

* * *

Assessing effectiveness of recent raids, a daylight reconnaissance aircraft crossed Norfolk on 23 December to photograph the Midlands, turning at Sheffield and flying over to Duxford before changing course for its base. The next night incendiaries fell at Clacton, and the big question being asked was — would the incessant raids continue during Christmas? Within the 24 hours from 06:00 on the 24th to 25th only two red alerts sounded in the entire country. One was at Truro, the other at Norwich from 13:29 to 13:32, the latter arising from mistaken identity of a friendly aircraft. As for the rest of Christmas, there was great relief that the bombs did not come.

Christmas was barely recognizable.

True, extra rations were on hand and, barely noticeable, a few 'goodies' possibly obtainable on 'points'. Ever-increasing shipping losses meant food shortages. Gone the traditional 'orange in a stocking' for every child, the icing sugar on the cake. Missing, too, many an unfortunate, backyard pet chicken or cockerel and long gone the lights and colour of Christmas. Many people by now had lost everything — loved ones, homes, pets, and there was the worry of how one's dearest were faring far from home. Without doubt this was the worst wartime Christmas, and very bad times lay ahead.

That the Luftwaffe had not forgotten us was plain on 27 December when two mines were unloaded near Chelmsford, and the Leiston area was bombed . At midday on the 29th seven bombs reached Lowestoft, and there was activity around Cromer. And then, early in the evening came the first major incendiary onslaught, upon the City of London. Again, the fires were visible from Cambridge — hardly surprising because, within a small part of London, ten conflagrations and ten major fires took hold, along with 28 serious, 137 medium and 569 small fires making an assessable 708 fires in all. Fire quenching was impossible, all that could be attempted was to prevent the unbelievable from engulfing all.

Thick drizzle covered East Anglia during 30 December. A Ju 88 following the Norwich-Thetford railway broke cloud near Attleborough and, spotting the distinctive shape of Gaymers Cider factory, released five HEs and an oil bomb which hit the factory and seriously damaged it. An old part of the factory was soon aflame. One employee was wounded and his leg had to be amputated. Mainly, though, it was airfields that between 10:00 and 14:00 were targeted. At Stradishall two were killed, four injured.

Above *At 11:56 on 29 December 1940 seven HEs fell on London Road South, Union Place, Salisbury Road and Beaconsfield Road, Lowestoft, killing five civilians. From shattered homes in Beaconsfield Road, as much as possible is salvaged* (Ford Jenkins Photography).

Below *In place of Tudor House, Surrey Street, Lowestoft — destruction* (Ford Jenkins Photography).

Top *Wreckage of the bottling department at Gaymers cider factory following the attack by a Ju 88 on 30 December 1940.*

Above *Photographs of bomb-damaged airfields are rare. This shows bomb damage to a hangar at Stradishall at the beginning of 1941.*

Shortly after 13:30 a neighbour rushed in calling, 'A Dornier, Mike, come quickly'. I heard it coming low and at first thought it was an Anson. But as it hurried close by, the under gunner firing, I could see this to be one of the rare Do 215s. It had circled Marshall's aerodrome making at least two strafing passes. Spent cartridges falling around discouraged the study of its identity letters. Presumably it was this machine which unloaded bombs along the apron at Waterbeach.

In many respects that sudden strike, with crowds in the streets watching and little military reaction, was a microcosm of so much of the 1940 air raids upon East Anglia. We heard and distantly witnessed the sort of assaults we had been led to expect. The man with his piles of sand had the right idea after all, but by now few carried gas masks, let alone assumed their need likely. So many times the raider didn't raid that the vast majority of people were staying in bed and ignoring the Luftwaffe, until after the bombs fell. And when they did it was nearly always in open country, or when the siren had not been sounded. Would things change, an invasion come, a repeat of last summer's raids south? There was no need to worry about such treats for by now it was incredibly cold. Best to indulge in a large Horlicks, curl up with a stone hot water bottle, put out the light and dream — for this was indeed a cruel, bleak midwinter.

Chapter 13
Unhappy New Year

Bleak, icy, alarmingly waterless was the start of 1941. Food was short, news bad and the scene to hand grim. Borrowing our low cloud, the Luftwaffe for three months daily mounted a campaign against East Anglians, pestering their streets, their farms and fields. To London, the Midlands and the north-west streams of aliens roamed, crossing our countryside and rooftops in moonlit impunity, etching our sky with vapour trails on icy nights. 'Twas then that fire bombs burnt brilliantly, the flares hovered brightly and the high explosive bombs burst with exceptionally loud, hollow bangs. Life was bitterly hard and worrying, our '80s joyful by comparison. After all, one might be but a memory by dawn; many were, in one's own kitchen, by the hearth or near the back door. Yet, no one seemed faint-hearted.

On all but three January days East Anglia was attacked, poor weather restricting activity on another five. Coastwise shipping twenty to forty miles out became increasingly pursued while further seawards Zenit (weather reporting) sorties were daily mounted, single aircraft (Do 17s, '215s and Ju 88s) venturing into the Midlands on long reconnaissance sweeps which usefully indicated areas of enemy interest.

New Year's Day was relatively quiet, night activity commencing as six Dutch-based Ju 88Cs skirted the Norfolk coast prior to landfall, placing bombs close to a Wittering hangar. From about 19:20, seventy bombers of KG2, KG3 and KG53 headed in between Dunwich and the Humber to the Midlands, Yorkshire and East Anglia, over which others travelled to Liverpool, among them fifteen Soesterberg-based He 111s of I/KG4 proceeding to mine Liverpool Bay. A Do 17Z of KG3 dropped eight HEs in South Cambs RD, and Samford RD received an unexploded mine.

In strong winds next night another two mines fell, the first exploding over Breydon Water at 00:55 and causing little damage. At 02:35 Grove Farm, Harkstead, received the second, its impact marked by a crater 40 ft across and 12 ft deep.

Airfields and bomber operations were attracting more enemy attention than any other targets. Sometimes the raids started just after dusk, as on 2 January when six raiders crossed the East Anglian coast at 17:00. Possibly He 111s of I/KG53 from Lille/Vendeville, they achieved little, nor did Do 17Zs of I/KG3 operating over Norfolk the next night. Seven bombs fell in Hartismere RD and three each in Gipping and Thedwastre.

A daytime reconnaissance machine circled the Blackwater Estuary at about 15,000 ft on 3 January before venturing to Lowestoft. In mid-afternoon another entered over Clacton and, although fighters were scrambled at 15:52, the raider escaped.

The Fourth of January brought 1941's first unusual incident. No firm conclusions were drawn about what fell at Valley Farm, Wherstead, by the Manningtree Road and in Blue Gate Lodge garden. Nine craters resulted, probably from a Do 17Z of II/KG3. Four craters 12 ft across and 3 ft deep resulted, but in the drive of Blue Gates Lodge was a smaller crater 6 ft wide by 2 ft deep, like one in a meadow. A dozen windows were broken at the Lodge, and its roof was damaged. In three craters, aluminium-like tubes were found and burnt calcium carbide. Fierce fires observed at those craters suggested use of combined HEs and incendiaries. Special interest had arisen because confirmation came in October 1940 that 1 kg incendiary bombs fitted with explosive components were being dropped, with charges sufficient to hurl a person at least five feet. The tail disc was replaced by a steel adaptor and steel box carrying the explosive charge and detonator. Usually torn off upon penetrating a building, the tail was ripped away revealing the explosive charge, ten per cent wax and ninety per cent *petnpentaerythri-toltetpanitrate* contained in a small, thin, aluminimum case. Detonation by *leadazide leadstyphnat* and primer of PTN was caused by burning thermite elektron metal, the explosion coming about $1\frac{1}{2}$ minutes after bomb ignition. The spread of burning particles was enhanced by the weapon's ability to penetrate a thick wooden floor. Widespread use of such weapons could have resulted in very serious incidents and evidence suggested their early use at Wherstead.

Three armed-reconnaissance flights penetrated into East Anglia between 08:00 and 08:30 on 4 January. One entered at Orford Ness and flew to Southwold via Harleston and Bungay. The second came in over Southwold and flew to Winterton via Diss, over Watton whose guns opened fire shortly before 09:00, then over Norwich and Coltishall. Over Ipswich, Sudbury, Lavenham, Stowmarket and Diss toured the first intruder before it left over Dunwich. Much more activity came when two patrolling Hurricanes of 242 Squadron were, at 14:20, vectored south-east and, at 9,000 ft east of Dunwich, engaged a Do 215 which fired back before entering cloud. An hour later a Ju 88, possibly of 3.(F)/122, machine-gunned Southwold's High Street.

Midnight brought the unmistakable tones of Heinkel 111Hs high over the Norfolk and Suffolk coasts for I and III/KG53 were making unconventional approaches to Bristol. More Heinkels heard later were I and II/KG4 returning to Wittmundhafen and Westerland. Dorniers of II/KG2 headed for Merville. Two bombers each dropped ten HEs in Clare and Samford RD regions.

The Fifth of January brought 35 enemy daylight sorties to the Thames Estuary and East Anglian coast as bombers searched for shipping. Some raiders ventured inland to bomb Norwich, Bishop's Stortford and Saxmundham. At Clacton two HEs fell at 11:00 in the Old Road car park, a punctured gasometer being set alight. The fire was soon extinguished, slight casualties amounting to two. Honington had been attacked at 10:35 by a very low-flying Do 17Z whose ten bombs killed one and injured another Serviceman. Ju 88Cs of I/NJG2 penetrated to the East Midlands ahead of nearly fifty Dutch-based bombers (mainly of KG4 and KG30) using Harwich as their entry point for London.

Low clouds on 6 January encouraged low-level raids. At 09:30 one of KG3's Do 17Zs passed over Lowestoft and flew to Swaffham where it broke cloud then placed nine HEs on the railway station, killing five soldiers and injuring civilians. An Observer Corps post near Bircham Newton was machine-gunned when another KG3 Dornier circled Stiffkey very low, replying to ground fire before dropping ten HEs on a road near Docking. Bircham Newton aerodrome came under attack two hours later when one of four Dorniers of III/KG3, active from St Trond, appeared at 300 ft to release four bombs on to the flying field and three more near the control tower before escaping over Lowestoft. Heinkel 111Ps of III/KG27 were operating over Essex and one, tracking along the Blackwater Estuary at 15:15, flew over Colchester, bombed Pitsea then retired over Clacton. Bad weather brought a relatively peaceful night. Ju 88A *3Z+GT* of KG77, busy off the East Anglian coast, managed to reach Schiphol just in time to avoid the atrocious weather.

Cloudy conditions pervaded eastern England next day, 7 January, making it ideal for sneak raids. An early penetration by one of seven Dorniers of I/KG3 was to Cambridgeshire. By noon a second phase of activity was under way, two lines of aproach being over the Thames Estuary and Harwich. More than fifty bombers operated, only seven entering the London IAZ leaving the remainder operating over Essex, Suffolk and Norfolk. Four bombs fell at Debden and fourteen in Samford RD, airfields being the main targets. Two attempts to bomb Newmarket Heath were made, but eight bombs fell 1,000 yd wide. At Honington, also raided twice, bombs burst near Station Sick Quarters, SHQ and the guardroom. In a raid on Stradishall a Do 17 released its bombs half a mile away. At Feltwell no damage was done and conditions were so poor that a dense snowstorm forced Coltishall's fighters home.

Notwithstanding, the Luftwaffe was intent upon making this a special day. With so many enemy aircraft roaming among the clouds, more than four warnings sounded in most towns during the day. At Cambridge the Rustat Road Waterworks' siren was even sounding the 'All Clear' as others gave a warning. Sirens wailed at 14:04 in Ipswich, the 'All Clear' coming at 15:35. But all was far from clear for, three minutes later, a Heinkel 111 flying very low over the town dropped two HEs before machine-gunning the Rushmere area. There, at 15:50, a companion, probably of I/KG53 from Lille/Vendeville and flying a northerly track, slipped below the clouds and, when over the river, released an enormous bomb which buried itself 30 ft into Holywell Park without exploding. Seven minutes too late, sirens warned of the foe. By then the Heinkel had machine-gunned Wickham Market and the Glemham area, causing widespread damage. Initially its large weapon was classed as a 1,000 kg bomb, the biggest yet to fall in East Anglia. But when the Bomb Disposal Team, displaying great courage, reached the weapon, after digging through a morass of mud and water, they discovered a gigantic SD1700 heavy fragmentation bomb, one of few dropped on Britain. Not for six days was the A45 (which had been closed at Bishops Hill) re-opened to traffic, by which time the BDS had reduced the brute to impotence. Heinkel 111s of KG53 were specially modified to carry these large bombs externally.

Shortly prior to the Ipswich attacks, a particularly pernicious raid had been made upon the small hamlet of Market Weston where at 15:25 ten HEs were dropped along The Street. They demolished a shop, seriously damaged three houses, blocked the road and damaged GPO lorries in the depot. Conditions permitting such daytime activity again prohibited night operations.

Of 21 bombers located by radar around the eastern shores on 8 January, only three came inland. After circling off Cap Gris Nez, a Do 17 flew to the Thames Estuary searching for shipping, a quest leading it to Harwich. At 2,000 ft it flew to Aldeburgh, back-tracked to Martlesham Heath then chose Ipswich as target. Ten 50 kg bombs (one UX) fell at 10:15 on No 6 Romney Road, where a child was killed, and on 16 Fletcher Road where one person died. The Dornier's crew then machine-gunned Foxhall Road, Rushmere. Of the other aircraft, two which crossed the coast circled Harwich at 09:55 before going to attack Broadstairs. The other crossed the coast near Winterton at 12:40 then turned to direct its load at an Army parade in the grounds of a Happisburgh hotel. Luckily, the bombs overshot into the sea. An attempt to sink a ship off Orford Ness at 10:03 was unsuccessful. Afternoon plotting showed a further 29 enemy bombers mainly out to sea, but at 13:20 a Dornier flew inland north of Orford Ness, then over Saxmundham to Halesworth where it circled prior to releasing five HEs south of the town. Night operations over East Anglia were still impossible due to inclement weather.

Ascertaining the possibility of evening operations on 9 January, three reconnaissance Dorniers crossed East Anglia during the afternoon, one from Wells-next-Sea flying to Littleport and Duxford, and out over Shoeburyness. Favourable reports of a pause in snowy, intensely cold conditions encouraged 300 bombers to operate between 17:35 and 02:30, mainly against London and the central Midlands to which KG3 and KG53 made their way over East Anglia. At 18:50 nine HEs fell on Clacton — four in Lancaster Gardens, East Clacton. Four houses were badly damaged and casualties numbered five. Two parachute mines fell on South House Farm, Frinton, Essex, at 20:05, one exploding and damaging two empty cottages. Yarmouth at 21:25 received its first attack in the year when it was savagely assaulted by the Luftwaffe. Fourteen HEs fell at South Denes, Riverside, Gorleston, injuring two people. Clacton was again attacked at 23:02, a Heinkel unloading incendiaries across the town starting numerous small fires between Jaywick (where four HEs also fell) and Old Road, Clacton. Damage was slight and no casualties were sustained. The night also saw four bombs each in St Ives, in Blyth RD and Gipping RD. Six fell in Freebridge/Lynn RD without causing much damage.

Activity on 10 January was restricted to reconnaissance flights including an afternoon sortie to Harwich by Ju 88A *F6+EH* of 3(F)/122. Next morning He 111H *A1+CH* of 1/KG53 under Villacoublay's control checked the East Anglian conditions. No 257 Squadron was ordered at 13:56 on 15 January to patrol Honington. Reported enemy aircraft were not seen but, about to land at Coltishall, they spotted over Sheringham at about 20,000 ft a reconnoitring He 111. Closing, they opened fire, saw smoke issue from the enemy which then produced some wild return fire and was soon lost in cloud. This was the nearest that fighters had yet come to bagging a 1941 East Anglian raider.

Better weather on 15/16 January brought the enemy out in force. Activity commenced around 19:50 and continued until 08:00. Two entry zones were evident, firstly between Harwich and Flamborough Head through which about 100 bombers penetrated to the East and South Midlands, and secondly between Harwich and the Thames Estuary. Included in group one were Dornier 17s of

Above *Bf 110s of 1./ZG2 about to take off for a 1940 escort mission. 3M+DH nearest and 3M+LH wear mottled grey-blue camouflage, 3M+AH and 'GH have the earlier dark green-black upper surfaces* (Bundesarchiv 403/333/16).

Below *Ju 88As preparing for night operations* (Bundesarchiv 388/968/33).

Bottom *Sharp attacks were carried out upon shipping and coastal towns by Bf 110 fighter-bombers of Erpro 210* (Bundesarchiv 405/585/15).

Above *Familiar at night was the rattle of the engines of Do 17Zs like this example, possibly of KG3* (Bundesarchiv 345/766/170).
Below *Flying pencil-like Do 17Zs like these of KG2 pestered East Anglians in early 1941* (Bundesarchiv 342/603/18).
Bottom *Suddenly they had all gone, the flying pencils. From Yarmouth to the Acropolis. From the chill of Norfolk to the sun went these Do 17Zs of KG2* (Bundesarchiv Bilol 141/105/1031).

II/KG2 which operated between midnight and 05:30 over East Anglia and the East Midlands. At 00:45 *U5+MM* was over Wisbech, and *U5+HP* was still over Bedfordshire at 05:11 like *U5+DM*, also returning to Merville. *U5+GM, 'KM, 'LM, 'PM, 'PN, 'DN, 'HN* and *'CP* had been among fifteen Dorniers of the Gruppe operating. For company they had twenty He 111s of KG4, twelve Dorniers of II/KG3, twenty of I/KG53 and twelve of II/KG53. Between them they bombed Felixstowe (four HEs), Debden (ten HEs), Samford RD (seven), Downham RD (23), Smallborough RD, Erping RD (eight), Godmanchester (three), North Witchwood RD (two) and Forhoe/Henstead RD (three). At 03:20 He 111H-5 W Nr *3638:A1+JK* flown by a crew of 2./KG53 sank by a buoy at Wholehaven, Essex.

It was at 03:55 on the 16th that a very low flier, by sound definitely a Ju 88 and thus almost certainly of I/KG30, placed a container of incendiaries over the Hyde Park Corner area of Cambridge. About 250 bombs rained down, several slithering across the southern part of the Catholic church roof, slightly damaging it. Others clattered on to Flinders store, which was soon engulfed by a major fire. Most of the bombs, though, burst on the Perse Boys' School Hall, an imposing chapel-like strucure containing many wooden beams and trimmings which burnt fiercely, the whole impossible to save. As the fire brigade arrived the Ju 88 made a second, north-south strafing run, its gunners firing into both blazing buildings.

The Perse School Hall was still burning furiously at 08:30. Despite the devastation, and the multitude of hoses necessary because, due to the icy conditions, water had to be widely tapped, buses were still passing close to the huge fire. Sitting atop a double-decker I watched as much of the hall roof, or its remains, suddenly collapsed into remnants of the familiar form and erupted into a tremendous burst of flame, the blaze showering sparks widely. The conductor leaned across and said 'I think we've had enough excitement for one day'. We all agreed, especially as fragments rained on to the roof during as exciting a bus ride as one could expect, and survive! Presumably the target had been Cambridge station, but airfields were also listed, a Ju 88 dropping its load on Feltwell's dispersals and a He 111 trying to damage Marham.

It was Saturday, 18 January, before the Luftwaffe returned, about fifteen Dorniers of II/KG3 from Antwerp/Duerne, to attack airfields. First to be raided was West Raynham, then at 14:20 ten HEs at Watton damaged Married Quarters and the NAAFI; another forty HEs were used against Great Massingham where half landed on Hill Farm. Ten minutes later Moggs Farm and Black Dyke, Feltwell, received thirteen HEs and Hockwold was machine-gunned. In thick cloud one intrepid Dornier crew flew to Macclesfield and left over Orford Ness. Fighters from Coltishall and Wittering unsuccessfully tried to intercept. Another Dornier tried unsuccessfuly to sink the Sunk LV.

After facing Bofors guns at Horsham St Faith, a Dornier broke cloud over West Raynham and was again made unwelcome. Then, at tree-top height, it raced across Great Massingham, machine-gunning and dropping sixteen bombs — twelve falling on the landing ground. Soon afterwards, a Dornier broke cloud machine-gunning Halesworth before dropping eight HEs across the railway installation. The station house, booking office and track were hit and the signal box was badly damaged. Three were killed, four injured.

At 15:25 the crew of Do 17Z *5K+BN* signalled that they had reached Colchester. With disastrous results for civilians aboard, the Saturday afternoon train from London was approaching Chitts Hill crossing when the Dornier slid from snow clouds, its machine-gunners raking the entire length of the train at which were aimed the bombs, the first bearing organ pipe screamers, before the aircraft turned and the whole train was again machine-gunned. Luckily the bombs missed, but gunfire seriously injured six passengers and the guard, Arthur Pike of Ipswich who, like Florence Knowles, a 24-year-old passenger, died later. Aboard the train a nineteen-year-old pianist about to commence his career as a professional lost all of the fingers on one hand. One of the luckiest survivors was Mr H. G. Meadows, crossing gate keeper, who quickly lay flat to escape bullets whistling through the window of his hut — and out through its door.

The Luftwaffe concentrated upon coastal shipping on the 19th, a Dornier 17 of I/KG2 attacking five merchant vessels and their naval escort twenty miles off Lowestoft. After an unsuccessful attempt they landed back at Epinoy at 11:25, just as another bomber was dropping four HEs on Connaught Gardens, Clacton, where the Army was much in evidence. Four soldiers billeted in requisitioned houses were killed. Meanwhile, the FS convoy had attracted II/KG53, one of whose six aircraft operating selected a ship off the Naze at 13:20 for attack. Next it was the turn of aircraft call-sign 'CP3'. The crew spotted what they estimated to be an 8,000-ton merchant ship. They claimed a successful attack at 15:24 in position 51° 40'N/01° 30'E. In the evening, operations against shipping were continued by nine aircraft of II/KG53, while Soesterberg's II/KG4 had a dozen Heinkels operating over Essex, near Colchester and against Debden.

Throughout 20 January, clouds hung low and the search was resumed for yesterday's convoy. Mid-morning three crews of Gestab. III/KG2 and others of II/KG53 sought in vain, the ships being in the Thames. Both units operated about two dozen aircraft in the afternoon, and one of KG2's aircraft (which included *U5+BA*, in the Lowestoft area at 14:11, *U5+AR*, *'EF* and *'ER*) flew from Orford Ness to Royston looking for a target of opportunity. Fighters scrambled from Duxford failed to engage the bomber which turned north and fired upon Little Barford power station before hurrying into the safety of clouds. Another crew dropped bombs near Kimbolton.

One of the busiest days of the period was 21 January. Defending fighters, despite awful weather, managed 47 sorties, 22 patrols over East Anglia, facing KG2, KG3 and KG53. The first enemy aircraft, a reconnaissance machine located at 14,000 ft over Dunkirk at 09:25, flew to Yarmouth then at 1,000 ft made for Ramsey, Baldock and north-east London before bombing Hatfield and Cheshunt and leaving via the Thames Estuary. Shorter incursions followed between Felixstowe and Southwold. At 11:01, using cloud cover, a bomber from Shoeburyness flew to Saffron Walden and Bishop's Stortford before leaving over Aldeburgh. Another 'tourist' came in over Aldeburgh at 11:30 and made direct for Mildenhall before leaving over Orford Ness. Another raider was discovered near Coltishall, Feltwell was bombed and machine-gunned and ten HEs fell near Swaffham railway station. Additionally, enemy aircraft searched for shipping.

Afternoon sorties were made by seven He 111s of II/KG53 from Lille/Vendeville. The most noteworthy sortie came in over Walton-on-the-Naze for a deep penetration via Sudbury to Bury St Edmunds, Newmarket, south of

Peterborough to Melton Mowbray, north-east of Derby and thence to Uttoxeter. Then it returned over Derby, Leicester, Market Harborough, Wellingborough, Baldock and Rayleigh, leaving via Southend. Fighters trying to engage it were thwarted by thick cloud.

There had been numerous bombing incidents, Aldeburgh being attacked by Do 17s four times. At 10:45 four HEs were dropped and another six soon afterwards. A dozen HEs (two UX) at 11:12 hit the north-west side of Brick Kiln, and at 14:25 one bomb exploded at Aldeburgh Lodge, another in the sea. Victoria Road church, as well as houses in Crescent Road and Park Road, were also damaged. Roof tiles were damaged at 14:20 by machine-gun fire from a Dornier which bombed Aldeburgh and dropped three HEs on Thorpeness.

At Harwich two HEs exploded close to a Trinity House Examining Vessel in Harwich, the bomber firing at protecting barrage balloons. A sharp attack by Do 17 '*A*' of III/KG3 resulting in machine-gunning of Frinton and Walton at 11:50. It placed nine HEs (one UX) near Megling Green, Old Road, Clacton, causing five minor casualties, demolishing five houses and damaging 38 more. Ten bombs were also dropped near Swaffham and nine in Downham RD.

On 22 January Luftwaffe activity was restricted to armed reconnaissance over Essex by I/KG53 in the morning and by III/KG3 later along the coast. Six Heinkels of I/KG53 searched for shipping in the morning and afternoon of 23 January. At 11:11 one crew attacked Yarmouth, their HEs dropping in Caister Road and injuring Florence Wharton. Despite bad weather, Oakington was raided late on the 24th resulting in two 38 ft by 8 ft craters.

Ju 88As of III/KG30 carried on the anti-shipping war during 25 January. One of four operating — probably *4D+BR* — came across a large convoy, warship-escorted, off Yarmouth at 15:26. An escorting trawler opened fire, seriously damaging the Ju 88's starboard engine. Getting home was a slow task and an hour later the '88 had only reached Smith's Knoll LV. Eventually it limped into Schiphol. Others, possibly discouraged by the convoy's defences, sheered off.

At 14:35 two HEs fell in the Harbour Mouth, Yarmouth, before at 15:19 a far more damaging attack developed. A very low-flying aircraft dropped twelve bombs between Messrs Sacrets and across Middlegate Street, Queen Street and South Quay, over the river to Southtown. The Sacrets' bomb did not explode, but both the Police Station and Central Fire Station had to be evacuated quickly. This incident cost the lives of seven and injured thirteen more civilians.

III/KG30 operated on the following afternoon and evening, laying mines and seeking shipping. *4D+BC* at 13:30 attacked a merchant ship fifteen miles east of Cromer, and left it blazing. Another unit working off the Suffolk coast late in the afternoon assaulted a convoy without results. Next day the crew of Ju 88 *4D+NT* reported weather too bad for such ventures.

On the 29th, a weather scout from Holland flew from London to Debden, dropped two HEs (one UX) near Dunmow and climbed out over Clacton, its crew able to report better weather approaching. Five Dutch-based bombers came in high over the Harwich-Clacton front at dusk. Forty-five minutes later ten of I/NJG2's Ju 88C-2 intruders (including *R4+BH*, '*GH*, '*SL* and '*AL*) positioned themselves over East Anglian bomber bases. Unable to contain their imagination the crew of *R4+MK* called Gilze Rijen with an astonishing claim to please their superiors, that they had shot down six Blenheims already! The reality was entirely different.

A third phase of activity began at 18:43, 25 bombers from Holland turning in off the Stour Estuary at between 6,000 and 16,000 ft heading for London. Meanwhile, a Ju 88 attacked Mildenhall, another flew to the Bury area and others were recorded over Royston and Norwich. Shortly before dawn, radar located several Ju 88Cs patrolling off Lowestoft unsuccessfully seeking RAF bombers.

The activity of 30 January had started and proved considerable as German bombers widely conducted nuisance raids. II/KG3 from Antwerp/Duerne, and KG2 twice raided East Anglia between 09:00 and 17:30 during the day while Heinkel 111s of KG4 bombed London and the south-east. Fighter response was very strong, and sirens wailed repeatedly over wide areas, coastal regions enduring long alert periods.

The first offensive action in East Anglia occurred at Kesgrave when at noon a Do 17Z deposited two HEs then went on its way firing upon Rushmere, Woodbridge Road and Felixstowe Ferry. Soon afterwards, 222 Squadron Spitfires engaged a Ju 88 reconnaissance aircraft thirty miles off Yarmouth. At 12:40 a Do 17 dropped three HEs at old Newton-Haughley Street, damaging Red House Farm and injuring a horse.

Over Great Clacton at 13:12 a Ju 88 appeared, from which two parachute mines leisurely descended. One exploded in Chilburn Road, extensively damaging property but causing only slight casualties. The other touched down on open ground north of Clacton-on-Sea. Ten minutes later the aircraft, Ju 88A-5 W Nr *6053:4D+CK* of 2./KG30, its ordered task to attack shipping in the Thames, crashed near Wyer's Hall, St Osyth. Apparently it succumbed to flak, almost buried itself in soft ground and the crew of four died. Black under-surfaces showed more usual employment for night mining.

At 13:15 three HEs were aimed at the chicory factory, Lakenheath, near the railway station. Strafing killed a workman and two other people were injured. There was, luckily, no fire for a UXHE lodged in the factory washing plant. Crossing Diss, the aircraft dropped a strange, small canister, unidentified, attached to a parachute. Seven HEs fell at Great Whelnetham and other incidents occurred at Mildenhall, ten HEs (one UX) in Downham RD, ten at Dunmow, Melford and Halstead.

Both KG3 and KG2 were operating during the afternoon phase, aircraft of the latter including *U5+AM, 'BM, 'CM, 'DM, 'HM, 'IM, 'LM, 'NM, 'PM, 'BN, 'GN, 'HN* and *'DS*, one of which nearly destroyed Cambridge railway engine sheds. Creeping in from Ely at low level during the dull, dreary Thursday afternoon, it dropped nine 50 kg HEs at 15:57 straddling Mill Road Bridge. Bombs burst in the Corporation store yard, and No 130 Mill Road and the next house were shattered by a direct hit. Other bombs exploded in the rail yard. Although the undershoot meant that the locomotive maintenance area escaped destruction, two civilians were killed and ten injured, for the bridge was being used by many pedestrians and cyclists at the time.

In the obliging weather the Luftwaffe continued its offensive next morning bringing confusion so widespread that Colchester, for instance, was under alert for six hours while cloud-clad raiders roamed Essex and Suffolk skies. Twelve bombs fell between Barrow and Kentford at 12:26 and at about the same time three 250 kg HEs landed in a wood near Elmswell. Bombing was reported at 12:30 from Whepstead and Chevington where four cottages were partly demolished; at Hargrave where five HEs and incendiaries fell on farm land; at Rede and at Chedburgh where more incendiaries spread over Bird's Farm and Gooches Farm. Twenty HEs were reported from Cosford RD.

January had seen extensive cloud cover raids, but not until February did they reach their climax. The month began as Heinkel 111s of I/KG4 crossed East Anglia to sow mines in Liverpool Bay before returning to Soesterberg. At least nine Do 17s of II/KG2 also crossed, to the Midlands, in company with III/KG53. A small contingent from II/KG2 attempted to interfere with shipping. During the morning of 1 February Merville's Dorniers of II/KG2 again used glowering skies, six singly crossing the coast between Felixstowe and Hunstanton. Raid 28 attacked Honington at 11:43, bombs falling in woodland. Mildenhall was then attacked by Raid 473 from an incredibly low level. Bofors and machine guns forced it off track, six HEs dropping on the south side of the aerodrome causing damage in Beck Row. Then the aircraft went to Honington, placing three HEs among dispersals and once more getting a hot reception. Nine localities were machine-gunned including Hempstead Hall, Knapton Hall, Hanworth Hall, Hill Farm, Great Hockham, and Manor Road, Heacham. At Bacton a horse was killed by a Dornier's gunner. Bombing also took place at Sheringham where eight bombs fell on the town, Little Fakenham, Shropham, Baconsthorpe Rectory, Hargham Heath, Leiston (ten UXHEs) and effectively at Yarmouth where an earlier attacker with navigation lights 'on' dropped a dozen 50 kg HEs on allotments off Boundary Road, Southtown, damaging several houses and a factory which made slippers. The Luftwaffe returned at 12:21, a Dornier delivering from very low level a stick of twelve HEs from Kitchener Road to the junction on Princess Road, scoring three direct hits on the five-storied south mill of Grout's Silk Factory in St Nicholas Road, involved with yarn preparation and weaving. A hideously fierce fire soon engulfed that section of the works. Elsewhere the raid had been equally cruel, bombs from an extremely low altitude ricocheting off road surfaces into upper stories of buildings. Although the warning siren had sounded at 11:35 it had been deemed safe for those in the factory to work on. Great Yarmouth, as much Britain's premier front line town as any, was open to attack on every second of every day so that the decision as to when to take cover posed problems. It was partly solved by the use of a cuckoo-sounding crash warning which sounded moments prior to certain bombing. Had Yarmouth been better defended, by guns and balloons, it might have been fairer. But the authorities could point to a largely evacuated population, and limited value in the overall war effort — adding that equipment and men were in limited supply. It was fortunate that the casualties on 1 February were not higher, amounting to two killed (George Green and the seventeen-year-old Robert Dennis), one seriously injured and nine less so. Additional of course was damage to the general fabric of the community — and its cumulative effect.

Damage at Grout's was not the only success celebrated over late lunch at Merville. Another crew using the railway leading to Great Blakenham cement works, near Claydon, dropped eight bombs and machine-gunned on racing by. They narrowly missed scoring direct hits on the factory although there was some damage and an employee was killed. Strafing attacks were also carried out in Suffolk, against Allwood Farm, Botesdale (12:15), the main street through Melton, at Stowmarket where at 12:38 a Dornier hurried across, guns blazing,

Grout's Silk Factory at Yarmouth after being bombed by II/KG2 on 1 February 1941.

and at Leiston where one of a group of soldiers was wounded. Shots were also taken at Clopton Hall and Orford.

Afternoon operations on 2 February were preceded by Raid 76, a Do 17 whose bombs damaged the railway and gasworks at Wymondham at 10:25. Coming in alone over Lowestoft, its successful interception was judged feasible. Three sections of fighters were scrambled from Coltishall but none had any success. Neither did the machine-gunners of searchlight posts CS073 and CS076.

At 13:50 a lone reconnaissance aircraft off Cromer turned south, then upon reaching Southwold headed inland, heralding the afternoon phase. After changing course at East Harling it bombed Leiston. A lonesome attacker had all but pulled off another worthwhile assault by placing ten HEs around the Garrett Engineering Works before making another pass, at about 300 ft, to machine-gun the factory. Luckily, none of the bombs exploded. As they headed for home the aircraft's crew poured machine-gun fire into the Halesworth area.

Aerodromes were main targets throughout daylight hours. Raid 11 placed HEs by a line of six Wellingtons at East Wretham without much effect, and was engaged by gunners at CS077 and CS093. Raid 16 dropped ten HEs from 2,500 ft, causing damage to two Wellingtons at Newmarket. Raid 21 was driven off by gunners at Honington, its stick of six bombs damaging power lines and three Wellingtons before it flew to Feltwell and faced more heavy AA and Bofors fire making the crew wisely jettison their load and make off. Raid 72 ran in on Mildenhall from Thetford to place eight HEs on the landing ground and four on the Technical Site. Nine bombs fell across Waterbeach in the most damaging of the attacks. One burst was on a hangar annexe, another on a runway. Flying glass caused injuries and one fatality. Raid 75 which passed over Coltishall was engaged by searchlight post gunners at CS046 and CS068 then intercepted over Yarmouth. Bombs were jettisoned then the Do 17Z escaped into cloud depriving Flight Lieutenant van Mentz of 222 Squadron of a kill. Both KG2 and KG53 had been active.

Shielded by low clouds and snow showers, nine Ju 88s of III/KG30 directed their operations, on 3 February, against Feltwell, Honington, Newmarket Heath, Mildenhall and Waterbeach with, yet again, little damage being caused. A Ju 88 was, at 13:30, located off Harwich by two Hurricanes of 242 Squadron, trying to interfere with a quartet of naval ships which were firing back at the bomber; it escaped in cloud despite attacks by the fighters. Evening operations began at 19:45 as the first of eight Ju 88C intruders of 1/NJG2 appeared over the Wash. Their sorties continued throughout the night as they sought, unsuccessfully, British night fliers.

The weather showed a marked improvement on 4 February, allowing the defenders to fly 168 defensive sorties. Luftwaffe interest was centred upon Convoy 'Arena' spread along thirty miles between Southwold and Harwich. Early morning attacks were also delivered against Alderton, Bawdsey and Reydon shortly before Raid 4, a Dornier, headed for Mildenhall. In the clearer conditions, Pilot Officer Barnes (*V7137*) and Sergeant Brejcha (*P3705*) of 257 Squadron were ordered to intercept. Possibly aware of that, the Dornier Do 17Z-2 W Nr *1132:U5+LM* of 4./KG2 turned to Lowestoft, its secondary target, dropping eighteen HEs across Lowestoft's Herring Market, Harbour, Battery Garrison Road and St Peter's Street, killing two and injuring nine others. Anti-aircraft guns blazed away as the raider turned out to sea, machine-guns firing. But the clearer weather assisted its downfall, 242 Squadron Hurricanes shooting down the bomber into the sea half a mile off Corton. Only one injured crew member survived.

By mid-morning, by which time four He 111s of 1/KG53 which reconnoitred the East coast were landing at Vitry, the day's centre of activity for over fifty Luftwaffe crews was Convoy 'Agent' causing standing patrols to be placed over Clacton. Two Hurricanes of 249 Squadron came across Bf 110s of Gruppe 210 nosing around the ships. Bf 110C/W Nr *3852:S9+EH* was soon shot down from 10,000 ft, and a second was put into the sea after a chase. Others operating against the convoy included six of I/KG1 from Achiet, three of III/KG30 active during the morning, and elements of I, II and III/KG2 and KG3 providing 24 aircraft.

Between 18:00 and 01:00 sixty aircraft, 37 from Dutch bases, were active over the east and south-east, London being the main target. Two went to Upwood while a third flew from Clacton to Gloucestershire then returned to Southwold via Aberdovey, the Irish Sea, Birmingham and Ely, keeping many areas under 'Red' alert. In bright moonlight bombs were reported from Lincolnshire, Yorkshire, Derby and Birmingham, the approaches to which were later switched from the east to the south coast. As Ju 88s of KG30 mined off the East Coast, overland operations were conducted by KG2, 3, 4 and 53. The clear night provided ideal conditions for Sergeant Bodian of 151 Squadron and his gunner in a Defiant. Patrolling west of Wittering at 21:40 they came upon a Do 17Z. Two devastating blasts from the Defiant's turret guns fired the centre of the bomber. A small explosion and it fell to its doom. Sufficient remained to show the aircraft to be an unusual Dornier 17 night-fighter conversion, W Nr *2859:R4+GM* of 2./NJG2 and supplementing Ju 88Cs also active from Gilze Rijen. During the evening bombs fell at Lowestoft damaging a relay station and shop, killing three and injuring six people; at Feltwell where the operations room was damaged; near Ramsey, King's Lynn (six), in Depwade RD (two), Deben RD (seventeen), Chesterton RD (ten), Norwich, Frinton and Ely where three HEs fell near the RAF Hospital.

Felixstowe received the most interesting attention. Facing searchlights and nearby balloons, a raider arrived at 22:20 to unload seven containers of incendiaries totalling 288 (78UX). Rosemary Avenue, Park Avenue and Quilter Road were the main recipients. When the official investigation ensued, many unexploded bombs were found. All had a warning letter 'A' on their noses. This was undoubtedly the first occasion when such a high proportion of explosive incendiaries was used.

Chapter 14
Clouds, clouds, go *away!*

Low clouds and intense cold persisted throughout most of February 1941, so that the pattern of Luftwaffe operations changed little from that of January. During daylight hours on 5 February two Dorniers of III/KG1 searched for coastal shipping and, acting upon their reports, nine crews of III/KG2 carried out afternoon searches 25 miles offshore between Felixstowe and Winterton, and also around the area of the Sunk LV. Although limited night action followed, it was nonetheless terrifying. Twelve HEs fell near Newmarket and Raid 29's two parachute mines came down near Bradwell, Suffolk, one exploding in a field by Gipsy Lane and damaging six cottages. The other fell at Church Farm 200 yd west of the Beccles Road. Yet again, Yarmouth endured the worst incident.

Flying low in a north-south pass, its attacker dropped a line of ten HEs between the town centre and the Regal Cinema. They burst by Ormond Road, Pelgrave Road and on a surface shelter at the Hospital School entrance. Amazingly, although some people were sheltering, there were no casualties. An even more potentially horrific event took place at the Regal Cinema, Regent Road, which received a direct hit. Fortune favoured those enjoying the performance for the bomb, in a dangerous blast enclosure, did not explode. Neither was there panic as the building was evacuated. St Nicholas Church, too, had a lucky escape for another HE grazed one of its west end spires in falling, was deflected from the building and amazingly broke up as it crashed on to the concrete path leading to the church. Casualties amounted to four killed and 23 injured. The evening attackers had been Heinkel He 111s of KG53 supplemented by nine Ju 88C night intruders, some of which spent two hours in their patrol areas. By the time they had returned to Gilze Rijen the weather over Britain was so bad that few Luftwaffe operations were undertaken against East Anglia until darkness fell on 9 February.

To this there had been a glaring exception for, shortly after 13:00 on the 7th, the crew of an He 111 of 3./KG53 on an armed reconnaissance lost their position, suddenly broke cloud, and from 1,000 ft dropped twenty HEs and a small container load of incendiaries across Lowestoft's dock area, achieving considerable success. All the bombs fell on LNER land and the railway station was closed, but most of the HEs exploded around the Customs House and Lowestoft's well known swing bridge whose power house received a direct hit. For the enemy that was a notable success and for the defenders a major annoyance. Direct hits were also scored on North Quay, the harbour blacksmith's and the Harbour Master's quarters. Casualties amounted to eight killed and 32 injured (24 seriously). Light flak put one of the Heinkel's engines out of action, and the second failed off Zeebrugge, forcing the aircraft to ditch. Despite the heavy sea, the crew was rescued. In an attack the following day, a Dornier 17 of III/KG2 dropped fifteen HEs wide at Aldeburgh.

Reconnaissance reports indicating improved weather, the Luftwaffe mounted some sharp inland attacks on the night of 9/10 February which commenced at dusk with five crews of Staffel 4./KG2 (flying *U5+DM, 'HM, 'OM, 'PM* and *'AM*) slipping across the coast between Southwold and Orford to operate against airfields in the Cambridge area where they met frustrating weather conditions. Seven HEs were dropped in Ely RD. A second phase involved II/KG30 whose '88s mined off Cromer before early on the 10th ten Do 17s of KG2 (including *U5+BN, 'DN, 'HN, 'EA, 'ER, 'ES, 'GS, 'AS* and *'AT*) penetrated to the Bury St Edmunds area to attack surrounding bomber bases during the two hours following midnight. Their incendiaries caused a huge blaze among Forestry Commission trees west of Thetford. By 03:29 all were safely back at their bases near Lille, leaving four Ju 88s of NJG2 roaming in the Upwood-Peterborough area and making such lengthy patrols that it was 08:27 before the last landed at Gilze Rijen. One of the Ju 88s had mistaken Wittering's Q-Site for the real airfield, and bombed it.

Daylight hours saw last night's attackers preparing for more night operations. Ju 88s of III/KG30 attempted to bomb a convoy off Happisburgh, then dropped several mines before leaving the area. Another six Ju 88s, of I and II/KG30, were later involved in mining, but the main effort of the evening was, again, upon airfields in the Bury area to which nineteen Dorniers of III/KG2 (*U5+BN* leading, with *U5+CN, 'DN, 'EN, 'GN, 'HN, 'MN, 'RN, 'BM, 'HM, 'KM, 'MM, 'OM, 'PM, 'AS, 'ES, 'AT* and *'KT*) directed their attention. Overcome by misguided exuberance, the crew of *U5+BN* excitedly called to their Lille controller at 18:55 that they had 'set Honington ablaze', an over-estimation of success! Others homed in, bombing the area in quick succession and unloading 41 HEs and a few incendiaries followed by eight more and an oil bomb at Bury St Edmunds. Despite *'BN's* foolish and revealing chatter all had landed back at Merville by 20:30, leaving the night free for ten Ju 88Cs of I/NJG2 (*R4+AH, 'CH, 'AK, 'EK, 'LK, 'HL,* and *'SL* included) to roam widely over bomber bases.

Back home their pilots made claims as inflated as that of KG2, with Hauptmann Jung telling of a Wellington shot down at West Raynham and Oberleutnant Semrau of two Blenheims destroyed at Feltwell. Jung was totally mistaken, Semrau was just confused. Forty 2 Group Blenheims had been sent to Hanover and he came across Squadron Leader Sabine's Blenheim homing on Bodney. After a long chase and exchange of fire Sabine crash-landed at base. Semrau cruised around Bodney — well away from Feltwell — and as Sergeant Chattaway circled in Blenheim *Z5877*, Semrau opened fire. Chattaway was killed, Pilot Officer Cherval died later and Sergeant Burch, the gunner, was wounded. Feltwell was, however, twice bombed, by Raid 73 which crept in from Sheringham and by Raid 61 which dropped two salvoes.

Operations were resumed, after poor weather, on 13 February when a lone aircraft (possibly a Ju 88 of II/KG30) machine-gunned Syderstone, then flew to Hull making weather observations. Afternoon brought four He 111s of I/KG53 from Vitry-en-Artois to venture briefly into East Anglia. One flew low over Yarmouth at 15:10, machine-gunning North End and injuring two people before placing nine HEs in the harbour mouth. A cloudless evening enticed II/KG2 with seventeen aircraft, and III/KG2 with at least four, to operate over East Anglia between 18:30 and 21:00. Included in nineteen minor Norfolk incidents were attacks on the Barford, Kimberley and Reepham areas. Increasing fog prompted the radio operator of *U5+KM* to suggest that it could well spread to Merville. Some raiders flew low, machine-gunning several localities, and bombs were again aimed at Bircham Newton, Marham and Mildenhall, and in North Witchford RD.

Many flares were dropped over Cambridgeshire during the evening of 13/14 February, but bombing took place mainly in Norfolk. Searchlight CS031, near Little Snoring, held a bomber whose crew turned, dived and dropped three bombs close to the site. Evidently encouraged by their skill they promptly tried to bomb CS035, CS037 and CS077 — without success.

Under the control of Cambrai, three phases of bombing occurred on the evening of 14 February, 25 raids being plotted. First entries came over Southwold at 18:30 from the Dunkirk area, a second contingent arriving from the Royston-Buckingham section before the third group came from the south to operate over Cambridgeshire. Drawn again from KG2, they had, as an alternative to East Anglian airfields, aiming points in London which *U5+GN* for one attacked. Overall control of the operation was handled by the captain of *U5+KM*. Machine-gunning of fifteen Norfolk localities took place in the early evening, four HEs falling at Breydon Bridge and Coleman's Wharf, Yarmouth. Two HEs fell at Blakeney harbour, five were aimed at Bircham Newton and another eight missed Horsham St Faith. As the Dorniers left, seven Ju 88Cs replaced them, operations being conducted over and off Norfolk. They carried out a concerted attack upon Marham, their 34 bombs dropping around Swaffham, Hilborough and South Pickenham. RAF territory at Tuddenham, Norfolk, was also attacked, at 23:45, using three HEs and one of the rarer oil bombs.

It was late on 14 February that the Luftwaffe paid a very special call upon the RAF, in one of the most remarkable events of the war. At 22:55 an aircraft circled Debden and on orders from Group HQ the flarepath was lit and permission given for it to land. Showing a full array of navigation lights it did just that, then taxied to the Watch Hut. The Duty Pilot went to the aircraft and to his amazement identified it as a He 111, its tail Swastika blacked out. One of the crew jumped out and addressed him in German so, being unarmed, he hurried back to the Watch Hut and told the Controller who ordered the local AA gunners to open fire. Too late: the aircraft vanished into the night. Or had it? At Feltwell, where Wellingtons were returning, an unscheduled aircraft joined the circuit and, with a bright landing light 'on' it touched down on the flare path, taxied back and quickly took off again. Staff were certain this was a Ju 88. There are also reports that an enemy aircraft, presumably the same one, sampled Newmarket's high quality turf. Who, what and why never seems to have emerged ... yet!

To the civilian population enemy aircraft seemed free to deliver short, sharp, shocking attacks at will, in daylight too. There were constant cries of 'Where are the fighters?', especially from those who had begrudged even a penny for 'defence'. With the clouds low and detection of low fliers in any case difficult, fighters were at a grave disadvantage and much of their effort was pointless. Given better weather and a load of luck the situation could quickly change; and change it did, on 15 February.

Coastal operations, mainly, took place although on 14 February HEs fell in marshland, Oulton Broad, at 15:47. Fighters had already been busy; Squadron Leader Turner and Flight Lieutenant Donaldson of 242 Squadron on patrol spotted a reconnaissance aircraft and climbed to 29,000 ft but it was still above them. Such machines, usually Do 215s of Ob.d.Lt but sometimes Ju 88s, were regular passers by, their routes giving clues to areas of particular enemy interest. Unable to intercept the intruder, they resumed their patrol until told that it had descended to 25,000 ft. Again they climbed and were amazed to find their quarry was a Messerschmitt Bf 109 operating at extreme range, and which quickly used its speed advantage to carry it from Norfolk to safety. This may have been the furthest north over Britain that a Bf 109 had so far ventured.

Later that day Flight Lieutenant Milling engaged a Ju 88, setting fire to its port engine and chasing it forty miles off Aldeburgh. He returned with a damaged fuel tank and shattered windscreen on his Hurricane. The final engagement on the 14th was more satisfying. Pilot Officer Klee, 222 Squadron, spotted a low-flying bomber creeping south from the Yarmouth area. He dived from 7,000 ft, closed to 300 yd and poured in machine-gun fire, receiving the satisfaction of seeing it fall into the sea off Lowestoft.

Early evening of 15 February brought many flares, and the first contingent from KG2 fielding about twenty aircraft in two phases. Feltwell was subjected to a sharp attack at 21:42, bombs hitting the RAF Station and also demolishing a cottage, possibly as a result of one of the Ju 88s of NJG2 operating. *R4+EH* had at 19:01 signalled its base that it had shot down a British aeroplane. Bircham Newton was also attacked, but a more unusual event overtook a pair of large semi-detached houses, Nos 341/343 Cherry Hinton Road, Cambridge. Presumably it was a Dornier which, just before 23:00 made a fast run towards the south-east over Cambridge, perhaps attempting to bomb the airport or the distinctive Eastern Tank Trap. Almost along the latter it released an unusually assorted bomb load. First to explode was an HE, immediately in front of the two houses whose frontal sections it tore away. Eight occupants escaped without injury and, even more strangely, hardly anyone heard the explosion. Sensing something unusual was going on, Dr Hanton — whose surgery was just across the road — went to investigate and was amazed at what he saw. Also living close was Alan Wright, author of Ian Allan's popular *Civil Aircraft Markings* series who, unusually for such occasions, slept throughout the event! Another 'silent bomb' crater was soon discovered on waste ground by Perne Road, while more evident had been incendiaries burning on fields stretching between Queen Edith's Way and Lime Kiln Road.

Dr Hanton called the police who were most surprised to know of the event, to the extent that a Chief Inspector was brought along by Special Constable Williams. More investigation revealed a burnt-out oil bomb, six complete containers of unignited incendiaries and parts of three other containers along with 58 unignited bombs. Since no enemy aircraft was known to have been in the area at the time, no warning had been sounded to accompany Cambridge's quietest raid of the war. Some of the bombers which had been attacking

*A most surprising arrival at RAF Steeple Morden early on 16 February 1941 was this Ju
88 whose pilot, mistaking his position, erroneously landed in Britain* (IWM CH2104).

Merseyside were returning that night across East Anglia, and one of these may
have been involved.

In Norfolk between 01:11 and 03:20 a number of small scale, sharp raids were
delivered. Sixteen HEs were dropped on Suffolk Road, Yarmouth, and
Gorleston North railway station. At 02:20 another dozen HEs fell on marshland
at Southtown, Yarmouth, where a quarter of an hour later four HEs were
dropped on August Road and Queen's Place. Casualties totalled three dead and
six injured. Over the same period five attempts were made to damage Bircham
Newton aerodrome, but despite the use of 35 HEs, most of which fell near
Cockley Cley, nothing worthwhile was achieved. Not only that, the night also
brought another very disheartening event for one bomber crew.

Among those who had bombed Birmingham were the four men aboard Ju
88A-5 W Nr *6214:4V+GS* of III/KG1. Although it was a moonlit night, the crew
became uncertain of their bearings. Short of fuel and with landing lights on, they
made a cross-wind landing on Steeple Morden's flare path, the starboard
undercarriage leg collapsing in the process. The Duty Crew could scarcely
believe their eyes and raced across in their 'armadillo' to capture the strangers.
The all-black Ju 88 with dark green spinners and *GS* in small white characters on
the fin, Jumo 211G-powered and armed with five MG 15s, had been accepted by
the Luftwaffe on 11 November 1940. It was too badly damaged to be flown
again. The constructor's plate suggested it to be *6217*, but the Germans recorded
the loss of W Nr *6214*. Such inconsistencies are quite common in these cases.

Somewhat better weather on the 16th made RAF fighter operations possible,
most of the opposition being provided by I and II/KG53 which, from Vitry-en-
Artois, operated about a dozen He 111s (including *A1+AD, 'AH, 'BA, 'BC, 'CE,
'CG, 'DH* and *'KH*) off the coast. A few Do 17s were also active, one being

encountered by Pilot Officers Kay and Mctyre below 10/10 cloud covering Yarmouth at 1,500 ft. One of the Heinkels was encountered at midday over Sheringham by Pilot Officer Bedford of 257 Squadron, but neither engagement was successful. Many raiders flew exceptionally low, presumably to reduce the risk of discovery.

KG53 was mounting a two-phase operation around midday; at Hunstanton, five bombs fell near the Green and three in the sea, while Cromer was machine-gunned, as were Salthouse and Weybourne. During the afternoon HEs dropped at Pulham, Buxton Heath, Haveringland Park and machine-gunning of East Winch and Grimston took place. Raid 418 was active along the Norfolk coast before crossing Sheringham for West Raynham where at 16:18 eighteen HEs were released, six on the aerodrome. The airfield AA gunners gave the foreigners a spectacular welcome, 21 rounds of Bofors fire and three of 3-in shrapnel of which one hit the aircraft's nose. As it left, violently rocking, machine-gunners at searchlight posts CS022 and CS061 also fired at the bomber. It did not reach the coast until 18:03, by which time it was in perilous state. What went on aboard can but be guessed. Luftwaffe records refer to a Ju 88A-5, W Nr *4170:F1+JP* of II/KG76 not returning from an attack on West Raynham on 17 February; that seems to have been the aircraft engaged the previous day, and if so it came down in the sea.

At least a dozen aircraft delivered low-level evening strikes on airfields including Swanton Morley and Coltishall, bombs also landing at Haverhill, Cromer, Orford, Lowestoft, Horsey and Hemsby Hall. About six Ju 88s of II/KG30 mined off the coast, *4D+KN* venturing inland and at 19:55 being located west of Norwich heading for Orford Ness and home.

An interesting feature of daylight activity on 17 February was the unusual appearance, during shipping attacks along the East Coast as far as Yorkshire, of Ju 88s of II/KG76. First daylight bombing came at 12:35 with Bengate Bridge the target. Around midday 222 Squadron chased and damaged a Do 17 over Martham. Another Section of 222 Squadron found a Ju 88 five miles east of Cromer and shot it into the sea, and Ju 88 *F1+DY* of KG76 forty miles east of Yarmouth at 13:15 was engaged by fighters and forced to return to Châteaudun. Among the enemy aircraft searching for shipping between 13:15 and 21:38 were Ju 88s *F1+AC, 'AD, 'AE, 'BC, 'BF, 'BG, 'CC, 'CD, 'CE, 'CH* and *'CJ*. One of these at 15:10 dropped bombs off Overstrand, and Cromer where Cliff Avenue was machine-gunned.

Evening and night operations on the 17th/18th followed an increasingly familiar pattern with 27 Dorniers of I, II and III/KG2 active over East Anglia between 00:50 and 03:25 while twenty He 111s of I/KG4 from Soesterberg mined off shore and both I and II/KG53 had aircraft night bombing, for the first time in many weeks. Night operations extended to 06:00 on the 18th. Participants included six Ju 88s of NJG2 (among them *R4+AL, 'EL, 'KL* and *'LL*) all concentrating on attacking Norfolk's airfields. Yarmouth was under attack from 03:01 to 05:54, bombing being centred around the Fish Wharf, Suffolk Road to Malthouse Lane, Admiralty Road to Southgate Road and on Cobholme Marshes. Several hundred incendiaries and 28 HEs were dropped and, as the last bombs fell, the most frightening part of the raid commenced, when hot bomb splinters perforated a Yarmouth gas holder. Instantly the gas caught fire, long tongues of flame issuing from the punctures. Immediate

Top *The corner of Walpole Street, Norwich, smashed on 18 February 1941* (Eastern Daily Press).

Above *Attempting to strafe Watton, Heinkel He 111H-3 3349:A1+CM of 4./KG53 was brought down by parachute and cable fire, wires ensnaring the unmarked raider* (RAF Museum P11827).

concern arose over a possible explosion and whether bombers would stoke the fire. At breakneck speed the fire service skilfully hosed the metal uprights supporting the gasometer, preventing them from buckling and causing a sudden loss of gas if the holder toppled. Thus the gas burnt from a container, slowly lowering itself into its water-filled base. Working under such frightening conditions, the fire service earned enormous admiration which was richly deserved. Despite the intensity of the raid, casualties amounted to only one killed and twelve injured.

After a brief respite the bombers returned, led by five He 111s of I and II/KG53 operating off the coast soon after daybreak. W Nr *3349:A1+CM* of 4./KG53 dropped sixteen HEs at 07:37 near Attlebridge, and another attacked a small merchant ship at 10:41 in a convoy twenty miles south-east of Harwich where aircraft *A1+CB* was also operating. For *A1+CM* things seemed to be going well as it headed inland. At 07:48 it was driven off by Mildenhall's Bofors which fired nine rounds of FAS, the novel Parachute and Cable shell. Losing height, it flew to East Wretham, where it damaged a Wellington and put shots into the Sergeants' Mess. Gunners at searchlight DX063 fired some shots into its fuselage as it turned for Honington. There, two more aircraft were damaged and

Honington aerodrome photographed at 13:25 hours on 29 October 1940 from a Dornier flying westwards. Painted 'hedgerows' across the landing ground have failed to disguise it, for a line of bomb craters cross it (Bundesarchiv 74/55/16).

bomb craters temporarily put the airfield out of commission. Doing splendidly, the He 111 approached Watton at 300 ft and there the AA gunners fired eight rounds of shrapnel and 27 rounds of FAS. Running in at 100 ft, the bomber was struck three times, the first cable ripping into the wing 15 ft from the tip and through to the spar to jam the aileron control rods. A second cable cut into the wing nearer the tip and the third one, 12 ft from the starboard tip, also whipped back to the spar. Within seconds the aircraft made a forced belly landing at 07:55, almost intact, at Ovington four miles north-east of the airfield. On this aircraft the fuselage 'Balkenkreuz' as well as the Swastikas had been blacked out. Of even more interest was the backwards-firing gun fitted in the tail cone.

Rumour-mongers would doubtless have been delighted to elaborate upon the downfall of this German bomber, but the events of the following afternoon would certainly have brought no jubilation. III/KG53 sent along three He 111s—*A1+JB* to the Clacton area, *A1+JC* to make a nuisance of itself over east Norfolk and the third, *A1+JD*, to Honington. All were home at St Trond by 16:45. By then it was the turn, yet again, of the Dorniers.

First to cross the coast, between Clacton and Yarmouth and flying very low, was the five-aircraft contingent of III/KG2 comprising *U5+NA, 'NC, 'NE, 'NF* and *'NI*. Following were a dozen fielded by I/KG2, all making again for the bomber bases. Honington was attacked three times during the day, the most effective raid coming at 15:55 when two HEs each smashed into hangars and two exploded on the landing ground. Other bombs fell near Feltwell and alternative targets were attacked — notably Southwold Harbour and the swing bridge at Aldeby which luckily escaped the three bombs aimed at it. Not so the centre of Newmarket.

Probably it was a Dornier Do 17Z of I/KG2, perhaps *U5+BA, 'BC, 'BD, 'BE* or one which around 15:00 radioed a weather report detailing conditions five miles north of Bury without identifying itself, which perpetrated an appalling deed. It had entered 12 Group area near Duxford and flown south of Newmarket. Turning west, it flew along the line of an Army convoy, machine-gunning the lorries. Newmarket certainly teemed with soldiers and many things akin to their world, while to the west, on the Heath, was based 99 Squadron and its Wellingtons. What happened was surely intended for the military; instead, the aircraft's bombs undershot by a mile or more because the aircraft, running in from the direction of Bury, met thirteen rounds of 40 mm Bofors shots.

Well do I remember that day, the Cambridge sirens wailing on a dreary afternoon. My father, whose work took him widely around the county, came home later than usual from his customary Tuesday call in Newmarket Hospital where he attended to the needs of pensioners. Often he went for a haircut at a High Street barber, then usually walked around the lively street market. As he put away his cycle in the garden shed (for the car was garaged elsewhere) he turned to me. Clearly, something was very wrong. Through the darkness he was almost crying as he quietly said, 'They've got Newmarket, boy, the "Bs"have got Newmarket.'

As soon as he was indoors, behind the blackout boards, he poured forth to Mum and I the ghastly details in a manner most unlike him. He had indeed witnessed a catastrophe. 'Far worse than anything I saw "in the last lot"', he said; 'all so sudden.' 'Give us the details', we asked — by which time I noticed his hand shaking. That certainly was not like him. We sat down to a wartime hot, cooked 'tea' — parsnips, turnips, swedes, potatoes and, to make it much more exciting, the hidden meat. There was, of course, no evening paper to give the details and for 'security reasons' the radio carried no reference to 'it'. In any case we could hear from a serious official eyewitness who would never forget the scene. His story went something like this.

'I was near Newmarket just before 3 o'clock when I heard the siren. I had intended to call at the barber's shop but instead made two calls on the Exning Road. At ten past three, as I stood talking to an old lady, I happened to glance to the left and there over the Clock Tower, was one of "your" Dorniers, and from it I then saw bombs dropping. It was flying right along the High Street, very, very low and fast. Poor devils had no chance, and as it was Market Day, the High Street was packed full of people. I could see the bombs bursting and the rubble being hurled high. The noise was terrible and into all the ghastly horror the bastards poured machine-gun fire, into all those ordinary people. He'd put down ten HEs and a few incendiaries and they all fell just behind the fronts of the buildings on the Exning side of the Street.'

'Didn't the guns on the Heath open up, Dad?' 'Yes, and I reckon that made him panic. It was all so quick, and he was away, banked south, into the clouds.' 'What did you do then?', asked my mother. 'I got into the car and parked it as near as I could to the Clock Tower and, and ... ' I don't think I'd ever seen my Dad cry before. He carried on: 'There were hundreds of people dazed, not knowing where to go, what to do. Some were on their knees, heads cupped in hands—and many had nasty cuts. I could see already that the Freeman Hardy and Willis shoe shop half way along the street was blazing furiously. People were trapped in there. It then occurred to me—had I been in the barber's shop, the car outside... I walked towards the centre of it all — the barber's had been sliced in two, the front blown away with some of those inside. The "White Hart" hotel was battered, but what shocked me most was — well, there wasn't a pane of glass intact anywhere. I don't know how many people were hurt, but wherever I looked people were staggering aimlessly, bandaging their hands with handkerchiefs, wiping blood from their faces and beginning to try to help. Eight bombs scored direct hits on buildings, people said, and two, opposite the Memorial Hall and outside the Doric Cinema, had splattered the fronts of the

Above *'They've got Newmarket, boy, the "Bs" have got Newmarket ...' In the 1980s it is almost impossible to stand in the High Street and believe it was as bad as this — and only part of the damage is seen here.*

Below *The most serious casualties occurred at the Post Office, yet next door J.A.S. Smith's unprotected front window remained intact.*

Bottom *'To think', my father said, 'I nearly went for a haircut.' The shop where he and I used often to go was completely wrecked, and there were fatalities there too.*

Inspectors carrying gas masks in tins can see that Bryce & Rogers to the right is amazingly intact, unlike the 'White Hart' Hotel along the street which was badly mutilated.

buildings with shrapnel. The Post Office got it worst, full of people. Terrible there, boy. Everyone kept calm and soon there were people everywhere trying to help others even though many were suffering terribly from shock.

'A soldier came up to me — he had cuts on his hands — and he was leading an old man who had lots of small wounds so I took him to hospital. Small place, Newmarket, hadn't enough ARP people and ambulances to cope. The High Street is in a terrible mess, really has wrecked the whole street. I stayed a while, but like so many others I just felt too upset to do much. Lots of soldiers and RAF chaps came to help.'

Next day more details filtered through. So awful had the bombing been that it was to be three days before the bodies of the eleven killed were found, and there was the possibility of more. That there wasn't great panic, with street and shops teeming with people, was amazing. Many had miraculous escapes, as ever, and the seriously injured were lovingly cared for by total strangers. If only we could all act in that manner on *every* day of our peacetime lives. Ambulances took ten minutes to arrive due to the general confusion throughout the street where people were strewn around in large numbers, many half stunned, before a first aid post was established in the Jockey Club. Four fires had broken out, but only one was of major proportions, and that was soon under control.

By Thursday the total number of casualties recorded was 110 including thirteen dead. Eighteen shops or business premises and three houses had been completely wrecked and another eight badly damaged. Blast damage was to be found on probably every High Street building and even on the following Sunday, by which time the extensive blood stains (many caused by flying glass) had been washed away, the street was littered by vast quantities of glass. By any measure this was one of the worst wartime incidents East Anglia endured. Well do I recall my father saying, as we ate our late tea, 'I wonder what tale they told when they got back to their station?' Probably 'they' had no idea of what they had done to a little town, and sincerely believed they had struck mostly at soldiers. We listened to Lord Haw-Haw that evening, but he had nothing to say on the subject.

Soon the very bad weather was back, it being 20 February before limited bombing was resumed. A fresh feature was offshore involvement of III/KG3 from St Trond. I/KG53, and I and III/KG2, operated in small numbers too, six enemy aircraft flying overland in the morning, one in the afternoon. A small damaged merchant ship beached near Yarmouth attracted particular attention. Apart from two mid-morning, unsuccessful, attempts to bomb Wattisham, it was coastal areas that received the bombs, Fakenham, Leiston and Lowestoft. Colchester's railway station was machine-gunned, also Harwich. A Ju 88 made a low-level strafing attack on Coltishall, putting a shot through the wing of Hurricane *W9306*.

Apart from two deep penetration reconnaissance flights by Ob. d. L. aircraft and a brief strafing incursion into Norfolk on the 21st, there was little night activity until the 23rd. Earlier, there had been an incursion into Cambridgeshire by a Dornier of II/KG2 which was chased off by fighters. At night four Ju 88Cs operated, one unsuccessfully attacking Wittering.

An improvement in the weather commenced late on 24 February and, although daylight activity was slight, it was noteworthy. At 09:45 an enemy aircraft made landfall at Cromer. Two Hurricanes of 257 Squadron were sent to investigate and located a Do 17 of 8./KG3 at 8,000 ft fifteen miles east of Happisburgh. Pilot Officer E.H. Atkins (*P5186*) fired before his Hurricane was so badly damaged that he had to bale out and was not seen again. The Dornier later crashed in the sea. Also engaged that morning was Ju 88 *F6+HK* of 2.(F)/122. Despite its crippled state the Ju 88, which had reconnoitred the Wash and Humber, flew back to the Brussels area where, flying on one motor, it performed a wheels-up landing. Another Ju 88, probably of II/KG30, at 15:05 attacked a group of five small ships 26 miles north-east of Yarmouth and was observed doing so by the crew of a Coastal Command Blenheim. They engaged the Ju 88, but it escaped into cloud.

By evening the weather had much improved and 27 aircraft of the three Gruppen of KG2 again swung into action, the first coming into East Anglia at 19:35 at 8,000 ft over Southwold. They made deep penetrations, one to Bedford and another around Thame. Attacks were also made upon Norwich, Peterborough, Brandon and Felixstowe where, at 23:02, six HEs and over 200 incendiaries (many of an explosive type) were distributed over Grange Road, Rosslyn House School and the southern area, and at Methwold Hythe where at 20:13 five HEs, two oil bombs and incendiaries fell. Machine-gunners at Bawdsey damaged a passing Dornier, and HEs dropped on Oakington aerodrome forced operating Stirlings to be diverted. Two 50 kg HEs were dropped on Ipswich at 22:15, one demolishing the rear sections of Nos 6, 8 and 10 Bloomfield Road while the other fell in a nursery garden. Throughout the evening the Dornier crews passed their positions to Merville, their homing station, *U5+BN* being over Wisbech at 20:25, and both '*BN* and '*GT* were near Harwich at 21:30 and heading homewards. The unit's aircraft operated over Britain for three hours, during which they delivered one concentrated attack, possibly unique in technique. Target, Cambridge.

Exactly what happened during the raid is never likely to be fully unravelled, but it was certainly no ordinary operation. A few days after, a dead German agent was found in an air raid shelter on Christ's Pieces, his pistol alongside. He had lodged in Montague Road, and later Glisson Road close to Hills Road — upon which the attack in question was directed. What part he played in the night's accurate bombing remains conjectural.

There were a variety of military targets for legitimate attack in the area including sprawling rail yards close to Hills Road Bridge where tanks and military vehicles were being unloaded in darkness, Army personnel billeted in houses south of Cherry Hinton Road and a military convoy passing through Cambridge to the south. Either the first or third, maybe both, were selected for attack. No similar attack on Britain was as accurate on a dark night, when only a bundle of red-green-white target markers was dropped.

Reports of the order of events are confusing, but it appears that the first HEs and incendiaries fell at 22:00. On the spot was Dr J. A. Charles, who had been evacuated to Cambridge from London.

'One bomb', he recalls, 'fell in the front garden of a house in Rustat Road and another in Flamsteed Road, on the path adjacent to the garden fence of No 26 Rustat Road, occupied by Mr and Mrs "Jimmy" Bain. My aunt and I had taken refuge in the half-cellar of No 28, under the stairs, and my uncle was just coming down the steps to join us when the bomb in Flamsteed Road exploded. His descent down the stairs, thus aided, was accompanied by a pan and other utensils falling on his head from fixings above, leaving him in a dazed condition! There seemed to be a very strong smell of gas, but it was of course that of the explosive detonated only some 40 ft away across Bain's garden. All the windows had been blown out and getting back to bed was a somewhat hazardous business. The other bomb in a front garden in Rustat Road uprooted a tree, part of which rested on the roof of the house.'

Incendiaries fell in the Cattle Market and close to the railway area. Whether those bombs were part of a specially controlled attack is open to question; the bombing of a house, No 91 Grantchester Meadows, which at 22:55 received a direct hit, and where Olive and Florence Barker were killed, was almost beyond doubt unrelated. The main raid came at 23:15 and was the work of II/KG2, maybe a mixture of about six aircraft drawn from Staffel 4, *U5+AM, 'BM, 'DM, 'GM, 'HM, 'IM, 'MM, 'NM* and *'OM,* and Staffel 5, *U5+AN, 'CN, 'DN, 'HN, 'IN* and *'MN.* If the attack was conventional, then employment of a pincer movement with bombing from either end of the target area was novel.

Marker flares hovered over Coe Fen, their appearance causing wardens to call people to shelter for already a number of Do 17Zs were flying around very low. As we crossed to the public shelter, Mum shepherding the elderly ones, a Do 17 rattled in fast from the north, low enough for its shape and twin fins to be clear. On its second run, small track and speed corrections evident, the bombs fell. My suspicion will always be that there was contact with a ground controller.

In bed at 48 Hills Road, above Dewhurst's butchers' shop, Mr H. Ashman was asleep. Suddenly there was a shattering explosion, one of three in rapid succession. Bombs had burst on the roadway (which the military convoy was to pass along), very close to the shops. One was later reckoned to have smashed a marble counter in Bull's Dairy shop before skidding to explode outside. Another wrecked Nutt's Garage at the corner of Coronation Street. Between them, these and other HEs were supplemented almost immediately by a shower of incendiaries which damaged the Catholic church and particularly the rear of the Eastern Counties bus garage. The convoy was at once diverted along Lensfield Road, to Brooklands Avenue.

Mr Ashman had been hurled into a glass-fronted cabinet in which he was held.

In another room his fourteen-year old sister experienced equal horror for a five-inch piece of the bomb had impaled her long hair deeply into a wall. Their mother had to free them both, although it was difficult and later brought on a hernia. Such later, serious complications were never reflected in casualty listing.

Mr Ashman's mind was then upon one thing. Moments before the bomb exploded his father left home to join firewatchers using the 'Globe' public house opposite as base. Recalling those traumatic moments, he says, 'I rushed out into Hills Road which was in quite a mess; I had to find my father. What was, perhaps, most surprising was that nobody else was about — except for someone very seriously injured, probably dead and lying on the pavement at the corner of Coronation Street. It was uncannily quiet too. I just did not know where to start looking for Dad.'

The horror in the 'Globe' one may surmise. Some had died and many were injured, the building displaying its shrapnel scars until very recently. Among those who did not make the 'Globe' in time were Mr and Mrs Woodcock. He was felled by the blast and soon found himself lying most uncomfortably. Although he lost an arm he miraculously survived and is now in his eighties. His wife died in the street near her home. Such first aid as could be given was administered by those on the spot; it was some time before anyone else arrived. Fires at the bus garage and GPO tyre depot were dealt with by fire-watchers, by which time more bombs had fallen, dropped by aircraft attacking from the south-east and possibly using Cherry Hinton Road as their lead-in.

Mr and Mrs Cowell were wardens in Lichfield Road at the time. Mrs Cowell recalls how they 'went into the gardens and heard a diving plane, then explosions. We had just got into the hall of our house, 11 Lichfield Road, in time when a bomb fell on to a shed in a corner of the garden of a house opposite. All our front windows went and the back door was blown open, although it had been locked. A mother with two children, who had an indoor Morrison shelter, had an arm badly cut by flying glass, and the room was in a mess. In the next house Mr and Mrs Clennett were suffering shock and Mr Clennett had an injury to his knee—he had been standing at his back door opposite the bombed shed. From the Cherry Hinton Road warden's post, Mr Cowell summoned help and the two injured were taken away for treatment. My task already was to make the recommended cups of sweet tea! Mrs Gould returned to the children, but Mr Clennett was more badly hurt than we had thought. Metal had entered the back of his knee and he had a spell in hospital.

'Next morning the windows were attended to, but my biggest problem was how to clean my carpet. In the bombed shed there had been an oil drum, and people coming into my house had oil on their shoes. It now seemed to be everywhere in the house, including the WC. When my husband returned from the Post he said that several bombs had fallen, one on Nutt's Garage in Hills Road. This worried me terribly as my brother worked there, and often very late. He and his fiancée were to marry in a fortnight. A flat over the garage had been offered to them, and they had spent much time redecorating it and that week had put in the furniture. There was nothing we could do that night, but the next day my brother said he had been there up to about ten minutes before the bomb fell, but had decided to go home earlier than usual. The flat was more or less a write-off, although some items were recovered. My brother, incidentally, had a close friend killed, along with his father, in the Vicarage Terrace bombing.'

While the Cowells sorted out their problems the rescue services, Police, AFS and a number of soldiers were busy. KG2 seems to have made six bombing runs and whilst the Army convoy had been diverted and none of the tanks were hit, 28 HEs and many incendiaries from both aiming points had produced many problems. None, though, could ever exceed those of the small group so traumatically engulfed in Hills Road. Kathleen Thaxter (24) and Ivy Woodcock (29), both fire-watchers, had died together with P. Robertson and Lucy Gent (60), an ARP Warden. Sidney Brittain (50) and Fred Negus (19) died in hospital next day, also Maurice Lambert (34).

Well into the early hours Mr Ashman sought news of his father, close to home, among the ARP workers, at the Police Station, at Addenbrookes Hospital — and all in vain. 'No official seemed to want to be involved' he recalls, 'and nobody seemed to help us, for some time.' Not long before dawn a visitor came, to inform the family that it was now assumed Bertie Ashman had been killed and was probably in the street when the bomb fell.

He was found in the shop, now Peter Dominic's. 'What was most difficult to come to terms with,' Mr Ashman says upon looking back, 'is the thought that the last time I saw my father was when he hurried off firewatching. He just disappeared from our world. We were never asked to identify him; we just never saw him again. I recalled that he had that day drawn some money for me from a bank. It must, I thought, have been in his wallet when he was killed. After a few days various items he was carrying were returned to us — including the wallet. It contained no money. He had been wearing a pocket watch which his father gave to him — only its chain was returned. I like to think the watch was too badly damaged to be of further use.'

Morning scenes in the attack area were quite incredible. The entire strip between the Catholic Church and the War Memorial had been terribly battered. Windows, roofs and doors had been wrecked in profusion, and this was also true of parts of Cherry Hinton Road. The accuracy of the bombing would have done credit to any unit at any time of the war. Planned, it certainly was. How much special guidance was to hand remains a mystery. For an air force whose bombing accuracy was repeatedly poor, this was something quite extraordinary.

Next day my mother and I paid a call on her Aunt Emily who lived in Cherry Hinton Road. 'Terrible night', I recall her telling us. 'We haven't got ANY windows left. In all my 75 years I haven't seen anything like it. But that Hitler has gone too far this time. Look in my garden, he's blown up my "Vic"'. By that time she was waving a vicious looking umbrella. I looked in her garden. There was a huge hole where once her plum tree stood. The tree was going to present a big problem too, for quite intact it was standing entirely upside down filling her neighbour's garden. What cruelty, anguish and everlasting remorse had been achieved for no useful purpose.

Chapter 15
Into the spring

As winter passed, the improving weather gradually led to reduced Luftwaffe daylight cloud cover activity and extended night bombing, clearer skies bringing increased accuracy. Improved aircraft and more advanced operational techniques remained far off, allowing few changes in tactics, although alterations in emphasis were increasingly apparent. There was no sudden change in the pattern of attacks on the Eastern Counties, but a change in emphasis was apparent at the end of February.

After hectic night activity on 24 February 1941, the daylight period was quiet. Then Ju 88s (including *R4+FK, 'GK, 'KL* and *'SM*) of NJG2 interfered with RAF bomber activity. The main evening effort involved twenty He 111Hs of I and II/KG53 (including *A1+HB, 'DK, 'HK, 'BN, 'AP, 'CP, 'DP* and *'DR*) operating from Lille/Vendeville against targets in Suffolk. One bomber had a container of SD2 'butterfly' bombs for Ipswich and at 21:50 went in so low that searchlights trying to illuminate it played instead upon tree tops and the large house in Chantry Park. There the bomber unloaded its vicious weapons, the first falling on the edge of the garden. Most air burst over a 400-yd trail destroying telegraph wires. In the park were found 37 small craters, and only one bomb had not exploded. The Heinkel was again after the Ipswich dock area. Mid-evening brought an unexpected arrival, one of twenty KG2 Dorniers participating in a London raid. Their aircraft too damaged to reach home, the four-man crew of Do 17Z-2 W Nr *1134:U5+PM* of 4./KG2 baled out. One died when his parachute failed to open and two had bullet wounds. The aircraft crashed at Little Waldringfield, near Lavenham, an area well acquainted with KG2.

Also busy that evening were the Ju 88Cs of NJG2. Near Marham an intruder fired upon Wellington *R1009 'L'* of 218 Squadron, fracturing fuel pipes. During its crash landing near Swaffham the bomber burst into flames, and miraculously only one crew member was seriously injured. The Ju 88 at 21:45 put eight HEs on Marham's Q-Site. Duxford, too, was assaulted when at 20:09 seven bombs and incendiaries fell, mainly to the west, during three attacks, and killed two men. At Caxton Gibbet RLG where Tiger Moths were night flying, and at Watton and Wittering, Ju 88s were active.

At 22:13 a sharp attack was carried out by III/KG2 led by *U5+IR* and supported variously by *U5+AT, 'CT* and *'GT* upon flare-lit Harwich. Five houses and a shop were demolished, 100 houses damaged, the A136 road was blocked and a UXB rested by the Civil Defence Report Centre where two HEs burst. Due to their style and proximity many buildings suffered serious blast damage. Gas pipes and sewers were fractured too, the population being ordered to boil all drinking water after flooding occurred. Fourteen bombs hit the town, and another six fell in Una Road, Parkeston, where the golf club's pavilion was fired. When at 21:30 fifty HEs fell near Stanbourne no casualties were caused, but at Harwich five were killed and nine injured. Other notable incidents that night included the dropping of ten HEs near Cockley Cley, twenty at Mattishall blocking a road, three at Wymondham and twenty explosive incendiaries on fields near Kerdiston. Nine Do 17s of II/KG3 operated against coastal targets.

KG2 was responsible for much East Anglian bombing. Operating mainly against airfields, on ten of the last seventeen nights all three Gruppen had been active. On most nights Ju 88A minelayers of II/KG30, from Gilze Rijen, operated well out to sea, where operations constantly took place.

Better weather favoured fighter defence, yet patchy cloud seemed always ready to shield the attackers. At 07:50 on 26 February when Hurricanes of 257 Squadron located a Do 17Z six miles south-east of Cromer, Flight Lieutenant Hanks (*V7296*) fired several bursts without success. Similarly, two Hurricane IIs of 242 Squadron engaged a Bf 110 off Orford Ness before it escaped into cloud.

On 26/27 February about thirty raiders visited East Anglian airfields and others crossing between the Blackwater Estuary and Southwold headed for London. Evening bombing occurred in Norfolk at Coxford Heath, Docking, Heveningham (where four cottages were badly damaged and one person was killed) and near Rackheath. Bombing also took place on the London route, ten HEs and incendiaries falling at Clay Hall, Clacton and another twelve nearby. Shortly after midnight a dozen Ju 88s of NJG2 headed inland. Steeple Morden received nine HEs across its runway, two Wellingtons being damaged. Night effort had, however, been less than of late, the reason soon becoming clear as the Luftwaffe launched its biggest cloudy day onslaught since 18 February.

Rain and 9/10 cloud at 400 ft gave ideal cover, as doubtless was reported by an enemy aircraft from Holland which, at 07:45, roared across Felixstowe and at tree top height flew via Bury to Oundle before returning via Peterborough and March where the rail yards were machine-gunned. As it left over Happisburgh widespread bombing had commenced with an 08:15 low level raid on Yarmouth. Two 250 kg HEs (larger than usual) exploded at the junction of Euston and Nelson Roads, between the 'Garibaldi' Hotel and the Beach Station, demolishing the 'Aquarium' Hotel. Swanton Morley was fired upon and two HEs fell at Horstead Heath. At 10:20 the first of sixteen Do 17s of II/KG3 from Schiphol began strafing and bombing Norfolk and Suffolk. During an east-west pass over Stowmarket at 10:38, machine-gun bullets rammed into houses including 10 Church Walk and 59 Newton Road. Three bullets penetrated a gasometer from which fierce flames belched and were not extinguished until the afternoon. Eight HEs dropped on or near Mousehold's hangars and two on Barnard's. Swanton Morley received twelve HEs and Bury's sugar beet factory attracted further bombing, this time in the form of three HEs and incendiaries. The RN Hospital at Yarmouth was strafed, Feltwell bombed and strafed, Hockwold received one HE, Beechamwell five more. By noon one aircraft had reached Molesworth to drop four HEs and incendiaries. At 12:40 Honington aerodrome, Lopham, Lime Tree Farm at Shelfanger and Yarmouth were machine-gunned.

German cloud cover operation maps

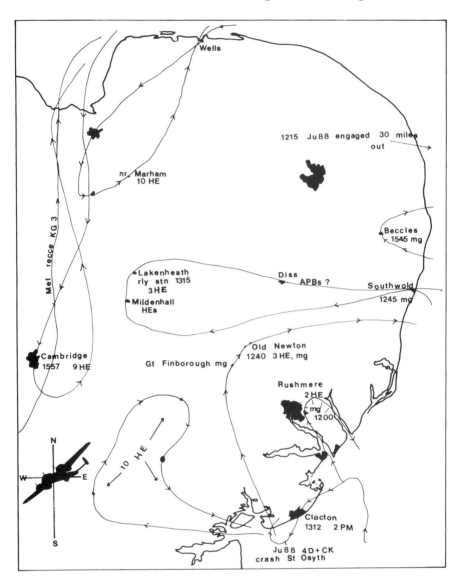

A. Cloud cover operations, 30 January 1941, with approximate routes of aircraft which committed hostile acts — dropping high explosive bombs, machine-gunning and the release of two parachute mines at Clacton.

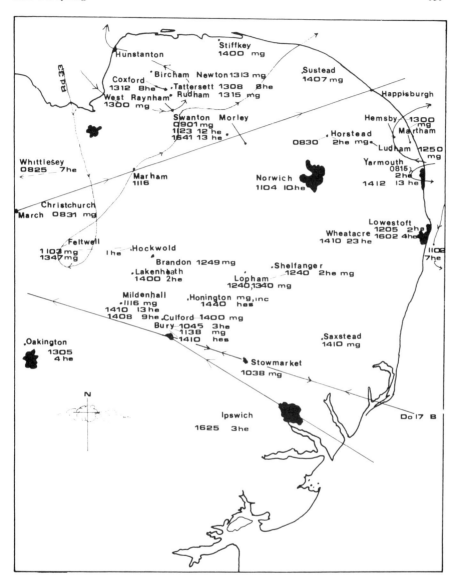

B. Cloud cover operations, 27 February 1941. Effective use of cloud cover was such that in many cases radar and Observer Corps tracking of raiders was not possible. Shown is the early morning weather reconnaissance to Cambridgeshire and Peterborough, after which activity occurred widely in Norfolk and Suffolk, between 10:20 and 17:00. Precise timing of attacks was variously recorded — depending upon time of the receipt of messages. Sixteen bombers of II/KG3 (including eleven identifying themselves as B, C, D, F, G, H, N, P, Q, AMI and HVQ) operated over East Anglia from Dutch bases. 'P' was off the Naze at 14:25, 'Q' thirty miles east of Maldon at 13:55 also going home, 'R' was thirty miles inland at 13:35. At 11:45 'D' reported the second pilot injured by AA fire. He 111s of KG53 also operated, and certainly bombed Norwich and Ipswich. During the day 23 bombers entered the IAZ, ten from the Netherlands and thirteen from the Pas de Calais.

Bombing at Lowestoft demolished four houses and shops, damaged twenty more and killed two civilians. A low-flying Dornier raced over Brandon firing at the town at 12:49 and at 13:00 a banking Dornier dropped three HEs and an incendiary container just outside Oakington's airfield boundary. A Stirling was damaged by machine-gunning. West Raynham, Bircham Newton, East Rudham, Hunstanton, Martham and South Lopham were similarly assaulted and eight HEs dropped near Tattersett.

Although the afternoon brought less activity, in which the Gesch. Stab. III/KG2 and probably I/KG30 played a part, there was more action than usual. Feltwell was four times strafed and at 14:00 a Do 17 crew had the temerity to fire at Stiffkey Light AA School. Again the Bury beet factory was a target, HEs slamming on to cottages nearby and killing three and injuring nine people. At the same time, 14:10, thirteen HEs were unsuccessfully aimed at Mildenhall aerodrome which was four times attacked during the day, but without the slightest success. Saxstead was machine-gunned, 23 HEs fell around Wheatacre Hall and a few moments later a stick of thirteen HEs was dropped across Yarmouth from Apsley Road to King Street, demolishing Reynold's Garage and a number of houses and damaging the Girls' High School, the Manual School, a number of utilities including the fire station and killing two and injuring eight people. A final burst of fury developed at 16:02 with another attack upon Lowestoft when four HEs demolished nine houses, killing four and injuring nine civilians; and at 16:25 when a machine-gunning He 111 broke cloud over the Orwell then returned flying very low over Ipswich docks to drop a stick of four 250 kg HEs. The first hit the road by St Mary's, the Quay Church, ricocheted and holed a two-foot thick stone wall, allowing a staggering 500 tons of barley to pour forth which quickly filled Keith Street and fractured a low pressure water main. Within the debris was found a solitary, stifled 1 kg Elektron incendiary unable to ignite, which had been strapped to one of the HE's fins. A direct hit on the bakery of Messrs Kerridge, Quay Street, was scored by bomb number two, and a five-year-old boy seriously injured later died. Bomb number three entered No 1 Malting, Messrs R. W. Paul, through a roof ventilator and wrecked No 3 Kiln. Behind No 74 Fore Street, the fourth bomb exploded trapping a man and woman. The other two bombs fell close to where bombs had landed on 8 July 1940. At 16:41 a He 111 rounded off the daylight operation at Swanton Morley and narrowly escaped being ensnared by FAS shells. Not until 1/2 March did the enemy return, night fighters patrolling while KG2 tried again for airfields.

On 2/3 March a parachute mine which fell at Birch Hall, Tendring RD, at 17:20 and damaged a cottage, was probably dropped by a Ju 88 of Eindhoven's I/KG30. During this period new units were operating from Holland including KG53 whose Heinkels' range allowed them to prowl even off Northumberland. A dozen were engaged in such activity on 3 March, when attacks were also made upon shipping off Lowestoft. At night on the 3rd/4th Yarmouth was twice bombed, first with incendiaries which set alight commercial premises. Ten HEs fell near Crowhall Farm south-west of the town shortly after midnight, then a container of incendiaries was distributed over the Lowestoft Road-Marine Parade-Bridge Road area leading to Gorleston without causing much damage. Dorniers of KG2 had yet again attacked bomber stations, and six Ju 88Cs sought RAF bombers. One managed shots at Wellington *KX:G-T2972* of 311 Squadron during its approach to East Wretham where ten bombs were delivered. At Feltwell a Ju 88 followed a Wellington in and dropped HEs and incendiaries as it landed.

The anti-shipping offensive off East Anglia was flourishing, general reconnaissance sorties by 1.(F)/122 from Lille/Vendeville and 3.(F)/122 from Leeuwarden being daily flown about thirty miles off shore and followed by armed reconnaissances by KG2, KG3 and KG53 which carried out strikes, and in the evening of 4 March a dozen Dorniers of II/KG3 sought ships off Yarmouth. Clouds at 800 ft on 6 March brought attacks by II/KG3, the first at Sheringham at 11:12 where two HEs injured two people. At 12:45 Raid 403 placed nine HEs on Feltwell where a hangar was hit and two aircraft damaged. Wattisham's ground defences claimed hits on a Do 17, probably that from which a message informed Schiphol that the aircraft's observer had been wounded. Oulton landing ground was bombed in the afternoon when machine-gunning took place over Norfolk and two Do 17s attacked Horsham, one being chased off by a Spitfire. Those later intrusions over Norfolk were by I/KG2, but KG2's main interest lay in shipping about twelve miles north-east of Yarmouth. U5+AA and 'CD tried to bomb a convoy whose defensive fire had driven away U5+CA. Near Cromer Knoll LV, U5+CB also attacked a ship.

Early evening brought a score of Ju 88Cs making East Anglian patrols, and a Do 17Z of II/KG3 dropped thirteen HEs at Lowestoft. Only one exploded, damaging a library and some houses, killing three people and injuring thirteen. If shipping was not located, then factories, airfields and ports served as alternatives. Three bombs at Brightlingsea quayside which on the 7th damaged the 'Anchor' Hotel, probably fell in that category. Cloud had again allowed bombers to penetrate inland, but the main operations area lay off Essex, Suffolk and Norfolk. KG3 first sought the ships, off Essex, thick cloud making the task difficult. Six He 111s (including A1+FM and 'FK) of I/KG53 also operated in the morning, the first crossing in over Yarmouth at 10:47 and en route to King's Lynn, machine-gunning Rollesby and Martham before sweeping round to leave over Southwold. A second Heinkel crossed Yarmouth at 11:00 and journeyed almost directly to Chester, whence it returned to the Wash which it left at 13:00. Another He 111 attacked Feltwell. Afternoon anti-shipping operations were undertaken by I and II/KG30 whose Ju 88s roamed as far north as Scarborough, and again by KG3 which delivered attacks upon a convoy off Yarmouth. Its defenders blazed away and brought down Do 17Z-2 W Nr 3391:5K+MK of 2./KG3, from which two of the crew were rescued and put ashore at Yarmouth. Six aircraft of KG2 also operated during the afternoon, and one probably of III/KG2 at 15:26 bombed Page Road, Clacton, damaging several houses and killing three and trapping two people.

After dark Ju 88 F6+PH flew by about ten miles offshore, and located Convoy 'Agent' north-east of Southwold then dropped red and white flares guiding E-Boats to attack.

Several early morning raiders visited Norfolk on 8 March. At 08:40 fighters from Coltishall tried intercepting a Dornier (either U5+BA or 'DA) circling Norwich, but it left before they could engage it. Six Dorniers of I and II/KG3 were active off Yarmouth mid-morning, one producing no worthwhile effect from a load of ten HEs and a few incendiaries at Bircham Newton. Morning activity included Ju 88s of II/KG30 which drew 222 Squadron into precautionary patrols over Yarmouth. On arrival, Pilot Officer B. P. Clee

(*R6596*) witnessed a Ju 88 dive through cloud and drop four bombs in the sea off Britannia Pier. He closed, pouring his ammunition into the enemy as it climbed to 7,000 ft. As his number two, Sergeant R. G. Morland (*R6684*), made three attacks a gunner in the '88 scored hits on the engine of his Spitfire. The Ju 88 had been badly mauled and, low over the sea, Morland fired the rest of his ammunition into Ju 88A-5 W Nr *3198:4D+DN* which plunged into the sea off Gorleston. *4D+FM,* another Ju 88 of KG30 damaged by AA fire, was meanwhile flying home in poor state and had to divert to Abbeville/Drucat.

Next night brought further attempts to disturb airfield activity, mainly in Cambridgeshire and Bedfordshire. Alconbury was twice attacked, and Marham's Q-Site attracted interest. One bomber put four HEs and a few fire bombs on to Lowestoft, demolishing one house and damaging eighteen more.

The Ninth of March saw reduced activity, two Do 17s, *U5+BA* and *'DA*, searching for shipping between 08:00 and 09:00. In mid-afternoon several aircraft of KG3 (*5K+AN* and *'AM* included) flew armed reconnaissance flights off Yarmouth and attacked a ship off Sheringham. Another aircraft flew along the coast to King's Lynn and on return dropped a bomb at 16:55 on Cliff Road, Sheringham, which destroyed two houses. During the evening three Dorniers of KG3 attacked Convoy 'Agent' off Happisburgh while I and II/KG2 sought success at aerodromes.

The now customary early reconnaissance by KG2 followed next morning and in the early afternoon five He 111s (*A1+EJ, 'EM, 'EP, 'CP* and *'HM*) operated offshore before returning to Leeuwarden. Heavy bombing elsewhere occupied much of the Luftwaffe's effort, it being left to 25 Dorniers of II/KG3 to conduct evening anti-shipping operations off Norfolk while six of I and III/KG3 operated inland. Mainly over Lincolnshire roamed nine Ju 88Cs of I/NJG2, one of these providing the night's highlight when it crashed at Terrington St Clement, south of King's Lynn.

That unheralded arrival proved most exciting. Home Guard Corporal Buffham was on foot patrol at 23:40 and saw the silhouette of the Ju 88 before it crashed near Hay Green. He quickly sent a colleague to telephone Platoon HQ for help as he and three others hurried to the crash site. There they were surprised to find an almost intact Ju 88 and two Germans coming towards them, hands raised, calling 'Doc' and pointing to the aircraft. On reaching it they saw another of the crew was injured, and carefully freed him, then two of them hurried off to find a gate to serve as a makeshift stretcher. They then noticed that one of the crew edging nearer to the aircraft had taken out a cigarette. Fumbling in his pocket for matches and furtively looking over his shoulder, he clearly had one intention so Corporal Buffham snatched the cigarette and ordered 'Hands up!' Then he told three of the patrol, bayonets fixed, to mount close guard until both prisoners were in police custody. The injured man was taken to the 'Plough' Inn.

While the Home Guard were guarding their trophy, an array of ARP wardens, police, special constables and 'the military' — not to mention locals — soon homed in. The Home Guard had captured the aircraft and by prompt action saved it for others to enjoy. Harsh words were quickly exchanged as the regulars ordered a hand-over, so much so that an official complaint was lodged by the Home Guard, to which higher echelons meanly responded '... not much substance in the complaint'!

But if there was dissatisfaction at Hay Green, such was not so in London, that a Ju 88 with nose guns, and intact, had decided to stay. Even better, its crew of three — Oberleutnant Kurt Herrmann, Unteroffizier Engelbert Bottner and Feldwebel Wilhelm Ruppel — had become prisoners and might throw some light upon their activities. What was revealed merely confirmed the already known.

Not until 29 January 1941 did the British discover for certain that Ju 88 night fighters were making specially organized night intruder sorties over bomber bases in England, yet they had been flown since the previous summer. When RAF bombers began night raids on Germany in May 1940 a night fighter force was needed to halt such activities. Its formation commenced in June and its expansion was ordered by Göring in July. Even before the war some Ju 88A-1s had been converted into Ju 88C-0 long-range fighters and placed in a Staffel of KG30 usually referred to as 'Z/KG30'. That unit and part of ZG76 amalgamated in July 1940, forming II/NJG2, Schiphol-based, and commenced operations late in the month. In August the unit moved to Gilze Rijen, by which time it was equipping with Ju 88C-2s and under the command of Hauptmann Karl Heyse. On 11 September the unit was renamed I/NJG2.

Ensuing months found the unit still quite small with resources only allowing one Staffel to operate, and on two or three nights a week. Coastal patrols were flown by day, night operations only when the weather was suitable. On 23 November NJG2's commandant was shot down over the North Sea, his place taken by Hauptmann Lutzow, ex-Staffel Kapitän of I/NJG2. To be of value the unit needed enlarging and on 12 December 1940 Göring had promised that it would be raised to full Geschwader strength. That aroused much opposition and showed a total lack of realization of the great potential of extensive night intruder operations. Ironically it was just at this time that in Britain the decision was made to undertake very similar activities which were to expand in scope throughout the war and lead to Bomber Command's own fighter support force, No 100 Group. All that I/NJG2 had added, for the present, was 'M' Staffel, Staffel 4 of II Gruppe.

Throughout 11 March 1941 technical intelligence personnel combed the Terrington trophy, a fine treat. Ju 88C-4, marking (barely visible) *R4+CH*, W Nr *0343*, had been sprayed overall very matt black. International identity markings had all but disappeared, while the unit's lettering was small and in slate grey, the 'C' outlined white. Fitted in the 'solid' nose was a belt-fed 20 mm MG 151 cannon with three MG 17 machine-guns installed above. All fixed guns, they could be fired simultaneously from one button on the pilot's control column. Ammunition was stored behind an 11 mm armour plate, and cockpit glazing ahead of the pilot was three inches thick because return fire from British bombers could be quite devastating. The rear gunner had a belt-fed MG 15 machine-gun and the upper gunner a magazine-fed MG 17. Internal racks could carry up to eight 50 kg bombs, but absence of provisioning for external loads suggested range was important. Unlike the Ju 88C-2, the main type on strength, the C-4 had the lengthened wingspan of the Ju 88A-5 from which it was derived. Also operating during the night of the aircraft's arrival were Ju 88Cs *R4+AK, 'EK, 'LK, 'AH, 'CH, 'HL,* and *'SL.*

That the pattern of operations was to change became apparent over the next few days as German units changed bases. Three Gruppen of KG3 were using Schiphol, but Stab.II/KG3 now moved to the Mediterranean Theatre. I/KG4 settled in at Soesterberg which was used by II Gruppe who also operated from Eindhoven, while III/KG4 was based at Leeuwarden with I and II/KG53, a unit which also used Wittmundhafen. I and III/KG2 were still at Merville, some of their Do 17Zs recently having been fitted with underwing flotation gear, better suiting them for maritime operations. Most important, it was discovered that the long range bomber force now planned to concentrate upon attacking shipping by day and airfields by night. That was apparent on 12 March when four of II/KG3's aircraft sought Convoy 'Arena' off Clacton. Seeing it well protected, they pressed on northwards to attack a ship at 10:34 and, a mile off Raugh Buoy at 12:03, to bomb the *Milford Queen*. That night two 250 kg bombs fell on Ipswich, and Pilot Officer Stevens in a 151 Squadron Hurricane claimed a probable Ju 88 25 miles off Orford Ness. At 04:00 ten HEs hit a small gelignite dump at King's Lynn's Bentinct Dock.

Eighty per cent of the night effort on 13/14 March was devoted to anti-shipping activity emphasizing the profound changes taking place. KG2 had thirty aircraft off the coast with orders to sink ships, land targets being alternatives. Throughout the night such activities were carried on by units new to the area, I/KG51 flying fifteen aircraft from the Amiens area and I/KG77 operating twenty aircraft from Schiphol. Heinkel 111s of I and III/KG4 were also active over the sea, producing an uneasy night for many a sailor. Ships, though, were notoriously difficult targets at any time, a near miss being a complete miss. Not all of the bombers had it easy either for, at 21:45, south-east of Skegness Point, the crew of a 29 Squadron Beaufighter located Dornier Do 17Z-2 W Nr *4248:U5+DA* (flying with a Stab./KG2 crew) which was intending to search for shipping as far north as the Humber. It did not succeed and was shot into the sea. The same night I/NJG2 lost another Ju 88C-4, W Nr *0604:R4+GM,* and Waterbeach received eight HEs from a bomber making a precision attack from 16,000 ft.

After daylight spy flights along the coast by Lille/Vendeville's Ju 88s, the Luftwaffe conducted a night operation against a convoy off Lowestoft in which 3(F)./122, Gilze Rijen, took a leading part. Lowestoft also came under very sharp attack for nearly an hour before midnight, probably from a fair proportion of the twenty active Dorniers of II/KG3. Incendiaries ignited between Sycamore Avenue and Oulton Broad. Then seven HEs exploded in the Giselham area. Half an hour later seven more HEs burst south of Notley Road, near to which incendiaries were also dropped. Others burnt in Beaconsfield and Salisbury Roads, and two HEs fell in the Mutford Lock Bridge area. Another shower of incendiaries drifted over Park Hill, Gorleston. A further phase developed at midnight, incendiaries spreading over North Town causing fifteen fires. Six HEs fell into a huge collection of wooden boxes at Bloomfield's Fish House, tearing them apart. On Whapload Road more bombs fell, making this Lowestoft's heaviest raid so far. Was it a portent of things to come?

Inland, I/NJG2 was exceptionally successful. A Ju 88 crept quietly upon Wittering then roared across unloading six HEs and about 100 incendiaries. The first HE smashed through the roof of 25 Squadron's hangar, breaking the wing of a Beaufighter, but amazingly did not explode. A second bomb did, and in the hangar roof which was seriously damaged. A third exploded on the Airmen's Mess and another by the gas decontamination centre. A fifth burst alongside the Officers' Mess and incendiaries fired a hangar, destroyed the Station Cinema and started blazes at two barrack blocks. Fires raged for almost two hours, yet surprisingly did not attract other raiders. Three RAF men were killed and seventeen injured, two later dying.

As Wittering's fires were tackled Yarmouth was being bombed, incendiaries and four HEs being slammed on to the northern centre, damaging an ambulance station, two garages and houses. Damage was also caused to a ship repair yard. Incendiaries were also dropped near RAF Stradishall.

Two Heinkels of II/KG53 operated off Cromer during the evening of 17 March before activity increased next morning. At 05:27 the Luftwaffe was back over Yarmouth, and placed eight 50 kg HEs between Vauxhall Street and the River Bure. Sufficient afternoon cloud permitted I/KG53 to patrol over East Anglia, and two Spitfires patrolling east of Sheringham spotted an unidentified aircraft contrailing. As they climbed the quarry dived away south-east. Flight Lieutenant van Mentz (*P7697*) and Pilot Officer Clee (*P7699*) chased it, making rear and quarter attacks and driving the enemy aircraft close to the water. Mentz made two more passes then the bomber plunged into the water 25 miles east of Sheringham.

On the night of 17/18 March Mildenhall's lighting was on when an aircraft showing navigation lights joined the circuit. Following 149 Squadron's Wellington *OJ:M-R1474* it soon opened fire, the bomber falling in flames. Subsequent bombing did no damage though. Marham was more fortunate for yet again it was the Q-Site which attracted the bombing. Certainly such distractions were a worthwhile development for the British, but an experienced NJG2 crew would not be easily deceived.

Throughout the evening of 18 March KG53 again operated from the Norfolk coast northwards. Ju 88 *F6+FH* conducted a lengthy reconnaissance from Lille/Vendeville and several Heinkels of III/KG26 made their way back to Le Bourget across Norfolk to the safety of the sea over which shipping beats were flown throughout 19 and 20 March. Squadron Leader Stanford Tuck (*V6864*) was off Happisburgh at 08:25 on the 19th when he spotted a Do 17Z. This he stalked and at 08:25 despatched it into the sea four miles south of Cromer Knoll LV. Another, unidentified, aircraft, unusually from Le Culot, operated along the coast. Evening patrols were flown from Lille by 1.(F)/122 and it may well have been one of their Ju 88s which was badly damaged off Southwold by Flight Lieutenant Blatchford of 257 Squadron. Fighter interceptions increased with the clearer weather although often it was hazy at sea. Despite such conditions 4.(F)/122 flew seven shipping searches along the East Anglian coast on 20 March. The evening was marked by the dropping of two parachute mines in fields at Wissett near to 'Rydal Mount' which was damaged, like houses over a three-mile radius — hardly surprising for one crater was 45 ft across and 20 ft deep. Two more mines came down at Hollesley. The sea claimed one, while the other produced a crater on the shore north of the Coast Guard Station.

III/KG2 was again in action on 21 March with eight aircraft (including *U5+AT, 'CT, 'GT, 'HT, 'IT* and *'KT*), one of Stab.1, resuming airfield attacks from Nierguise. Three Dorniers crossed Yarmouth at 17:30 to bomb near Stoke Holy Cross and Aylsham. But next day it was business as usual, KG4 flying sixteen sorties against shipping while Eindhoven's Ju 88s of I/KG30 mined further out to sea. One of the latter encountered engine trouble and crash landed at Soesterberg, terminal of another spectacular return.

Did that policeman see a Dornier Do 26 flying-boat? Shown is the fourth example, used by 1./Ku.Fl.Gr.406 and possibly, then, the machine seen off Felixstowe. (Bundesarchiv 85/17/2).

Heinkel 111 *5J+JM* was fired upon from shipping and shortly after 17:30 its radio operator was injured and the aircraft, one engine stopped, was limping back only 350 ft above the sea. Power was lost from the remaining engine just south of Kentish Knoll LV. Miraculously the Heinkel's engine kept going and at 18:18 the crew told control that they intended to crash land near Zandvoort. At 18:48 they had reached Schouwen and were still airworthy, although only at 500 ft. 'Please have an ambulance ready', they called, and at 19:03 crash landed at Soesterberg after an epic return. Two other crews repeatedly called by their control never responded.

While that drama was unfolding, PC Bannister at the 'Cavendish' Hotel, Felixstowe, was writing a report which, IF accurate, was of a sight which many then and certainly now would have thrilled (and shivered) to see. At 17:13 a low-flying aircraft dropped two parachute mines in Harwich Harbour, one near the boom and another, which exploded five minutes later, nearby. The large perpetrator swung, machine-gunning the Landguard area as it roared by. The Constable, no aircraft enthusiast, merely recorded what he saw — an aircraft that 'had two engines forward and two behind the wing, a seaplane' — and he had a second opportunity to check its appearance when, at 17:35, it flew by again. This time he observed something fall into the sea. He reckoned it was a man, but it was one of two parachute mines dropped east-south-east of New Pier as the aircraft left. Assuming PC Bannister's report accurate, the aircraft could only have been a rare Dornier Do 26D flying-boat.

Germany's Lufthansa airline in 1937 ordered the Do 26, a shoulder wing seaplane with retractable wing floats and four 600 hp Junkers Jumo 205 diesel engines fitted in tandem — two tractors and two pushers as the Constable had recorded. Their intention was to operate Do 26s between Lisbon and New York but the war halted that plan. Only six examples were built, the last four modified before completion into transport/reconnaissance aircraft, a bow turret supplementing waist gun cupolas. The aircraft entered service in 1940 and were active during the invasion of Norway, three being destroyed in action. The remaining three were drafted into 1./Ku. Fl. Gr. 406, Norway-based, and presumably it was one of those which operated over Harwich Harbour. No other such sighting around Britain seems ever to have been made.

On 24 March the Luftwaffe now uncharacteristically launched early morning raids into East Anglia. Some fifteen Ju 88Cs had been active during the night, then two Do 17s (probably of III/KG2) machine-gunned Shotley and at 06:18 made a very low level raid on Martlesham Heath, scoring direct hits on two hangars, demolishing one end of No 4 Hangar and damaging two Hurricanes. Two HEs landed at the north end of the aerodrome, causing small fires. Four minutes later six Hurricanes of 605 Squadron chasing the raiders were confronted by two Heinkel 111s heading out to sea from Felixstowe, and reckoned then to have joined two Bf 109s. A couple of 250 kg HEs had fallen on Felixstowe Road, two more on Nacton Road by Ipswich Airport. As they fled the bombers machine-gunned Alderton. By the time the Hurricanes caught up with the bombers they were all well out to sea. During the day KG3, supported by 3.(F)/122, operating from Schiphol and Lille/Vendeville, maintained search for shipping which task, to the end of March, represented about 75 per cent of the Luftwaffe effort in the area. Night activity between 24 and 27 March was prevented by inclement weather over German bases, but small-scale daylight operations continued, mainly around coastal areas.

Late afternoon on 25 March a pair of Hurricanes damaged a Bf 110 east of Orford Ness and at 09:06 next day two Spitfires of 602 Squadron claimed a Do 17 in the same region. Hunstanton was machine-gunned mid-morning of 27 March, possibly by one of the reconnaissance flights flown daily by 1., 2., 3. and 4. (F)/122. Observations by one resulted in shipping attacks off Norfolk during 29 March when 3./KG1 and 2./KG77 were found to be lending a hand.

A few minutes after 13:00 a bomber raced across Walberswick very low, dropping four bombs on to the small town. One demolished Short Lane Cottage from which, very surprisingly, Mrs Elizabeth Taylor crawled despite her injuries. Another bomb fell near, two exploded at Manor Farm and between them they damaged over thirty houses. Twice during the day Yarmouth's guns fired at aircraft trying to interfere with shipping in the Roads, and east of Norwich a civilian was killed and two more injured when a train was strafed between Postwick and Brundall. During the evening I and II/KG53 operated and at 17:10 one of their He 111s dropped five HEs on Heath Farm, Kessingland. One bomb burst on the beach setting off land mines and producing a 45 ft crater. Other unexpected operators also appeared off the coast after dark, a few of II/KG76 from Châteaudun searching for shipping. They did surprisingly well for, at 20:48 off Happisburgh, one of their Ju 88s managed a hit on a fair sized merchant ship. Two other ships were claimed as damaged. Small numbers from II/KG4 and II/KG30 also operated.

From all this activity one formation was, however, very obviously missing, East Anglia's particularly unwanted visitor, KG2. It was already known that the whole Kampfgeschwader had assembled recently at Merville, and it was soon obvious that KG3, too, was also no longer with us. They were in fact already on their ways, forsaking grey skies for the blue of the Balkans and their share in the campaign against Yugoslavia. Thus, the attack on a ship fifteen miles north-east of Skegness at 15:35 on 29 March marked the end of a memorable phase in the air war above East Anglia. KG2 would be back, but things would be very different by then. On the evening of the 30th about 24 Heinkel He 111s of I and II/KG53 operated over East Anglia, and that day 12./KG2 managed to crash one of its new toys at Achmer, Do 217 W Nr *5055*, though operational employment of what was heralded, wrongly, as a wonder bomber was a long way off.

Chapter 16

On the move

Transfer of KG2 and 3 to the Balkans punched a sizable hole in the long-range bomber force available for attacks against East Anglia. Harassing raids upon bomber stations were NJG2's responsibility and would continue, whereas cloud-cover inland operations would all but cease and the main area of attack be off-shore... with one or two outstanding exceptions. Bombs would now often fall in coastal areas, secondary to shipping operations or considered as ports worthy of attention. Daily reconnaissance flights would continue, 3.(F)/122 moving to Schiphol for the purpose. For the defenders this meant that engagements would usually be out to sea with chances of success even more reduced unless standing patrols were undertaken.

Activity in the first week of April 1941 was restricted while the Luftwaffe reorganized. Twice in the late afternoon of 1 April pairs of Hurricanes of 242 Squadron engaged Ju 88s and at 17:15 shot down a Ju 88A-5 at Worlingham. *3Z+LN* of I/KG77, it dived vertically into the ground after two of the crew baled out. An interesting discovery, in the hedge at Sandy Lane, Blythburgh, was an unusual-looking 'explosive incendiary bomb' (or an SDI?) left over from a raid of 26 February when six HEs and fire bombs fell at Mile Field, Walberswick. Quite unlike the usual weapons, this was a canister of 2 in diameter, $5\frac{3}{4}$ in long. Attached was a six-fin tail, making the bomb 9 in long overall. The use of explosive incendiaries was still unusual.

From the Stour to the Humber KG53 presently was conducting anti-shipping operations, its He 111 operating at between 1,500 ft and 3,000 ft from three to six miles off shore, generally singly and making five-hour sorties. The unit also came inland if clouds permitted and 2 April witnessed II/KG53 mount two such sorties. The He 111s came in at around 09:00, one being hotly engaged by Norwich guns which claimed hits. But Luftwaffe concentration remained upon shipping and the Gruppe homed in at 10:56 to heavily attack a minesweeper a mile off Walberswick. Three more Heinkels joined them and at 12:30 attacked HMS *Lorna Doone* off Lowestoft. Aldeburgh, a secondary target, was bombed at 14:35, two 250 kg HEs overshooting into marshland to the north and one producing a 40-ft-wide crater. At the same time a fast-flying aircraft, possibly an Erpro. 210 Bf 110, crossed the coast at Tostock to put two 250 kg HEs on to Norwich, one scoring a direct hit on Thorpe Station goods yard and causing a fatality as well as destroying five trucks. Not for over a year would the city again be bombed in daylight, such activities over Norfolk temporarily halting on 16

April after an HE bomb was dropped mid-afternoon at Kenningham Hall.

Making an armed reconnaissance, a raider causing Hurricanes to be scrambled approached Martlesham Heath at 06:06 on the 3rd. The crew clearly was filled with alarm for they fled as fast as possible, jettisoning nine HEs in the River Deben. The measure of the Luftwaffe's reduced front line strength was shown when only twelve raids entered UK air space during the entire day. Off East Anglia mines were laid and 4.(F)/122 sought targets, one of their Ju 88s being attacked by 222 Squadron north-east of Cromer. Slipping inland, a raider deposited HEs along the Beccles-Bungay railway late in the evening, and another was responsible for interrupting Marham's night activity. Wellington *R1470:'H'* of 115 Squadron was in contact with base when radio calls ceased for it had been shot down north of King's Lynn and crashed on mud flats. Two of the crew were killed, the others lost without trace. Then the intruder circled Marham low as Wellingtons were returning from Brest. Seven UXHEs were subsequently found, one in a hangar, and a barrack block was damaged. Another Ju 88 penetrated to Henlow and, flying via St Neots, dropped two HEs near Upwood before looking for trade at Bassingbourn and Debden.

Between 4 and 7 April most activity remained over sea apart from NJG2's activities and the bombing of alternatives. The Yarmouth raid late on 4 April, heavier than usual, may have been specially designed to cripple what the Germans always considered a major port. Activity over Yarmouth extended for more than two hours, two HEs exploding in the Harbour Mouth while about 500 incendiaries, some explosive, were scattered over the north end of the town, from Newtown to Runham Vauxhall. Many small fires were extinguished by the police, wardens and those first on the scene. Inland, a Ju 88C (possibly *R4+FM*) wasted its munitions by attacking Wittering's Q-Site, and another used five HEs to close East Wretham temporarily. Mines were still being regularly sown, off Orford Ness, Harwich and on the 6th/7th, by II/KG30 off Yarmouth.

Activity began increasing on 7 April, a busy few days following. At midday, shipping attacks developed off Orford and Clacton. Pilot Officer R. G. Marland of 222 Squadron, spotting bomb splashes off Yarmouth among ships in convoy, called his number two, Pilot Officer Ramsey, and they both sped through defending AA fire to shoot down an attacker from which the crew baled out but could not be saved.

Shortly after dusk enemy activity rapidly increased to become the most widespread for some time, raids from the south-east making landfall over Norfolk and between the Wash and Humber. Glasgow was their main target, but the townsfolk of Yarmouth must surely have concluded otherwise. For the first time an East Anglian town came under sustained heavy bombardment, initially from eight He 111s comprising Raid 83.

A few minutes after midnight incendiaries west of Yarmouth opened the operation, then came a mighty blast when, at 00:32 two parachute mines were released over the north end of the town. They came down in the Collingwood Road area. Luckily, many who dwelt there had already moved to safer places so that, although a great number of houses were very badly damaged, casualties amounted to 'only' two killed and seven injured. The incident was being thoroughly dealt with when an unexpectedly huge load of incendiaries showered down. From the Market Place southwards across the Rows, and along South Quay to Gorleston, they ignited so that within moments the whole southern part of Yarmouth and much of Gorleston seemed to be on fire. Tackling hundreds of small incidents was very hazardous because a fair proportion of the bombs included explosive components. Nevertheless, the task was very courageously tackled by all, but the fires were numerous and some soon assumed huge proportions. Shortly after 02:00, and with local firemen unable to cope, an urgent call was made for brigades at Beccles and Lowestoft to help out. So vast were the fires that by 03:00 desperate pleas went to Cromer and Norwich for further urgent help. While the fires were being attended to, in came more of KG53 dropping incendiaries to extend the burning. Then, on to Southtown Road, two heavy calibre bombs dropped, huge craters halting the passage of urgent traffic between Yarmouth and Gorleston. Luckily, there were enough personnel at Gorleston to cope with the fires, the fighting of which had been made more difficult by broken water mains which greatly reduced levels of pressure in Yarmouth. Even so, good progress in stemming the raging furnaces had been made when, at 05:02, an act of great barbarity was perpetrated. Two mines were parachuted into the burning southern area of Yarmouth. One exploded at the junction of Blackfriars Road and Queen's Road, the other in the highly congested and already blazing Row Area at the southern end of Middlegate Street. The havoc wrought was simply tremendous. In the first blast five special constables were killed when their sub-station felt the enormous effect of a mine blast. In the Rows the second mine produced appalling destruction, so bad that Norwich was desperately asked to send rescue parties.

Raid analysis showed that 65 major fires and 200 smaller had been caused, most fire bombs having been sown over known combustible areas. By next morning the extent of the damage was quite incredible. Boots Chemist's shop, Rose's Fashion Centre, Hill's Restaurant, Johnson's Clothing Factory, Marks and Spencer's, the Museum and Library, Education Offices, Science School and the Seamen's Mission had all been seriously damaged or gutted, so that urgent demolition was called for despite the tired state of the available military and civilian personnel. All had, throughout the raid, shown enormous bravery in fighting fires while shoals of bombs rained upon them. Casualties amounted to seventeen killed and 68 injured, and would have been even higher had not almost half the town been evacuated.

'Human memory is short', wrote Farra Conway, the Town Clerk, in recollection of that horrific night, 'but I shall never forget the appalling sight that Yarmouth presented and, with the additional fires that continually broke out, it seemed that nothing could prevent the destruction of the Town and South Quay.' But when day broke, owing to the untiring efforts of all concerned, all fires were under control and their situation, although bad, was saved from becoming any worse. It was estimated that over 4,000 incendiaries had been dropped.

Not only had the Luftwaffe wrought havoc at Yarmouth, but it had also successfully attacked the BX Plastics factory at Brantham, East Suffolk. Nine of the ten HEs dropped there had exploded, causing extensive damage. Two craters, nearby at Burstall Hall, were of the 45-ft variety — suggesting the use of 250 kg bombs. HEs also fell in Third Avenue, Frinton, at 23:40, damaging a dozen houses. Ju 88 night fighters were active throughout the night as well.

Eight HEs fell in Castlegate St, Harwich at midday on 8 April for no ships were at hand. But if the enemy had little to occupy his time, that was far from true of those working desperately to bring some order back to Yarmouth. They did so, they recall, in many cases with a sense of foreboding which proved well founded. Soon after dusk a hoard of German bombers crossed East Anglia, to and fro, for a share in a six-hour Coventry onslaught. Horsham St Faith was bombed but little damage was caused, while at Yarmouth it was all starting once more.

At 21:30 on 8 April, the raid began with four HEs smashing into the southern end of the Borough. Almost two hours later a second large-scale incendiary attack was launched, clearly directed at buildings along both sides of the River Yare. This time the fires were tackled with even greater alacrity and most were almost immediately extinguished, although there was insufficient time to prevent the Salt Union premises from being burnt out.

At 02:32 the second phase opened with HEs, most of them on the beach at the south end of the town. Ten minutes later, more dropped, this time in the river. The final attack opened at 03:07, proving to be the most damaging. Four HEs which fell on Nelson and Upper Cliff Roads at Gorleston destroyed ten houses and damaged many others. They also killed six and injured five more people. But the fire torture, at least, was not repeated.

Unfortunately, Yarmouth was a town very easy to find, its layout leading to attack along the north-south axis. Thus its misfortune was its geographical position. In addition, there was much sentimentality connected with Yarmouth — the grand scenic railway, the kipper to bring home and literally all the fun of the fair — with two piers thrown in. This combined to make it somewhere very special for many people, a town which the enemy mistakenly might have decided to destroy in some insane bid to lower morale. All that hideous bombing has ever achieved is the strengthening of willpower. Far more productive for the foe was the compelled landing of Wellington *P9230* of 311 Czech Squadron. Pilot Officer Hrnair was instructing a pilot, and the aircraft's lighting was on, when a Ju 88 engaged and fired, forcing a crash landing at West Toft. Bombs on incomplete Bourn airfield — one on the runway, another on a dumper truck — were another reminder that the enemy had good information sources.

The Ninth of April was also the date of a successful attack on Trinity Pier, Harwich. Lying alongside was the *Darcy Cooper*, an Examination Vessel, sunk by a direct hit. All six aboard were lost. Bomb blast also fired the *Marnione*, a supply vessel alongside. Quickly it took on water and began settling by the bows but soon the fire was extinguished and the vessel prevented from sinking, although it was in a very bad state. Casualties aboard the second ship amounted to sixteen. All had been achieved by just two bombs. Three other HEs dropped, one on Harwich football ground, one on a bowling green and one which penetrated the footpath to the railway station without exploding. Another passing enemy aircraft machine-gunned a searchlight post. Four 250 kg HEs were also dropped, near Belstead Road, Ipswich, at 03:00. Casualties by the end of the raids totalled nine killed, thirteen seriously injured and nine slightly.

Apart from usual coastal reconnaissance flights, 9 April was a quiet day — meaning that the omens for the night ahead were not good. Tragically it lived up to expectation, the first notable incident being HEs at 21:15 near Ramsey by the Stour which showed that the enemy was about again. Where the main attack would be it did not take long to discover, for at 21:45 a high-flying Heinkel headed west across Lowestoft unloading about 300 incendiaries over the St

Pauls Street-Beresford Road section of the town and lighting a beckoning beacon. A dozen houses were soon seriously damaged along with the 'Havelock' public house in Cove Road. Much of that area soon suffered worse for at 21:50 the aircraft unloaded hundreds more incendiaries over a large part of Lowestoft. A huge fire immediately engulfed the LNER goods station, Denmark Road had several fires and the social club in Commercial Road was burnt out. Fire raged at the Palace Cinema, and Austin & Wales' wholesale grocery store was burnt out. At County Electrical Services, and at Matthews and Durrant Garage, fires destroyed most of the contents.

Then it was the turn of the German Main Force which hurled its HEs into the fires after the Yarmouth manner. No 25 Cathcart Street, Bevan Cottage in Clapham Road and 78 Milton Road, disappeared into a 45-ft crater caused by a bomb which smashed six more houses and badly damaged another 25, all receiving direct hits from the first salvo. No 152 Raglan Street was yet to go, for the large bomb there did not explode until 22:42 when a 36-ft hole swallowed the house, as was the case with No 107 Clapham Road. Behind No 93, another bomb took away the rear of the house, and Clapham Road 'Co-Op' was damaged by a bomb in Gordon Road. At 10 The Prairie, a small HE exploded on an Anderson Shelter, luckily unoccupied. Dr Boswell's Tudor Lodge disappeared from Surrey Street, and a gigantic hole 50 ft across and 12 ft deep occupied Suffolk Corner at the east end of Denmark Road where fires had earlier been started. All this was merely from the first HE drop.

More incendiaries came at 22:35, over the Stradbroke Road area, but causing less damage than earlier ones. Twenty minutes later a Heinkel delivered ten HEs at the west end of Lowestoft. Again a direct hit was scored on an Anderson Shelter, in the garden of 100 Rotterdam Road. A crater 30 ft by 12 ft deep marked the spot. Another of similar size erupted in the Phillips fish curing yard.

Then came a break in the bombing, but for those who had fought the fires and faced the bombs with — in the words of the official report of the events — 'fearlessness and energy', the night was young. They had, like those in Yarmouth, to contend with high explosive bombs bursting among the very fires they were trying to douse. While they did so how many dared spare a thought for those whom they loved, close at hand or far? For rescue services trying to ensure the injured were found and cared for, the ever present risks were enormous. Some, at least, had recent practice at a task often demoralizing but sometimes so worthwhile. The stench of burning, the clouds of dust, the aroma of wood, masses of smoke, plenty of smashing glass and, for good measure, many unexploded incendiaries, were common features which all, on many nights, came to accept as part of living. How easy life now seems.

That the Heinkels would keep coming was an horrific certainty and they did not disappoint anyone. A few moments past midnight, a bomber from the north scattered six HEs on to Normanton Drive, demolishing 'Skamacre', to the rear of Rotterdam Road's isolation hospital, and hitting the railway line. Ten minutes later six more made short work of Roberts & Son, the Milton Road grocer's. Morlin's Radio and Music Store would provide no more pleasure, and in London Road North, Nos 142 and 144 were destroyed. A quarter of an hour later another ten HEs arrived from a west-east run. This time they hit Stevens Street and Clemence Street. No 194 Denmark Road was demolished and at the same time in a fiery, final gesture, III/KG76 sowed yet another load of incendiaries on to Wollaston Road, Bevan Street, Denmark Road and Flensburgh Street. Stretching the fire services to their limit, an enormous blaze engulfed Eastro's fish yard.

All through, the moon beamed brilliantly on this calm night baring Lowestoft like an unprotected virgin with no means of escape until the 'white' All Clear sounded at 05:25. By comparison with loads released upon London, Birmingham and Coventry, Yarmouth and Lowestoft might seem to have received a small share. But these were much smaller places with limited resources to cope with their traumas. Countless empty buildings were easy to fire, and it must be emphasized that the East Anglian experience was always that it was not the number of bombs which fell that caused the greatest problem, but the positions in which they exploded.

There was another East Anglian town which constantly received Luftwaffe attention — Ipswich, which had been raided while Lowestoft burned. Here, though, mainly high explosives rather than incendiaries were used. The town was under 'Red Alert' from 23:00 to 05:01, during which period HEs fell over a wide area, but mostly around the docks, emphasizing the German intention to neutralize East Coast ports. Being relatively small, and built so much around their harbours, Lowestoft, Yarmouth and Ipswich fared very badly.

The approach in moonlight to Ipswich Docks along the Orwell is well defined, and it was easy for the Luftwaffe to produce scars at Brown's Timber Yard, at Three Cranes Wharf (where a fireman was killed), the Dock Commission yard, Jepson's in Cliff Road, Ransomes & Rapier, Cliff Quay, Lower Orwell Street, Paul's Maltings, Fairfield Road and Pipers Vale. Although fires resulted, the absence of fire bombs in the enemy loads brought nothing like the damage inflicted upon the other ports.

Yarmouth had not escaped further attention for at 00:12 on 10 April two HEs caused damage in Nelson Road, Springfield Road and Lowestoft Road, casualties amounting to two killed and three injured. Later, two more HEs hit the Front, and a further fourteen dropped in a line from the south end of Nelson Road Central to North Drive, one striking the Royal Aquarium but causing minimal damage.

Throughout the night, Ju 88Cs sought RAF aircraft over East Anglia, and next night, 10/11 April, succeeded in destroying one of 11 OTU's Wellington 1s (*L4253*) which was shot down at 00:40 near Ashwell, Hertfordshire. Its Steeple Morden base was subsequently attacked, and the same night Feltwell's No 1 Hangar was set on fire and three craters marred tarmac alongside. That night, Birmingham was the main target but enough other aircraft were available to drop incendiaries at Parkeston Quay, causing a small fire and injuring three. Walton, too, was bombed and at Yarmouth the George Street Row area received another resounding blow from four very large HEs which hit houses, trapping a number of their inmates. One burst upon a communal shelter from which seven bodies were retrieved. Casualties totalled thirteen killed and twelve injured.

Shortly after dawn on 11 April Cromer was bombed by a reconnaissance aircraft which dropped six bombs, the last two, as George Baker recalls, hitting two houses in Runton Road and Alfred Road, killing twelve soldiers billeted in 'Lyndhurst'. In the strange twists of fate so prevalent during air raids, from the very top of a large heap of rubble Brian Durrant picked up an electric light bulb which, despite its experience, continued to do its duty. Three of the bombs shot across tennis courts, and another penetrated the cliffs and lodged there until discovered after the war. What possible value might tennis courts have been in wartime, one might ask? These were serving well, as parking grounds for lorries and Bren gun carriers — few of which happened to be there at the time.

While other large towns in Britain suffered terribly in the night Blitz, enemy activity over East Anglia continued to be mainly coastal. There was ample evidence too that, despite the sharp raids on Yarmouth and Lowestoft, the local bomber effort was declining while more effort was expended against shipping. Late on 13 April an attempt was made to sink trawlers off Lowestoft, and an HE fell at Waveney Dock and two (UX) in the Trawler Dock. Next morning a Ju 88 put two bombs into Harwich Harbour. There, at 04:10, excitement had arisen within 928 Balloon Squadron when a He 111 coming from the north at only 1,000 ft entered the balloon barrage at Site 8 — but it emerged unscathed between balloons 3 and 4! Thereafter activity even seawards declined — perhaps the shock of that crew's passage discouraged others. More likely the continued movement of the long-range bomber force was responsible.

An interesting raid took place on 14 April when, just before 15:00, a Ju 88 at 1,000 ft was discovered obviously engaged on a precision raid. Its target may have been the Unicam Instrument factory in Cambridge, but instead its seven HEs were aimed at Chivers jam factory, Histon, after which the Ju 88 climbed into cloud on a reciprocal course back to the Wash. Shortly before the bombing there was much concern south of Cambridge when a 'He 113' was reported at 1,000 ft heading easterly. Such a type, of course, never ventured over Britain, but there remains the distant possibility that it was a Bf 109 — or more likely an American-built fighter from Duxford.

Further raids on Yarmouth followed, the first between midnight and 05:00 on 16 April during which five attacks were delivered. First came two HEs on the Front, followed by an incendiary shower on to the centre of the town which set two large stores on fire as well as a shop, houses and an office, all of which were extinguished by firewatchers, AFS and police. Two parachute mines then arrived, one exploding on marshes west of the River Bure and the other at Palgrave/Alderson Road junction, to damage many houses. Four HEs then fell at Row 132 and on South Quay before two more burst in Bells Marsh Road, Gorleston, and two very heavy bombs near Crabtree's Yard, Southtown. Rounding off another night of misery in which two people died and nineteen were injured, a raider machine-gunned the town. At about the same time, two HEs in Una Road, Parkeston, demolished two houses killing two and injuring two. A further five people were trapped for some time in the wreckage. Out to sea, where III/KG77 was currently boosting the effort, KG30 had been busy mine laying.

Beccles Road, Gorleston, received a salvo of eight HEs early on the 17th, the night seeing a delivery of German propaganda leaflets which, unfortunately for the 'postman', scattered uselessly on marshland near North Cove, Suffolk. A determined attempt was made at around 04:00 to bomb Bawdsey, six HEs and three incendiary loads falling quite close to the radar station.

Repeated attacks on Lowestoft and Yarmouth had begun to produce prudence to the extent that many residents were sleeping away from the ports. Some went nightly to friends, and from Bradwell and Burgh additional buses brought them to work. Most were seeking temporary respite, and with good reason for, at 05:19, a group of five aircraft flying very low over Yarmouth dropped eight very heavy bombs, two on the Coronation-Elsie Roads district, Cobholm, causing serious damage. Twelve people were killed, thirteen injured, three of whom were in an Anderson Shelter which almost received a direct hit.

Dovercourt was also rocked by a deafening blast when, at 04:12 on the 17th, two parachute mines landed on the foreshore, at New Hall Farm and Brookman's Farm, damaging a number of buildings.

Occasions upon which enemy aircraft were even glimpsed when about their business were relatively few despite the number of incursions. Those brought down were often found as almost unrecognizable strewn wreckage, like Ju 88A-5 W Nr *5131:3Z+BS* of 3./KG77 which crashed in unravelled circumstances at 21:23 on 17 April at Hurns Farm, Thorney, near Ely. Markings had been entirely over-painted, and whilst no battle damage was found the aircraft appeared to have been on fire when it dived in vertically to bury itself deep in wet ground.

Should the raider be flying, a brief glimpse was usually all one had, but not at Harwich at lunchtime on 20 April. In and out of cloud could be seen an astonishing procession of Heinkel 111s of III/KG4 from Soesterberg, possibly as many as eight being chased out to sea and dropping bombs in the harbour as they fled from fighters. In circumstances unknown, *5J+IR* never reached home.

Suffolk was now bearing the brunt of enemy activity against East Anglia. At 22:05 next night, at Hobland Hall, Bradwell, a container of incendiaries was quickly followed by a giant explosion caused by a bomb producing a crater 40 ft wide by 20 ft deep. Then, as Stradishall's Wellingtons were landing back from Cologne, a Ju 88 joined the circuit to crater the active runway.

If those taking refuge from Lowestoft raids were having second thoughts they need not have done so, for at 21:41 the Luftwaffe opened another fire raid on the town. Again, a high level fire raiser opened the operation, distributing incendiaries over the Stradbroke Road-Pakefield Street-London Road South area. Four huge fires were lit at stores in Walmer Road to The Avenue, mainly among fishing gear. Thatch on the roof of Pakefield church caught fire, followed by most of the church, and a bungalow in Walmer Road was destroyed. A second incendiary load was distributed over the Lorne Park-Richmond Road-Claremont Road-Kirkley Cliff area.

Activity during the last week of April 1941 took on a slightly different look for the enemy was re-organizing his anti-shipping campaign. Evidence of activity over Suffolk attracted the attention of the crew of an 85 Squadron Debden-based Havoc late on 24 April. As Squadron Leader Wheller and Flying Officer Maton in *VY:A* fired upon a Ju 88, their aircraft was hit by return fire. Over Stradishall the Havoc pilot fired once more, damaging the raider. Flying Officer Evans and Sergeant Corton (*VY:D*) raked an He 111 off Felixstowe without making any claim.

During this period operations were much reduced, although intruder activity at Bassingbourn soon after midnight on 24 April was spectacular when Wellington *N2912* was shot down and crashed on to *R1404* which was on a dispersal. Two Ju 88s in the early hours of 26 April damaged water mains and a hangar at Marham, cratering the airfield and causing returning bombers to divert to Honington, where the Q-Site again effectively attracted another eight bombs. Horrific was the bombing of Horning 'Ferry Inn' at 21:46 on 27/28 April in which 22 died. Among those killed was 222 Squadron's Flight Lieutenant B.

Left *Enormous damage was inflicted upon Yarmouth in April 1941, as this picture of Middlegate Street following the raid of the 8th/9th shows.*

Left *There is not the slightest doubt that Their Majesties King George VI and Queen Elizabeth cared very, very deeply for the victims of air raids. The visits they made to quite awful scenes needed special courage and were great morale boosters. Here, the King talks to Yarmouth's Chief Constable in Middlegate Street, Yarmouth, on 25 April 1941.*

von Mentz who had tried hard on a number of occasions to drive away the foe. The squadron's Adjutant, H.P. Robertson, also died, alongside the Medical Officer. It was suggested that exposed lights attracted attention — and might have been mistaken for RAF Coltishall. Three bombs had been dropped, from 500 ft and probably from a Ju 88C.

At dusk on 27 April, Squadron Leader Tuck (*Z3152*) of 257 Squadron poured cannon fire into the wing root of a Ju 88 attempting to bomb shipping off Yarmouth. His aim, however, was not to the normal standard because AA guns were firing and their flashes all but blinded him. Next evening another Ju 88 in the same area attacked trawlers. Earlier, 257 Squadron had come near to bagging a He 111 when Pilot Officer Kay (*Z3070*) and Pilot Officer Cowen (*Z3175*) intercepted it over Yarmouth, firing only as it escaped into cloud. The squadron had received cannon-armed Hurricane IIcs mid-April. Yarmouth endured five more attacks in April, during which 35 HEs were dropped, twenty at the south end of the town and in Gorleston High Street during the evening of 23 April.

Rounding off the month quite daringly, Epro Gruppe 210's Messerschmitt Bf 110s once more ventured into East Anglia off whose shores they had recently been working. Three approached Martlesham aerodrome from the north-east, line abreast, at 1,000 ft at 21:18 on 29 April, each performing a cheeky pass and dropping a 250 kg bomb. They had followed a landing Hurricane, and the first bomb burst in 'B' Flight dispersal, wrecking a Hurricane and damaging three others. The second bomb exploded close to a house in RAF hands and the third overshot into Ipswich Borough. Hardly an effective performance, it highlighted the vulnerability of fringe targets to low-flying surprise raiders. That feature the Luftwaffe often exploited.

The first ten days of May 1941 brought the Luftwaffe's night campaign against the British Isles to its climax. It was an almost final, furious, desperate gesture. Within days many aircrews who had found their way through the clouds over the eastern counties were heading for their part in the German onslaught upon the USSR.

Since the effort was now mostly against large towns, East Anglians watched mainly from the sidelines. There was, however, a noticeable change in intruder activity with RAF night fighter bases receiving particular attention as the Luftwaffe decided their activities must now be curbed. The British were equally concerned about German intruders currently having more success. On 1 May authorization was given for the formation of a mobile AA force under the 'Scarecrow Scheme'. One of two batteries would spend a few days at a vulnerable airfield, then move its four 20 mm cannon and four .303-in guns to another site. After ten days four raiders had been engaged successfully, so the scheme was extended. Two mobile searchlight Troops were now to follow, and mobility of guns was increased so that they could give cover to active flare paths.

Nevertheless, East Anglia's airfields continued to suffer, six HEs and ten explosive incendiaries falling from a Ju 88, flying at 300 ft, on to Waterbeach's dispersals at 23:05 on 2 May. Possibly the same aircraft proceeded to Oakington, following 7 Squadron Stirling *N6012* upon which it fired as the large bomber lowered its undercarriage. Soon it was burning and hit trees as it approached over Dry Drayton. Flight Lieutenant Cruickshank and crew were all killed.

On the same day a Ju 88 came down intact on Welney Wash. Its arrival was due to double engine failure during a Liverpool raid. Three of the crew of Ju 88A-5 W Nr *4269* (originally *DE+ES* and now *3Z+CL*) of I/KG77 had baled out, leaving the pilot to crash land and destroy the aircraft, which he was unable to do.

Early on 3 May fifteen HEs fell on Lowestoft. Among those operating was Ju 88A-5 W Nr *8180:4D+BH* of 1/KG30. Flying high at 23,000 ft, it skirted the north of the Wash and near Skegness was fired upon, almost certainly by a Defiant of 151 Squadron. Although there was no evidence of battle damage, the Ju 88's port engine lost power and the compass went haywire, so the weapon load was jettisoned and the pilot turned south. Over Norfolk the starboard engine stopped and the crew decided to belly land on Sheringham's shore. Their capture brought a great surprise for the gunner was a 53-year-old Major making his first operational flight, so his possession of the Iron Cross 2nd Class award was, to say the least, surprising. Asked how he had spent his time he replied, 'Signing "Ausweise"' (identity cards)!

Although shipping off Cromer was attacked late in the evening of 3 May, a trawler being sunk and one badly damaged, there was more concentration than before around Harwich where Cliff Road, Dovercourt, was bombed. At 23:34 a bomb demolished a Harwich home, trapping three people and injuring others. Further bombs hit the railway track to Parkeston. Only after three days could rescue workers remove those killed from the shattered houses, a most arduous duty. Losses had not apparently been one-sided, though. Around 22:00 Flying Officer Hemmingway and Sergeant Bailey in an 85 Squadron Havoc (*VY-P*) engaged a raider near Halesworth, probably a He 111H of KG26, which crashed in the sea three miles off Dunwich. About the same time Flight Lieutenant Marshall and Sergeant Hollett (*VY-R*) engaged another He 111 in the same area.

For Norfolk residents, 4 May was another night of excitement. Heinkel 111s of KG53 were operating, and at 21:00 W Nr *3235:AI+LL* belonging to 3./KG53 set off from northern France to bomb Liverpool. After unloading, it made for the Wash over which it was suddenly raked by machine-gun fire, in a classic attack — for which it had been designed — from a Boulton Paul Defiant turret fighter of 151 Squadron operating from Coltishall. Bullets poured into the Heinkel's underside and the wireless operator was killed instantly, shot through the chest. Oil loss caused the Heinkel's port engine to heat dramatically, then the other engine lost power, giving the crew no choice but to belly land the aircraft, which came down at Brinton, near Holt, at 01:04. Immediately, the crew dragged their dead companion from the Heinkel which they promptly set on fire. Then they burnt their documents and were nearly eight miles away before capture. Talking of their dead colleague, they related to interrogators how terrified of night fighters the dead man had been, and that all too often he would scream through the intercom that they were being followed when such was not the case.

From PoWs it was deduced that improved RAF night fighting techniques were causing the Luftwaffe concern, making deep penetration more dangerous and forcing it to route bombers over water where possible — hence that of the KG53 Heinkel. Thus, continuance of raids upon the east coast gave no surprise, and at 22:40 on 4 May a sharp attack was made upon Ipswich. Eighteen 250 kg bombs fell, making this a very noisy and quite severe onslaught. Four bombs landed on Cranes', two each in Christchurch Park, on Crane Hill Farm, in the Orwell, Elmhurst Drive and Hall. Single bombs were dropped on Westerfield Road, Park Road — killing a man and woman, Salisbury Road and Nacton Road where two more people in a shelter were also killed.

Total exposure of the private world of home in Unthank Road, Norwich, on 5 May 1941 (Eastern Daily Press).

Above left *Problems for any business following bombing were considerable. Here, the staff search for documents at the smashed High Street premises of a Lowestoft accountant* (Ford Jenkins Photography).

Above right *Even a steel framed building like Lowestoft's Woolworth's could not defeat 5 May 1941's incendiaries* (Ford Jenkins Photography).

A high proportion of 4/5 May activity was again over Norfolk, Ju 88Cs aiming HEs at West Raynham, East Wretham and Great Massingham. Four HEs fell near the Happisburgh Coast Guard Station. Wittering, Watton, Coltishall and Martlesham Heath were also subjected to intruder attention, but it was Debden that experienced the smartest of these raids. At 01:25 a low flier raced across the aerodrome, fired the correct identity colours, flashed its landing lights, made a mock approach and flared out at a mere 15 ft to become momentarily visible in the airfield's Chance light. Immediately it climbed and slipped behind a Hurricane on circuit upon which it opened fire, then in a parting gesture raked the airfield during a low pass.

Clacton too had been bombed, three HEs falling at 22:47 on Gorse Lane. Yet again the enemy was warned about over-confidence, for 25 Squadron's Beaufighters had twice fired upon raiders over Norfolk, near Watton and Attleborough. Anti-aircraft gunners, too, had their successes, as proven by the arrival of Ju 88A-5 W Nr *6027:3Z+EC* soon after 04:00 on 5 May off Waxham, Norfolk. It had left Schiphol at 22:42 for Belfast, anti-aircraft fire on the English west coast putting the port engine out of action. Bombs were jettisoned and the crew headed for base, albeit it with most instrumentation out of use. Trying instead to land on the shore, they hit sand dunes and the aircraft broke up, injuring three of the crew and killing one. Out to sea, though, it was a different story. During the night — when nearly 400 sorties had been directed against the UK — seven ships had been attacked and one was left sinking.

Enemy night intruders again operated on 6/7 May, attacking Oakington, where five HEs fell on the airfield, Methwold where a Wellington was set on fire, Bircham Newton, Great Massingham and particularly Feltwell, where, at 23:57, incendiaries fell along with three HEs, setting an aircraft ablaze. Wellington *R3227* was at 02:10 shot down on approach to Bassingbourn while at 03:01 a Ju 88C glided towards Wittering to attack a landing Beaufighter, the second such attack.

More attacks upon airfields occurred on 7/8 May, during one of which eight HEs were misplaced across Fakenham. Wittering again came under particular attack, a Ju 88C, orbiting for over thirty minutes at 10,000 ft before diving to 800 ft and dropping eight HEs, one of which killed four men and injured eight others in a barrack block. Unusual was the use of oil bombs, four of which were deposited, harmlessly, at Gissing, Norfolk. At Stowmarket about 100 incendiaries were dropped plus three HEs. For night fighters it proved another rewarding night when, at 22:20, a Hurricane of 257 Squadron shot down off Lowestoft a Schiphol-based Ju 88A of 2. Gr106. Later, He 111 5*J+CB* of KG4 was engaged off Felixstowe by Flying Officer Snell and Sergeant Cummings in *VY-V*, an 85 Squadron Havoc. Another 85 Squadron crew, Flying Officer Hemmingway and Sergeant Bailey (*VY-P*), damaged a HE 111 over Mildenhall at 23:30. Perhaps the most interesting battle was over the Wash between a 25 Squadron Beaufighter and what was claimed to be a Do 17Z. The possibility of this gave added credence to the news that I/KG3 had recently come from Germany to Le Culot, and that III/KG3 was installed at Chievres. Merville, KG2's old lair, was currently the home of at least part of Erpro Gruppe 210's Bf 110s.

On 8/9 May Wittering's night fighters again attracted Luftwaffe attention. Two Ju 88s were involved, the first gliding in to put ten HEs and a few incendiaries among dispersals, killing one airman and damaging two Beaufighters. A second intruder later placed five bombs close to the watch office, in an attempt to disrupt night fighting. Bombs were also dropped on Oakington and Honington aerodromes. Bombers were active off Norfolk where an interesting and relatively unusual feature was a procession of Heinkel 111s of III/KG26 crossing the coast over Lowestoft. Heinkels of another unit operated over East Anglia that night — one was damaged at 00:10 by an 85 Squadron Havoc (*VY-K*) off Felixstowe — and were responsible for dropping incendiaries and four HEs in Railway Street and Coldham's Lane, Cherry Hinton, at 00:45 on the 9th; and at 01:50 delivered a very sharp incendiaries-only attack over much of southern Cambridge.

Two targets there presented themselves, the rail complex and more fleetingly a large array of Army vehicles which were for some weeks parked along the sides of most of the streets between Hills Road and Mowbray Road. Troops of the 27th Lancers attending them were billeted with families in many of the houses alongside, an uncommon feature. Presumably the Army presence attracted the Heinkels, which carried out a very accurate attack using exclusively 1 kg incendiaries. Showered over the Coleridge Ward-Hills Road area roughly in the triangle between Hills Road Bridge-Mowbray Road-Worts Causeway, with spillovers on to Brooklands Avenue and Newton Road, the bombs started fires in fifty houses, but most were quickly subdued although not without bringing residents uneasy moments.

Mrs Pickford was in bed at 58 Marshall Road. Being deaf, aged and resilient, she like many more took a chance and slept on during the 'alert' in her upstairs bed. The proximity of the railway meant that many living in this section of Cambridge were supplied with Morrison Shelters, but they were not necessarily occupied whenever the siren sounded! And so it was at 58 Marshall Road.

Fire bombs were generally delivered in oblong containers, commonly called 'Molotov breadbaskets', designed to burst open shortly after release allowing the incendiaries to spread with slightly forward trajectory. Realization of their falling came from a widespread clatter as they smashed tiles and slates. Often they penetrated ceilings, and usually burst in the first upstairs room. Unfortunately for those staying in bed, the incendiary could land on the eiderdown with a thump and burst into life showering brilliant sparks, spewing masses of greyish smoke and creating a foul smell. That almost happened at No 58. Mrs Pickford not surprisingly left her bedroom somewhat hastily when she found an incendiary bomb which had bounced off a mirror and landed on her bed, although fortunately it did not ignite.

At No 26 Marshall Road another incendiary landed on a wardrobe top, and again was promptly tackled. What amazed the residents of the street, where quite a number of bombs were burning, was that, as they were tackled in the broad moonlight, a warden was shouting to his fellow citizens to 'put that light out!'.

Bombs were burning brilliantly on Mowbray Road, on the pavements and in the houses. From No 20 Mrs Rayner, her husband away in London's Fire Service, was advised to leave with her young daughter. That meant a dash through the bombs burning, converting the street into a frightening spectacle. Such personal moments of alarm were for many in East Coast towns almost a daily feature of wartime life.

Despite their quantity, most of the incendiaries were soon extinguished. Holes in the roofs of houses in Blinco Grove marked entry points. Others had fallen in the grounds of the large house now known as 100 Blinco Grove, and which in recent years has served as a school annexe offering an idyllic learning environment. Others burnt themselves out in Morley Memorial School playground, but at Nos 8 and 10 Cavendish Avenue, and 224 and 226 Hills Road, fires were serious enough to warrant visits by the fire service even though damage was limited. The worst was at Homerton College where a number of bombs in the high roof of the main hall quickly set fire to many timbers after the manner of the Perse School blaze. By the time the NFS arrived much of the roof was burning, and had later to be rebuilt. No other Cambridge residents had that problem, but instead they had to cope with clouds of grey ash produced by burnt thermite. Everything in affected rooms, often beyond, looked as if a volcanic eruption had taken place. But cleaning the house after the incendiaries was a wartime chore — often repeated because the annoying little blighters did strike twice!

Simultaneous with the Cambridge raid had come other sharp attacks, yet again, on Ipswich and Yarmouth, the likelihood being that KG26 was responsible overall. These two raids were unusual for the inclusion of heavier calibre HEs, also evident in April's attacks on Yarmouth and Lowestoft. The Ipswich raid began at 00:15, lasted 25 minutes, and embraced very mixed loads, all of which were directed on to the docks flanking the River Orwell. Four 250 kg HEs fell in meadows of the Orwell Lodge, Belstead Road, a dairy farm west of the Ipswich-Colchester main rail line and killed a Jersey cow and six chickens. Two bombs fell close to craters caused on 4 May, in front of 17 and 19 Beech Grove, and to the rear of 27 Cliff Lane. Another four 250 kg HEs dropped in a line a quarter of a mile long across a Corporation housing estate and the main road leading to the dock area, scoring a direct hit on No 20 Bonington Road, killing four people and demolishing four other houses. Like those on the farm, all these 250 kg weapons had a marked splinter effect. Craters in the gardens of Nos 44 and 55 Fletcher Road, and in Raeburn Road, were made by 50 kg bombs. Throughout the bombing Heinkels passed over the dock region delivering eight loads each of about 280 1 kg incendiaries. Woodland west of Ipswich airfield, and Nightingale Road, where Nos 19 and 24 were damaged, suffered. The highlights, though, were the two 500 kg bombs. One may have included a delaying device for not until 03:40 did it explode, on the airfield's west side. Messrs Fison, Packard and Prentice felt the tremendous power of the other which scored a stunning hit on their acid store situated near the higher land at the south end of Cliff Quay. By bursting on the girder-supported roof, it blew away the stanchions and seriously shook the building. A medium fire was started and spread to the sulphur store. On to this and the wreckage around, more incendiaries were unloaded.

Casualties totalled four killed, nine injured. Four houses were completely destroyed, three more were later demolished, fifteen were seriously damaged and eighteen had to be evacuated. Another 465 houses suffered various degrees of damage.

Harwich, like Yarmouth, was also attacked the same night, firstly at 23:20 when ten HEs fell on waste ground. A further nineteen HEs fell near Ramsey church, and an hour later incendiaries and an HE landed in Fonts Road, Dovercourt. After a pause, more HEs and incendiaries came at 04:03 and had a considerable effect. Falling in George Street, they set fire to Bernard's clothing factory. Subsequent demolition of houses nearby resulted in twenty families being made homeless. Casualties amounted to fifteen injured.

As Harwich was raided so Clacton was bombed with 250 kg bombs, two of which hit Pier Avenue and the A133 road east of Grosvenor Road. Extensive damage affected Barclays Bank and shops.

Yarmouth was bombed three times between 00:31 and 01:51. First came ten HEs north of the Borough, damaging Churchill Road Rescue Depot and the Isolation Hospital. Second came a stick of eight HEs, including some 250 kg bombs, dropped at Mill Road, Cobholm, causing much damage to houses, a post office, a small furniture store which caught light, two public houses and a saw mill. The third attack was directed at a small beached vessel which the enemy persistently bombed. Casualties at Yarmouth amounted to six killed and ten injured. It had been one of the busiest nights for East Anglia's Civil Defence workers, facing some of the 280 bombers known to have operated against Britain.

German night fighters were particularly active, and Wittering was attacked for the fourth night in succession, one Ju 88C orbiting the station for forty minutes. Responding Bofors crews fired off 57 rounds before the enemy left, to drop four HEs at Peterborough where two people were killed.

Not surprisingly, the following night's activity showed the enemy mainly resting. Bombs were dropped at Colchester, a Havoc of 85 Squadron fired at a Ju 88 25 miles east of Cromer, and at Norwich at 02:27 four HEs fell without causing casualties. At 03:30 25 Squadron claimed the destruction of a HE 111 over the Wash.

Analysis showed that 121 airfield attacks had been carried out between the Humber and the Stour since 1 February, 32 by day and seventeen against fighter airfields — twelve since 10 April. On nights when the bomber effort was less, though, NJG2 still attempted to disturb bomber stations. By mid-May enough was known to enable an outline of the activities of the intruders to be drawn up. Some mystique always surrounded their raids. Aboard a Ju 88C brought down on 8/9 April, which had set off from Gilze Rijen at 20:00, was a mixed load of 50 kg HEs and incendiaries. After crossing Lowestoft it headed for Leicester, but near Oakham a Beaufighter using cannon at extreme range delivered a mortal blow to both the Ju 88 and its pilot, and badly wounded the bomb aimer. Only slightly injured, the radio operator baled out, losing his boots on the way down before landing in a field. Quickly he buried his radio and notebook (later recovered) and walked in stockinged feet to Langham. He later recounted how a passing soldier bade him 'goodnight', and that a crossing gate attendant had opened the gates so that he could go on his way. Others just ignored him until he enquired the way to the police station. He was told to wait, and within a few moments was in Home Guard custody.

Pooled intelligence information showed that NJG2 was indeed a specialized organization under General Khumhuber's Flieger Division 10. Expansion of NJG2 was coming along slowly, Major Branck appointed to increase its strength having only formed five Staffeln. The fifth was quickly removed to create the basis of home defence NJG3. Pilots of NJG2 made some extraordinarily inflated claims relating to RAF aircraft shot down, the ace of the 3rd Staffel laying an impossible claim of twelve. Hauptmann Hultzow was still commanding I/NJG2 and effectively the whole unit. The 4th Staffel, from which the latest arrival came, was under Oberleutnant Bohn. Its fourteen aircraft and slightly fewer crews concentrated on training others, although every crew of three men would rely very much upon their personal tactics. They were given a free hand for a given time in one of four fighting zones over England drawn up by the Gruppe intelligence staff. Usually they patrolled just below cloud base, operations generally taking place when that was between 200 and 9,000 ft, although preference was for a low base of around 6-700 ft.

Patrols extended inland to about 100 miles searching for aircraft in flight. On making a sighting an attempt would be made to close to about 600 ft to assess the situation, then the fighter would move in even to 150 ft before firing, hopefully in surprise and often when a bomber, its crew weary, was landing after an operation. Cannon were fired only when it was impossible to close the range. Rarely was a direct astern attack made, for a bomber's turret guns could in a second destroy the attacker. Tactics had changed over the months and by April 1941 incendiary loads were common and used both to illuminate airfields and to fire targets prior to strafing with machine-guns.

Take-off, anything from every ten to thirty minutes, involved three or four aircraft. A similar number would be despatched about an hour and a half later, flights lasting five hours so that at one time as many as sixteen Ju 88Cs could be active. Usual patrol time was about four hours, permitting three operations on many nights. Following take-off, climb was made to about 10,000 ft, the patrol being controlled by the radio station/beacon at Schouwen. Course would then be set, transit height being anything between 3,500 and 13,000 ft, but on return the Dutch coast would be crossed below 3,300 ft for safety.

An interesting feature was the armament variation in the Ju 88Cs. The Terrington example had three machine-guns and a cannon fixed in the nose, while one which crashed at Market Deeping, Lincolnshire, had two nose cannon, forcing deletion of the rear under gun. Another variation was two 20 mm cannon and a 15 mm cannon, all fixed in the nose.

To aid the night's intruders the Luftwaffe monitored British radio chatter and by mid-afternoon enough had been heard to know whether operations would be on that night. With British airfield call signs and frequencies known, all that was left to discover was the recognition signal of the day, which was radioed to base as soon as observed. In so doing, though, the intruder risked a D/F plot being obtained, revealing his whereabouts.

Chapter 17
Towards a respite

London's heaviest raid occurred on 10/11 May 1941 when, in brilliant moonlight, the Luftwaffe despatched much of its strength, over 350 bombers, against the Capital. Although unrealized at the time, it was indeed a bass chord sounding the finale of massive night raids which East Anglia had mercifully missed. Forthwith, there would be increased 'novelty' in the air assault.

East Anglia endured few daylight attacks by bomber formations because it lay beyond the effective combat range of the Messerschmitt Bf 109 escort fighter. But IF the fighter carried a long range tank, and avoided battle, it could just reach Norfolk, certainly Suffolk. Proof of that potential was displayed on the evening of 11 May when, at 21:45 and literally at roof top height, a yellow-nosed Bf 109F of JG51 roared along Aldeburgh's front, firing its machine-guns and distributing chippings into 'Brudenells' Hotel where Miss Iris Denny was injured. Blue Section, 257 Squadron, was already after another three Bf 109s which strafed Oulton Broads before the Aldeburgh attack. Evidence of the confusion engendered is illustrated by the fact that Coltishall's Operations Controller stated that the '109s were at 15,000 ft instead of 150! Slightly earlier, seventeen Bf 109Fs had dived from such a height on to Rochford, possibly promoting confusion. Many an East Anglian had endured strafing, but not previously by a single-seat fighter; that was quite novel, heralding new techniques, some due to expediency, for the war was changing direction.

On 12 May '109s came again, very low and in force, in an effort that showed hallmarks of considered attack. Out to sea three Bf 109s awaited RAF response while two of their colleagues strafed Southwold. Concentrating fire along North Parade, their shots notched a number of buildings used as Servicemen's billets. At the 'Craighurst' Hotel the porter received thigh injuries, and a house was damaged in Dunwich Road. The heavy thump of cannon fire was also heard as heavy rounds ricocheted along the Parade. Such attacks were extremely frightening; couple them with bombing and they would be extremely physically and mentally damaging. For the moment, though, night raids were the norm — with the worst yet to come.

Around the Clacton area at 03:16 on 11 May, the last night of the 'big blitz', incendiaries fired a number of evacuated houses, and St Michael's Church was damaged. Eleven HEs were dropped around Great Holland and Frinton, but it was Walton-on-the-Naze where the most serious event took place when two parachute mines fell, one in the sea, the other in a boating lake, without

'The Craighurst', on Southwold's North Parade, once a hotel and now self-catering flats, holds the unwanted distinction of being one of the very few East Anglian buildings to have been fired upon by a Messerschmitt 109 which strafed it on 12 May 1941.

exploding. Residents of over 100 houses around the High Street had to evacuate the street rapidly for at any moment the mine was likely to explode. Fortunately, neither did, and that ashore was made safe next day. Not long before the bombing, Havoc *VY:E* flown by Flight Lieutenant Raphael and AC1 Addison found a He 111 going north-east from London and destroyed it near Chelmsford.

Night intruders were also active again, visiting Waterbeach and Oakington to deliver incendiary raids as well as Feltwell where No 1 Hangar suffered a direct hit. It was empty and the fire was soon extinguished, but craters needed filling.

Early on 12 May intruder Ju 88s were once more in action, making three bombing attacks on Marham and raiding West Raynham, Stradishall, Waterbeach (where a dozen bombs burst by the perimeter track), Oakington (where a Stirling was damaged) and Marham, whose Sergeants' Mess suffered badly along with the Equipment and MT Sections, three Wellingtons and an Oxford. Bodney was attacked, and Watton, where AA defences scored a bull's eye, crippling a Ju 88A which crashed on Rectory Farm, Scoulton, at 01:45. Three of the crew were killed, the other taken prisoner. Among the bent metal the aircraft's rear fuselage was found, marked *EM* in small characters.

While Watton's defenders celebrated, Yarmouth was again a centre of Luftwaffe interest. Between 00:48 and 03:43 six attacks were made, during which 38 HEs fell upon the town. Although only two people were injured, widespread damage involved the Trawl Market, Yacht Station, Addison Road, Beaconsfield Road, Cemetery Lane, Caister Road, Highfield Road, Northgate Street and Westbrook Avenue.

Ipswich, too, was attacked, HEs severing its rail link with Felixstowe and falling in Campbell Road, Nacton Road and Rydal Walk. Incendiaries burnt in Kingsway, Bantoft Terrace and Howe Avenue. At Southwold a raid at 03:02

brought more damage than might be expected. Four HEs in the town centre caused casualties in York Road, two bombs fell in St Edmunds Gardens and one at the rear of No 26 High Street, damaging Nos 6 and 30. Southwold Cinema was damaged, one house demolished, twelve seriously damaged and another 85 affected. Three people were injured.

The night of 11/12 May gave proof of improving defences, however. Difficult as it remained for a single-seat fighter without radar to find an enemy bomber at night, Squadron Leader Stanford Tuck (*Z3070*) took off at 23:15 to try his luck and near Sheringham inconclusively engaged a Ju 88. Twenty minutes later he intercepted another Ju 88 and, after receiving two bursts from 200 yd, with its starboard wing burning, the bomber crashed in the sea. Flight Lieutenant Blatchford, too, flew a night patrol. After chasing two enemy aircraft he came across a He 111 arriving from the east. First he fired an engine, then the fuselage and soon that too was burning on the water. Later, 25 Squadron damaged a He 111 near West Raynham and Flying Officer Carnaby with Flying Officer Cordingly in Havoc *VY-D* were credited with a probable Ju 88 off Felixstowe. Records suggest that two Ju 88A-5s were destroyed, for by dawn W Nr *5168: F1+BS* of 3./KG76 was missing from Leeuwarden and *6203:M2+DL* of 3./Gr106 from Schiphol.

Already, there were indications of change. Whereas around 230 bombers were tracked over Britain on 11/12 May, the number fell dramatically to about sixty on the 12th/13th when Wittering's guns damaged a Ju 88 and eight HEs at Hunstanton injured three people and damaged over 120 houses.

A similar amount of night activity occurred over the whole of Britain on each of the ensuing seven days. At sea, however, interest in East Coast convoys continued to be displayed with a burst of activity by KG4's He 111s (challenged three times unsuccessfully by 222 Squadron's Spitfires on the afternoon of 14 May) and resulting at 14:10 in the sinking of the *M.A. West* off Yarmouth. Bombs twice fell in the Yarmouth area, seven in the sea, and in the early evening at Blackwell Reach, Gorleston. At night on the 15th 25 Squadron again claimed a He 111 off Cromer, but Squadron Leader Pleasance had to nurse his Beaufighter (*T4634*) back to base with an engine damaged by return fire. More HEs later fell at Gorleston and off Yarmouth.

Twice in the early hours of 16 May Yarmouth was subjected to attack, a stick of ten HEs extending from Cemetery Lane to Balill Road, Gorleston, while others exploded in the sea. Further attacks on the evening of 24 May brought damage to Great Yarmouth Hospital Nurses' Home and houses in Alexandra Road and St George's Park. Certainly the intensity and style of attack was changing, though. On 17 May an unusual evening fighter sweep off Essex involved about 100 Bf 109s from the Pas de Calais, as two Ju 88s operated off Brightlingsea without bombing. A raid on Southwold the same day using incendiaries and HEs (all UX) was, however, of the 'traditional' type.

Untraditional, and rare, was the delivery to Norwich late on 17 May of two enormous 2,500 kg HEs, of which only four were ever brought to East Anglia. (The other two landed in the Isle of Ely.) Both came down on waste ground near Lakenham Swimming Baths, on the edge of Norwich. Roofs and windows of over 400 houses were torn apart by blast. But by just how much the bombing offensive was to be reduced was evidenced by the fact that only one more bomb exploded in Norwich in the next 11½ months.

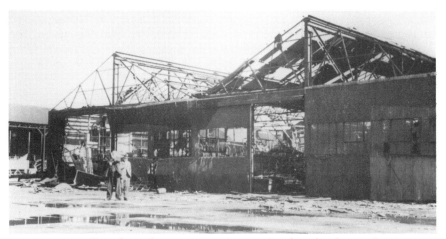

Among Lowestoft's industrial premises was Eastern Coachworks, damaged on 24 May 1941 (Ford Jenkins Photography).

Harwich, too, was subjected to the blast from a powerful weapon on May 17, probably a Type 'G' mine (only eight fell in Region 4) which hit an ordnance store damaging ARP buildings and vehicles nearby. Blast damage was widespread, casualties totalling 34. Distributed along the foreshore were pieces of the bakelized-paper tail unit of this mine variant which resembled in appearance a conventional HE bomb. Yet again, this was a sort of hefty parting shot; only five more bombing incidents involved Harwich before January 1943.

Because of its close proximity to RAF West Raynham, Fakenham received the residue of some attacks upon that airfield. Nearly always it involved incendiaries which were extinguished before they could cause much harm. The Airfield Repair Depot on the northern side of the town received similar attention, and the only bomb damage the town can claim as its own was caused on the night of 18 May 1941. About 01:30 a lone bomber, thought to have been fleeing from night fighters, dropped nine bombs on Fakenham, very close to the town centre. One fell near Mrs Needs' house in Queens Road, four in Lover's Lane, two in Church Yard, one on the old Wesleyan Chapel (used then by the Salvation Army) and one on the opposite side of Oak Street in front of the Rectory. The Salvation Army was instantly without a home for the Chapel was totally demolished. Superficial damage was caused to adjacent property, but there were no civilian casualties.

Even shipping attacks declined. Erpro Gruppe 210 had recently participated, and lost an aircraft off Felixstowe — credited to Yarmouth's guns — on 19 May. Minelaying was reduced when Ju 88s of II/KG30 moved to Scandinavia late in May, but at the same time back came our old adversaries, KG2, the 'Hochhammer' Kampfgeschwader, returning from the Balkans to resume service in north-west Europe. About two months later it completely re-equipped with Dornier Do 217Es.

The German invasion of the USSR necessitated the use of as many long-range bombers as possible. Involvement in the Balkans campaign, and North Africa, drew off much of the bomber force from attacking Britain, and RAF day raids on northern Europe meant that fighter-bomber forays against fringe targets needed to be restricted as Bf 109s went on to the defensive. But two facets of the Luftwaffe's air war would linger, the almost nightly intruder missions by NJG2 and the anti-shipping campaign including that against East Coast convoys. When no trace of the latter could be found, loads continued to be unloaded upon coastal targets.

Yarmouth received 77 HEs and was attacked nine times in June 1941, and additionally was subjected to two small scale incendiary attacks. Only one raid took place in daylight, at 13:38 on 15 June when seven HEs were scattered over Gorleston's High Street and Western Road. At 02:05 on 23 June, firebombs fell at Newtown, setting houses ablaze and damaging Smith's Potato Crisp factory. Three times Yarmouth was raided on 24 June, twenty HEs exploding in the harbour mouth and 22, along with 200 incendiaries, falling in south-west Gorleston. The final phase brought eight HEs across the River Yare between Gorleston and Southtown where the gasworks retort house and PCB Wharf suffered serious damage. Yarmouth remained a regular target, whereas Clacton, a garrison town without a port, was only six times attacked between June and the end of the year.

Shipping north of Cromer attracted the bombers on 2/3 June, a repeat following next night, and on 4 June Sergeant Gigny flying Beaufighter *R2157* of 25 Squadron engaged a He 111 over the Wash. Far less likely adversaries appeared on 11 June, when a highly surprising, fast strike against Cromer was carried out by a handful of Bf 109s operating very far from home. Equally surprised by the appearance of three Bf 109s was the crew of a Blenheim on convoy escort. A fierce, necessarily short fight ensued, but the Blenheim escaped while a fighter was claimed by an escort vessel's AA gunners.

Scattered operations over the Midlands and East Anglia by fifty long range bombers followed after dark on 11 June. At Diss nine HEs were dropped, on Victoria Road and the railway arches in Station Road. Other Norfolk targets

Mercifully, this unwanted stranger did not explode. The highly courageous Army team which defuzed what looks like an SC1000 give scale to its enormous size — and potential. Photographed in Frederick Road, Gorleston, on 12 June 1941.

were King's Lynn – where casualties were high at sixteen killed and eleven injured, at Docking where ten HEs fell, and in the Snettisham-Sedgeford area.

Nightly, NJG2 was now operating about fifteen aircraft, some overland and others awaiting RAF bombers at sea. A Ju 88C was shot down over the Wash early on 14 June, the crew of three being killed. Another Ju 88C placed five delayed action bombs on to Alconbury at 00:55 on the same morning and fired at a Wellington taking off, then revenge was again exacted. Participating in a late night phase, Ju 88C *R4+DM* of 4./NJG2 was patrolling when, over Narborough, a 25 Squadron Beaufighter intercepted, the German crew being lucky to bale out in time. Another Ju 88C of the same Staffel was shot down on 21/22 June at Haines Farm, Deeping St James. Next night NJG2 disfigured squadron offices at Oakington, damaged a Stirling and killed an airman.

Concentration on shipping targets was obvious throughout June, at the start of which Lille/Vendeville's Heinkels of I/KG53, and others of II/KG53, briefly lent their weight. Mining remained a regular activity, usually undertaken by KG30 and I and III/KG4, all of which also carried out shipping raids. But at the end of June this anti-shipping force began to disperse and KG3, Schiphol-based, was briefly seconded to assist in operations. Maritime reconnaissance flights were still performed by 1.(F)/122 from Lille or 3.(F)/122 from Schiphol. Generally they operated well out to sea, and sometimes carried bombs. Minelayers also dropped their weapons ashore, as on 17 June when two exploded at Holt damaging the Lodge and breaking windows and tiles in the town. Another mine exploded at Warham. At 01:20 that night Squadron Leader, R. Atcherley in Beaufighter *R2251* of 25 Squadron shot down a He 111 near Sheringham. During the night of 18/19 June a convoy was twice attacked off Norfolk, an escort ship being damaged. At night on 20/21 June another convoy attack took place off Cromer, one ship being sunk. Three attacks on shipping off Sheringham on 22/23 June resulted in a further sinking. Late on 29 June a Hurricane of 151 Squadron shot down near Happisburgh Ju 88 W Nr *5241:7T+HK* of Gruppe 606 operating from Schiphol, the base also for Gruppe 106's anti-shipping sorties.

July 1941 brought to Yarmouth more heavy raids. Five in which bombs caused little damage were followed by two devastating attacks, the first between 01:04 and 02:59 on the 7th, and in which four phases were evident. Opening the operation, four heavy HEs exploded on the Frederick and Kitchener Roads area. Casualties amounted to seven killed in five Anderson Shelters, all of which were hit. Five houses, a shop and a public house were destroyed and many houses damaged. Next, four HEs landed on Southgates Road, battering a house and a ship chandler's store, luckily without casualties. Thirdly, another heavy bomb landed in Row 127. Eight houses and the foundry of Messrs Brett were demolished, and again houses were seriously damaged. Finally, four bombs fell west of Southtown Road, damaging a public house and more homes. Casualties amounted to twelve dead and six seriously injured. During the night Squadron Leader R. Atcherley (*R2251*) claimed a Ju 88.

The raid of early 9 July, when fifteen raiders concentrated over the town, turned out to be Yarmouth's heaviest so far. Twenty-one bombing passes were made against the town between 01:04 and 03:45. In the course of them eighty HEs were dropped, totalling about 31 tons and ranging in calibre from 50 kg to 1,800 kg. Well over 1,000 incendiaries also arrived, along with a load of leaflets.

Extensive damage befell hundreds of homes, shops, public houses, a shoe factory, a chapel, timber yard and quay. Railway lines received direct hits closing traffic at Southtown Station where carriages were overturned. Spectacular was the bombing of a gasometer for, after it received a direct hit, there was a tremendous rush of water from the container upon which it floated. A surface shelter holding thirty people all but received a direct hit, yet nobody was hurt. Fires were soon extinguished although all public services suffered badly. Casualties amounted to three killed and 29 injured. Shortly before the bombing a Ju 88 (probably of Gruppe 106 which lost three aircraft during the night) was shot down off Happisburgh by a 257 Squadron Hurricane.

July raids upon Yarmouth were far from finished even now. Four attacks came early on the 11th, the nine HEs used including a very heavy bomb in Bells Marsh Road. Other areas hit were Lowestoft Road, Church Road, Duke Road and the East Anglian School, Southtown and Granville Road, Cobholme. One person was killed and seven injured. Three nights later four 250 kg bombs fell across the Mill Road-St Lune's Terrace residential area, destroying twenty houses, a school room and St Luke's Church. Six were killed, twelve injured, and in other raids 22 HEs fell in nearby waters.

Such bombing operations were the exception, as the effort remained mainly against shipping. There was an evening raid off Sheringham on 11 July, and when 'He 111s' operated on 14 July a Havoc of 85 Squadron (Pilot Officer Howitt) shot down one off Clacton and Flight Lieutenant Raphael and AC1 Addison, also of 85 Squadron, engaged another near Martlesham Heath. Whether these claims can be substantiated is difficult to decide for during the night two Ju 88s were lost in action over the North Sea, W Nr *8191:M2+GK* of Gr. 106 and *3238:7T+HH* of Gr. 606. More anti-shipping operations on 17/18 July were followed by day raiders from France, and three dusk raids on 25 July resulted in a ship being damaged off Aldeburgh.

Ju 88 intruders of NJG2 completed about 250 sorties during July. On two nights diverted from their primary role, they participated in bombing raids upon London. Otherwise, roaming widely over Eastern England, they attacked sixty airfields. Extravagant claims were made by the pilots who really damaged only two aircraft, a Wellington and a Stirling. Docking was attacked on the 10th/11th and 12th/13th, and at Caxton Gibbet on 16 July a Tiger Moth in the circuit was shot at. Next night Wellington *X3169* about to land at Steeple Morden was raked with fire, before HEs dropped on East Wretham where the next night two strafing attacks accompanied the arrival of eight HEs. Eight airfields were assaulted on 25/26 July, but the most memorable of the JU 88s' activities took place at Bassingbourn on 22/23 July.

The intruder arrived as 11 OTU's Wellingtons were night flying, joined the circuit and followed *R1334*. Warned of the foe, the Wellington pilot decided to go round again. Leutnant Heinz Volker flying Ju 88C-2 W Nr *842:R4+BL* was obviously unaware of this, and as the Wellington banked to port over Ashwell he suddenly crashed into the bomber. There was a tremendous explosion and fireball as the aircraft locked themselves together to crash in Ashwell village. Investigation of the wreckage revealed that the fighter had three MG17s in its nose and a cannon, supplemented by a second one carried in a detachable pack installed in the belly gun tunnel. The same night there was considerable consternation when seven SD2 anti-personnel bombs were found in a field just west of Oakington. Others had apparently damaged a Stirling, and an airman in a tent was also killed by one. At Ferry Farm, Reedham, bombs from another intruder demolished a farmhouse, killing two and injuring two people.

August 1941 found the Luftwaffe holding up to 120 aircraft for operations against the UK, although the activity level was far less than possible. Only on six nights was there any concentration upon land targets, none East Anglian. Night intruders continued almost nightly and despite German claims only two Wellingtons were shot down over Britain in the entire month, one near Grimsby on 14/15 August, the other – credited to Oberfeldwebel Laufs – on 12/13 August near Coltishall. Ten other aircraft were fired upon. A new ploy first tried over the Wash on the 12th/13th was to expose a bright light to illuminate British aircraft, a Wellington being thus engaged near Marham. Current tactics included firing colours of the day during a slow glide approach, in the course of a wide circuit allowing time for aerodrome lights to be exposed prior to a sudden attack, as at Marham on the 12th/13th. A variation at Caxton on the 6th was to circle, call up control, then flash the correct colour. Two Tiger Moths were damaged by the ten HEs following. Confusion was caused around Marham early on the 13th when an intruder operated at higher speed than usual leading to the belief that it must be a Bf 109 which attacked a Blenheim and Anson north of Thetford, then a Wellington approaching Marham which was itself bombed and strafed. NJG2 was surprisingly ready to attack the same airfields on consecutive nights. At Feltwell early on 15 August a Wellington was followed in, then the airfield was bombed and machine-gunned. A fighter patrol was mounted and two nights later an intruder tried a repeat attack. This time an 85 Squadron Havoc was waiting and drove off the enemy. No protecting fighter was at hand on 19 August when Wellington *N3005* was shot down near Barrington. Next night the new aerodrome being constructed at Little Staughton was raided, then incendiaries were aimed at Waterbeach.

To strengthen East Anglia's night defence, a detachment of 604 Squadron under Wing Commander John Cunningham arrived at Coltishall on 22 August. Flying with Pilot Officer C. F. Rawnsley, the night fighter ace bagged a He 111 35 miles north-west of Coltishall later that day.

The persistence with which NJG2 attacked insignificant Caxton Gibbet landing ground was astonishing, the next raid coming on 23/24 August, ten HEs dropping from 500 ft and killing two Marshall employees. Three HEs and a few fire bombs were dropped at Caxton on 3 September when the intruder made two dummy approaches and bombed on a fourth run, damaging five Tiger Moths.

Throughout East Anglia there were much smaller, but irresistible targets, though: the searchlight sites. The value of searchlights, ground or airborne, was repeatedly reviewed. A large number of men was necessary to man effective searchlight defences which, for most of the time, played no active part. The introduction of airborne radar seemed to further reduce their usefulness, yet there was one feature of searchlights largely overlooked – their dazzle capability. That was well demonstrated at 23:30 on 6 August 1941 when the 310th Searchlight Battery illuminated a Ju 88 off Clacton. Although promptly fired upon by Frinton's B Troop, 16 Battery RGA, it seemed that the pilot was so dazzled that the aircraft was already diving out of control. Whatever happened, the next few minutes were even more remarkable for, on its way down, it collided with another Ju 88 and both went into the water off Clacton. The presence of Ju

88s in the area may have been connected with two mines dropped at Colliers Wood, Ardleigh, which slightly damaged farm buildings.

Late July had seen further changes in forces available for raids on East Anglia. Although depleted by the departure of I and III/KG4 to the Russian Front, II/KG2 had arrived at Evreux after conversion training at Bramsche, Germany. Still flying Do 17Zs, it was expecting a full complement of Do 217s at any time. The latter already equipped II/KG40 at Soesterberg, the unit operationally training with them over the North Sea early in August. III/KG30's minelaying Ju 88s recently at Gilze Rijen were now at Melun/Villaroche, south of Paris. Reconnaissance for the anti-shipping force was supplied by Ju 88s of 1. and 3. (F)/122 and Gruppe 106, usually operating from Schiphol.

Employment in the anti-shipping role against East Coast convoys continued into the autumn. The extent of ships sunk or damaged remained low, but the number of RAF fighters required to give convoy cover was considerable because of their short patrol times. Escort vessels were necessary, so that the expense of convoy defence forces was high in terms of manpower and equipment.

Bombing of coastal towns continued, Yarmouth being subjected to attack eleven times in August and three in September although on only five occasions were bombs dropped. Provision of extremely strong AA defences would probably not have prevented sudden, fast attacks. Nor would balloon barrages. The latter was more feasible at Harwich, where the establishment of 928 Squadron (still based at Felixstowe) stood at nineteen low zone (LZ) MK VII balloons on land and thirteen waterborne, to be supplemented by twelve of the new and smaller Mk VI balloons on barges. At this time there were 2,401 LZ balloons in use throughout the UK and only fourteen Mk VIs. While balloons discouraged the bombers, they did not stop them.

The persistence with which anti-shipping forces operated was very evident on 3 and 4 August when small formations of Dorniers raided a convoy off Orford Ness. The American Eagle Squadron, No 71, destroyed one of them on the 3rd, but successful interception was chancy. When the clouds were thick, as on 8 August, it was virtually impossible. On that day more attacks were made, off Harwich and Happisburgh. At night on the 8th/9th the failure to find shipping led to the bombing of Cromer where ten bombs fell in Hall Road, as well as Caister, where four houses were badly damaged and five people injured, and Yarmouth and Lowestoft. Due to the nature of the intended raids most of the bombs were relatively small and HEs. These did not give the authorities a chance to assess the effectiveness of fire-watching forces now that they were established on a compulsory basis.

Only two German aircraft were known to have been shot down in the latter part of the month. Both were He 111s, one brought down by 266 Squadron twenty miles off Winterton at 20:10 on the 19th, the other by 257 Squadron sixty miles east of Winterton at 08:16 on 22 August – some hours after a ship had been sunk off Yarmouth.

September 1941 witnessed a further decline in enemy activity, even the recorded 125 sorties by Ju 88 intruders showing about a fifty per cent reduction in effort. Offshore and inland they prowled, shooting down Wellington *LN:N-R1411* of 99 Squadron as it was landing at Mildenhall on the 1st, and firing at our aircraft on three other occasions. One Ju 88 crept across the coast at 21:17 on the 16th and near Coltishall fired upon a Beaufighter before hurrying out towards Felixstowe where it unloaded its incendiaries. There, waiting, was a Havoc of 85 Squadron which soon shot down the raider as it crossed out over Clacton. Intruders seemed this month to keep more to East Anglia, operating particularly over Cambridgeshire and against Suffolk's bomber bases. They were busy on 2/3 September, ten operating overland and dropping bombs at Thaxted and Debden. On 8/9 September a Ju 88 followed a Wellington to Stradishall, firing upon it as it landed. The station's ground defences opened up and seriously damaged the German aircraft. Next night a Ju 88 circled Cambridge aerodrome and then, following a low pass towards the south-east, dropped, at 03:12, a 250 kg HE on Ditton Walk and six smaller bombs on the western side of the airfield, damaging parked Oxfords. On five nights the intruders, significantly, did not appear; those upon which the RAF bomber force was raiding Brest or northern Italy which made the time of their homecoming hard to predict.

A decline was apparent in the number of shipping attacks. On the 6th/7th two raids were directed at a convoy off Yarmouth, and another two later at shipping off Sheringham. Similar night operations followed on the 9th/10th, the raiders possibly including an element of Gr. 606 which was then operating from Schiphol. One of their Ju 88s shot down by anti-aircraft fire on 19 September was found to have two free-mounted 20 mm Oerlikon cannon in the nose, presumably for ship attack purposes. Another enemy aircraft was shot down in the course of its anti-shipping crusade off Happisburgh by a Hurricane flying a dusk patrol on the 15th. This was, though, one of the quietest months for a long time and even Yarmouth, easily East Anglia's most bombed town, suffered only three attacks. On 7 September four HEs fell near Breydon railway bridge and at 02:44 a small incendiary load was distributed over South Beach Parade plus eight HEs in the York Road area, causing one casualty. The third raid resulted in four bombs hitting the water off Gorleston.

Inland bombing was also on a small scale, an HE and incendiary night attack of 13 September on Colchester resulting in damage to the North railway station, a carriage and Prior's, the rose nursery. Foulsham aerodrome being built in Norfolk received four HEs on the 9th, an additional four dropping at nearby Wood Norton. Overland sorties, some lengthy, were mainly by NJG2. One on 6/7 September sent sirens wailing over a very wide area as the Ju 88 crossed in over Orford Ness and flew to Rugby and back searching for trade. A companion flying the Leicester-Grantham beat left via the Southwold-Lowestoft area passing, en route, a third fighter scouring between Harwich and Newmarket. Annoying, small-scale operations were a far cry from even recent experience, and insufficient for 604 Squadron's fighter detachment to be retained at Coltishall. It was replaced on 20 September by 255 Squadron from Hibaldstow, which watched over shipping at night by facing III/KG3, then operating off Yarmouth. Increased activity against Yarmouth, raided another nine times at night and thrice shortly after dusk, was again a spin-off from the absence of shipping for attack. Potentially most serious was the arrival of a mine at 03:20 on 16 October. Along with an HE, it fell at Wood Farm Lane, Gorleston, causing less damage than expected though. Two people were injured on the 19th when at 18:51 four HEs exploded between Blake Road and Raleigh Avenue, another being injured on the 30th when four bombs exploded between Admiralty Road and Micawber Avenue.

Layout of air defence of East Anglia
showing Sectors, aerodromes and radar defences

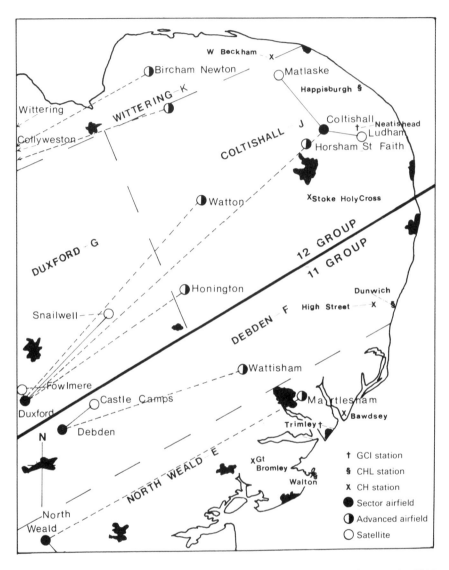

Chain Home (CH) and Chain Home Low (CHL) radar stations came into use by 1940, GCI stations in 1941. Satellite airfields can into use in the spring of 1940. Squadrons were at first based at Sector stations and moved daily to Advanced Airfields, often bomber bases, to protect coastal and shipping targets. From the fall of France squadrons often moved completely to those and satellite airfields, while remaining under Sector Station control. By 1943 some satellite airfields had assumed self-accounting status and Sector control was less rigid as the speed of attack increased. Many squadrons after 1942 were mainly engaged in offensive operations, home defence being a secondary employment.

General arrangement — LZ Kite Balloon

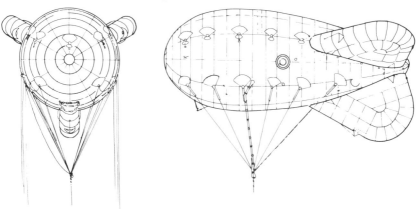

Apart from the Mk VI, the Low Zone balloons flown in East Anglian barrages were of similar shape and generally when inflated had a gas capacity of about 19,150 cu ft. Overall length was 64.2 ft, maximum diameter 25.2 ft, overall height 31.8 ft, overall width 33.7 ft. Such balloons, designed for use to 5,000 ft, were operationally placed at heights of up to 6,500 ft. The balloon's upper section contained hydrogen, the lower air which entered through the wind scoop. On rising the expanded hydrogen forced out the air, which returned as the hydrogen contracted when the balloon was winched in. This, and the air-filled stabilizers, made the balloon controllable.

The Harbour Master's office roof bearing new slates following the destruction of Lowestoft swing bridge power house. In this 1944 view, Mk VI kite balloons protect shipping and the harbour (Ford Jenkins Photography).

Enemy aircraft were now more absent from southern England than East Anglia. In the former region one of the most cost-ineffective schemes of the war was awaiting trial, the absence of the foe causing the novelty to be brought from Middle Wallop to Coltishall. It was LAM, the Long Aerial Mine appropriately code-named 'Mutton'.

Aerial minefields were a pre-war notion. A large number of HE canisters, each connected by a long wire to a parachute, would be sown ahead of approaching bombers. Should one strike the cable its parachute would immediately whip the weapon against the aircraft, blowing it apart. Sounding simple and effective, LAM's protracted development absorbed scarce resources. Research was particularly connected with arming the weapon, preventing premature bursts and development of operating techniques. Winston Churchill found the idea much to his liking and was very instrumental in its development, which resulted in the wire being lengthened to 2,000 ft – and the 'Long' version with a predicted fall rate of 1,000 ft/min and a lethality of two minutes.

Everything concerning wire weapons was simply staggering. Aerial minefields needed to be extensive for the sky is so gigantic, and in March 1941 monthly production was set at 16,560 units involving a mind-boggling 34 million feet (6,440 miles) of 19 gauge wire. That was a mere start for simultaneous plans called for 40,000 parachute and cable shells monthly, and other schemes whereby kites and balloons would trail wire and lethal charges. Each month 163,000 wire weapons were scheduled for production, the wire for which would have encircled the world several times. All grand stuff for rumour-mongers, not to mention spies!

Success with aerial mines being limited, an ultimatum was issued in autumn 1941 – make a success of them or switch to more productive ideas. There being little trade over the South, 12 Group was approached to include mining over its territory, to which it agreed – adding a cautionary note concerning considerable RAF night traffic over Eastern England. Accordingly, two LAM Havocs of 93 Squadron nightly stood by at Coltishall from 7 September. Neatishead radar would control them within their strict radius of 35 miles from the GCI station.

Following four unproductive night missions, the Havocs stood ready on 16 September when take-off was ordered. The defenders were being misled by a 'friendly' not expressing itself correctly. At 23:14 the second patrolling Havoc, *DG554*, call sign Waddle 23, flown by Pilot Officer Porter and Sergeant Edwards, was informed of the approach from the south-east of Raid 20. The latter was on a course of 340⁰ at 8,000 ft and flying at 160 mph. *DG554* then positioned itself two miles ahead of the enemy and, following careful checks that no friendlies were about, was ordered at 23:24 to 'FIRE!'

Aboard the Havoc were 92 of the very latest AD Type A Mk VII mines, now being operationally used for the first time. Seven immediately refused to leave their carriers – vital items in triggering the weapons. As the remainder fell several prematurely exploded, signalling the enemy pilot to change course to 250⁰, thus evading the field.

The curtain was intended to be effective for about seventeen minutes. That assumed the mines were correctly functioning; on this occasion faulty initiators and detonator strikers of incorrect shape prevented seventy of them from ever becoming 'live'! They had been sown to the south-west of Norwich and by the time the Havoc crew landed at 00:03 no mean alarm had overtaken the City authorities who were unaware of what had been going on. 'An ancient City has been put in jeopardy', commented one official most correctly. By 23:35 reports were reaching the police of strange canisters, parachutes without parachutists and masses of 19 gauge wire festooning trees, telephone lines, roofs and chimneys. The mines had landed in an arc from Eaton Golf Course to the City centre, arming pins which should have been pulled out as the weapons deployed remaining firmly in safe position. Between them the police and Services made 'safe' 69 useless mines, and exploded an unsafe one.

'Childhood tells us the City of Norwich
Has people most strongly addicted to porridge,
The Law denies them the treat,
They get Mutton to eat,
A disastrous event to acknowledge.'

Thus commented 93 Squadron's historian, for the drop near the City had dire consequences. Temporary Police Sergeant Alfred Wheatley went with PCs Godbolt and Scott to West Pottergate where a 'UX bomb' had been reported. There they discovered ARP Warden Herbert Batley, his horrific leg injuries being attended by Dr Soothill, Medical Officer for Norwich. Receiving a report of a parachute bomb, the warden had investigated and on touching a spiral cable caused the canister to explode. Sadly, he died of his wounds.

Special Constable 279 went to Unthank Road, by Park Lane, where a Ford HP car GME591 had been damaged by an explosion and the Czech pilot driving it was being cared for nearby. PC Thomas Archer with Temporary Sergeant Kemp went to 8 Wellington Street and found wire in its garden, windows blown out and wire protruding from a hole in the roof and connected to a yard long spiral. The occupant, Henry Bulldeath, told how at about 23:45 he was in bed when he heard something fall through the roof. He had, apparently, then returned to bed!

Archer went to Nelson Street, finding plenty of wire in the garden of No 4, tiles having been stripped from the front roof. He awoke George Bales and together they inspected the damage. There was no sign of an explosion, and Mr Bales then said that he would move anyway into the back bedroom. Subsequent searches located assorted mine items at, among many others, 179 Dereham Road, 87 Nelson Street, 18 Neville Street, 4 Essex Street, 74 Rupert Street, Glaston Street ARP post, 38 Melrose Road and 5 and 8 Upton Road. It had been a disastrous event, the outcome being that on the 18th the order was given that mines must never again be sown overland. Further sorties were flown out to sea, but no drops were made in the area and on 26 October the detachment returned to Middle Wallop where, soon afterwards, the squadron ceased mining.

A far more profitable use for the Havocs would have been for them to join their companions intruding, and with considerable success, on German airfields in Occupied Countries. The German NJG2 was less successful, particularly on 16 September when *R4+NH* came to Patrol Area C, carrying eight 50 kg HEs and two AB36 containers of incendiaries, a usual load. Crossing the coast at 8,000 ft, it roamed the Stradishall area, attempting to bomb the aerodrome. Exit was about to take place over Clacton when a warning of fighters came simultaneous with searchlight beams illuminating the Ju 88. Almost at once the guns of a patrolling 85 Squadron Havoc tore into the intruder which came down in the sea half a mile offshore.

While the fight was on, little or no thought was given to the predicament of enemy airmen falling to their doom in blazing bombers, or being cruelly savaged by the freezing North Sea. It is difficult in a bitter conflict to succour he who has lately killed one's dearest; such is largely a peacetime luxury. Hard, too, was the realization that overhead flew many with no desire to commit grotesque deeds which scheming, detestable politicians had ordered and from which there was no escape. Many of those young warriors showed immense courage, and higher ideals than any politicians seem capable of displaying. On both sides there was grand comradeship which sadly only war generates, and which seems utterly unobtainable in peacetime as each populace allows itself to be repeatedly bullied by pathetic, worthless leadership.

Certainly the worthy crew of Ju 88 *7T+LK* of 2./Gruppe 606 showed supreme courage far from their Lannion lair. On 15 September, four 500 kgs aboard, Staffel Kapitän in control, they left Schiphol at 18:45 to attack a northbound convoy sailing off Yarmouth. Searching at 4,000 ft, they then discovered six escorted merchant ships, and delivered a steep, diving beam attack. AA fire greeted the bomber and suddenly a fighter raked it from astern, seriously injuring the gunner. Quickly the observer took his place, but the starboard engine coolant tank had been punctured, forcing the aircraft to ditch. Their dinghy was found to be badly holed, forcing the crew to rely upon life jackets and prayers. The Kapitän seized the wounded gunner, holding the unconscious man's head above water for over an hour before a minesweeper mercifully saved them. How many more, unheralded, deserved their country's recognition?

Bravery and ill-will are often inextricably linked in war, and so it was over Bourn on the night of 3/4 October. As Squadron Leader D.I. McCleod flew his Stirling *N6085* back from Brest and into the circuit, a Ju 88C attacked, no less than six times. From the burning bomber the second pilot baled out, the front gunner doing likewise, only to find his parachute failing to deploy. By then Feldwebel Köster's Ju 88 was diving low over Oakington dropping its bombs and damaging Wellington *X*-Xray of 101 Squadron which had just landed, and injuring three people. Four night fighters ordered to destroy the raider had no success.

Clacton received attention during the month when one of the mining force at 19:55 on the 19th released two mines and a UXHE at Bocking Elm, making two farm houses uninhabitable and bringing blast damage to houses wherein two people were slightly injured. At Colchester on the 12th SD2 anti-personnel bombs, presumably intended for the garrison, fell between Berechurch Road and the cemetery, breaking only the windows in Queen's Hotel.

Shipping raids continued, III/KG30 busily minelaying of late, fielding 29 aircraft during one night. Ships were attacked off Yarmouth on 2/3 and 11/12 October – the latter being one of the busier nights of the month – and off Norfolk again on the 16th/17th. The most interesting fall-out from these operations was obtained on 2 October when confirmation came that II/KG2 was operating the Dornier Do 217E-1. One, *U5+GN*, had been shot down into the sea at 21:30 on 2 October by a Beaufighter eight miles east-north-east of Teignmouth, then on 12 October came the chance to examine an example. *U5+DN* of 5./KG2 which had set out from Evreux to attack the Dorchester area flew over Pembroke making for Tenby then Barnstaple. A dog-legged course led to a crash landing around 05:05 at Jury's Gut near Lydd, Kent. After four hours the pilot had thought he

Instructions relating to markings of German aircraft for particular roles were precise, especially about the time when the Dornier Do 217E entered service. Shown here in standard day bomber colours is Do 217E-4 U5+ZN of Staffel 5, II/KG2, in the summer of 1942 (Bundesarchiv 362/2212/38).

must be over France and with fuel low attempted a belly landing. His was one of the first batch of 100 Do 217s, delivery of which commenced in March 1941. Being an E-1, replacement of which by the E-2 was already under way, it lacked a dorsal turret, had a larger cabin than later E variants and different armament. More important, its performance was well in advance of the Do 17Z, for it was powered by two BMW 80ls which gave 1,480 hp at 14,700 ft – 1,600 hp for take-off – and promoted a top speed, fully loaded, of 290 mph at 17,000 ft – about 320 mph after bombing. Operating at 35,300 1b – plus 650 gallons of fuel and a 6,500 lb bomb load – its range was around 1,000 miles when cruising at 225 mph at 10,000 ft.

Examination of the 20-ft-long bomb bay of *U5+DN* showed racks for four 500 kg HEs and the possibility of alternatives including one or two 1,000 kg HEs internally supplemented by a 500 kg beneath each wing, or 500 or 1,000 kg mines or a torpedo. A 15 mm MG 151 fixed gun was fired from the bottom of the cockpit and mounts for four fixed MG 15s in the tail cone were intended for the Do 217E without tail dive brakes. In the top position were two 7.9 mm guns, and another was in the ventral position. All were naturally subject to modification and few Do 217Es seem to have operated with tail 'scare' guns *in situ*. No glittering performer, the Do 217 was, however, clearly a major advance over its predecessor and soon became a regular visitor to East Anglia.

Presently, change of a very different sort was to come. Since mid-September the activities of NJG2 had noticeably declined in the face of demands that the German night force defend the Homeland rather than indulge in what were erroneously termed 'wasteful excursions' over England. On 13 October, in Berlin, orders were given to NJG2's commander to halt intruder operations and immediately transfer his fighters. He returned to Gilze Rijen too late to stop that night's activity, during which intruders penetrated to Cambridgeshire and attacked Mildenhall airfield, damaging a hangar.

Stopping intruder operations was a mammoth blunder. Their largely unproductive nature came about because they had been carried out on too small a scale, and on a highly individualistic basis at a time when the British bomber offensive was barely under way. Although resumed during 1943 in desultory style, they were never intensely pursued in the effective, British manner.

With the intruders gone, ever-improving night fighters, more sophisticated identity/interception radar devices and the Russian campaign sucking in more and more German effort, the amount of enemy activity continued its decline and after 21 October 1941 there was barely any enemy effort against East Anglia. Colchester was bombed on 3 November, but such raids were very few. From mid-May to November 1941 front-line Harwich was free of air attack. A raider dive-bombed the harbour on 6 November, and a few HEs fell in the sea off Dovercourt on 18 November. But in 1942 there were only three incidents in that area, and in much of East Anglia there was little enemy activity to report for some six months.

Off shore the offensive continued, but there too on a limited scale, conducted mainly by II/KG40's Soesterberg-based Do 217s, II/KG2's Do 217s from Evreux, Schiphol's reconnaissance Ju 88s of Gr. 606 and Ju 88 mine-layers of KG30 operating from the Paris area. On 31 October and 1 and 3 November, afternoon operations were flown by Gr. 606 seeking shipping for follow-up forces of II/KG2 and II/KG40, such combined activities continuing into the spring of 1942. KG3 was no longer available, having in October returned to Germany. Very few Heinkel 111s remained available either.

From time to time bombing raids did occur, King's Lynn dock area for instance being subjected to attack on 10 November when, at 04:54, an attacker roared in at 100 ft above the Ouse and from the south, to first hurl a 500 kg HE through the roof of a wharf. After bouncing along the quay the bomb exploded on railway lines. A second 500 kg HE hit a detached house, No 2 Loke Road, and damaged the premises of the Eastern General Transport Co. Before the Dornier left it deposited three Flam 250 oil bombs (by now uncommon), four containers and eight AB36 containers from which nearly 800 incendiaries fell without causing much damage.

Yarmouth was attacked upon five November days, bombs only twice falling on land. At 10:14 on the 7th four HEs cut the MGN rail line at Cobholme and on the 18th bombs fell west of the town. For once Yarmouth was luckier than usual since this was the busiest time in November. Two convoys had been attacked between Cromer and Southwold on the 17th/18th and a 1,200-ton ship sunk, HEs falling in the sea off Yarmouth and Dovercourt. Frinton at 19:55 on the 17th felt the blast of a mine dropped in Eton Road where houses were variously damaged, yet only four people were injured. Another mine landed 100 yd off shore between Frinton and Walton, resulting in the demolition of five houses, damage to another 300 and caused six casualties. Two mines exploded in Bradwell village by the Blackwater Estuary damaging yet more houses. The afternoon of the 18th brought three 250 kg HEs on Lowestoft. One damaged buildings in Denmark Road injuring three people, the second fell in the harbour 300 yd west of the swing bridge adjacent to Rich's iron works, damaging the quay and piling at the base of a 25-ft crane, and the third exploded behind No 56 Waveney Drive, wrecking an Anderson Shelter. Both occupants were unhurt. Four more bombs fell early in the evening, but Lowestoft was being spared a part in an operation during which mines were dropped overland at selected points between Canterbury (close to which fifteen people were killed) and Harwich. At the latter a small ship suffered bomb damage on 22/33 November. Farm houses were wrecked at Carrington's Farm and Walnut Tree Farm when two mines were dropped from a very low-flying Ju 88 near Bromley, Essex at 19:00.

Most of December's activity took place off the coast, particularly on the 1st/2nd and 7th/8th when minelayers were active and two aircraft made brief landfalls, and on 21/22 December when an enemy aircraft flew inland over Norfolk. At 17:40 it passed Norwich before dropping its load near Walsham and leaving over Yarmouth. What then happened remains obscure for it ended in the sea at 18:08 off Winterton where, later that night, two bodies were washed ashore.

Ship searches on 23/24 December resulted in bombs falling at Holland-on-Sea on both sides of the main road around detached houses. Unprotected by fire-watchers, all the houses were burnt out. About six out of sixty 1 kg bombs were found to have been fitted with explosive components. Three brief incursions overland were also made near Lowestoft, and Christmas Eve was marked by more than usual activity off Essex. No 71 Squadron damaged a Ju 88, and three Spitfire Vbs of 19 Squadron, Ludham, brought down a Ju 88 at sea. Christmas Day 1941 was disturbed at 18:30 when a container of fifty 1 kg incendiaries (about six explosive) was opened over a meadow north of the B1034 road leading to Walton. Some fell on bungalows near Kirby, and one which penetrated a roof and ceiling, bounced on the floor, hit the ceiling, bounded back then ignited much to the amazement of troops sitting around the fireplace. It surely was the ultimate in Christmas Day indoor fireworks, which they soon dealt with.

Since that sudden appearance of Bf 109s in early summer there were no more such sightings until 29 December. Two Spitfires of 485 Squadron which left Matlaske at 14:00 saw, fifteen minutes later, a Ju 88 at 2,000 ft over a convoy. As they engaged it two Bf 109s 'bounced' them. Shots soon wrecked a Spitfire's engine, and the pilot, who baled out, was soon picked up by a launch.

Inland bombing had now all but ceased. For some parts of East Anglia it was all but over. This list shows dates upon which the most recent incident had taken place, and the date upon which bombing was resumed in main towns and vulnerable areas – in some cases a year or more later:

Aldeburgh 21.7.41-27.8.42; Bedford 29.11.40-29.6.42; Chelmsford 21.5.41-18.7.42; Chesterton RD 11.10.41-6.8.42; Clacton 23.12.41-23.7.42; Clare 2.10.41-29.6.42; Colchester 12.10.41-10.8.42; Cosford RD 13.6.41-29.7.42; Docking RD 22.10.41-24.6.42; Dunmow RD 2.9.41-7.9.42; Felixstowe 25.10.41-21.7.42; Gipping RD 21.9.41-12.8.42; Halstead RD 29.6.41-28.7.42; Harwich 17.11.41-17.2.42, after which the next attack came on 13.5.43; Ipswich 11.10.41-1.6.42; Melford RD 30.8.41-16.4.43; Mildenhall 13.10.41 when the last Ju 88C intruder attack took place using six 50 kg HEs and 36 incendiaries-6.8.42; Newmarket 13.10.41-12.5.42; Saffron Walden RD 16.8.41-21.12.43; South Cambs RD 16.9.41-2.8.42; Southwold 12.6.41-9.2.43; Swaffham RD 7.9.41-29.5.42; and Wymondham UD 22.9.41-27.7.42. Not listed are Lowestoft and Yarmouth, against which bombing continued unabated.

* * *

Introduction of the Do 217 meant that larger calibre bombs could be more often

Lowestoft's highest loss of life came on the cold, snowy afternoon of 13 January 1942. The dead comprised 51 civilians and eighteen Service personnel. Seriously injured were 92 civilians and 22 Service personnel. Among well known premises destroyed were Aldertons, Morlings, Hepworths, Fifty Shilling Tailors, Boots' Arcade, Cooper's, Bonsall's, part of Marks and Spencer and Waller's Shop and Restaurant where many of the casualties occurred (Ford Jenkins Photography).

Of Boots' Arcade virtually nothing was left after four hefty bombs from a Do 217 smashed London Road North, the heart of the town. The attackers machine-gunned the street as they raced over very low (Ford Jenkins Photography).

A view reminiscent of Newmarket High Street a year before. Opposite the totally demolished shops, extensive blast has caused widespread damage to, among others, the town's main cinema, the Odeon. A girl roof-spotter on a shop roof was killed and a young shop assistant, rescued after being buried for 24 hours in a cellar, died soon after. Rescue workers toiled at the site for four days and nights dealing with East Anglia's most ghastly single bombing incident (Ford Jenkins Photography).

used, as happened at 16:27 on 13 January 1942 when four 500 kg HEs fell from a cloud-skimming Do 217 on to London Road, Lowestoft. At 15:06 eleven enemy aircraft were plotted offshore, and Raid 643 made a run in from the south-east. Bofors guns challenged it with eight rounds, two of which burst ahead of the bomber whose course might then have been diverted. Whatever the facts, the outcome was horrific, as Mrs V. M. Swaine who worked in a grocer's shop in the street vividly remembers.

'I was about to leave the shop to visit a restaurant some thirty yards away on the other side of the road, to purchase cakes for tea. Just as I was going to leave, a customer (known to be the owner of eight ration books) entered the shop. Needless to say, the rest of the staff disappeared leaving me to serve this one – and it undoubtedly saved my life. As I commenced serving the air raid warning sounded, and almost immediately came the scream of bombs falling which left only time to dive under the counter. Within a flash thirteen shops were completely demolished – including the restaurant which I was about to visit. Casualties amounted to 54 killed and eighty injured, the majority of whom were Wrens and Naval ratings in that restaurant.

'It was an extremely cold afternoon and snow was falling heavily. As I looked out, with all our windows smashed, the outside was as dark as night for paving stones and earth were still floating about in the air. As this cleared it gave me an everlasting, vivid memory, of two airmen carrying a terribly wounded child, blood pouring from a back injury, to the hospital nearby. Many bodies were found later, on the roof of the Odeon Cinema and covered in snow.' This incident without doubt brought the highest casualty figures arising from a single East Anglian incident, and they take no account of minor injuries.

On the evening of 19 January two 250 kg HEs fell on the town, one hitting the rear of 152 Denmark Street and the other causing damage close by. A Ju 88 dropped a flare over Yarmouth on 21/22 January at 18:05 before making a mere 50 ft south-north pass to slam four HEs on to the town. Next evening it was again Lowestoft's turn. Four 500 kg HEs fell, one at the Till and Summer Roads junction, tearing down the front of a building, and the others in Stanley Street in the garden of 48, on 46 and the fourth at the front of No 55.

Raids continued on both towns in 1942, their geographical locations largely their problem. In this predicament they had company on 6 January at 14:42 when four HEs fell in a field at Ramsey, near the Stour, killing two cows. As the raider headed home the crew apparently could not resist machine-gunning Harwich where some bullets penetrated the Regal Cinema. One of those there later came out saying, 'Yes, I was injured. Good film, wasn't it? Sort of different.'

On the night of 10/11 January as 25 bombers which had operated over north-west England headed for home across Norfolk and Suffolk, another six raiders, probably Do 217s of KG2, came in from Holland. From one, four HEs fell around Horning School; and later that day the few civilians remaining in Aldeburgh were showered with propaganda leaflets.

Each day, reconnoitring Ju 88s of 3.(F)/122 sought shipping. On 14 January II and III/KG2 followed up with attempts to cripple ships off Lowestoft. Bombs which fell on that town on 14/15 January were also the work of I or III/KG2, the latter operating from Schiphol searching the North Sea late afternoon on 15 January for maritime targets.

For 928 Squadron, Harwich Harbour, this was a busy time, balloons being

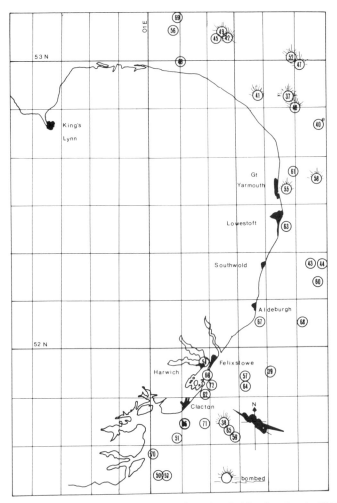

British merchant ships sunk by bombs or mines (probably air mines) off East Anglia during 1941–43. Day/month follows map key number. Tonnage (bracketed) follows name. Ships mined unless otherwise indicated.

1941 36 8.1 *Strathearn* (Trinity House vessel; 683); **37** 26.1 *Meriones* (7,557); **38** 2.2 *The Sultan* (824); **39** 27.2 *Old Charlton* (1,562); **40** 11.3 *Treverthroe* (sunk by E-Boat, possible air support; 5,257); **41** 14.3 *Artemisia* (6,507); **42** 4.4 *Salvus* (4,815); **43** 21.6 *Gasfire* (3,001); **44** 21.6 *Kennetts Hawksfield* (1,546); **45** 23.6 *Hull Trader* (717); **46** 23.6 *Trelissick* (5,265); **47** 25.6 *Dashwood* (2,154); **48** 28.6 *Barrhill* (4,972); **49** 1.7 *Homefire* (1,262); **50** 3.7 *Rosme* (sprit sail barge; 97); **51** 9.7 *Blue Mermaid* (sprit sail barge; 97); **52** 9.8 *Cordene* (2,345); **53** 19.8 *Golden Grain* (barge; 101); **54** 24.8 *Skagerak* (1,283); **55** 7.9 *Marcrest* (4,224); **56** 15.9 *Birtley* (2,873); **57** 21.9 *Vancouver* (5,729); **58** 12.10 *Glym* (1,134); **59** 18.10 *Mahseer* (7,911); **60** 6.12 *Greenland* (1,281).

1942 61 1.1 *Kentwood* (2,180); **62** 3.1 *Corfu* (1,848); **68** 3.1 *Robert Trader* (1,272); **64** 6.1 *Norwich Trader* (217); **65** 12.1 *Quickstep* (2,722); **66** 25.1 *Swynfleet* (1,168); **67** 1.3 *Polygarth* (794); **68** 16.3 *Cressdene* (4,270); **69** 1.4 *Robert W Pomeroy* (1,750); **70** 2.5 *Unique* (barge; 51); **71** 27.12 *Gertrude May* (barge; 72).

1943 72 13.11 *Cormount* (2,841).

Above *Mining was conducted on a widespread basis in 1941–1942. Mines like these awaiting delivery by I/KG54 were sown in shipping lanes and off major ports like Hull and Harwich* (Bundesarchiv 375/2710/30).

Below *Mines (MA1) being loaded on to a Ju 88A-5* B3+AK *of 2./KG54. Ju 88s undertook most of the mining off East Anglia in 1941-1942, assisted by Do 217s* (Bundesarchiv 375/2110/22).

flown whenever shipping raiders were near. Not until around 17:40 on 18 January did raiders come close to the barrage area. One selected a balloon flying just below cloud from site 28/6, into which a gunner poured his fire before the Dornier made off northerly. Moments later North Weald Spitfires were vectored towards the raider which jettisoned its load on the shore at Orford Ness before heading out to sea spewing smoke.

A feature of 1942 was the reliance by the Luftwaffe on reconnaissance-bomber units to swell the strength of its long-range strike force. This became evident on the evening of 19 January when seven Ju 88s of KGr.506 set off from Leeuwarden on a widespread search for East Coast shipping. Finding none, one of them, at 18:09, dropped two 500 kg HEs on Cremer Street, Sheringham (which town had not been attacked since 9 July 1941), demolishing four houses, killing four people and injuring four more. Soon after, four HEs were harmlessly donated by KGr.506 to Halvergate Marshes.

Dusk operations were also a feature of this period, as on 20 January when two raiders slipped across the coast, swept round climbing, and aimed five bombs from inland towards Southwold. Offshore dusk fighter patrols were at once increased to thwart such activity, but the weather prevented the chosen aircraft, Defiant turret fighters of Wittering's 151 Squadron using Coltishall as a forward base, from much success. They failed to prevent a raid at 18:06 on 21 January when two HEs caused extensive damage to a shoe factory at Gorleston. A few minutes later one of KGr.506's Ju 88s savaged the trawler *Arkwright* minesweeping twenty miles north-east of Yarmouth.

More hectic activity off Norfolk commenced at 17:00 on the 22nd, directed against Convoy 'Brest'. Although seventeen fighters were used to protect the ships, German bombers sneaked through to damage the 'Kingfisher' Class sloop HMS *Sheldbroke* off Hornsea. Despite good use of cloud, not all of the raiders went unscathed, a KGr.506 Ju 88 being damaged by Spitfires of 19 Squadron. Around 19:30 several Ju 88s circled off Harwich, and one of them was thought to have dropped a mine off Felixstowe Pier. There was by then a lot of AA fire from Landguard Fort and at 19:40 exhilaration as an enemy aircraft fell sideways into the sea and for two minutes floated, burning, two miles off Landguard Point. Come breakfast time next morning and the bombers had another go at the convoy. One, a Do 217, deprived of the sight of a ship, approached Lowestoft from the north-east, dived to 500 ft to release four HEs then hurried into cloud, its crew probably unaware of the havoc they had wrought around the railway station.

Two 'tip and run' raids were made upon Yarmouth on 26 January during which AA sites fired ninety 40 mm rounds. Five sites engaged a Ju 88 which then faced a furious barrage from naval ships in harbour. They opened up just as a Defiant fighter came into the GDA. Guns or fighters? There were constant problems as to which was best suited to engage any raider.

Although the number of ships being sunk was few, many had narrow escapes — unlike the trawler HMS *Loch Alsh*. In the low level style of attack generally used, whereby the bombers attacked from seaward or, as in this case, from astern, the ship was, at 09:50 on the 30th, sunk by a Ju 88 thirty miles east of Happisburgh. Gunners on other escorts bagged the bomber which, in the rain and sleet, soon became a shivering tomb from which two bodies were retrieved.

A combination of snow, low clouds and exceptionally low flying permitted a

Ju 88 to slip across the coast into Norfolk, at what was reckoned to be no more than 30 ft, mid-morning on 31 January to place four HEs near Reedham, Norfolk. Another crew unloaded their bombs on Cromer despite attempts by seven fighters to prevent such activity, the raider creeping out over Wells shortly before midnight.

On cloudy 2 February the Luftwaffe launched two operations, directed against two east coast convoys. As usual 3.(F)/122 flew the preceding search before attack phase one (09:30-10:15) in which six bombers participated after the reconnoitring Ju 88 had damaged a trawler in Yarmouth Roads. By the time of the second phase (12:40-14:31) a convoy off Norfolk was the centre of attraction. Two Dorniers made brief landfalls, bombs falling at Southwold. During the day protecting fighters flew 94 sorties and in the course of seven combats a Dornier was damaged. After dark bombs fell in Lowestoft Harbour.

More cloud cover attacks came mid-morning on 6 February and this time some eight Do 217s faced severe low icing levels inland, one to drop four HEs south of Coltishall. Even worse weather followed, severely limiting operations — and giving the German Navy the opportunity to move its capital ships from Brest in the 'Channel Dash' episode. On Valentine's Day, however, a Ju 88 came across a group of drifters off Landguard Point, climbed, and then dive-bombed them. As it did so the crew of an escorting balloon barge let slip their balloon, discouraging any repeat attack in the face of the straying object and fierce AA fire.

Three HEs were dropped in cloudy, snowy weather near Mutford, south-west of Lowestoft, on the 17th, and next day one of the sixteen aircraft seeking shipping dropped four HEs on Yarmouth. Then came the month's major event. Between 18:42 and 19:20, five raiders were sighted off Norfolk preparing to attack a convoy when they were bounced by four Defiants of 151 Squadron. Had these been front-gun fighters the RAF's score might have been higher. As it was, though, they soon shot down Do 217E-4, W Nr *5342:U5+KR* of 9./KG2, damaged two more as well as a Ju 88 and saved the convoy from being bombed. A little later, landfall by a bomber of unknown type resulted in the dropping of a large calibre bomb near Beccles. As for the night's activity, destroyers caught a force of E-boats mining off Yarmouth, promptly sank three and took seventeen PoWs.

That evening's activity proved that the bombers were far from invulnerable although so few had been successfully engaged during their anti-shipping sorties. Twenty-four patrols (56 sorties) were flown on 24 February and while two Spitfire Vbs of 266 Squadron were patrolling a convoy near Happisburgh they spotted four Do 217s of III/KG2 barely above the water and hurrying in to attack. There was only time to deal with Do 217E-4 W Nr *1166:U5+AD* before the others escaped. The defenders did not always have it their own way, as witness a Beaufighter pilot flying Mk II *R2333:B* of 255 Squadron off Norfolk on the evening of 28 February. He called Coltishall announcing that he had shot down an enemy aircraft at sea. Then, at 20:30, he again called, stating that his starboard engine had 'gone' and that the wing was ablaze. The crew baled out of their blazing fighter, but were not found.

March saw no let-up in the anti-shipping campaign, the 4th being the first busy day during which seventeen Dornier 217s of Soesterberg's II/KG2 and II/KG40 operated in atrocious weather. Brief landfalls were made by six aircraft in the

Winterton-Lowestoft area, bombs falling at Bradwell south of Yarmouth where anti-aircraft guns challenged the raiders. North of Happisburgh damaged $U5+MP$ was seen creeping home in battered state. No fighters challenged the enemy in the bad weather.

The evening of 8 March saw the Luftwaffe, again using cloud cover, attacking shipping between Montrose and Orford Ness, six convoys being vulnerable. Night fighters were despatched, 406 Squadron destroying a raider off Lincolnshire and 68 Squadron damaging another. Interestingly, Heinkel 111s were once again active, III/KG26 Poix-based operating in the southern area. Although that Kampfgeschwader specialized in anti-shipping operations, it had lately been operating on the Russian front. This was its first operation since returning.

Whilst the Harwich balloons protected shipping they were a hazard to friendly aircraft which, when in distress, often flew off intended track. On 10 March a Hudson returning from operations with flak damage and radio useless impacted a cable at 22:08. After hitting the starboard propeller, the cable sliced into the wing striking the main spar before snapping. The crew were lucky to land safely at Martlesham.

E-Boats were now launching damaging night assaults on East Coast convoys as on 14/15 March. Closing upon a convoy off Norfolk at 04:30, they sank the destroyer, HMS *Vortigern*, and seriously damaged a merchant vessel. Heading homewards they were spotted and attacked by Spitfires of 412 (RCAF) Squadron. By the time 137 Squadron's Whirlwinds from Matlaske reached the E-Boats they found them under attack by British MTBs. The enemy was not giving up that easily, though, and as soon as a spy Ju 88D of 3.(F)/122 landed in Holland that afternoon details of the convoy attacked, now off Harwich, were flashed to II and III/KG2. Consisting of four destroyers, five escort vessels and 36 small merchant vessels, it was too good to miss. During mid-evening on the 15th 28 Do 217Es attempted, unsuccessfully, to destroy the ships. As the latter progressed there was the ever-present risk of striking mines, laying of which was a regular feature and undertaken by KG2 and KG40. This activity often produced brief landfalls as on 19 March when six minelayers were known to have crossed the coast whilst mining.

Reduction in Luftwaffe operations was now becoming apparent even off the East Anglian coast. Overland barely one aircraft ventured. Demands on the Luftwaffe in other areas were so heavy that by late March only a handful of aircraft were available for attacks on Britain where night fighter defences were far more effective and about to be vastly improved by the introduction of the first two Mosquito II squadrons, 151 at Wittering and 157 at Castle Camps. There was also another increasingly worrying problem for German night bomber crews — British intruders.

Just what this could mean was illustrated on 26/27 March. At least five Do 217Es of II/KG2 and a few of II/KG40 left Soesterberg to conduct maritime operations over the eastern end of the English Channel. At 22:42 Leeuwarden was advised of an air raid warning. Twente was warned at 22:56, Soesterberg at 23:36. All aircraft would have had to land away from these airfields, eventually homing in on Eindhoven. III/KG2 had seven aircraft operating off Dover, these having to land at Evreux. Alterations at the end of dangerous operations no longer due just to weather conditions were disturbing to any crew. That the

Ju 88s of reconnaissance units for much of the war carried out lengthy flights along the East Coast. Depicted here is a Ju 88D-2, one of the types used (Bundesarchiv 402/270/5A).

Luftwaffe, which launched intruder activities in summer 1940 and halted them in October 1941, acted foolishly in withdrawing them was repeatedly proven. Also about to be displayed was RAF Bomber Command's vast increase in striking power, and when its aircraft landed there were no intruders with which to contend.

Some idea of what was in store for Germany was revealed on 3/4 March when, in testing the effectiveness of the 'Gee' radio navigation aid, 223 bombers carrying a high percentage of incendiaries, ample flares and some 4,000 lb bombs, raided the Renault car factory at Billancourt, near Paris. By packing the attack into about two hours, they reduced their loss rate dramatically, repeating the style at the Matford factory, Poissy.

On 28 March 234 bombers set off on a clear moonlit night for Lübeck, beyond the range of 'Gee' but easy to identify by its coastal features. Only 191 crews claimed to attack using 300 tons of bombs — almost half of them incendiaries—which laid waste to over 200 acres of Lübeck. German records list the total loss of 1,918 buildings with serious damage to another 5,928. Homeless numbered 15,707 in a town and port which was put virtually out of use for three weeks. No German city had previously so suffered, and the raid sent shudders throughout the German Establishment. What effect would it have, they asked, if the British repeatedly launched such onslaughts? But the RAF's five per cent loss rate demanded an interval prior to another operation; and the German population was about to show itself as stoic as that of its enemy. Bombing would never quench their spirit any more than it had demoralized the British. What it always did achieve was a grand morale boost for the nation backing the raiding force. It was 'good' to at last be giving 'them' a dose of 'their own medicine'. Post-war criticism of the tremendous assault which Bomber Command made upon Germany rarely takes note of what was, at the time, a great tonic to millions who stood in the streets to watch with pride the bombers setting off for distant places few had visited, with strange sounding names.

The effect that those RAF heavy raids would have upon 'the enemy' was predictable, but it would take time for any response so run-down was the Luftwaffe's long-range bomber force which, for much of April, continued only anti-shipping activities. On 7 April, 32 Do 217s operated, twenty of them mining off the Wash. A few bombs fell on the north Norfolk coast. A Beaufighter of 68 Squadron had a radar contact over Yarmouth on the 11th, and when E-Boats were active later that night 137 Squadron's Whirlwinds again went after them. King's Lynn was bombed on 19 April, when III/KG2 had seven aircraft operating, I Gruppe had four and III/KG40 nine.

Although operational flying had been drastically reduced, over France, the Low Countries and Germany there was suddenly a lot of activity by RTUs, the IVth Gruppe of each Kampfgeschwader and the Luftwaffe's equivalent of British OTUs. Stung to fury by the fierce and highly damaging RAF raids, the Führer decided to reply, in kind, viciously and with as much horror as his depleted bomber force could muster. On 14 April 1942 the Führer's order for retaliation was issued: 'Accordingly, when targets are being selected, preference is to be given to those where attacks are likely to have the greatest possible effect on civilian life. Besides raids on ports and industry, terror attacks of a retaliatory nature are to be carried out against towns other than London. Minelaying is to be scaled down in favour of these attacks.' The brief respite was over.

Preparing for a night take-off, Do 217E-4 (5383?) F8+KP of 6./KG40. If this is 5383 then it was the aircraft lost by I/KG2 on 16 June 1942 (Bundesarchiv 372/2596/17).

Chapter 18
The sacking of Norwich

Visibility three miles, moon three-quarters, wind north-east gusting to 21 mph, cloud 2/10 at 10,000 feet. A fine, bracing, East Anglian evening spanning springtime's awakening and Norfolk's fields bordered by high, vibrant hedgerows. At the feet of myriads of song birds flowered cowslips in thousands,violets in millions, while in town and country gardens 'King Alfreds' swayed in yellow profusion. Such delights reminded all that life, precariously balanced in wartime, had still much to offer.

On Monday evening, 27 April 1942, many a mum would have been 'doing the ironing', still with a flat iron heated upon the stove. Cooking posed problems for by now food was in very short supply, the Ration Book a pass to survival. Lose that at your peril! 'Make do and mend', produce a smart frock from the remnants of the old, or an acquired parachute. 'Dig for Victory' – and keep quiet, 'walls have ears'. Still, there were trophies from the bad days, one the stirrup pump, the other the government bucket. Both had in many cases been placed 'somewhere safe' or 'lost' as far as any nosey ARP official was concerned. They could be very useful when the war was over and roses assumed their rightful importance. Not so that ugly static water tank that the Council called an 'EWS', and which held enough water to flood the town and was so unsightly!

No doubt about one thing though, food really was short. The week's butter ration was about as much as many of us now spread on one slice of toast. Cheese, meat, even tea were becoming increasingly shy, yet there was a bright spot, the clear feeling that those fighting the war were doing a lot better. It really did help to know that nasty Nazis were being dealt with by our bombers. For those bold enough to stand and stare there was, just outside Norwich, the possibility of seeing Britain's latest, very secret bomber, the Mosquito, fastest in the world, a real beauty and reckoned, by a handful who really knew, to be a world beater. Read the newspapers — far more accurate and reliable then than they are now — and one knew that our bombers were at last giving the Jerries a hiding. Well, they deserved it.

Despite the war, some shops were surprisingly well stocked. Certainly book paper was of pathetic quality, and liberally supplied with unpulped chippings. Although limited in choice, Norwich shoes continued to be made of real leather. Colman's still mass-produced mustard for invisible ham, while using an evocative word linked with gas attack which we had long awaited and which was no longer expected. Indeed, many admitted that they had 'lost' their gas masks.

Only the professionals always carried them. They included the Home Guard, by now a well-trained huge force even acquiring 'regimental traditions' along with quite sophisticated equipment. With the likelihood of invasion receding, the new role for what had become a reserve army, the manning of AA defences, had been under review since June 1941. Recruiting for men to man AA 'Z' rocket batteries began in some places during March 1942.

Gaze through the window at the long-haired non-nylon maiden next door already wearing a pretty, summery dress and lingering dreamily beneath trees blossoming as well as they had ever done in one of the warmest springs for some time, and one could fairly conclude that life wasn't so bad. How fast fair scene doth crumble! At 23:21 the Norwich sirens wailed, and over considerable areas of Norfolk and Suffolk too. Surely, a lone bomber had accidently strayed?

There had, lately, been disturbing news from then so distant south-west England where, with unexpected fury, the Luftwaffe had lashed Exeter and Bath. A glance now through many a window would have presented a scene greatly changed from recent times for by 23:30 searchlights were once more stabbing the sky. From the south-west was coming at around 13,000/14,000 ft a force of Dorniers, Heinkels and Ju 88s which, on reaching their action line, would turn west. Timing for this was critical because the aircraft needed to be strung out along the coast so that they were able to cross between Southwold and Hunstanton, and mainly over the north Norfolk coast, to bomb their targets singly, meticulously. To add confusion to the defences, about twenty Ju 88s of KG30 mined between Cromer and Southwold. By 23:35 there was scant doubt as to what was to happen, for the leading bombers were fast descending, and heading for Norwich.

Chief town for a large area, it centrally contained many mediaeval buildings. Each century had extended Norwich, assorted industries establishing themselves near the River Wensum by which the old city was situated, traditionally within a protective river curve. Built upon rising ground, its centre surrounded the market place. Building was nowhere as dense as in many ancient towns, indeed there were few completely built-up areas. Nevertheless, many central buildings were composed of timber, soft brick, pantile roofs laid upon reeds – and, like Lübeck's, highly combustible.

Considerable seventeenth-century expansion spread the town outwards, after

Top *Starting point for the first 'Baedecker raid', City Station Norwich was completely destroyed* (Eastern Daily Press).

Above *The only way to defeat to an incendiary raid was prompt reaction. Facing the potentially very hazardous situation required cool courage, knowhow and team work. Good knowledge of the building at risk was necessary to ensure one's escape and the structure's survival. This Norwich Woolworth team has another most vital element, wartime cheerfulness which saw the country through bad times* (Eastern Daily Press).

Left *A sight unlikely to return? How wrong that belief was. The machine shown was used by KG40* (Bundesarchiv 369/2520/6).

which industrial and supporting residential districts were established in the early and mid-nineteenth century, particularly by both the lower and upper reaches of the river. Construction of small terraced houses was followed between the last two wars by extensive housing estates on higher ground. Some open spaces had surrendered to factory buildings, Caley chocolate and Colman mustard being among their widely known productions. Norwich's unsuspecting population on this fine, clear evening was officially recorded as 126,236.

The first hint of enemy activity over the North Sea was picked up by radio at 20:15, and on a greater scale than of late. It seems probable that the leader of what was assessed to be 25 crews detailed to incinerate Norwich may well have been flying a Heinkel 111 of KGr.100, the Luftwaffe's special pathfinder force. Whatever he was flying, the task was to mark the vulnerable city centre.

At 23:40 as the first crew opened the attack, by diving steeply to improve marking accuracy, a Ju 88 simultaneously raced over Horsham St Faith where

Bofors gun battery L1 banged off five rounds rapid fire, by which time the first incendiaries were burning at the City Railway Station. From several low-flying aircraft machine-gun fire raked the central city streets, which were fairly well vacated by this time of night except for the many people who very quickly had assessed a potentially serious raid and were racing for home or communal shelters.

Shoals of incendiaries rapidly overtook the station surrounds where buildings with felt roofs covering wooden ceilings, partly timber-supported, rapidly became the intended beckoning beacon. Fire soon engulfed a grain store and station offices. Passenger coaches blazed by the platforms, the whole amounting to 'the best firework display since Queen Victoria's Jubilee in 1897' according to one cynic.

Once the principal fire started there was a pause before the main force crossed the city, singly, from the west, dropping mixed loads. Horsham's guns had fired three times, then at 23:50 all guns were ordered to cease fire. Fighters — nine Beaufighters of 68 Squadron from Coltishall, ten Spitfires of 610 Squadron from Ludham and, operating for the first time, a trio of Mosquitoes of 157 Squadron from Castle Camps — were instructed to fly a layer patrol with 500 ft vertical separation between operating heights and fourteen aircraft active at any one time. They could do nothing to halt the bombing and were not in position when the first HE burst to the rear of Nos 144 and 146 Drayton Road. Others followed almost immediately in Valpy Avenue and Shorncliffe Avenue.

Thereafter the bombing spread fast and as well as in the city centre there were noticeable concentrations in the west and north-west with much damage being caused in the Dereham and Hailsham Road areas. Barely was the raid under way when alarm was expressed about the very rapid spread of fires and development of new ones. Showers of 1 kg bombs had already been distributed over the Westwick Road region, while others fell upon Clark's shoe factory, which was built mainly of reinforced concrete, and set it alight, the incendiaries having crashed through glass roofing. Another brick and steel factory close by was also burning, and more incendiaries fired the front of St Mary's Silk Mills east of the station, although concrete floors at least prohibited downward spread of the blaze. Fortunately, areas being hit were reasonably well spaced, except around City Station where further incendiaries were hurled into an enormous fire which was soon out of control, a conflagration which eventually engulfed 120 acres.

What also alarmed the authorities early in the raid was the apparent absence of many 'fire-watchers' from their posts. Since the great London fire raid of December 1940, 'fire-watchers' had been deemed an essential force. Each Warden Area was organized to have six to eight fire guard parties, and 12,000 people in Norwich had been registered for the task. Despite the fact that compulsory enrolment notices for another 2,500 had been issued, only 180 had been returned. Fire prevention for business in the City centre, and elsewhere, had been devised on a 'block system' of which 123 existed along with 120 individual schemes. Each block had a central rest room to which personnel reported for duty on a rota, and there was a 'spotter's post' from which communication by a warning bell or telephone was made with the central rest room, giving valuable assurance to those on duty. The task of training vast numbers in basic fire fighting had been difficult, many insisting that it should be done in working hours. Lectures were in any case no substitute for the experience.

When that engulfed them many fire-watchers took cover, and it needed courageous wardens to encourage their less experienced companions to action. It was not a question of fearing the attackers, more it was a case of realizing an inability to cope with multiple shoals of fire bombs. Many had insufficient knowledge of the inner recesses of the aged buildings they were expected to save. There was no case of the fires getting out of hand because 'fire-watchers' had failed to attend for duty. Indeed, many were public spirited enough to serve in the Home Guard as well. Throughout the country the fireguard scheme had proven the weakest part of the Civil Defence scheme and it was again the case in Norwich, for many reasons.

For the NFS the greatest problem quickly came with an acute shortage of water when mains were seriously damaged early in the attack. Plenty of water was available in the Rivers Wensum and Yare, but pumping out and delivery under sufficient pressure to reach the fires was difficult. Static water tank supplies were totally inadequate, and at Caley's the fire-guards made full use of theirs in an attempt to quench a fire at adjacent premises so that, when it spread to their own factory, adjacent to which the mains were shattered, there was insufficient water to halt a catastrophe. That was unfortunate for there was general agreement that the 1 kg bombs being dropped burnt far less fiercely than in previous times, and were easier to deal with. New techniques had also been developed for tackling them with a water jet instead of a spray. Although equipment was available in many places, there was usually no uniform point of storage, making availability limited. Little wonder, then, that fires were quickly taking hold despite courageous attempts to quench them as the bombs were falling.

From their dwellings people had in droves taken shelter, naturally locking their houses in which remained the buckets of sand and water and the very necessary stirrup pumps. No effort on the part of the NFS could now quell the infernos, fires gaining hold at 79 sites, some of which rapidly joined together. Ultimately, 179 fires — slight to serious — were recorded.

Tactics born in London during December 1940 were clearly being repeated, and improved upon by the addition of various HE components. Norwich, like other cities recently attacked on both sides of the North Sea, was being terribly burned and soon it was clear that 500 kg and 250 kg HEs were also being hurled upon the city. Although the effects of heavy calibre bombs were not directly proportional to their size, larger weapons usually produced greater blast effects in semi-open areas. Tightly packed buildings in narrow streets were readily, utterly demolished since they absorbed the full power of the weapons.

Although quite a high proportion of HEs burst in gardens, on roadways and open land, there were disastrous direct hits. Nos 47-49 Elm Grove Lane, succumbed to a 500 kg HE, another of which fell elsewhere in the road. A 500 kg exploded at the junction of Earlham Road and West Parade and others at 39/41 Elizabeth Road, which was machine-gunned, and at the 'Rainbow' public house, North Palace Road. Unexploded 500 kg HEs were found in St Giles Street, in a garden shed at 2 Merton Road, at 21 Bond Street, 17 Balthorpe Road and one at 114 West End Street, which rested undiscovered until 16 June 1942. A 250 kg bomb mutilated Nos 1, 2, and 3 View Terrace and Nos 144 and 146 Drayton Road were hit by a 500 kg. Bomb number thirty, a 50 kg, demolished Nos 7-9 Margaret Pattison Avenue. Direct hits by 250 kg HEs were scored on 7 West

Parade, 115 Elizabeth Fry Road, 121, 123 and 127 Newmarket Road, 29 Alexandra Road and 213 and 129 Dereham Road. Other bombs exploded at 2 Grant Street, 49/51 Northumberland Street, in the Jewish Cemetery, Beaufort Road, and the 'Horse Barracks' public house. The rear of the Wincarnis factory received a direct hit, shops in St Stephen's Street and the 'Woodcock' Inn too.

A large bomb hit the CWS warehouse in Victoria Goods Station yard resulting in the loss of all the food stored therein. During the attack three food wholesalers' premises were totally destroyed, although stocks were rapidly replenished. At least four 1,000 kg bombs were thought to have fallen during the raid, two certainly, for they did not explode, one falling by 15/17 Angel Road and the other at Heatral, St George's Street. Another scored a direct hit on the Swan Laundry, Heigham Street, and one which did explode landed behind Woodlands Hospital, Dereham Road, where the Institution Site received a direct hit on one of its wards, the damage being extended by fire. It cost the lives of twelve inmates, and others had to be moved to different institutions in the area for the damage was serious.

One of the most disturbing developments was the destruction by fire of the Civil Defence depot at the City Engineer's Westwick Road premises which were gutted and demolished by three HEs and incendiaries. A direct hit on a surface shelter there killed four. Burning of the depot meant the loss of vital rescue equipment and the aftercare resource centre.

For the first time an East Anglian city's ARP plans were being totally tested. Norwich had been divided into three Wardens' Divisions, each consisting of four Groups with a total of 78 wardens' posts, most specially prepared either on or below the surface. Manning the service were 179 paid and 760 voluntary personnel, the operational strength of the corps being swollen by other CD workers to 179 paid and approximately 1,400 volunteers at the time of the raid. Skilfully, the Chief Warden had devised a good level of decentralization and the individual posts had been organized on a 'specialists' basis. Thus there was a special corps of female telephonists and specially trained officers to maintain and update lists of people living within the area — vital if rescue services were needed, and medical services. Between them the personnel were quite able to take charge at any site until the police and the local Incident Officer arrived, and to give both advice. The youngest wardens were given a special job, as messengers. Their role was as dangerous as it was vital, for they supplemented the available telephone system. In a final Ministry report it was recorded that 'They did extremely well, were very effective...' The Wardens turned out at almost maximum possible strength and 'performed indispensable duty', among their unenviable tasks being the inspection of 100 possible UXBs, of which only 21 were eventually thought to be such. Such activities by those whose daily tasks were far removed from anything so frightening, and so often involved arrival at tragic events, must always be regarded with enormous admiration. Gone forever the figure who shouted through the keyhole that the kitchen light was beaming. In the real war he performed bravely and usually most calmly.

By the end of the first raid the five main stand-by rescue party depots were being manned by 109 men, the ARP service rescuing 84 trapped people and ultimately recovering the bodies of 63 who had died. To cope with the injured, Norwich had available 28 whole-time ambulances and 36 sitting-case cars in action, driven by 26 full-time and 46 part-time drivers.

At 00:22 on 28 April the bombing became so intense that at Norwich Telephone Exchange the night supervisor ordered the evacuation of the top storey switchboard room. The telephone system, and indeed the City, suffered a major blow when very heavy bombing engulfed the Eaton Exchange area and then the trunk lines to Cambridge (site of the Regional CD HQ) and Cromer were severed. Not for twenty hours were the links reinstated.

Not the least of the problems immediately facing the authorities was the restoration of public utilities. Water, before the attack, was pumped from the river at Heigham at the rate of four million gallons daily into a ring main extended around much of the City in 1935-36. During the bombing the main pumping station was put out of action, but at no time was there complete loss of water although many mains pipes were smashed. Using up to 170 pumping points, the NFS extracted 8,370,000 gallons from the rivers in 24 hours, and reservoirs on Mousehold Heath and Lakenham were completely emptied over the next few days. Gas services suffered less for the gas works escaped damage apart from its No 2 gasholder, although over 100 gas mains had leakages, giving a hazardous loss of 100,000 cu ft of gas an hour. Electricity escaped reasonably well although two high tension cables were cut. The most dangerous risk to supplies came when the fire at Caley's extended under the street, burning out all the cables in a building on the opposite side of the road, threatening major damage to the large Sub-Station at St Stephens which, luckily, escaped damage. Fractured sewers caused concern, for the City's sewerage system was complicated and vulnerable. Compressed air extraction was via eight ejectors controlled from the damaged Westwick station, the difficulty arising due to the sewage having to be pumped up to a level of 100 ft for final treatment. Over twenty sewers suffered leakages, some at major junctions.

The bus depot escaped the bombing, so that an excellent source of transport was still intact. Thorpe Station remained undamaged, whereas the City Station was burnt out. Its importance was less, it being the terminus for the old MGN line to King's Lynn.

At 00:45 the last bomb fell and the raiders, all of them, headed for home individually. Perhaps surprisingly, they had suffered no losses. Fighter Command had certainly responded, 32 aircraft having tried to engage the bombers, but it was far from easy and to a considerable extent the defenders had been taken by surprise. Six radar contacts were obtained and two visuals, and there was one combat. Five other pilots spotted bombers and three more inconclusive combats evolved.

The constitution of the bomber force was interesting and in keeping with that of other 'Baedecker' raids. Prominent was the long time adversary, KG2, fielding four aircraft of Gruppe I from Gilze Rijen, nineteen of Gruppe II and eight of Gruppe III, the latter under Schiphol's control and supplemented by a trainee crew of Gruppe IV, all flying Do 217Es — mainly E-4s. II/KG40 had three Do 217s operating, and also taking part were ten Ju 88s of KGr.506 and a dozen of IV/KG30 from Evreux. The most unusual feature was the appearance of a dozen Heinkel 111s of IV/KG55, Soesterberg, and two of IV/KG4. Employment of the IVth Gruppe of long-range bomber units for operations readily boosted the Luftwaffe's bomber strength in Holland and France to about 150 front-line aircraft, half of which operated against Norwich. Seven 'RTUs' were at present on the Western Front and Gruppen IV of KGs 4 and 77 had recently operated.

With this strength mustered, the likelihood of a further raid was a distinct possibility; Norwich had but a short wait.

During that pause, initial assessment of the results of the raid showed that about 450 incidents could be identified, 41 rescue operations had led to the recovery of 58 bodies and 1,200 homeless people were being accommodated in Rest Centres. Many more were lodging with friends. A report from the mutual aid/good neighbour association indicated that the magnitude of the raid had upset preconceived ideas about neighbours accommodating the homeless of their own streets, but it was done where possible. Whole streets, indeed whole areas, had often suffered severe damage, and in those cases local leaders had been found to organize help for those in need and some accommodation in less affected zones. Over 400 shocked, bombed-out people were thus housed.

Feeding the homeless, and indeed the rest of the population, was a daunting task with supplies lost, shops severely damaged and large outlets still smouldering. Within a short time of the raid ending, 23 mobile canteens were supplying tea, food and succour to the needy, and field kitchens were operating within half an hour of the 01:19 'All Clear'. To the NFS alone 800 suppers were supplied, and the Church Army could be phoned for particular aid.

During the ninety-minute attack the ARP Control Centre had been advised of thirty major incidents, another eighteen just after the raid and 75 more by daybreak. By then the citizens of Norwich, between pouring out to each other their countless stories of the night, could see that the heart of old Norwich had been brutally destroyed in nothing short of a terrorist attack. Fires were still burning, many a well-known landmark was reduced to a smouldering skeleton and the main thoroughfares remained festooned with hose pipes. The amount of glass, dust and rubble was simply colossal, and thousands of giant wooden beams, many charred and mostly very old were sadly languishing, their working days done. Damage to shops with household names was enormous. Gone, too, many of those very 'individual' shops that in days long gone one adored in childhood and dreamed of in adulthood. Perhaps most amazing of all was the amount of destruction caused by some fifty quite small bombers — the precise number was never established because some of the force bombed rural areas that night. In a month's time Cologne would be visited by 1,000 large capacity RAF bombers, so that anyone who can recall the state of Norwich on 28 April must

Left *In a scene reminiscent of the 1940 blitz, ARP workers receive 'char and wads' from a YMCA mobile canteen. Even at the time, 1942, such a scene seemed quite unbelievable in an East Anglian town* (Eastern Daily Press).

Right *The remains of Curls, Rampart Horse Street, Norwich. Firemen are damping the wreckage of the popular department store gutted by incendiaries. Debenhams now stands on the site* (Eastern Daily Press).

still but marvel at what such a gigantic force could do to a city of similar size and precious quality.

The reaction of the authorities to the Norwich raid, by far the most punishing any East Anglian town had undergone in one night, was rapid. Within hours it became a Gun Defended Area, a battery of eight 3.7-in 'M' (Mobile) guns arriving. With Regimental HQ at 221 Beccles Road, Gorleston, the 106th HAA Regiment, RA, placed its 270th Battery HQ on Mousehold Heath where the two Sections of guns forming 'NH2' were sited. Of the other four Sections, NH1 was placed at Horsham St Faith and NH3 by Church Lane, Eaton. In action the crack of brightly exploding shells from the 3.7-in guns was spectacular — and alarming, as the shrapnel fell around. But they were about to be outclassed as a spectacle which never palled, following the order for a 'Z' Rocket Battery to fire. That, the residents of Norwich would shortly witness for the 13th Regiment AA'Z' was quickly establishing its HQ in Unthank Road and hastily deploying three Sections of 'twin ' rocket projectors — NH1 at Horsham, NH2 on Mousehold Heath and NH3 at Broomhill, Church Lane, Eaton, thus supplementing the 3.7s on site.

Those arrivals rapidly gave a boost to morale in the city, over which there had been some concern by the authorities. It was further improved as builders set to making repairs, sometimes makeshift but often incredibly complete in record time, to the thousands of dwellings needing windows, tiles, slates and doors. By nightfall on the 28th they could be proud of their achievement while the population prayed that ....

There were still pale glows above major fires which had not been fully extinguished. An enormous fire had engulfed the Coburn-St Stephens-Chantry Road-Rampant North Street-Brig Street-Oxford Place-Red Lion Street-St Stephen's Street area. Famous names like Boots, Curls, Woolworth and Caleys were being badly treated, and incendiary loads had seriously damaged Earlham Road, Christchurch Road, Portisfield Road, Unthank Road, Chapel Field and Victoria Street. Little surprise, then, that from the city as dusk approached long lines of people were moving to the countryside around seeking safety either out of doors or with nearby friends. Some spent the night in buses dispersed outside Norwich, but for much of the area it was far from quiet or peaceful as the Luftwaffe mounted another Baedecker raid, this time upon York. En route and upon their return the bombers, some of which had been involved in the Norwich raid, partly progressed across north-east Norfolk. That brought into action the heavy guns now protecting the area and particularly those at Lowestoft where, in response, HEs were dropped at 23:55. Some of the raiders upon their return flew low to escape detection, one of them at 02.38 dropping HEs south-west of Lowestoft and two on Gun Site 412. Low flying was a new ruse at once countered by the redistribution of AA light machine-guns. Thus, although the citizens of Norwich were not under attack, it was clear that the new offensive was far from finished. After dawn, as they returned home, it was to a city most vividly, terribly scarred, and whose wounds were too bad to mend.

Evening on 29 April brought a further exodus, although inactivity of the previous night encouraged fewer to leave. Many must have regretted staying when, at 23:10, the sirens sounded again over Norfolk. That was a commonplace event, but now it was far more emotive on a fine, cloudless, clear and moonlit night accompanied from the north by a fresh breeze rising not above 20 mph. Fortunately nearly all the fires were out, several still smoking not producing sufficient smoke to give the slightest screening to the city upon which, at 23:25, the first bombs fell. Norwich was about to face a second round of torture.

This time the raiders came mainly from the north-east, attacked, and retreated on reciprocal courses avoiding Yarmouth guns. The pattern of attack was similar — marking, back-up flares during the raid, shoals of 1 kg incendiaries and then widespread use of heavy calibred HEs. No mines, no oil bombs, for they were largely superseded by 1942. Now it was incendiary raids which had everything to commend them, caused massive destruction over wide areas and did not call for accurate aiming. They also permitted, even encouraged, short concentrated attacks, and this time Norwich was savaged in just over half an hour and probably by a larger bomber force drawn from about 75 aircraft operating that night. Since bombs were also dropped around Ely, March, Ipswich, in Forhoe RD and St Faiths RD, the precise number of attackers could not be ascertained.

There was no doubt who was leading, seven crews of 7./KG100 flying Heinkel 111s from Chartres. Their task was to mark and illuminate the city with flares and incendiaries. Then came the main force, seventeen Do 217s of II/KG2 from Soesterberg and eleven of III/KG2 from Schiphol; another eight Do 217s of I and IV/KG2 from Gilze Rijen; nine crews of IV/KG55 and nine of II/KG40 from Soesterberg; five of IV/KG4 and fifteen Ju 88s drawn from the IV Gruppen of KG3, KG30 and KG77, all operating from Chievres. Bombing, mainly from around 2,000 ft, commenced at 23.25 and when it ended at midnight 39 tonnes had been unloaded on to Norwich. Some aircraft again machine-gunned the city, and this time the fires, fanned by the strong wind, many among damage produced by HEs in the first raid, were even more intense. Fortunately being separate, though, they did not produce any conflagration.

The principal seat of the fire was close to the city centre which was completely burnt out. Shops and offices, high risk buildings, from Orford Place to Rampanthall Street burnt furiously, and soon the flames swept across to Woolworth's and the flanking flammable shops. Those with floors of concrete again showed some resistance and at Pontings only the timber attic flat caught alight — until an HE smashed windows. Early in the attack more water mains burst and the NFS was unable then to stop the fire spreading to St Stephen's

Right *St Stephen's Street, badly damaged during the second Baedecker raid. The censor ordered that prior to publication the name 'Peacocks' on the shop, needed removal for it could have shown where the picture was taken. Of course, the whole of East Anglia — and Germany — knew of the Norwich raid!* (Eastern Daily Press).

Below right *Shot from a circling Lysander, Rowntree Mackintosh (coloquially 'Caley's chocolate factory') still burning after the previous night's fire bomb onslaught* (Eastern Daily Press).

Below *Enormous heat at 'Caley's' bowed the factory walls and dealt grotesquely with the metal window frames. The northern facade facing Chapel Field survives as part of the present factory, along with some of the original window frames. From the burning factory ran into the street rivers of burning chocolate and sugar. After it cooled children brought up never to waste things chipped away chunks of the chocolate, a precious commodity in wartime* (Rowntree Mackintosh).

Below right *The central factory block, reduced to an empty tomb* (Rowntree Mackintosh).

Church. Caley's works fire brigade tried to halt the terrifying, engulfing blaze at Cuthbert's Printing Works, the narrowest point of the fire, but they used all their water to no avail and had no mains supply to turn to. Caley's was a high multi-storey metal-framed brick building but that did not thwart its incineration and a huge store of chocolate melted and, like an horrific lava flow, made its way, burning, into the street. Only a few outbuildings standing on their own survived, but the fire was halted at Caley's Stores behind Boots and Buntings Stores.

In the hours since the first major raid, loudspeaker vans had toured Norwich telling people to make their stirrup pumps and water and sand buckets readily accessible. They had also implored fire-watchers to attend their posts, and this time some potentially serious fires were frustrated by teams of fire-guards. At Norwich Training College, a sturdy building with a steep tiled roof which was struck by many fire bombs and badly damaged, combined efforts by the students certainly prevented a large fire. But the number of buildings badly burnt was still high and included Clark's Shoe factory, Barker's Engineering Works, two laundries, St Mary's Silk Mills and Bishop Hall's Palace. Many smaller fires raged in residential areas which, in the opinion of the authorities, could have been dealt with had fire-watchers been more ready to tackle them. The NFS attended 179 individual fires and the number would have been higher had reporting been more efficient. A report summarizing the effects of the raids commented that there were 'very few people in Norwich streets, but the stout hearts that were did excellent work'.

Who, though, could blame anyone for taking shelter? For a population reckoned at the time as being over 126,000, domestic shelters provided for 94,050. Of these, 58,250 had access to an Anderson Shelter (easily the most popular type), 4,725 could use a Morrison Shelter reckoned suitable for three adults and a child, 27,950 were provided for by surface shelters and the remaining 3,125 were reserved by a variety of trenches and basements. Additionally, public shelters comprised trenches for 5,175, surface shelters for 5,150, basements for 5,725 and a tunnel bored into a 'cliff' face able to hold 200. Thus, there was shelter available for 110,150 — 87 per cent of the population if all were present.

Considering their importance to all, the part played generally by the shelters needs to be recorded. About 1,500 Andersons and Morrisons were indeed destroyed in the Norwich raids, but replacements were rapidly delivered. Boulton & Paul's Norwich factory (which, incidentally, produced miles of Sommerfeld steel tracking for airfields) built 85,400 Morrison Shelters, producing over 2,000 a week at one time, so help was close at hand. Some 8,400 of the surface shelters were constructed of reinforced brickwork, but this had already been found to afford insufficient protection and already 1,400 of this type of shelter had been strengthened with lime/mortar brickwork, leaving 20,300 shelters awaiting attention. Prior to that the typical public surface shelter held 50 persons in each compartment, protected by brick walls 18 in thick. The floor was sunk 2 ft below ground level while the 8 in thick concrete roof was placed upon angle irons 4 x 3 in thick placed 3 ft apart. The roof spanned 5 ft and the compartment was 69 ft long. Soil excavated during building was set against the shelter walls. Later surface shelters spanned 10 ft, had reinforced concrete roofing stressed to accept a debris load of 300 lb/sq ft and had 13 ½ in thick walls but were only 40 ft long. In addition there were small surface shelters for only a dozen people. Strengthening was being achieved using a $4\frac{1}{2}$ in brick skin and a 1 in mortar intermediate skin with $\frac{1}{4}$ in rods tying roof to floor.

The protection such shelters could give was shown in countless incidents. A reinforced brick surface shelter in Ethel Road, though, suffered a direct hit, three sections being demolished with the fourth proving strong enough to withstand the blow, even though it was slewed 3 in out of true. In Northcote Road a 500 kg HE fell 31 ft away from the end of a reinforced brick shelter, and although it demolished four houses and rendered twelve more beyond repair, the shelter suffered only a cracked roof.

In Exeter Street a massive 1,000 kg HE instantly disposed of six houses and damaged ten more so badly that they had to be demolished. Some thirty feet away was an unreinforced shelter, but only one compartment suffered serious damage. When a 250 kg HE burst about 25 ft from a $13\frac{1}{2}$ in walled four-compartment shelter in Lothian Street, the shelter's rear walls collapsed letting down the roof, but the two central compartments remained intact.

Just what level of safety could be achieved was shown by a four-compartment shelter in Nicholas Street. With 14-in thick mortar reinforcement, a $4\frac{1}{2}$ in skin in cement mortar and $\frac{1}{4}$ in steel rods in cement mortar between the old and new bricks, and the header bonding bricks in every course at 3 ft, centres horizontal, the shelter was 62 ft long. About 30 ft away a 500 kg HE burst on the roadway, and so effective was the structure that only the compartment nearest the blast showed any effect, being shifted 12 in out of alignment. The wall facing the bomb was smashed by a hail of splinters. The old brick wall fell in, bonding bricks were sheared off, but the mortar stuck to the new work and the roof and other walls remained in position.

Nothing could sustain a mighty direct blow, but many shelters proved extremely protective. In Chapel Field one trench shelter received such a hit and four people were killed, but nevertheless it had stood up very well to the blow. Destruction of city centre buildings deprived the populace of 350 basement shelters, largely due to the collapse of superstructures above. No one was killed in any of these basements, which were well protected against fire, usually by 3-in floorboards.

From the Anderson Shelters there were some astonishing escapes. Huge 1,000 kg HE craters in Millers Lane and Nicholas Street had, upon their edges, such shelters which were generally undamaged except for their doors. In Miller's Lane five shelters were on the crater edge and out of 27 people using them only two were killed and one seriously injured. Of those, one who died was in a normal six-person shelter holding nine adults and two children. The door faced the crater and one occupant was buried by the hurled debris. The other occupants were unaware of just what had happened until long after they had left the damaged shelter. What was apparent was that many Anderson Shelters were not covered by enough earth, something soon remedied.

Morrison Shelters, which resembled tough metal cages suitable for use as tables when their wire mesh was not *in situ*, were less popular. Understandably so, for by sheltering in them one risked injury or worse by a building collapsing on to the shelter. Indeed, there was one instance in Norwich of the occupants of such a shelter in a burning building being beyond rescue. Another Morrison Shelter was hurled from a house which received a direct hit, and its occupants died. Yet set against these were many instances where houses collapsed around

the sturdy little shelter but it saved its occupants. Before the first raid, 1,349 Morrisons had been delivered in Norwich and after the attacks another 600 were.

An unusual item was the tunnel shelter driven into a chalk 'wall' and strengthened with corrugated lining and timber. With bunks for 75, it withstood a hit on the quarry face some 30 ft above the entry, those inside being unaware of the bomb. On 6 April a survey had shown that only 46 people were sleeping in shelters for safety. On 1 June, long after the big raids, there were still 1,062 taking cover for the night, some because of loss or serious damage to their homes.

There were about 37,000 houses in the city in April 1942. During the raids 1,487 were damaged beyond possible repair and another 19,600 variously damaged were repairable. It was to take five weeks to repair 15,500 of them and even then for nearly 3,000 it amounted to mere 'first aid'. Finding sufficient workmen to effect repairs was difficult. Immediately following the first raid, 150 Corporation workers, 100 local builders and 119 outside workers frantically coped with the damage. Most were above call-up age, or unable to serve in the Forces, and many were also ARP workers or in the Home Guard. Thus, for many the task was extremely difficult. Over 200 Corporation workers and 400 local builders were employed after the second raid, another 742 arriving from outside Norwich. The Ministry of Works special mobile repair squad boosted the total to 2,082. On 2 May all local builders were asked to lend a hand, providing another 300. Fine weather coupled with ample material available helped, but enormous problems confronted them. Each air raid had its own characteristics, the Norwich 'Baedecker' raids producing much fire damage and the results of the use of mainly larger calibre HE weapons combining to produce more wreckage than the number of attacking aircraft might imply.

No key war factories were battered. Machine tools at Caley's, a Mackintosh subsidiary, were so damaged that such as survived were passed to any who could use them, and Caley's needed new premises. Three shoe factories were rendered useless, along with a few small engineering works, laundries and small businesses. In all 54 works premises (43 having Government contracts) were put out of action. Three were abandoned, seven transferred production elsewhere, three were badly damaged and production was halted at another six. By June 75 per cent were back in business although 29 had roof, window and door problems. Damage extent varied enormously. Whereas Messrs Hind and Hardy's Silk Mills were almost destroyed by fire and HEs, having suffered in both raids, Baker Engineering had only a single crankshaft wrecked by fire.

Feeding the population was another major problem. Emergency ration cards were issued to 14,000, and 8,000 customers had to re-register at a grocer's of their choice. Rapid analysis indicated that 105 food shops had been variously hit and

Top left *It was amazing how some survived vicious assaults upon their homes. From this Norwich house an Old Age Pensioner was blown out of his room and found unhurt still in bed. His eighteen-year-old granddaughter, Eileen Warnes, was killed and his daughter, Mrs Howard, was injured. Sticky paper on windows opposite has saved them, and slates remain intact. Blast played peculiar tricks* (Eastern Daily Press).

Above left *Woodland's Infirmary, Norwich, a Poor Law institution, was hit by a heavy calibre HE* (Eastern Daily Press).

Left *Vast amounts of food were destroyed during the 1942 Norwich raids. Salvaging useful remains was essential and soldiers are stacking cans of baked beans following the 26 June 1942 raid* (Eastern Daily Press).

seventeen warehouses or depots. At the City Railway Station 8,500 14 lb tins of biscuits had perished, but twenty tons of food were saved at Norwich CWS store. At the Ministry of Food buffer supplies depot half the 400 tons of flour held was rescued. But only 300 tons out of 1,000 tons of stored chocolate, so scarce in wartime, was saved along with 300 tons of sugar.

Many aged landmarks had received a hammering. Of the fifty churches, St Bartholomew's was gutted, St Benedict's half demolished although its round tower had survived, and windows in St Stephens' were damaged. Special glass in the Roman Catholic Cathedral, donated by Dunstan Powell of Birmingham, was smashed, and the 1699 Guilden Croft Friends' Meeting House became a memory, as did Bishop Hall's Palace (converted into the 'Dolphin' Inn), the only truly mediaeval building completely demolished. The only 'military' building hit was the Old Horse Barracks.

Mercifully spared was the Norfolk & Norwich Hospital although it endured blast damage often in both raids, the Ophthalmic and Throat Ward losing its windows, and fifty beds needed to be vacated. Superficial damage affected the carpenters' store, while windows, doors and ceilings in the private patients' section were blast affected and another 35 beds lost.

Of the most poignant cost of these two heavy raids, and indeed many others, there can be no precise record as many bore their wounds for ever. What ultimately took them from their loved ones could well have remained attributable to wartime catastrophe. By mid-June the known loss of life and injuries were officially collated as follows:

	27/28 April	29/30 April	Total
Killed	158	68	226
Seriously injured	161	86	247
Less seriously wounded	262	112	374
Totals	581	266	847

Two ARP wardens had died and seven were injured. Nine fire-guards were killed, all in business premises — five in one building and all in shelters provided. Many casualties, higher in the first raid due to its surprise nature, arrived at hospital covered in soot from burning buildings.

Estimates of the number of houses unsuitable for continued occupation were at times as high as 5,000. To leave a shelter and find one's home and all its loving connotations vanished provided the most tragic moments in life. To have to pick through the remains of one's personal life, maybe seek in vain for the mere trace of a deeply loved pet, could but scar many forever. No reckoning of the emotional effects of such traumas, nor of their ultimate toll, can ever be established or remotely imagined by those spared such horror.

At Earlham Road Cemetery came the most ghastly moments of all. Three times assembled were groups of those closest to those held dearest. On 4 May the burial took place, in a mass grave, of 47 who had died. Another 42 were buried on 5 May and thirty others on 7 May for by then all the bodies found had been identified. Their misfortune had been that they lived in an attractive, ancient city near enough to the coast to allow its attackers to almost all escape ... for the time being. The war saw many a small town brutally savaged, and by all warring parties. Familiar faces, friendly old places were the casualties, but rarely the pathetic political instigators of the fight. Such, sadly, is a constant.

Chapter 19
Many targets, great and small

Military response to the Norwich raids was rapid. At 07:18 on 30 April two spying Ju 88Ds of 3.(F)/122 reconnoitred the City from 22,000 ft, but they arrived too soon to learn of imminent changes. The 3.7-in AA guns which had fired 315 rounds and the the 'Z' Battery which had loosed off 465 3-in UPs were now to be strengthened with the arrival during the afternoon of 30 April of Fighter Command's requested barrage balloon protection for the city. A mere 48 hours later 35 balloons had been deployed ready to fly. On the night of 30 April/1 May the Luftwaffe operated north of the Wash, but as its bombers proceeded homewards Wing Commander Max Aitken claimed a Do 217 and another 68 Squadron pilot two HE 111s, with a 29 Squadron Beaufighter damaging another, off Orford Ness. At 02:10 bombs fell on Lowestoft, and two raiders from the north made a short cut home across Norfolk. But the increased Norwich defences were not put to the test until 00:30 on 9 May when enemy bombers crossed the Norfolk coast, obviously heading for the City.

Marring the fine, clear starlit night, wind 12 mph east-north-east, sirens sounded at 00:40 and within a few moments four hostiles were plotted heading in at between 3,000 and 18,000 ft. These were probably among six He 111s of 7./KG100 from Chartres operating as pathfinders, and already warned of RAF fighters. Following came I, II and III/KG2 from Gilze Rijen, Eindhoven and Schiphol respectively, seven Do 217s of II/KG40 and eight Ju 88s of KGr.506 from Leeuwarden. Balloons were immediately raised to 3,500 ft, preventing KG100's marker force from low flying. In all 37 fighter sorties were despatched before, at 01:04, the three heavy AA sites commenced a thirty-minute non-stop barrage just above the balloon level and along the approach line of the confused bomber crews, well shielding the city. Between them, they fired 186 rounds. Additionally, three 'Z' projector batteries firing in salvoes loosed off 227 3-in rockets. Further out were three 40 mm Bofors gun Troops of the Field Force sited at Thorpe, Hellesdon and Stoke Holy Cross which between them fired off another 101 rounds. Placing balloons within the Gun Defended Area had, however, restricted predicted AA fire so that only geographical and local barrages could be fired.

The outcome was as planned, the Luftwaffe being forced to unload flares and bombs on the outskirts of Norwich and beyond, the brunt of them occurring at Bramerton, Caister, Kirby, Stoke Holy Cross, Hellesdon and Thorpe. No civilian casualties were sustained in Norwich, but beyond four were killed and five injured. Although shrapnel from the guns fell widely, the sound of their firing and the balloon barrage flying proved grand boosters to public morale. Dive bombing was prevented and the raiders kept above 3,000 ft. By intent or chance three bombers attacked Stoke Holy Cross, under flare illumination, and markers fell over Horsham St Faith whose guns responded. At 01:29 an unsuspecting Do 217E-4, W Nr *5375:U5+EH* of I/KG2, rammed the armed cable of the Site 33 balloon flying at 4,525 ft. Then the bomber was hurled into the balloon which burst into flames. *U5+EH* dived, flattened out at 200 ft and then was hit by LAA fire before crashing near Stoke Holy Cross. Such spectacular success was rare; and more important, the defenders had prevented all but two bombs from falling on the city centre.

Investigation of the remnants of the Dornier, three of whose crew died in the crash, showed that it was fitted with 'Kutonaz' cable cutters protected by a thin metal layer which evidently did not give way sufficiently. The aircraft also had a jettisonable, power-operated turret and bomb rack for a 1,000 kg HE. Rumour raced through Norwich that the raid leader had crashed, although this was not so. The population naturally clamoured for the extensive defences to remain, stating that their morale would otherwise fall in the knowledge that the enemy could attack with impunity.

It would be wrong to dismiss the third raid as having no effects. Indeed 21 premises were fired, eight being gutted and another six seriously damaged within four distinct areas. But all available evidence suggests that Norwich had missed its heaviest intended raid, a survey concluding that 63 metric tonnes of HEs had fallen from forty raiders, including seven parachute mines. Bombing incidents were reported from Loddon, Forhoe and Erping RDs. Many conflicting HE bomb census reports were raised relating to the three raids, the following being the figures finally compiled by the Ministry of Home Security raid research team.

	27/28 April		29/30 April		8/9 May	
Attack time	23:00 – 00:45		23:25 – 00:00		–	
HE weapons:	Expl	UX	Expl	UX	Expl	UX
1,000 kg	2	–	6	1	14	?
500 kg	31	2	24	4	53	?
250 kg	53	–	44	–	57	?
50 kg	35	–	5	–	?	?
Para mine	–	–	–	–	7	–
Unclassified	32	2	23	6	?	?
Totals	153	4	102	113	?	?
Tonnage		40 MT		39 MT		63 MT

No count of the number of incendiaries dropped was possible, and clearly the established figures showed far, far fewer UXBs than likely.

Personal memories of Norwich 'Baedecker' raids of course abound. Mrs V.M. Swaine who had witnessed the Lowestoft raid of 13 January 1942 moved to Unthank Road, Norwich, in March. There she and the family lived and took shelter, with many others. After the raid she and the family found that they had to put out a fire which was overtaking one of their beds. Going outside for fresh air they spotted a burning rabbit hutch, and managed to put that out before moving it to safety. Such activities were legion — then the problem was to find where everything had been taken! 'One thing I must mention,' she pointed out to me, 'and that is the services of the Salvation Army who appeared soon after the raid to provide endless cups of tea and encouragement, which I am sure that those present would never forget.' Indeed, the selfless service that the Salvation Army always rendered after raids was magnificent.

Probably it is true that all air raids provided an astonishing mix of pathos and humour, not to mention incredible situations. Few, surely, experienced anything as alarming and bizarre as did Gerald Sambrooke-Sturgess. Throughout the war, he served as an Inspector in City Division, Norwich City Special Constabulary, but was probably better known as a dental surgeon with a practice in Unthank Road where he lived with his family.

'On the night of the "Baedecker" raid,' he recalls, 'I was returning by car from a meeting in Stalham when, just as we reached the outskirts of Norwich, a large area around the City Station was illuminated by chandelier flares. I reached home just as the bombs began to fall, and changed into uniform while my wife and four children went to the cellar, and then walked towards St Giles' Gate. Just as I reached St John's Catholic Church I saw a plane only a few hundred feet up drop a stick of four HEs at the top of Grapes Hill, about a hundred yards away. I threw myself on the ground and the blast blew me backwards along the pavement.

'At HQ I was told to investigate a report that four people living in a caravan at the back of the Hippodrome were trapped there. The Hippodrome had been hit and was on fire. Its entrance doors had been blown open and the place was dark and full of smoke. I groped my way in and found myself on the stage. As I was looking round there was a terrifying noise almost in my ear, and my tin hat rose at least an inch off my head! I thought it must have come from one of the trapped people. Imagine my surprise at finding it was the roar of a sea lion in a cage on the stage; and consider its effect upon me while bombs were still dropping around. Eventually I made my way through to the yard at the back, where I found four people in an Anderson Shelter very dead, jammed together like sardines and covered with dust and rubble. As I could do nothing for them, I returned to HQ, reported the incident then went back to await the Rescue Services collecting the bodies.

'Preparations were next day made to bury the raid victims in a mass grave. The regular Station Sergeant phoned me, saying that the relatives of the dead had learned the sad news and told him that the married couple who owned the sea lion probably had some valuables on them. I told him that I had not seen any. The police then located their coffins, opening them just before interment. They found that the woman was wearing a large solitaire diamond ring and had £600 in bearer bonds stitched into her corsets, while the man carried £11,000 in a body belt.

'Coping with that large, excited sea lion in an air raid was not an everyday event. Since its owners were dead a new home was needed — other than the river! Eventually it was transported to a zoo at Scarborough where it soon appeared to be recuperating well. Evidently, like the residents of Norwich, it found the sound of the "Baedecker" raids unforgettable for it later died of heart failure — during a thunderstorm.'

* * *

On 10/11 May the Luftwaffe resumed attacking East Coast shipping, with small-

Above *Incredible was the discovery at the Norwich Hippodrome of a live sea lion whose owners had perished in the bombing. The remains of the wrecked dressing rooms at the variety theatre are depicted here* (Eastern Daily Press).

Below *A target of frequent enemy attention was RAF Newmarket Heath whose Grandstand complex (central in this picture) served as quarters for RAF units and squadrons* (RAF Museum W7/3/2).

Bottom *Also often in the enemy's sights, but almost entirely unscathed, was Mildenhall, seen here in June 1942* (RAF Museum W7/3/7).

scale searches being flown by III/KG2 and II/KG40 acting upon information from 3.(F)/122. Apart from this, the only East Anglian bombing to the end of the month took place near Soham on 12/13 May, when a lone raider appeared to be seeking Mildenhall, off the coast on the 20th/21st where I and III/KG2 operated with KGr.506 mining, in Lothingland RD on the 23rd/24th, on Yarmouth beach and race course and Caister golf course on the 27th/28th when four raiders operated, and in Swaffham RD and Mitford RD on the 29th/30th. Overland flights were an off-shoot of operations at sea. II/KG40 was also active that night over Essex. On the night of 29/30 May two convoys were twice unsuccessfully attacked, Yarmouth guns claiming a raider. Coltishall's Beaufighters had sought out passing bombers, damaging a Do 217 five miles north of Cromer early on the 29th and, when an estimated eighteen aircraft laid mines off the Wash early on the 30th, 12 Group flew 24 night fighter patrols and claimed three Do 217s and a Ju 88, Yarmouth gunners again claiming one.

Flying Spitfire Vbs from Ludham at this time was 610 Squadron which had several successful engagements. On 27 April Pilot Officer Hokan (*H:BL267*) and Sergeant S.G.Creagh (*K:BL484*) had at dawn put Ju 88D-5 W Nr *430215:F6+HL* of 3.(F)/122 into the sea off Yarmouth. During the evening of 14 May another two of their Spitfire pilots, Squadron Leader G.S.K. Haywood (*E:BL564*) and Sergeant F. Mares (*B:W3128*) found some Ju 88 minelayers close to Convoy 'Smilax' and sent one off in distress. Next day in cloud and rain six of the squadron's pilots destroyed two Do 217s of 3./KG2 (*5378:U5+CL* and *5373:U5+BL*) while Whirlwinds of 137 Squadron damaged a Ju 88. Early in the evening of 16 May Hayward (again in *BL564*) and Mares (*H:BL267*) were patrolling off Lowestoft when they saw a low-flying Ju 88 coming head on. Long bursts hit the nose and tail and then Wing Commander Hanks in a third Spitfire from Coltishall joined the fight. The Ju 88 was last seen entering mist with a silent rear gun and both engines belching smoke. Another Ju 88, probably of 3.(F)/122, was damaged off Lowestoft at dawn on 21 May by Pilot Officer P.B. Wright (*E:BL564*) and Sergeant J.H. Turner (*L:BL262*).

June was relatively quiet, eight periods of bombing taking place. On 1/2 June about eight enemy aircraft crossed in between Clacton and Orford Ness, one going towards Colchester, another to Bury. Bombing was centred around Ipswich where fires were started, and near Aldeburgh. An 85 Squadron Havoc engaged a Ju 88A-4 of II/KG77, but the only known loss that night was of *U5+CK*, a Do 217 which failed to return to Schiphol. On 4/5 June Lowestoft was bombed by a Ju 88 (which 68 Squadron claimed out to sea), and King's Lynn on the 12th. Wainford, Loddon and Downham RDs were visited on the 24th, Deben and Wainford RDs the next night when 68 Squadron claimed a Do 217 of II/KG40. On 29/30 June there was more widespread activity when Bedford, King's Lynn and Peterborough were visited along with Deben, Downham, Depwade, and Clare as well as North Witchford and Mitford Rural Districts.

Although airborne radar was rapidly improving, searchlights continued to play an impressive role at night. At Bradwell, Coltishall, Duxford, Matlaske, Marham, Martlesham and Wittering, six lights around the airfields played their part in 'Canopy', assisting LAA gunners locate attacking aircraft. Because such were now so few in number a new use for the searchlights, usually in a clutch of four, was devised. Under the 'Sandra' scheme their beams would from May 1942 intersect above bomber airfields marking places for safe havens. Had NJG2 not

Left *As part of the 1942 summer terror raids, Yarmouth came under attack on 25 June during which St Nicholas Church was reduced to a shell.*

Above *Middlegate Street suffered yet again, on 25 June 1942.*

Below *The sharp raid of 25 June dealt viciously with Lacon's joiner's shop.*

been withdrawn from its night intruding, such a plan would have been fraught with enormous risks. A count on 13 June had shown that Coltishall Sector (CO) had 44 searchlight sites, Debden (DN) 86 and Wittering (WT) over forty, its strength increasing. One of the latter's searchlights was probing when, at about 800 ft, a Do 217 hurried north-west across Peterborough at 03:35, sowing 1,480 incendiaries. Half an hour earlier a Mosquito had fired at a Do 217 nearby, and about ten minutes later searchlights illuminated another Dornier whose gunner promptly fired down the beam, a more unusual and difficult act than always rumoured. A second Dornier dropped HEs in the Thorney district and the Isle of Ely. Then, at 03:20, another was circling Peterborough with a Mosquito attempting to close in.

During the cat and mouse game, the bomber was four times chased over Peterborough before it lined up on the North Station area to release four ABB500 containers, their contents spilling over a quarter of a square mile, mainly over the west end of Cowgate including the Cemetery, Nelson Street, St Leonard Street and around the station. By the time of release LAA guns and Peterborough's 'Z' battery had fired several salvoes.

A very high proportion of the incendiaries ignited, probably due to correct ejection, about sixty per cent being of an explosive type. The NFS rapidly dealt with several fires, but top floors of Robert Sayle's stores in Cowgate were burnt out, and the Salvation Army HQ was badly damaged. Large fires quickly overtook the 'George' Hotel and adjacent Bowering's Motor Garage. Others occurred in St Leonard's Street, in offices, a public house and a potato store. Much water and fire damage was caused at Brown, Son & Co's clothing factory. The only injury was to a young man who received leg burns.

The raids on Bedford and King's Lynn took place simultaneously, at 02:30. At Lynn a Do 217 made an eastward pass dropping incendiaries which fell on the Edward VII Grammar School, circled Wootton and dropped more. Three areas were affected, 480 firebombs scattering around Gayton Road and some over West Lynn. Six ABB500 and eight AB36 containers had carried usual 1 kg weapons.

Four Dorniers performed the bombing of Bedford from 500 ft, two 500 kg HEs bursting in Broad Avenue and Willow Road just before the first of 1,000 incendiaries ignited on a meadow by Cardington Road. Others burnt in Russell Avenue and Park, Castle Road, Pembroke Street, South York Street, South Denmark Street, South Dudley Street, George Street and Greenshiels Road.

The choice of such targets was interesting. Bedford, King's Lynn and Peterborough all contained specialized industrial undertakings contributing usefully to the war effort. Part of a major bombing policy switch from 'Baedecker' terror attacks, they were important enough for the formation of mobile, independent LAA Troops raised specially to defend them.

June's heaviest raid came on the 26th/27th, Norwich once more being the target. A bright moon and flares floodlit the city for about thirty bombers, including examples from 7./KG100, KGr.106 and 1, II and III/KG2, which cunningly ran in from the north-west to mill around over a wide area, many showing navigation lights in attempts to confuse the defenders. The raiders came from two distinct regions: Lille, climbing via Ostend and Flushing to 15,000 ft and attacking from around 6,000 ft; and from North Holland to attack at between 6,000 and 12,000 ft. Forty minutes' bombing took place from between 3,000 and 9,000 ft, starting at 02:05. Balloons were soon flown over Norwich at 6,000 ft and there was intermittent AA fire. Also operating were 44 fighters of 12 Group, eighteen of which were committed to a clear fighter night. Mosquito *DD609* of 151 Squadron claimed a Do 217, and a Spitfire of 610 Squadron was credited with a Ju 88.

A careful incendiary count suggested that 7,764 had been used. Later, more detailed investigations suggested 8,500, even 9,000, among them some of aged French origin, steel-nosed German examples and some of the soda type. The conclusion was that maybe 500 container loads had been released, one of the rare three-leaved variety, the others the conventional two-leaf type, starting 663 fires — seventy major, five of which developed into conflagrations. Flare cases

Above *Dornier Do 217E-4s* F8+DM *and* F8+AM *of Staffel 4, II/KG40 operated against shipping and overland in 1942* (Bundesarchiv 365/2342/15).

Below *A Dornier 217E-4 of II/KG40 prepares for its load at Soesterberg. Note the folding bomb doors* (Bundesarchiv 483/2882/18).

Bottom *By 1943 the Dorniers had acquired wave-like upper surfaces or grey blotching on a dark green or black base.* 'HN' *of KG40, Soesterberg, has anti-shipping markings* (Bundesarchiv 483/2882/10).

Above *Do 217E-4s of KG2 were common sights in 1942. U5+FS shown may well be training for low level precision operations* (Bundesarchiv 358/1921/27).

Below *Mostly the '217s operated at night. U5+BS has its hockhammer badge overpainted, but retains a coloured nose stripe* (Bundesarchiv 358/1922/37).

Bottom *Constant problems with the engines of Heinkel He 177s were encountered. Undergoing a change is a coupled powerplant of a KG100 aircraft* (Bundesarchiv 676/7972/14).

totalling nineteen were discovered, and casings of three BLC50 flash bombs. Twenty-six incendiaries fell at the transept-tower junction of the Cathedral and 28 on Lower Close. It was estimated that 34 HEs had fallen, one 1,000 kg, nine 500 kgs and 24 250 kgs. The large weapon landed on the east side of Junction Road, producing a clear, perfect crater and causing eight houses to simply disappear. A 500 kg HE hit the south-west wall of Norwich Prison, damaging the main hall roof and the precincts with blast and fragmentation effects. The back garden of 6 Vincent Road acquired a 500 kg HE, with others falling in Harvey Lane and in the road outside 'Hillcrest', Telegraph Lane East. A 500 kg bomb hit the tower of St Julian's Church which was completely demolished. Seriously damaged Norwich Maternity Home was also the recipient of a 500 kg HE, another of which exploded outside Nos 9 and 11 Hatton Road, damaging a school gymnasium.

Among targets for 250 kg bombs were 39-43 Spittalfields, Ketts Hall, Harvey Lane where two fell, Norwich Corporation's water tower, No 14 Catton Road which received a direct hit, Cinder Oven Row, St Mark's churchyard where the church was damaged too, a large block of flats in Brook Place and the garden of 42 Unthank Road where the crater lip touched the rear of the house. The signal telegraph office in the LNER Thorpe goods yard was hit, a 250 kg HE burst in a tree by the river and similar bombs dropped in gardens, one behind 167 Dereham Road, another behind 77/79 Aimes Street and at 23/25 Goldsmith Street. No 8 Barker Street received a direct hit.

A constant fear was that the cathedral would sooner or later be hit. Nobody surely would ever forget the sight of Coventry's memorial, and there was deep concern that more might be lost. For Norwich, fortune or Great Might prevailed and, although fire bombs hit the roof, the cathedral again escaped much damage. Fire destroyed the churches of St. Paul and St Michael and the Synagogue was damaged. Eighteen fires were burning many hours after the raid. Severe was the damage to shops, and two hospitals were damaged — one so severely that it had to be evacuated. Industrial premises hit included Lawrence Scott Electro Motors Ltd which escaped serious damage because incendiaries fell mainly in its yard and on the canteen. As a result of the attack nine people were killed and 22 injured.

Margaret Lindley, a second year student nurse at the Norfolk and Norwich Hospital at the time of the raid, was awoken by the 'crash warning'. For her a night to remember was approaching, as she recalls:

'Norwich had so many false alarms when the siren sounded that a system was devised whereby if the raiders were within three minutes' flying time of Norwich, the factory hooters sounded. On this particular night when I awoke to the crash warning there was also a very bright orange light showing through my curtains. I put my head out of the window, and discovered incendiary bombs raining down. As I was on the third floor of the Nurses' Home I made haste downstairs. It was not on fire, so we were told to return to our rooms, dress and collect any essential clothing. As the main hospital was on fire we were asked to help with the evacuation of the patients. These were all moved in their beds on to the front lawn — 500 in all. Ambulances and every sort of vehicle — military and civilian — which could transport patients were already queueing in St Stephen's Road.

'Men from the Scottish Horse Regiment stationed nearby helped remove as much equipment as possible from the burning hospital. I had been working on a Male Surgical Ward, and all my poor old men had left their false teeth on their lockers. We were not supposed to go back into the hospital, but my patients persuaded me and I crept back into the smoke-filled ward and collected several mugs of teeth — they had to sort out which belonged to who! The nurses escorted the patients to outlying hospitals, and I travelled in an Army truck through burning Norwich. I particularly remember going past Bonds shop which, being half timbered, was like an enormous bonfire.

Twice during June Luftwaffe attention was directed against Yarmouth. Early on the 10th sixteen HEs fell across South Denes, High Street and Riverside, Gorleston, Burgh Road to Beccles Road and several in the sea. II/KG2 was probably responsible, having recently moved from Soesterberg to Eindhoven. More punishing was the second attack, between 01:30 and 02:50 on the 25th, carried out possibly by four aircraft either of KG2 or KGr.106. The 'red' was received in the Borough at 23:58 and the bombs, eight HEs and about 1,500 incendiaries, were laid across the town centre. Lacon's workshop and store were gutted, Palmer's furniture store was hit and Brett's Furniture Store on North Quay, where the contents of 22 houses had been put in 'safe keeping', was completely burnt out. The 'Wrestler's Arms', British Restaurant, Liberal Club and Fordes furniture warehouse were all badly damaged. A group of HEs further smashed the Row area, between Nos 107 and 128, which had suffered previously like Greyfriars' Cloisters which had been partly rebuilt. One of the first HEs at the foot of the GNM railway embankment caused subsidence of the track by Breydon Bridge. Superficial damage was caused to the Central Police Station, Town Hall and the Free Library and the question arose as to whether any remained safe for occupation. Windows were smashed in 25 shops, and 35 houses were of no more use. Another 200 were damaged. In the Row area 300 houses had now been destroyed or were beyond repair. A gas main fracture caused a sharp fire and the NFS, called to ten sizeable blazes, summoned outside assistance.

Dawn brought the sad sight of St Nicholas' Parish Church, largest in the country, gutted, although its reredos was almost untouched. St Nicholas' was to Yarmouth what the Cathedral was to Norwich. The raid cost the lives of three people, two had serious injuries and nineteen were slightly wounded. A further 117 needed rest centre accommodation.

Individual style attacks peculiar to this period involved lone bombers coming in at 7,000 ft and diving to 1,000 ft despite fire from ground defences.

The first three dark-night weeks of July saw little enemy activity over land, although early on the 3rd enemy aircraft penetrated from the Wash to unload incendiaries near Peterborough and HEs near March, Bedford and West Dereham. Peterborough's heavy guns fired 34 rounds at a marauding Ju 88. Off the East Anglian shore Dorniers followed reconnaissances by 3.(F)/122 with anti-shipping raids, but with little success while the Luftwaffe awaited the next moon period. Intelligence assessments of Luftwaffe strength in mid-June 1942 suggested that it held 1,470 long-range bombers, including 800 Ju 88s (54.5 per cent), 490 He 111s (33.4 per cent) and 120 Do 217s (8.17 per cent). In the Netherlands from where most East Anglian raids were being mounted there were 177 bombers. On 13 June, one of these, a Do 217, carried out a daring, low-level attack on the Lockheed Hydraulics factory in Leamington Spa. Entering over the Wash, it placed HEs on three workshops before leaving on a cloud-clad reciprocal course. A repeat occurred on 16 July, the bomber orbiting west of Wittering to put defenders off the scent. Beaufighters, unusually operating in daylight, located the Do 217 north-east of Wittering but it was skilfully flown and evaded them to drop four 500 kgs again on the Leamington factory. German radio claimed extensive fires, although the small one caused was soon extinguished. This raid, and another on 3 July in which a Do 217 in daylight bombed the main Rolls-Royce factory store at Derby, causing heavy casualties in a nearby street, proved that the Germans were indeed attempting very worthwhile specialized operations. That specific targets were listed was further shown when Chelmsford (home of Marconi radio and Hoffman ballbearings) was attacked on 19 July from low level.

Whether the bombing of Yarmouth's Corporation Destructor Plant fell into a similar category seems highly unlikely, but when two Do 217s — the first one dropping incendiaries, the second two 500 kg HEs — attacked at 01:45 they performed for Yarmouth's population an act providing much satisfaction. Long had it been argued that the plant's tall chimney was a beacon for bombers, and so after the furnace was destroyed, and the salvage plant crushed, the authorities demolished their chimney to the relief of many in New Town.

Yarmouth was bombed again early on 12 July, and this time a direct hit was scored on the Eastern Counties Omnibus Depot. A 500 kg bomb flattened their office and a restaurant in RAF hands. The four HEs killed two and injured seven people. At the same time that night Lowestoft was raided without any alert. One HE burst on the Naval Commander's office, Hamilton Dock, the other in clinker and sand at Messrs Overys' in Battery Green Road. Three workshops were damaged, casualties amounting to one killed and five injured.

Throughout the year the Luftwaffe had been minelaying off the East Coast, but these operations had by now fallen from about fifty per cent of total effort to around thirty per cent. There had been no more fighter strikes along the coast although at 05:45 on 20 July a Bf 109 was reported near Lowestoft by a Beaufighter crew.

Scattered Dornier raids developed over East Anglia on 21/22 July, during which Do 217 E-4 *4260:U5+IH* probably fell to Mosquito II *W4090* of 151 Squadron. The first bombing incident occurred at 23:37 when 500 kg SC HEs fell on Cromer, one demolishing 13 Garden Street, one exploding on the Kursaal Fun Fair in Church Square where also Messrs Rounce & Wortley and Clarke's the tobacconist, were hit. Eleven civilians were killed and fifteen injured, nine houses were destroyed and 189 variously damaged. Another Do 217 from 300 ft delivered two ABB500 container loads of incendiaries over King's Lynn's dock area. About 170 ignited in St Anne's and North Street, but without causing fires.

Ten minutes later another Do 217 three times circled the Felixstowe Dock area before dropping an ABB500 container carrying about 360 Type 36 and Type 41 incendiaries. Balloons at 3,000 ft kept the raider at around 5,000 ft and heavy AA guns fired about fifty rounds. The attack was directed upon the Boom Defence Depot, 47 incendiaries falling in the naval zone, the remainder on adjacent meadows. Although there were no casualties, a lot of equipment was damaged, suggesting again an operation of a specialized nature.

Another took place on 23 July around 08:30. Do 217 *U5+LP* from the Wash followed the Old Bedford River, periodically checking its position by coming out

Yarmouth's Royal Naval Barracks were badly battered on 24 July 1942.

of the cloud, to aim, from the south, four 500 kg HEs at the railway installations or industrial targets at Bedford. They fell on the approach to Ford End Bridge, Grafton Assembly Rooms and partly demolished the 'Grosvenor' Hotel. About 250 houses and shops suffered superficial damage.

After dark on 23 July bombs fell in eight East Anglian areas, two of the four 250 kg HEs at Yarmouth exploding at the RN Barracks causing blast and splinter damage. Two Dorniers made low level passes over King's Lynn Docks, dropping four ABB500 containers carrying 480 incendiaries, only thirty of which ignited, and an hour later four HEs. As a result a tug in dock was sunk and a coal tip wrecked although most of the bombs fell wide. Other incidents took place in Ramsey UD and Huntingdonshire while patrolling fighter crews, including ten of 68 Squadron, claimed to have destroyed seven raiders. Of these Wing Commander Aitken claimed a Ju 88 and a Do 217, while Sergeant Truscott, Warrant Officer BeBeh and Squadron Leader Vesely, also of 68 Squadron, each reckoned to have shot down a Do 217. Known losses were one aircraft of III/KG2 and two of II/KG40.

By day Ju 88s of 3.(F)/122 were making on average three North Sea searches daily. One of the aircraft from Creil, Ju 88A *5649:8H + KL* (on loan from 3.(F)/33) was shot down on 25 July near Smith Knoll LV. Much more unusual was the extensive daylight operation mounted during the morning of 27 July. Raids developed over a wide area as 25 aircraft drawn from I, II and III/KG2, II/KG40 and 7./KG100 (two He 111s) took advantage of cloud and drizzle to bomb Derby, the Gloucester area and penetrate even to Birmingham. Once more, radar-equipped Beaufighters were deployed without success. Relying upon visual navigation, the bombers flew between fifty and 11,000 ft. In the poor conditions the enemy did not have it all his own way for three times the Do 217s impacted barrage balloon cables, although they survived.

Sheringham received bombs from Raid 639 in Priory and Beeston Roads at

07:45, nine people being killed and two injured. Eleven houses were destroyed, two badly damaged and over 300 more needed repairs. Around midday Do 217s of III/KG2 crossed into East Anglia, HEs from Raid 648 directed at RAF Docking at 12:38 destroying a Wellington and damaging buildings and three cottages. Another raider in that wave was engaged by Lowestoft's LH2 3.7-in guns which fired six rounds, and at 12:15 four HEs were dropped at South Repps before warning could be given. Off Aldeburgh four bombs exploded in the sea opposite the lifeboat station, the gunner in the Do 217 answering fire from soldiers in a blockhouse. Another Do 217 in low cloud and rain hedge-hopped to Pulham where at 13:55 four 500 kg HEs ricocheted, three air-bursting and one ramming into a metal shed. So low was the '217 that it literally climbed over a small hut and skimmed over the large airship shed, then machine-gunned Thorpe Abbotts airfield, which was being constructed.

After dark a major effort was mounted, about sixty aircraft of four RTUs and front line units entering over the Wash at between 500 and 1,500 ft. II and III/KG2 headed mainly for Birmingham and a low-level return, leaving a few others going southerly. Peterborough guns fired once, and a Heinkel 111 was heard over Duxford., That terror and spoiling attacks upon historic places were nevertheless continuing, despite recent specialized raids, was proven when Raid No 464 penetrated to Cambridge.

Flying incredibly low, a Ju 88A-5, possibly of KGr.106, arrived from the east in moonlight. Frequent claims that cockpit lights in low fliers were visible are often made. Possibly, but in this case with the bomber at no more than 100 ft above me I saw none but I picked out the oil trays beneath its engines, as featured by later Ju 88As. As it roared overhead, engines emitting their characteristic, Ju 88 smooth sound, I watched from outside the Brunswick School shelters, a splendid vantage point from which I tried always to observe events. The aircraft had astonishingly to rise to clear elms by the River Cam, and as it did so the LAA mobile Bofors Troop on Midsummer Common fired two rounds, to which the '88's crew hopefully responded with a Very light. A power surge carried the climbing aircraft into a very steep turn which resolved itself into a dive. Hurrying south, it released twelve bombs along the east side of Bridge Street. Against the red and yellow explosions masonry could be seen hurled high. Quickly following more muted 'cracks', bright fires burnt too. I was held transfixed, this was a once in a lifetime experience for rarely was it possible to see such an event so clearly unfold. Rapidly the sky reflected a fierce fire, and next morning's discoveries were equally memorable.

Gone first had been the 'Blue Barn' Restaurant, an aged two-storey building in Ram Yard removed by a 250 kg HE, another of which scored a direct hit on the repair shop of Allins' Garage at 5 Jordan's Yard, causing the collapse of adjoining houses. At the Bridge Street/Jesus Lane junction a 50kg HE smashed its way through a 2½-in concrete step to explode in a cellar and damage the nearby 4-in gas main. The next HE hit a parapet on No 3 Jesus Lane, richocheting on to the opposite wall before exploding in the basement of No 4 Jesus Lane. Scars caused by fragmentation from these incidents may still be found on the wall of Trinity College opposite.

Most unfortunate was the effect of a 50 kg HE which penetrated a flanking wall of the Union Debating Society's first floor writing room, causing much damage. Nearby, the British Restaurant had a narrow escape for a bomb there did not explode, whereas two other 50 kg HEs in gardens burst, one behind No 22 Portugal Place and the other demolishing a shed in the Union Debating Society's garden. No 4 St Clements Garden received another which, upon exploding on the ground floor, caused partial collapse of a partition wall.

Fortunately, apart from the Union building, the precious College buildings had very narrowly escaped for, had the bomb line been a mere 50 ft further west, there would have been loss of famous places. Luckiest of all must have been the irreplaceable Round Church, close to which the bombs had fallen. Its escape was a relief.

The fire bombs ignited to a curious cracking sound, and soon after the raid, with the top of No 4 Jesus Lane burning, likewise the Union Society building, it was apparent that unconventional explosive incendiaries had been used and their precise nature was soon discovered. Into 13 Portugal Place, eight feet up, had come an unusual bomb akin in shape to a 50 kg HE weapon. After bouncing on to the front hearth, and leaving appropriate skid marks, it had penetrated into the basement's party wall and failed to burst. A policeman investigating by torchlight cautiously entered the room into which the bomb was poking through the wall. His arrival apparently coincided with the moment when a lodger in the room also awoke ... to the accompaniment of two unexpected ambassadors! Disbelieving, he informed the Constable that he would sleep on — until the extent of his danger dissuaded him.

Another of these unusual weapons rested unexploded within outbuildings in 'The Mitre's' yard. Disarming them revealed that within the casing was an explosive head charge behind which were three conical shaped bombs. In a third, aft compartment was a package of 67 small incendiaries. The explosive device should have scattered them all over quite a wide area with considerable penetrative force. Suspicion at the time that these were new explosive incendiaries, IBSEN type, was ill founded. What had arrived, possibly for the first time in East Anglia, were Sprengband C.50s, the first 'Firepots'. They were being confirmed as such for the first time, although some may well have been previously used even though the very distinctive bursting sound had not apparently been previously noted.

Raid casualties totalled three killed and eighteen injured, six seriously. Three houses and seven other buildings were badly hit, 127 more variously damaged, and far more havoc might have been wrought at Norwich the same night. Another Ju 88 crossing the city at 8,000 ft — well above the balloons — launched a 1,000 kg HE which detonated in an orchard between Trafford Road and Rowington Road close to Southwold Railway goods siding, the likely target. It damaged about forty houses, not many considering the might of the bomb. Other loads fell at Wymondham, near Ely and in Lothing and Mitford RDs.

Over the closing nights of July it was obvious that the enemy was concentrating most of his effort on Birmingham and the Midlands. Pincer operations were mounted, and some lengthy round flights. High percentages of fire bombs were released, among them Sprengband C.50s and elaborate explosive incendiaries. Early on 29 July a small force operated over the eastern counties. Raid N1N flew from the Wash to drop four 500 kg HEs which demolished three houses at March, killing six people. Other bombs fell in Deben, Wainford and Halstead RDs. Over Norwich 36 balloons were flying at 6,500 ft when at 02:38 one of a number of Dorniers flying back to the Netherlands very

Above left *Houses were hit on the corner of Palgrave and Alderson Roads, Yarmouth, on 29 July 1942.*
Above right *Royal Avenue, Yarmouth, was also bombed on 29 July 1942.*

low nearly hit Cable 6. It then nearly clouted Cable 12. Over ten Do 217s passed close to Norwich, flying very low to escape fighters.

At 08:56 a 'tip and run' Dornier, Raid 452, placed four HEs, probably 500 kgs and intended for Vauxhall Station, across a residential area of Yarmouth from Royal Avenue to Palgrave and Alderson Roads, killing two and injuring fifteen. Damage amounted to two shops demolished, 42 houses seriously damaged and another 306 less so. Lots of light guns blazed away, but they had been given insufficient warning.

On 29/30 July many fires developed as over 100 bombers raided Birmingham, Wales, London and ten East Anglian localities. As it approached into Norfolk Do 217E-4 W Nr *1213:U5+DP* carrying four ABB500 containers was shot down. The night was, however, more memorable for the many bombers, including those of II and III/KG2 and its 11th Staffel operating from Deelen, which flew home to Dutch bases at exceptionally low heights, often not above 50 ft. Many were challenged by guns at Peterborough and Norwich as they headed for their exit north of Yarmouth. Searchlights involved in 187 engagements managed twenty illuminations. Cambridge HAA guns fired seventeen rounds at 01:29, and at 01:42 five 250 kg HEs and explosive incendiaries demolished three houses at Bedford, killing four people.

Between 02:30 and 03:30 there was intensive activity as Dorniers and Ju 88s hurried home, literally at treetop height. A Ju 88 fired at a Feltwell Wellington and was engaged by the station's 'canopy', Bofors LAA guns L2 and L3 hurling fourteen shots at the attacker which was passing at below 100 ft. Honington and Newmarket LAA at 02:45 engaged a Ju 88 and Do 217 respectively. During the 01:30-03:45 Cambridge alert three enemy aircraft flew over low facing LAA guns on Midsummer Common, by Long Road and Luard Road. Unlucky was a passing Wellington Ic which was fired upon. Bofors at Sites L4, 8 and 9 fired eight rounds at a Do 217 flying easterly at 200 ft, then at 03:10 the Cambridge reinforcing light guns L6, 10, 15 and 19 fired seventeen rounds at another low-flying Dornier. A Ju 88 which at 02:45 passed over Oakington was too low even for the Bofors there, but 94 rounds SAA were fired. Lit by 'canopy', the bomber left with a smoking engine.

So far the East Anglian returners had escaped, but for no longer. Trouble first engulfed Ju 88A-4 W Nr *2086:1H+CR* of III/KG26, one of sixteen aircraft despatched from Rennes by the unit at about 22:50. Heading for home via Soesterberg it was brought down near Peterborough, the crew all dying. At 03:07 Ju 88A-4 W Nr *3810:1H+KT*, also of III/KG26, crashed into the sea. It had flown to Birmingham over the south-west carrying an ABB500 and one BSB700 container, headed at sea level over Cardigan Bay, climbed to 15,000 ft then came down to 4,500 ft to bomb. Its low-level run home commenced near Coventry and over Norfolk misty weather was encountered. So low was the aircraft that it clouted telephone wires at Norwich then was hit by gunfire from L9, L20 and L30 at the coast. The crew was lucky to survive the crash.

Gruppe 106 likewise flew a similar route home, making use of the Huntingdon-Ely-Thetford-Norwich railway for navigation. Also flying low were KG 100's He 111s, one of which was claimed, and confirmed to come down three miles off Southwold, by Bofors of Site L2 there. Lowestoft's LH1 gunners were the others to have confirmed success when they brought down Do 217E-4 W Nr *5469:U5+GV* flown by the 11th Staffel of KG2, and which came down 44 miles off the Dutch coast. Bodies of the crew were washed ashore near Lowestoft.

Next night, although the only bombs in the area fell near St Ives, there was plenty of flying. Four Gruppen operating from the Netherlands all attacked from the east and nearly all flew home at rooftop height. Among them were examples from III/KG26, five RTUs and He 111s of KG100 heading, ultimately, for Chartres. Twice around 02:00 the Cambridge 3.7-in guns fired, loosing off 27 rounds at 6,800 ft. At 03:33 it was the turn of the town's Bofors (Field Force) to shoot six times at a Do 217. At 02:20 Upwood defenders fired 125 rounds SAA at a bomber 80 ft above. Incendiaries fell at Glatton airfield site, and searchlight WT104 gunners shot at a Do 217. The night's eastern highlight, though, came at 03:10 when Ju 88A-5 W Nr *4293:3Z+HU* of IV/KG77 from Creil was engaged by searchlights DX072 and DX072B, then hit at a mere 50 ft over Oakington by one of the seven 40 mm Bofors shells fired. Already it had sustained night fighter damage, and now immediately dived to total destruction at Rampton. IV/KG77 also lost W Nr *5123:3Z+BW* and KG2 three aircraft — *5422:U5+FP, 5427:U5+IR* and *5470:U5+ET*.

Strong momentum established, the Luftwaffe was active on most days in August, I, II and III/KG2 attacking Norwich on the 1st/2nd from around 9,000 ft. A 1,000 kg HE fell in the centre of Brandford Road, badly damaging nineteen houses near its 69-ft crater. A UXHE rested nearby, another in Spencer Street. A 500 kg HE scored a direct hit on Clarkes' factory in Northumberland Street, falling on the reinforced concrete roof and penetrating the top three floors before exploding. Another destroyed houses in Napier Street. Six people were rescued from a damaged public house. Six times the 'Z' rocket battery fired, releasing 487 rounds in all. Another 120 shells were fired by 3.7-in guns. Off Norfolk twelve Do 217s of II/KG40 mounted an anti-shipping foray, during the course of which *F8+GN* crashed into the sea and eight aircraft made landfalls.

Next day was August Bank Holiday. Low cloud and drizzle provided ideal conditions for sneak raiders which had twofold tasks — destroy military targets and deliberately spoil the holiday over a wide area. Late afternoon raids developed during the third phase. Eight Do 217s of II and III/KG2 operating very low strafed the Watts Naval School and at 17:10 placed four HEs on rail

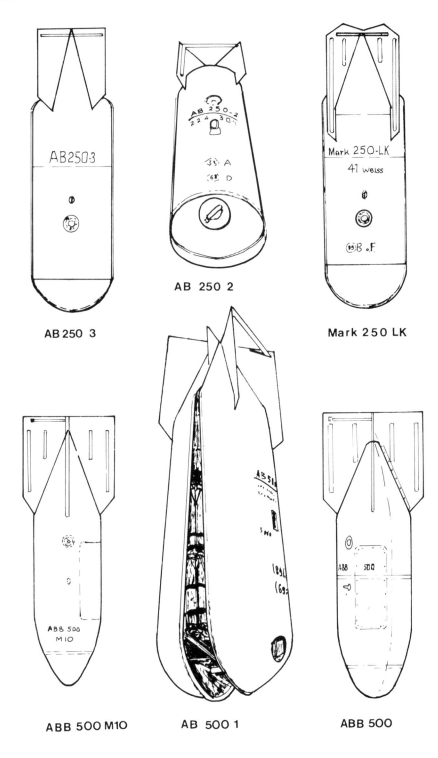

AB 250 3

AB 250 2

Mark 250 LK

ABB 500 M10   AB 500 1   ABB 500

A wide assortment of containers were used for the carriage of incendiary bombs, flares and anti-personnel bombs. Many were marked 'AB' meaning Abwurf Behalter ('throwing out container'). These were released intact and fuzed to open at a chosen altitude. Where the container corresponded with an HE bomb in size, it was designated appropriately, eg, AB250 occupying the space taken by a 250 kg HE. Many variations in design and tail structure existed, the ABB series having the additional 'B' for 'Brandbomben' (fire bomb). Containers known to have fallen on East Anglia included those illustrated and others listed here.

German designation	Contents	Length (in)	Max diameter (in)	Colour	British designation
(Carried in 50 kg stowage space)					
AB23 SD2	23 SD2	43.5	8	Dark green	J
AB36	36 IB or 24 IBSEN	42	8	Green	B or C
BSK36	36 IB or 16 IBSEN	43	8	Aluminium	A
AB70D1	50 SD1	43.5	8	Grey	M(i)
(Carried in 250 kg stowage space)					
AB250-2	224 SD1 or 17 SD10A	63.6	14.7	Khaki	N
AB250-3	108 SD2	63.7	14.7	Dark green	N
Mark 250 LK	41 small flares	49	14	Khaki	N
Mark 250 BK	Single-candle flares and 3 SD2	49	14	Khaki	N
(Carried in 500 kg stowage space)					
ABB500	140 IB or 2,200 crowsfeet	69.6	18.4	Grey/red band	F(i)
ABB500 M10	10 small flares	69.6	18.4	Grey/red band	F(ii)
(Mark 500 similar)					
AB500-1	184 IB or 116 IBSEN or 37 SD10A	82	19	Khaki	H
BSB320	320 IB	93	20	Black	E(ii)
(Carried in 1,000 kg stowage space)					
AB1000-2	620 IB or 372 IBSEN or 238 IB+ 248 IBSEN	118	26.5	Khaki	G
BSB700	700 IB	123	26	Light blue	E(i)
BSB1000	620 IB	104	24	Khaki	P

The illustration of an AB500-1 shows the common style of splitting apart. Neither the Germans nor the Allies aimed incendiary bombs in the conventional manner, but dropped them in shoals. Note the assorted types of tails fitted — according to the required spread and type of load carried.

sheds at Melton Constable. HEs were also dropped south-east of Harpley, east of Haddiscoe Street and at Great Ryburgh Maltings which, it will be recalled, had previously been the scene of a memorable incident. Close by the 'Crown' Inn and railway installations were also hard hit. A train was fired upon at North Wootton, likewise Edgefield School. My own recollection of that afternoon is clear, posing an interesting question. At 18:05 Cambridge sirens sounded and moments later, doubtless like many others, I was amazed to see at about 150 ft a Heinkel He 111 emerge from the mist over Chesterton. It promptly banked towards the north, opening fire on the Arbury Road searchlight site which answered with LMG fire. A He 111 over Britain in daylight seemed even then an unlikely event and seems even more so now, but there is no doubting the unusual sight. Was it of IV/KG55? Even more interesting was the target area which was evoking particular German interest. Was the Heinkel on a special 'spotting' venture?

The extent of low flying, especially in daylight and cloud cover, was bringing ever increasing concern. Lack of LAA guns was known by the enemy, many Bofors having gone overseas. Home defences needed 4,410 40 mm guns — and held only 941. Clearly the Luftwaffe crews were attacking important, precise targets, at first on the south and south-east coasts and now by skilled crews flying far inland. Forces of up to forty aircraft sometimes operated these raids, in one case fanning out after entry to include the bombing of an ammunition factory at Hereford, Shorts at Swindon and Marconi at Chelmsford. Of 216 Vital Points scheduled for Bofors, none yet had them.

Not only were guns short and searchlight sites likely to be too, manpower was an equally grave problem. There was of course an obvious answer, woman power. On 9 August a senior official gave his opinion of that most clearly. Night after night searchlight crews had been inactive until lately. In his opinion that was 'the sort of life that suits women but demoralizes men. The women will spend their hours of waiting knitting, gossiping, busying themselves in a multitude of small matters. Men will lie on their beds reading "Edgar Wallace" novels and getting more demoralized as time goes on. Busy women of common sense will find on the other hand a virile appeal if you promise danger, and hard work; and opportunities for real service will receive an enthusiastic response. Practical experience in the WAAF has shown that in general women are calm, well balanced and efficient in action, but that they may flop a bit when the party's over.' Luckily, few women are likely to have read his report! In AA Command, women did indeed come to play an impressive part.

At 00:50 on 7 August, another round of specialized activity took place after sirens again sounded in Cambridge. Barely had I time to organize my spotting activity when the tell-tale sound of Dorniers, not very high, was with us. According to my diary they crossed the town then circled to the west, each crew awaiting its turn for a level bombing pass. Searchlights were probing and to my amazement found in their beams what I recorded as a 'light blue, four-engined bomber, a Fw 200'. Believing this quite impossible I later renamed my Condor a He 111. But in the light of post-war knowledge I have concluded that, since II/KG40's Dorniers were active at this time, a Condor of I/KG40 seems a likely possibility.

Being mounted was a precision attack on the Unicam Works, a small factory in Arbury Road (over which that Heinkel had recently been) which specialized in optical equipment for guns and submarines. That a target finder was leading there is no doubt. Certainly the bomber force operating at between 2,000 and 8,000 ft numbered over ten aircraft — Fighter Command reckoned on fifteen raiders from Holland, and Coltishall sent up six 68 Squadron Beaufighters (*V8283, V8524, V9255, V8249* the veteran *R2148* and Flight Sergeant Adam in *X7583* who fired at one of the bombers).

The raid opened with the launch of single-candle flares, then came Dorniers from the north-west dropping at 01:05 about 360 incendiaries, initially very close to the target, over Leys Road, Orchard Avenue, Arbury Road and College land adjacent, then more in Histon where a timber yard was set ablaze. They returned, bombing nearer the target, another incendiary load igniting within the area between Shirley School-Scotland Road and Kendal Way. From my usual vantage point at Brunswick School's shelters I watched the marker flares drifting easterly, and bombing to the south-east followed after the crump of three 250 kg HEs which fell at the sewage farm and one in a cornfield. A third shoal of incendiaries ignited in Chesterton Road where, in the gutter outside G.P. Hawkins' shop next day, an ABB500 container lay occasioning much public interest. Four 50 kg HEs exploded in the Stourbridge Common/Garlic Row area injuring an ARP warden, before the final incendiary shower guided by the markers was scattered just to the east of Barnwell Bridge, on Newmarket Road, Ditton Walk and Ditton Fields. Among this load were a few explosive incendiaries. Throughout the raid the 78 HAA's two 3.7-in Troops were awaiting the order to fire, but they only managed a few rounds because of the presence of fighters. Impressive, as ever, were those hollow bangs not all that high. When the raid ended at 01:55 a count showed 114 Cambridge properties with fire or blast damage, but only two houses untenantable. Eight ABB500 containers were found.

The possibility of a repeat attack was not ruled out, but when the Cambridge alert was in force from 00:55 to 01:45 on 10 August it was connected with a precision raid elsewhere. Flying through wind and rain a Do 217 had located its target, Peterborough's imposing 1928 power station, whose three 160-ft chimneys had always been thought by the public to make it an attractive target. Again, a level pass was in keeping with most recent attacks, the first being made at 10,000 ft at 23:51, the second a few minutes later lower from 5,000 ft. Three 500 kg SD HEs were used and about 250 incendiaries, but none hit the power station. Instead, a pair of houses in Oundle Road, Woodston, suffered. The second bomb skidded across a garden and the other at 8 Wharf Road did not explode. Six containers of incendiaries fell within the area of Fengate Pumping Station-Power Station-Cross Street causing fifteen fires, the most serious being at the Bridge Street City Picture House.

Early on 11 August a 10,000-ft level raid developed on Ipswich with clouds, 4/10 at 4,000 ft racing across. As at Peterborough no flares were dropped, but four ABB500 containers of fire bombs fell, mainly in the Derwent Road zone, and 21 fires developed, five needing NFS attention. Of fourteen HEs dropped, eleven fell on playing fields in Raeburn/Landsear Roads damaging the school. A 250 kg HE scored a direct hit on 269 Landsear Road, one fell between two Anderson Shelters behind 282 Landsear Road and the third, of 50 kg, hit an unoccupied Anderson behind 17 Derwent Road. More incidents were reported in East Anglia that night than upon any other in August, bombs falling in

Hartismere, Lothing, Deben, Wainford and Downham RDs and also at Colchester. Next night bombs fell in Frinton and Gipping RD, and Do 217 *U5+DT* of III/KG2 was brought down.

At 22:43 on August 13 Norwich received a 'red' warning and shortly afterwards the first of sixteen bombers approached the city. Norwich was no longer an easy run. It was well defended by guns, and with ever more effective fighters to contend with, only five of the bombers managed to cross the city, at around 8,000 ft. Flares were wasted, only about eighty incendiaries fell at 22:57 within the city area, and only three HEs. One 250 kg HE punched a hole 29 ft across in the grounds of Mousehold Avenue Infants' School, Gertrude Road, damaging that and fifty terraced houses around. A 500 kg bomb made a 36-ft crater on nearby allotments while another on Mousehold Heath caused slight damage to twenty houses. Whether two Ju 88A-4s of 2./KG54 shot down during the night were involved in the raid is not known.

Attacks, generally on a small scale, continued to the end of August. On the 14th/15th when a dozen enemy aircraft operated mainly over Suffolk, incendiaries and HEs again fell on Ipswich causing little damage. Next night brought unsuccessful attempts to bomb two airfields in Norfolk. Little was achieved by fifteen Dorniers operating on the 16th/17th when Colchester was raided. Norwich was singled out for bombing on the 18th/19th, but the four aircraft, flying high, instead distributed most of their loads over four rural areas. While most of the Dutch-based Dorniers were thrown into a loss-producing attempt over the English Channel to interfere with the Dieppe landing on 19 August, II/KG40 mounted an unprofitable diversionary shipping sweep off Norfolk. Whirlwinds responded, shooting down a Dornier of 5./KG40.

Not until 22/23 August was activity over East Anglia resumed, a lone Dornier dropping four 500 kg HEs at Yarmouth. One scored a direct hit on 102 Baliol Road, and others doing no damage produced 30- and 36-ft diameter craters. Activity on the 22nd also brought the loss of Do 217E-4 W Nr *1152:U5+LP* of II/KG2 at Worlingworth. At 20:00 this and four more aircraft had left Eindhoven to make a repeat raid on the Cambridge Unicam works. Instructions from the Gruppenkommandeur had been explained by No 6 Staffelkapitän. Large-scale maps were carried to make sure of target marking, with Chesterton Fen Road viaduct, which Walter Horn's Home Guards were still guarding, a special pin-point during the bomb run. But *U5+LP*, carrying four 500 kg HEs, was caught over Orford Ness by Mosquito *DD612* of 157 Squadron and set on fire. No bombing took place at Cambridge that night but bombs fell in Forhoe, Hartismere and Walsingham costing I/KG2 *U5+CK* and *U5+KH*.

Another small-scale raid, this time on Ipswich,took place on 25/26 August, and it produced one of the most distressing tragedies the town endured. A 500 kg HE exploded on an Anderson Shelter at 501 Moulton Road, killing a mother and no less than eight children sheltering. One HE fell at the Nacton Road/Lindberg Road junction, another on a recreation ground.The residents of 21 Harmony Square had a lucky escape when a 500 kg HE crashed into their roof — and did not explode. A mixed load had fallen and next night flares preceded the fall of nine HEs backed by the dropping of two ABB500 container loads during a low-level pass. Ipswich guns fired, and further incidents occurred near Saxmundham and in Samford RD and Frinton.

On 26 August a dozen Ju 88s of I/KG77 set out from Creil for Colchester and

Built 1884, reduced to a shell 1942. Perrides, The Chemist, at the south end of London Road North, Lowestoft eventually stood alone (Ford Jenkins Photography).

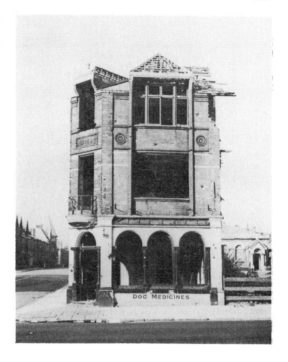

nearby industrial targets. Of the two leaders carrying flares, one released its load on a decoy nineteen miles west and flares from the others did not ignite. It was a disastrous raid, *3Z+CB* suffering badly from AA fire and *3Z+OH* being completely unable to locate the town. Another aircraft was brought down four miles offshore.

The final notable raid in August 1942 came late on the 28th when a Do 217 delivered a diving pass across Lowestoft, dropping two ABB500 loads on 65 Avondale Road and causing damage also at Nos 53 and 57. At Ipswich Airport a C500 Flam (oil bomb) burnt itself out that night.

Once more the enemy did not escape entirely for I/KG2 lost Do 217E-4 *U5+FH*, II/KG40 lost another — W Nr *4233:F8+EN* and I/KG77 Ju 88A-4 W Nr *144146:3Z+CB*. The latter Gruppe had been active on 26, 27 and 28 August, II/KG40 on the 28th/29th with III/KG2, I/KG2 on the 27th/28th and II/KG2 on 27, 28 and 29 August. Gone from the offensive were II/KG53 (Chartres-based) and II/KG54 (Beauvais) for in mid-August they had departed for Germany and the Eastern Front. The outcome had to be a reduction in activity even though KG6 was arriving to replace other Gruppen. At the end of August 1942 the Luftwaffe summarized its night operations against Britain. Sorties flown totalled 909 in April, 637 in May, 791 in June, 639 in July and 556 in August. All were directed against land targets. Apart from a memorable morning's maximum effort, spasmodic night activity and offshoots of 'The Baby Blitz', and the appearance of Heinkel 111s carrying V-1s, the conventional bombing campaign as we had known it since May 1940 was all but over. There was, however, an element of novelty in the current proceedings.

Chapter 20
Facing the unexpected

Throughout the war certain ideas and scenarios gripped public or official imagination. Tales of giant springs entangling bombers originated in mines which ensnared Norwich chimneys. 'You can tell Italian bombers by the sound — there's one', went the unlikely tale. 'Don't go near that mine, it's magnetic' — all mines were supposed to be so! German parachutes attracted amazing notions, and as for flares....

British fighters willed the appearance of a He 113 or a Fw 187 Zerstörer. Although neither was truly fictitious, even few Germans saw them. For years one awaited the He 177 to trundle by, while every spotter dreamed of his Ju 89, every coastal watcher an Ha 138.

Me 109 and '110 we'd seen, but what about the Me 209 and the Me 210? And where had all those Ju 86Ks gone? The answers, and viewing for some, albeit highly distant, were surprisingly close.

At 19:36 on 13 August 1942 off Yarmouth Me 210A-1 *2H:VA* (or possibly coded *VN+AV*?) which, unarmed, had left Soesterberg at 18.30, was conducting a low-level dusk search for shipping. Following its detection by radar, four Typhoons intercepted the rare bird and attacking in line astern from the beam soon set one of the Me 210's engines and fuselage on fire. Its radio operator baled out whereas the pilot drowned in the ensuing crash. Into his dinghy climbed the survivor where, injured and without food and water, he spent six days before being unexpectedly found, taken ashore and rushed to hospital.

Not for another three weeks was it discovered that he was a survivor from that Me 210, a member of 'Erprobungs Staffel Me 210', alias Versuchsstaffel 210. By then he was not the only Me 210 crewman in Britain, and quite a lot had come to light about the newcomers to our skies. Erpro.Kdo. had also lost W Nr *2322:GF+CB* during operations on 10 August.

Design of this twin-engined fighter-reconnaissance-bomber commenced in 1937, 1,000 being ordered off the drawing board. Novel were its two MG 17 machine-guns in remotely controlled barbettes on the rear fuselage sides. First flown in September 1939, centre of gravity problems soon revealed themselves. The aircraft's inability to recover from a spin demanded various modifications, the most obvious being wing leading edge slats. In October 1941 the Me 210 became available for tactical trials, with a view to its introduction in ZG1 as a multi-role fighter. Assessment continued until April 1942 when an operational trials unit formed at Lechfeld and Bf 110 crews arrived for six-week conversion

An unexpected high flyer, the Me 210A operated over East Anglia in summer 1942. Shown is W Nr 063:2H+HA, photographed over France (Bundesarchiv 363/2270/29).

courses. Early in July the unit, 'Erpro. 210', arrived at Evreux but after two weeks moved to Soesterberg for operations at the start of August. Soon it became the 16th Staffel of KG6.

Its employment remained unsettled since it suited no particular role. High hopes were pinned to the aircraft, but it was much inferior to the Mosquito bomber with which it came to be compared. Initially, employment was on maritime reconnaissance, mainly off the English East Coast. The first sortie probably took place on 2 August, and next day an attempt was made to attack a convoy off Yorkshire. By mid-August pairs of Me 210s were making twice-daily reconnaissance sorties off East Anglia, and one of these was intercepted on the 13th. Five such sorties were flown on the 26th, by which time sorties were despatched from Schiphol and sometimes controlled from there and/or Creil. On the 27th flights were mounted after dark, then came the Luftwaffe's decision of 2 September allowing Me 210s over the UK. The first reconnaissance over East Anglia is believed to have been flown at night.

During the morning of 5 September 1942 two Me 210A-1s set out to bomb Norwich. At around 25,000 ft, they slipped in unnoticed until thin vapour trails caused a crash warning to be sounded at 10:35 — just as four 250 kg HEs fell. Identity of the raiders was impossible at their height, and it was suggested that they were He 111s. But no, Me 210s were precision bombing, their HEs scoring a direct hit on Frazer's Joinery, St Martin's Palace Plain, killing four and injuring three; falling in the yard of Batson & Websters, Fishergate shoe factory killing two more and wounding fourteen; in the rear of Boots in Magdalen Street and on already damaged premises in Carbutt Street. Houses, too, were damaged and since it happened on a busy Saturday in town the casualties were remarkably low.

Early in the afternoon, another two Me 210s were found by 610 Squadron at 25,500 ft 25 miles south-east of Southwold. One immediately dived away, but Pilot Officer S.G. Creagh (*EP253:K*) and Sergeant H.R. Gregory (*AR509:H*) using full boost closed. As Me 210A-1 W Nr *173:2H+LA* of 16./KG6 dived for Holland, the Spitfires set its starboard engine on fire. Then it turned on to its back and crashed into the sea thirty miles east of Southend. Its companion dropped two UXHEs on Eastwood Lane, Leigh-on-Sea, during a rapid flight

On 5 September 1942 two very high flying Me 210s bombed Norwich. The boiler house at Frazer's Joinery works was destroyed (Eastern Daily Press).

home. Next day two Me 210s reconnoitred Middlesbrough and the Tees. Typhoons of 1 Squadron intercepted them and both (W Nr *2348:2H+CA* and W Nr *2321:2H+HA*) were brought down, one yielding technical information supplementing that revealed by its pilot, the Staffelkapitän. Limited traverse and difficult aiming of barbette guns meant that the Me 210s were ill protected.

Nevertheless, operations continued, six sorties being flown on 7 September. Dawn reconnaissances were conducted off East Anglia on 9 and 10 September, and probably on successive days. At 17:25 on the 15th an Me 210 was off Walton. A morning flight between 07:00 and 09:00 on 11 October seems to have been the last reconnaissance by 16./KG6. Major Walter Storp, unit Kommodore, then played his strong hand in keeping the Me 210 going, for he had come from Göring's Staff and made use of his association.

While few glimpsed the secretive Me 210, even if many knew of its existence, another new form boasted of its presence to the East Anglians. On 29 August 1942, a fine clear summer day and ideal for aircraft spotting, over Cambridge had been seen a rare Brewster Bermuda, Skua target tug and around midday a low, labouring Halifax II towing 'Experimental Aeroplane No 153', alias the Hamilcar tank-carrying glider undergoing load trials from Rowley Mile. Barely had the thrill of that sight abated when, at 13:45, the siren unexpectedly sounded. I immediately went into the garden, binoculars in hand. Vividly white against the cloudless sky, and coming from a southerly direction, was a vapour trail headed by a strange looking twin-engined aeroplane. By its long, narrow, tapered wings and twin tail I reckoned it to be an Me 110 ... yet surely not, at that height. Flying very slowly and labouring at about an amazing 40,000 ft, possibly flying higher than any other operational aeroplane so far, it was an eerie sight.

Abruptly, it was all change, the aircraft was turning left as, with an astonishing clatter, a 250 kg bomb tumbled to the north of Cambridge into a field on Chivers' Farm just to the east of Arbury Road's Unicam Works and north of the Mere Way. A loud explosion preceded a lot of black smoke, as slowly the perpetrator headed home. Cambridge had been attacked by a 'stratosphere bomber', a Ju 86R, whose sole bomb, unstable when dropped from great altitude, had turned head over tail in falling. A Ju 86 had at last called!

Protecting bombers by flying them very high was no new idea. Pre-war RAF plans were for a fleet of modified Wellington bombers fitted with specially sealed metal cylinders in which air pressure would be maintained, permitting crew safety and efficiency at exceptional altitudes. Nowadays, pressure cabins are a common feature of jet airliners. Early versions had been difficult to build, hard to make work satisfactorily and reckoned highly vulnerable. Like the British, the Germans adapted a few ageing bombers, their Ju 86Ks. A small capsule installed in the nose allowed the aircraft to fly higher, likewise the wing tips which were extended from 73 ft 9¾ in first to 83 ft 11⅞ in, and later to 104 ft 11⅞ in as in the case of the Cambridge raider. Engines were, unusually, diesels — 950 hp Jumo 207As fitted with exhaust-driven centrifugal superchargers. These changes formed the basis of the high raider which was first flown in February 1940, and were followed by modifications for operations of forty Ju 86s, the P-1 being a photo-reconnaissance version, the P-2 a bomber. That several were flown on reconnaissance flights over Britain in 1941, and at around 41,000 ft, seems certain, although there is no evidence to show that they ever came over the Eastern Counties — likely as it is. After operations over the USSR and in the Mediterranean Theatre, a handful of Ju 86Ps and 'Rs (the -1 having short span wings and the -2 the long span) arrived at Beauvais in August 1942 where they joined 4./F.Ob.d.L which soon became 14./KG6. Four were there on 10 August, five on the 20th and six at peak strength. The Ju 86R-2s, the most sophisticated, had 1,000 hp Jumo 207B-3 engines, GM-1 nitrous oxide power boost for escape and four-bladed propellers.

Operations commenced mid-August, but cloud and hazy conditions prevalent over Britain as summer wore on limited the extent of high altitude visual bombing. That tempted the British to assume the Germans would use the new weapon for damaging radio/radar-controlled operations, although apparently they had no such intentions. Two Ju 86s roamed over southern England on 24 August; on the 28th Cardiff and Bristol each received a high flown 250 kg bomb and next day visits were paid to Cambridge and Swindon.

Clearly, these precision attacks fitting neatly into the recent pattern needed to be halted. At 08:05 on 29 August two Spitfire IXs of 401 Squadron tried to engage a Ju 86 over Horsham, Surrey, but reaching it at 39,700 feet was beyond their means. To bring down the later East Anglian attacker whose target was the Unicam Works, two high-flying pressure cabin equipped Spitfire HF VIs (not yet in full working order) were positioned over Clacton at 26,000 ft by 13:35 and told to engage the raider which was then fifteen miles west. At 37,000 ft their IAS was a mere 105 mph, and they were about two miles behind the raider which was at least 2,000 ft above them... and was climbing away. If specialized high-altitude interceptors could not reach the Ju 86 there was little hope for two Spitfire Vbs of 121 (Eagle) Squadron whose pilots spotted the Ju 86 at 40,000 ft, 18,000 ft above them. Their only hope was to catch it descending, so they climbed to 31,000 feet and followed. Too late for them to catch it, the bomber dived away.

Tempting Chelmsford, home of Hoffman and Marconi, was next day's target for a Ju 86R first reported at 39,000 ft thirty miles east of Ramsgate by two Spitfire pilots of 611 Squadron, and identified as both a He 177 and Do 218! In bright clear weather, the German bomb aimer managed to place his single bomb through the slate roof of a warehouse in Baldon Road, Chelmsford, which needed skilful aim. This time, however, the unexploding bomb broke on impact. A pipe screamer was found a mile away.

Before the brief campaign faded, a Ju 86R on 5 September bombed houses in Midland Road, Luton, and headed home over Colchester and Clacton. Again fighters challenged it, two Spitfire VIs of 124 Squadron closing to 500 yd over the Thames Estuary then firing without success. As the Ju 86 crossed Hatfield, de Havilland's design staff decided to develop quickly a suitable Mosquito fighter to bring the high flier down. In a mere week they had it flying. It was too late, for unsuitable weather halted the raids.

Meanwhile more conventional activity continued, although during the rest of September only thirty inland incidents occurred. Apart from offshore activity, Ju 88s of KG6 and Do 217s of KG2 and II/KG40 conducted nuisance raids, mainly on airfields. At night on 7/8 September, their targets were in South Cambs, Dunmow, Clare and Hartismere RDs. Next night Do 217E-4 W Nr *5502:F8+AP* of 6./KG40, which dropped HEs on University Farm, Cambridge, and annoyed RAF Bourn, was caught by a 151 Squadron Mosquito (*DD669*) and shot down in flames near Orwell. That ended Luftwaffe activity over Cambridgeshire in 1942 where incidents had occurred on only seven days and only 51 HEs had been dropped. On 11/12 September six Do 217s of II/KG40 sought shipping off Harwich-Southwold and on the 14th a Ju 88 ventured briefly over Norfolk. Typhoons of 56 Squadron claimed its downfall off Cromer.

Proving it could still bring trouble, the Luftwaffe delivered a 'reprisal raid' on Ipswich. Bombing through cloud breaks using flares during the 15th/16th, a handful of Do 217s of I and III/KG2 attacked just after midnight, facing barrage balloons which had recently been installed, to drop sixteen 50 kg HEs. They caused damage around railway sidings, and on allotments fell three UXHEs plus thirteen Firepots, all of which exploded. One aircraft released four ABB500 containers each carrying 180 incendiaries. Next night Colchester was raided. Coming in at 6,000 ft, the eight bombers reduced height to 2,000 ft for release on their initial pass. In the moonlight they dropped three HEs and 39 Firepots. Again there was little damage although fires were caused in Ipswich Road, at the Royston NFS Station which was being built in Eastgate, at 13 St Andrews Avenue , 27 Harwich Road and at Grinstead Hawk Farm. Three Firepots fell alongside a house in St Andrews Avenue, others in Lexden Road and Mersea Road. One crew crossed in too far north and after facing Harwich guns decided to jettison their dozen Firepots. In so doing it appeared that they had delivered a precision raid on Great Bromley RDF Station No 24, a most prominent landmark with three 360-ft steel pylons and four 240-ft wooden ones. At 21:20 their flares ignited at 3,000 ft before the dozen 50 kg Firepots were unloaded from only 500 ft. They fell on Goughs and Thicks Farms. Flares damaged Elmstead Hall.

Attention was on 17/18 September directed at King's Lynn. Four crews of 7./KG2 and five from the rest of its Gruppe had been detailed for the raid, mounted from Deelen where III/KG2 (now with only fifteen Do 217s instead of the establishment of 27) had arrived in mid-July. At the briefing King's Lynn was described as 'small fry', and Yarmouth given as the alternative. Instructions were to 'aim at the centre'. Each aircraft carried two 500 kg HEs and eight 50 kg

Firepots. As a result of the raid part of the load, four HEs (three of them UX) and 27 Firepots (three UX), caused damage to a quay and dock buildings, Holkham Avenue, the main Ely-Lynn railway line 100 yd south of the town crossing gates and by firebombs on allotments in Cooper's Chase. One of four Firepots which fell on Moses Field did not explode, likewise those in Harwicke Narrows and another at Dennison Mells Nursery. The sharp attack had seen nine Dorniers around King's Lynn, and it cost them one of their number, Do 217E-4 W Nr *4265:U5+UR* of III/KG2 shot down by Mosquito *DD610* of 151 Squadron. The bomber, last to take off, made a north-south bomb run on King's Lynn where fires were beckoning. Just after a partial bomb drop the Do 217 made a sharp left turn, the fighter fired, the rest of the bombs were released and from the crippled Dornier the crew baled out near Docking.

Meanwhile, along England's south coast fighter-bomber raids were a daily part of life. Difficult to halt because radar could not locate them in time, these operations tied down considerable AA defences and defending fighters. Such raids upon East Anglia's shoreline towns meant a lengthy journey well out to sea and were far more risky, but their feasibility was proven again on 16 September when a pair of fighter-bombers strafed and bombed Aldeburgh. Possibly they were Bf 109Fs attached to 3.(F)/122 and used for reconnaissance off Harwich and Yarmouth in support of E-Boats.

Despite reduced enemy strength, anti-shipping operations continued, Schiphol's Ju 88s of 3.(F)/122 daily searching for likely targets while for most of East Anglia the offensive had again petered out. No more intensive raids would take place, although some extremely alarming and distressing events lay ahead. Westleton on 28 September received four 250 kg HEs at 14:50, probably intended for the nearby RAF D/F Station. Earlier, four 500 kg HEs were dropped on Colchester by a very low-flying Do 217 of III/KG2.

Only on the 1st, 10th and 13th of October was there any enemy activity over land, one of three Do 217Es of III/KG2 operating being claimed off Felixstowe, around 08:00 on the 10th, by two Spitfire Vbs of 132 Squadron.

Much daylight low flying training by three Geschwader available for operations against eastern England had, however, been taking place, bringing suspicion of something special. Dawn on 19 October 1942 brought the revelation. Shortly after 06:00 the first of six Do 217s of I/KG2 set forth from Gilze Rijen bound for Norfolk. In 10/10 cloud at 600 ft, rain and visibility 2,000 yd, the Dorniers flew just above the cloud base making it extremely difficult for day fighters to intercept them. Any response had to include Beaufighter and Mosquito night fighters. During the day 12 Group operated seventeen patrols of 35 aircraft fielded by Nos 56, 68, 151, 167, 268, 303 and 411 Squadrons. At 06:54 the crash warning at Yarmouth sounded with four raiders closing in. At 07:16 came the first hostile action, four 500 kg HEs crashing on to North River Road, Yarmouth, injuring one person. Raid 459 was the only one to penetrate much inland, meeting Horsham St Faith's LAA guns before dropping bombs near Wymondham. At 07:50 the Do 217 aimed four 500 kgs at Norwich power station. Foulsham was machine-gunned, as was a train at Spooner Row aboard which two passengers were injured. Three HEs fell on Winterton's beach at 07:30 and Gaymer's Attleborough works was damaged again. Worstead was machine-gunned at 07:45 then came a lull. Very little had so far been achieved, six raiders landing back at Gilze Rijen by 10:06.

Within the next phase were seven crews of III/KG2, from Deelen, three of II/KG40 from Soesterberg and Ju 88A-4s of II/KG6. At 08:30 they approached the Yarmouth-Lowestoft front to launch an ineffective attack on a train between Lingwood and Acle. By now a larger operation than lately seen was under way, Essex, too, being violated. Four HEs fell at Pond House Farm, Clacton and another four at Faulton Hall Farm, Ramsey, both at 09:05. Soon afterwards, one of the raiders was engaged offshore by an 11 Group 157 Squadron Mosquito. Four 500 kg bombs exploded in a beet field at Carlton Colville, another four at 09:05 at Chapel Road and Market Place, Kessingland. Eleven houses were badly damaged, 78 less so, a grocer's shop was smashed and a school damaged.

Norwich received a 'crash' warning at 10:15 with Raid 461 circling north before placing four HEs in the city centre producing a large crater in the Jenny Lind Playground, scattering parts of the gutted St Mary's Baptist Chapel in Duke Street, placing a UXHE through the roof of 1 Oak Street and scoring a direct hit on Edward & Holmes shoe factory in Westwick Street. Fortunately, the staff had taken shelter. By circling the raider minimized its safety, allowing Norwich HAA guns and 'Z' Battery to open fire. South of Cromer Knoll LV a Dornier 217 of III/KG2 was engaged by Squadron Leader Vesely, a Czech, flying a Beaufighter 1 of 68 Squadron. Highly successful though were the gunners at Lowestoft who, using three 40 mm rounds and 139 rounds LMG, brought down a Ju 88 which blew up on striking the perimeter of gunsite H2. By then, five Ju 88 crews of II/KG6 were airborne from Beauvais/Tille and ten of I/KG6, some of the latter seeking East Coast shipping. Both units homed on Leeuwarden after operations — until bad weather forced them elsewhere.

The third phase lasted from 10:20 to 13:05, eleven aircraft entering between Dunwich and Cromer. Two raids crossed Orford Ness to operate around Martlesham at 10:20 and then, over the twenty minutes prior to 11:00, came the busiest period. As Raid 461, a Ju 88, passed by Lowestoft, Gunners at H1 fired seven rounds of 3.7-in, scoring some shrapnel hits on the bomber. Cranfields and Belstead Road, Ipswich, then received two 500 kg HEs from Raid 92. Sproughton was fired upon, six buildings being damaged including the blacksmith's, Hall Farm and a garage which was set on fire. Crowfield and Stonham Aspel between them received four 250 kg HEs (two UX) which damaged eighteen houses, the church and the school. Two more HEs fell in fields by Coddenham and Hemingstone, then came the most serious incident so far, at Needham Market. Although the Ju 88 dropped only two 500 kg SC HEs, the first exploded in the High Street killing four people and seriously injuring nine in Nos 32, 41, 43 and 45. It demolished nine houses, seriously damaged another fifteen and the Congregational Church and caused damage to another 100 houses. The second, in Stowmarket Road, partly demolished Needham Market Area School, damaged thirty houses and the nearby junior school and caused seven more casualities.

Simultaneously, Cromer was bombed, a house and hotel being hit by two HEs which caused the death of one and injuries to three. At 10:55 as St Allright's Hospital at Standay was being strafed, five 250 kg HEs exploded in trees at Eyke damaging a cottage and injuring Mrs A. Skinner. Stratford St Andrew and Marlesford were bombed and machine-gunned too — just as Raid C2 was commencing its bomb run at Colchester.

That the crews had all been given specially selected targets was certain but successfully attacking them was beyond the capability of most, who had chosen alternatives. What others might have achieved was now demonstrated at Mason's Arclight works on the east side of Colchester, 600 yd south-east of Colchester North railway station. Four HEs were dropped and two scored direct hits on the factory, completely demolishing its machine and fitting shop, tool room, maintenance section and metal stores. Of its 100,000 sq ft floor area, 17,000 sq ft was destroyed. Six workers were killed. Fortunately another engineering section in the factory escaped destruction, and tools and fixtures were partly recoverable, 75 per cent production of MoS contracts being under way by the end of October. The other bombs damaged seventy houses and blocked the major A12 road. A Rest Centre for the homeless was opened at East Hill.

The day's activity was far from over, and at 11:10 another six bombers (possibly of I/KG1; one certainly arriving off Lowestoft from Villacoublay) came in north-west of Felixstowe. This time airfields were certainly targets, four 250 kg HEs being dropped at 11:25 on the new 'Holton' airfield being constructed near Halesworth; it was again bombed equally ineffectively at 12:55. Harwich was machine-gunned at 11:39, then there was another pause in the proceedings.

The final attacks commenced with a Ju 88, which had evaded detection, bombing Snailwell airfield at 12:10. Another dropped four 250 kg HEs at Snape killing two cows before turning to deliver a punishing blow upon Wickham Market where one 500 kg and two 250 kgs wrought considerable havoc within the winding, narrow High Street. Buildings Nos 110, 112, 114, 116, 120 and 122 were immediately demolished, Nos 119, 124, 126, 128 and 130 received severe damage and the A12 through the town was of course blocked. Casualties — three killed, seven wounded — could very easily have been much higher.

Last to be raided, eight houses at Tiptree were rendered inhabitable, sixty seriously damaged, church windows broken, an ambulance depot battered and 23 people injured. Lincolnshire had been similarly attacked, Wainfleet being bombed. Southend was raided, and a Ju 88 which crossed Hornchurch fired on Bradwell Bay aerodrome during exit.

Radar-equipped night fighters had busily sought the raiders, Flight Sergeant N. Munro in Mosquito *W4094* of 157 Squadron destroying a Ju 88A of I/KG6 off Southwold. Mosquitoes of 85 Squadron damaged a Do 217 over the sea near Clacton and a Ju 88 off Harwich, while near Cromer Knoll Flight Lieutenant Winward of 68 Squadron shot down a Ju 88. Luftwaffe records indicate two Ju 88A-4s of II/KG6, W Nr *14439(?):3E+CM* and *142224:3E+DP* as lost, noting that damaged Ju 88A-14, W Nr *4141*, managed to make Leeuwarden. However, other records state that a Do 217 of III/KG2 which had bombed Norwich was lost without trace, and that both I and II/KG6 each lost a crew. Between 07:15 and 11:15 seven aircraft were engaged by AA guns which fired 31 40 mm rounds (24 of PC and FAS type), 1,086 rounds LMG and 133 20 mm shots. During the evening three aircraft of 3./F33 (ie, 3rd Staffel, Gruppe 33 Erprobungstaffel) flew reconnaissance sorties over Suffolk and off shore. At least 36 bombers operated during daylight and seven reconnaissance aircraft after dusk.

Never again would the Luftwaffe launch in daylight against East Anglia a medium bomber attack in such strength, but there would be peaks of night activity. Thirteen towns likely to receive 'retaliation-Baedecker' raids were still within GDAs, including Cambridge, Colchester, Ipswich, Norwich and Peterborough, each defended by eight 3.7-in guns and lighter AA weapons. The large number of guns manned in the face of no attackers was a constant, costly concern. The best solution seemed to be to protect such towns with mobile 40 mm Bofors, etc. Most of these towns were really too small to support Home Guard manning, and in emergencies reservists would never be in action quickly enough. Although there were reductions in manpower, the heavy guns remained into spring, 1944, the 'knock-on' effect of reprisal raids thus being more than was expected.

On 21 and 22 October, and at night, I and III/KG2 were active, bombs falling in Walsingham, Deben and Erping RDs. At 08:07 on the 22nd four 500 kgs dropped on Market Hill, Orford, demolishing a draper's shop, warehouse and Manor Cottage where five were killed. The other two HEs fell in gardens – at 104 Front Street, and at the Council Houses, seriously damaging Nos 3, 4, 7 and 8. Do 217E-4 W Nr *4289:U5+JS* was missing from operations over the North Sea on 26 October. North Walsham was raided at 08:20 on 31 October when a Dornier of II/KG2 bombed Bacton Road and Mundesley Road, sixty houses being damaged. On the last day of the month four HEs (one of 1,000 kg) fell on Hall Farm, Parham.

Several more daylight raids occurred before 1942 ended. Shortly before dawn on 3 November, relying upon rain and cloud cover, a Do 217 set off to bomb a factory to the south of Thorpe Station, Norwich. This was to be a precision attack, the crew having specially studied the route. Erroneously they crossed in at '0 feet' two miles north of Yarmouth instead of the planned Cromer entry point. This caused them confusion, and flying as ordered 'not above 150 ft', they entered a heavy rainstorm just before Norwich where, at 07:50 the crash warning was sounded. Holding course, and realizing a second run far too dangerous, the gunner opened fire as they swept in. Aiming their bombs 'at a factory', they left, machine-gunning the city 'at random'. The first of four 500 kg HEs actually fell on to Surrey Street Bus Station. The bomb, which did not explode, spectacularly penetrated a single-decker bus to rest upon its floor. Other UXHEs positioned themselves behind No 53 All Saints' Green. As it was leaving, the Do 217 crossed Coltishall from where a Beaufighter unsuccessfully tried to intercept it. Each crewman was decorated with the Iron Cross 2nd Class, but glory soon expired for all were shot down on 2 January 1943.

Mid-morning of 3 November saw further reconnaissance flights off Yarmouth by Bf 109s before, at 11:34, a Do 217 was plotted thirty miles east of Happisburgh headed west. Following landfall over Hornsea it bypassed Norwich, machine-gunning, before leaving over Southwold. At 13:05 on 6 December another Dornier crossed the coast at Pakefield, then circled Rentum to check its position. By then a Section of Typhoons of 56 Squadron had been scrambled. Three minutes later the Do 217 aimed four 500 kg SD bombs at Oulton Broad, hitting Swan Maltings and Lea Robinson's boat yard where two wherries were sunk and a beached MGB was damaged.

At 12:15 on 12 December Norwich heard its sirens for the 106th, and last time, in 1942. Balloons took station, and guns fired to drive off a Do 217 which flew in over Mundesley to south of Norwich, before returning on a reciprocal course and unloading bombs ineffectively by Heartease Lane.

Removal of unexploded bombs, a dangerous engineering feat, needed infinite patience and sustained courage. In this picture taken on 24 October 1942 excavation close to battered houses on Yarmouth's South Quay is being aided by a dewatering plant.

On the 15th Aldeburgh suffered from a small scale, highly destructive and demoralizing raid. Flying at 500 ft, the machine-gunning Dornier placed four 500 kg HEs in the High Street, scoring direct hits on No 105 and the Post Office where the telephone exchange was destroyed. Seriously damaged were Nos 103 and 107 High Street, 150 ft away. Another bomb fell in the roadway outside No 72, further damaging houses and the Cottage War Emergency Hospital. The other, a 500 SD, produced a 28 ft-wide crater at the base of a wall in the gardens of No 39 High Street and Wymondham House. Heavy casualties of course resulted, nine being killed at the GPO – five of them soldiers with the 5th Royal Berkshire Regiment. Two others died elsewhere while 29 people were injured.

For the last damaging raid of 1942, on 22 December, the Luftwaffe chose what had now become almost symbolic with the cry 'air raid', the terribly battered town of Great Yarmouth. Surely, had not its prefix already been bestowed, it would by now have been richly deserved. During 1942 Yarmouth was bombed 26 times in the course of which 27 of its people died and 95 were injured. It received 69 HEs, five of which did not explode, two parachute mines, ten phosphorus incendiaries, six Firepots and something like 2,000 incendiaries. Sirens had sounded 324 times under standard 'red alert' procedures and in addition 291 'crash' warnings were given, a staggering 651 alarms. The low-flying Dornier this time dropped two HEs at 09:27 between Higham Place and Isaacs Buildings and Albion Road as well as ten phosphorus 'Brand C50' bombs. The latter contained a dark, very viscous, liquid comprising phosphorus, oil and rubber solution scattered by an explosive charge. Between them the bombs damaged St Mary's Catholic School and caused fires in several homes. The 50 kg phosphorus incendiaries were new weapons making their initial appearance in an East Anglian raid. For the townsfolk came satisfaction in knowing that the raiding Dornier had been caught by Yarmouth's gunners and crashed in the sea. Perhaps the dusk raider in the area on New Year's Eve was considering avenging lost comrades; his four HEs, two not exploding, formed the only hostile activity in the area since Christmas, and brought an inauspicious ending to 1942.

Chapter 21
Six faces of the foe

Seemingly unstoppable was the frightening increase in weapon effectiveness, but luckily the Luftwaffe was too stretched to much exploit that situation in our direction. Gone forever the amateurism of the air raid warden, his world of sandbags — and even the searchlights were radar-guided. Blackout remained, but 'put that light out' was an ancient war cry losing out to sophisticated navigational aids. The war being waged in 1943 made that of yesteryear seem quaint, antique. As the vast majority of the population slept relatively peacefully, fighters arrived as fast bombers, rocket weapons were reality and luckily the Germans never developed anything like the Lancaster. Second generation bombers never came, and long alert states vanished as high flying, fast aircraft made hit and run raids. One bomber's fire bombs could burn out the centre of a town, and the depleted Luftwaffe was attempting more meaningful precision strikes. There were still the lone rangers, anti-shipping operations by medium bombers, Main Force raids, 'rhubarbs' and hazardous night operations by Fw 190 fighter-bombers, and airfield attacks. Each required some specialization. Late 1943 also saw increased activity as operational training led towards 'The Baby Blitz'.

* * *

At a further reduced level, anti-shipping and mining operations continued during 1943. Single aircraft finding no shipping made secondary attacks on fringe towns, and specialized targets were attacked. On the afternoon of 1 January a Do 217 raided Norwich, crossing in at Happisburgh and, following a circuitous route, braved the Norwich guns and balloons, missed its factory target and instead placed nine 50 kg HEs in a densely populated area already bombed. St Barnabas Church and Mission Hall in Russell Street were damaged, along with houses nearby, before Hellesdon and the Salthouse-Neatishead areas were machine-gunned.

Another Do 217, on 6 January, strafed Harwich from The Haven. Flying at about 30 ft it machine-gunned Beacon Hill Fort, injuring two soldiers, a sawmill, the Regal Cinema and the house next door, 'Cartref', where a bullet smashed a mirror and dressing table ornaments. Suddenly, the aircraft was among balloon cables and to ease escape the crew jettisoned four 500 kg HEs which landed on Brick Kiln Farm, Ramsey Wash, killing three animals.

The Lowestoft area was attacked by two Ju 88s at midday on 11 January.

From seven bombers operating offshore these two detached themselves, selecting Lowestoft's silk works, being modified for the Navy as HMS *Mylodon*, one stick of their bombs hitting a corner and the remainder exploding in marshes. The second attacker dropped a mixed HE load (nine 50 kg SDs, one 50 kg SC and one 250 kg SC) across Kessingland and Oulton Broad, mainly in the Marsh Lane area, and damaging Brookland House.

A specialized attack was delivered at 19:47 on 25 January by two Dorniers, one of which was reckoned to descend as low as 50 ft despite dark, wet conditions. Probably trying to damage Orford Ness research station, it released a parachute mine which produced a 54 ft by 15 ft crater at Broomhouse Farm, Gedgrave. A large bomb was dropped off Orford Quay. Few mines were falling inland, making arrival of two at Brightlingsea on 4/5 February unusual. Both were 'G' Type, only one exploding, at Morse's Farm.

Increased activity came on 9 February, a dark and wet morning when Southwold saw the first daylight use of Firepots, seven of which were released from a Do 217 which put a 500 kg HE and a 46-ft crater behind No 61 Pier Avenue. Firepots extensively damaged two houses, set fire to a boarded shop at Pier View and hit the roof of 'Pier View', setting rafters alight. Stradbroke and Field Star Roads received the others, one Firepot bouncing in the road to clout the chimney from a house before exploding. Seven people were injured and nineteen houses damaged. Incidents also took place in seven other areas of Suffolk about the same time, four Firepots dropping at Hintingfield and eight at Melton where two 500 kg HEs also fell. A large crater was produced at Spex Hall, and machine-gunning took place at Darsham and Metfield.

A daylight reconnaissance was undertaken around Felixstowe and Harwich on 28 February, mines being laid the following night off Orford Ness. Although less spectacular than other activities, minelaying was a constant annoyance to the Allies, and the Germans were ever improving their mine technology and sowing tactics. About this time the Ankertau mine began to be air-laid off East Anglia. A heavy carriage dragged mine and anchor to the sea bed, fuzes releasing

Quiet residential Stradbroke Road, Southwold, upon which in February 1943 in daylight a Firepot burst raining incendiaries around.

the mine which then rose attached to its cable of pre-set length. At least five basic air-delivered types of sea mines were available, viz: LMF — parachute mine with contact fuze: Ankertau mine, moored; BMC — mine dropped without parachute, with contact fuze: Ankertau mine, moored; LMA — 750 kg parachute mine, with contact fuze (LM = Luft minen); LMB — 1,000 kg parachute mine, with non-contact fuze; and BM — mine without parachute (alias Type 'G').

Typical characteristics of these mines were:

	LMB	BM1000	BMC
Total weight	975 kg	680 kg	540 kg
Charge	705 kg	?	55 kg
Release height, min	350 m	50 m	?
max	2,000 m	2,000 m	200 m
Release speed IAS/km/h	310	500	300

Troops were stationed at most coastal towns for anti-invasion purposes, vacant holiday accommodation being ideal for billeting while the surrounds provided training grounds. Not until 1943 was a German invasion finally deemed unlikely. Presence of Servicemen at coastal towns therefore rendered them legitimate target areas, the bombing of Sheringham, on 6/7 March possibly falling under that category. Certainly Yarmouth suffered because of the Royal Navy presence, although that did not warrant the attention it received.

A memorable attack on Yarmouth took place at 06:35 on 18 March 1943, a Do 217 dropping seven HEs across the southern part of the Borough. No 37 Queen's Road received a direct hit, a bomb fell opposite South Denes Lodge in King's Road fracturing gas and water mains, another exploded nearby and an unexploded 50 kg HE was deemed unusual because of its light alloy tail, red comb and cardboard 'whistles'.

More concern surrounded the direct hit on Mason's Laundry and even more an awful incident at a large house at the Queen's Road/Nelson Road junction, occupied by the WRNS. For the rescue parties that presented an enormous challenge, especially when fire broke out in the debris. Unstintingly the rescuers worked, retrieving thirteen trapped people. Among the dead were six Wrens and seven more were listed missing. Injured totalled 29, and one civilian was killed. Over 500 houses suffered damage.

* * *

Bombers available for Main Force raids in 1943 were Do 217Es held within KG2, II/KG40 Soesterberg-based and controlled by KG2, and Belgian-based Ju 88As of KG6. Autumn 1942 had found each Gruppe of KG2 (I at Gilze Rijen, II at Eindhoven and III at Deelen) with an average of nine crews. In November 1942 KG2 was suddenly ordered to Carcassonne, southern France, in a panic measure to prevent the French Fleet from defecting. They returned to Dutch airfields and by January 1943 high losses meant that only III/KG2 remained operational, other Gruppen merely training.

Do 217E operational loads were usually four 500 kg HEs or ABB500 incendiary containers. The latter employed the casing of the unsuccessful Flam C500 oil bomb, into which was packed a load of 140 lkg incendiaries. Container burst could be preset, or selected by the pilot. Modern AB36 containers carried 36 lkg incendiaries. Anti-personnel bombs could now be delivered from containers which allowed single SD2s to fall, although cluster bombs were increasingly favoured by the Luftwaffe.

With clearer weather and tactics refined, the Luftwaffe was bullied by Hitler into resuming small-scale night attacks in March and he directed them against industrial towns for several nights of considerable activity. The first occurred on 3/4 March when 117 bombers (six of which did not survive) operated mainly against London, although Chelmsford's Crompton & Parkinson, Hoffman and Marconi factories were also listed targets. All in the town area, they were heavily defended by AA guns and a balloon barrage which prevented raiders from placing even one bomb upon the factories. Nevertheless the spectacular, noisy night saw very mixed loads distributed widely. Around Dunmow thirteen ABB 500 containers of incendiaries burnt in fields, other bombs falling even as far away as Bradwell. Within Chelmsford fell six 500 kgs, eight 250 kgs, sixteen 50 kgs, four UXHEs, five uncertain types of HE bombs, plus five 50 kg phosphor incendiaries supplementing twelve ABB500 container loads of 1 kg types. To mark and light the target area six sets of flares were used. An AB23 container load of twenty SD2 'butterfly bombs' was also released, and all soon exploded.

Readily, the enemy responded to any interesting stray light, intentional exposure at Wattisham's Q-Site dummy airfield at 20:27 diverting one crew from Chelmsford. Two flares were positioned, then at 21:02 two ABB500 and two AB36 incendiary loads fell on Peyton Farm from a circling second aircraft. Attempts to illuminate raiders flying just above cloud were made by a number of local searchlights. The night's activity cost KG2 three Do 217E-4s, W Nr *5581:U5+KL, 4361:US+OM* and *5438*, the latter crashing near Antwerp.

Bright moonlight on 18/19 March brought the next Main Force raid. Frustrated particularly by fighters, some 24 enemy aircraft crossed the Norfolk coast between Yarmouth and Hunstanton at heights between 3,000 and 9,000 ft. Half reached the Norwich area from differing directions, releasing their loads from 15,000 ft, in a disorganized attack delivered even before flares fell. Eight markers placed east of the city and falling fast were quickly wafted away in the strong wind. Another two landed on 185 Newmarket Road and Eaton Golf Course. Most of the load intended for Norwich was distributed over rural areas and the city outskirts.

Old Catton at 22:50 received the first bombs, nineteen Firepots and a UX example. Two parachute mines dropped on Stoke Holy Cross five minutes later while three Firepots, two HEs and two ABB500s fell on to Mulbarton. By 23:00 IBEN, four HEs and explosive incendiaries had arrived at Raveningham, two mines (one UX) at Oulton, a mine at Kirby Kane, three Firepots and two ABB500s at Cringleford, five ABB500s at Toft Monks, three AB500s and four explosive incendiaries at Halesworth, four ABB500s and three 50 kg HEs which camoufletted (burst underground without causing the ground above to collapse) at Seething, seven explosive incendiaries on Norfolk Farm, East Bradenham and two mines plus two containers and a phosphor bomb in Sutton. A brief pause, then two mines came down near Swainsthorpe station, a mine damaged fifty houses at Hemsby, seven Firepots exploded at Hainford and one of two mines at Cawston. Bilney was treated to an unusual C500 Flam, phosphor bombs, two Firepots and two UXHEs, Ormsby to 300 incendiaries, eleven phosphor bombs and two ABB500s. On Benlah Farm, Bedingham, two ABB500s fell, Colkirk received three C500s, two mines (one UX) landed on White Horse Farm,

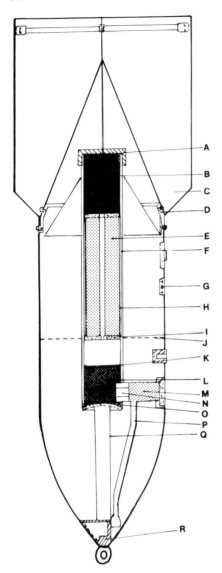

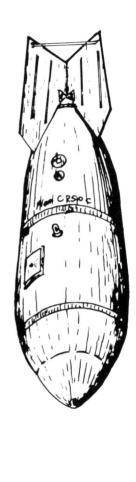

Oil bombs (Flammenbomben to the Germans) surrounded themselves with an aura quite undeserved. The layout of the early KC250 GB weapon with explosive burster is shown here. Weighing about 110 kg, it had similar dimensions to a 250 kg HE. A—the steel cap over the central filling area; B—wood shavings and petrol filling; C—metal vanes; D—alloy fastening ring; E—charcoal and magnesium powder; F—steel tube 29.5 in long and 4.75 in in diameter; G—filler cap; H—thin metal tubes with caps (I) soldered in place; J—steel diaphragm with central core hole and four large radial holes cut through; K—brown paper packing discs; L—1.25 kg of TNT; M—fuze; N—perforated picric acid pellet; O—wood wool; P—soft steel tubing; Q—steel tube; R—nose section and hoist point. Length overall 63 in, diameter 14.5 in. Volume of central case, about 16.1 gallons. Later oil bombs were the Flam C250C Above right and C500, the latter based upon a 500 kg case.

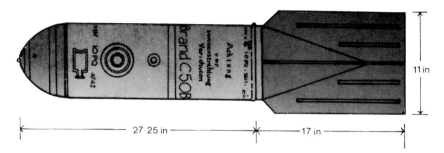

The phosphorus oil bomb (Brand C50 A) used in the later period of the war was similar in appearance to a 50 kg HE. The one-piece, case, 30 in long and 8 in in diameter, contained a dark, very viscous mixture of 86% benzine, 10% rubber and 4% phosphorus, and was split apart by a conventional fuze. The spreading mixture ignited spontaneously. Other variants included the C50 B with a welded case and a larger edition, C250 A, in a 250 kg bomb casing in which the reduced phosphorus content was kept separate in glass vials which broke upon impact. This was a very dangerous weapon whose fumes could easily cause an explosion, yet surprisingly few of the many dropped (mainly C50s) functioned.

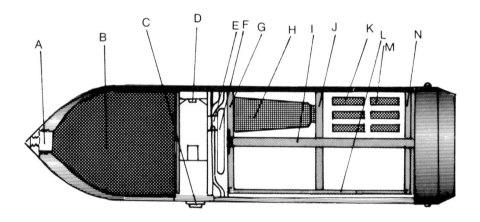

Above The Sprengband C50 Firepot incendiary bomb, combining HE and incendiary elements in a casing similar to the 50 kg HE's. Upon impact, after the base-plug has been blown off six pre-ignited magnesium-electron tumbler-shaped Firepots, together with 67 small magnesium incendiary units, were widely ejected. Then detonation of the 17 lb TNT charge in the nose followed. Some examples had flare-type fuzes actioning air bursts. Items marked are: A—filling plug; B—TNT charge; C—fuzing item; D—Penthrite exploder; E—flash hole; F—gunpowder bag; G—J and N—igniter plates; H—large Firepot (5.75 in long, 2.25 in across base, 3.75 in at top and tumbler shaped); I—central pillar; K and M—small incendiary magnesium items triangular in section and 2.5 in long. A complex weapon probably first used in July 1942.

Runham, and Kettlestone, Colney and Heckingham each received two more. Seven Firepots (and five UX) dropped at Tittlesham and fourteen more at Spooner Row. Another five ignited in Rainhill Wood. A UX mine drifted down at Stockton, two HEs exploded at Intywood and others at Brisley, East Raynham and Mount Farm, Hempnall, the last four targets also receiving incendiaries. A phosphor incendiary and two 500 Flams landed at Stratton Strawless before activity ended around 23:30.

Meanwhile, Norwich City had received a mixture of weapons including 48 SBC50 (Firepots), three 50 kg phosphor bombs (and fifteen UX) and two incendiaries of uncertain type. All were more potent than the 1 kg variety, and started a large fire at Harmers, St Andrews St, lasting many hours, and another at 99 Pottergate along with minor fires. Several were started by flying embers. An SBC50 hit an outhouse of the Lothian Street malting, and others exploded in Cardigan Street, Devonshire Street, Russell Street, Old Palace Road, Armes Street, Douro Street, at 65 St Phillips Road, 182 Drayton Road and 2 Woodcock Road. Crutch, the plasterer's, was damaged and Firepots burst through the windows of the Norwich Union Office to pass through sandbag protection and land in the basement, putting the lift out of action. The Telephone Exchange was scorched, and damage also occurred at 40 Bethel Street, in St Giles Street and in front of 19 Sunnyhill, City Road. Less than half of the force had bombed anywhere near its main target, a wide spillover resulting, partly due to defences including decoy fires. Norwich recorded 39 incidents, mainly from Sprengband (Firepot) weapons, leaving most HEs, incendiaries and para-mines falling in rural Norfolk.

Norwich gains, though, meant misfortune for alternative targets. The first bombing at Lowestoft came at 22:45. Although marker flares were destroyed by AA fire about six raiders placed HEs and three ABB500 containers of 1 kg bombs, explosive versions and SNIBS on to the town. A rick fire by Oulton Road and blazes due to 50 kg Firepots were started at 'Woodberry', Mill Road, in a yard at Hervey, Wilson and Osborn and on North Quay. Notable fires overtook houses in Prince's Road, Water Lane, Rotterdam Road, St Margaret's Church and Pickford's furniture store, which was burnt out.

Yarmouth was twice attacked, the first resulting in an incendiary raid on Gorleston High Street and South Dienes causing fires which were soon extinguished. During the second attack a para-mine scored a direct hit on Watney, Combe and Reid's Southtown maltings, completely demolishing 18,000 sq ft floor space of the building. At the same time a sea mine landed six yards east of the southernmost building, the Fishwharf. After its parachute broke away the weapon became almost completely embedded in the ground. A major fire engulfed the area, splinters damaging a coal conveyor 40 yd from the mine crater. Two more mines on marshes west of Caister Road caused blast damage to Smith's Potato Crisp factory. Incendiaries were deposited in the naval area, the power station was damaged and so were about eighty houses in the north Borough area. Throughout the raid ground defences gave an impressive welcome to the Luftwaffe. From the night's activity it did not escape intact, for Flying Officer Williams (Mosquito *HJ936*) of 410 Squadron destroyed Do 217E-4 W Nr *5523:U5+AH* over the Wash, aided by AA guns. Flying Officer Deakin (Mosquito *W4099*) of 157 Squadron shot down Ju 88 A-14 W Nr *4322:3E+AK* of I/KG6 into the sea.

On 18 March 1943 a parachute mine exploded at Watney, Combe and Reid's Southtown Maltings, Yarmouth, creating enormous destruction over 18,000 sq ft floor space.

A most unusual raid developed inland when, at 22:46, and again at 23:00, pairs of Type C para-mines were released north-west of Oulton aerodrome's bomb dump, where one exploded. The others burst two miles south of the landing ground which certainly did not warrant such hefty attention.

A specialized night operation on 28/29 March resulted in 22 incidents. Six involved HEs, one the dropping of two para-mines at Limpenhoe and the rest conventional incendiaries and Firepots mainly between Halesworth and Loddon. Mosquito *W4079* of 157 Squadron and Pilot Officer Bobek in a Beaufighter of 68 Squadron shared the destruction off Southwold of Do 217E-4 W Nr *4345:F8+MP* of II/KG40.

Major activity followed on 29/30 March. Clearly attacking a target east of Norwich, twenty Do 217s on their run-in encountered intense anti-aircraft fire at Yarmouth which forced them to scatter bombs over a wide area. Night fighters had also to be faced and bombers flying too near to Norwich ran again into a heavy defensive barrage. Decoy fires were lit at Braberton and Great Plumstead, but it soon appeared that the Luftwaffe's target was shipping in the River Chet. A number of moderate sized cargo ships had recently unloaded there and had probably been observed doing so in daylight by the Ju 88s which often reconnoitred the region. On to the area where they believed such activity took place the crews unloaded 26 HEs, ten ABB500s, four mines, 78 Firepots and three phosphor incendiaries. On to Hulver Street, 33 phosphor bombs were dropped and 200 incendiaries. Despite the quantity of munitions used little damage resulted, most landing in fields, including the mines at Alderton and Felton.

Another concentrated attack was launched on 14/15 April by at least fourteen Ju 88s of I, II and III/KG6 from Beauvais, Creil and Cormeilles, and Do 217s of II/KG40 from Gilze Rijen, I/KG2 from Eindhoven and III/KG2 from Coulommiers. (Gruppe II was, incidentally, at Soesterberg and Deelen, the training Gruppe IV at Melun/Villaroche.)

The Battle of the Atlantic is being lost!

The reasons why:

1. German U-boats, German bombers and the German fleet sink and seriously damage between them every month a total of 700 000 to 1 million tons of British and allied shipping.

2. All attempts at finding a satisfactory means of defence against the German U-boats or the German bombers have failed disastrously.

3. Even President Roosevelt has openly stated that for every five ships sunk by Germany, Britain and America between them can only build two new ones. All attempts to launch a larger shipbuilding programme in America have failed.

4. Britain is no longer in a position to secure her avenues of supply. The population of Britain has to do with about half the ration that the population of Germany gets. Britain, herself, can only support 40 % of her population from her own resources in spite of the attempts made to increase the amount of land under cultivation. If the war is continued until 1942, 60 % of the population of Britain will starve!

All this means that starvation in Britain is not to be staved off. At the most it can be postponed, but whether starvation comes this year or at the beginning of next doesn't make a ha'porth of difference. Britain must starve because she is being cut off from her supplies.

Britain's losing the Battle of the Atlantic means Britain's losing the war!

Relatively few propaganda leaflets were delivered to Britain by the Luftwaffe, but the example illustrated was dropped on Yarmouth in spring, 1941. Its style and accuracy suggested compilation by a traitor. Such leaflets, also brought to East Anglian coastal area by small balloons, are rare possessions.

Their target was Chelmsford where at 00:07 sirens sounded and barrage balloons of 993 Squadron were raised to 4,500 ft. Intelligence gatherers had already located the bases from which the enemy was operating and at 00:24 the first of seven RAF intruders, Boston IIIs of 418 (Canadian) Squadron, set off from Bradwell Bay to Beauvais, Creil, Cormeilles and Evreux leaving Mosquito IIs of 605 (County of Warwick) Squadron based at Castle Camps to await the Luftwaffe's return to Eindhoven, Gilze Rijen and Soesterberg.

Coming from Gravelines, the bombers had skirted the coast, turning in at Harwich, fanning out about 25 miles inland to concentrate their attack on Chelmsford. At 00:29 marker flares were dropped, and promptly fired upon by Bofors. A minute later Chelmsford's 101 Essex 'Z' Battery fired from its recreation ground site as incendiaries began falling from a Ju 88 held in searchlights. Outside the 'Roseberry' Hotel a Firepot burst and within moments much of the city's telephone network was out of use, forcing ARP communications by messenger. Incendiaries fell over the north-east area at 00:47, and the Home Guard 'Z' Battery fired again. Although the balloons went to 6,000 ft, Bofors, machine-gun and rocket defences busily engaged bombers, exploiting a gap above balloon level. Around 00:49, 33 phosphor bombs were dropped alongside 31 Firepots, HEs, mines and incendiaries. Since the balloons were tightly clustered over the town centre only the perimeter was negotiable. By steeply banking following bomb release, the aircraft placed their loads centrally. Attack alleviation might have come had decoy fires at Little Baddow been lit, but telephone communications to the site had been cut. Luckily the phosphor bombs (only 28 of which fired) fell wide, and ABB containers were released too low, no spread resulting. The thirty target markers either did not ignite or burnt out on the ground in misleading positions. About 2,500 incendiaries in sixteen groupings were dropped, eight ABB500 containers being found, and nineteen HEs reckoned to be two 500 kgs, four 250 kgs, four 50 kgs and nine others, type not known. Two para-mines landed, one in a field by Victoria Road, the other by Second Avenue east of Broomfield Road.

Early incendiaries fell on the prison, setting the brush-making workshop ablaze. Doubtless the inmates took satisfaction when the Governor's house also caught fire. Some, along with the staff, put out the blaze using stirrup pumps. Extinguishing the main fire took the NFS, using 25 appliances that night, five hours. Hoffman's, Victoria Street, had a fire in a single-storey building and at Marconi the canteen and club room were hit. At Denham & Archers' store a small shed was set on fire. The main damage, though, involved the County Offices, Old Court and Archers' suet factory, upon which much of a container load of incendiaries ignited. Fire broke out at the west end of the factory's first floor, then spread rapidly to engulf the entire building. Melted fat poured into the road, although 1½ tons of shredded suet and 52 tons of fat were salvaged, along with five lorry loads of damaged paper and cartons. All those commodities were, of course, in short supply during wartime.

Bofors guns at the Arbour Lane and Emery Road sites had fired 447 rounds by the end of the raid, and Site 25 found their balloon deflated on the ground after being hit by an enemy aircraft.

Attacks were also attempted the same night upon the explosives and chemical plant on Bramwell Island, and Wrabness mine depot. Between them these attracted 76 HEs and SBC50s, C50 phosphors, fourteen ABB500 containers of incendiaries and ten flares which landed on farmland around Great and Little Oakley some five miles south-west of Harwich. A 16-ton stack fired early in the operation burnt very brightly, undoubtedly attracting much of the attack. Arriving initially in line astern and then in pairs, the bombers circled prior to attack and immediate departure. Taken by surprise, 928 Squadron's 32 balloons remained close hauled around Harwich. During the whole night's activity 3.7-in AA guns were very busy, those at Harwich and Landguard firing 675 rounds, Clacton's 195 and Ipswich's 173. 'Z' batteries fired sixty rounds at Chelmsford and 199 at Colchester. Fourteen HE bombs also fell near Kelsale, at the Hall and Trust Farm. Plans for replacing the 3.7-in gun cover given to Marconi and Hoffman by Home Guard-manned twenty 20 mm Hispano cannon, which were under discussion, were now abandoned. Three Dornier 217s of II/KG40, including W Nr *4287:F8+EN* and *5593:F8+AM*, fell that night to Mosquitoes. Two were brought down by guns of Mark NF XIIs for the first time. The other fell to *DD730* of 157 Squadron. Remains of one black Dornier in a field at Sewell's Farm, Bockings Elm, occasioned much interest; the others crashed in the sea.

For the surviving bombers there was indeed trouble ahead. Wing Commander J. H. Little of 418 Squadron, prowling around Beauvais, selected one of seven Ju 88s returning home and soon despatched it. Squadron Leader Tomalin of 605 Squadron saw two Dorniers join the Soesterberg circuit and fired upon one before intense ground fire drove him off. Six bombers were seen in the Creil area where attacks were not possible, whereas at Evreux the night was undisturbed so the intruders contented themselves by attacking trains. Another nuisance was perpetrated on 1 May when Ju 88s of 2./KG6 laid mines off Harwich and Lowestoft.

Mingling with returning RAF bombers, Do 217s of KG2, II/KG40 and fourteen Ju 88s of I and III/KG6 intended to operate against Norwich between 02:34 and 03:34 on 5 May. Several pilots accepted as friendly turned about on reaching Winterton, arousing the defenders' suspicions, and other attackers exposed navigation lights making identification difficult. Their listed targets in Norwich were Thorpe Railway Station, Boulton & Paul, Lawrence Scott Electric Motors, the power station, Reckitt and Colman & Co — and none was hit. About fifty parachute flares were at 02:38 released in error too far north-west of the city, among them a novel red target indicator which ejected two green stars to either side, each of which then shed a white flare attached to a parachute. Most bombing took place in that area. Balloons were flying and fighters active, and AA gunners were unable to engage the enemy who persisted in firing correct colours of the day. A balloon flying at 5,000 ft was shot down, and soon after the order was given to raise them as high as possible.

By the end of the raid 157 bombs in addition to incendiaries were reckoned to have fallen, among them eighteen SC50s and 27 SBC50s. Many landed between Mundesley and Norwich, the released load upon the latter thought to be eighteen 50 kg phosphor (all UX), 27 50 kg SBCs and, judging by found containers, about 600 1 kg mixed incendiaries. Four major fires were extinguished by 04:20, including those at St Audrey's Church, a metal merchant's and Revington the antique dealer's. A surprising number of parachute mines were dropped, falling at Tavenham (three and one UX), Blakeney Farm, Croxton, Welbourne, Bizwell Farm, Mattishall, Shropham (one UX), Hockering (two), Moltesham (two), Sevilthorpe, Trunch, Knapton, Storygate, Aylsham, Brandon Parva, Kerdiston, Horsford and Tuddenham, making a total of 22, the largest in one East Anglian raid.

Among buildings hit during the night was the school at Little Melton, the only one in 'rural Norfolk' to be demolished during the war, along with the adjacent School House occupied by the Head, Mrs Barbara Buckton. Well isolated from the village, it was a curious target, but windows may have reflected Norwich fires. Mrs Buckton and her young had been 'down the garden' in the shelter and were indoors again after the 'All Clear' when the bombs came. She carried her son from the house to the village, whence he was conveyed by the only available transport, a bicycle, to the nearest doctor for attention to his head wounds. As for resumed schooling, that meant conveying stock and equipment into the village inn and Parish room where lessons took place until a corrugated roofed building became available later in the year. Of course, buildings are not the heart of a school. What Mrs Buckton remembers most was the tremendous help the children rendered in rebuilding their school, the way the parents, Rector and School Managers weighed in, and the total honesty that everyone showed. That was a strong feature too whenever homes were wrecked, for the level of looting was extremely low and the deluge of kindness, even to total strangers, stupendous.

For KG2 it had been an equally sobering night. Just after a Do 217 of I/KG2 took off from Eindhoven an RAF intruder shot it down twenty miles away, all aboard dying. On return another Dornier crash-landed. Aboard was Major Walter Bradel, Geschwader Kommodore, who was killed along with the pilot,

Top *During 1943 the final form of the Dornier range entered service, characterised by a much revised nose form. Possibly '4582', this version with BMW 801s is a Do 217K-1, the fin 'G' being its individual identity* (Bundesarchiv 372/2598/31).

Above *The only school in rural Norfolk to be bombed was Little Melton* (Barbara Buckton).

Leutnant Andreas. Bradel, a 31-year-old, had served in the Condor Legion, operated over Norway, Greece and Crete, was credited with the sinking of a British destroyer, accepted the surrender of Athens Airport and was awarded the Knight's Cross in September 1941 for service in the USSR. Summer 1942 saw him take command of II/KG2 and March 1943 of KG2. Many Luftwaffe officers enjoyed scant popularity; Bradel was an exception. He died as I/KG2 was about to re-equip, for its first three Do 217M-ls — faster and with a 25,000 ft ceiling — arrived at Eindhoven mid-May 1943, although it had yet to receive Do 217K-ls. Mining was still carried out by KG2 whose aircraft crossed the North Sea very low, climbed to 6,000 ft off our shore then made their drops from 3,000 ft at 300 km/h before returning home at low level.

On 14 May at 02:06 the Luftwaffe opened another attack on Chelmsford, at least 27 aircraft participating including 21 Ju 88s of I, II and III/KG6 and six Do 217s of II/KG2 and '40 which bombed from between 5,000 and 8,000 ft, their crews diving between balloons to drop six mines and 69 assorted bombs. In bright moonlight, flares were first released to the south, generally marking Chelmsford. At about 01:00 incendiaries ignited, 300 yd north of the Hoffman factory. Then Marconi became the centre of attraction.

The factory, in a large field by Broomfield Road, assembled radio components, and to achieve its destruction several crews flew very low to ensure good aim. Many flares — red, white and green — were dropped, then clusters of red and green flares in groups of three, probably marking Marconi. Coming in at 4,500 ft, one raider dropped two mines, one hitting the factory and the other a residential area to the north. Blast and hurled debris badly damaged the assembly shop, and the new testing shop was completely flattened. Walls collapsed at a third building, and a boiler house was demolished. Production was halted for nearly a month. In Sunrise Avenue two parachute mines caused extensive damage to houses.

Duke Street's modern, camouflaged bus station was hit by a 250 kg SC bomb which exploded 20 ft above the floor, completely blasting the roof from supporting girders. Shattered glass and asbestos tiles made 28 buses useless. Fire destroyed the south-east corner of the building, a strong northerly wind spreading the inferno to the contents of houses opposite. In the garage — where there had been 43 buses — 250 tyres caught alight and all fitters' tools were destroyed. Behind the garage four houses were badly damaged. Six medium fires were started. Meanwhile, at Broomfield and Little Waltham four parachute mines fell.

Brightly moonlit, Chelmsford's defences had stoutly defended it. Guns of 8 Troop, 415 Heavy AA Battery, fired 81 rounds while night fighters sought the raiders. Further HEs and incendiaries fell that night near Ipswich, along with two para-mines at Antham, two at Great Leigh and another which did not explode.

From now there was a switch to attacking airfields, causing numerous incidents in rural areas. The proximity of Ipswich to its airport similarly brought damage on 27/28 September. A homing searchlight apparently attracted the raider which then dropped eleven 50 kg HEs. A Walrus amphibian was set on fire and a Spitfire damaged. Some bombs landed in gardens and fields near the aerodrome. Inaccurate bombing on 2/3 October caused eight 50 kg HEs to fall near Histon and another near Roseford Road, Cambridge, all from an Me 410 flying at 14,000 ft, and ten 50 kg HEs at Aldeburgh on 3/4 October, one of which landed on the lawn of Warren House, and were probably a jettisoned load.

Summer 1943 had seen KG2 re-arm with Do 217Ks and 'Ms, since when the Geschwader had mixed precision attacks with new tactics. Following sea crossings at between 50 and 150 m, they would head for a sea marker about thirty to sixty miles from Britain, such turning points being constantly lit over twenty minutes by drops of white or coloured LC50 flares, or modified 'See-Lux' ASR flares. Relying on the 'Knickebein' beam system, the aircraft would head for target at about 3,500-4,500 ft. Leading would be the 'Zeilfinder' (target pin-point crew) which would release marker flares about ten minutes ahead of Main Force, three 'backers-up' supporting. The first would act as target marker dropping incendiaries, followed by two target illuminators dropping LC50s. Typical Dornier bomb loads were four 500 kg Trialen HEs and four 50 kg phosphor bombs. Prescribed tactics required precise timing — which meant much practice

General development of the Ju 88 resulted in the Ju 188 introduced in summer 1943. First to enter service were Ju 188 Es, like 1730:3E+KL of 3./KG6, a Ju 188 E-2 photographed at Chartres (Bundesarchiv 505/363/27).

which the Luftwaffe lacked badly, some very disorganized attacks therefore resulting. Losses were high too, caused particularly by inexperience and intruders awaiting the bombers' return.

While KG2 mastered its latest acquisitions, KG66, the pathfinding pioneers, brought the Junkers Ju 188 into front-line use. Based upon the Ju 88, it had long span wings with pointed tips, BMW 801 radial engines, a dorsal turret and a 3,000 kg bomb load. Its top speed was about 310 mph, cruising speed around 230 mph at 16,400 feet and its ceiling about 30,500 feet. Nevertheless, it never supplanted the faithful Ju 88A-4 which figured in operations against the UK until mid-1944. The Ju 188 was introduced by the 4th Staffel of I/KG66, itself formed from 15/KG6, at Chartres, joining the Ju 88s and Do 217s also serving as pathfinders. I/KG66 took its Ju 188Es into action for the first time during the Lincoln raid of 18 August. By October I/KG6 had equipped with Ju 188s and soon commenced operations, its aircraft usually carrying two 500 kg HEs and, for target-marking, eighteen 50 kg LC50s or incendiary loads.

That the new type was present over East Anglia was proven on 15 October when Mosquito XII *VY:E* of 85 Squadron destroyed a bomber over Suffolk, thought to be an Me 410. Examination of the wreckage, near Woodbridge, revealed it to be Ju 188E-1 W Nr *260179:3E+BL* of I/KG6. Two other claims were subsequently reckoned to involve Ju 188Es, one being *260173:3E+RH* thought to have crashed off Clacton on a night that saw III/KG6 making its first Ju 188 sorties from Munster/Handorf. Not until January 1944 did II/KG2 begin to use Ju 188s.

On 23/24 October came the last major 1943 raid upon an East Anglian town, possibly thirty Ju 88s and Do 217s being used in a carefully planned attack concentrating between about 22:58 and 23:55. Bombing from 5,000 ft, they dropped two 500 kg and seven 250 kg HEs along with 35 SBC50s and many incendiaries (carried in seventeen AB36, fifteen ABB500 and two ABB1000 containers) on marshland north of Lowestoft. First came a flare dropper who then delivered incendiaries, and was quickly followed by six 'backers-up' producing a circle of flares about sixteen miles in circumference between Yarmouth and Lowestoft within which they dropped many more fire bombs. Then came the Main Force whose tactics were similar. They fed the flare circle, dropping their loads within it, sometimes gliding and weaving. Balloons on the flanks of the raid were at 4,500 ft, guns and searchlights engaging the attackers whose raid was well off target. Nevertheless, incendiaries made a mess of Oulton Broad's Poor Law Institute, gutting the nurses' home and damaging 100 nearby homes. An unexploded HE also took the welcoming sign outside 'The Rest Awhile' Inn in Market Lane, Blundeston, very literally!

Not until midnight did the driver of a light NFS car travelling away from Oulton Broad realize something was wrong with his vehicle. Then, shortly before 00:30, the tyre of a fire tender was punctured and moments later the car used by the CO, 63rd AA Brigade, also acquired an unpleasant puncture. In each case the vehicle was difficult to control. Before dawn there had been thirteen such incidents and some close accidents. Their particular concentration around Crossway, Gorleston, led to an investigation showing that from an ABB500 container, partly opened in mid-air, had fallen about 100 'Crowsfeet'. These triple-pointed, tyre-puncturing metal objects had seen widespread use in the Middle East. Used in towns they would bring havoc — even more so on airfield runways. Luckily most had fallen in a field north-east of the crossroads, but the incident was enough to cause the Ministry of Home Security to at once warn the country of the danger these seemingly inoffensive objects could present. Surprisingly, in view of that, their use was far less widespread than might have seemed likely, although some were dropped during later raids on East Anglian airfields. It was, once more, those tempting targets which attracted most of the bombing between July 1943 and the end of the war.

November and December 1943 saw a dramatic reduction in enemy operations, training for the 1944 offensive being more important. Nevertheless the operation which developed at around 19:00 on 3 November in East Suffolk settled into a very sharp attack on Ipswich and its surrounds. At Rushmere St Andrew two houses were demolished, nine people dying and four being injured when a shelter received a direct hit. Four HEs and many incendiaries had already fallen at Yoxford, and a house was blazing in Eyke where APBs also dropped. Bramford received over thirty HEs and incendiaries which damaged electricity supplies, plunging much of West Suffolk into darkness. Sixty Bramford houses were destroyed, a hundred damaged and a large fire overtook the chemical works of Fison, Packard & Prentice before, at 19:25, bombing of the main target, Ipswich, commenced.

The first indication of attack came when white flares were released east of the town. A red and white mix north, and red and green east, were then released to guide Main Force in. A four-candle flare then marked the town and incendiaries commenced falling, shoals of 'Düppel' protecting the raiders against radar location. Bombs landed in Westerfield and Henley Road, damaging cottages at the Dale and the Brooke Nursing Home, and killing two. South-west of Henley bridge railway lines were smashed, and more bombs fell upon Norwich Road, Leopold Road, Colchester Road, Yarmouth Road, Brookfield Road and Bramford Lane. All Hallows Church was hit and some of the houses damaged in the raid had previously been hit and repaired no less than five times. Fifteen small fires were caused, 199 people were made homeless and a bomb count showed that nineteen 500 kg HEs had fallen plus over 1,000 incendiaries.

Sustaining operations even on that scale was impossible, only two aircraft bombing Norwich on 6 November, dropping incendiaries and four HEs in the Bluebell Road area, damaging four houses by fire. Raiders ventured over East Anglia in small numbers on 3, 4, 6 and 7 November. On only two nights in December was there notable activity, nine HEs being dropped at Wrabness at 20:00 on the 10th, a night when numerous incidents occurred in Essex and four HEs in Castle Park, Colchester, caused four casualties. But if the medium bombers were largely absent for much of the year, that certainly was not true where fast intruders were concerned.

* * *

Since October 1940 south-east England had been subjected to bombing and strafing by Messerschmitt 109s, and in 1942 the Luftwaffe introduced fast Fw 190s during attacks on South Coast towns. Flying low to avoid radar detection, they delivered fast strikes to such an extent that the defenders were compelled to devote fighters and guns to defeat the raiders who, in February 1943, extended such operations to East Anglian towns.

Sea mist and rising sun on 17 February 1943 gave excellent cover to five Fw 190s flying low and out to sea before turning west. At 07:58 they hurtled across Clacton, releasing five 500 kg SC HEs (one fell on a minefield and did not explode) while firing machine-guns and cannon. Completely unheralded, Clacton's residents were unaware of what was taking place until the raiders were escaping. Clacton, packed with about 8,000 troops mostly occupying evacuated houses, had streets full of Army vehicles. Light anti-aircraft guns were much in evidence too, for the Army Light AA Training School was sited here.

Although the enemy claimed to be attacking military targets, all had strong civilian content. Release, from exceedingly low levels, caused many bombs to skip, skid and bounce unpredictably. That happened to the first Clacton bomb which jumped 400 yd at very high speed off Bedford Road, Holland-on-Sea, and over house tops before exploding behind No 233 Harwood Road. The second also ricocheted over house tops after skipping off Oxford Road, to score a direct hit on No 1 Herbert Road. Similar devastation also occurred at Nos 31/33 and Nos 7/9 Church Road. Marine Parade East, St Albans Road and Victoria Road were all closed, 200 houses had been damaged and twenty families needed accommodating. Five casualties included a dead civilian. The next appearance over East Anglia by Fw 190s came on 12 March when, as an off-shoot to an attack on Ilford, several Fw 190s tried unsuccessfully to bomb factories at Chelmsford.

With incredible suddenness six Fw 190s arrived over Frinton at 14:15 on 14 March, cannon and machine-guns chattering, to place 500 kg HEs on Greenway, the level crossing area, Turpin's Lane where two houses were demolished, and in Fourth Avenue. Two soldiers died, 800 houses were damaged and the '190s then released two HEs on Walton, one in Round Gardens and the other on to Station Street, killing two civilians. To warn of these strikes was difficult, stopping them impossible.

Far more unconventional was the arrival of a pair of Fw 190s during late afternoon on 16 April. Radar tracking located their landfall over Bradwell Bay at nearly 30,000 ft, on a course taking them over Chelmsford — presumably to assess the effectiveness of the recent night raid before leaving for Dover. Apparently they were unsuccessful, and the High Command was determined to know the result of the Chelmsford raid. Therefore, the Luftwaffe mounted another reconnaissance using *T9+FH*, a specialized and rare photo-reconnaissance Ju 88B (a Ju 88A with additional nose glazing but without an under-gun position and only a 20 mm dorsal gun). Powered by BMW 801s, it also had GM-1 injection gear to greatly increase their power output. After special briefing on 18 April by Oberst Dietrich Pelz, the newly appointed Angriffsführer England, the three-man crew left Orly/Villeneuve at 08:30 on 20 April, refuelled at Schiphol and took off again at 10:30 for the Essex coast. Of the elite Versuchs-Verband Ob.d.L. (Experimental Staffel of the Commander in Chief of the German Air Force, ex-Sonder Aufklärungs-Gruppe Ob.d.L.), their task was to photograph both the Blackwater Estuary and damage at Chelmsford.

Crossing in near Harwich at 34,000 ft and 270 km/h IAS, they were greeted by the five Harwich gun sites which in ten minutes fired 96 3.7-in predicted fire shells for, since the time they had flown over Rotterdam, the British had been tracking their Ju 88. At once the crew operated the methanol injectors, increasing speed to 310 km/h IAS. Already they were being warned by their controllers of fighter response. Watchers on the ground, in plenty, were meanwhile observing their contrails, and from Colchester four more AA shots were fired. Again warned to watch for fighters, the pilot applied more boost, taking the speed to 360 km/h IAS as he hurried away from the target area. From Clacton another 23 3.7-in shells were hurled at the impertinent visitor, then at 11:45 the German gunner opened fire on two Spitfire IXs of 332 (Norwegian) Squadron flown by Second Lieutenant M. Erikson, DFM, (*EN177*) and Sergeant K. Herfjord (*BS401*) who had been ordered off from North Weald at 11:30. Under Trimley Radar control, they began closing on the Ju 88 ten miles west of Clacton. Erikson fired three punishing bursts which soon had the Ju 88B's port engine blazing. When smoke filled the cockpit the pilot baled out, *T9+FH* taking the other crew members to a watery grave in Barrow Deep. At 13:30 the pilot was rescued by a lifeboat.

The next noteworthy Luftwaffe intrusion came on 7 May when Focke-Wulfs delivered another stinging attack on that irresistible target, Great Yarmouth, their brief to aim for Vauxhall Station. Very low, out to sea, the twenty Fw 190s flew unnoticed until 07:11 when, below 250 ft, they roared across the Horsey shore. Seven immediately swung south to take Yarmouth from the west and within a few extremely noisy moments their attack was over, the fighters strafing Yarmouth whilst whistling across.

Again the bombing was spectacular, a 500 kg HE ricocheting over 600 yd before performing an amazing air burst behind 15 Neville Terrace, and demolishing ten houses along a 120-ft frontage. Another destroyed a public house and two shops, and yet another produced a crater in Northgate Road School's playground. Close to Vauxhall Station a bomb grazed a road, twice cut through railway lines, then soared into the air to burst on a refreshment kiosk and set ablaze a large lorry. After hurtling through a malting house one bomb reached the station, to rest unexploded between railway lines beside a platform.

Awaiting a train was a naval bomb disposal officer who, with enormous courage, promptly defuzed the terrifying arrival! Two others scored direct hits, one on an ARP post, the other destroying eleven houses in Olive Road. Four houses were flattened by another 500 kg SC. Casualties amounted to thirteen killed, 51 injured.

The remainder of the force created northern diversions, four strafing and bombing Winterton. Achieving complete surprise, they caused twenty casualties — two fatal — and seriously damaged seventeen houses. Simultaneously, Hemsby was attacked, two of the five HEs performing air bursts, and 47 buildings were damaged. Firing widely, the attackers sprayed a searchlight camp and fishermen's homes near the Newport and Scratby cliff edges. At this point the force suffered their only casualty when at 07:12 Fw 190A-5, W Nr *2526*, flying too low clipped a 30-ft electricity pylon three feet from its top, then hurtled into the sea. By then others were shooting at cottages, bungalows, shops and two radio masts nearby. Passengers on the 07:00 train from Yarmouth to Ormsby had a lucky escape whereas at Filby an HE in open country bounced into the air, then burst damaging many windows.

Six Fw 190s flew south, line abreast, firing at opportune targets and hurling two HEs on to Caister before turning out to sea and leaving plenty of cannon cartridge cases, unusual treasures in the area. In a mere three minutes all was over.

Having proven a relatively long distance operation possible, the Fw 190s struck again four days afterwards, and later than the defenders had been primed to accept. Of the force comprising 28 aircraft, eight attacked patrol boats while providing cover for the bombers. In two groups, the others attacked around 08:45, bombing and strafing and then strafing again on their outward run. There were more people in the streets than in the previous raid, including children going to school, errand boys and tradesmen making deliveries. Many still have all too vivid memories of those terrible moments, including a mother whose boy was feeding chickens in the garden before leaving for school, and who would always remember a bomb bouncing close before killing friends nearby.

Some incidents like the one involving a packed ATS billet, where casualties were high, were horrific; others were nothing short of unbelievable. The seventh bomb bounced in a garden before crashing through a house from which it emerged to cross Blake Road still in level flight. On the east side of the road it careered through a window and across a breakfast table, emerging into the back garden to explode, damaging three houses. Equally amazing was the eighth bomb's track for, after landing on the west side of North Denes Road, hitting part of a semi-detached house on the east side of Blake Road and ricocheting, it passed through a house in West Road before crossing to another on the east side of North Dienes Road about 15 ft above ground level before exploding.

The next bomb shot along a railway track, climbed into the air for a 220-ft flight then entered a house on the east side of North Dienes Road before detonating on the opposite side of the road. Bomb number ten initially passed through a house on the east side of Windsor Avenue, and continued along The Avenue before passing through a brick garage to end its journey at the rear of a house in Royal Avenue and damage another house. Among other places to suffer were Seymour Avenue and the Onsley Avenue/Berisford Road corner where a shop was demolished.

Left *So low and fast came the Fw 190 fighter-bombers when they attacked Lowestoft that some bombs flew, bounced and, with almost horizontal trajectory, passed clean through buildings before exploding. One 500 kg bomb hurtled through the bedroom of a house on North Parade* (Ford Jenkins Photography).

Left *It then ricochetted off a tennis court, before finally exploding on houses in Corton Road* (Ford Jenkins Photography).

Again, the suddenness of attack made effective engagement impossible, although one aircraft crashed. The ease with which the town could be found due to prominent, tall landmarks and narrow layout parallel to the coastline made it easy to attack at high speed when flying low. In less than a minute the raid was over, and even before the crash warning sounded, for which reason the figure of 49 killed and 41 injured is hardly surprising. Yarmouth was never hard hit again, probably because balloons were at last provided for its defence. It had endured its 175th and penultimate bombing raid. Next day Lowestoft was the target.

Attacking early in the day Fw 190s, possibly thirty in number, concentrated upon small ships at sea, leaving only three pilots to fly inland. Only one dropped a bomb, which skipped from Belview Park to Royal Avenue, there damaging houses, sheds and a school, killing five people.

Surprise and nuisance were again achieved when at 21:01 another 24 Fw 190s (many with yellow rear fuselage bands and partly yellow cowlings) returned to Lowestoft at dusk, sweeping in line-abreast from the north-east, shooting and bombing as they came. They flew away south leaving two fires engulfing Watson's Garage in the High Street and No 3 Gasholder. No warning sounded; it could not, for a bomb disconnected the power line to the crash siren.

Plentiful damage was caused to houses, the sudden raid killing seventeen civilians and fourteen Servicemen, and seriously injuring 81 civilians and three soldiers while leaving another 23 people wounded. Two bombs broke upon impact, some fell into the sea off Waveney Dock, three dropped at Kessingland and one by London Road brought down telephone lines. In one house a resident was killed, whereas a dog sheltering was rescued alive. From another house a Morrison Shelter was hurled into the next one, to settle alongside another shelter in a house where the dwellers were all killed.

After keeping the defences alert for little purpose, 26 fighter-bombers (mainly Fw 190s) arrived at around 22:00 on 15 May operating in the Felixstowe-Southwold sector, and lost two of their number, one being Fw 190A-5 W Nr *0842* of Stab./SKG10. One bomb fell at Felixstowe and four on Southwold, demolishing three houses from one of which a mutilated Morrison Shelter was thrown 50 ft into a churchyard. Parts were discovered on the church roof; luckily the house was unoccupied. Nearby, another Morrison Shelter among debris in a room held eight people who had quickly taken shelter. All were rescued, uninjured, within ten minutes. Typhoons of 56 and 195 Squadrons chased the raiders, Sergeant Hough of 195 Squadron claiming a Bf 109.

On 30 May the fighter-bombers struck yet again, three Bf 109s being spotted along with nineteen Fw 190s, and all bombed. Completely thwarted from bombing intended targets in Colchester, the attackers (two of whom were shot down) unloaded 500 kg HEs on to Walton and Frinton. The one-minute attack, line-abreast, came at 19:25, no warning being sounded. Six bombs did little damage, but the rest were widely distributed causing incidents in Martello Road, at 'The Briars' in Kirby Road and near the junction of Church Street and West Street, from where it ricocheted on to the lawn of a house in Mill Lane. Frinton's water tower also received a hit, a bomb embedding itself in a supporting girder. Another, after hitting a house in Third Avenue, bounced through a garage roof into the next garden, then skipped into the space between two detached houses near Holland Road junction. Three HEs landed in Third Avenue, one in the 'Beach' Hotel. Others exploded in a back garden in Norwood Old Road, and at the Esplanade/Connaught Avenue corner. At Walton the police station and Catholic Church were destroyed. Four people were in all killed, 21 injured. Six houses were demolished, twenty seriously damaged and 800 in all affected, making 200 people homeless.

The final Fw 190 daylight East Coast bombing raid came on 2 June. Thwarted by balloons at Harwich, the seventeen attackers turned to their alternative targets, Felixstowe and Ipswich. Nine Fw 190s at 05:25 attacked Ipswich from Felixstowe Road heading for the docks, the first bomb passing through a house roof in Prettyman Road, before wrecking two houses in Hamilton Road then exploding in 29 Hamilton Road, killing four occupants. A second bomb bounced near Alan Road junction, shed a fin which clouted a shop in Alston Road, passed through trees in Holywells Park, rammed its way through a house in Myrtle Road, smashed tarmac and exploded outside No 42.

Fw 190A-5 W Nr *2529* 'Green R' of II/SKG10, some way behind the others, appeared to be caught by the Myrtle Road hefty blast, was possibly damaged, and steeply dived into ground east of the lock gates. Apparently its bomb became detached and exploded in Ransome and Rapiers' corrugated mixer test house in Napier Road. Casualties totalled four killed and nineteen injured. Eight other Fw 190s from seawards raced over Bawdsey as light AA guns went into action. At Felixstowe they dropped three 500 kg HEs, the first bouncing from the beach to explode on grass in front of the Coastguard Cottages. The second exploded just below the cliff top, the third resting UX by a hedge in Marcus Road.

Daylight fighter-bomber raids on Britain ended on 6 June. Then the aircraft used were sent to the Mediterranean Theatre. Perhaps to disguise this move two Fw 190s made a brief, machine-gunning incursion at Winterton at 21:30 on 6 July. Four Typhoons gave chase, and Flight Sergeant Chisas did not return. Next evening the pair of '190s returned, and one crashed a few miles out to sea. Remaining Fw 190 penetrations of East Anglia came at night for, despite their total unsuitability for such missions, they participated in nocturnal operations with airfields as primary targets.

*   *   *

The first 1943 night airfield intruding took place on 13/14 February. A Ju 88 used HEs and incendiaries against Lavenham, still under construction, then another aimed four 250 kg HEs at Bradwell Bay. By then it was clear that the ten aircraft, which had first been active off Southend before being joined by fifteen more and moving northwards, were searching for shipping. Three had detached themselves, at differing times, to bomb airfields. HEs were aimed from 2,000 ft towards Bradwell where the raider was engaged by Bofors guns, some of whose 29 rounds brought it down at Twinglefoot Bridge, Burnham-on-Crouch. Then the airfield lights were briefly switched on, allowing Mosquitoes to depart on 'intruders'. Around their likely landing time the airfield was marked by chandelier flares, then four incendiary canisters were released which overshot on to Denghie Flats, producing a huge blaze. Next night another Ju 88 visited the station, sixteen SBC50s falling wide.

On 3 April came a decision that the RAF Regiment must man 300 Bofors guns protecting UK airfields, reducing AA Command's manning commitment. Next night incendiaries fell at Boxford, Suffolk, and more portentously four containers of SD2 butterfly bombs were showered on to Thameshaven's refineries, killing four workmen. If extensively used they would have brought

Me 410s normally came in fast, high and singly. The examples here were uncharacteristically formating (Bundesarchiv 489/3156/30).

enormous problems, and that gave justified concern. Instead, raids on airfields faded until 13/14 May when an incendiary container and three HEs were aimed at Debach. On 17/18 May a 500 kg HE intended for RAF Lavenham exploded in a barley field west of Willow Bridge. This bomb had been brought by the first night-flying Fw 190 of SKG10 to attack an East Anglian target.

Focke-Wulf Fw 190A-4 and 'A-5 fighter-bombers began night nuisance raids against London and the Home Counties on 16 April. Based at St André l'Eure, men and aircraft of I/Schnellkampfgeschwader 10 (I/SKG10) about a week prior to each moon period moved to Poix, the forward base, for two weeks of operations. Far from a happy organization, SKG10 not being a fighter unit was staffed by ground and air crew drawn from bomber and Stuka formations with little Fw 190 experience.

Using mainly the Fw 190A-5, reckoned the 'finest '190 variant', the pilots took off individually, their aircraft usually carrying one 250 kg HE and two wing-mounted drop tanks. On special missions a 500 kg HE was carried, but it produced critical handling conditions for night operations. After crossing the English coast at about 12,000 ft these flights often became alarming experiences for it was easy to become disorientated. Not surprisingly they were unpopular ventures. For safety the aircraft had to climb to 20,000 ft, bombing from 12,000 ft after a 50⁰ dive homewards. Gruppe I/SKG10 held about forty Fw 190s and pilots for these operations.

On 15 June at least three Fw 190s made the second journey to East Anglia. Glem Lights were on at Castle Camps and its Mosquitoes busy when at 03:07 a Fw 190 slipped along the airfield's east side to about four miles north then returned to drop a bomb which fell in a wheat field near the 'Marquis of Granby' public house. Five houses were damaged. Another Fw 190 five minutes later strafed Chedburgh then, flying at 1,000 feet, machine-gunned Stradishall, before turning left to release its bomb which exploded in a ploughed field east of Stradishall village. Again it raked the station, cannon fire damaging a Stirling and setting a hay stack on fire. A third Fw 190's bomb fell harmlessly near Helions Bumpstead. To bring a Fw 190 so far at night with scant navigational aids, then find far from easy targets, required both skill and strong nerves.

Who was responsible for operations on 23 June remains uncertain. At 03:17 on this dark, cloudy night, the moon in its last quarter, two HEs fell in fields north of Linton, Cambs, not far from the railway line. At about the same time another two HEs were delivered to Welwyn Garden City. Probably they fell from a new aircraft type, the Me 410.

A refined, high-altitude and faster version of the Me 210, powered by DB 603As, it was the nearest aircraft in performance, size and general capability to the Mosquito that the Luftwaffe ever possessed. Four machine-guns along with two MG131/13s in barbettes and two MG151/20 cannon defended it. A top speed of 388 mph at 21,982 ft, ceiling of 32,810 ft and range well loaded of 1,447 miles made it potentially a good performer, although its usual load was only eight 50 kgs or two 250 kgs which could be supplemented by four more under the wing centre section. Technical problems beset the aircraft, and its ammunition storage layout rendered survival in combat unlikely. The Me 410A-1 came into front-line service with KG2 at Lechfeld in April 1943. About this time II/KG40 amalgamated with KG2 forming Gruppe V/KG2, Me 410A-1s equipping its three Staffeln — 14, 15 and 16 — for high-speed high-level night operations. A

Usually, Me 410As crept in singly at night, intruding upon East Anglian airfields. The '410 was a more potent version of the Me 210 and difficult to catch because it was almost as fast as our Mosquito (Bundesarchiv 489/3156/30).

few were also supplied to 4.(F)/121 for photo-reconnaissance flights over eastern England.

Not until 13/14 July did the next airfield raids come about, Me 410s preceding a Do 217 raid on Hull. One Me 410 journeyed at 18,000 ft to Mildenhall, circled, then bombed at 00:23 on a northerly heading, trying to evade 317 Battery's probing searchlights. Outer markers had revealed the station's position, seven 50 kg HEs being spread over Howe Hill, by plantations and — the only three to explode — a sugar beet field. A further six 50 kg HEs directed from 10,000 ft at Stradishall fell near Helions Bumpstead, and two 500 kg SC HEs were dropped by a Ju 88 near Boreham, Essex. Another HE fell at Finchingfield.

Me 410A-1 W Nr *238:U5+KG* had taken off from Cambrai/Epinoy and crossed in over Dover heading for Essex. Flight Lieutenant Bunting flying Mosquito XII *VY:T* of 85 Squadron spotted its glowing exhausts and chased it, using full boost. He closed to 200 yd, identified it then shot it into the sea off Felixstowe. This was the first Me 410 shot down near Britain.

A two-part intruder operation was mounted by Me 410s on 10/11 August, a very dark night. In each phase, three Me 410s flew fast into Norfolk scattering over Caston Ricklands and Northwold eight 50 kg HEs and fourteen Type 23 containers estimated to have been loaded with 332 SD2s. Many failed to explode, which led to an intensive search involving 935 man hours over twelve days before it was decided that 13½ loads of butterfly bombs had craftily arrived, along with three UXHEs at least one of which had a 1 kg Elektron incendiary fastened to its tail after the manner of the still common pipe whistles. Near Downham 75 per cent of the APBs burst in the air, but only seven per cent at Didlington where 40.5 per cent exploded upon impact. Near Feltwell, where two

Me 410s dropped five container loads (probably 115 SD2s) along the flare path line, 24 per cent were UX, only one per cent being unaccounted for. A farmhouse had suffered damage and three cows were badly injured by APBs.

Ten Me 410s were active over Suffolk on 12/13 August, bombs falling near Ipswich. On 17/18 August, Me 410s and Fw 190s flew another diversionary phase while Do 217s conducted a poorly executed raid on Lincoln. Operating particularly in the Colchester area, a Fw 190 placed a 500 kg HE on the town, damaging four houses and railway lines. Fw 190s also attacked Langham airfield, alias Birch. Four flares at 23:55 hrs preceded a dive attack in which three HEs were aimed at the very incomplete aerodrome. A load of APBs settled around Wells before an Me 410 released seven 50 kg HEs at Burnham Market at 00:15. From other aircraft loads fell at Kenton, East Suffolk, and near Methwold.

Another busy night was 22/23 August, ten Me 410s of 16./KG2 setting off from Cambrai/Epinoy intent upon raiding five airfields and operating widely over Norfolk and Suffolk, part of an uncoordinated venture between Sussex and The Wash. The first incident occurred at Ardleigh where 23 SD2s were distributed in a field by Wick Lane 400 yd from the A12 road. From three AB23 containers, 69 SD2s spread along a runway and on to grass at Boxted, others being placed south of the main runway. Witnesses identified a Fw 190 by sound, another example of which (or the same one) at 02:18 deposited SD2s over aircraft on eastern dispersals. All exploded but caused little damage.

Parham was also subjected to a Fw 190 attack, the aircraft making three low runs and dropping 46 SD2s during the last two passes. The first load fell on dispersals, some bombs detonating, others being dealt with *in situ*. More landed just north of the main runway. It is tempting to suppose that the single 500 kg SC HE dropped from a low level at the north-east end of Waterbeach's main runway, damaging two Stirlings, was also from a Fw 190. Another aircraft which dropped three 50 kg HEs from 15,000 ft, in the North Walsham area after raiding Coltishall, was certainly an Me 410. At 02:10 it released a load of seventeen SD2s, only six of which exploded, in a meadow behind the 'Three Horseshoes', Scottow. Another three were found 100 yd south-west of Coltishall's control tower. Me 410 W Nr *10120:U5+HF* which crossed the coast over Clacton was intercepted by Flight Lieutenant Howitt and crashed near Chelmondiston at 02:02, the first of its type to fall on land.

As a diversion to a well concentrated raid on Hull on 23/24 August, airfield diversionary attacks again took place, one upon Downham Market using a 250 kg and two 50 kg HEs, one of which hit the centre of a runway. Of 106 SD2s planted, only 36 exploded. At Shipdham, three 50 kg HEs accompanied four containers of SD2s. At Hall Farm, Raveningham, and Aitken Farm, Kirby Cane, APBs fell around 22:50 and at Weybourne seventy APBs were dropped at 03:30. No 29 Squadron destroyed three Me 410s as they crossed the South Coast heading for home. Briefed to engage bombers returning from Dusseldorf to an airfield near Cambridge, Me 410 W Nr *287:U5+EG* took off from near Lille at 01:20, but a Mosquito crew soon despatched the brand-new machine.

Me 410s followed RAF bombers home on 31 August trying to engage them off Yarmouth and dropping APBs near East Dereham. A similar operation was mounted on 3 September. Another intrusion upon Castle Camps came a week later. As two Mosquitoes were about to land a 250 kg SDX was dropped, bomb

A wide assortment of German bombs: from left to right an SC50 with screamers attached, SC250, PC500 armour-piercing bomb, SC500, SC1000 (or SC1200?) with Kopfring and an SC1800 above which an SC50 rests to give scale (Bundesarchiv 388/995/9).

fragments setting fire to a dispersed Mosquito whose burning wing was soon extinguished. At Downham Market Drem Lights were on when Operations advised the tower of a 'bogey'. Visiting aircraft were in the circuit in the bright moonlight when at 22:08 the Me 410 roared in at 400 ft, first placing a 250 kg HE on the intersection of Runway 16/21. From its second pass a 50 kg SDX landed 52 ft from the runway controller's caravan, as the raider had evaded four rounds of Bofors fire. Two airmen were slightly injured.

Repeated attacks on the same airfields would have been worthwhile, but the Luftwaffe had to switch for safety and on 7/8 September, incomplete Wethersfield was bombed and strafed. One bomb bounced and air burst. No military personnel had yet reached the station, although they were using Snailwell which was itself hit by a 250 kg SC HE at 22:25 on 8 September. After a low-level run from the south-east, the raider circled then dropped a bomb which produced a 22 ft by 4 ft crater east of The Avenue leading to Chippenham Park. Two lorries were burnt and Nissen huts damaged. During the night Wing Commander John Cunningham, flying Mosquito XII *VY:R* of 85 Squadron, destroyed a Fw 190A-5 off Aldeburgh, one of three destroyed that night.

Low-level mining was carried out between Cromer and the Humber on 21 September, probably by about twenty Do 217s of KG2. Very likely it was a Do 217M-1 of III/KG2 and not an Me 410 which was shot down off Orford Ness on 22 September. Next night the intruders came again, giving the returning crew of 620 Squadron's *A*-Apple an unforgettable experience. As they touched down at Chedburgh, three 50 kg HEs and a few SD2s exploded just behind them, the gunner of the intruder overhead firing too. Several of the ten Me 410s operating had been in the area, but 'all clear' had been given just before bombing at 00:45.

The enemy had circled for some minutes to the north. One of its bombs exploded 800 ft from a runway intersection, the other two near the active runway where eight UX SD2s were also found. Others were on the grass alongside the runway and dealt with by 621 BD Flight, Waterbeach. Of the 115 SD2s dropped, 112 had not exploded, probably because of a low release height. Next evening Me 410s prowled off East Anglia awaiting RAF bombers setting out for operations.

A mixture of fifteen Ju 88s and Me 410s was active on 27/28 September when Coltishall was visited. Some 6-700 RAF bombers were crossing the area at around 12,000 ft, prohibiting defenders from firing, when from the north-west at 00:35 came a low-flying attacker to put three 50 kg HEs on the landing ground, along with 43 SD2s (fifteen UX) distributed mainly south of Oak Grove. Another fourteen exploded in the north-east corner of the aerodrome as a Halifax, returning from Hanover on two engines, made an emergency landing.

Operations over a wide area on 2/3 October included attacks on five East Anglian airfields, between 01:50 and 02:15. Tuddenham received eleven 50 kg HEs from a high flier. All overshot into fields and woodland, and eight 50 kg HEs at Mildenhall exploded in a sandy plantation south-east of the landing ground.

Gransden Lodge was attacked from 10,000 ft, nine 50 kg SC HEs all missing the airfield. The first exploded in Longstowe Park, breaking windows and damaging the Hall's north gable. The second fell in a small paddock, the third on the edge of a pond, the next in marshy ground and others in fields as 405 Squadron's Lancasters were landing after operations.

Warboys suffered more when, unheralded, a Ju 88 dropped the customary three HEs and four containers of SD2s as 156 Squadron's Lancasters landed at the fully lit station. Not until bombs began exploding was the intruder discovered in the circuit, and by then it was strafing too. One 50 kg bomb hit a barrack hut, and an SD2 exploded on a Lancaster's wing. Three others clouted a small brick building, others falling in three groups on northern parts of the airfield.

Cambridge's sirens wailed at 01:30 and soon a Ju 88 was heard to the north. Two bursts of AA fire and a salvo of 'Z' rockets greeted the foe, and searchlights sought it as Lancasters continued landing at Bourn and Oakington. After unloading ample flares, the Ju 88 bombed at 02:00 from 14,000 ft, its ten bombs exploding in fields north-east of Oakington station. It was a busy night, small bomb loads over a wide area dropping for little apparent purpose. Incidents, too many to completely list here, included 50 kg HEs near Braintree, Halesworth and Westhall.

High-level night precision bombing of airfields had featured in recent airfield raids. In response to them, four Mosquitoes of 151 Squadron were moved to Coltishall. Such attacks were in evidence again on 3/4 October when Me 410s penetrated even to Northamptonshire and a few Ju 88s mined off Yarmouth at the opening of the moon period which lasted until 10 October. A busy night saw attacks coinciding with the return of British bombers to their bases.

Realizing that military targets were being sought, few people now bothered to leave their beds when sirens sounded. For those keenly interested in the events taking place there was usually local action. On this particular night a quite astonishing number of red and white flares fell to the north of Cambridge, and I recorded 'in all twelve HEs west'. Searchlights were busily sweeping the sky and at 02:06 an HE was heard (one of four) exploding on No 2 Dispersal, 'C' Flight area at Waterbeach and another in a Milton beet field, after which the circling Me 410 left us. That may have been the example destroyed, after a long chase, by Beaufighter *V8619* of 68 Squadron.

That night some effort was wasted against USAAF Gosfield where HEs and three SD2 loads fell in fields. Metfield also received a group of 'butterflies' which damaged four aircraft. Nine HEs dropped from 12,000 ft landed in fields at Knettishall at 23:35, possibly intended for nearby Rushford Heath bombing range which was in use at the time. Containers of SD2s were already being widely distributed, at Clare (23:15), Shaker's Lodge, Brandon (23:25), Houghton Hall, Cavendish (23:27), Crown Farm, Leiston (23:29), Elvedon (23:45) and Burnt Fen, Isle of Ely (23:50). Four HEs exploded near Burwell at 23:30, another four on Park Farm, Stetchworth, and two near Fakenham at 23:40, indicating the wide extent of operations.

Enemy aircraft followed a Mosquito into Castle Camps and from 500 ft dropped a trio of 50 kg HEs and five containers of SD2s, one of which rested near the north-east end of the main runway, to the southern side of which were found 296 UX SD2s. There was no consistency among loads dropped.

Wyton's Mosquitoes had landed when six HEs fell, including four on the airfield grass and one on the perimeter track. The last exploded near a hangar, damaging a Mosquito. Twenty minutes later Wyton's Lancasters landed without interference.

Graveley came under attack at 23:37 just as the first returning 35 Squadron Halifax was approaching. The pilot was warned just before two HEs fell. Landing lights were doused, but not those of the attacker who released two more HEs and 46 SD2s which were heard exploding in fields near Toseland four minutes later.

Attempts to disorganize 405 Squadron's midnight return to Gransden resulted in fiasco for the foe and alarm for Caxton village. From a north-south pass the raider deposited four 50 kg HEs and two full and four half-full AB23 SD2 containers. All undershot, half loads of SD2s being distributed on the 'Red Lion', behind two bungalows, in a field east of St Andrew's Church and variously in fields. Some exploded, but not those by the church. Disposing of them was not easy, especially if the nasty little bombs hung on trees, or in hedges — in which case they were virtually 'fished for' using poles and nets.

A few intruders operated on 4/5 October, APBs falling at Kesgrave (23:40) and Dereham (00:04) and a solitary 50 kg HE on New England Farm, Wickhambrook. Mainly Fw 190s dropped bombs in Suffolk and Essex on 6 October, Stowlangtoft Hall and Walsham le Willows each receiving one bomb at 20:25 while six HEs landed upon Great Ashfield. During the evening of 7 October, 75 enemy aircraft operated over East Anglia as well as penetrating to Bedfordshire and North London. Activity was the most extensive for many months, incidents occurring particularly in Norfolk where a large HE fell at 20:50 on Bush Farm, Loddon, killing one and injuring five, and others at Wroxham, in the river bank at Buckenham, Shottisham, Heckingham and at Langley where six houses were set ablaze and one person died. APBs were sown near 100 Group HQ at Bylaugh Hall and incendiaries were widely distributed. About forty miles off Yarmouth the crew of a 68 Squadron Beaufighter (*MM850*) claimed a Do 217. HEs also fell in Essex.

A raider being chased was ever likely to jettison its load, as happened over Chedburgh at 21:17 on 12 October. Five HEs were dropped when Flight Lieutenant Allan of 68 Squadron in a Beaufighter fired at the enemy which unloaded fourteen 50 kg SCs at Whepstead, damaging five houses. The bomber escaped — only to be again engaged by Flying Officer Boyle, in a Mosquito of 151 Squadron (Coltishall Detachment), who shot the aircraft (likely to have been of III/KG6) into the Wash.

Among places bombed on 15 October were Bentley (ten HEs) and Leiston (six HEs) in East Suffolk and on the 17th Langley, Norfolk, suffered once more when at 20:50 four 1,000 kg UXHE, and six containers arrived, severely damaging eight houses, a farm and a school, an unusually heavy load. Fourteen HEs and some incendiaries damaged the school vicarage and cottages when they exploded on Moat Farm, Cowlinge, at 19:28 on 22 October. Whether these incidents arose from misplaced airfield attacks it is not possible to be certain. Next night eighteen enemy aircraft roamed over East Anglia, eight heading for London. October's last noteworthy airfield attack came on the 24th/25th, an unusual load of nine 50 kgs and three SBC50s falling around Matlaske and Toft's Monk from two high-flying aircraft. The airfield had closed to flying in August for development. No night work was in progress, so it must be supposed that the raid was possibly intended for Coltishall. Shortly before, Ludham had received six HEs and nine Sprengband C50s one of which failed to function.

November saw notable activity on only five nights. Wing Commander Hayley-Bell (*MM844*) of 68 Squadron shot down an Me 410 six miles north of Happisburgh, and when on the 8th an Me 410 was shot down off Clacton the Mosquito Mk XIII was achieving its first combat success. *HK367* of 488 Squadron was the aircraft involved. Three Me 410s were destroyed that night.

On nights of good visibility Fw 190s of SKG10 continued their activities, making use of British searchlights to guide them and usually calling for fixes two minutes prior to bomb release. Staffel II had been using St Omer/Fort Rouge but for safety moved to Brussels then Rosières-en-Santerre. Allied bombing in September had driven the third Staffel out of St André and into Beauvais where yet more bombing drove it to Rosières. Amiens/Glisy too had been used — and bombed — so that the unit made use of Dreux, Caen and Poix. Its strength was being much depleted, as was that of KG2 when Typhoons dealt with nineteen of its Dorniers at Eindhoven on 4 December.

December's decline in activity was even greater than November's, with only two nights of activity. Of all night attacks upon eastern airfields none was more amazing than that which developed around Gosfield, one of the largest airfields in the area, on 10/11 December. There was immediate questioning about the whole astonishing affair until intelligence sources confirmed that the raid was intended for Chelmsford. So intense was the bombardment that it could be heard from Cambridge, over which a Do 217 and Ju 88 circled, apparently lost.

Covering four square miles, Gosfield was unusually large. About a quarter of a mile south was a large lake, in moonlight a mirror. Runways were uncamouflaged, and the ammunition dump was easily visible. Defending Gosfield were a few 20 mm guns, and no aircraft had arrived. An astonishing 65 HEs (18.55 tonnes) fell around the aerodrome from about ten aircraft — Do 217s and Ju 88s — engaged by Bofors in the Braintree area and by light fire from Southey Green searchlight site (NW 0334) tackling low level attackers. Plentiful flares preceded the bombing, during which forty HEs were apparently directed against the airfield. Raid results were poor, many bombs falling wide and damaging houses and roadways. The load of 26 500 kgs, eighteen 250 kgs and 21 50 kgs was the heaviest ever directed — or, more accurately, misplaced — against an East Anglian airfield apart from that hurled at Debden in 1940.

Wethersfield the same night received twelve HEs north of its main runway, from a Do 217 and a Ju 88, both illuminated by searchlight beams. Earl's Colne was also subjected to an early evening raid, yellow flares marking it. An unusual assortment of four 50 kg and four 500 kg HEs was dropped in a peculiar sequence, causing little damage.

At Birch two 250 kg and two 500 kg bombs straddled the runway, upon which one burst, in an attack made from below 100 ft. The most successful intrusion was at Chedburgh which had been attacked three times in the previous three months. Each time the raider pursued an almost identical track — but increasingly nearer the control tower. This time the first three bombs from a Do 217 landed close to a hangar, the next four among administrative buildings. Each salvo, consisting of almost evenly spaced bombs, shattered the control tower's windows and injured two WAAFs.

Beaufighter and Mosquito night fighters were ordered to intercept the intruders as a result of which Flying Officer R. Schultz in *DZ292* of 410 Squadron achieved astonishing success by shooting down three Do 217M-1s of I/KG2 off Clacton. In addition to these (*56059:U5+IK, 56157:U5+BB* and *722747:U5+CK*) a Do 217K-1, *4476:U5+AS*, was lost by III/KG2. Mosquito *HJ944* of 410 Squadron had damaged a Do 217 near Chelmsford, perhaps *U5+AS*. Shots from Beaufighter *MM844* damaged two Do 217s, but 68 Squadron also lost an aircraft, *V8619*.

Attacks upon East Anglian airfields in 1943 had now finished.

All change indeed — even the mines looked different. Seen here is what the British knew as 'Type G' (Bundesarchiv 342/605/30).

Chapter 22
From Capricorn to Overlord

By January 1944 the question was not who would win the war, merely when the Allies would do so. Processions of East Anglian Mosquitoes and Lancasters and trios of searchlights welcoming them home, these were the sights and sounds of the night. Gone the 'oom-pahing' Heinkels, chattering Dorniers, mines, incendiaries in the gutter, stirrup pumps and evacuees when, shortly after 21:00 on 21 January air raid warnings sounded throughout much of east and south-east England. More intruders? Indeed not, the Luftwaffe was launching a new 'Baby Blitz' on London.

Around 20:00 about 115 German bombers and twenty fighter-bombers began take-off, one group from Germany and Holland, others from France and Belgium. Off the Foreland the streams merged, ninety bombers and fifteen Fw 190s making landfall slightly north of Southend. Pathfinders of KG66 preceded Heinkel He 177s, with I/KG54, II/KG54 and KG2 following. Approaching our coast each crew, every thirty seconds, dropped radar-confusing metallic strips — 'Window' to us, 'Düppel' to them — and no revealing incendiary line-leads or sky markers. Part of London south-east of Waterloo Station, code-named 'München' to encourage crews to retaliate against Allied raids on the German city, was their target.

Entering at 18,000 ft did not protect Do 217 U5+LN of II/KG2 which was brought down in Essex. Typically carrying two AB1000s containing mixed type 1 kg incendiaries, and ten 50 kg phosphorus incendiaries, it emphasized that this was to be very much a fire raid. Each I/KG54 aircraft had aboard one AB1000, one ABB500 and ten 50 kg phosphor bombs, while II/KG54's Ju 88s each carried two AB1000s supplemented either by two 500 kg HE or ten phosphor bombs which had largely superseded Sprengband C50s and oil bombs. About to be used for the first time were many examples of the IBSEN (incendiary bomb, separating explosive nose). Similar to the IBEN, the new version carried an explosive charge to blow the incendiary/high explosive sections apart after about eight minutes' burn. Container Type AB1000-2 had been specifically designed to carry 360 examples of IBSEN which could be identified by its three-fin tail unit, longer than the usual 1 kg bomb type. The first examples of IBSEN in East Anglia were reckoned to have fallen at 04:22 on Moors Farm, Assington, setting four stacks on fire and killing a calf.

As the bomber stream leaders swung east, running in across London at 13,000 ft, they were frantically swamping radar defences with Düppel. Then at 22:02

they commenced the attack, each dropping coloured flare clusters and two 500 kg HEs on to the intended area. Backers-up followed to release white or amber flares, correcting drift error. High percentages of fire bomb loads (AB1000, ABB500 and 50 kg phosphor) were dropped while about fifteen of Châteaudun's Heinkel He 177A-3s of 3./KG100 and 1./KG40 each delivered four 1,000 kg HEs, surprisingly small loads, before returning to Rheine. One, hit by flak over the coast, had aborted.

At 21:05 the first of eight bombers, all flying above 20,000 ft, strayed into the 12 Group area near Bury. Raid H19A, thought to be a He 177, was believed to have deposited two exceptionally heavy SC 2,500 kg HEs in a field 270 yd from railway lines south of March, one exploding 300 yd from a farmhouse. H24D flew to St Neots and Henlow, while H129 was at 26,000 ft over Bedford by 21:19. X45C journeyed to Marham then Newmarket over which Raid 44C passed en route for Ely then Stradishall. Around 21:30 another aircraft flying along the boundary of the 41st AA Brigade area released masses of Düppel which drifted north-east, extensively blotting out defensive radar. Six Mosquitoes of 68 and 409 Squadrons sought the raiders, largely prohibiting AA gunners from firing, but at 21:51 Cambs 101 'Z' Battery released a salvo and Cambridge CH5 fired ten rounds of 3.7-in at a bomber over the town at 16,000 ft. All was clear by 22:05.

Not since 1942 had such a large operation been mounted, and it was far from over. At 05:00 East Anglia's sirens wailed again as a second attack headed our way. At 04:16 the first of forty bombers which had left France between Le Havre and Dunkirk made landfall over Selsey Bill while more entered over the south-east coast. Flying at between 10,000 and 20,000 ft, fourteen penetrated the London area, but most of the 95 arriving circled the London IAZ before flying to Aylesbury or towards Cambridge. The first two entered 12 Group area at 04:57 twelve miles south of Cambridge, whose sirens were sounded at 05:00. A Dornier Do 217 circled the town before leaving south to drop flares, a 250 kg HE and incendiaries. At 05:05 the machine, then at 12,000 ft and near Debden, abruptly turned for Ely before leaving near Southwold at 05:25. Another crossed Bury heading for Lowestoft, and west of Cambridge Raid H198 dropped chandelier flares at 04:55 before turning about near St Ives. H57A passed over Duxford at 05:04 tracking north at 10,000 ft before leaving via Southwold at 05:26. Again, a clever attempt to disorganize defensive radar was being carried out, H33E managing disruption of East Anglia's cover for seven minutes around 05:15 while positioning yellow and white route markers, to assist aircraft leaving the country.

No specific targets seemed identifiable among the bombing incidents in Dunmow RD (two 500 kg HEs and nine 50 kg UX phosphor bombs), Braintree (two 50 kg UXHEs and two 250 kg HEs), Melford RD (two AB1000s) and Newmarket RD (two 250 kg UXHEs). Six Beaufighters (three each from 68 and 409 Squadrons) tried to challenge the bombers, but were prevented from achieving much by the effectiveness of Düppel. As twenty raiders left East Anglia between 00:05 and 00:56 at around 15,000 ft, heavy anti-aircraft guns gave them a noisy send-off, Harwich batteries firing 274 rounds, Clacton 136 (and 97 earlier), Ipswich 43, Colchester ten, and its 'Z' battery twenty rockets despite fire being much restricted by the presence of fighters.

Although the raids were not unexpected, the effectiveness of German anti-radar foil — especially against centimetric radar-equipped Mosquitoes —

produced a shock. Well disguised, attacking in one group and at very varying heights, then diving fast for home, the bombers largely evaded the defenders. Although the bombing results were unimpressive, they provided a nasty jolt to complacency and gave a glimpse of the modern bombing techniques so massively and effectively being used by the RAF.

Behind Operation 'Steinbock' was Oberstleutnant Pelz, personally selected for the role by Göring with whom he had ingratiated himself. Pelz had spent months planning the revenge offensive. After masterminding 'Jabo' Fw 190 attacks on England he acquired bomber units from Italy, organizing the re-equipment of his force with new aircraft. Do 217K-1s, Do 217M-1s, Ju 88S-1s, Ju 188Es and the long-expected but troublesome He 177 four-engined bomber — all came into front-line use. Hope was soon dispelled that new Do 217s would raise morale after the disappointment the Do 217E had generated, for performance improvement was minimal.

Italy's fall spread gloom, to counteract which rumours were deliberately launched within the bomber force during September 1943 that southern England was about to be laid waste by bombardment with eighty-ton rockets. Further boosting the claim, it was said that a large bomber force was to assemble to support the rocket onslaught — and 'Angriffsführer England' Pelz was suitably promoted to Generalmajor. So secret was the 'build up' that fortunately very few of those involved knew much about the others' activities and few appear to have known that the rocket offensive was imaginary. It had been hoped to make the flying-bomb offensive part of 'Steinbock', but the weapons were not yet ready. All that could be achieved would be revenge bombing of London, Baedecker-style by an air force lacking the training and discipline now required for effective and safe concentrated fast bombing operations.

Since summer 1943 the Luftwaffe had been copying RAF bombing tactics, and experimenting with a pathfinder force. Initially, KG2 was given the task, sending a few crews ahead to mark the target and indicate any necessary route changes. Late in August 1943 KG6, which had been target-marking in the Mediterranean Theatre, moved to Belgium for rest and re-equipment. It took over KG2's role, Gruppe I soon operating Ju 188Es over Britain. By October III/KG6's Ju 188s were also operational, along with some Ju 88s high-flying GM-1-boosted aircraft for pathfinder trials during attacks on eastern England. Testing of 50 kg flares and phosphor bombs, target markers and navigational aids was carried out by 8./KG6 until late December 1943 when it reverted to normal bomber operations. Then I/KG66 at Montdidier adopted the pathfinder role, 1 and 3 Staffel using Ju 88S-1s and 2 Staffel the Ju 188E, each holding about fifteen aircraft.

While final touches were put to the new force, small-scale night training operations took place, 91 sorties overflying England in the course of five nights, in December 1943, the fewest since February that year. During the chaotic Chelmsford attack of 10/11 December, 35 crews of the new bomber force flew in between Orford and Southend and tried out new tactics in a raid erroneously centred almost 25 miles from the intended target. Such a fiasco must have shocked the Luftwaffe management. Mining took place on nine December nights but only fourteen reconnaissance sorties had appeared near or over Britain.

Not until 12/13 January was there again more appreciable enemy activity

Top *Tail of Me 410A1-1 10120:
U5+HF of V/KG2 shot down
on 23 August 1943 at Shotley by
Mosquito XII VY:V.*

Above *Late Ju 88Ds reconnoitring offshore were fitted
with BMW 801 engines and had
no gondola (Bundesarchiv 607/
1837/25A).*

Left *Slimmer nose and BMW
801s, features of the Ju 88S
possibly first seen over East
Anglia in the Chelmsford raids
of 1943 (Bundesarchiv 489/
3159/30).*

Right *German diagram of the
A-4/V-2 long-range rocket and
its mobile launch vehicle (Bundesarchiv Bilol 141 (LOC)
1896).*

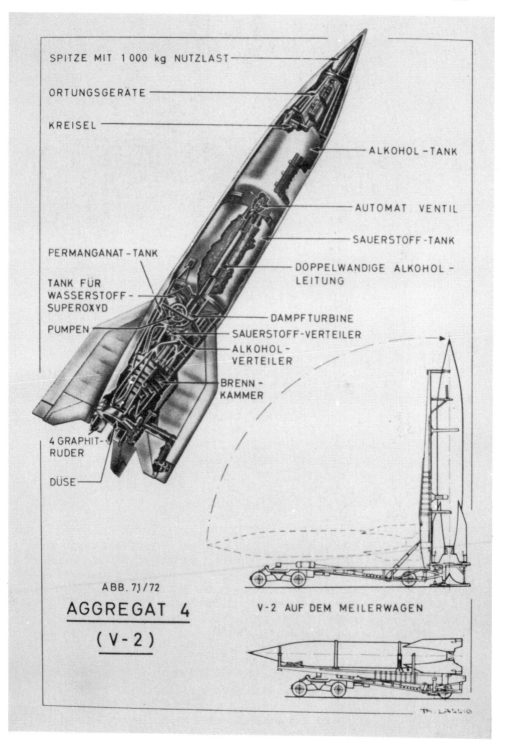

SPITZE MIT 1 000 kg NUTZLAST

ORTUNGSGERATE

KREISEL

ALKOHOL –TANK

AUTOMAT. VENTIL

SAUERSTOFF -TANK

PERMANGANAT – TANK

DOPPELWANDIGE ALKOHOL – LEITUNG

TANK FÜR WASSERSTOFF – SUPEROXYD

DAMPFTURBINE

PUMPEN

SAUERSTOFF-VERTEILER

ALKOHOL – VERTEILER

BRENN – KAMMER

4 GRAPHIT- RUDER

DÜSE

ABB. 71/72

AGGREGAT 4
(V-2)

V-2 AUF DEM MEILERWAGEN

Petal cowlings open on the engine, bomb doors apart and the hefty twin wheeled undercarriage units are clearly seen as 'whistling bombs' await to board He 177A-3 6N+HK 'Helga' of KG100 at Châteaudun early in 1944 during Operation 'Steinbock' (Bundesarchiv 668/7164/36A).

when seven aircraft approached the East Anglian coast very high and then headed towards London. One was claimed by Harwich AA guns. On the 15th/16th eight operated over the Home Counties, five reaching London.

By mid-January 1944 a revised order of battle had been realized, each Gruppe nominally having thirty aircraft. Gestab. KG2 with three aircraft was based at Soesterberg with II/KG2 split between there and Münster/Handorf working up on Ju 188Es. Dornier Do 217Ks and (mainly) M-1s equipped the rest of KG2, I Gruppe being at Eindhoven and III at Gilze Rijen. An oddity in the Lille/Cambrai area was V/KG2, the only bomber unit in the west flying Me 410As.

Gestab. KG6 was at Brussels, Gruppe I being at Chievres, II at Le Culot and III at Melsbroek flying Ju 88s or Ju 188s. Gestab. KG54 was in Germany, along with I/KG54 at Wittmundhafen and II/KG54 at Marx, both operating Ju 88A-4s. The dozen Ju 188 pathfinders of I/KG66 were still at Montdidier, and a similar number of He 177s of I/KG100 based at Rheine were detached to Châteaudun for operations. Reconnaissance was still provided by Soesterberg's 3.(F)/122, lately equipped with Ju 188s. On the Western Front the Luftwaffe held about 280 long-range bombers, a fifth of its total strength. If Fw 190 fighter-bombers were included that amounted to about 336 aircraft.

The importance of Operation 'Steinbock' — 'Capricorn' to the British — was personally impressed upon the He 177 crews by 29-year old Pelz just before they took their prestigious bombers into action for the first time over Britain. He seemed to have forgotten the rockets, but he stressed the importance of precise courses and timing. Unlike many, the He 177 crews had long been in training. Indeed, it was 1942 when I/KG4 began converting from He 111s to '177s at Lechfeld. Coupled engines driving a single large four-bladed propeller produced endless transmission and cooling problems making the large bomber most unpopular. By August 1943 the He 177A-3 was arriving and on 1 October I/KG4 was reconstituted as I/KG100. Staffel 3, the first operationally fit, moved to Châteaudun on 18 December and was immediately joined by He 177s of I/KG40.

The assumption after 21/22 January 1944 was that the enemy would keep the momentum going. But not until 28/29 January was another raid launched, a small-scale effort by about fifteen Me 410s, a few Do 217s and fifteen Fw 190s. The twin-engined bombers made landfall over East Anglia, the others the south-east, operations taking place over Kent, Sussex, Suffolk and Norfolk by 22 aircraft at between 10,000 and 20,000 ft. Only one penetrated to London and a Mosquito (one of which was shot down) destroyed an Me 410. Mosquitoes of 264 and Beaufighters of 68 and 409 Squadrons patrolled.

A larger operation took place on 29/30 January, over 100 bombers operating between Suffolk and Hampshire and particularly over the Thames Estuary. Included again were He 177s of 3./KG100 and I/KG40 operating entirely from Rheine, the latter unit to be withdrawn from the raids on 1 February.

Activity over East Anglia commenced at 20:27 when Ju 88A-4 W Nr *300228:B3+AL* of KG54 entered over Lowestoft heading for Bury. Flight Sergeant Neal of 68 Squadron in a Beaufighter followed it at 16,000 ft for ten minutes before twice firing. After jettisoning its incendiaries the Ju 88 crashed at Barham, north-west of Ipswich, where its remains were widely scattered. Only one of the six raiders destroyed during the night came down on land, and fewer than ten penetrated into East Anglia, to drop bombs as follows: in Halstead RD three AB500s; in Clare RD one AB100-2 and ten 50 kg phosphors; in Deben RD four 50 kg HEs one 500 kg HE and two Firepots; and at Brightlingsea four containers and one AB1000. HEs fell at Stansfield, West Suffolk.

Statistics for January 1944 included an estimated 611 enemy night sorties directed against southern England and East Anglia. A known 377 crossed the coast and 85 reached London, target for two-thirds of them. Fighter-bomber Fw 190s operating on five nights managed 79 sorties and lost three of their number. Such statistics as survive show that 36 enemy aircraft (5.9 per cent of sorties flown) were lost, twelve crashing on land and two falling to AA guns. In all, 201 fighter defence sorties were flown.

On six February nights German bombers operated over East Anglia. One occasion was 3/4 February when among the fifty to sixty invaders over the area, the south-east and the IAZ was a supposed Ju 88 which proceeded to Cambridge where, at 20:40, I recorded an aircraft sowing a string of sixteen flares. A white one spectacularly cascaded into an astonishing marker comprising white, blue, green and red elements. At the same time, Cambridge Site 2, Grantchester's HAA 3.7-in guns loosed off a dozen rounds before it was discovered that a passing Lancaster was heading roughly north-west, and failing to reveal its identity, had been accosted.

It was a dark, misty night with much cloud and no moon, thus the bombers were well shielded. Phase 2's activity on 4 February began as raiders from Holland and Belgium collected off the Orford Ness-Aldeburgh area, sowed large quantities of Düppel and headed inland. At about 04:20 the leader crossed Aldeburgh at around 8,000 ft and was followed by about twenty entering widely between Lowestoft and Deal. Others headed for the Home Counties, fifteen

He 177A-5 6N+SK *of KG100 wearing black under surfaces for night operations*
(Bundesarchiv 668/716A/33A).

flying into the London area at between 8,000 and 16,000 ft, and all operating
south-east of a line Winterton to Buckingham. Nine aircraft from Essex
distributed themselves between Lowestoft and Yarmouth and fourteen raids
crossed the coast between Aldeburgh and Yarmouth under much Düppel cover.
Yarmouth's guns engaged six, and three raiders which left the 2nd AA Group
area passed through Cambridge GDA at between 05:03 and 05:13 before turning
about. Against H123 the Cambridge guns directed five rounds before a closing
fighter caused the shooting to stop. H423, a Do 217, was engaged by both
Cambridge sites which fired 111 rounds. Beaufighters of 68 Squadron were in the
area and prevented guns engaging H422. Pilot Officer Seda (with Pilot Officer
Hrandsky) of 68 Squadron were vectored to Raid H112, a Ju 188 which they
shot down off Southwold. Before East Anglia was clear at 05:52 bombing had
occurred as follows; Dunmow RD nine 50 kg phosphor bombs; Chelmsford one
50 kg HE and two phosphor bombs; Deben RD thirteen 50 kgs, four 500 kg HEs,
a phosphor bomb and a container load; Halstead RD three phosphor bombs
and two AB500s; Melford RD four 50 kg and one 500 kg HEs with five
phosphors and four AB1000s; Samford RD two 50 kg and two HEs; Wainford
RD two containers of incendiaries; Lothingland two AB1000s and six UX
phosphor bombs, with Lowestoft and Southwold each receiving two incendiary
container loads. Incendiaries also fell at Clacton, Lexden and Tendring, most of
the bombing taking place around 05:00-05:30. Anti-aircraft gunners during the
night had been very heavily engaging the attackers, with 3.7-in guns firing 1,080

rounds from Harwich, 712 from Clacton, 1,090 from Ipswich and 388 from Colchester, whose 'Z' Battery also fired sixty rounds. Additionally 4,051 smaller rounds were fired.

Not until Sunday, 13/14 February, did the next major activity unfold, and mainly south of East Anglia. Pelz again reiterated the need for accurate timing, and played down the RAF's night fighting capability in the face of Düppel before watching the He 177s of 2 and 3 Staffeln, KG100, start off. Intensely cold conditions meant cold starts for the thirty aircraft detailed. One crashed on take off due to a tyre burst, and eight soon turned back with engine trouble due to the cold. Only four reached their target, and one of these was badly mauled. Over Norwich the Gruppe leader was forced to abort ... and not till over the Zuyder Zee did the crew remember to jettison their bombs. Only three He 177s touched down, after the operation, at Rheine as expected. Hardly an impressive performance.

It was at 19:55 that the first of about forty bombers had begun to leave France and some 110 took off from Dutch airfields. Flying high, the forces converged east of the Thames Estuary, 99 aircraft making landfall between Lowestoft and Deal, the remainder having participated in a feint before returning to their bases. Most of the others pressed on to the Home Counties, fifteen entering the London area. Most of the East Anglian bombs fell along the Suffolk and Essex coasts. At 21:06 an AB1000 container opened distributing 600 incendiaries over the Dovercourt holiday camp (now Warner's and recently featured in the popular TV series, *Hi-de-Hi*). Many incendiaries fell into the sea off Felixstowe, and more in Deben RD along with phosphor bombs, four 50 kgs and a 500 kg HE. In Samford RD three 250 kg HEs were dropped, but the main area of attack lay along the north Essex coast. Over and around Frinton and Walton two 50 kg HEs, five 500 kg HEs, two 1,000 kg HEs, three 50 kg phosphors, two AB1000s, two AB500s and six other HEs were dropped, and at Brightlingsea a 50 kg HE, two 500 kg HEs, four phosphor bombs, two AB1000 containers, an AB500 and an unclassified HE.

The heaviest bombing, though, overtook Clacton where at 21:15 a hefty consignment of fire bombs (six AB1000s, three AB500s and eighteen 50 kg phosphors—thirteen of which did not ignite) was showered upon the town centre. The warning had sounded at 20:25 and soon afterwards AA guns in the area were engaging several enemy aircraft. Brilliant white flares illuminated the town centre which became engulfed by fire as burning incendiaries littered roads and pavements in Pier Avenue and Station Road. Catling's roof burst into flames, Fairbairns too, and combustible 'Marks and Sparks' living up to its latter name was gutted. The upper floor of Smith's blazed furiously, and incendiaries pelted through the floor of Woolworth's. At the Odeon fire-watchers bravely extinguished the bombs, while Butlins and houses in Park Way were on fire. More incendiaries burnt around the 'Grand' Hotel in what for Clacton was a minute taste of how the Royal Air Force was operating over Germany, for Bomber Command literally delivered incendiaries by the million. The composition of the Clacton load suggests that a He 177 was responsible, for more HEs and firebombs also fell at Little Clacton, two HEs near the 'White Hart', Weeley, while incendiaries ignited in fields causing stack fires near the 'Bee Hive', Weeley Heath. Further HEs and incendiaries fell around St Osyth, cattle were killed at Pump Hill, HEs fell by Thorpe railway bridge, buildings on Giles

Farm, Holland, were destroyed and residents in the area found great quantities of Düppel. Decorating trees and hedgerows, the metallic strips were much larger that ours and matt black. By the time the 'All Clear' sounded over 20,000 incendiaries had fallen from one or two bombers around Clacton — more, and far more efficient types, than those delivered by a fleet of bombers on Norwich in a Baedecker raid. How much all had changed since the first incendiaries fell at Newton.

Relatively few noteworthy attacks were ever carried out upon USAAF bases in Britain, but one of them was delivered on Martlesham at 20:48 on 13 February when an AB1000-2 and two ABB500-1 incendiary container loads were dropped. The first opened, the smaller loads landing on the north side of the aerodrome and mainly they consisted of steel nosed 1 kg bombs. Probably from a Do 217, the delivery amounted to about 1,000 bombs, at least 100 not exploding.

At 20:50 the residents of Elsenham had become the first in the area to be treated to the arrival of the latest German HE weapon, an SB1000 parachute bomb of the type introduced at Brooklands, Romney Marsh, on 4/5 January 1944. Crudely welded, this was a thin walled purely blast weapon classified as a 1,000 kg HE. Of strange elliptical cross section, it had a charge/weight ratio of 75/80 per cent, the explosive being a mixture of ammonite nitrate, dinitrate-benzine, calcium nitrate and RDX. A red or green 5-ft diameter parachute of thin carpet-like material ensured a fairly fast delivery, for the weapon's fuzing demanded strong surface impact to function. Only nine bombs of this type were dropped in East Anglia.

Again, the AA gunners had been busy, Clacton's 3.7-in batteries firing 423 rounds and the Bofors there another 548 rounds. Colchester's 3.7-in guns had fired another 793 rounds and the rocket battery 59.

Essex again suffered, on 18/19 February when, soon after midnight, the first bombers (mainly from Holland) joined a force of about 45 from France thirty miles east of Harwich and began at 00:30 to pass over Felixstowe at between 12,000 and 25,000 ft. They were followed by about 120 more which entered between Winterton and the Thames to be greeted by 1,487 rounds of 3.7-in AA fire. Nearly all were here to participate in a very sharp attack on Greater London before diving for home over the South Coast. About five aircraft flew to King's Lynn, several to Luton and all of these left via Suffolk. In eight localities there and in Essex HE bombs fell, including an SB1000 para-bomb in Deben RD and four 250 kg HEs at Clacton. Containers of fire bombs and 50 kg phosphor bombs dropped in Mitford RD, Dunmow RD, Saffron Walden RD and near Braintree. Over Cambridge many enemy aircraft — Do 217s, He 177s of 2. and 3./KG100 from Rheine returning to Rennes, and Ju 88s including 26 of KG 54—progressed towards London, dropping flares to the south of the town and phosphor bombs at Fulbourn. Before the country was clear at 01:50 a sharp attack on Earl's Colne airfield took place. Firstly, fifteen HEs and an AB1000-2 load of incendiaries fell, a second attack being made using six HEs and another incendiary load.

The night of 20/21 February saw departure from the Dutch coast at 21:00 of sixty bombers which crossed our coast between Hythe and Harwich. Mosquitoes of 25 Squadron were active, *HK285* claiming a Ju 188E and *HK255* a Do 217 off East Anglia, but most of the raiders penetrated to London.

Incidents occurred at Clacton (two AB1000s), in Chelmsford RD (four 250 kg HEs), Dunmow RD (two AB500s), Halstead RD (where four out of five 50 kg HEs were UX), and in Deben (five 50 kg HEs, four UX phosphor bombs and a container of incendiaries). Second phase activity was confined to southern England and London.

From Rheine the first of fourteen He 177A-3s of I/KG100 started off at 20:37 on 22/23 February. Attempting to improve their timing, all were airborne in ten minutes. Most carried four 1,000 kg HEs, experienced crews taking two 1,800 kg and two 1,000 kg bombs. A few aircraft had Neptun tail warning radar. Over Harwich the leading bomber arrived at 23:55, others entering between Yarmouth and North Foreland. Two were shot down by Mosquitoes, *HK283* of 25 Squadron destroying a Do 217 over Norfolk and *HK521* of 410 Squadron a Ju 88 at Earl's Colne. A two-pronged operation against London and the Home Counties evolved using about 100 aircraft mostly from Montdidier/Creil and fifty from the Merville region. All left via the Thames Estuary or south-east coast.

About a score of bombers detached themselves to operate over Bedfordshire and Huntingdonshire. Three entered Yarmouth GDA. Intrusions south of Cambridge at 00:12-00:23 encountered 151 rounds of 3.7-in fire from the two batteries, and salvoes from Cambs 101 Home Guard 'Z' Battery, in response to which two sticks of bombs and incendiaries fell. More HEs than usual were dropped on Suffolk and Essex coastal regions, and between 00:20 and 01:00 many incendiary loads were released over Orford, Falkenham, Pakefield (five 50 kg phosphor bombs, two UX, with 1,186 incendiaries from two containers), Claydon, Boyton, Kirton, Street Farm, Bucklesham (on to which a 50 kg UX phosphor bomb fell), Cauldwell Hall at Hollesley and on Bramford police station, all in Suffolk. Mixed loads dropped upon Essex included two HEs at Dedham, three UXHEs at Yoxford, two HEs and two phosphor bombs at Sudbourne, two HEs off Dovercourt, three 50 kg phosphor bombs and two AB1000 containers over Dunmow RD, and incendiary loads at Fingringhoe, Frating, Great and Little Warley, Great Canfield and Great Saling. Two AB1000 incendiary container loads east of Clacton damaged fourteen houses and caused four casualties. Mostly the fire bombs burnt in open country — with one major exception.

Colchester's sirens sounded at 23:53 and very soon a lone bomber circled. At 00:20 flares were dropped then, making a single run at about 13,000 ft, the raider released two 50 kg phosphor bombs and an AB1000 container carrying around 600 SNIBs. Functioning well, it spread its load over 75 acres — an area about 230 yd in diameter. Instantly, buildings around St Botolph's were engulfed by fire caused by steel nosed bombs which easily penetrated roofs. The Britannia Works were gutted, and after machinery crashed into furious fires Hollington's and Leaning's clothing factories were reduced to unsafe shells. H. L. Griffin's furniture store burnt fast and furiously, many firemen having a lucky escape when the building collapsed.

Blomfield and Coy's shop and ironmongery store was burnt out too. The 'Plough' Hotel, J. W. Bare & Co's shop, J. Damponey's in St Botolph Street, Moore & Roberts', Cheshire's China Stores and Hancock & Co were soon beyond saving. More shops were burning in Mersea Road, houses were ablaze at Blackheath and other shops were damaged in Calver Street and Arthur Street.

Above Crowsfeet were first reported to have fallen on the west side of Lowestoft. Others were dropped on East Anglian airfields, but official records appear to have overlooked the recording of these annoying objects which were intended to puncture tyres. Consisting of segments of green- or khaki-painted metal arranged with four barbed points, they were so devised that upon landing one point would always face directly upwards. Two sizes were known to have been dropped, one with its upright point 2.5 in above the ground and the other measuring 2 in.

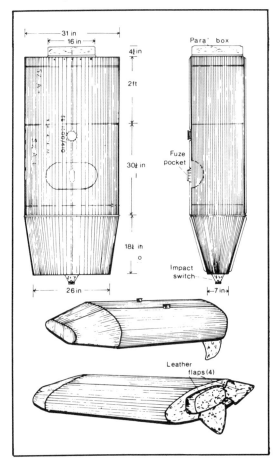

Left Almost as strange a weapon as the crowsfoot was the SB1000 parachute bomb. Of most unusual shape, its parachute was packed in a box at its stern and kept in place by leather flaps. A thin skin ensured maximum blast effect. It was a late-war weapon and only a few examples fell on Britain.

Above *Loading 500 kg HEs into a Heinkel He 177 was difficult because of its low 'sit'. Putting the intended German atomic bomb aboard would have been even more so* (Bundesarchiv 676/7970A/23).

Below *Fuzing a 500 kg bomb. Netting covers the KG100 He 177 for the risk of intruder attack was high* (Bundesarchiv 668/7162/9A).

Firemen at Griffin's were very lucky to escape when the building collapsed. Many incendiaries were nevertheless doused, fire-guards and two schoolboys climbing a steep iron ladder on to the roof of St Botolph's Church while carrying buckets of water with which they put out the fire. More bombs entered the Empire Cinema, and they too were extinguished. During the first eight hours of fire fighting the NFS used two million gallons of water. Eventually another million were drawn leaving Colchester very short of water. For the NFS and the fire-guards that one aircraft had created an immense problem laced with great danger which they all faced with enormous courage. Had they realized at the time, they might have had some satisfaction in knowing that at Stebbing, near Braintree, Ju 188E-1 W Nr *260312:U5+HP* had been hit by AA fire and dived steeply into a field, part of its bomb load exploding.

Analysis of the Colchester raid showed that as a result of over 130 reported fires, fourteen properties had been completely destroyed. Only one serious casualty was recorded, seventy-year old Bertha Nunn who was burned when an incendiary fell on her bed. The Colchester raid produced the most serious incident in East Anglia during Operation 'Steinbock'; but it was certainly not the most remarkable.

Operations Orders issued to the Luftwaffe for the night of 23/24 February outlined an attack on the Isle of Dogs, code-named 'Hamburg'. Bombing from 13,000 ft between 22:30-22:42 was to follow the pathfinding lead of KG66. The units involved were:

Take off base	Unit	Aircraft	Approx effort
Melun/Villaroche	Stab./KG2	Do 217M-1	2
Melun/Villaroche	2./KG2	Do 217M-1	6
Melun/Villaroche	3./KG2	Do 217M-1	7
Coulommiers	4 & 5./KG2	Ju 188E	13
Coulommiers	6./KG2	Ju 188E	7
Unknown	III/KG2	Do 217M-1	?
Brussels/Melsbroek	7./KG6	Ju 88A-4	5/6
Brussels/Melsbroek	8./KG6	Ju 88A-4	4/5
Brussels/Melsbroek	9./KG6	Ju 88A-4	5/6
Unknown	Rest of KG6	Ju 88/188E	?
Unknown	KG54	Ju 88A-4	?
Montdidier	2./KG66	Ju 188E	2?
Montdidier	1 and 3./KG6	Ju 88S-1	?
Châteaudun	I/KG100	He 177A-3	?

Operational Staffel IV/KG101 and Fw 190s were to operate together with a few Me 410s, three of which flew north of London, one to Debden, another to Bedford.

The Battle Order and load prescribed for KG2 was: *U5+AK* (Leutnant Burgart), four SC500 and four BC50 fuze 38 (delay); *U5+BK* (Oberleutnant Tamm), one AB1000 and two AB500s, also carried by *U5+LK* (Leutnant Tamm), *U5+MK* (Unteroffizier Jakob), *U5+HK* (Leutnant Boettger), *U5+AL* (Leutnant Ott), *U5+CL* (Feldwebel Spiering), *U5+IL* (Feldwebel Möbins), *U5+ML* (Oberfeldwebel Jäger), *U5+OL* (Leutnant von Parpart) and *U5+CB* (Feldwebel Kuester). *U5+EL*, '*BA* and '*CA* carried four SC500s and four

BC50s, instantaneous fuzing. In addition to them was Oberfeldwebel Stemann flying Do 217 *U5+DK* carrying an AB1000 and two AB500s. His journey was most unusual.

KG2 was ordered to fly at 500 ft to St Valéry en Caux then climb fast to 16,500 ft, cross the coast over Eastbourne at 16,500 ft then gradually descend to 13,000 ft for bombing, unloading HEs between 22:30 and 22:33. Incendiaries would be dropped by the 2nd and 3rd Staffeln during the following nine minutes. A left turn on to a reciprocal course was prescribed and a crossing into France at 650 ft. Düppel would be released every thirty seconds from 25 miles off the English coast to target and back, one packet being thrown out over the IAZ every four to five seconds. Flak star shells fired over France and the coast would serve as route markers.

On time KG2 set off for London, Oberfeldwebel Stemann, taking off at 20:20, being fourth or fifth to leave. *U5+DK* headed for Evreux, climbed, passed St Valéry and made landfall over Beachy Head. Arriving early, Stemann took the Dornier over north London and circled. Suddenly a stabbing searchlight beam snatched the aircraft from the darkness over Ealing, and an AA 'Z' battery at once fired a box barrage which encased it. In the aircraft the noise was undoubtedly terrifying and believing *U5+DK* to have received damage to its starboard engine, wing and cockpit, the crew baled out over Acton. The bomber, however, was still in very good state and headed north-easterly, very slowly descending.

Sirens sounded in Cambridge at 22:30 and, already recording at my usual vantage point, I noted in my diary 'two red flares south-south-west, red shell bursts, three large explosions, many incendiary loads south before siren'. Just before the 'All Clear' there came 'an incredibly quiet, low flying "Lancaster" going north-east over town'. The sound disappeared in the Chesterton direction. I noted it and gave it no more thought. Identification of most aircraft by sound was still possible, although some of the new German aircraft were not so easy to identify since one did not have the chance to link sight and sound in daylight.

By dawn the news had spread throughout the town, a Dornier had come down last night on allotments close to St George's Church, Chesterton. It had by inches missed the roof of Chesterton Institution to belly land in the extreme north-east corner of the open ground. Only the second Luftwaffe aircraft to visit Britain in such style, it had arrived almost completely unharmed carrying plentiful petrol and its full bomb load. How, just how, did it come to make an almost perfect belly landing? If that was never to be explained one thing was obvious. Here was a splendid item to view.

Many had similar thoughts and throughout the day crowds swarmed to the area, only to be held well back from the allotments by the Law in all its splendour — well, the Dornier had delivered itself on official land. But, what of the private gardens into which it had almost poked its unusual nose? Ah, the value of private enterprise showed itself, as householders with an eye to business and a thought for war charities offered for sixpence a most splendid look at the Dornier at the bottom of the garden. Just imagine that moment when surely someone cried 'Dad, we've got a Dornier poking through our fence', then Dad's disbelief! For my part I was somewhat disappointed because my father owned a moderate piece of land in Green End Road where I (but certainly not *he*) would have readily accommodated the visitor!

Above *Bomb doors open, Do 217M-1* U5+LK *during the 1944 'Baby Blitz' keeps an eye on a sophisticated BSB700 incendiary bomb container being wheeled across the snow at Melun/Villaroche to a companion aircraft* — U5+DK? (Bundesarchiv 489/3166/17).

Below *After an incredible flight, Do 217M-1* U5+DK *of 2./KG2 slid to an intact end on a Cambridge allotment* (RAF Museum).

By the weekend the authorities had, as ever, been worn down by the sheer number of those who wanted a close look at the first Do 217M-1 to land intact in Britain. Three of us thus made our cautious way, early on the Saturday, to the scene of the misadventure.

I have never seen a more ugly, roughly finished aeroplane. Over its matt black lower surfaces there was a sort of greyish wash, and on to its pale blue-grey upper surfaces had been sprayed many patches of darker grey and a few splodges of black, colouring fairly usual and almost impossible to record except on colour film which was then impossibly inaccurate. Only the white areas of the national identity markings remained, and also white and low on the fuselage just ahead of the tail unit was *U5*, identifying it as originating from 'East Anglia's Own', KG2. Aft of the white cross on the fuselage port side, and forward on the starboard, was *DK* boldly in grey, linking the aircraft with 2./KG2, and both spinners had white tips. Outer faces of the fins, the port one dark green mottled grey, bore a large white *2* with *5574* in yellow at their tips and *U5* with *DK* lower on the base of the rudders. A maker's plate identified the tail constructor as *DORNIER/ GMBH/ FREDERICH*, beneath which was *CER:T N/R 8.217.356* and then *WERKE 5574*, a likely Dornier Werke Nr. However, a maker's plate in the cockpit referred to *56051*, and *51* was also painted on the nose in 9-in white characters. The officials, I learned years later, were mystified and like myself concluded that the aircraft had been repaired and consisted of an amalgamation of Dorniers.

Lying by the little-damaged machine were two khaki coloured containers which I recorded as Type H AB500-1, basing the title upon an inscription carried. Alongside was a large yellow container, presumably the AB1000. Also alongside were many unusual-looking incendiaries with curious fins and curved noses, and when I asked one of the quite talkative investigating team what they were, he reckoned 'IBSEN'. I think it was when I referred to 'the AB 1000-2' that, while suppressing astonishment, he recognized a kindred spirit! That large container was unusual in that it had four compartments, two for IBSEN and two for normal 'IB 1 kg', and could accommodate 590 bombs. Also aboard the aircraft were two cardboard boxes each carrying forty bundles composed of 350 strips of Düppel 79.7 cm long by 20 cm wide. In each of the nose, dorsal turret and ventral positions were fitted an MG 131 machine-gun, and two MG 81s poked from the sides of the top of the cabin.

Everyone, though, was asking the same question and getting no sensible answer. How *did* the bomber manage the flight so far then land without exploding, with so much fuel and weapon load aboard? True, it was twisted upon impact and could never fly again. But its strange arrival continues to make it a fascinating wartime memory. If he is still around maybe Oberfeldwebel Stemann might like to offer his suggestions?

A week later I watched it leave for Farnborough, in large pieces on a 'Queen Mary' trailer heading along Maid's Causeway. When that wonderful exhibition of German aircraft was held in October-November 1945 one of the fins of *5651* (or whatever it was) could be seen looking lonely and dejected in a corner of 'A' Shed. What a splendid museum exhibit that would now make!

On the night the Dornier arrived, 3./KG2 and III/KG6 each lost an aircraft, matching three successes claimed by AA gunners. Of those, only *U5+DK* came down on land; but there was another German aircraft to be viewed, near

Yoxford. A few cannon shots from a 25 Squadron Mosquito flown by Wing Commander Wight-Boycott had proven lethal to a He 177A-3 of I/KG100.

Both Staffel 2 and 3 were operating He 177s from Châteaudun against London when the fighter killed the unorthodox, legendary bomber whose service career had been four years in limbo. This example, individual identity *Q*, almost instantly disintegrated when hit, its wreckage extending for a quarter of a mile with the tail unit bearing the W Nr *322(7?)* dropping two miles away. Considerable investigation into the He 177 was producing valuable information, showing that the aircraft had a very ordinary performance which was not aided by its exceptionally heavy aramament. The small bomb load being carried was thought to be due to the aircraft's limited lifting capability, brought about by heavy engines and a structure which therefore had to be strengthened. Wing span of 103 ft and an all-up weight of 68,000 lb (72,500 lb at maximum overload) put it in the Stirling class, but not its bomb load. By now it was known that the first example brought down was carrying an 11,000 lb load and 9,360 lb of fuel. The maximum bomb load possible was two 1,800 kg HEs and two 1,000 kg HEs internally and two 1,000 kgs externally coupled to a range of only 400 miles. With a 7,900 kg load it was 550 miles. Normally the aircraft would carry only a full internal load. Questioned must be the precise nature of the two huge bombs dropped near March supposedly from a He 177. Could they have been 1,800 kg and not 2,500 kg weapons?

For defence the tail gunner had a huge MG 151 20 mm cannon, another of which could be installed in the nose. Without power traverse, these were useless items. Elsewhere five MG 131 and one MG 81 machine-guns were carried. Great had been the problems with the He 177A-3's DB 610 (Duplex DB 605) engines which, when working properly, gave 2,580 hp for take off and 2,468 hp at 19,000 ft. Again, when functioning, one of the pair could be shut down for economic cruise – which facility added to complexity. The bomber's top speed was an unimpressive 280 mph at 13,000 ft, and KG100 lost six aircraft between 21 January and 2 March 1944. Four were shot down making night sorties, one was shot down near Antwerp by the Germans themselves and the other was destroyed by a P-51 Mustang in daylight.

During February seventeen enemy aircraft crashed in Britain, among them Ju 188 *Z6+HK* of pathfinding KG66. Most interestingly, it was fitted with British ARI 5083 'Gee' navigational equipment. Although Gerät 'Benito' beams operated on most nights, few bombers carried equipment enabling use of the system. Instead, they relied upon British Gee transmissions. One aircraft examined had FuG 25A IFF apparatus used by a ground station to ascertain the aircraft's position. Few bombers had FuG 214 or '216 tail warning radar; Do 217 *U5+DK* was merely wired for it. But use of Düppel had indeed created havoc with British defensive radar. All the German aircraft brought down carried bundles of one type or another. About 35 bundles each of 300 strips could be packed in an AB36 container.

February raids on London continued on a small scale, and a few raiders flew as far north as Debden and Harwich on the 24th/25th. But the raids were taking a steady toll of the bombers, III/KG 2 moving its Ju 188s to Münster/Handorf at the end of February. Part of II/KG2 vacated Soesterberg due to RAF bombing.

Apart from nuisance attacks by Fw 190s and Me 410s – now also being operated by KG51 – the next major operation involving East Anglia came on 14/15 March. First off were Montdidier's pathfinders of I/KG66, behind which came the representatives of I, II and III/KG2, I and II/KG3, I, II and III/KG6, II and III/KG30, I and II/KG54 and KG51. Diversionary sorties were flown by Fw 190s of SKG10. About 130 aircraft in all, they had set off in three groups for the collecting point (52° 21'N/03° 08'E), from which they made their ways into England. For disguise they infiltrated a stream of returning Mosquitoes and made much use of Düppel. The first landfalls took place at 22:11 between Cromer and Clacton, most aircraft crossing the coast between Yarmouth and Southwold at heights between 14,000 and 24,000 ft then heading for London. By then Mosquitoes were challenging them, Squadron Leader Green and Lieutenant Havington of 410 Squadron each claiming a Ju 88, another of which was shot down by 12 Group. Thirty bombers penetrated the IAZ leaving the remainder scattered widely south-east of a line Cromer-Oxford-Isle of Wight before they headed home across the South Coast. Typical of the night's activity was that undertaken by KG6 which commenced taking off at 21:11 and flew over Rotterdam en route for Norfolk. Its track lay south of Norwich to a turning point south-east of Cambridge, where the sirens were sounded at 22:45. My diary mentions 'three flares, and incendiaries seen to the south-east, Ju 88s/188s about' just after the warning. Some of the Ju 88s were probably of the large KG54 contingent, one third bringing HEs and the rest two AB 1000s per aircraft.

Authorized run-in was on a track of 246° True leading to the turn in for the attack. Some of the bombers crossed over Chelmsford whose gunners responded with 1,530 rounds of 3.7-in and 64 rockets. After aiming their loads of two AB1000 and ten BC50s from 21,000 ft on to ground markers, and enduring a tremendous reception from London's 'Z' batteries, the KG6 Ju 188s made for Calais and home. For many there was the ordeal of Mosquito intruders to face, and within hours a number of KG6's aircraft were destroyed in sharp attacks upon their bases.

Night fighters claimed seven of the night's raiders, AA gunners four and another crashed due to unknown causes. One was Ju 188E *U5+B*? of 5./KG2 brought down by Mosquito *MM476* of 488 Squadron at 23:03 on White House Farm, Great Leigh. Mosquitoes *HK466* and *HK521* each destroyed a Ju 188 off the coast. Bombs fell widely over East Anglia but caused very little damage. Extremely mixed loads were used, including about 10,000 incendiaries brought in AB1000s and AB500s, AB23s and 27 50 kg phosphor bombs, four of which failed to ignite. There were 50, 250 and a single 500 kg HEs, the latter near Dunmow. An oil bomb reported near Shudy Camps was probably a phosphor weapon.

When, on 19/20 March Hull was the target, some flights crossed Norfolk. Crews of 25 Squadron, which had replaced 68 Squadron at Coltishall after that squadron's long stay from 8 March 1942 to 5 February 1944, claimed three bombers, *HK255* a Ju 188, *HK278* an He 177 and a Do 217. The raid dissolved into random bombing of the eastern counties, incendiaries coming down at Horsham St Faith and Aylsham, four container loads near Walsingham and two 500 kgs in Erping RD. Inaccurate navigation and late marking, probably due to strong winds, was largely to blame.

Operations orders had stressed low and medium transit across the North Sea to the collecting point, followed by a straight leg to Hull for bombing then a left

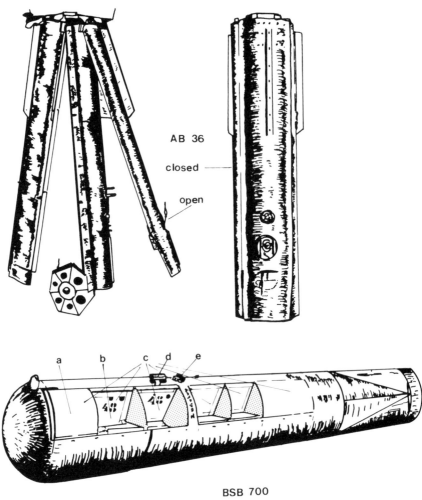

AB 36

closed

open

a   b   c   d   e

BSB 700

Type 'E'

The early AB36 container split in a different manner to other containers. BSB700 came into use in 1942 and was used to deliver heavy incendiary showers, during 'The Baby Blitz', upon Clacton and Colchester. Incendiaries were ejected from compartments in a quite sophisticated manner. 'a' is the door in place, 'b' the rotating inner door, 'c' the bomb compartments, 'd' a bomb release unit/timer and 'e' the automatic distributor. Tails were often not fitted to these containers which could carry up to 700 1 kg incendiaries, or slightly fewer explosive incendiaries.

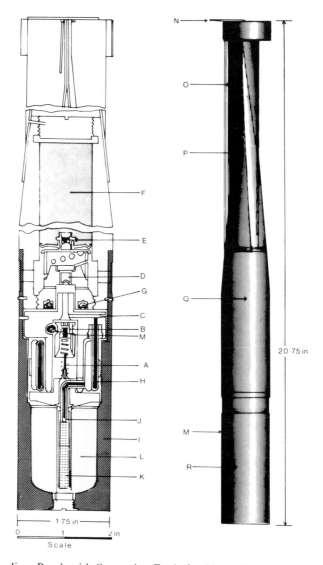

The 2 kg Incendiary Bomb with Separating Explosive Nose (IBSEN; B2 E.Z. to the Germans) used during the 1944 'Baby Blitz'. A 2 oz nose charge was hurled from the main bomb by a charge, the conventional 1 kg incendiary portion was shorter than normal but the tail unit was longer at 9.75 in and had three instead of four fins. The arming wire and safety pin were as for the IBEN. On falling from the container the safety pin (M) was withdrawn by air pressure on the arming rod plate (N). On impact the striker (A) fired the detonator (B), igniting the chemical in the flash chamber (C) and the relay pellet (D). The flash from that started the igniter (E) which fired the main incendiary filling (F). Whilst that has taken place ignition of the flash chamber (C) has set off the separate charge (G) which blew the incendiary and HE components several yards apart. The delay fuze (H) burned then ignited the flash pellet (J) which initiated the detonator (K) and blew the main nose explosive charge (L). O—one of the triple fins; P—the tail unit; Q—the main incendiary portion; R—the explosive component.

turn for Grimsby, KG54 leading the exit to a new assembly point, 53^0 32'N/02^0 35'E, where Ju 188 *Z6+EK* was to place Lux buoys on the water. From there the force was to head to Terschelling and dispersal. So persistently bad was route marking that a specially equipped night-reconnaissance Me 410 of 1.(F)/121, on detachment from Paris/Buc, accompanied each raid. Normally, photographic reconnaissance over East Anglia was undertaken by Ju 188s of Soesterberg's 4.(F)/122.

On 21/22 March another determined attack upon London was launched, about ninety bombers from Holland heading in at between 10,000 and 23,000 ft, the first entering over Southwold at 00:25. Again a turning point was established south-east of Cambridge where markers burnt for an hour. A smaller force of Fw 190s and Me 410s from France approached London from the south, sixty bombers entering the IAZ and bombing 41 London boroughs. Tactics were quite different for instead of low flying over the North Sea the Main Force climbed over their own territory. Operational heights were now between 13,000 and 16,000 ft for Ju 88s and Do 217s, 20,000 and 23,000 ft for Ju 188s and He 177s with Fw 190s and Me 410s operating between 26,000 and 30,000 ft. A diversion group came in between Felixstowe and Yarmouth and fanned out towards Norwich, Cambridge, Bedford and roamed east of a line Yarmouth-Bedford-Reading-Portsmouth at heights between 14,000 and 26,000 ft before leaving between Clacton and Selsey, all being clear at 01:50. An enormous quantity of Düppel was dropped, between Holland and England and over the east and south-east, and more during the return over the Channel. Night fighters were very busy, 11 Group mounting 44 patrols during which 410 Squadron from Castle Camps destroyed an enemy aircraft, one of the Group's claim to seven. Another two fell to 12 Group and the AA gunners claimed another. Known to have taken part were I, II and III/KG2, II/KG30, KG51, KG54, I/KG66, I/KG100 and Fw 190s.

Nine areas of East Anglia were bombed. Southwold received 300 incendiaries, Lothingland RD UX phosphor bombs and incendiaries, Chelmsford RD three AB 1000s, Dunmow RD two AB1000s and ten phosphor bombs, Halstead two 500 kg HEs (one UX), Saffron Walden RD four 500 kg HEs, Mitford and Wainford four AB1000s and eight UX phosphor bombs. At Colchester, where 395 rounds of 3.7-in AA fire greeted the raiders, an AB1000 hit a public surface shelter before rolling on to the road and exploding. Its mainly explosive load produced a crater 15 ft across and 6 ft deep, demolished 6 ft of the shelter and damaged houses close by.

At 00:44 bombs fell at Long Melford and Glemsford where, at Blackland Hall a minute later, a Ju 88A-4 crashed. At 22:55 it had left Varelbusch and was shot down by Mosquito *MM476* of 488 Squadron. *4D+AT* of 9./KG30 dived in steeply, its fuel tanks exploding on impact and the engines burying themselves deeply. Three jettisoned 50 kg phosphor bombs exploded, damaging a bungalow, but a further five of these temperamental bombs refused to operate even in these circumstances. From the wreckage it was deduced that the machine was W Nr *088 301522*.

Almost simultaneously 488 Squadron scored a second victory when *HK380* shot down another Ju 88A-4, *3E+GS* of 8./KG6 operating from Melsbroek. Searchlights illuminated the bomber, cannon shots hit it and the Ju 88, with a 500 kg HE aboard, smashed into a B-26 Marauder on Earl's Colne aerodrome, fragments of the two aircraft littering the flying field. A third Ju 88, W Nr *088 300500*, was set on fire by a Mosquito's guns when over Chelmsford and dived steeply into the ground near Latchingdon. For East Anglians it proved to be another hectic, noisy night, Chelmsford's AA gunners firing 787 rounds of 3.7-in, Ipswich's 151 rounds and Harwich's 323.

Several high-flying enemy aircraft visited East Anglia on 24/25 March, detaching themselves from the eighty or so attacking London from the south and retreating across Essex. Mosquito *HK293* of 25 Squadron shot down a Ju 188 45 miles off Lowestoft.

There followed a pause in Luftwaffe activity over East Anglia until 11/12 April when about a dozen Me 410s of V/KG2 operated over Cambridgeshire, Lincolnshire and Norfolk. By dawn it was clear that activities against airfields and aircraft had been resumed, and that Operation 'Steinbock' was ending. Bombing had been restricted to eighteen 50 kg HEs dropped in Loddon RD.

The next busy night was 18/19 April, ninety aircraft raiding London, scoring a direct hit on the North Middlesex Hospital and producing a forty-pump fire in Romford, while ten Me 410s intruded widely against East Anglian airfields.

At 00:50 Cambridge sirens sounded and almost immediately a Do 217 could be heard circling. I went into the garden in the hope of seeing the aircraft when I heard distantly the heavy thump of cannon fire. Moments later there was the tell-tale sudden glare of an aircraft crashing. Mosquito *MM456* of 410 Squadron had been finishing off He 177A-3 *6N+AK* of 3./KG100 which crashed at 01:03 on Butler's Farm, near Little Walden airfield. Four of the Heinkel's crew of six survived the engagement and from their interrogation, and items found in the wreck, an account of *6N+AK*'s venture was compiled.

According to the crew they were bringing from Rheine twelve 250 kgs to be dropped upon Tower Bridge. At 20:00 on the 18th three crews of 2./KG100 and two of Staffel 3 were briefed by Hauptmann von Kalkreudh, the Gruppen Kommandeur. A captured flight plan had the five aircraft taking off between 23:18 and 23:34 and setting course between 23:34 and 23:39. They climbed out over the Dutch coast at Noordwyk, and checked position over six Lux sea buoys. After landfall just north of Orford Ness *6N+AK* was flying at 18,000 ft and heading for a turning point just east of Newmarket, marked at 10,000 ft by four red flares. *6N+AK* had been ordered to bomb between 01:03-01:07 an area marked by a cluster of seven red flares, bombs to be released during a glide to 11,500 ft. Return to Rheine would be via Boulogne and Arnhem, the French coast being crossed at 2,500 ft — but not by *332379:6N+AK*.

Soon after crossing in slightly south of Orford the crew was taken completely by surprise when a burst of fire from a Mosquito tore into the fuselage side putting the intercom out of use. When the rear gunner saw the fighter coming in a second time he fired a white Very signal warning his pilot, then fired his 20 mm cannon. Decades later one of the spent cartridges was picked up by a schoolboy, Sean Munro, and it occasioned considerable interest, a rare trophy indeed. Following a third assault the Heinkel was too disabled to survive so the bomb load, which failed to explode, was jettisoned near Saffron Walden. Four of the crew managed to bale out and one evaded capture for some days by hiding in the Little Walden countryside. When eventually found he was in a highly dishevelled state, and despite his ordeal still proudly proclaimed the certainty of a Nazi victory. Perhaps he had believed Pelz.

The night of 18/19 April was also special for other reasons — there would never be another of so much bombing of East Anglia. Incidents were reported from nineteen areas. As well as the Heinkel's arrival, sinister events took place near Ely. After creeping in unobserved, an Me 410 joined the circuit at Witchford, its arrival coinciding with the return of 115 Squadron from Rouen. A few bursts of fire and two Lancaster IIs had been shot down. To nearby Mepal an Me 410, probably another one, directed its attention. Five Stirlings and ten Lancasters of 75 (RNZAF) Squadron were due to land between 02:00 and 03:00 from operations during which Bomber Command dropped about 4,110 metric tonnes, a quite astonishing figure when set against the Luftwaffe puny effort against East Anglia.

At 01:57 the pilot of Lancaster *M* returning from Rouen asked for landing permission and was told to follow *V* whose navigation lights were showing. An Me 410, circling unobserved, then slipped in behind *V*-Victor. Just as the Lancaster touched down on the 1,950-yd SW/NE runway several dull thuds were heard, also bursts of cannon and machine-gun fire. Delivered on to the runway from 50-75 ft had been 34 SD10A APBs — brought in two AB250 containers — being used for the first time in this area. Unlike 'butterfly bombs', they resembled in appearance conventional weapons. A few exploded on impact and the Lancaster was lucky to escape. Other aircraft of 75 Squadron were diverted to Tempsford and Newmarket, but luckily not Tuddenham where, at 02:45, another Me 410 deposited 34 SD10As in a field north-east of the village. Little Snoring, too, was raided at 02:10, SD10s (eight exploding) landing close to the main runway.

Among other incidents the same night was the firing of buildings on Heath Farm, Sheringham; damage to 59 houses at Westleton by an SB1000 para-bomb which exploded on Grange Farm, injuring three people and killing several cattle; dropping of three 50 kg HEs on Lilac Farm, Hockwood, Norfolk, five UX bombs at Mickfield and Stonham, Suffolk, and a UX 500 kg HE at Earl Soham. Incendiaries were particularly numerous in the Hollesley-Leiston-Hasketon part of Suffolk. Analysis of the total load dropped suggests it amounted to: fifteen 50 kgs one 250 kg, four 500 kgs and one 1,200 kg HE; 25 50 kg phosphor bombs, seventeen AB500s and at least twenty AB1000 containers, and in addition 102 SD10As. A conservative count suggests at the most delivery of 24 metric tonnes. On 21 April an unusual find was of the remains of thirteen small SD1 APBs which had fallen in Wood Road, Brandon.

One of the aircraft operating on 18/19 April was Ju 88A-4/Trop *1214:B3+GP*. At 12,000 ft over the North Sea the crew concluded that their aircraft was so badly damaged by AA fire that it could never make home. Accordingly, they turned about and crash landed it at Bradwell Bay.

On 20/21 April the Luftwaffe again attempted a raid on Hull, ten Me 410s roaming over East Anglia providing diversions. One of the Hull force dropped six 500 kg HEs near Lowestoft at 01:50. One fell at Elm House, Normanton Drive, Oulton Broad, one behind Betty Cottages, another on the LNER's track sleeper depot and one in a field off Hall Road. Another refugee from the Hull raid was probably the 50 kg phosphor bomb at Stebbing. At 04:25 Horsham airfield was bombed — its lighting on for an RAF aircraft in distress—six HEs dropping on the funnel approach. Shipdham, also displaying lights, was receiving a Wellington when an Me 410 caught up with the bomber and opened fire. The Wellington dived away and escaped, but 34 SD10As were dropped as the intruder machine-gunned the airfield. Almost simultaneously Lakenheath was bombed by a very low flier which released eight 50 kg HEs, cutting field telephones, damaging a funnel light and producing a shrapnel hole in the flare path caravan. Two other 50 kg HEs, which fell on Beach Farm, Benacre, were the last to drop in Lothingland RD.

Late on 12 April a new type of operation evolved, possibly rapidly devised. About twelve night fighters followed home some late-flying B-24s, firing upon one landing at Framlingham. They also found a Spitfire of 64 Squadron about to land and fired at that. Flight Sergeant Maunders felt the shock of the aircraft being hit and put on power. Engine temperature rapidly rising, he turned the aircraft upside down then it rapidly went into a spin. He was lucky to be able to bale out.

On 22 April a repeat of this style of intruder took place. It being obvious that B-17s and B-24s would be landing after dark, six Me 410s set off to attack Liberators landing in Norfolk and Suffolk, arriving among them at 21:30. Great was the confusion among eleven Bomb Groups, all 125 bombers showing navigation lights, when the Me 410s opened fire. Five B-24s were shot down off Norfolk, two more as they tried to land at Rackheath. AA guns fired, unfortunately bringing down another B-24 near Norwich, and the intruders shot down a ninth machine. Another two Liberators were destroyed on the ground, and American casualties totalled 38 killed and 24 injured. The intruders did not all escape, though, for gunners in a 448th Bomb Group B-24 shot down one Me 410, which at 22:10 crashed at Ashby St Mary killing its crew of two. But for the loss of one German aircraft over twenty B-24s were eventually written off. Amazing, surely, that the Luftwaffe never mounted more assaults against battle weary American crews. During the operation 34 SD10As were dropped in Mitford RD, and later about fifty enemy bombers approached the coast. Only two made landfall, suggesting the others might be mining. Seven 50 kg HEs were dropped on the grass of Rackheath airfield, probably from a Ju 88.

Major bombing raids on Britain were all but over. Only the novel attack upon Plymouth by KG100 using remotely controlled Fritz-X bombs on 30 April, and the Bristol raid of 14/15 May, were to come. For the rest, it would be intruders operating pathetically against Allied bomber bases. Splendid opportunities to cause enormous havoc to our bomber operations had been missed — and at enormous cost to German life and property.

Six 50 kg HEs — three on the perimeter track—landed on Bourn at 03:23 on 23 May, and seven 250 kg HEs on Great Ashfield's grass at 03:35. A UX 500 kg HE fell in Forhoe and seven 50 kg HEs on Denham Hall Farm, Aylsham. Eight 50 kg HEs in a wheatfield near Tuddenham on 24/25 May were not going to alter the course of the war, nor the eight which on 29 May fell on grass near Oakington's No 1 Hangar or the other eight which Deopham received, nor indeed the sixteen dropped there on 1 June. Lone missions were dangerous for the Luftwaffe, too, and fifty miles east of Cromer on 29 May Mosquito *HK257* of 25 Squadron claimed an Me 410.

There was still the unexpected novelty in enemy activity as demonstrated on 15 May when, early in the evening, a Luftwaffe deserter attempted to belly-land a Messerschmitt Bf 109G-12 of 1./Jagdfliegerschule 102, Zerbst (near Dessau) at Herring Fleet, Lowestoft. Instead, his aircraft hit a tree and was badly smashed.

From a training unit, the Bf 109 had been converted into a rare two-seater for blind flying training. On its fuselage was the identity *22GD+NR* and near the tail unit *CDR BST TEF 870/71*. Its cowling, fin and rudder were yellow, trim tabs red. Much more notoriety was to surround another arrival, the Ju 88G *712273:4R+UR* at Woodbridge at 04:25 on 13 July which gave the Allies a great amount of information about German AI radar.

Luftwaffe response following the Allied landings in Normandy was insignificant. On 5/6 June 409 Squadron claimed a Ju 188 off the East Coast and on 7/8 June a B-17 landed at Tuddenham shortly before 32 SD10As exploded. At Framlingham an example of the curious SB1000 para-bomb was delivered. An intruder attacked three night-flying B-24s, and a 25 Squadron Mosquito destroyed an Me 410 forty miles east of Southwold.

Possibly the rarest type of bomb dropped upon Britain fell a few moments after midnight on 7/8 June, and just after Mendlesham-based B-24 *42-94911* had been shot down by an intruder. Seven of the crew baled out before the bomber fired three cottages at Joe's Road, Wetheringsett. The first of the new-type bombs hit the road between Wickham Market and Framlingham, the next exploded in a spinney near Marlesford Hall and the third by the road to Parham. One dropped 70 yd north of Mill Lane, Wickham Market, breaking windows, and another in the garden of The School House, Easton, again causing blast damage. Immediate investigation showed two unusual features, very small, shallow craters caused by moderately powerful bombs and traces of red parachute. Discovery of an unexploded example confirmed belief of yet another new blast weapon. This was the SD70 para-bomb fitted with a Type B air-burst fuze. Into the usual 8-in diameter bomb case had been welded brackets to take the parachute fitting. A thin, 18-in long steel tube replaced the usual tail unit, this housing the unusual 5-ft square parachute. Unlike the SB1000, this bomb could be fitted with a short delay fuze. No further use of the weapon against East Anglia was ever ascertained.

Into June the Luftwaffe continued its pathetic attacks on airfields. On 12/13 June two Ju 88s each dropped eight SD50 kg HEs, one load on Hall Green, Wattisfield, the other at Cley, and Me 410 *9K+HP* which had been active over Essex crashed on marshland at Barking. At Rattlesden on the 14th/15th, 34 SD10As (eighteen UX), two 50 kg HEs and six 250 kg HEs distributed themselves over Haywood and Model Farms. Three HEs at Little Tey on 21 June caused little damage. Four 50 kg HEs were dropped on 22/23 June, one at Bawdsey and three in the sea and at Holme Hill Farm, Felixstowe. Another seven fell in open country in Deben RD next night. Slight activity also took place early on 26 June, HEs dropping at Boreham, Bures and Peasenhall. Then, on 27/28 June, three incidents closed the 1944 bombing offensive against East Anglia. Bungay and Seething each received four 50 kg HEs, and fifteen fell in Deben RD.

By then East Anglians had experienced the arrival of the missile age. We were entering a dark age — at high speed.

Chapter 23
Final fling

Pilotless aircraft, cruise missiles, are nothing new. Britain devised a 'flying bomb' in the 1920s, but control problems — not to mention unreliability — halted development. Only recently have these been largely mastered.

Cruise missiles have long been considered cost effective, lacking interfering intelligent aircrew who are expensive to train. For decades they have fascinated politicians of all shades, amateur and professional, on account of their aura of mystery and cheaply promoted terror. Post-war British governments have accordingly competed with each other by ordering Blue Boar, Blue Steel, the Red Rapier bomb and more, after Hitler found similar curious, spooky 'toys' worth acquisition. In wartime such 'secret weapons' were feared, revered and pondered upon. Exactly what these rumoured contraptions were, few knew. Some shrewdly guessed, and many pontificated, revealing delightfully unreliable and impressive authority. Ironically, secret weapons seemed good for morale.

Work was under way in Germany on rockets and jet propulsion when Hitler seized power, but not until November 1939 did the Argus aero engine firm have a working pulse jet. This was a primitive device in which fuel was injected into a grid, burnt, then exhausted to provide reaction propulsion. Applying this or a piston engine to an unmanned aircraft was considered, but accuracy and the necessary range of at least 350 miles were deemed impossible to achieve and development was shelved.

Enraged at the 1942 destruction of Lübeck, Hitler sanctioned both the Baedecker raids and development of terror weapons with which to attack British towns. Radio control for those devices was envisaged, but soon discarded for the proximity of Britain to France made jamming too easy. Application of the pulse jet to a fast, short-journey, pilotless, primitive winged bomb, easy and cheap to build, seemed the best scheme. Design of an 'aircraft' using the Argus pulse jet was quickly made the responsibility of the Gerhard Fieseler firm and on 19 June 1942 given high priority. Guidance system design was undertaken by Askania, drop trials later that year being made from a Peenemünde-based Fw 200.

Fieseler's FZG-76 (ie, Flakzielgerät or Anti-aircraft artillery apparatus 76) design proved protracted and difficult. Although production commenced in September 1943, the flying bombs and launch systems were unready for a part in Operation 'Steinbock'. Troops needed to learn how to handle, maintain and fire the ground-launched weapons, and many ramps needed to be built — in the face of watchful Allied eyes.

Summer 1943 had brought to the Allies long-awaited details of the 'winged mine' and 108 launching sites were confirmed by photo reconnaissance. The possibility of wasting too much effort upon them concerned the Allies, but there was also the possibility that the bombs would interfere with invasion preparations. On 5 December 1943, bombing of the launching sites commenced, causing the Germans to replace them with simple, hard to spot launch ramps. Thei intention remained to combine firing as part of Operation 'Steinbock', but the flying bombs were not ready in time.

The Allied decision was that the easiest way to defeat the flying bombs was to destroy their launch sites, stores and support depots. When the offensive was launched, fighter standing patrols would form the front line defence, HAA and LAA guns backing vast numbers of balloons to give defence in depth for London, the Solent and Bristol.

Between 7 and 16 June 1944, 873 FZG 76 flying bombs (V-1, or Vergeltungswaffe 'revenge weapon' 1) were positioned at launch sites, about eighty of which were reckoned ready to fire a salvo at London, in an ideal response to the Normandy venture. Abteilung Flakregiment 155(W) awaited orders to fire in the full knowledge that the V-1 was far from ready for operations, and that launch safety had been alarmingly ignored. Late on 12 June, 55 sites were pronounced 'ready' although only a third had even practised a launch sequence. Nevertheless, the order to fire was signalled for a salvo to fall upon London at 23:40. With firing to continue until 04:45, about 500 V-1s would be despatched. But at 23:00 not one site was ready to fire, and it was 03:30 before the first ten flying-bombs were whirring their ways to England. Five crashed almost immediately and one disappeared into the Channel leaving four to cross the British coast. The first exploded at 04:18 at Gravesend, one fell in Sussex, another at Sevenoaks and the other killed six people and injured nine at Bethnal Green. The first salvo had been a fiasco and firing was halted until after dark on 15 June.

Tracking these small, low flying aircraft — faster than almost all Allied fighters and flying in busy areas — proved very difficult. Giving warnings enabling civilians to take cover also posed problems. When launching was resumed around 22:00 on the 15th the defences were more prepared and realized that each weapon would behave similarly — unless it malfunctioned, which they often did. By noon on 16 June 244 V-1s had been fired towards London from 55 operational sites, and at least another fifty had been despatched towards Southampton. Many had gone astray. AA gunners destroyed fourteen, fighters seven and one was claimed jointly. Only eleven penetrated London's IAZ.

Throughout the war, the Royal Observer Corps (the Royal title being awarded in April 1941) kept a constant watch on air activity over the region. Observation and accurate identification of aircraft was a very important back-up to radar plotting, which was very difficult where low-flying V-1s were concerned. During the flying bomb offensive, the ROC came to play a particularly important role.

Quirks exhibited throughout the campaign by the bombs, aptly nicknamed 'Doodle-bugs', were many. Their range was limited by fuel load — less fuel, shorter flight, and the maximum journey normally took the V-1 a little north of London. Should, however, the fuel flow be slightly slowed, by intent or by poor engineering, or should the weather interfere, a V-1 would continue further northwards which explains why at 00:28 on 16 June the residents of Peasenhall,

Most of East Anglia's airfields at some time were defended by 40 mm Bofors AA guns, and in 1944 a host of them helped form part of the anti-diver (V-1) coastal box which defended the region and London (AB Bofors, Sweden).

Suffolk, where once a land mine had been bravely defuzed, heard overhead an enormous bang. A flying bomb, not content with its record flight, was ending life in an air burst over Lodge Farm, spectacularly announcing the arrival of East Anglia's first V-1 and causing blast damage to houses. At 10:19 another V-1 exploded at Cold Norton, not far from Bradwell Bay, and at 16:14 a third landed in a field at Woolverstone, Suffolk. By midnight on the 16th 144 V-1s had reached England — but at least another 45 crashed soon after take-off. Defending guns and balloons were already in position, and the country had been told of the arrival of a new stage in warfare. Had these cruise missiles been an Allied development they would probably have had a more favourable presentation! Instead, their horrific, indiscriminate nature was cynically disclosed by an official whose dedication to ruthless bombing of German towns — not to mention concentration camps — shocked even our tough Prime Minister. German hopes for the creation of great terror in London failed, although the flying bombs forced plentiful evacuation. Every V-1 landing in a town created much devastation and heavy casualties, and after little warning. As frightening weapons the strange-sounding V-1s were effective, most eerie when the engine cut-out came for one could never be quite sure what the bomb would do, where it would come down. Some glided considerable distances, others just dived steeply in — and the carnage was often created on a fine summer's day. 'Buzz bombs' demanded respect.

By 30 June, seventeen V-1s had reached 'East Anglia' including three in Suffolk and one in a barley field at Fowlmere, Cambridgeshire. Only two caused much damage, at Crow's Green, Great Saling, where on 25 June eleven houses were damaged, and on the 30th near Braintree where a cottage was fired. The latter bomb carried radio gear, presumably signalling its activity. Coltishall's first V-1 alert came on 1 July, in response to which 316 Squadron destroyed a flying bomb five miles off Lowestoft.

On almost every day in July and August an average of about 100 V-1s crossed the South Coast, fighters destroying about thirty daily. Few V-1s were able to reach East Anglia, only eighteen managing it in July, thirteen in August. At the start of September the V-1 campaign petered out due to the Allied advance into northern France and the German decision to re-orientate the attack upon Continental targets.

Any notion that the V-1 had passed into memory was, however, blown away when, between 05:00 and 06:00 on 5 September, nine V-1s approached the country from the east. They had been air-launched. Knowledge of such activity was already to hand for, between the end of the first week of July and 31 August, III/KG3 using adapted, aged He 111s had air-launched 300 V-1s towards London, directed ninety at Southampton and twenty towards Gloucester. The loss of French bases meant that only air launching could prolong the campaign, and East Anglia was then placed in the front line for V-1 attacks. Four of the 5 September launch fell in the region and one ominously penetrated to Eyeworth, Bedfordshire. Theoretically, much of the country was thus in range.

An eleven-day lull followed as III/KG3 quit its Dutch base for the safety of Varrelbusch, Aalhorn, Münster/Handorf and Zwischenahn in Germany. More crews and aircraft were posted in and the organization then re-formed as I/KG53.

* * *

At 18:40 on 8 September 1944, to the accompaniment of two enormous bangs, a 40-ft crater without the slightest warning replaced buildings in Chiswick. A few seconds later another such crater appeared by trees at Epping. V-2, the long-range A-4 rocket, was reality. The world would never be the same again. Small missiles carrying their own propellants had seen plentiful use, but V-2 was in a different category and opened the way to the ICBMs of today. Despite the enormous fear the thought of missile attack now generates, general concern at the time was less towards the 46 ft long rocket than the V-1. Perhaps the total lack of knowledge that a rocket's arrival was imminent had something to do with this? Certainly there seemed no apparent concern at the fact that without any warning a giant rocket could wreak enormous destruction.

By 18 September another 25 12.7-ton A-4s were known to have reached Britain, sixteen falling in the London area, six in Essex, one in Kent, one off Shoeburyness and one off Clacton. At least another eight had failed to make landfall, and then, in the middle of the V-2 assault, He 111s of III/KG3 on the 16th resumed launching of V-1s. Three of those landed in Essex damaging Bradwell's sea wall, causing blast damage at French's Green and slightly damaging Saffron Walden Isolation Hospital. Probably fifteen Heinkels had operated and managed to launch only nine bombs successfully, of which naval ships shot down two, fighters three.

Halting the new revenge weapons posed major problems. Each Heinkel flew extremely low to avoid radar detection when releasing its flying bomb about fifty miles off shore. There was no possibility of shooting down a V-2, little prospect of even warning of its approach. The best that again could be hoped for was destruction of launch sites, stores, communications and factories. Locating launch sites was very difficult, and eventually only by capturing them would the menace be halted.

Most early V-2 launches were undertaken by the 1st and 2nd Batteries of Art. Abt. (mot) 485, from sites in the suburbs of Wassenaar, north-east of The Hague in the Netherlands. A few, from 14 September, were fired by Lehr und Versuchs

Batterie 444 from Walcheren Island where the unit settled after firing V-2s at Paris. Their aiming point for both formations was set at 1,000 yd east of Waterloo Station.

When the Arnhem airborne landings took place Art.Abt.(mot) 485 quickly moved near Burgsteinfurt, north-west of Münster, the other formation going from Walcheren to Zwolle on 18 September, only ten days after starting the rocket offensive. Batterie 444 was then ordered to maintain the campaign by firing at Norwich and Ipswich, although German records suggest that only one rocket was aimed at the latter target. Batterie 444 moved to a woodland site near Staveren, Friesland, and recommenced firing on 25 September.

The first rocket to fall in East Anglia exploded on Castle Farm, Hoxne, Suffolk at 19:05 on 25 September, slightly damaging twelve houses. The second, which landed at 16:30 next day, cratered a stubble field at Ranworth, eight miles north-east of Norwich. Between 25 September and 12 October, the period of this phase of V-2 attack, the 444th Batterie fired 44 rockets, thirty of which landed in East Anglia and four malfunctioned over or near land. First to have much effect was that which fell at Corporation Farm, Whitlingham, Norfolk on 27 September which damaged houses, a farm and the railway. On the 29th 25 houses were slightly damaged at Thorpe when a V-2 exploded in a beet field. On 3 October, the peak day, five rockets arrived including one at Hopton whose blast affected 28 houses in the first major incident. Five hours later a rocket at Hellesdon, Norwich damaged 400 houses within a two-mile radius. On 4 October eight people were injured by a V-2 at Rockland St Mary.

Failure of the Arnhem landing allowed Batterie 485 to resume the bombardment of London, evident when late on 3 October a V-2 landed at Leytonstone. Hitler had been dissatisfied with rockets being wasted upon the 'side targets' and on 12 October the offensive fully switched to the bombardment of Antwerp and London. Many V-2s fell wide of their targets, coming down in northern Essex and on the coast. One strayed as far as Mundesley on the north Norfolk coast, another close to Mildenhall and that at Valley Farm, Fulbourn, Cambridgeshire, produced the usual re-entry sonic boom and its 1-ton warhead exploded making the normal 40-ft crater 25 ft deep in the adjacent field to that in which, on 19 June 1940, a He 111 had crashed.

The campaign was strengthened on 20 October when the 444th joined the 2nd Batterie of '485 and for a time their 3rd Batterie, although for most of the remainder of the attack two batteries conducted operations from wooded areas near The Hague. Their rate of fire was largely controlled by V-2 delivery (constantly harassed) and the time taken to fuel the rockets. Difficult to store, many had been around for some time and their corroded parts needed careful attention. Eventually, though, it was common for a V-2 to be fired within three days of completion at the factory.

In the third week of October, Fighter Command commenced armed reconnaissance cover of The Hague, that task being carried out by Spitfires of Nos 229, 453 and 602 Squadrons operating from the Coltishall Sector. Over 600 sorties were flown during the first five weeks of the operation. V-2 firings towards London totalled about three a day at the start of October. After reinforcement they not only increased but became more accurate. Between 26 October and 4 November, 44 V-2s landed in England, 33 in London which meant much higher casualty figures which exceeded 1,400 in one month.

Devastation in the Essex village of Ardleigh where a V-1 landed in the early hours of 27 September 1944 demolishing a row of cottages and killing four people.

To cover up introduction of the long-range rocket the term 'explosion' was given in reports relating to V-2 incidents, or as the official explanation stated, in place of 'Big Ben', the code name for A-4. Officials also attributed the explosions to bursting gas mains. Those in fields were caused by bombs. But the secret could not be kept for long and by October it was general knowledge that the 'LRR' was the culprit, confirmed publicly by the Prime Minister on 10 November.

What could not be disguised was the almost nightly firing of V-1s from Heinkel 111s off Suffolk and Essex which reached its climax in October-November. The attackers had been reorganized as I, II and III/KG53, and to help defeat the V-1s the 'Diver Box' which defended the Thames Estuary during the summer offensive was re-orientated. A coastal gun belt extending to Yarmouth was added so that when, on 28/29 October, it became operational, 1,107 guns were in position, many of them 3.7-in guns firing in an 'intermediate' height role to destroy the low-flying bombs. Achieving that was difficult, for the East Coast area teemed with friendly aircraft. Considerable concern arose as to how the thousands of gunners could be housed in a very cold winter — certainly not in tents.

That the gunners were an invaluable force was proven night after night. Of 23 V-1s plotted heading in between 19:09 and 19:58 on 4 November only three made landfall. One was destroyed by Southwold's guns and another six fell in the sea to AA fire which, during the phase, amounted to 1,364 3.7-in rounds, 193 40 mm Bofors and 278 0.50-in rounds of machine-gun fire. On 5/6 November 26 V-1s were plotted after launch, and twelve almost immediately dropped into the sea. Ten achieved landfall, six were brought down by the defences. On 6 November the only ten V-1s to come in range of gunners between Southwold and Bradwell were all destroyed.

Increased firing took place, in two phases, on 10/11 November. Phase one involved the launching of 26 V-1s, most of which headed for the Southwold-

Felixstowe front. This time, every one which reached the coast was destroyed by AA guns — except for one which, held by Walton's searchlights, was chased nearly to Chelmsford and shot down by one of the four Tempests on patrol. Phase two occurred between 01:27 and 01:59, twelve launches being plotted. Six V-1s were claimed by gunners between Aldeburgh and Clacton, one V-1 exploded in the River Blackwater, one crashed at Great Warley, a fighter destroyed one near Dagenham and another came down near Southwold, destroyed by a fighter aided by searchlights. During the night 475 rounds of 40 mm and 962 of 3.7-in ammunition were expended.

An even more intensive operation took place on 14/15 November, its first phase, 18:49-19:25, involving the launch of eighteen V-1s, eleven of which came in range of the guns and nine of which were destroyed. In phase two, 00:01-00:49, twelve flying-bombs were plotted. Two fell in the sea, four were destroyed by guns and six managed to head inland. The third phase came between 05:29 and 05:50 when, of the seven bombs released, four faded at sea and three went inland towards London. Gunners had destroyed thirteen of the 37 bombs known to have been sent on their ways.

During the last half of November, when conditions allowed, it was usually eighteen He 111s that set off to attack, flying low over Holland and turning to their launch areas off the Dutch islands. Releases took place about fifty miles off England, many of the bombs malfunctioning or being badly directed and crashing into the sea shortly after release. On 17 November, for instance, when eighteen He 111s operated, only eleven bombs lasted long enough to be plotted, three were shot down by guns and only five headed inland. Flying-bombs proved highly unpredictable in their behaviour, one on 22/23 November taking nine minutes to proceed a mere sixty miles. That made interception very dificult, but not on 7/8 December. Between 18:27 and 19:15, 21 V-1s were plotted out of which seven crashed into the water. Of the nine which reached the Essex coast, AA guns destroyed eight and a night fighter destroyed the other near Laindon. Four more fell to the Clacton-Aldeburgh guns, the other bomb being destroyed by naval gunners. Total success had been achieved for which gunners in the 'Diver Box' fired 775 3.7-in and 28 40 mm rounds and those in the strip 764 rounds of 3.7-in. A splendid evening's firing, whose success was repeated when, on the evening of 4 December, nine bombs out of ten were destroyed at the coast and the final one over East Malling. Only when the defences were outflanked by the Christmas Eve assault towards Manchester were gunners cheated of almost total success.

Over half of all the V-1s which approached the shore were brought down by AA gunners. No precise figures detailing air launches have survived, but estimates of 1,200 seem reasonable although only 638 were recorded by the defenders as running up on shore.

Well out to sea, AI-equipped Mosquitoes aided by 'radar picket' warships bagged twenty V-1s at night and were ultimately credited with sixteen He 111s. Between 16 September 1944 and 14 January 1945 (when only 205 V-1s aimed at London evaded the defenders and 66 reached the Capital), 41 He 111s were lost during operations and four on the ground. Losses due to all causes during the entire air-launching phase totalled 77 He 111s, some undoubtedly the result of launch explosions and flying into the sea. Tempest V night fighters from Bradwell Bay and Manston did well to destroy fifty V-1s, because estimating

The ultimate German weapon, the A-4 rocket alias V-2 was 46 ft long. It weighed 12.7 tons at operational take-off when carrying a one-ton warhead (including 1,650 lb of explosive). Taking off on 25 tons of thrust generated by alcohol-water and liquid oxygen mixing at 2,700° C, it attained 3,600 mph climbing to about twenty miles during the combustion phase. Peak of trajectory was at about sixty miles, horizontal range just over 200 miles and velocity on impact between 2,200 and 2,500 mph. It heralded the space age, and our era of hideous giant ballistic missiles. Its development and operation was without doubt a most stupendous achievement (Bundesarchiv 78/Auh.26/5).

range at night was extremely difficult. Naval ships bagged another ten. It was not these losses which halted operations though, but the fact that bases and necessary operational routing became quite impossible to use. At 02:00 on 14 January 1945 the last air-launched V-1 came down at Hornsey.

By January 1945 V-2s were arriving at the rate of about two a day, many launches taking place in darkness to avoid air attack. Despite repeated attempts, RAF fighter-bombers failed to halt the rocket offensive, although points of launch were frequently pin-pointed and bombed. In view of present plans to use particle beam weapons to destroy ICBMs it is interesting to recall that in 1945 suggestions were made for predicted AA fire to be placed in the route of an incoming rocket. By firing 150 shells it was reckoned the chance of success was 1:1,000, with 400 shells the success ratio might reach 1:30. Before any such activity could take place, though, the rocket needed to be located by radar — no mean task. When, on 27 March, the last V-2 headed for England, there was still no means of destroying it. Luckily, German atomic warheads planned for rockets were not available.

After the air-launched V-1 campaign faded in January 1945, a lightened version of the V-1, with a range of about 250 miles and the ability to fly along a slightly curved track in a primitive attempt at defence evasion came into use. Three ramps — at Delft, Vlaardingen and Ypenburg — were built for launches against London, another three being built for the bombardment of Antwerp. Home-based fighter defences were accordingly re-arranged to meet the threat, with three Mustang squadrons and Meteors of 616 Squadron responsible for day interceptions and a Tempest squadron at night, along with three Mustang and one Mosquito squadrons out at sea.

On 3 March the first firing took place, and was combined with the first extensive operational flying over East Anglia by manned German aircraft since

June 1944. There had been rare intrusions, as on 21 February 1945 when Stirlings were operating from Shepherd's Grove. Flight Lieutenant Campbell was on final approach when an Me 410 attacked, setting the Stirling on fire. The crew, except one, baled out safely. Flight Sergeant Payne's aircraft was attacked four times over the same airfield. Such rare events paled into insignificance, however, compared with the operation of 3/4 March. The German intention was to knock out British night bombers landing at their bases, in a modified form of the noteworthy Operation 'Bodenplatz' delivered against 2TAF on New Year's Day 1945. Hitler's preference for having Allied aircraft shot down over the Continent had for so long prohibited intruder raids over British airfields that it was far too late for them to have much effect upon the war. Had the effort in 1942 been directed against British airfields, and unceasingly, then it might well have altered the course of the bomber offensive, but now?

A few minutes after midnight the first of about sixty enemy aircraft, mainly Ju 88Gs with a few Me 410s, was discovered by radar off the north Norfolk coast. Picking them out was no minor task for they had cleverly put themselves within a stream of returning bombers, and were followed by many more although only about 100 of the 140 despatched crossed the English coast, operating until about 04:50 between Norfolk and Blyth and as far inland as Banbury. Six of the intruders were destroyed, three over land. By comparison, Bomber Command the same night had 210 aircraft dropping 696 tons of bombs on Kamen, 213 releasing 1,053 tons on the Dortmund-Ems Canal at Ladbergen, 58 Mosquitoes bombing Berlin and 31 attacking Würzburg. In support were 77 aircraft of 100 Group and 83 bombers making diversionary sea sweeps. Another 29 Lancasters mined off Norway, during this night of relatively reduced RAF effort. After roaming widely, and attacking thirty bomber bases, the Luftwaffe shot down 22 RAF bombers in Lincolnshire and Yorkshire in the most effective of any German intruder operations.

Hostile activity over East Anglia commenced at 00:23 on 4 March when three HEs fell in a Rendlesham field. At 00:30 two 250 kg HEs dropped at Seymour Road, Ipswich, killing nine people. Six houses were demolished, six seriously damaged and 250 slightly affected. Bury St Edmunds was strafed at 00:54, an ARP warden of Post 41 being injured. Machine-gun bullets hit windows and roofs of Shores Mill, Nos 42, 52, 53, and 54 St Andrews Street, and Lee's shop at the junction with Woodhall Street. Also damaged was the front of The Playhouse, Pretty's, Capur House, Felton's Cornmill and 'Everard's' Hotel where ceilings and windows were hit. Two HEs fell at Little Cressingham at 01:00 and at 01:05, 34 SD10As at Fulmodestone killed six bulls and damaged three houses. East Rudham was strafed at 01:15 and Hemsby at 01:50. Further machine-gunning of the King's Lynn road at Lexham at 02:00 killed an American, then a 50 kg HE exploded by East Rudham station. At 00:32 Botesdale, Rickinghall Inferior and Superior were showered with 784 SD 1 small grenade-like APBs, released from two AB500-1 containers. Locating the unexploded ones was a mammoth, hazardous task and fourteen seem never to have been accounted for. At 00:44 the same aircraft machine-gunned Wetheringsett, killing an American airman and injuring four other people. Reepham had been machine-gunned at 00:40, Cringleford soon afterwards. Another American was injured and over fifty houses damaged when more SD1s were dropped south-east of Thetford over Botesdale and Rickinghall, Norfolk,

With the war almost over, the Luftwaffe in March 1945 too late launched sharp intruder raids upon returning British bombers using, among others, some of its sophisticated Ju 88G-7 night fighters (M. Olmsted).

at 02:50, while at Docking three 50 kg and three 250 kg HEs fell plus one UXHE. At 01:55 the Norwich road near Chippenham was machine-gunned and a Jeep was damaged. Four more 250 kg HEs dropped in Swaffham RD, and at Turner Road, Colchester, a solitary 1,000 kg HE decided to remain dormant, as did a 500 kg HE at Great Bromley. Bodney was the only East Anglian airfield actually attacked, a strafing Ju 88 dropping two 250 kg HEs on swampy land. At another airfield, though, an attempted intrusion proved horrific.

A USAAF transport Liberator was on final approach to Metfield when, at 02:00, Ju 88G-6 *621805* of 5./NJG4 slipped below, the crew intending to bring down the large aircraft using their twin upward firing MG 151/20 cannon. The American pilot spotted the aircraft below and quickly manoeuvred to avoid it. This forced the Ju 88 into a very tight turn in which its wing tip touched the ground. Wreckage was immediately hurled over several fields around. Fragments were all that remained of one of the most sophisticated German night fighters, carrying Naxos radar and the strange sting-like radar tail attachment of FuG 220 designed to give warning of enemy aircraft to the rear. To have crept under that Liberator was a courageous act of flying, perhaps too risky to have been tried?

Response to this outburst of night activity already included 22 Mosquitoes intruding on German night fighter airfields. Others of 68, 125 and 456 Squadrons were scrambled. Mosquitoes *NT368* and *NT381* of 68 Squadron each claimed a Ju 88, one ten miles north-east of Cromer. *NT415* of 125 Squadron destroyed a Ju 88 further east. At Twente 406 Squadron shot down a Ju 88, and 307 Squadron claimed a Ju 88 fifteen miles west of Bonn. Both 68 and 406 Squadrons each lost a Mosquito.

Next night, 4/5 March, the Luftwaffe managed only eleven intruder sorties, seven over Lincolnshire, Norfolk and Suffolk between 19:40 and 21:18. One raider at 20:10 released two AB250-2 containers, each carrying 28 SD10Cs (fifty of which were accounted for), over the Derby Road area of Beccles. Eleven houses were damaged. Over Potter Heigham, Norfolk, an intruder at 20:00 intercepted a Mosquito, whose crew safely baled out.

Not until 17/18 March did the Luftwaffe return, despatching eighteen intruders, eleven of which operated over Yorkshire and East Anglia where evening raids were concentrated upon the Coltishall-Swanton Morley-Swannington area. At 20:46 a twin-engined aircraft came in over Yarmouth at 2,000 ft, and commenced bombing at Buxton after circling. Then it placed an AB500-1 container of 24 SD10As over gardens and Coltishall airfield's south-west corner, damaging two cottages. Circling at 5,000 ft, the raider attacked Coltishall and Tunstead around 21:00, this time releasing an AB500-1 over open fields between Watering Pit Lane and World's End Lane, on to which 34 SD10As fell. At 21:20 the crew evidently spotted a brightly lit civilian bus near Hevingham and this they strafed twice, luckily without causing injuries. Before leaving over Yarmouth they placed a few shots into huts at Swannington at 21:25.

Metfield was also assaulted again, at 21:22 by a Ju 88 which released two containers of SD10Cs, one bomb exploding on the main runway and another on the grass. Shots from the aircraft penetrated a hangar, the Officers' Mess and the theatre. As the bomber came in through the dark night, a transport aircraft was about to take off; it had a very lucky escape, especially as only two APBs exploded and the container contents did not scatter.

Potentially the most alarming incident occurred around Alexandra Road, Wisbech, where a load of SD10s was dropped at 21:58. A few minutes later Swaffham was machine-gunned, similar strikes having involved the East Dereham area and Wickham Market.

The last major night activity came on 20/21 March, the first of ten arrivals being discovered at 20:20 sixty miles east of Orford Ness, making landfall there at 20:49 among Mosquitoes and followed by others crossing in as far north as Cromer to roam singly over Norfolk, Suffolk and Essex, the last leaving our shores at 22:43. First to be attacked, at 20:51, was Parham where an AB250-2 container of 34 SD10A/Cs fell on the airfield's grass and caused no damage. Next it was Langham's turn, and at 21:05 224 SD1s and twenty SD10Cs were dropped, all except four landing in fields south of the Langham-Bingham Road and killing 28 cattle while the SD10s came down on Cottage Plantation. One of the other SD1s penetrated the roof of 524 Squadron's office, three more exploding nearby. At Wendling a Ju 188 placed two AB 250-2 containers over eight dispersed B-24s which it raked with cannon and machine-gun fire. Fragments from 45 exploding SD10Cs seriously damaged three Liberators, peppered a 4,000-gallon fuel trailer and ignited fourteen empty B-24 bomb bay fuel tanks.

Shipdham was strafed at 21:12 and then what was believed to be a Ju 188 in the Swanton Morley area (originally thought by sound to be a UC-64 Norseman, which this type did somewhat resemble) made three attacking runs upon the airfield, dropping nearby two containers of SD10A/Cs, 35 of which exploded. During the subsequent two strafing runs a bullet hit a Mosquito's tail and a hanger was fired upon. The supposed Ju 188 left for home at 21:40, having dropped some of the last bombs to fall upon East Anglia. While it was bombing, another raider put shots into an inoffensive barn at Terrington St Clement, and another machine-gunned Sustead. Around 21:53 machine-gunning took place south of Cromer over quite a wide area, shots being fired at Gunton, Cresham, Roughton, Wendling, Langham and South Repps in the last machine-gunning attacks on East Anglia. That had been a particularly frightening aspect of the war for rural areas. White alert states were declared at 22:34. During the activity 22 Mosquitoes were on patrol and a Ju 88 was claimed. Come the morning and Walsingham reported that 448 SD1s and 180 SD2s had been found following the raids, Mitford and Launditch RD reporting the dropping of 83 SD10s (thirteen UX).

Throughout the period of the intruder raids the long-range V-1s were still being fired at the East Coast. Although 275 were despatched towards London before the campaign ended, only 125 were seen to approach Britain. Of those, 86 fell to AA guns and only 34 eluded the defences, thirteen managing to enter the London area. At 12:43 on 29 March AA gunners at Orford destroyed the last V-1 to approach the coast and the V-weapons' attack passed into memory.

Of the two the V-1 was undoubtedly the more effective. Cheaper, more annoying and more efficient as a terror weapon, it had the added virtue of diverting a vast amount of Allied air power from both attacking and defending forces. About half of all V-1s launched reached our shores, a quarter of them landing in London where ninety per cent of the 6,000 killed and 18,000 seriously injured lived. For those living on the East Anglian coast the nightly sound of the pulsating, spooky din coming ashore and the fantastic reception given by the guns — particularly around Aldeburgh, Orford and off the Orwell Estuary — was unforgettable.

With bombing all but over, the time to look back had come and Mr I. G. Crane of Ipswich was hailed as something of a record holder. In all probability his boyhood home, 518 Nacton Road, Ipswich, was East Anglia's most bombed homestead. First came a high explosive bomb which fell upon two Anderson Shelters opposite the bungalow, where the Nunn family tragically lost their spastic children. The blast blew down 518's front fence and wrecked the front bedroom. Then came two anti-personnel bombs in the garden almost exactly where an incendiary arrived later. Both splendid treasures to have kept, but too dangerous. Only the harmless leaves from the butterfly bombs were good for swopping in class! One of the many strafing events next overtook No 518, although it was reckoned more likely that a Lewis gunner had put a bullet into the house instead of a bomber. One bullet had passed through a picture of Mrs Crane, which gave more fuel for a story. Then came the late war event, for the bungalow was twice damaged by flying bombs in Maryon Road and Campbell Road. Mr Crane had been with a girl friend when the V-1 crashed and, walking home, he could see Campbell Road illuminated by searchlights. By his front garden there was a congregation — and on the lawn was the 'exhaust tube' of the flying bomb. Few houses could have been the subject of such a wide array of Luftwaffe attention!

The enemy did not finish with the East Anglians until late on 30 March, when five enemy aircraft operated off shore. Three of them then came inland to attack four Norfolk airfields and a Mosquito landing at Coltishall was fired upon. Almost certainly there were several very high altitude photographic reconnaissances by Arado Ar 234 jets at this time too. But as far as the bombing was concerned it was all over — bar the reckoning.

Chapter 24
The reckoning

Something like 5,000 tons of bombs were directed against East Anglia in five and a half years of war. Quantity, type and indeed even where they landed are not, and cannot ever be, precisely recorded. Neither can the damage they caused be placed upon exact record, although clearly a very high proportion landed in open country causing annoyance more than material loss.

Certainly of the number of casualties caused there can never be a full count. Many still bear their wounds, some grievous, to this day. Others injured in a host of ways, died many years after official statistics were compiled. They had suggested that over 1,000 died and more than 4,000 were seriously injured as a direct result of enemy action. There can be no complete record of those whose lives forever carry the burden of sorrow, of terrible memories of events quite unforgettable — and certainly unimaginable by those who have only known peace. Let there never be the slightest doubt that the war years were times for many of great poverty, deprivation, fear, shortage and enormous remorse. They were times when the flash of a bomb could deprive one instantly of all that made life worthwhile, release enormous all-engulfing fear. Destruction of people and places revered, the sudden capitulation of personally precious things to a monstrous ugliness, these were commonplace occurrences which by comparison make the 1980s seem like paradise.

In many important respects the quality of life has faded far since those distant times for, out of carnage ever arose strong sincere friendship in a profusion so lacking in peacetime. Most of the time enemy action was absent. Then, with unbelievable swiftness, the seemingly most unlikely neighbour was showing supreme courage as the street that was home became impossibly changed with incredible speed into a blood-stained battlefield. As a result, all were immediately fortified by ordeal which strengthened the will and made one true to the great Churchillian cry, 'we will never surrender'. The strengthening of character, within fleeting moments, was quite astonishing and was to remain part of one throughout life. That strength of will was particularly clear when, come the dawn, home perhaps gone, many still made their ways to work, often walking or cycling miles. There was no thought of excuse, of bemoaning one's misfortune. All really did pull as one against evil with no regard for class structure, and pomposity and privilege were swept away. Splendid indeed was the comradeship born in those hours of adversity which paradoxically generated such magnificent humour in abundance. Prejudice vanished in an instant, yet

Above *It is still possible, just, to come across a bomb crater in a field. Two may be seen by the A45 road about seven miles to the west of Bury St Edmunds. Nitrates from bomb filling usually encouraged shrubs to grow well and thus mark the spot. Near Southwold's Harbour a fence surrounds a reed-lined deep pit. Actually, this large crater was produced by one of two parachute mines which burst thereabouts.*
Below *Just the countryside? Actually the farm near Peasenhall where two mines landed. Nearby, a flying bomb burst overhead. How unlikely it now seems.*

within a few weeks of the end of the bombing that fine spirit which had carried us through terrible days was rent by a disastrous dose of class-doped politics.

* * *

I had all but finished *Air Raid!* when I found myself in the German city of Cologne. On that February day, inside the city's colossal cathedral which had witnessed scenes of ghastly barbarity, the cold was almost unbearable. Shivering, partly at the thought of all that its blackened pinnacles had witnessed, just like those the magnificent spire at Norwich had likewise been compelled to view, I could not help but weep upon the paper in hand on which I had intended to place my feelings for my diary.

As if by magic the sun, hidden from view by days of once protecting smog, suddenly penetrated the southern windows to flood the nave with the intensity of fire. Sweeping upwards, it raced along the magnificent verticals which must so often have cried to the Heavens for mercy — just as must the spire at Norwich.

Alongside then came company, clad in a robe rich red. He and I were minding the mammoth building, empty apart from hundreds of candles glowing by a shrine which held a billion, billion memories. Soon we began exchanging our thoughts. He told me of terrible days, and I told him of the bad moments that came our way. How appalling the carnage had been. Perish the thought that those who write of war, sensibly demand strong defence, want anything less than its total abolition.

Wandering soon by the Rhine I recalled much that I associated with my recent writing. My mother shepherding the aged to the shelters, the rubble of Vicarage Terrace, that terrible day at Newmarket and the survivors of Hills Road. Some of those around me in the bustling city could well have caused such events, yet I had met so many to whom such things would clearly be totally alien, like the blind ex-Luftwaffe man in a cafe. Vivid was the memory, too, of my father — most upset on that Saturday when we discovered through someone's indiscretion that 1,000 bombers were about to destroy Cologne that very night; he was praying that a magnificent building he knew very well would survive.

Had the freedom to travel in Europe that the European Community now offers its members been possible long ago, and as a result more friends been made in 'foreign' places, it would certainly have been much harder for any of us to have been forced to fight the wars which politicians created. Companionship between ourselves and the ordinary people of Eastern Europe would undoubtedly achieve more for the common good than any number of government conferences.

I once had good proof of this as I was entertained for afternoon tea as never before. A smart young man married, post-war, into the family was introduced to me. Shyly, privately, he admitted that he was one of those 'Sudetenland Germans' that Hitler once worried us all about. He then admitted that he had, indeed, been a warrior. 'Not in the Luftwaffe?' I hopefully enquired, facing black looks from my relatives for raising a delicate issue. 'Indeed', he answered affirmatively, adding that he was an 'engineer. Captured at Melun/Villaroche'. That being so he could have been but one of … 'So, you were with KG2', I probed. His look was one of total amazement. How could this fellow deduce that? It was pleasing. He nodded his thunderstruck admiration.

'Great to meet you', I said. 'I think the family has had some dealings with quite a lot of your friends.' There was no question that here was someone with great charm who, like so many more, was forced into deeds for which he could not really be held responsible.

Yet, all evil is wrong, there can be no amnesty for heinous crimes. Our best hope lies in personal friendship overcoming the remoteness and cruelty of government.

'Tell me', I said to my new friend, 'do you like gardening? I know of an old lady who has long had trouble with a plum tree which one windy night became completely uprooted, and wants the right person to help her replant it. Do you think we two could try, together?'

Appendix 1: Ministry of Home Security assessment of German weapons thought to have fallen on East Anglia May 1940—May 1945

High Explosive (kg)

	50	SD70	250	500	1,000	SB1,000
Bedfordshire[1]	46(5)[2]	—	35(3)	18(5)	1(1)	—
Cambridgeshire	198(15)	—	43(4)	15(4)	—	—
Essex	980(138)	—	401(43)	398(50)	59(25)	7(2)
Huntingdonshire	58(6)	—	15(2)	11(1)	—	—
Isle of Ely	32(1)	—	17	10	(1)	—
Norfolk	926(43)	—	555(9)	445(68)	42(5)	—
East Suffolk	537(61)	5(1)	283(2)	309(24)	19(6)	2
West Suffolk	235(16)	—	28(2)	8(3)	(1)	—
Totals	3,012(285)	5(1)	1,377(65)	1,214(155)	121(39)	9(2)

	1,200	1,700	1,800	2,500	Unclass	PM	Mine	V-1	V-2
Bedfordshire	—	—	—	—	1,161(129)	8(3)	—	10	3
Cambridgeshire	—	—	—	—	1,399(38)	4	—	5	1
Essex	5(1)	—	—	2	11,439(1,401)	418(116)	5(2)	420(1)	382(3)
Huntingdonshire	—	—	—	—	390(63)	—	—	2	—
Isle of Ely	—	—	—	2	426(12)	6(1)	—	3	—
Norfolk	(1)	—	(1)	—	5,172(515)	81(26)	1(1)	18	29
East Suffolk	—	1	—	—	3,340(351)	46(11)	—	202	11
West Suffolk	—	—	—	—	1,384(116)	11(4)	—	20	3
Totals	5(2)	1	(1)	4	24,711(2,625)	574(161)	1(3)	680(1)	429(3)

Incendiary and other weapons[3]

	1 kg Inc	Oil	50 kg Phos	250 kg Phos	FP	APB
Bedfordshire	2,870	50	9(1)	—	—	—
Cambridgeshire	2,558	25	11(2)	—	39(4)	192
Essex	55,189	476(10)	403	10(1)	333(42)	1,459
Huntingdonshire	1,714	24	—	—	—	182
Isle of Ely	1,252	1	—	—	6(1)	194
Norfolk	41,967	30(1)	63	—	391(90)	222
East Suffolk	43,394	36(6)	53	—	170(33)	2,398
West Suffolk	3,260	43	10	—	5(0)	327
Totals	152,204	685(17)	549(3)	10(1)	944(170)	4,974

Notes: [1] Figures relate to entire counties including population centres, but do not include weapons dropped on to military property, for which statistics appear not to have been collated. [2] Bracketed figures are additional UX items. [3] No precise figures for incendiary loads could ever be listed, those given being very conservative. No German load figures survived.

Prior to 1 August 1941 precise weapon drops were unclassified, and identification later was often not possible.

Abbreviations: Oil = oil bomb, phos = phosphorus incendiary, V-1 = flying bomb, V-2 = A-4/V-2 long-range rocket, APB = Anti-Personnel Bomb—all categories, PM = parachute mine, FP = Firepot, Unclass = unclassified.

	Alerts	Killed	Injured	
Colchester	1,094	54	100	Casualties resulting from attacks
Ipswich	?	73	412	on major towns. For further
Lowestoft	2,047	266	690	details see Appendix 4.
Cambridge	329	39	71	

Appendix 2: Metric tonnages of bombs dropped on East Anglia (number of days of attacks bracketed). Excludes unclassified bombs

Bedfordshire	UDs	Bedford (5) 6.09 MT	
		Biggleswade (3) 1.89	Sandy (4) 3.47
	RDs	Bedford 46.07	Biggleswade 27.28
Cambridgeshire	MB	Cambridge (21) 17.76	
	RDs	Chesterton (77) 81.97	Newmarket (46) 47.60
		South Cambridgeshire (79) 37.20	
Essex	MB	Chelmsford 58.98	Colchester 39.69
		Harwich (41) 31.65	Saffron Walden (6) 8.38
	UD	Clacton (56) 52.06	Frinton & Walton (59) 72.16
	RD	Braintree 112.64	Brightlingsea 4.00
		Chelmsford (142) 289.56	Dunmow (105) 156.66
		Halstead (78) 118.99	Lexden & Winstree 69.96
		Maldon 267.59	Saffron Walden (49) 105.04
		Tendring 164.92	
Huntingdonshire	MB	Godmanchester (4) 2.60	Huntingdon (3) 0.48
		St Ives (1) 0.16	
	UD	Old Fletton (2) 4.04	Ramsey (12) 10.20
		St Neots (1) 3.42	
	RD	Huntingdon (20) 21.23	Norman Cross (11) 12.36
		St Ives (15) 12.77	St Neots (20) 23.31
Isle of Ely	UD	Chatteris (5) 5.36	Ely (7) 7.78
		March (11) 16.64	
	RD	Ely (23) 7.78	North Witchford (16) 25.43
		Whittlesey (1) 8.20	Wisbech (6) 7.70
Norfolk	Boros	Gt Yarmouth 185.83	King's Lynn (15) 17.09
		Norwich 154.26	
	UD	Cromer 8.32	East Dereham (5) 2.29
		Diss (3) 2.08	Downham Market (3) 2.81
		Hunstanton (2) 2.56	Sheringham (10) 7.38
		North Walsham (3) 2.13	Swaffham (3) 4.80
		Wells-next-Sea (4) 1.44	Wymondham (13) 19.21
	RD	Blofield & Flegg (105) 137.82	Depwade (57) 51.37
		Docking (65) 72.67	Downham (60) 108.94
		Erpingham (64) 69.18	Forhoe & Henstead (50) 141.85
		Freebridge & Lynn (33) 34.89	Loddon (51) 67.11
		Marshland 32.12	Mitford & Launditch (63) 97.63
		Smallburgh (81) 84.13	Swaffham (30) 46.69
		Walsingham (65) 73.77	Wayland (48) 45.90
East Suffolk	Boros	Aldeburgh (32) 41.17	Beccles (6) 1.65
		Eye (2) 0.64	Ipswich (50) 68.60
		Lowestoft (83) 116.29	Southwold (25) 36.93
	UD	Bungay (6) 6.49	Felixstowe (48) 58.66
		Halesworth (3) 2.60	Saxmundham (3) 1.55
		Stowmarket (9) 4.86	Woodbridge (7) 7.62
	RD	Blyth (126) 134.82	Deben (176) 338.02
		Gipping (76) 68.35	Hartismere (63) 57.39
		Lothingland (91) 130.53	Samford (65) 74.50
		Wainford (34) 28.53	Leiston-cum-Sizewell (13) 15.21
West Suffolk	Boros	Bury St Edmunds (3) 5.23	Sudbury (6) 3.30
	UD	Hadleigh (4) 1.40	Haverhill (4) 2.21
		Newmarket (9) 11.63	
	RD	Clare (42) 52.42	Cosford (42) 34.64
		Melford (32) 26.85	Mildenhall (51) 72.77
		Thedwastre (19) 23.07	Thingoe (43) 75.11(?)

Appendix 3: Areas most heavily attacked

Towns

HE(kg)	50	250	500	1,000	1,200	1,800	PM	Mine	V-1	V-2
Yarmouth	76(9)	71	74(2)	—	(1)	—	7(2)	—	—	—
Norwich	111(2)	168(1)	103(20)	14(3)	(1)	(1)	—	—	—	—
Lowestoft	31(2)	27(2)	45(4)	1(1)	—	—	6	—	5	—
Ipswich	76(9)	54(7)	29(7)	4	— 1 × 1,700		1(1)	1	2	—

Others	1 kg Inc	50 kg Phos	FP	Oil	APB	Unclass HE
Yarmouth	1,590	7(1)	10	1	—	653(60)
Norwich	19,620	2(22)	76(8)	2	—	121(18)
Lowestoft	4,169	5(2)	5(2)	1	—	395(42)
Ipswich	866(39)	—	13(2)	3(6)	232(78)	116(13)

Rural areas

HE(kg)	50	70	250	500	1,000	1,200	SB1,000	1,700	PM	V-1	V-2
Deben	183(25)	1	62	97(20)	6	—	1	1	15(4)	67(1)	5
Chelmsford	88(6)	—	36(5)	47(5)	5(1)	—	—	—	47(10)	26	39
Blyth	50	5	22(2)	38(8)	5	—	1	—	5(2)	18	1

Others	1 kg Inc	50 kg Phos	FP	Oil	APB	Unclass HE
Deben	3,939	4(10)	36(17)	16	18	900(40)
Chelmsford	7,301	24(53)	44(1)	43	46	605(61)
Blyth	10,043	6(6)	14(2)	3	264(7)	379(59)

Note: Whilst the figures relating to weapon/tonnage deliveries are very likely to be underestimates, they give good indications of the relative intensity of attacks on the region. For abbreviations see Appendix 1.

Appendix 4: Attacks on major East Anglian towns

Inevitably the question arises — which towns, and their populations, suffered most from bombing? Statistics detailing casualties and damage are conflicting in precise detail, and depend upon varying levels of notification, and the dates when summaries were compiled. Therefore the following from official sources can give only a reliable indication.

	Norwich			Great Yarmouth			
	Killed	Injured	Alerts	Killed	Injured	Alerts	Alarms
1940	60	190	580	9	40	574	68*
1941	21	104	673	109	329	767	1,328
1942	258	784	106	27	95	324	291
1943	1	14	95	72	124	217	97
1944	—	—	76	—	—	139	62
1945	—	—	?	—	—	23	8
Totals	*340*	*1,092*	*1,530*	*217*	*588*	*2,044*	*1,854*

* Commenced 16 December 1940.

Houses destroyed:	Norwich	2,082		Great Yarmouth	1,639
seriously damaged:		2,651			1,509
slightly/moderately damaged:		25,621			18,303
Totals:		30,354			21,451
Last raid:		6.11.43			
Last warning:		?			

1.6.44, bombs on S. Denes foreshore.
30.4.45, 13:23–13:29, possibly in connection with an Ar 234B jet reconnaissance aircraft.

Appendix 5: Fieseler Fi 103/FZG-76/V-1 flying-bomb incidents in East Anglia 1944–1945

Month	6.44	7.44	8.44	9.44	9.44	10.44	11.44	12.44	1.45	3.45
Bedfordshire	—	—	—	—	1	6	—	3	—	—
Cambridgeshire	1	1	—	—	1	—	—	—	3	1
Essex (as defined)	11	6	4	1	23	25	21	8	4	5
Isle of Ely	—	—	—	—	1	2	—	—	—	—
Norfolk*	—	2	—	—	1	4	2	3	3	—
Suffolk*	4	9	9	1	11	32	12	10	8	—
Crashed/destroyed close to shore	1	2	—	—	—	45	97	45*	21	10
Totals	17	20	13	2	38	89	132	69+	39	16

*Number coming down close to shore uncertain on many occasions.

Prominent incidents, June 1944: 16th—first arrivals 00:28 Peasenhall, Suffolk (airburst); 10:19 Cold Norton, Essex; 16:14 Woolverstone, Suffolk. 25th—23:25 eleven houses damaged at Crow's Green, Essex (first major damage). 28th—14:10 Fowlmere, first falling in Cambridgeshire. 30th—10:56 Braintree, cottage fire, three slight casualties (the first) and V-1 carrying radio gear. July: 10th—03:13 Southborough, first in Norfolk. 27th—02:25 Great Warley, Essex, first fatality, four injured, two houses demolished. 28th—06:32 Benhall, Suffolk, three houses seriously damaged, fourteen slightly. August: 13th—06:20 Cockfield, Suffolk, 25 houses severe blast damage. September: 1st—02:20 Meryon Road, Ipswich, one killed, 31 injured four bungalows demolished, 500 buildings damaged.

Phase 2. September: 5th—first drop 05:08 Felixstowe, Hill Farm and three at 05:30 at Langham and Dedham, Essex and Eyeworth, Bedfordshire. 20th—01:45 Little Baddow, Essex, one killed, two injured, seven houses seriously damaged. 27th—03:52 Ardleigh, Essex, Redbury Farm, four killed, five injured, nine houses demolished, nine seriously damaged. October: 7th—20:20 Little Yeldham, Essex, two cottages and church seriously damaged; 20:28 Greenstead Green, Essex, three cottages seriously damaged, sixty houses and school slight damage. 14th—20:00 Southwold, blast damage to 357 houses, 68 shops, three churches, nine business premises, cottage hospital and fire station yet no casualties reported. 16th—20:05 Kirby-le-Soken, Essex, seventy houses damaged. 18th—23:35 Ipswich, rear of No 5 Halton Crescent on shelter, four killed, eight seriously injured, fourteen houses demolished, 400 damaged, Crane Ltd of Nacton Road and Wrich's furniture store damaged; 23:27 Thorrington, Essex, sixty houses damaged and church. 19th—05:11 Oulton Broad, Suffolk, two houses demolished, 268 houses damaged. November: 5th—20:20 Gorse Hill, Aldeburgh, shot down and warhead fell on AA site injuring three. 17th—19:23 Hadleigh, Essex, eleven serious and five slight casualties, widespread damage. 19th—Coastal AA guns very successful (21 V-1s shot down off Harwich/Felixstowe). 23rd—25 shot down same area. 24th—eleven shot down off Felixstowe and seventeen more on 18th December. Uncertain numbers destroyed on 24, 27, 28 and 30 December, and twelve on 3 January 1945. Phase 2 faded on 13 January, guns bringing down a V-1 unexploded at 06:05 at Capel St Andrew, Suffolk, and one exploding at 0:09 on Manor Farm, Great Holland, Essex.

Phase 3. March 1945: 3rd—first arrival 04:56 near Frinton Essex, airburst over Walton cliffs releasing unfuzed incendiaries. 17th—second arrival 02:55 Somersham, Cambs, and only four more exploded on land as intended—all on 29th—00:04 at Great Holland with incendiary load; 08:56 at Datchworth, Herts, damaging six houses; 09:40 Little Oakley, Essex, damaging 31 houses, two farms and the church; and 09.58 on a farm at Great Wigborough, Essex. Final V-1 approached at 12:43, shot down off Orford Ness, Suffolk.

Appendix 6: Heinkel He 111 FZG-76 launchers claimed in combat by Mosquitoes

Date	Squadron	Aircraft
25.9.44	409	*MM589*
25.9.44	25	?
29.9.44	25	*HK357*, destroyed two
5.10.44	25	*HK239*
25.10.44	125	*HK310*
30.10.44	125	*HK240*
5.11.44	68	*TA389*
10.11.44	125	?
19.11.44	456	?
25.11.44	456	*HK290*
23.12.44	125	*HK247*
?.12.44	68	*TA389*
6.1.45	68	*HK296* (Mosquito missing)

Few details appear to have survived relating to the loss of Heinkel He 111 V-1 launchers of KG53, the 'Legion Condor', but the following are the total losses for the period 9 November to 25 November 1944:

9.11.44   He 111 of 6./KG53 written off after belly landing.
10.11.44   He 111 W Nr *162080:A1+AB* of 3./KG53 missing from operations.
11.11.44   He 111H-16 W Nr *161924:A1+NM* and He 111H-16 W Nr *700862:A1+BM*, both of 4./KG53, missing from operations.
14.11.44   He 111H-16 W Nr *161756:A1+KP* of 6./KG53 abandoned operational flight due to trimming trouble, and crashed near base; two killed.
19.11.44   He 111H-16 W Nr *162377:A1+NN* of 5./KG53 probably shot down by 456 Squadron into the Ijsselmeer, off Stavoren.
22.11.44   He 111H-20 W Nr *700638:A1+KH* of 1./KG53 during operational sortie crashed from 300 ft at Ostenrode, near Bramsche; two killed.
25.11.44   He 111H-16 W Nr *110304:A1+BH* missing from operations, probably came down off Texel to a 456 Squadron Mosquito.

Both the He 111H-16 and H-20 had an MG 131 machine-gun in a dorsal turret. Some sources quote the designation of the He 111 V-1 carrier as the H-22, but Luftwaffe records appear to give earlier variants as being used, over seventy of which were lost during the period July 1944-January 1945.

Appendix 7: A-4 long-range rocket incidents in East Anglia 1944–1945

Date	Time	Site	Remarks
1944			
September			
25	19:05	Castle Farm, Hoxne, Suff	12 houses slightly damaged.
26	16:30	Ranworth, Norf	Stubble field.
27	10:48	Horsford, Norf	Botany Bay Farm.
	16:25	Whitlingham, Norf	5 houses, Corporation Farm, railway damaged.
	17:55	Beighton, Norf	Acle Hall Farm.
29	13:11	Hemsby, Norf, on shore minefield	6 houses, 2 shops, 60 bungalows damaged.

	19:44	Coltishall, Norf	In meadowland; 2 slight casualties.
	20:41	Thorpe, Norf	In beet field; 25 houses slightly damaged.
30	12:14	Damgate, Halvergate, Norf	Staithe Farm; in open country.

October

1	17:55	Bedingham, Norf	Sycamore Farm; serious damage to farmhouse.
3	09:31	Heeton St Lawrence, Norf	Slight damage to church and hall and 5 houses.
	14:40	Valley Fm, Hopton, Norf	Damage to 28 houses, much blast damage; first major incident.
	16:55	Gt Witchingham, Norf	Slight damage to 2 farms.
	19:49	Hellesdon, and Norwich, Norf	Golf course damaged, damage to 400 houses over 2-mile radius.
	20:00	Denton, Norf	Slight damage to Durrow Farm house.
4	13:41	Rockland St Mary, Norf	Rectory, 'pub', 26 houses damaged; 8 injured.
	16:48	Crostwick, Norf	Farm house and 2 cottages damaged.
	17:37	Spixworth, Norf	Church and 4 houses slightly damaged.
5	09:04	Tavenham, Norf	Hall Farm.
	13:28	Surlingham, Norf	36 houses slightly damaged.
	16:10	1½ miles NE Acle, Norf	3 houses slightly damaged.
	17:44	Little Plumstead, Norf	Heath Farm.
6	09:25	Shottisham All Saints, Norf	In wood SW of church, 42 houses slightly damaged.
9	10:46	Cantley, Norf	House damaged, 2 bullocks killed.
	10:50	Brooke, Norf	Brooks Hall slightly damaged.
	18:03	Between Orford and Shingle Street, Suff	2½ miles off shore.
10	07:27	Frinton, Ex	Suspected air burst 6 miles off.
	16:00	Harwich, Ex	Suspected air burst.
	17:55	Bramerton, Norf	In meadow; cottages damaged.
11	08:10	Haddiscoe, Norf	4 cottages and Hall damaged.
	10:53	Rocklands St Mary, Norf	15 houses and glasshouses damaged, acre of beet destroyed.
	14:25	Playford, Suff	In stubble field.
12	02:47	3 miles SE Clacton	Air burst warhead fell in Denghie Flats.
	07:40	Ingworth, Norf	In stubble field.
15	05:04	Chelmsford, Ex	4 houses in Belcross Road seriously damaged.
17	15:50	Little Baddow, Ex	6 houses seriously damaged, 2 slight casualties.
23	04:01	Off St Osyth	In sea.
24	05:00	Rushmere St Andrew, Suff	SE of Church.
26	10:14	Welborne, Norf	School and 15 houses damaged.

November

10	15:04	Fulbourn, Cambs	In field at Valley Farm.
22	13:27	Bradwell Marshes, Ex	

24	11:00	Braughing, Herts	6½ miles NW of Bishop's Stortford. Slight damage.
29	15:10	Bradwell, Ex	
	19:50	Poslingford, Suff	In field.

December

2	07:35	Ramsholt, Suff	On mud flats.
3	09:30	Burnham-on-Crouch, Ex	In river ¼ mile W of Whitehouse.
6	04:47	Woodham Ferrars, Ex	Slight damage.
7	02:10	Gt Saling, Ex	In field at Anker's Farm.
	14:43	Chediston, Suff	Unexploded; 2 miles W of Halesworth.
14	05:05	Nuthampstead airfield	Air burst, 2 craters.
	23:43	Writtle, Ex	In field.
18	16:32	Clacton, Ex	Hit cliff face ¼ mile SW of pier.
19	01:30	Chelmsford, Ex	Major damage to one Hoffman's factory shop, serious damage to another, 39 killed, 152 variously injured, damage to Marconi works, also serious damage to 60 other properties and slight to 340.
	11.30	Bradwell Marshes, Ex	
21	09:45	Bradwell-on-Sea, Ex	
23	23:50	West Row, Suff	Air burst, fragments fell widely.

1945

January

3	03:30	Chelmsford, Ex	SW of town; slight damage.
5	09:25	Layham, Suff	Air burst, fragments fell widely.
7	18:10	Brightlingsea, Ex	80 houses slightly damaged.
8	00:34	Bacton, Suff	
	02:18	Cley, Norf	
9	17:20	Lt Hallingbury, Dunmow, Norf	In field at Monksbury Farm.
10	14:20	Henlow, Beds	
12	17:37	Trimley St Mary, Suff	In field by railway.
	17:58	Writtle, Ex	In meadow.
13	03:42	Halstead, Ex	280 houses slightly damaged.
	16:40	Depden, Suff	Farmhouse damaged.
15	16:00	Mundesley, Norf	Slight damage.
17	17:00	Hatfield Broad Oak, Ex	S of Lancaster's Farm.
20	08:58	Takeley, Ex	In field NW of Frimhall Priory.
	09:57	Earl Soham, Suff	
	10:05	Bishop's Stortford, Herts	Slight damage.
22	07:04	Brightlingsea, Ex	Slight damage.
	20:10	Clacton, Ex; edge of sea wall	7 houses badly damaged, 200 variously, 27 casualties.
23	10:50	Mayland, Ex	6 houses and 6 greenhouses damaged.
	17:00	Chelmsford, Ex	Timber yard and Canyard Iron Foundry, 9 houses badly damaged, 218 slightly, 1 killed, 16 injured.
25	12:10	Hatfield Heath, Ex	N side of 'Stortford–Chelmsford Rd, Lancaster's Farm.
28	07:30	Kirby Creek, Thorpe-le-Soken, Ex	In mudflats by Horsey Isle.

29	05:55	Bradwell-on-Sea, Ex	1 slight casualty.
February			
1	02:30	Gt Leighs, Ex	
	09:15	Gt Leighs, Ex	Slight damage to houses.
5	23:43	Tollesbury, Ex	In R. Blackwater.
8	03:25	Writtle, Ex	Reeds Farm.
March			
7	14:50	Brundish, Norf	Clutton's Farm.
12	11:15	Lower Kirby, Ex	2 houses demolished, school and 11 houses damaged; 1 killed, 1 injured.
21	05:30	Boreham, Ex	Slight damage.
	21:35	Bardfield Saling, Ex	Slight damage.
	23:52	Stansted, Burton End, Ex	Slight damage, stack fire.

Appendix 8: Locations of anti-aircraft guns and searchlights in East Anglia

No detailed, complete, comparative records of the positioning of these defences remain, if indeed they were ever compiled. The first of the following listings gives, for the regions involved, details of Troop dispositions at airfields.

1 Light Anti-Aircraft (LAA) defences gradually positioned following the outbreak of war.

108 LAA Battery (8 officers, 116 men): 218/293 Troop, Marham; 230/294, West Raynham; 239/295, Bircham Newton.

117 LAA Battery (8 officers, 116 men): 119/326 Troop, Debden; 236/327, Duxford; 239/328, Bassingbourn.

118 LAA Battery (10 officers, 150 men): 517/329 Troop, Cranfield; 430/330, Henlow; 220/331, Upwood; 223/332, Wyton.

119 LAA Battery (6 officers, 82 men): 117/333 Troop, Stradishall; 118/334, Wattisham.

120 LAA Battery (8 officers, 116 men): 221/335 Troop, Mildenhall; 222/336, Honington; 219/337, Feltwell.

121 LAA Battery (10 officers, 150 men): 231/338 Troop, Watton; 249/339, Swanton Morley; 244/340, Coltishall; 247/341, Horsham St Faith.

2 Positioning of AA guns and searchlights, 2 AA Division, 18 May 1940.

32 Brigade (HQ Wittering). Defending areas mainly to north of region, but included was the 27 LAA Battery defending Peterborough, Wittering, Corby steel works and Cottesmore.

40 Brigade (HQ Duxford). Controlling five components administering searchlight companies each managing searchlight sites usually also armed with at least one LMG.

36 AA Battalion, RE, controlling searchlights: 346 Battery/201 Company, Royston area; 424/202, St Neots; 345/203, Ely area; 317/204, Newmarket.

60 Searchlight Regiment, RA: 306 Battery/205 Company, Barton Mills; 441/215, Bauper Hall, near Wisbech; 442/216 Ramsey; 443/217, Thrapston.

65 Searchlight Regiment RA: 446 Battery/One Section 72 AA Regiment, Aylsham; 444/211 Company and two Sections 352 Company/38 AA Regiment, Aylsham; 445/212, Guist (with two Companies 352 Company/38 AA Regiment).

69 Searchlight Regiment, RA: 457 Battery/208 Company, Cavick (Wymondham area); 458/209 with Section of 466 Company, Raveningham; 456/210 with 2 Sections of 466 Company, Brundall.

41 Brigade (HQ Debden). Controlling AA guns.

29 LAA Regiment (operating in 'J' Sector, Coltishall, in June): 108 Battery/295 Troop, Bircham Newton; 293, Marham; 294, West Raynham; 465 West Beckham, Honington. 121 Battery, guns at Watton, Denver Sluice, Coltishall, Horsham St Faith and Stoke Holy Cross.

30 AA Regiment: 117 Battery/326 Troop, Duxford; 329 Cranfield; 327 Bassingbourn; 330 Henlow. 118 Battery/331 Troop, Upwood; 332 Wyton. 119 Battery/328 Troop, Debden; 334, Darsham experimental station; 418, Wattisham (and 333, Ipswich soon added). 120 Battery/473 Troop, Stradishall; 337, Feltwell; 335, Mildenhall (and 339, Denver Sluice, soon transferred).

32 Searchlight Battalion: 328 FD Company, Bildeston; 329 FE, Framlingham; 330 FF, Saxmundham.

33 Searchlight Battalion: 332 FC Company, Yeldham; 333 FB, Stansted; 334 FA, Collier's End.

78 Heavy AA Regiment: HQ Stradishall. Providing guns at listed airfield sites. 243 Battery, Wattisham 'A' and 'B', Watton 'B', Duxford 'B'; 244, Marham 'B', Sutton Bridge, West Raynham, Feltwell 'A'; 245 (HQ Debden), Ipswich, Honington, Sutton Bridge. 409 Battery was presently attached to 5 Brigade.

By 20 June 1940 30 LAA was under the control of 40 Brigade and units controlled by 60 Searchlight Regiment were with the 64th. 26 Regiment, 116 Battalion, now controlled 323 Troop, Honington 'A' and 'B'; 336, Watton; 340, Coltishall; 338, Horsham St Faith; and 341, Stoke Holy Cross. 32 Searchlight Battalion now controlled 320 FD Company, Friars Hall, Hadleigh; 329 FE, Monewden Hall, Woodbridge; and 330, Saxmundham. 60 Searchlight Regiment (HQ Thetford) now controlled 429/206, Thetford; 430/207, East Harling; and 431/214, Narborough. 65 Searchlight Regiment (HQ Brundall) now controlled 457/208, Cavick; 458/209, Raveningham; and 456/210, Brundall.

3 6 AA Division was responsible for AA defence of Essex and the south-east. Its anti-aircraft dispositions on 8 July 1940 included the following.

99 HAA Regiment: Battery 318, Site 'H1', Landguard; 'H3', Dovercourt (both having four 3.7-in static guns); 303, Site 'H2', Trimley (four 3.7-in), 'H4', Shotley (three 3.7-in); 302, Site 'H9', Martlesham (two 3-in), 'H10', Brightwell (two 3-in); and 'H12', Ipswich (four 3-in).

17 LAA Regiment: Battery 93, Bawdsey (three Bofors); 59, Chelmsford (eight LMGs); 49, Gt Bromley (three Bofors and six LMGs); 49, 'H5', Harwich (one 3-in); 49, Wrabness (seventeen LMGs); 95, 'H8', Landguard (one 3-in and twelve LMGs); 95, Martlesham (on three sites, four Bofors, two 3-in, ten LMGs). Its searchlights were sited as follows. 29 AA Brigade, 74 AA Battalion, RE: HQ Springfield House, Hatfield Peverel: 335 AA Company (HQ Roxwell), controlled sites EBO with EB11–16 (ie, 1–1 to 1–6 centred on Waldringtree Farm; EB21–26, Good Easter; EB31–36, Lt Leigh; and EB41–46, Faulkbourne. 357 AA Company (HQ Stanway), controlled ED11–16, Earl's Colne; ED21–26, Tolleshunt D'Arcy; ED31–36, Mile End, Colchester; and ED41–46 Peldon. 469 AA Company (HQ 'Gunhouse' Hotel, Felixstowe), controlled EF11–16, Kirton; EF21–26, Trimley; EF31–36, Chelmondiston; and EF41–46, Gt Oakley. 310 AA Company (HQ Mistley), controlled EE11–16, Mistley; EE21–26, Thorpe-le-Soken; EE31–36, Burnthouse Farm; and EE41–46 Fisher's Farm.

4 Frequent variations in Battery strengths took place, and by 11 October while the heavy guns around Harwich remained, Martlesham, Brightwell and Ipswich each had only two 3-in guns. Layout of 6 AA Division included: 11 HLA Regiment, 31 Battery, Debden, manning Sites 1, 2, 4 and 7, each with one Bofors; 49 LAA Regiment, 119 Battery; 328 Troop manning Bofors on Sites 3 and 6 and LMGs on remaining sites; 418, Wattisham, manning two LMGs at Crowfoot, two at Sunnyside, one at Moat Farm, four at the Officers' Mess, two at Bryce and two on a hangar.

The placing of searchlights in the Division was now: 33 Regiment: 333 Battery FB Company, FB11–16 respectively sited at Debden Common, Clavering, Lodge Farm, Wendons Ambo, Lt Chesterford and Widdington; FB21–26 sited at Bentfield Inn, Bishops St, Lt Bustard, Themerhill Priory, Gaunts End and Takeley; FB31–36 at Holmstead Hall, Bartlow, Ashdon, Partridge's Farm, Steeple Bumpstead and Hatcher End; FB41–46 at Gt Dunmow, Leggett's Farm, Tilty, Cranage Farm, Bardfield End and Lashley Hall. 332 Battery FC Company, FC11–16 at Ruse's Farm, Ridgewell, Hundon, Leas Farm, Assington Green and Wake's Farm; FC21–26 at Pouches Hall, Gt Bardfield, Gt Saling, Whole Farm, Oliver's Farm and Bovington Hall; FC31–36 at Boxted, Cavendish, Rowney Farm, Burton's Farm, Shimpling and Bradfield Combust; FC41–46 at Castle Hedingham, South Ney Green, Halstead, Belchant Mordale, Twinstead Green and Sudbury.

32 Regiment: 330 Battery FD Company, FD11–16 respectively sited at Felsham, Hessiet, Mt Farm, Hitcham, Woolpit and Park Farm; FD21–26 at Newton, Slough Farm, Workhouse Green, Milden, Leavenheath and Wicker St; FD31–36 at Coombs, Haughley, Charles Tye, Mendlesham Lodge, Barking and Bull's Farm; FD41–46 at Hadleigh, Semer, Stoke by Nayland, Elmstead, Hintlesham and Branford. 329 Battery FF Company, in the Saxmundham area, FF11–16 at The Grove, Uppbeston, Knoddishall, East Bridge, Sibton Green and Town Farm; in the Wickham Market area, FF21–26 at Black Hall, Sudbourne, Benhall, Snake Warren, North Green and Aldeburgh; in the Hollesley area, FF31–36 at Hollesley Heath, Sutton, Bawdsey, Alderton, Butley and Rendlesham; in the Wangford area, FF41–46 at Henham Park, Wrentham, Hinton, Brampton, Halesworth and Frostenden. 328 Battery FE Company, in the Stonham area, FE11–16 at Four Elms, King's Farm, Creeting St Mary, Brames Hall, Kenton and Debenham; in the Grundisburgh area, FE21–26 at Grundisburgh, Barham, Whitton, Isle of Wight, Rushmere St Andrew and Martlesham; in the Framlingham area, FE31–36 at Tannington, Chediston, Dennington, Horham, Poplar Farm and Bredfield Hall; in the Wickham Market area, FE41–46 at Charles Field, Elm Farm, Earl Soham, Lampard Farm, Bredfield, and another unknown site.

74 Regiment: 310 Battery EE Company in the Wrabness area, EE11–16 at Mistley, Birchhouse-Copdock, Bentley, Wrabness, Stour House and Rith Farm; in the Naze area, EE21–26 at Thorpe-le-Soken, Beaumont, Kirby-le-Soken Quay, The Naze, Composite 'o the Naze and Hodhill's Farm; in the Frinton area, EE31–36 at Burnthouse Farm, Walton Cliff, Frinton Golf Course, Holland Haven, Lt Holland and Clacton Cliff; in the Clacton area, EE41–46 at Fisher's Farm, Bocking Elm, Clacton Golf Club, Martello Tower, Brightlingsea and Hiskey's Farm. 335 Battery ED Company, in the Colne Valley area, ED11–16 at Earl's Colne, Colne Engine, Aldham, Copford, Langley Green and Bradwell; in the Tiptree area, ED21–26 at Tolleshunt D'Arcy, Ruckstead Park, Lt Totham, Tiptree, Goldhanger and Tollesbury; in the Colchester area, ED31–36 at Mile End, Wormingford, Gt Horkesley, Langham and Colliers Wood Farm; in the Mersea area, ED41–46 at Pelden, Middle Field Hall, Maypole Farm, Fingringhoe, West and East Mersea. 469th Battery EF Company in the Martlesham area, EF11–16 at Kirton, Falkenham, Morston Hall, Martlesham, Sheperton Dock and Levington Heath; in the Felixstowe area, EF21–26 at Trimley, Felixstowe Golf Course, Brackenbury, Q Tower, Landguard Point and Walton Ferry; in the Chelmondiston area, EF31–36 At Chelmondiston, Bloody Point, Erwarton, Sutton, Freston and Hill House; in the Gt Oakley area, EF41–46 at Gt Oakley, Poplar Farm, Ray Farm, Harwich, Brookman Farm and Fulton Hall.

5 Location of AA and searchlight defences, 28 February 1941: 2AA Division.

40 Brigade (HQ Pampisford Hall, Cambs).

30 LAA Regiment (HQ Newmarket): 117 Battery/326 Troop, Duxford; 327, Bassingbourn; 329, Cranfield; 330 Henlow. 118 Battery/331 Troop, Upwood; 332,

Wyton; 414, The Manse, Fenstanton (HQ); 473, Oakington. 120 Battery (HQ Ely), 333 Troop, 'A', 'B' Sites, Stradishall; 335 'CC' Site, Mildenhall; 337, Feltwell; 339 'A', 'B' Sites, Newmarket Heath.

44 Searchlight Regiment: 374 Battery, Wittering Sector, WT05/220 Company in area of Terrington St Clement.

36 Searchlight Regiment (HQ Militia Camp, Ely): 317 Battery/DX08/204 Company in area of Newmarket; 345/DX07/203, Ely; 346/DX09/201, Royston; 424/DX06/205, Barton Mills.

64 Searchlight Regiment (HQ Ramsey): 441/DX05/215, Outwell, Wisbech; 442/DX04/ 216, Ramsey Militia Camp; 443/DX03/217, Thrapston.

72 Searchlight Regiment: 467/DX10/202, St Neots Militia Camp.

78 HAA Regiment, RA (HQ Stradishall): 243 Battery (HQ Watton with two gun Sections), one gun section each at Marham, Feltwell and Duxford.

29 LAA Regiment: 108 Battery (HQ S. Creake): 293, Troop Marham; 294, West Raynham; 295, Bircham Newton; 465, West Beckham. 122 Battery (HQ Norwich): 336, Stoke Holy Cross; 340, Coltishall; 341, Horsham St Faith. 126 Battery (HQ Reepham): 357, Honington; 359, Watton; 360, Swanton Morley.

60 Searchlight Regiment, RA (HQ Thetford): 429/CSO9 2 Essex Company, Thetford area; 430/CSO8/207, East Harling; 431/CSO1/214, Narborough; 444/CSO4/211, Aylsham; 445/CSO3/212, Giurst; 446/CSO2/213, South Raynham.

69 Searchlight Regiment, RA (HQ Raveningham): 456/CSO5/210 in the Brundall area; 457/CSO7/208, Cavick (Wymondham); 458/CSO6/209, Raveningham.

78 HAA Regiment: 245 Battery, HQ Horsham St Faith, with gun sites there and by Norwich.

2 AA 'Z' Regiment: 131 Battery, HQ Framlingham, Norfolk. One troop attached to 245 Battery, two with 60 Searchlight Regiment and two with 69 Searchlight Regiment. 6 AA Division.

99 Regiment: 302 Battery, sites 'H1', Landguard and 'H3', Dovercourt (both with four 3.7-in guns); 'H2', Trimley; 'H4', Shotley Street; 'H9', Martlesham and 'H10', Brightwell (each with two 3-in guns); and 'H12' Ipswich.

49 Regiment: 119 Battery/334 Troop (five sites) and 536 (two sites) at Debden; 418, Wattisham (four Bofors).

48 Regiment: 98 Battery/449 Troop, Landguard (twelve LMGs, Site 'H8A'); 253 and 448, Martlesham (eight sites, Bofors and LMGs); 254 split at Bawdsey Cliff, Ferry and Marsh (three Bofors, four LMGs). 49 Battery/120 Troop, Wrabness; 490, Wrabness and Shotley (three Bofors, six LMGs); 255, Gt Bromley (four sites each with a Bofors and five LMGs). 491 Battery 'H5' Harwich E and NE of Parkeston (two naval guns — 3-in?), Bofors and mgs at west end, Central Control one LMG, Hamilton House two LMGs, Mistley Place three LMGs).

32 Regiment (LMGs on searchlight sites): 330 Battery: DNO41, Hitcham; DNO42, Slough Farm; DNO43, Woolpit; DNO44, Cosmos; DNO45, Workhouse Green; DNO46, Wicker Street; DNO47, Helmscott; DNO48, Borham; DNO4A, Hadleigh (airfield). 329 Battery: DNO51, Four Arms; DNO52, Kenton; DNO53, Rushmere St Andrew; DNO54, Chediston; DNO55, Laxfield; DNO56, Elm Farm; DNO57, Lampartbrook; DNO58, Redingfield; DNO5A, aerodrome. 329 Battery in the Saxmundham area: DNO61, The Grove; DNO62, Knoddishall; DNO63, Black Saw; DNO64, Hemp Green; DNO65, Sudbourne; DNO66, Hollesley Heath; DNO67, Henham Park; DNO68, Brampton; DNO6A, Bawdsey.

74 Regiment: 469 Battery: NWO61, Kirton; NWO62, Landguard; NWO63, Chelmondiston; NWO64, Copdock Hill House; NWO65, Oakley; NWO6A, Felixstowe Golf Course; NWO6B, Brackenbury; NWO6C, Felixstowe Q Tower; NWO6D, Bloody Point; NWO6E, Harwich; NWO6F, Brookman Farm 'H1' Gun Site on Landguard Common.

Note renaming of some searchlight sites, arising from re-alignment of Fighter Sectors.

Considerable re-deployment of searchlights took place in the mid-war period too, along with major reductions, especially in the west of the region. In November 1942, following reorganization into AA Groups, Wittering (then placed in 5 AA Group) lost eight sites. Coltishall's were then placed: CSO11, South Wooton; CSO28, Holme Hill; CSO32, Waterden; CSO41, Saxthorpe; CSO51, Horning; CSO63, Bungay; CSO71, Runhall; CSO78, Pulham; CSO81A, Reymerston; CS1B, Shipdham; CS2A, Hingham; CS2B, Deopham; CS3A, Stow Bedon; CS3B, Ovington; CS4A, Horham; CS4B, Rockland; CS5B, East Harling; CS93A, Rowdhams; CS7A, Stayhall; CS7B, Ixworth.

6 By 1942 AA and searchlight defences were much reduced, as this layout of 2 AA Division in East Anglia shows.
41 Brigade.

82 LAA Regiment: 275 LAA Battery, Troops A and B at Bircham Newton and C at Gt Massingham; 192 LAA Battery (HQ Weasenham), Troop A at Honington, B at Watton and C at Bodney; 287 LAA Battery (HQ Marham), Troop A at Feltwell, B at Marham and C at West Raynham; 282 Battery, A, B and C Troops at Gt Yarmouth; 230 Battery, Troop A at Swanton Morley, B at Lowestoft and C at Attlebridge.

45 LAA Regiment: 142 Battery Troops A and C at Yarmouth and B at Gorleston.

38 LAA Regiment: 230 Battery at Lowestoft; 216 Battery, Troop A at West Beckham, B and C at Mousehold and Norwich; New Battery forming, A and C Troops at Horsham St Faith, B at Lowestoft.

7 Following the Baedecker raids there was a considerable change in AA defences as this listing for mid-May 1942 shows.
40 Brigade (HQ Pampisford Hall).

77 HAA Regiment: 218 Battery, Troops A and B at Newmarket Road, Cambridge.

79 LAA Regiment: 470 Battery at Ely, with Troops at Mildenhall, Newmarket and Stradishall.

469 Independent Battery (HQ Manor House, Royston), Troops at Duxford, Fowlmere and Waterbeach.

111 LAA Regiment: 348 Battery, Troop A at Upwood, B at Wyton and C at Oakington; 368 Battery, C Troop at Henlow.

36 Searchlight Regiment: 317 Battery, DX06, DX08; 345 Battery, DX05, Newmarket; DX07, Ely; 346 Battery, DX09, Royston; 424 Battery, DX10, St Neots.

30 Searchlight Regiment: 323 Battery, Troop 4 at Cambridge.
41 Brigade (HQ Coltishall).

72 Searchlight Regiment: 465 Battery, CS02, South Raynham; 466 Battery, CS08, Old Buckenham; 467 Battery, CS03, Guist; 501 Battery, CS01/9, Thetford.

69 Searchlight Regiment: 457 Battery, CS04/5, Brundall; 458 Battery, CS06, Raveningham; 456 Battery, CS07, Cavick House, Wymondham; 561 Battery, Aylsham.

30 Searchlight Regiment: 567 Battery, Brundall.

106 HAA Regiment (HQ Gorleston): 270 Battery, HQ Mousehold, with Sections NH1 at Horsham St Faith and NH3 Eaton. 331 Battery, four Troops, YH1, Caistor and YH3, Yarmouth. 332 Battery, four Troops at Lowestoft. 327 Battery, YH4 Troop at Yarmouth with NH2 at Norwich and LH3 at Lowestoft.

78 HAA Regiment: 468 Battery, two Troops BNH1 at Bircham Newton.

13 Regiment AA 'Z': 188 Battery, Norwich (NH1 Horsham St Faith, NH2 Mousehold, NH3 Broomhill, Church Lane, Eaton).

113 LAA Regiment: 368 Battery, A and B Troops at Wellington Esplanade, Lowestoft, and C Troop at Stoke Holy Cross. 369 Battery, Troop A at West Beckham; B at Matlaske and C at Oulton. 370 Battery, Troops A and C at Coltishall and B at Ludham. 371 Battery, three Troops at Yarmouth.
42 Brigade.

126 LAA Regiment (HQ Thetford): 415 Battery, Troop A at West Raynham, B at Marham and C at Feltwell. 429 Battery, Troop A at Swanton Morley, B at Attlebridge

and C at Horsham St Faith. 430 Battery, Troop A at Bodney, B at Honington and C at Watton. 431 Battery, Troops A and B at Birçham Newton, C at Gt Massingham.
43 Brigade.
    45 LAA Regiment: 142 Battery, Troop A in the 32 Brigade Area, B and C at Marine Parade/Crescent, Yarmouth.

8 Frequent adjustments to AA defences were brought about as enemy air activity declined. Home Guard-manned 'Z' Batteries operated at Cambridge, Colchester, Chelmsford, Norwich and Peterborough, and the 1944 'Baby Blitz' caused reinforcement. The most dramatic change came in September/October 1944 with the establishment of the Diver Strip to prevent the arrival of V-1s. The layout within this strip in 9 AA Group on 18 November 1944 was as follows.
5 AA Brigade.
    138 HAA Regiment: 419 Battery, Lambert's Grove, Orford (three sites); 437 Battery, Thorpeness Overmere (three sites); 438 Battery, Aldeburgh area (three sites).
    119 HAA Regiment: 372 Battery, Thorpeness (three sites); 422 Independent Battery, near Orford (three sites); 433 Independent Battery, Aldeburgh (three sites).
    135 LAA Regiment: 447 Battery, Aldeburgh (two sites); 450 Battery, Leiston (two sites); 432/131 Battery, Aldeburgh (one site).
37 AA Brigade.
    142(M) Regiment: 488 Battery, Bradwell (one site); 261 Battery, Gt Baddow (one site); 433 Battery, Stanford le Hope (one site); 196 Independent Rocket Battery, Colchester; 211 Independent Rocket Battery, Chelmsford.
40 AA Brigade.
    126 HAA Regiment, Clacton area: 423 Battery, Ramsey–Dovercourt (three sites); 425 Battery, Harwich (two sites); 426 Battery, Thorpe-le-Soken (three sites); 431 Battery, Clacton (two sites).
    136 Regiment, Walton area: 182 Battery (three sites); 409 Battery, (two sites); 432 Battery (two sites); 468 Battery, Felixstowe (two sites).
    150(M) HAA Regiment: H2/Battery 489, Felixstowe (two sites); H3 and H4/492 Batteries, Shotley (three sites); 515 Battery, C3/C4, Jaywick/Frinton (three sites); 456 Battery, Ipswich/Nacton, H12 and H18 sites; one Troop of 439 Independent HAA Battery attached to 492 Battery at H5, Lt Oakley.
    19 LAA Regiment, Frinton area: 221 Battery, Clacton (one site); 263 Battery, Walton (three sites); 294 Battery, K16, Frinton; 434/131 Battery, Harwich.
    81 LAA Regiment, Parkeston area: 199 Battery (two sites); Felixstowe (one site); one Troop, 261, at Felixstowe.
    171 Independent Rocket Battery, Frinton.
    50 Searchlight Regiment: 401, 402 and 403 Batteries, Frinton.
56 Brigade.
    32 Searchlight Regiment: 328, 329 and 330 Batteries at Woodbridge, Saxmundham and Manningtree respectively. 453/64 Battery attached, Ipswich–Belstead.
43 detached Brigade.
    32 Searchlight Regiment attached, 314/58 Battery, Frinton.
57 Brigade.
    188 Independent Rocket Battery, Halesworth.
    48 Searchlight Regiment: 391 and 392 Batteries, Southwold.
    437/132 LAA Battery, Leiston.
102 AA Brigade, Ipswich area.
    378 Independent HAA Battery, Ipswich.
    134 LAA Regiment: 192, 275 and 457 Batteries around Eyke, also 1514 Regiment with 449, 472 and 478 Batteries.
    28 Searchlight Regiment, Bawdsey area: 309, 312 and 438 Batteries.
    53 Regiment, with searchlight Batteries 408 (Ipswich), 409 (Colchester) and 410 (Harwich) — construction units.

Appendix 9: Regional maps showing Rural Districts, airfields and main centres of enemy activity

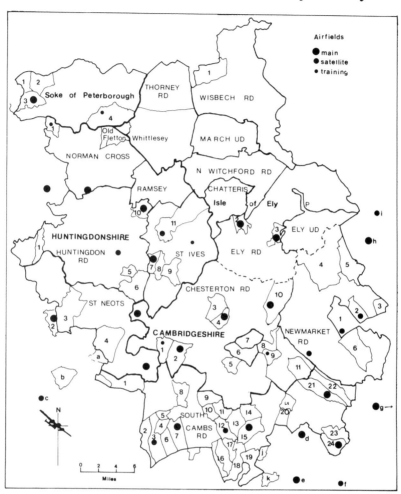

A. Cambridgeshire, Isle of Ely, Huntingdonshire, east Bedfordshire and Soke of Peterborough

Soke of Peterborough 1—St Martin Stamford Barron and Wothom, 2—Barnack, 3—Wittering. **Wisbech Rural District** 1—Newton. **Isle of Ely** 1—Parson Drove, 2—Mepal, 3—Witchford. **Norman Cross RD** 1—Sibson. **Huntingdon RD and border** 1—Molesworth, 2—Little Staughton, 3—Great Staughton; 4—St Neots and Aynesbury: a—Little Barford, b—Great Barford, c—Cardington; 5—Huntingdon, 6—Godmanchester; St Ives: 7—Wyton, 8—Houghton, 9—St Ives, 10—Upwood, 11—Warboys. **Newmarket RD** 1—Exning, 2—Snailwell, 3—Kennett, 4—Soham, 5—Isleham, 6—Wood Ditton: h—Mildenhall, i—Lakenheath. **Chesterton RD** 1—Caxton, 2—Bourn, 3—Longstanton, 4—Oakington, 5—Grantchester, 6—Cambridge Borough (independent), 7—Chesterton UD, 8—Fen Ditton, 9—Teversham, 10—Waterbeach, 11—Great Wilbraham. **South Cambs RD** 1—Gamlingay, 2—Guilden Morden, 3—Steeple Morden, 4—Abington Pigotts, 5—Shingay, 6—Litlington, 7—Bassingbourn, 8—Wimpole, 9—Barrington,

10—Shepreth, 11—Foxton, 12—Fowlmere, 13—Thriplow, 14—Whittlesford, 15—
Duxford; border area: 16—Great Chishall, 17—Heydon, 18—Chrishall, 19—Elmdon;
20—Little and Great Abington, 21—West Wratting, 22—Weston Colville, 23—Shudy
Camps, 24—Castle Camps: d—Hadstock, e—Debden, f—Great Sampford, g—Stradishall.

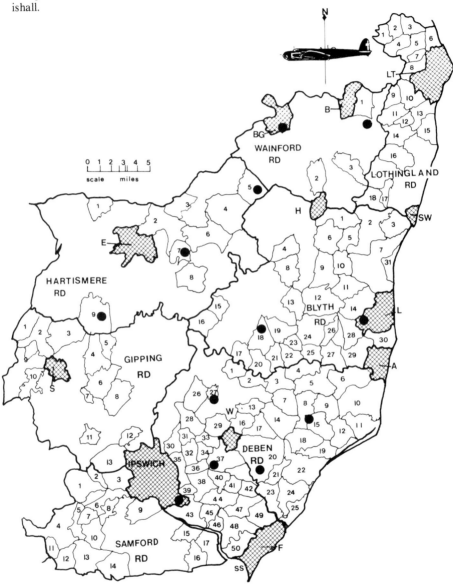

B. East Suffolk
Blyth Rural District 1—Wenhaston, 2—Blythburgh, 3—Walberswick, 4—Heveningham, 5—Thorington, 6—Bramfield, 7—Westleton, 8—Peasenhall, 9—Yoxford, 10—
Darsham, 11—Middleton, 12—Kelsale, 13—Rendham, 14—Theberton, 15—Saxtead,
16—Earl Soham, 17—Easton, 18—Parham, 19—Great Glemham, 20—Hacheston,

21—Marlesford, 22—Little Glemham, 23—Stratford St Andrew, 24—Benhall, 25—Farnham, 26—Sternfield, 27—Snape, 28—Knodishall, 29—Friston, 30—Aldringham with Thorpe, 31—Dunwich. SW=Southwold, L=Leiston cum Sizewell, A=Aldeburgh. **Deben RD** 1—Letheringham, 2—Wickham Market, 3—Campsey Ash, 4—Blaxhall, 5—Tunstall, 6—Iken, 7—Rendlesham, 8—Wantisden, 9—Chillesford, 10—Sudbourne, 11—Orford, 12—Gedgrave, 13—Ufford, 14—Eyke, 15—Butley, 16—Melton, 17—Bromeswell, 18—Capel St Andrew, 19—Boyton, 20—Sutton, 21—Shottisham, 22—Hollesley, 23—Ramsholt, 24—Alderton, 25—Bawdsey, 26—Clopton, 27—Debach, 28—Grundisburgh, 29—Hasketon, 30—Tuddenham St Martin, 31—Culpho, 32—Playford, 33—Great Bealings, 34—Little Bealings, 35—Rushmere St Andrew, 36—Kesgrave, 37—Martlesham, 38—Foxhall, 39—Purdis Farm, 40—Brightwell, 41—Newbourn, 42—Hemley, 43—Nacton, 44—Bucklesham, 45—Levington, 46—Stratton Hall, 47—Kirton, 48—Trimley St Martin, 49—Falkenham, 50—Trimley St Mary. W=Woodbridge, F=Felixstowe, with SS marking the seaplane station (now the Port of Felixstowe). **Gipping RD** 1—Wetherden, 2—Haughley, 3—Old Newton, 4—Earl Stonham, 5—Little Stonham, 6—Creeting St Mary, 7—Needham Market, 8—Coddenham, 9—Harleston, 10—Great Finborough, 11—Nettlestead, 12—Claydon, 13—Bramford. S=Stowmarket. **Hartismere RD** 1—Palgrave, 2—Hoxne, 3—Syleham, 4—Fressingfield, 5—Metfield, 6—Stradbroke, 7—Horham, 8—Worlingworth, 9—Mendlesham. E=Eye. **Lothingland RD** 1—Herringfleet, 2—Ashby, 3—Lound, 4—Somerleyton, 5—Blundeston, 6—Corton, 7—Flixton, 8—Oulton, 9—Barnby, 10—Carlton Colville, 11—Mutford, 12—Rushmere, 13—Gisleham, 14—Henstead, 15—Kessingland, 16—Wrentham, 17—Wangford, 18—Henham. LT=Lowestoft. **Samford RD** 1—Hintlesham, 2—Burstall, 3—Sproughton, 4—Raydon, 5—Great Wenham, 6—Washbrook, 7—Little Wenham, 8—Copdock, 9—Wherstead, 10—Capel St Mary, 11—Higham, 12—Stratford St Mary, 13—East Bergholt, 14—Brantham, 15—Chelmondiston, 16—Erwarton, 17—Shotley. **Wainford RD** 1—Worlingham, 2—Spexhall, 3—Brampton. B=Beccles, BG=Bungay, H=Halesworth.

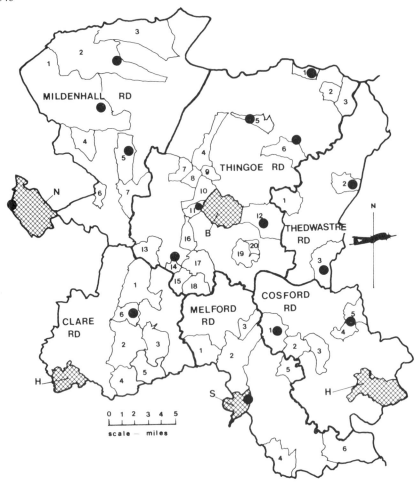

C. West Suffolk

Clare Rural District 1—Wickhambrook, 2—Hundon, 3—Poslingford, 4—Stoke-by-Clare, 5—Clare, 6—Stradishall. H= Haverhill. **Cosford RD** 1—Lavenham, 2—Brent Eleigh, 3—Monks Eleigh, 4—Bildeston, 5—Wattisham. H= Hadleigh. **Melford RD** 1—Glemsford, 2—Long Melford, 3—Alpheton, 4—Bures St Mary, 5—Little Waldingfield, 6—Stoke by Nayland. S=Sudbury. **Mildenhall RD** 1—Mildenhall, 2—Lakenheath, 3—Brandon, 4—Worlington, 5—Tuddenham, 6—Kentford, 7—Higham. N=Newmarket. **Thedwastre RD** 1—Thurston, 2—Great Ashfield, 3—Rattlesden. **Thingoe RD** 1—Knettishall, 2—Market Weston, 3—Thelnetham, 4—Culford, 5—Honington, 6—Ixworth, 7—Flempton, 8—Hengrave, 9—Fornham St Genevieve, 10—Fornham All Saints, 11—Westley, 12—Rougham, 13—Hargrave, 14—Chedburgh, 15—Rede, 16—Ickworth, 17—Whepstead, 18—Brockley, 19—Great Welnetham, 20—Little Welnetham. B= Bury St Edmunds.

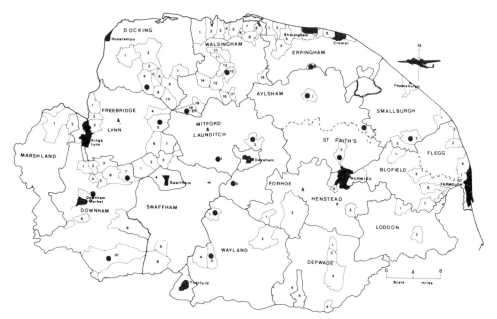

D. Norfolk

Docking Rural District 1—Sedgeford, 2—Docking, 3—Bircham Newton, 4—Great Bircham, 5—Tofts, 6—Bagthorpe, 7—Syderstone, 8—East Rudham, 9—Houghton, 10—West Rudham. **Walsingham RD** 1—Holkham, 2—Wells, 3/4—Warham, 5—Stiffkey, 6—Cockthorpe, 7—Morston, 8—Blakeney, 9—Langham, 10/11—Walsinghams, 12/13—Snorings, 14—Sculthorpe, 15—Fakenham, 16/17—Great/Little Ryburgh. **Erpingham RD** 1—Cley, 2—Salthouse, 3—Holt, 4—Kelling, 5—Runton. **Marshland RD** 1—Terrington St Clement, 2—Clenchwarton. **Freebridge & Lynn RD** 1—Wolferton, 2/3—North/South Wootton, 4/5—Little/Great Massingham, 6—West Acre, 7—Castle Acre. **Mitford & Launditch RD** 1—Wendling, 2—Swanton Morley, 3—Shipdham. **Aylsham RD** 1—Oulton, 2—Horsham St Faith. **Smallburgh RD** 1—Horsey, 2—Ludham, 3—Horning. **Downham RD** 1—Watlington, 2—Tattenham, 3—Wormigay, 4/5—Runctons, 6—Shouldham, 7—Marham, 8—Fordham, 9—Northwold, 10—Feltwell. **Swaffham RD** 1—Narborough, 2—Narford, 3—South Acre, 4—Swaffham, 5—Mundford, 6—Weeting. **Wayland RD** 1—Watton, 2—Attleborough, 3/4—East/West Wretham. **Forhoe & Henstead RD** 1—Deopham, 2—Wymondham, 3—Stoke Holy Cross, 4—Eaton. **Blofield and Flegg RDs** 1—Ranworth, 2—Winterton, 3—Hemsby, 4—Caister, 5—Acle, 6—Havergate. **Loddon RD** 1—Langley, 2—Raveningham. **Depwade RD** 1/2—The Strattons, 3—Pulham, 4—Thorpe Abbots, 5—Diss.

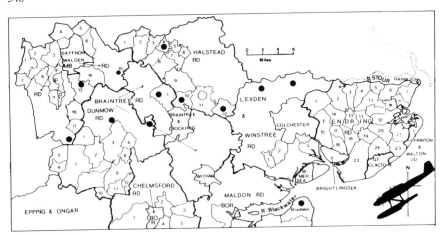

E. North Essex

Saffron Walden Rural District 1—Chrishall, 2—Wendon, 3—Littlebury, 4—Great Chesterford, 5—Hadstock, 6—Ashdon, 7—Langley, 8—Arkesden, 9—Wendons Ambo, 10—Newport, 11—Rickling, 12—Quendon, 13—Debden, 14—Wimbish, 15—Samford, 16—Henham, 17—Elsenham. **Halstead RD** 1—Helion Bumpstead, 2—Steeple Bumpstead, 3—Birdbrook, 4—Ridgewell, 5—Tilbury-juxta-Clare, 6—Little Yeldham, 7—Great Yeldham, 8—Toppesfield, 9—Sible Hedingham, 10—Gosfield, 11—Halstead, 12—Earl's Colne. **Braintree RD** 1—Wethersfield. **Dunmow RD** 1—Takeley, 2—Great and Little Canfield, 3—Great Dunmow, 4—Little Dunmow, 5—Great Hallingbury, 6—Little Hallingbury, 7—Hatfield Broad Oak, 8—Barnston, 9—High Easter, 10—Margaret Roding, 11—Good Easter, 12—Mashbury and Pleshey. **Clemsford RD** 1—Writtle, 2—Springfield, 3—Little Baddow, 4—Great Baddow, 5—Danbury. **Lexden & Winstree RD** 1—Layer Breton, 2—Layer de la Haye, 3—Fingringhoe. **Tendring RD** 1—Ardleigh, 2—Lawford and Manningtree (A), 3—Mistley, 4—Bradfield, 5—Wrabness, 6—Ramsey, 7—Dovercourt and Parkeston, 8—Little Oakley, 9—Great Oakley, 10—Wix, 11—Tendring, 12—Beaumont-cum-Moze, 13—Little Bentley, 14—Great Bromley, 15—Elmstead and Alresford, 16—Thorrington, 17—Frating, 18—Great Bentley, 19—Weeley, 20—Thorpe-le-Soken, 21—Kirby-le-Soken, 22—St Osyth, 23—Great Holland, 24—Little Clacton.

Select index

AA defence 25-27, 38, 62, 74, 76, 77, 80, 118-19, 146, 177, 179, 182, 206, 215, 219-20, 227, 233, 240, 242, 243, 246, 256-58, 263, 268, 269, 272, 276, 280, 284, 287, 290, 294, 296, 298, 302, 310, 316, 317, 320-1, 326

AIRFIELDS (UK): Alconbury 162, 189; Bassingbourn 107,123, 169, 175, 179, 190; Bentwaters 46; Bircham Newton 29, 33, 39, 41, 43, 47, 49, 57, 69, 73, 74, 124, 130, 143-45, 160-61, 179; Birch (Langham, Essex) 283, 288; Bodney 124, 142, 185, 324; Bourn 171, 198, 254, 313; Boxted 283; Bradwell Bay 84, 231, 268, 280, 312, 321; Cambridge 79, 84, 110, 127, 193; Cardington 58, 99; Castle Camps 208, 214, 268, 281, 283, 286, 310; Caxton 156, 190, 191; Chedburgh 281, 284, 287, 288; Coltishall 57, 58, 62, 66, 71, 97, 104, 107, 124, 130, 131, 139, 146, 152, 176, 178, 179, 184, 191, 192, 196, 206, 214, 231, 283, 285, 287, 317, 325, 326; Cranfield 93, 123; Debach 281; Debden 26, 29, 33, 39, 43, 50, 53, 57, 64, 75-84, 96, 98, 110, 112, 122, 124, 130, 134, 143, 169, 179, 193; Deopham 313; Digby 33, 34, 41, 43, 49; Docking 69, 121, 130, 157, 190, 240; Downham Market 283, 284; Duxford 25-9, 32, 33, 47, 51, 57, 62, 68, 71, 74-85, 90, 98, 99, 103, 110, 112, 116, 125, 135, 156, 231; Earl's Colne 288, 298, 310; E Wretham 85, 139, 148, 160, 179, 190; Feltwell 47, 48, 74, 104, 130, 134, 135, 139-44, 157, 160, 161, 173, 179, 185, 191, 282; Foulsham 193, 255; Fowlmere 62, 76, 78, 82, 91, 98, 110; Framlingham 313; Glatton

243; Gosfield 286; Gransden Lodge 285; Graveley 286; Gt Ashfield 313; Gt Massingham 104, 134, 179; Halesworth 257; Henlow 83, 85, 99, 112, 169; Honington 49, 54, 58, 64, 71, 85, 97, 104, 106, 112, 120, 129, 130, 131, 138-9, 142, 148, 175, 180; Hornchurch 74, 76; Horsham St Faith 29, 46-7, 69, 110, 112, 134, 143, 161, 171, 212, 307, 312; Ipswich 167, 272; Knettishall 286; Lakenheath 313; Langham 325, 326; Lavenham 280-1; Lt Staughton 191; Lt Snoring 312; Ludham 201, 214, 287; Manston 34, 36; Marham 47-8, 51, 74, 84, 104, 120, 134, 143, 156, 162, 169, 175, 185, 191, 231; Martlesham 29, 33-6, 39, 41, 43, 57, 62, 64, 66, 68, 70, 82, 84, 104, 111, 124, 167, 176, 179, 208, 231, 298; Matlaske 106, 201, 231, 287; Mepal 312; Mendlesham 314; Metfield 286, 324-5; Methwold 179; Mildenhall 39, 47, 51, 54, 85, 87, 97, 99, 104, 107, 112, 120, 137-9, 143, 146, 160, 165, 192, 199, 230, 282, 285; Newmarket 58, 68, 74, 103-4, 106, 123, 130, 139, 143, 230; N Weald 28, 33, 66, 74, 83, 206, 276; Oakington 87, 136, 152, 177, 179-80, 185, 189, 191, 198, 243, 285, 313; Oulton 161; Rackheath 313; Shepherd's Grove 323; Shipdham 283, 312, 325; Snailwell 257, 284; Steeple Morden 145, 157, 173, 190; Stradishall 33, 51, 73, 110, 125, 127, 130, 165, 175, 185, 193, 197, 281, 282; Swannington 32; Swanton Morley 47, 146, 157, 325; Thorpe Abbotts 240; Tuddenham 58, 143, 285, 312-14; Upwood 74, 85, 97, 124, 169; Waterbeach 127, 139, 164, 177, 185, 191, 283, 286;

Wattisham 54, 68, 106-7, 110-11, 152, 161; Watton 27, 29, 69, 71, 129, 134, 148, 156, 179, 185; Wendling 325, 326; Westley 97, 104, 124; W Raynham 29, 33-4, 46, 62, 64, 74, 104, 120, 134, 142, 146, 160, 179, 185-87; Wethersfield 284, 288; Witchford 312; Wittering 26, 29, 32-3, 43, 49, 50, 57, 62, 68, 84, 97, 112, 122, 124, 128, 140, 142, 152, 156, 164, 179, 180, 182, 186, 206, 231, 238; Woodbridge 314; Wyton 74, 97, 124, 286

LUFTWAFFE UNITS: Aufkl.Gr.F/33 257; F/106 62, 180, 186, 189, 190, 192, 240; F/121 87, 282, 310; F/122 36-7, 41-2, 44-5, 66, 103, 129, 131, 152, 164-9, 189, 192, 203, 207, 227, 231, 237, 239, 255, 294, 310; F/126 62, 85; 3/Obdl 103; 4/Obdl 79; Erprobungsgruppe 210 69-71, 85, 120, 140, 168, 180, 187; JG51 184; Kampfgeschwader KG1 62, 95, 104, 140-1, 145, 167, 257; KG2 64-73, 76-9, 82, 97, 128-9, 134, 137, 140-2, 146, 148, 152-3, 156, 160-8, 187, 192, 198-203, 207-10, 217, 220, 227-8, 231, 233, 237, 239-43, 248-9, 254-8, 262, 267, 270-2, 281, 284, 287-94, 302-6, 310-11; KG3 64, 125, 129-31, 134-8, 140, 152, 157, 161-2, 167-8, 180, 189, 193, 200, 220, 307, 318; KG4 32, 36, 43, 49, 50, 57-8, 68, 69, 85, 128-9, 134-5, 138, 140, 146, 162, 164, 167, 175, 180, 186, 189, 192, 217, 220, 294; KG6 251, 256-7, 262, 266-7, 270, 271, 273, 287, 291, 294, 302, 305, 307; KG26 29, 32, 33, 36, 41, 42, 101, 165, 178, 180, 208, 243; KG27 32, 46, 49, 50, 57-8, 130; KG28 44, 62, 102; KG30 30, 33, 40-2, 68, 98, 101,

129, 134, 136-7, 140, 142, 146, 152, 157, 160, 162, 163, 165, 167, 169, 177, 187, 189, 192, 198, 212, 217, 307, 310; **KG40** 192, 200, 207-10, 213, 217, 220, 227, 231, 239, 243, 246, 249, 254, 256, 262, 267-71, 281, 290, 295; **KG51** 164, 307, 310; **KG53** 64-7, 69, 74, 104, 106, 128, 129-31, 134-41, 145-8, 152, 156, 160-1, 164-8, 178, 189, 249, 318, 320; **KG54** 95, 205, 248-9, 289, 294-8, 307, 310; **KG55** 90, 121, 217, 220; **KG66** 273, 289, 291, 294, 302, 306-7, 310; **KG76** 45, 46, 98, 104, 146, 163, 172, 186; **KG77** 59, 87, 97, 130, 164, 167, 168, 175, 177, 217, 220, 231, 243, 249; **KGr/KG100** 213, 220, 227, 233, 239, 243, 290, 294, 298, 299, 302, 306, 310-11; **KG101** 302; **Ku.Fl.Gr106** 37, 68; **406** 166; **506** 39, 62, 68, 206, 217, 227; **606** 36, 103, 189, 190, 193, 198, 200; **906** 37, 85; **Nachtgeschwader NJG2** 136, 140, 144, 156, 163-4, 168-9, 171, 173, 175, 177, 179-82; **NJG 4** 324; **SKG10** 275-81, 287, 307

TOWNS/VILLAGES: Acle 256; Akeham 122; Aldeburgh 41-2, 55, 74, 111, 121, 136, 168, 184, 203, 231, 255, 259, 272; Aldeby 148; Alderton 58, 167; Alwalton 69; Ardleigh 192, 283, 320; Arkesden 64, 77; Ashby St Mary 313; Ashfield 91, 190; Ashwell 173; Assington 289; Attleborough 125, 127, 255; Attlebridge 67, 147; Audley End 124; Aylsham 46, 165, 270, 307, 313; Babraham 74; Baldock 96; Balsham 98; Barford 143; Barham 29; Barnston 74; Barrington 81, 191; Bawdsey 27, 34, 66, 69, 152, 174, 314; Beachamwell 157; Beccles 169, 207, 325; Beck Row 138; Bedford 112, 120, 231, 233, 237-8; Bedingfield 71; Benacre 312; Bentley 287; Benwick 53, 92; Berner's Heath 53; Biggleswade 103; Bishop's Stortford 75, 85, 90, 101, 129; Blakenham 90; Blakeney 50, 143; Blythburgh 64, 168; Boreham 314; Botesdale 138, 323; Bourn 90; Boyton 299; Bradwell 57, 141, 174, 175, 208, 318; Bramford 299; Bramwell Island 269; Braintree 66, 84, 97, 101-2, 111, 285, 290, 317; Brancaster 73; Brandon 152, 286, 312; Branfield 57; Bressingham 51; Breydon 128, 143; Brigg 57; Brightlingsea 57, 82, 161, 186,

295, 297; Brinton 178; Bromeswell 114; Bromham 85; Broxted 70; Brundall 167; Bucklesham 299; Bungay 57, 107, 169, 299, 314; Bures 314; Burgh St Peter 46; Burnham 91, 103; Burnham Market 283; Burnham-on-Crouch 280; Burnt Fen 286; Burwell 123; Bury St Edmunds 50, 53, 54, 87, 92, 106, 112, 122, 142, 157, 160, 323; Butley 47; Buxton Heath 146, 325; Bylaugh Hall 286; Caister 192, 277; Caldecote 99; Cambridge 15, 18, 22, 39, 51-6, 75, 79, 80-3, 91, 93, 100-3, 111-12, 134, 137, 144, 174, 180-1, 240, 246-8, 252-4, 272, 285, 303-5; Carlton Colville 256; Castle Mills 83; Caston Ricklands 282; Cavendish 286; Cavenham 107; Caxton 286; Chatteris 53; Chedburgh 138; Chelmondiston 283; Chelmsford 50, 78-9, 85, 87, 90-1, 99, 110, 125, 238, 246, 253, 263, 268-9, 272, 275-6, 287, 291, 296, 311; Cherry Hinton 79, 180; Chevington 137; Chilton Street 92; Chippenham 98, 324; Chitts Hill 135; Clacton 29, 42-5, 50, 55, 58, 71, 73, 76, 82, 110-12, 116, 120, 123-5, 129, 131, 135-7, 148, 157, 164, 179, 182, 184, 188, 193, 197, 198, 256, 276-6, 290, 298, 299; Clare 286; Claydon 73, 110, 299; Cley 314; Clopton 62; Cockley Cley 145; Coddenham 98, 256; Colchester 28, 57, 66-7, 71, 82-3, 85, 112, 120, 123-4, 130, 134, 137, 182, 193, 198, 200, 248-9, 254-6, 275-6, 290, 297, 298-9, 302, 310; Colmworth 98; Corton 116, 140; Coventry 120; Cowlinge 287; Coxford Heath 157; Creeting St Peter 111; Cresham 326; Cringleford 263, 323; Cromer 28, 33-4, 40-1, 64, 84, 97, 125, 146, 165, 173, 177, 188, 192, 207, 238, 256; Crowfield 256; Croxton 270; Culford 51, 85; Darsham 261; Deeping St James 189; Dennington 111; Dereham 286, 325; Didlington 282; Diss 137, 188; Docking 189, 255, 324; Dovercourt 59, 84, 175, 177, 182, 200, 297; Downham Market 177; Duddenhoe End 77; Dunwich 58, 62; Dykemoor Drove 53; Earl's Colne 299; Earl Soham 312; E Dereham 48, 283; E Rudham 160, 323; Easton 317; Elder Street 78, 82; Elmdon 77; Elmswell 137; Elsenham 70, 298; Elsworth 121; Elvedon 286; Ely 40, 48, 53, 110, 140, 220, 241;

Erwarton 103; Exning 123; Eyeworth 318; Eyke 274; Fakenham 152, 179, 187, 286; Falkenham 299; Felixstowe 33, 36-7, 42, 57, 59, 66, 70, 82, 84, 110, 122-3, 134, 140, 152, 166, 192-3, 238, 279, 314; Felton 267; Fen Ditton 102; Filby 277; Finchingfield 78, 282; Fingringhoe 299; Fordham 53, 123; Foulden 48; Fowlmere 80, 98, 317; Foxton 80; Framlingham 69, 98, 111, 314; Frating 299; Freckenham 68; French's Green 318; Frinton 59, 97, 102, 122-3, 131, 136, 140, 170, 184, 200, 248, 275, 279, 297; Fulbourn 54, 110, 298, 319; Gedgrave 261; Girtford 103; Gissing 179; Glemsford 310; Godmanchester 134; Good Easter 78; Gorleston 73-4, 131, 144, 162, 170-1, 174, 176, 186, 188, 193, 206, 266; Gt Abington 124; Gt Ashfield 286; Gt Bentley 76; Gt Blakenham 138; Gt Bromley 200, 254, 324; Gt Canfield 50, 61, 299; Gt Chesterford 39; Gt Cornard 190; Gt Holland 124, 184; Gt Leigh 272, 307; Gt Plumstead 267; Gt Ryburgh 74, 246; Gt Saling 299, 317; Gt Tey 76; Gt Warley 74, 299, 321; Gt Whelnetham 137; Gt Yarmouth 29, 33, 40, 42-3, 48, 64, 67, 73, 79, 85, 97-9, 103, 110, 112, 116, 122-4, 131, 136, 138, 141, 143, 145-6, 148, 152, 157, 160-2, 165, 167, 169-76, 181, 185-93, 198, 200, 203, 206-7, 231-2, 237-9, 242, 255, 259, 262, 266-7, 274-7, 296, 325; Grundisburgh 62, 110; Gunton 326; Haddington/Dalkeith 39; Hadleigh 64; Halesworth 74, 78, 130, 134, 139, 263, 267, 285; Halstead 55, 85, 102, 137; Happisburgh 41, 62, 85, 130, 142, 167, 179, 189; Hardwick 99; Hargrave 50, 138; Harkstead 128; Harleston 46, 57, 66, 69, 73, 78; Harpley 246; Harston 53; Harwich 25-8, 37-9, 42, 45, 55, 57-8, 62, 66, 69, 71, 84, 97, 99, 103, 114, 123, 131, 136, 139, 156-7, 166, 170-1, 174-5, 177, 182, 187, 192, 200, 203, 206, 257, 260, 276, 279, 297, 311; Hatfield Broad Oak 78; Haverhill 146; Heacham 138; Heckingham 286; Helions Bumpstead 281-2; Hellesdon 319; Hemmingstone 256; Hemsby 263, 323; Hevingham 96, 157, 325; High Roding 61, 82; Hillborough 143; Hintingfield 261; Histon 174; Hockering 270;

Hockwold 134, 157; Hockwood 312; Holland-on-Sea 50, 201; Hollesley 165, 299; Holt 189; Hopton 319; Horning 175, 203; Horsey Is 62, 322; Horsford 270; Horstead Heath 157; Hoxne 319; Hunstanton 34, 146, 160, 167, 186; Ipswich 36, 56, 60-4, 85, 90, 104-6, 111-12, 116, 124, 130-1, 152, 157, 160, 171, 173, 177, 181-2, 185, 220, 231, 248-9, 254, 256, 272, 274-5, 279, 290, 297, 311, 323, 326; Jaywick 57, 131; Kelsale 105; Kentford 137; Kenton 283; Kerdiston 157, 270; Kesgrave 137, 286; Kessingland 67, 167, 256, 261, 278; Keysoe 83; Kimberley 142; Kimbolton 135; King's Lynn 24, 44-5, 51, 74, 122, 140, 164, 189, 200, 210, 231, 233, 238, 239, 254-5; Kirby Cane 253, 283; Kirby Cross 201; Knapton 270; Lakenheath 87, 122, 137; Landguard 26, 45, 47, 99, 206; Langley 46, 77, 286-7; Latchingdon 311; Laxford 122; Layer 74; Leigh-on-Sea 251; Leiston 71, 138-9, 152, 286-7; Lexham 323; Linton 98, 281; Lt Barford 121, 135; Lt Bealings 104; Lt Cressingham 323; Lt Hallenbury 78; Lt Henham 53; Lt Melton 270; Lt Staughton 83; Lt Tey 314; Lt Waldringfield 156; Lt Waltham 272; Loddon 167, 286; Long Melford 310; Longstowe 285; Lower Standon 93; Lowestoft 60, 67, 73, 84-5, 96, 102, 116, 122-6, 135, 137, 140, 141, 144, 146, 152, 160-4, 171-9, 180, 187, 200-3, 207, 220, 227, 231, 238, 240, 243, 249, 256, 261, 266, 274, 278, 296, 311; Manningtree 71; March 58, 122, 220, 237, 290; Market Deeping 183; Market Weston 130; Marlesford 256; Martham 160; Mattishall 157; Meldreth 80; Melford 124, 137; Melton 138, 261; Melton Constable 244; Mersea 122; Micklefield 312; Milton 98, 286; Mistley 45, 61; Monk Soham 49; Moltesham 270; Mundesley 319; Mulbarton 263; Mutford 207; Needham Market 256; Neatishead 196; Nettlestead 196; Newmarket 48-50, 54, 71, 73, 107, 141, 149-51; Newport 64; Newton 47, 99; Norman Cross 123; N Cove 174; N Walsham 258, 283; Northwold 282; N Wootton 246; Norwich 25-6, 45, 48, 62, 63, 66-8, 71, 84, 87, 112, 120, 124-5, 129, 147, 167-8, 178, 182, 186, 197, 211-33, 236-7, 241-3, 248, 251-2, 255-6, 258, 260, 263, 266, 270,

275; Oakham 183; Oakley 59, 97, 269; Offton 107; Old Catton 263; Orford 146, 258, 261, 299, 326; Orford Ness 29, 33, 40, 58, 66, 110, 116, 206; Orwell 254; Oulton 263; Oulton Broad 258, 261, 312; Ovington 148; Overstrand 142; Parham 258, 314, 325; Pakefield 299; Parkeston Quay 56, 66, 84, 107, 157, 173, 177; Peasenhall 96, 314, 316, 328; Pelgrave 58; Peterborough 49, 58, 152, 182, 231-3, 237, 243; Pitsea 130; Playford 104; Poslingford 92; Postwick 167; Potter Heigham 325; Rackheath 157; Rampton 243; Ramsey 140, 171, 182, 203, 256, 260; Ranworth 319; Rattlesden 103, 314; Raveningham 263, 283; Reach 97; Rede 51, 57, 138; Reedham 191, 207; Reepham 143, 323; Rendlesham 84, 323; Renhold 83; Rickinghall 323; Ringsfield 64; Rivenhall 55, 74; Rockland St Mary 319; Rougham 50; Roughton 326; Royston 91, 112, 120; Rudham 49, 50; Rushford 286; Rushmere 90, 111, 130, 274; Saffron Walden 71, 78, 82, 91, 93, 102-3, 122-4, 318; Salt Fleet 104; Salthouse 146; Sandy 97; Saxmundham 62, 105, 129; Saxstead 160; Scottow 238; Seething 26; Shelford 79; Shepreth 80; Sheringham 29, 39, 42, 93, 138, 161-2, 165, 189, 193, 206, 312; Shotley 102, 111, 167; Shottisham 286; Shropham 138, 270; Shudy Camps 99, 307; Snape 58, 257; Soham 98; Southwold 33, 69, 71, 73, 85, 103, 112, 116, 129, 148, 165, 184, 186, 207, 243, 261, 279, 328; S Repps 240, 326; S Lopham 160; S Pickenham 143; Spelling Minnis 112; Spixworth 47; Sproughton 73, 256; Spooner Row 255; Stagsden 83; Stanbourne 157, 295; St Ives 131; St Neots 58; St Osyth 137, 297; Stebbing 302, 312; Steeple Bumpstead 55; Stetchworth 286; Stiffkey 58; Stoke-by-Clare 47, 69, 78, 165, 228, 263; Stoke Holy Cross 47, 69, 78, 228, 263; Stonham 256, 312; Stowmarket 69, 90, 138, 157, 179, 256; Stradbroke 111; Stratford St Andrew 256; Strumpshaw 47; Stuntney 68; Swaffham 112, 122, 130, 135-6, 142, 325; Syderstone 55; Swainsthorpe 263; Takeley 124; Tattersett 59, 97; Tempsford 97; Terrington St Clement 162; Thaxted 76-7;

Theberton 96; Thorpe 319; Thorpeness 136; Tiptree 257; Tofts Monk 263; Toseland 286; Tuddenham 270; Tunstall 59, 97; Tunstead 325; Thorney 175, 231; Ufford 98, 104; Walberswick 59, 167-8; Waldringfield 70; Walsham-le-Willows 286; Walsingham 307, 326; Walton-on-the-Naze 42, 54, 59, 97, 107, 122, 124, 136, 173, 184, 279, 297; Wattisfield 314; Welbourne 270; Weeley 297; Wells-next-the Sea 49, 50, 283; Welney 177; Westhall 285; Westleton 255, 312; W Bergholt 123; Weston Colville 98; West Wickham 98; Weybourne 64, 146, 283; Whelnetham 54; Whepstead 76, 137, 287; Wherstead 28, 129; Wholehaven 134; White Roding 78, 93; Wickhambrook 74, 98, 286; Wickham Bishop 78; Wickham Market 130, 257, 314, 325; Wimbish 58, 77-8, 82; Winfield 97; Winterton 58, 64, 277, 280; Wisbech 110, 120, 325; Woodbridge 99, 104, 273; Worlingham 168; Worlingworth 248; Wrabness 26, 275; Wroxham 286; Wyboston 103; Wymondham 112, 124, 139, 157, 241, 255

RURAL DISTRICTS: Blyth 85, 90-1, 110-11, 120, 131; Chelmsford 124, 299, 310; Chesterton 96-7, 121-2, 140; Clare 69, 98, 129, 231, 254, 295; Cosford 69, 96, 124, 138; Deben 71, 73, 121, 140, 231, 241, 248, 258, 295-6, 299, 314; Depwade 48, 51, 73, 125, 140, 231; Docking 51, 57, 122; Downham 96, 112, 122, 134, 136, 137, 231, 248, 290; Dunmow 55, 61, 78, 102, 121-3, 254, 296-9, 310; Ely 120-2; Erping 134, 228, 258, 307; Forhoe 126, 134, 220, 228, 248, 313; Freebridge 124, 131; Gipping 75, 83, 111, 124, 128, 131, 248; Halstead 71, 111, 122, 124, 241, 295, 296, 310; Hartismere 49, 90, 122, 124, 128, 248, 254; Huntingdon 55, 97, 122; Launditch 61, 125, 326; Lothingland 124, 231, 241, 248, 296, 310, 313; Lexden & Tendring 296; Loddon 48, 228, 231, 311; Melford 90, 290, 296; Mitford 61, 106, 122, 231, 241, 298, 310, 325; Newmarket 111, 122, 290; N Witchford 92, 120, 134, 143, 231; Saffron Walden 55, 78, 82, 90, 102, 298, 310; Samford 106, 110, 112, 120, 123, 128-30, 134, 248, 296-7;

Smallborough 57, 134; **S Cambs** 102, 111, 121-2, 125, 128, 254; **St Faiths** 106, 220; **St Neots** 55, 75, 111, 122; **Swaffham** 231, 324; **Thedwastre** 98, 102, 128; **Wainford** 231, 241, 246, 296, 310; **Walsingham** 75, 248, 258; **Weyland** 73, 98, 100; **Woodbridge** 124

RAF SQUADRONS: 1 70, 103, 110, 252; **7** 177; **16** 79; **17** 32, 62, 64, 65, 66, 69, 70, 83, 87, 97-8, 103, 104, 106, 110, 112, 114, 122; **19** 25, 27, 32-3, 43, 50, 54-5, 62, 66, 68, 71, 75, 80-4, 91, 201, 206; **23** 27, 32-3, 39, 41, 46, 50, 55; **25** 121, 164, 179, 180, 186, 188, 189, 298, 299, 306-7, 311, 313-14; **29** 26-7, 32, 39, 43, 46, 50, 53, 55, 164, 227; **35** 286; **46** 84, 114; **56** 26, 33-4, 73, 75, 254, 255, 258, 279; **64** 26, 313; **66** 25, 27, 32-3, 41, 43, 50, 62-4, 67, 71, 73, 79, 83; **68** 210, 214, 227, 231, 239, 247, 255-7, 267,

286-90, 295, 297, 307, 324; **71** 192, 201; **72** 103, 112; **73** 26; **74** 27, 50, 69, 85, 93, 97; **79** 34; **80** 26; **85** 26-7, 33, 62-9, 104, 175, 178, 180, 182, 190-3, 197, 231, 257, 282, 284; **87** 26-7; **93** 196; **99** 192; **101** 198; **111** 76, 82; **115** 169; **121** 253; **124** 254; **129** 324; **132** 255; **137** 208, 210, 231; **149** 165; **151** 28, 66, 140, 164, 177-8, 189, 208, 233, 254, 255, 285; **157** 208, 214, 248, 256, 257, 266-9; **167** 255; **195** 279; **213** 26, 32, 34, 43; **218** 156; **222** 33, 43, 46, 123, 137, 139, 144, 146, 161, 169, 175, 186; **229** 43; **236** 33; **242** 62-8, 73, 102, 129, 139, 140, 144, 168; **249** 140; **254** 33; **255** 193, 207; **257** 73, 82, 84, 97, 112, 114, 120-2, 131, 146, 152, 157, 165, 176, 180, 184, 190, 192; **264** 43, 66, 295; **266** 123, 192, 207; **268** 255; **302** 87; **303** 255; **310** 75, 78, 83, 84; **311** 85, 171; **316** 317; **332** 276; **401** 253; **405** 285-6; **406** 208; **409** 290, 295, 314; **410** 266, 273,

288, 299, 307, 310; **411** 255; **412** 208; **418** 268; **456** 324; **485** 201; **488** 287, 307, 310; **504** 27, 33, 41, 43; **601** 39; **602** 167; **604** 28, 50, 191, 193; **605** 167, 268-9; **610** 41, 43, 214, 231, 251; **611** 27, 32, 73, 83, 253; **616** 322; **620** 284; **928** 37, 66, 174, 192, 203, 269; **952** 39; **993** 268

MISCELLANEOUS:
Balloon barrage 37, 192, 195, 203, 207, 208, 227-8, 233, 239, 241, 263, 268, 337
Convoy/shipping raids 29, 33, 34-7, 43, 61-70, 135-6, 140, 147, 162-71, 174-7, 189-93, 198, 200, 203, 206-8, 229, 243, 256, 260, 262, 284-5, 291
Flares 117, 272, 290, 295
Incendiaries/raids 16, 20, 47-8, 108, 116, 125, 129, 140, 169-72, 189, 214-15, 220, 233, 240-1, 247, 254, 261-2, 265, 269, 274, 289, 297, 299, 305, 308-9